McDougal Littell

Teacher's Edition

MIDDLE ▾ GRADES

MATH *Thematics*®

SENIOR AUTHORS **Rick Billstein**
Jim Williamson

About the Teacher's Edition

This annotated Teacher's Edition provides Warm-Up Exercises
and Closure Questions for each section in the Student Edition—
all conveniently annotated at point of use. Answers to questions
within lessons and to Practice & Application Exercises are
annotated directly on the student pages. Answers that do not fit
on these pages appear in an Additional Answers section
beginning on page A1.

SUCCESS THROUGH EXPLORING MATHEMATICS
The STEM Project

BOOK 3

McDougal Littell

Evanston, Illinois • Boston • Dallas

AUTHORS

SENIOR AUTHORS

Rick Billstein — Department of Mathematical Sciences, University of Montana, Missoula, Montana

Jim Williamson — Department of Mathematical Sciences, University of Montana, Missoula, Montana

CONSULTING AUTHORS

Perry Montoya — Teacher, Mesa Public Schools, Mesa, Arizona

Jacqueline Lowery — Teacher, Indian Queen Elementary School, Fort Washington, Maryland

Dianne Williams — Teacher, Booker T. Washington Middle School for International Studies, Tampa, Florida

THE STEM PROJECT — *Middle Grades Math Thematics®* is based on the field-test versions of The STEM Project curriculum. The STEM Project was supported in part by the

 NATIONAL SCIENCE FOUNDATION

under Grant No. ESI-9150114. Opinions expressed in *Middle Grades Math Thematics®* are those of the authors and not necessarily those of the National Science Foundation.

STEM WRITERS

Mary Buck, Clay Burkett, Lynn Churchill, Chris Clouse, Roslyn Denny, William Derrick, Sue Dolezal, Doug Galarus, Paul Kennedy, Pat Lamphere, Nancy Merrill, Perry Montoya, Sallie Morse, Marjorie Petit, Patrick Runkel, Thomas Sanders-Garrett, Richard T. Seitz, Bonnie Spence, Becky Sowders, Chris Tuckerman, Ken Wenger, Joanne Wilkie, Cheryl Wilson, Bente Winston

STEM TEACHER CONSULTANTS

Polly Fite, Jean Howard, Paul Sowden, Linda Tetley, Patricia Zepp

ABOUT THE COVER

The students shown on the back cover are from Frank Kellogg Middle School, in Shoreline, Washington.

ISBN 0-618-09805-4   23456789–VH– 04 03   Teacher's Edition: ISBN 0-618-09806-2

MIDDLE GRADES
MATH *Thematics*

WELCOME

COURSE GOALS

This course will help you:

▶ Learn all the important middle grades mathematics concepts and skills that prepare you for high school and beyond.

▶ Develop the reasoning, problem solving, and communication skills that enable you to apply mathematics to real-life activities.

▶ Value mathematics and become confident in using it to make decisions in daily life.

SUCCESS THROUGH EXPLORING MATHEMATICS

Theme Approach
You will be learning through thematic modules that connect mathematical concepts to real-world applications.

Active Learning
The lessons in this course will get you actively involved in exploring, modeling, and communicating mathematics using a variety of tools, including technology when appropriate.

Varied Practice and Assessment
The variety of types of practice and assessment will help reinforce and extend your understanding. You will learn to assess your own progress as you go along.

MODULE 1

AMAZING FEATS, FACTS, and FICTION

1

Connecting the Theme *Tall tales and towering talents will capture your imagination, as you see how mathematics can be used to describe incredible accomplishments both real and legendary.*

AT THE MALL

MODULE
2

80

Connecting the Theme *Malls combine shopping with entertainment. Mathematics helps store owners plan inventory, and helps shoppers compare prices. You'll learn the mathematics that operates behind the scenes.*

The MYSTERY of BLACKTAIL CANYON

160

Connecting the Theme *Be on the lookout as a mystery unfolds. As you read, you'll rely on mathematics to help you piece together clues to catch a thief. Then, you'll use rules of logic to try solving the mystery.*

PATTERNS and DISCOVERIES

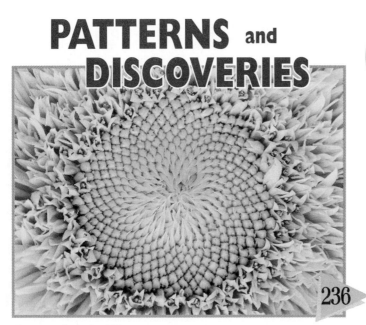

236

Connecting the Theme *Patterns found in nature, music, and geometric constructions have inspired mathematicians from Pythagorus to Fibonacci. You'll use observation of patterns to discover mathematical concepts.*

Module Features

Assessment Options

INVENTIONS

316

Connecting the Theme *How do inventors get new ideas? They brainstorm, experiment, and carefully calculate. You'll see how mathematics has helped in perfecting inventions from the tin can to the astrolabe to the Braille alphabet.*

ARCHITECTS and ENGINEERS

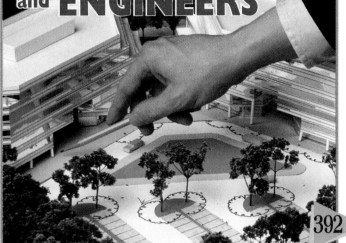

392

Connecting the Theme *From blueprint to model to construction site, a building takes shape. As you give form to your own constructions, you'll see how measurement and mathematics are tools of the construction trade around the world.*

Module Features

MODULE PROJECT
Creating a Model Town,
pp. 393, 416, 430, and 463

STUDENT RESOURCE
Bisecting an Angle, p. 407

CAREER CONNECTION
Surveyor, p. 439

TECHNOLOGY
Using Geometric Drawing
Software, p. 410

EXTENSION
Euler and Space Figures,
p. 415
Surface Areas of Cones,
p. 430

Assessment Options

PORTFOLIO ASSESSMENT
EXTENDED EXPLORATION (E²):
Mathematical Art, p. 441
REFLECTING ON THE SECTION:
pp. 402, 414, 429, 438, 449,
and 460

ONGOING ASSESSMENT
CHECKPOINTS: pp. 396, 397,
398, 406, 409, 420, 422,
423, 424, 435, 445, 446,
453, and 456
KEY CONCEPTS QUESTIONS:
pp. 399, 411, 425, 426, 436,
447, and 457
STANDARDIZED TESTING:
pp. 417, 431, 440, 450,
and 462

MODULE ASSESSMENT
REVIEW AND ASSESSMENT:
pp. 464 and 465
REFLECTING ON THE MODULE:
p. 465

MODULE 7

VISUALIZING CHANGE

466

Connecting the Theme *It may be impossible to see the future. Still, many professionals need to predict coming trends. From economics to environmental science, you'll learn how mathematical models can help people see patterns of change.*

MAKING an IMPACT

534

Connecting the Theme *When you care about an issue, numbers can help bring it into focus. Concerned citizens often gather and present information mathematically. You'll compile data and create visuals that make an impact.*

A1 Additional Answers
For each section in the book, answers that do not fit on the pages of the Student Edition are included in a special Additional Answers section at the back of this Teacher's Edition, beginning on page A1.

Module Features

MODULE PROJECT
Preparing an Investigative Report, pp. 535, 549, 575, 585, and 587

STUDENT RESOURCES
Choosing a Data Display, p. 566

CAREER CONNECTION
Market Researcher, p. 560

TECHNOLOGY
Using Spreadsheet Software to Display Data, p. 556

EXTENSION
Sampling Methods, p. 548

Assessment Options

PORTFOLIO ASSESSMENT
EXTENDED EXPLORATION (E²):
Making a New Type of Data Display, p. 577
REFLECTING ON THE SECTION:
pp. 548, 560, 575, and 585

ONGOING ASSESSMENT
CHECKPOINTS: pp. 537, 538, 539, 540, 541, 542, 543, 553, 555, 565, 568, 570, 579, 580, and 581
KEY CONCEPTS QUESTIONS:
pp. 544, 545, 557, 571, and 582
STANDARDIZED TESTING:
pp. 561, 576, and 586

MODULE ASSESSMENT
REVIEW AND ASSESSMENT:
pp. 588 and 589
REFLECTING ON THE MODULE:
p. 589

STUDENT RESOURCES
Toolbox, pp. 591–608
Tables, pp. 609–611
Glossary, p. 612
Index
Selected Answers

ORGANIZATION OF THE BOOK

This book contains eight modules. To get an overview of the modules and their themes, look at the Table of Contents starting on p. iv.

THEME APPROACH

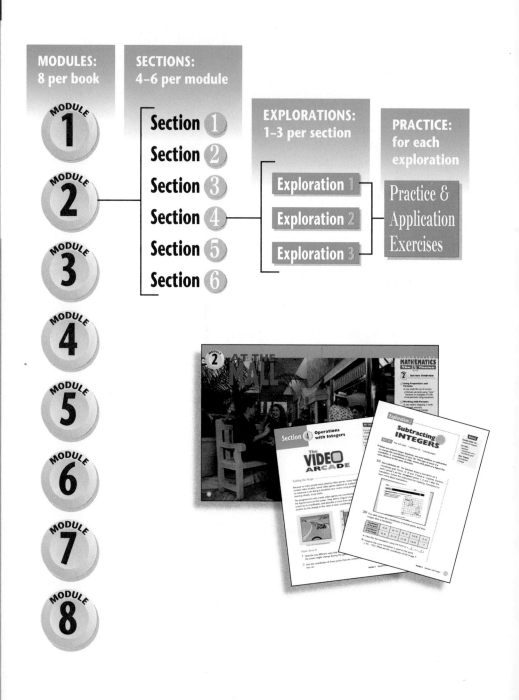

MODULES: 8 per book

SECTIONS: 4–6 per module

EXPLORATIONS: 1–3 per section

PRACTICE: for each exploration

MODULE 1

MODULE 2
- Section 1
- Section 2
- Section 3
- Section 4
- Section 5
- Section 6

- Exploration 1
- Exploration 2
- Exploration 3

Practice & Application Exercises

MODULE 3

MODULE 4

MODULE 5

MODULE 6

MODULE 7

MODULE 8

MODULE THEME & PROJECT

Each module's theme connects the mathematics you are learning to the real world. *At the Mall* is the theme of Module 2. The Module Project that you'll work on is introduced at the beginning of the module.

Connecting Mathematics and the Theme
The math topics you'll be learning and the settings in which you'll be learning them.

MODULE 2 · AT THE MALL

CONNECTING MATHEMATICS The & Theme

MODULE 2 SECTION OVERVIEW

1 Using Proportions and Percents
As you study the use of surveys:
◆ Estimate percents using "nice" fractions or multiples of 10%
◆ Find percents using equations

2 Working with Percents
As you explore shopping in malls:
◆ Estimate percents
◆ Find percents of change

3 Exploring Probability
As you find the chances of winning in a contest:
◆ Find theoretical probability
◆ Find experimental probability by repeating an experiment
◆ Construct tree diagrams

4 Operations with Integers
As you discover how video games are created:
◆ Add and subtract integers
◆ Multiply and divide integers

5 Operations with Fractions
As you explore a mall:
◆ Add and subtract positive and negative fractions

6 Inequalities and Box-and-Whisker Plots
As you read about T-shirt sales:
◆ Write and graph inequalities
◆ Construct box-and-whisker plots

The Module Project

Designing a Game

There are many games that imitate life. But who makes up these games and how much do they imitate? In this module you'll use mathematics to create your own board game about shopping in a mall. Then you'll play your game, refine it, and share it with your class.

More on the Module Project
See pp. 94, 104, 134, and 157.

INTERNET
To learn more about the theme:
http://www.mlmath.com

Completing the Module Project

Designing a Game

Playing the Game During this module you have explored mathematics as it applies to shopping malls. You have designed a game and made game cards, game pieces, and rules for the game. In order to make sure your game runs smoothly, you'll now play the game.

SET UP

Work in a group.
You will need:
• your game

7 With your group, assemble the game and game pieces. Review the rules.

8 Play the game.

9 After you have played the game, discuss each question below in your group.

    a. What math skills did you use while playing the game?

    b. What worked well in your game?

    c. What could you improve?

10 Make any changes necessary to improve your game. You may need to add or change rules.

11 As a group, prepare a presentation to give to the class. Each member of the group can present a part of the game. Include in your presentation the goal of the game, the rules, the mathematics used, the playing pieces, the cards, and your own experience playing the game.

Module 2 Completing the Module Project **157**

The Module Project
As you learn new math skills, you can apply them to your work on the Module Project. By the end of the module, you'll be able to complete the project and to present your results.

SECTION OVERVIEW

ACTIVE LEARNING

SECTION ORGANIZATION

The diagram below illustrates the organization of a section:

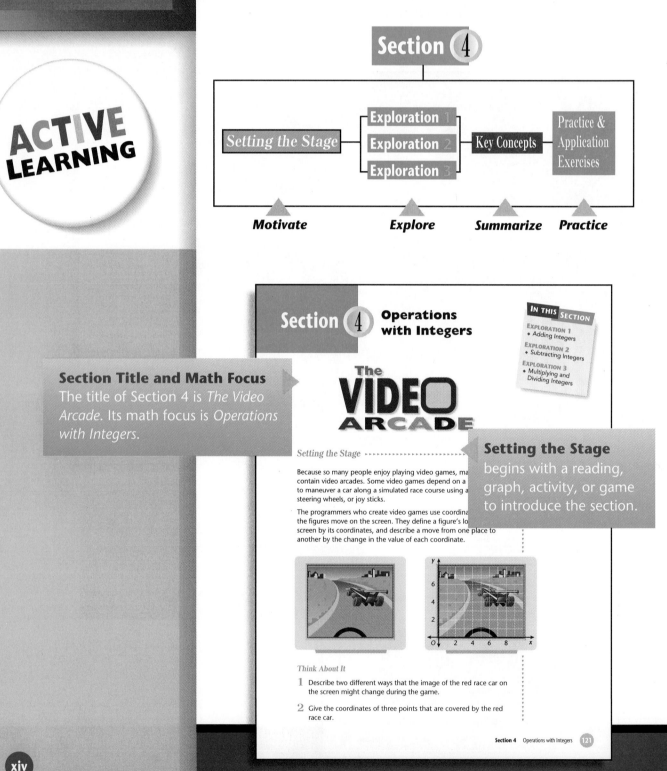

Section Title and Math Focus
The title of Section 4 is *The Video Arcade*. Its math focus is *Operations with Integers*.

Setting the Stage
begins with a reading, graph, activity, or game to introduce the section.

Section 4 Operations with Integers

IN THIS SECTION

EXPLORATION 1
◆ Adding Integers

EXPLORATION 2
◆ Subtracting Integers

EXPLORATION 3
◆ Multiplying and Dividing Integers

The VIDEO ARCADE

Setting the Stage

Because so many people enjoy playing video games, ma[...] contain video arcades. Some video games depend on a [...] to maneuver a car along a simulated race course using a [...] steering wheels, or joy sticks.

The programmers who create video games use coordina[...] the figures move on the screen. They define a figure's lo[...] screen by its coordinates, and describe a move from one place to another by the change in the value of each coordinate.

Think About It

1 Describe two different ways that the image of the red race car on the screen might change during the game.

2 Give the coordinates of three points that are covered by the red race car.

Section 4 Operations with Integers **121**

EXPLORATIONS & KEY CONCEPTS

In the explorations you'll be actively involved in investigating math concepts, learning math skills, and solving problems.

Exploration 2

Subtracting INTEGERS

SET UP You will need: • Labsheet 4C • tracing paper

GOAL

LEARN HOW TO...
• subtract integers

AS YOU...
• explore translations on a coordinate grid

KEY TERMS
• translation
• image

> When you played *Integer Speedway*, you used addition or subtraction to change the coordinates of your car. This type of move is a *translation*. A **translation**, or slide, moves each point of a figure the same distance in the same direction.

19 **Use Labsheet 4C.** The labsheet shows a translation on a coordinate grid. Points *A′*, *B′*, and *C′* (read as "*A*-prime, *B*-prime, and *C*-prime") are the **images** of points *A*, *B*, and *C* after the translation. Follow the instructions for *Exploring Translations* to learn more about translations.

20 This table shows the coordinates of several points and their images after a translation.

Coordinates of the point	(3, 2)	(5, –7)	(0, –3)	(–5, 6)	(x, y)
Coordinates of the image	(2, 5)	(4, –4)	(–1, 0)		

Goal

The math skills and key terms you'll learn.

This as a Class Suppose are programming a video e in which a jester is located int (x, y).

a. Write a translation in the form $(x + \underline{\ ?\ }, y + \underline{\ ?\ })$ that will move the jester to the right 2 units and up 1 unit.

b. Use the form $(x – \underline{\ ?\ }, y – \underline{\ ?\ })$ to write a translation that will move the jester to the left 3 units and down 5 units.

c. Rewrite the translation in part (b) in the form $(x + \underline{\ ?\ }, y + \underline{\ ?\ })$.

d. Explain how any subtraction expression can be written as addition.

22 Suppose the translation $(x – (–3), y – 4)$ is used on the jester shown in Question 21.

a. Write $1 – (–3)$ as an addition expression.

b. Suppose the jester is at point (1, 1). What is its new position after the translation $(x – (–3), y – 4)$?

c. Describe this translation in words.

> **Subtracting Integers** As you saw in Questions 21 and 22, you can write any subtraction problem as an addition problem.

EXAMPLE

Find the difference: $–8 – (–7)$

SAMPLE RESPONSE
$$–8 – (–7) = –8 + 7$$
$$= –1$$

Rewrite subtraction as addition.

Checkpoint

A pause to check for understanding of a math concept or skill.

✔ **QUESTION 23**
...checks that you can subtract integers.

23 ✔ **CHECKPOINT** Find each difference.

a. $23 – (–15)$ **b.** $12 – (–12)$ **c.** $–80 – 22$ **d.** $–65 – (–43)$

HOMEWORK EXERCISES See Exs. 21–30 on p. 132.

126 **Module 2** At

Homework Exercises

There are homework exercises for each exploration.

Section 4
Key Concepts

Key Terms

integer

absolute value

opposite

translation

image

Adding and Subtracting Integers (pp. 122–126)

The sum of two integers may be positive, negative, or zero.

Examples
$$-3 + 5 = 2 \qquad -4 + 1 = -3$$
$$12 + (-12) = 0 \qquad -1 + (-9) = -10$$

The absolute value of a number tells you its distance from 0.

$$|-3| = 3 \qquad |4| = 4$$

To subtract an integer, add its opposite.

Examples $3 – 5 = 3 + (–5) = –2 \qquad 7 – (–2) = 7 + 2 = 9$

A translation, or slide, moves each point of a figure the same distance in the same direction. A translation can be described by adding values to the coordinates of a point. The result of a translation is the image.

Original	Image
A(–4, 2)	A′(1, –2)
B(–3, 3)	B′(2, –1)

Translation: $(x + 5, y + (–4))$

Key Concepts Questions

37 The absolute value and the opposite of –12 are both 12. Is the absolute value of an integer always its opposite? Explain.

38 A negative integer and a positive integer are added. Describe the relationship between the integers being added if their sum is
a. positive **b.** negative **c.** zero

130 Module 2 At the Mall

Key Concepts

A summary of key concepts that can help you study and review the section, and develop note-taking skills.

XV

SECTION OVERVIEW ▶

PRACTICE & APPLICATION

Practice and Application Exercises will give you a chance to practice the skills and concepts in the explorations and apply them in solving many types of problems.

VARIED PRACTICE

Section ④
Practice & Application Exercises

Balanced Practice
These exercises develop numerical and problem solving skills, and the ability to write about and discuss mathematics.

Find each sum.

1. $-23 + (-8)$ 2. $91 + (-10)$ 3. $-15 + 7$
4. $12 + (-12)$ 5. $-88 + (-12)$ 6. $4 + (-10) + 7$

Find the opposite of each integer.

7. -15 8. 101 9. 74 10. -62

Find each absolute value.

11. $|-47|$ 12. $|53|$ 13. $\left|8\frac{1}{2}\right|$ 14. $|-0.42|$

15. Find two different integers with an absolute value of 7.

Solve each equation.

16. $|y| = 12$ 17. $-w = 2$ 18. $|z| = 0$ 19. $-x = -5$

20. Joe earned $15 mowing lawns, then bought a radio for $11. The next day he earned $5. He spent $3 on arcade games. Write an addition expression for his income and expenses.

Find each difference.

21. $5 - 9$ 22. $18 - (-13)$ 23. $2 - (-11)$
24. $-3 - (-3)$ 25. $-10 - 4$ 26. $-7 - (-19)$

27. **Weather** Suppose the temperature was $-18°F$ at 6:00 A.M. and 23°F at 2:00 P.M. What is the difference in the temperatures?

28. The translation $(x + 2, y + (-3))$ is applied to figure PQRST.

   a. Give the coordinates of the image points P′, Q′, R′, S′, and T′.

   b. **Writing** Describe in words a translation that moves PQRST to the opposite side of the vertical axis.

29. After the translation $(x + 5, y + 2)$, the image of a point is $(12, 16)$. What are the coordinates of the original point?

30. For each pair of coordinates, describe the translation in two ways, one using only addition and one using only subtraction. Then show each translation on a graph.

	Original	Image	Translations
a.	$L(2, 4)$	$L'(1, 5)$	$(x + \underline{?}, y + \underline{?})$ or $(x - \underline{?}, y - \underline{?})$
b.	$M(0, -7)$	$M'(2, -1)$	$(x + \underline{?}, y + \underline{?})$ or $(x - \underline{?}, y - \underline{?})$
c.	$N(-6, 3)$	$N'(-10, -3)$	$(x + \underline{?}, y + \underline{?})$ or $(x - \underline{?}, y - \underline{?})$

Find each product or quotient.

31. $8(-9)$ 32. $-16 \cdot 20$ 33. $-2(-7)(-4)$ 34. $-3(-8)(2)$
35. $-27 \div 9$ 36. $\frac{-56}{-8}$ 37. $-48 \div (-6)$ 38. $\frac{72}{-3}$

Algebra Connection Evaluate each expression when $a = -16$, $b = -4$, and $c = 48$.

39. ab 40. bc 41. $c \div a$ 42. $\frac{a}{b}$

43. **Football** On each of three consecutive plays, a football team loses 5 yd. Suppose lost yardage is represented by a negative integer. Write a multiplication expression that describes the total change in yardage and find the total number of yards lost.

Use this information for Exercises 44 and 45: On a test, each correct answer scores 5 points, each incorrect answer scores -2 points, and each question left unanswered scores 0 points.

44. Suppose a student answers 15 questions on the test correctly, 4 incorrectly, and does not answer 1 question. Write an expression for the student's score and find the score.

45. **Challenge** Suppose you answer all 20 questions on the test. What is the greatest number of questions you can answer incorrectly and still get a positive score? Explain your reasoning.

Reflecting ◀▶ on the Section

46. Suppose you multiply each coordinate of each point of a figure by -1. Describe the visual effect created by this operation.

Visual THINKING
Exercise 46 checks your understanding of opposites.

Spiral ◀▶ Review

A backpack contains 4 black pens, 2 blue pens, and a red pen. Find the theoretical probability of each event. (Module 2, p. 115)

47. pulling out a blue pen on the first try

48. *not* pulling out a black pen on the first try

49. pulling out a red pen after two black pens have been removed

Find each quotient. Write each answer in lowest terms. (Toolbox, p. 598)

50. $\frac{3}{8} \div \frac{1}{4}$ 51. $\frac{7}{12} \div \frac{5}{6}$ 52. $\frac{33}{39} \div \frac{11}{13}$ 53. $\frac{10}{21} \div \frac{7}{9}$

Replace each $\underline{?}$ with the number that will make the fractions equivalent. (Toolbox, p. 597)

54. $\frac{1}{5} = \frac{?}{30}$ 55. $\frac{1}{3} = \frac{?}{24}$ 56. $\frac{5}{8} = \frac{35}{?}$

57. $\frac{3}{10} = \frac{?}{110}$ 58. $\frac{3}{4} = \frac{21}{?}$ 59. $\frac{9}{16} = \frac{54}{?}$

Reflecting on the Section
helps you pull together what you've learned in the form of an oral report, journal writing, visual thinking, research, or a discussion.

ADDITIONAL PRACTICE

At the end of every section, you'll find Extra Skill Practice. You can use these exercises to check that you understand important skills before starting the next section.

Section 4
Extra Skill Practice

Find each sum.

1. –12 + 16   2. 27 + (–49)   3. –78 + 25 + (–4)   4. –130 + (–65)

Find the opposite of each integer.

5. 512   6. –43   7. –1   8. 38

Find each absolute value.

9. $|29|$ 10. $|-83|$ 11. $\left|-3\frac{3}{4}\right|$ 12. $|-1.45|$

Find each difference.

13. –32 – 45   14. 26 – (–13)   15. –16 – (–22)   16. 55 – (–55)

Find each product.

18. 4(–15)   19. –7 · 6   20. –12(–5)

otient.

22. –88 ÷ 22   23. $\frac{-54}{-3}$ 24. $\frac{95}{-5}$

expression.

26. 27 + (–33)   27. –24 ÷ (–6)

29. $\frac{-76}{19}$ 30. –41 + (–11)

32. 9 · (–7)   33. –13 – 13

Standardized Testing

develops your ability to answer questions in different formats: multiple-choice, open-ended, free response, and performance task.

Standardized Testing ▶ Open-ended

1. Give an example of two numbers that fit each description below. If no numbers fit the description, explain why.

d the product of 2 numbers are negative.

mbers is 0 and the product is positive.

mbers is positive and the quotient is negative.

f rectangle *ABCD* intersect the *x*-axis, and the ersect the *y*-axis. Give a set of possible , *C*, and *D*. Then write the coordinates of er the translation ($x - 4$, $y + 6$).

Section 4 Operations with Integers **135**

Reflecting ▶ on the Section

14. Find three sale ads in a newspaper or magazine that use percent discounts. Use estimation or mental math to determine the items on which you would save the greatest amount and the least amount. Do you always save the most with the greatest percent discount? Explain.

> **RESEARCH**
> Exercise 14 checks that you can apply percent of change.

Spiral ▶ Review

Use a proportion to find each percent. (Module 2, p. 90)

15. 28% of 5200   16. 2% of 485   17. 77% of 830

18. 100% of 61   19. 3.8% of 7900   20. 95% of 350

Find the greatest common factor and the least common multiple for each pair of numbers. (Toolbox, p. 596)

21. 10, 15   22. 12, 16   23. 9, 30   24. 21, 49

Replace each ? with >, <, or =. (Toolbox, p. 597)

25. $\frac{1}{4}$? $\frac{1}{3}$ 26. $\frac{3}{8}$? $\frac{1}{2}$ 27. $\frac{2}{3}$? $\frac{12}{18}$ 28. $\frac{7}{8}$? $\frac{5}{6}$

Extension ▶▶

Percent of Profit

Buyers are usually interested in the percent of decrease or increase in the cost of a product. Sellers are interested in how much profit has changed. Profit is based on the selling price, *s*, of an item and the cost, *c*, of making an item. Two ways to calculate the percent of profit are shown at the right.

Percent of profit on cost = $\frac{s-c}{c}$

Percent of profit on selling price = $\frac{s-c}{s}$

29. Suppose a candy bar costs 35¢ to make, and sells for 50¢. What is the percent of profit on cost? What is the percent of profit on selling price?

30. Which percent of profit in Exercise 29 was larger? Do you think this will always be true? Explain your thinking.

Extension

problems challenge you to extend what you have learned and to apply it in a new setting.

Section 2 Working with Percents **103**

CALCULATORS & COMPUTERS

There are many opportunities to use calculators, as well as mental-math and paper-and-pencil methods. Special Technology pages show you how to use computer programs and graphing technology to explore concepts and solve problems in the module.

TOOLS FOR LEARNING

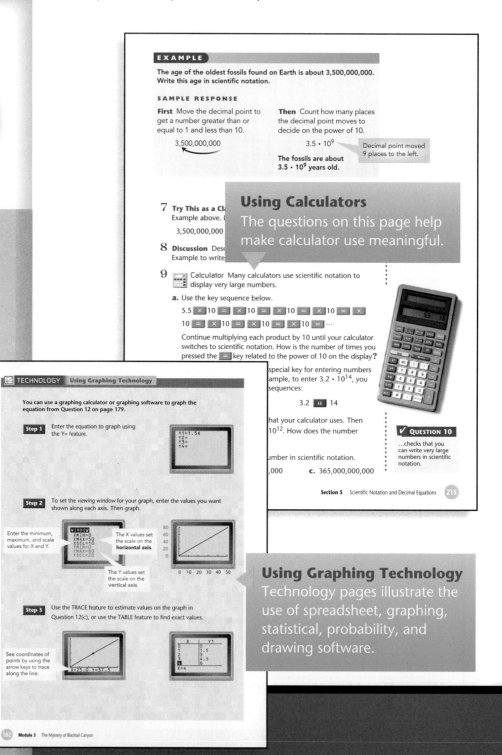

EXAMPLE

The age of the oldest fossils found on Earth is about 3,500,000,000. Write this age in scientific notation.

SAMPLE RESPONSE

First Move the decimal point to get a number greater than or equal to 1 and less than 10.

3,500,000,000

Then Count how many places the decimal point moves to decide on the power of 10.

$3.5 \cdot 10^9$

Decimal point moved 9 places to the left.

The fossils are about $3.5 \cdot 10^9$ years old.

Using Calculators
The questions on this page help make calculator use meaningful.

7 **Try This as a Cl**... Example above. ...

3,500,000,000 ...

8 **Discussion** Des... Example to write...

9 Calculator Many calculators use scientific notation to display very large numbers.

a. Use the key sequence below.

5.5 × 10 = × 10 = × 10 = × 10 = ×
10 = × 10 = × 10 = × 10 = ...

Continue multiplying each product by 10 until your calculator switches to scientific notation. How is the number of times you pressed the = key related to the power of 10 on the display?

...special key for entering numbers ...ample, to enter $3.2 \cdot 10^{14}$, you ...sequences:

3.2 **EE** 14

...hat your calculator uses. Then ...10^{12}. How does the number

...umber in scientific notation.

,000   **c.** 365,000,000,000

✔ QUESTION 10

...checks that you can write very large numbers in scientific notation.

Section 5 Scientific Notation and Decimal Equations   **215**

TECHNOLOGY   Using Graphing Technology

You can use a graphing calculator or graphing software to graph the equation from Question 12 on page 179.

Step 1   Enter the equation to graph using the Y= feature.

Y1=1.5X
Y2=
Y3=
Y4=

Step 2   To set the *viewing window* for your graph, enter the values you want shown along each axis. Then graph.

Enter the minimum, maximum, and scale values for X and Y.

WINDOW
XMIN=0
XMAX=50
XSCL=10
YMIN=0
YMAX=80
YSCL=20

The X values set the scale on the **horizontal axis.**

The Y values set the scale on the **vertical axis.**

Step 3   Use the TRACE feature to estimate values on the graph in Question 12(c), or use the TABLE feature to find exact values.

See coordinates of points by using the arrow keys to trace along the line.

X=25.0 Y=37.5

X   Y1
0   0
1   1.5
2   3
3   4.5
4   6
X=4

Using Graphing Technology
Technology pages illustrate the use of spreadsheet, graphing, statistical, probability, and drawing software.

ASSESSMENT & PORTFOLIOS

In each module there are a number of questions and projects that help you check your progress and reflect on what you have learned. These pages are listed under *Assessment Options* in the Table of Contents.

E^2 stands for Extended Exploration— a problem solving project that you'll want to add to your portfolio.

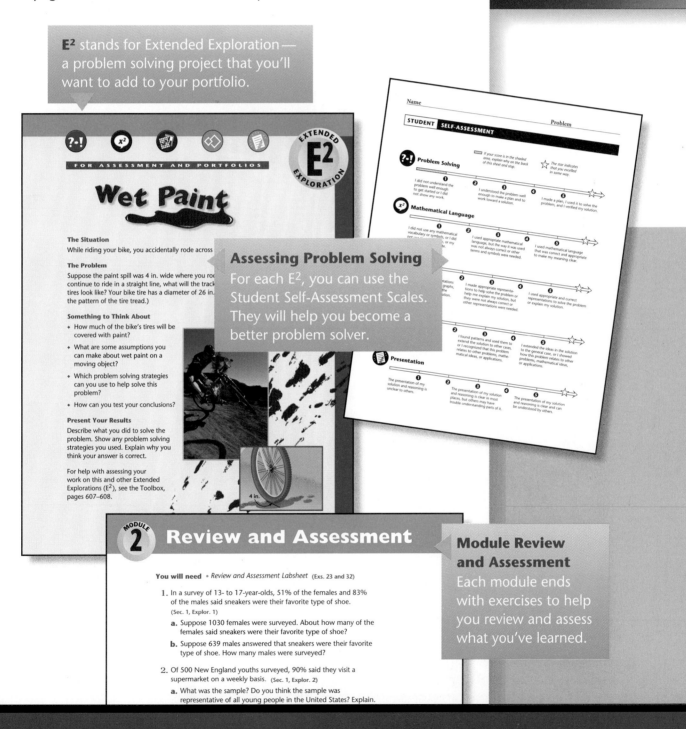

FOR ASSESSMENT AND PORTFOLIOS

EXTENDED E^2 EXPLORATION

Wet Paint

The Situation

While riding your bike, you accidentally rode across

The Problem

Suppose the paint spill was 4 in. wide where you ro continue to ride in a straight line, what will the track tires look like? Your bike tire has a diameter of 26 in. the pattern of the tire tread.)

Something to Think About

◆ How much of the bike's tires will be covered with paint?

◆ What are some assumptions you can make about wet paint on a moving object?

◆ Which problem solving strategies can you use to help solve this problem?

◆ How can you test your conclusions?

Present Your Results

Describe what you did to solve the problem. Show any problem solving strategies you used. Explain why you think your answer is correct.

For help with assessing your work on this and other Extended Explorations (E^2), see the Toolbox, pages 607–608.

4 in.

Assessing Problem Solving

For each E^2, you can use the Student Self-Assessment Scales. They will help you become a better problem solver.

Name

Problem

STUDENT SELF-ASSESSMENT

If your score is in the shaded area, explain why on the back of this sheet and stop.

☆ *The star indicates that you excelled in some way.*

?·! Problem Solving

❶ I did not understand the problem well enough to get started or I did not show any work.

❷

❸ I understood the problem well enough to make a plan and to work toward a solution.

❹

❺ I made a plan, I used it to solve the problem, and I verified my solution.

x^2 Mathematical Language

❶ I did not use any mathematical vocabulary or symbols, or I did

❷

❸ I used appropriate mathematical language, but the way it was used was not always correct or other terms and symbols were needed.

❹

❺ I used mathematical language that was correct and appropriate to make my meaning clear.

I made appropriate representations to help solve the problem or help me explain my solution, but they were not always correct or other representations were needed.

I used appropriate and correct representations to solve the problem or explain my solution.

I found patterns and used them to extend the solution to other cases, or I recognized that this problem relates to other problems, mathematical ideas, or applications.

I extended the ideas in the solution to the general case, or I showed how this problem relates to other problems, mathematical ideas, or applications.

Presentation

❶ The presentation of my solution and reasoning is unclear to others.

❷

❸ The presentation of my solution and reasoning is clear in most places, but others may have trouble understanding parts of it.

❹

❺ The presentation of my solution and reasoning is clear and can be understood by others.

MODULE 2 Review and Assessment

Module Review and Assessment

Each module ends with exercises to help you review and assess what you've learned.

You will need • *Review and Assessment Labsheet* (Exs. 23 and 32)

1. In a survey of 13- to 17-year-olds, 51% of the females and 83% of the males said sneakers were their favorite type of shoe. (Sec. 1, Explor. 1)

   a. Suppose 1030 females were surveyed. About how many of the females said sneakers were their favorite type of shoe?

   b. Suppose 639 males answered that sneakers were their favorite type of shoe. How many males were surveyed?

2. Of 500 New England youths surveyed, 90% said they visit a supermarket on a weekly basis. (Sec. 1, Explor. 2)

   a. What was the sample? Do you think the sample was representative of all young people in the United States? Explain.

AMAZING
feats
facts

CONNECTING

MATHEMATICS
The & Theme

and FICTION

The Module Project

Fact or Fiction

Every day you are bombarded with stories that seem amazing or incredible. In this project, you'll use mathematics to uncover the truth in some of these claims. Then you'll display your own amazing claims on a poster to share with your class.

More on the Module Project
See pp. 13, 25, 51, and 77.

INTERNET
To learn more about the theme:
http://www.mlmath.com

Section 1 Problem Solving and Rates

IN THIS SECTION

EXPLORATION 1
◆ Problem Solving Approach

EXPLORATION 2
◆ Using Rates

Warm-Up Exercises
See page 3.

We've Got a Problem Here

◂◂◂Setting the Stage

One of the most amazing and courageous feats of space travel occurred not because of success, but because of failure. Apollo 13 was the third manned space flight to the moon, but 56 hours into the flight something went wrong. Astronauts Jim Lovell, Fred Haise, and Jack Swigert were 200,000 miles from Earth when they heard a loud bang.

At first, Lovell and Swigert thought that Haise had released a valve, as planned, in Aquarius. But Haise, now back in the CM [command module], and scanning the instrument panel, saw that one of the main electrical systems of Apollo 13 was deteriorating. Just before 10:10 p.m., Swigert radioed the words that drew mankind together in a common concern: "Hey, we've got a problem here."

Apollo 13: "Houston, We've Got a Problem."
NASA

After checking the extent of the problem, NASA engineers at Mission Control in Houston decided there would be no moon landing. Now the mission was to get the three astronauts home alive!

Think About It ▸▸▸▸▸▸▸▸▸▸▸▸▸▸▸▸▸▸▸▸▸▸▸▸▸▸▸▸▸▸▸▸

1 Describe at least two problems that an astronaut in space might have that would not be a problem on Earth. **Sample Response: Supplies are limited to what has been stocked for the trip; having enough air to breathe.**

2 After the explosion, Apollo 13 was traveling at about 2000 miles per hour. If the crew could come straight home, about how long would it take to return to Earth at this speed? **100 h or 4 days and 4 hours**

▸ **In this module you'll read about some amazing people and use mathematics to investigate some amazing claims.**

WARM-UP EXERCISES

1. Name three different problem-solving strategies.
Possible answers: act it out, make a model, make a picture or diagram, make an organized list, try a simpler problem, examine a related problem, use an equation, guess and check, work backward, use logical reasoning

Write each fraction in simplest form.

2. $\frac{6}{32}$ $\frac{3}{16}$

3. $\frac{7}{49}$ $\frac{1}{7}$

4. $\frac{12}{3}$ 4

Exploration 1 ▸▸▸▸▸▸▸▸▸▸▸▸▸▸▸▸▸▸▸▸▸▸▸▸▸▸

Problem Solving Approach

SET UP | *Work in a group of four. You will need a bag of materials from your teacher.*

GOAL

LEARN HOW TO...
◆ use a 4-step problem solving approach

AS YOU...
◆ study a problem faced by the crew of *Apollo 13*

▸ **The first step in solving a problem is to understand it. Engineers at Mission Control in Houston worked together to understand and help solve the problems faced by the Apollo 13 crew.**

The News

VOLUME 252   25 cents

Oxygen tank explodes on Apollo 13

NASA engineers announced today that the loud bang heard on Apollo 13 was one of the oxygen tanks exploding. While the crew has enough oxygen to return to Earth, the air they breathe needs to be cleaned by air scrubbers. Without them, a deadly build-up of carbon dioxide will result. The air scrubbers in the lunar module will last only about 36 hours, but the crew needs 80 hours of clean air. The air scrubbers used in the command module are not designed for use in the lunar module.

3 Describe the problem in the article above in your own words.

The crew had 36 h worth of air-scrubbers that had to last 80 h.

▶ The article below describes the next steps in the problem solving approach used by NASA engineers.

Dangerous carbon dioxide levels threatened Apollo 13 crew

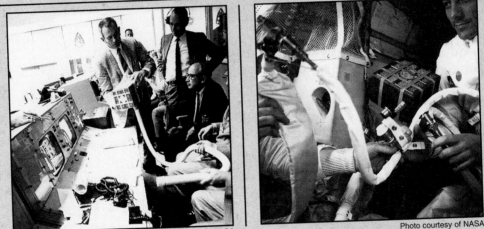

Photo courtesy of NASA

Photo courtesy of NASA

HOUSTON, TX- As carbon dioxide levels became dangerously high on Apollo 13, engineers in Houston had little time to make a plan. Their plan was to build a model of an air scrubber using items the astronauts had on board: cardboard, duct tape, and plastic bags. To carry out their plan, engineers tested the model air scrubber to make sure it worked. Since they could not show their invention to the astronauts, engineers explained in great detail to the Apollo 13 crew how to make an air scrubber.

"We want you to take the tape and cut out two pieces about three feet long, or a good arm's length,...The next step is to stop up the bypass hole in the bottom of the cannister....We recommend you use a wet-wipe or cut off a piece of sock and stuff it in there..."

Joe Kerwin *as told to* Andrew Chalkin in *A Man on the Moon*

When the air scrubber was in place, the NASA team and the Apollo 13 crew could look back at their solution. The carbon dioxide levels dropped - the air scrubber worked.

4 **Discussion** The problem solving approach used by the engineers at Mission Control can help you solve many problems. **See Additional Answers.**

a. Describe how the strategies *make a diagram* or *act it out* could be helpful in the situation described in the article.

b. Suppose the carbon dioxide levels did not decrease. What would be the next step for the engineers and the crew?

▶ Just as the NASA engineers worked together, you and your classmates will work together to solve many different problems. How well do you work in a group? What can you do to help your team? Think about these questions as your team uses the 4-step approach to solve the following problem.

A 4-Step Problem Solving Approach
- Understand the problem
- Make a plan
- Carry out the plan
- Look back

See🌱 Moving Problem

A deep gorge 10 ft across and 20 mi long separates your team. The teammates on one side of the gorge have 7 rare seeds that must be transported within 2 min to the rest of the team for delivery to a laboratory.

Your team must find a way to get the seeds across the gorge unharmed. The seeds cannot be thrown, rolled, or kicked. Like the astronauts on *Apollo 13*, you have a limited supply of materials.

5 Your team has 5 min to understand your problem and make a plan to solve it. Then you'll have 4 min to build your "seed mover" You'll use a bag of materials provided by your teacher.

   a. Your teacher will tell you when to start. Then discuss the problem and agree on a plan. You may alter any of the materials except the scissors. For example, you may cut the bag or the string, but you cannot take apart the scissors.
Check students' work.

   b. Build your seed mover.
Check students' work.

6 Now that your team has planned and built a seed mover, you have 2 min to carry out your plan by demonstrating it to the class.
Check students' work.

7 Write instructions for building your seed mover. The person following the instructions cannot see you or your invention.
Answers will vary. Check students' work.

8 **Discussion** Look back at your solution to the seed-moving problem. How did working in a group help you make a plan? Were you able to get all the seeds safely across the gorge within 2 min? What could you have done better? What did you learn?
Answers will vary. Check students' work.

HOMEWORK EXERCISES ▶ See Exs. 1–4 on p. 10.

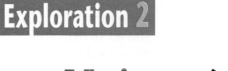

GOAL

LEARN HOW TO...
- ◆ use rates to solve problems

AS YOU...
- ◆ perform calculations related to space flight

KEY TERM
- ◆ rate
- ◆ unit rate

Using / RATES

▶ Imagine having to make mathematical calculations that affect your chances of getting back to Earth. Here is how astronaut Jim Lovell felt aboard Apollo 13.

> . . . he was seized by a momentary and unaccustomed uncertainty. . . 3 times 5 is 15, isn't it? 175 minus 82 is 93, isn't it? With the clock ticking down and so much riding on these rudimentary calculations, Lovell all at once found himself doubting his ability to add and subtract.
>
> *Lost Moon,* Jim Lovell and Jeffrey Kluger

9 Another problem for Apollo 13 was a shortage of water. The equipment on the spacecraft would overheat if it was not cooled continually by water.

a. It took about 6.3 lb of water per hour to cool the equipment. How much water was needed for 2 hours? for 4 hours? for 24 hours? about 12.6 lb, about 25.2 lb, about 151.2 lb

b. NASA engineers calculated that it would take Apollo 13 about 91 hours to return to Earth. How much water was needed to cool the equipment during the return flight? about 573.3 lb

FOR ▶ HELP

with *ratios,*
see
TOOLBOX, p. 597

▶ In Question 9, a *rate* was given to describe how much water was needed to cool the equipment on Apollo 13. A **rate** is a ratio that compares two quantities measured in different units. Rates describe how one quantity depends on another.

6.3 lb of water per hour

You can write this as $\frac{6.3\ lb}{1\ h}$ or **6.3 lb/h**.

10 a. Which two quantities are being compared in the rate above?
 amount of water and length of time

b. What does the amount of water needed depend on?
 the length of time

▶ When you use rates to solve problems, you may find it helpful to keep track of the units involved.

EXAMPLE

Apollo 13 had only **338 lb** of water on board. To see whether the crew had enough water to cool the equipment during the **91 h** trip back home, you can multiply:

$$\frac{6.3 \text{ lb}}{1 \cancel{h}} \cdot 91 \cancel{h} = 573.3 \text{ lb}$$

Notice that the **hour** units divide out. The answer is a number of **pounds**.

▶ If water was used at a rate of 6.3 lb/h, the crew would need more than the 338 lb. They did not have enough water.

11 The Apollo 13 crew was able to reduce the rate water was used for cooling to 3.5 lb/h. Did this solve the problem of having enough water to cool the equipment during the 91 h trip? Yes.

12 ✔ **CHECKPOINT** The astronauts also needed drinking water. On the final two days of the flight, each astronaut limited himself to 6 oz of water per day.

  a. What rate describes how much water the astronauts drank? Which two quantities are being compared? 6 oz/day; amount of water and length of time

  b. During the two final days in space, about how much water did the three crew members drink? 36 oz

  c. How many pounds of water is your answer to part (b)? (16 oz of water weighs about 1 lb.) 2.25 lb

✔ **QUESTION 12**

...checks that you can solve a problem involving rates.

▶ **Unit Rates** At one point in its journey, Apollo 13 was 12,000 mi from the moon. At the speed they were traveling, it would have taken them 4 h to reach the moon. You can use a **unit rate** to describe the speed of the spaceship.

EXAMPLE

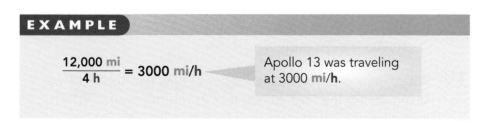

$$\frac{12,000 \text{ mi}}{4 \text{ h}} = 3000 \text{ mi/h}$$

Apollo 13 was traveling at 3000 **mi/h**.

13 Why is 3000 mi/h called a *unit rate*?

Sample Response: It describes a quantity in relation to 1 unit of another quantity.

14 ✔ **CHECKPOINT** The members of the Apollo 13 crew lost a total of 31.5 lb in 6 days, more than any other Apollo crew. This weight loss was due in part to food and water rationing on Apollo 13. What was the average weight loss per day for the crew? **5.25 lb**

▶ **The crew of Apollo 13 knew they were almost home when they successfully penetrated Earth's atmosphere.**

> . . . the steadily thickening layers of [Earth's] atmosphere had slowed their 25,000-mile-per-hour plunge to a comparatively gentle 300-mile-per-hour free fall. . . . [Lovell] looked at his altimeter: it read 35,000 ft.
>
> *Lost Moon,* Jim Lovell and Jeffrey Kluger

▶ **When the crew reached an altitude of about 20,000 ft, the spacecraft's parachutes opened, slowing the ship's speed to about 20 mi/h.**

15. a. Sample Response: There are 5280 ft in a mile and 20 times 5280 is 105,600.
b. less than an hour; They will fall 105,600 ft in one hour and 20,000 ft is less than that.

15 To get a better sense of how long it might take Apollo 13 to fall to Earth, you can convert the units of the ship's speed.

a. Explain why the rate 20 mi/h is equivalent to 105,600 ft/h.

b. Would it take Apollo 13 more or less than an hour to fall 20,000 ft? Explain why.

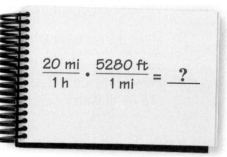

$$\frac{20 \text{ mi}}{1 \text{ h}} \cdot \frac{5280 \text{ ft}}{1 \text{ mi}} = \underline{\quad ? \quad}$$

16 ✔ **CHECKPOINT** Look back at your work in Question 15.

a. Convert Apollo 13's final falling speed of 20 mi/h to feet per minute. **1760 ft/min**

b. Estimate how many minutes it took Apollo 13 to fall 20,000 ft at 20 mi/h. **about 11 min**

17. Sample Response: mi/h; ft/min; From everyday experience I know how fast 20 mi/h is. I could estimate 20,000 ÷ 2000 to figure it took about 10 min.

17 Which units give you a better sense of how fast Apollo 13 was falling during the final 20,000 ft of its return voyage? Which units give you a better sense of how long it took? Explain.

HOMEWORK EXERCISES ▶ See Exs. 5–22 on pp. 10–12.

Key Concepts

Problem Solving (pp. 3–5)

In this section you explored a 4-step problem solving approach.

Understand the Problem Identify questions that need to be answered. Find the information you need to answer them. It may be helpful to restate the problem in your own words.

Make a Plan Choose a problem solving strategy. Decide what calculations, if any, are needed. Some problem solving strategies are:

- act it out
- make a model
- make a picture or diagram
- make an organized list
- try a simpler problem

- examine a related problem
- use an equation
- guess and check
- work backward
- use logical reasoning

Carry Out the Plan You may need to change your strategy or use a different approach, depending on how well your original plan works.

Look Back Is your solution reasonable? Is there another way you could have solved the problem? Are there other problems you can solve the same way?

Rates (pp. 6–8)

A rate compares two quantities measured in different units. It tells you how one quantity depends on the other. A unit rate gives an amount per one unit.

Example Suppose you pay $24 for 4 movie tickets. You can convert this rate to a unit rate of $6 per ticket. Both rates describe how the amount of money you pay depends on the number of tickets you buy.

CLOSURE QUESTION

What are the four steps in the problem solving approach? What is a rate?

Sample Response: Understand the Problem, Make a Plan, Carry Out the Plan, Look Back; A rate compares two quantities measured in different units.

rate

unit rate

18. Sample Response: Make a table to record the distance traveled by each student to school and the length of time it takes them to get to school. Establish a unit rate, then compare the rates.

18 **Key Concepts Question** Suppose you want to know which student in your class travels the fastest from home to school. Describe a plan for solving this problem. Be sure to talk about rates. What are some calculations you may have to perform?

Section 1

YOU WILL NEED

For Ex. 23:
♦ graph paper

1. Suppose an amateur astronomer wants to estimate the number of visible stars in the part of the evening sky shown at left.

   a. Describe a strategy for solving the problem. **See below.**

   b. Use your strategy to estimate the number of stars in the picture. **Sample Response: 196 stars**

2. Jupiter revolves around the Sun about once every 12 Earth years. Saturn revolves around the Sun about once every 30 Earth years. In 1982, Jupiter and Saturn appeared very close to each other. About when will Jupiter and Saturn appear together again? **2042**

3. Suppose you are studying 8 rocks brought back by an Apollo mission. Seven rocks weigh 1 lb each. One rock weighs more than 1 lb.

   a. Describe how you can use a balance scale to find out which rock is the heaviest one. **See below.**

   b. What is the least number of weighings you could use to find the heaviest rock?
   3 weighings

A balance scale is "balanced" when the weight of an object on one side equals the weight of an object on the other side.

1. a. Sample Response: Divide the photograph into equal sections, count the number of stars in one section and multiply by the number of sections.

3. a. Sample Response: Weigh 4 rocks on each side; take the heavier side, divide it in half, and weigh 2 rocks on each side; take the heavier side, divide it in half and weigh 1 rock on each side.

4. **Challenge** Suppose two identical tanks are to be filled with water. The first tank begins filling 5 min before the second tank begins filling. The first tank can be filled in 30 min. The second tank can be filled in 20 min.

   a. How much time will pass before both tanks hold the same amount of water? **15 min**

   b. Does your solution seem reasonable? Use another method to check your solution. **Yes. Alternate solutions may vary. Check students' work.**

Name the units in each rate. Then write a unit rate.

5. 360 mi in 6 h
   miles per hour; 60 mi/h

6. $30 for 6 pairs of socks
   cost in dollars for a pair of socks; $5/pair

7. 1.5 lb for $3.00
   cost in dollars per lb; $2/lb

8. $3.24 for 12 oranges
   cost in dollars of an orange; $.27/orange

Copy and complete each equation.

9. 1 mi/min = __?__ mi/h **60**

10. 59 in./year = __?__ in./month
about 4.9

11. 8000 lb/min = __?__ lb/h
480,000

12. $.03 per oz = __?__ per lb **$.48**

13. **Biology** The typical human heart pumps 0.023 gal of blood each second. Convert this to a rate that is easier for you to understand. Explain why you chose the rate. **Sample Response: 1.38 gal/min; It is easier to think of about $1\frac{1}{3}$ gal because gallon containers are used frequently.**

14. **World Records** The modern game of footbag is based on an old Native American game. The game involves keeping a small stuffed cloth bag in the air by kicking it with your foot. In 1996, Tricia George set a footbag record for women's singles at Eugene, Oregon, with 20,717 kicks in 3 h 15 min.

   a. Find Tricia's "kick rate" in kicks per minute. If necessary, round to the nearest whole number.
   about 106 kicks/min

   b. The overall singles record set in 1997 is 63,326 kicks in about 8 h 51 min. Compare this kick rate with Tricia George's kick rate. **At about 119 kicks/min, this rate is greater than Tricia George's.**

Open-ended For Exercises 15–18, write a word problem for each calculation. Solve the problem.

15. 55 mi/h · 6 h

16. $.99 per oz · 6 oz

17. $3.99 per day · 4 days

18. 19 mi/gal · 8 gal

19. a. In one year, as much as 120 in. of rain can fall on the Amazon rain forest in South America. On average, about how much rain falls per month? **10 in.**

   b. **Research** Find the amount of rain your state receives each year. About how much rain falls per month? How does your state's monthly rainfall compare with the rain forest's?
   Answers will vary.

20. **Challenge** A light-year is the distance light travels in one year. Light travels at a speed of 186,282 miles per second.

   a. Change the rate 186,282 miles per second to miles per hour.
   670,615,200 mi/h

   b. How fast does light travel in miles per day? **16,094,764,800 mi/day**

   c. How far does light travel in one year? **5,874,589,152,000 mi/yr**

   d. The sun is about 93 million miles from Earth. Estimate the amount of time it takes light from the sun to reach Earth.
   slightly more than 8 min

FOR ▶ HELP

with *relationships between units*, see
TABLE OF MEASURES, p. 610

For Exercises 15–18, Sample Responses are given.

15. The Taylor family drove on interstate highways at a rate of 55 mi/h for 6 h. How many miles did they travel? 330 mi

16. The unit price given for cinnamon is $0.99 per ounce. What is the cost of 6 oz? $5.94

17. Value Video rents newly released movies for $3.99. What is the total cost of the rental if a movie is rented for 4 days? $15.96

18. My truck averages 19 mi/gal of gas. About how many miles could I expect to drive on 8 gal of gas? 152 mi

21. **a.** It took about 21 months for the space probe Pioneer 10 to travel from Mars to Jupiter. This distance was about 620,000,000 mi. What was Pioneer 10's average speed in miles per month? in miles per day? in miles per hour?

b. Which rate gives you the best sense of how fast Pioneer 10 was traveling? Explain. **Sample Response: miles per hour; It is more common to measure speed in miles per hour.**

Reflecting ◀▶ on the Section

22. Suppose you are writing an article for a science magazine and need to describe the distance from Earth to Mars. You need to make this fact as interesting as possible.

a. Find out the distance from Earth to Mars. To make this fact interesting, you may want to compare the  distance to Mars to distances that are familiar to most people.

b. Once you have written your fact, describe how you approached the task. Be sure to talk about how you applied the 4-step problem solving approach outlined on page 9.

Spiral ◀▶ Review

23. Plot the points on graph paper and connect them alphabetically. Then connect point *N* to point *A* to see a rough outline of *Odyssey*. *Odyssey* included the command and service modules of Apollo 13. (Toolbox, p. 602) **See Additional Answers.**

A(4, 10)	*B*(6, 8)	*C*(6, 5)	*D*(5, 4)
E(4, 3)	*F*(5, 1)	*G*(4, 0)	*H*(3, 0)
I(2, 1)	*J*(3, 3)	*K*(2, 4)	*L*(1, 5)
M(1, 8)	*N*(3, 10)		

24. Find the mean, the median, the mode, and the range of the ice skater's competition scores shown below. (Toolbox, p. 606)

10, 10, 9.8, 9.8, 10, 9.9, 9.7, 9.8, 9.6
mean: about 9.84, median: 9.8, mode: 9.8 and 10; range: 0.4

Write each percent as a fraction in lowest terms. (Toolbox, p. 599)

25. 40% $\frac{2}{5}$ **26.** 80% $\frac{4}{5}$ **27.** 20% $\frac{1}{5}$ **28.** 35% $\frac{7}{20}$

Beginning the Module Project

Fact or Fiction?

Have you ever heard or read information that seemed too unlikely to be true? For example, "The average person eats 1095 lb of food a year!" or "The surface temperature of Venus is perfect for frying eggs."

Throughout this module you'll look at similar claims and check to see if they are true or false. Then you'll do research and gather data to write your own amazing claims. Finally, you'll share your claims with your class by making a poster to display the evidence that makes your claims true or false.

1 **Using a 4-Step Approach** Decide whether the following claim is reasonable. Use the 4-step problem solving approach shown below to organize your work.
See Additional Answers.

A stack of 200 billion pennies would reach from Earth to the moon.

Understand the Problem	Rewrite the claim in your own words. Decide what additional information you need to prove the claim.
Make a Plan	List some problem solving strategies you can try. Decide which strategy will be best.
Carry Out the Plan	As you carry out your plan, keep careful records of everything you do and the results of your work.
Look Back	Decide whether your solution is correct. If possible, check your solution by solving the problem another way.

Use the 4-step problem solving approach to solve Exercises 1 and 2.

1. Four different types of tents are being used on a camping trip. They include 12-person, 6-person, 5-person, and 2-person tents. Find a possible combination of tents to sleep exactly 26 people

    a. if only one 12-person tent is used. See Additional Answers.

    b. if the 12-person tent is not used.

    c. if at least one 5-person tent is used.

2. On a hike, a climber needs to measure 5 c of water to make soup. The climber has two pots, one that holds $3\frac{1}{2}$ pt and one that holds $1\frac{1}{2}$ pt. Explain how the climber can measure exactly 5 c of water using the two pots and a large container. (1 pt = 2 c)
   Sample Response: Measure two $3\frac{1}{2}$ pt pots of water then remove three $1\frac{1}{2}$ pt pots of water.

Copy and complete each equation.

3. 12 km/h = __?__ km/min 0.2

4. $6.00 per yd = __?__ per ft $2.00

5. $2.39 per lb = __?__ per oz about $.15

6. 111 gal/min = __?__ gal/h 6660

7. A hummingbird's heart beats 1260 times per minute. How many times does a hummingbird's heart beat per second? 21 times

---

Study Skills ◀▶ **Using Different Learning Styles**

People learn in different ways, such as by reading, listening, looking at pictures, and doing activities. Sometimes it is helpful to use two or more learning styles to better understand a topic.

1. Describe a topic in this section that you understood well. Tell whether it was presented through pictures or diagrams, a reading, an activity, or some other way. Answers will vary.

2. Describe a topic in this section that you had some difficulty understanding. How was it presented? Explain how you would change the presentation by adding pictures, readings, activities, and so on to help another student understand the topic. Answers will vary.

Section ② Displaying Data

IN THIS SECTION

EXPLORATION 1
♦ Stem-and-Leaf Plots

EXPLORATION 2
♦ Box-and-Whisker Plots

Amazing Musicians

Setting the Stage ▸▸▸▸▸▸▸▸▸▸▸▸▸▸▸▸▸▸▸▸▸▸▸

How would you like to have a hit record at the age of 13? What would it be like to release your first CD at the age of 121? Some people would consider Stevie Wonder and Jeanne Calment amazing musicians!

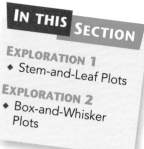

Jeanne Calment's CD, *Time's Mistress*, is a musical account of her life and was released in February, 1996, when she was 121 years old. ▶

▲
Stevie Wonder was 13 when his song, *Fingertips Pt 2*, made it to the #1 position on Billboard's Top 40 Chart in July, 1963.

Think About It

1 Estimate the years when Stevie Wonder and Jeanne Calment were born. **Stevie Wonder: 1950, Jeanne Calment: 1875**

2 How old do you think the typical musician is when he or she has a hit single for the first time? What information would help you answer this question? **Sample Response: In his or her twenties. Find a list of hit singles and recording artists, then determine ages by finding biographies.**

3 Who do you think is more amazing, Jeanne Calment or Stevie Wonder? Why? **Answers will vary.**

LEARN HOW TO...
- ◆ make and use stem-and-leaf plots

AS YOU...
- ◆ analyze the ages of famous pop and country musicians

KEY TERMS
- ◆ stem-and-leaf plot
- ◆ stem
- ◆ leaf

Exploration 1

STEM and LEAF Plots

▶ How unusual is it for a musician to have a #1 record at age 13? One way to answer this question is to look at the ages of musicians when they had their first #1 single.

4 As of 1996, the ages of the top 20 solo pop artists when they had their first #1 single were 26, 21, 20, 33, 28, 22, 19, 14, 25, 26, 29, 21, 25, 27, 21, 26, 32, 31, 26, and 13. What age were most of these musicians when they had their first #1 single? **in their 20s**

▶ To answer questions like the one in Question 4, it is often helpful to organize the data in a graph or find an average. The mean, the median, and the mode are types of averages.

FOR ▶ HELP

with *mean, median,* and *mode,* see **TOOLBOX, p. 606**

5 **a.** Find the mean, the median, and the mode of the data in Question 4. **mean: 24.25, median: 25.5, mode: 26**

b. Which average do you think best represents the data? Explain.
Possible Answers: the mode or the median because they represent numbers in the middle of the data

▶ Data can be organized in a **stem-and-leaf plot.** The stem-and-leaf plot below shows the ages of the top 20 solo pop musicians when they had their first #1 record. These musicians have had the most #1 hits as of 1996.

Each **stem** represents a tens digit.

Ages of Top 20 Solo Pop Artists When They Had Their First #1 Record

```
1 | 3 4 9
2 | 0 1 1 1 2 5 5 6 6 6 6 7 8 9
3 | 1 2 3
```

1 | 3 represents the data item **13.**

The **leaves** are written in order from least to greatest.

[Top 20 artists as of 1996]

6 The table lists the names and ages of four musicians from the stem-and-leaf plot. Find their ages in the plot. Write the ages that come right before and after each person's age in the plot.

Pop artist	Age
Mariah Carey	20
Whitney Houston	22
Barbra Streisand	31
Lionel Ritchie	32

6. Mariah Carey: 19 and 21; Whitney Houston: 21 and 25; Barbra Streisand: 29 and 32; Lionel Ritchie: 31 and 33

7 **Try This as a Class** Use the stem-and-leaf plot on page 16.

a. How were the numbers for the stems and leaves chosen?

b. Find the range of the data in the stem-and-leaf plot. **20 years**

c. Which averages (mean, median, and mode) can be found easily using the stem-and-leaf plot? Explain.

7. a. The stems are the tens digits of the numbers in the data set; The leaves are the ones digits.

FOR ▶ HELP

with *range*, see
TOOLBOX, p. 606

▶ **Comparing Data** You can use stem-and-leaf plots to compare the pop artists' ages with the top 20 country artists' ages.

8 Use the data in the table to make a stem-and-leaf plot. Be sure to put the same amount of space between the leaves. **See Additional Answers.**

7. c. Median because the numbers are already in order from least to greatest and mode because the numbers that are the same are placed together in the plot.

Ages of Top 20 Country Artists When They Had Their First #1 Record*					
Country artist	Age	Country artist	Age	Country artist	Age
Eddy Arnold	28	Reba McEntire	28	Marty Robbins	27
Earl Conley	39	Ronnie Milsap	28	Kenny Rogers	38
Crystal Gayle	25	Willie Nelson	42	George Strait	30
Mikey Gilley	38	Buck Owens	33	Conway Twitty	34
Merle Haggard	29	Dolly Parton	24	Don Williams	35
Sonny James	27	Charley Pride	31	Tammy Wynette	25
Waylon Jennings	36	Eddie Rabbit	31	*as of 1993	

9 ✔ **CHECKPOINT** Use the stem-and-leaf plot on page 16 and the stem-and-leaf plot you created in Question 8. **See Additional Answers.**

a. Compare the shapes of the two plots. What do the shapes tell you about the ages of the two groups of musicians?

b. Compare the ranges of the two sets of data. What do the ranges tell you about the ages of the two groups of musicians?

c. Linda Ronstadt had her first #1 pop hit and her first #1 country hit when she was 28. Is this age unusual for pop musicians? for country musicians? Explain.

✔ **QUESTION 9**

...checks that you can interpret stem-and-leaf plots.

HOMEWORK EXERCISES ▶ See Exs. 1 and 2 on p. 22.

GOAL

LEARN HOW TO...

◆ use box-and-whisker plots to analyze and compare data

AS YOU...

◆ investigate the achievements of famous musicians

KEY TERMS

◆ box-and-whisker plot
◆ lower extreme
◆ upper extreme
◆ lower quartile
◆ upper quartile

BOX and WHISKER Plots

▶ One way to decide whether musicians are amazing is to examine how many of their songs were popular. The stem-and-leaf plot below shows the number of #1 singles by the same top 20 solo pop artists from Exploration 1.

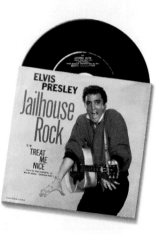

Number of #1 Singles by the Top 20 Solo Pop Artists as of 1996

```
0 | 5 5 5 5 6 6 6 6 6 7 7 8 9
1 | 0 0 0 1 1 3 8
```

10 Elvis Presley had 18 #1 singles, more than any other solo pop artist as of 1996. Based on data in the stem-and-leaf plot, do you think that Elvis Presley's achievement is amazing? Explain.

Sample Response: Yes, since the median number of hit singles by one artist is 7 and the mean is about 8.

▶ The **box-and-whisker plot** below is a display of the same data as the stem-and-leaf plot. Use the stem-and-leaf plot and the box-and-whisker plot for Questions 11–13.

Number of #1 Singles by the Top 20 Solo Pop Artists as of 1996

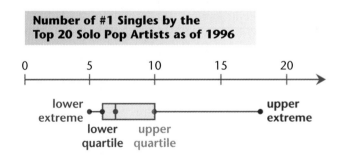

11. a. least: 5; greatest: 18; The least is the point labeled lower extreme and the greatest is the point labeled upper extreme.
b. 7; The point with a line passing through it inside the box is the median.
c. 5 and 6; to the left of the median: 6 and 7, to the right of the median: 7, 8, 9, and 10

11 **a.** Find the least and greatest data items in the stem-and-leaf plot. How are these shown in the box-and-whisker plot?

b. Use the stem-and-leaf plot to find the median of the data. How does the box-and-whisker plot show the median?

c. The upper whisker extends from 10 to 18. What are possible values in the lower whisker? in each portion of the box?

12 Try This as a Class The data items in the stem-and-leaf plot can be divided into four groups, as shown below.

5 5 5 5 6 / 6 6 6 6 7 / 7 8 9 10 10 / 10 11 11 13 18

a. How many items are in each group? What percent of the data items are in each group? 5 items; 25%

b. Find the median of the first 10 data items. Find the median of the last 10 data items. How are these values shown on the box-and-whisker plot? 6; 10; They are the points labeled lower quartile and upper quartile and are the east-west edges of the box.

c. Which group of data corresponds to the lower whisker on the box-and-whisker plot? Which group corresponds to the upper whisker? first group; last group

d. Where are the other two groups of data items located on the box-and-whisker plot?

12. d. The second group corresponds to the left portion of the box and the third group corresponds to the right portion of the box.

13 Try This as a Class A box-and-whisker plot is divided into four regions. Each of these regions represents about the same *number* of data items.

a. What percent of the data fall into each region of the box-and-whisker plot? 25% of the data are in each of the four regions

b. What percent of the data items are represented by the entire box portion of the box-and-whisker plot? 50%

c. Why is the upper whisker longer than the upper portion of the box? The range of data is greater in the upper whisker.

14 ✔ CHECKPOINT Elvis Presley had 104 singles make the Top 40 charts. The box-and-whisker plot below shows data about the highest position reached on the Top 40 charts by those singles.

a. Identify the lower extreme and the upper extreme. What information do these values give you about the data?
lower extreme: 1; upper extreme: 40; the range of the data

b. Find the median of the data. 16

c. About what percent of Elvis Presley's Top 40 singles reached positions 1 through 16? about 50%

✔ QUESTION 14

...checks that you can interpret a box-and-whisker plot.

Highest Positions Reached By Elvis Presley's 104 Top 40 Singles

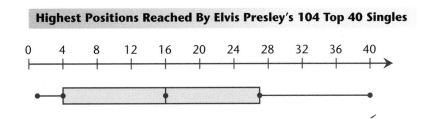

► **Comparing Data** As of 1996, Elvis Presley had more #1 singles than any other *solo* pop artist. But one *group*, the Beatles, had 20 #1 singles. So who is more amazing? One way to decide is to look at how long each of their #1 singles stayed at the #1 position on the Top 40 charts.

CLOSURE QUESTION

How are stem-and-leaf plots and box-and-whisker plots alike? How are they different?

Sample Response: Both plots allow you to make generalizations about the data, display data from a set, and make it relatively easy to find the median and the range of a set of data. A stem-and-leaf plot allows you to also find the mean and mode of a set of data, while a box-and-whisker plot does not. A box-and-whisker plot displays the ranges of the four quarters that the data fall into.

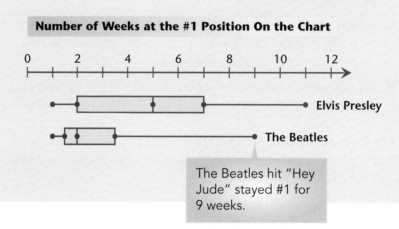

Number of Weeks at the #1 Position On the Chart

Elvis Presley

The Beatles

The Beatles hit "Hey Jude" stayed #1 for 9 weeks.

15 Use the box-and-whisker plots above.

a. What is the range for each data set? Presley: 10; Beatles: 8

b. What percent of the Beatles' #1 hit singles stayed at the #1 position for two weeks or less? What percent of Elvis Presley's #1 hit singles stayed at the #1 position for two weeks or less?
about 50%; about 25%

c. What percent of the data items for each set of data are represented by the box portion of each box-and-whisker plot? Why are the sizes of the boxes different?
about 50%; The ranges of the data within that 50% varies.

✔ **QUESTION 16**

...checks that you can use box-and-whisker plots to compare data sets.

16 ✔ **CHECKPOINT** 50% of Elvis Presley's #1 hit singles stayed at the #1 position for 5 to 11 weeks. 50% of the Beatles' #1 hits stayed at the #1 position for 2 or more weeks. How do the box-and-whisker plots above show this information?

17 **Discussion** Who do you think is more amazing, Elvis Presley or the Beatles? Use the box-and-whisker plots above to support your choice. Sample Response: Elvis Presley because 75% of his singles stayed at the #1 spot more than two weeks while only 50% of the Beatles singles had that record.

16. These are the data values that range from the line inside the box to the end of the upper whisker.

▶ **HOMEWORK EXERCISES** See Exs. 3–9 on pp. 22–24.

Section 2
Key Concepts ➤➤➤➤➤➤➤➤➤➤➤➤➤➤➤➤➤➤

Key Terms

Stem-and-Leaf Plots (pp. 16–17)

A stem-and-leaf plot displays data in an organized format. The data items are usually ordered from least to greatest.

stem-and-leaf plot

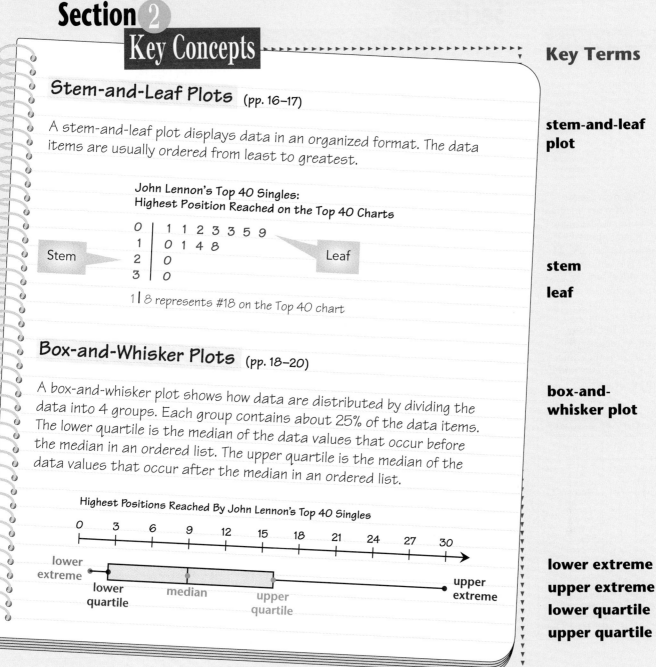

John Lennon's Top 40 Singles:
Highest Position Reached on the Top 40 Charts

```
0 | 1 1 2 3 3 5 9
1 | 0 1 4 8
2 | 0
3 | 0
```

Stem ◀

Leaf

1|8 represents #18 on the Top 40 chart

stem

leaf

Box-and-Whisker Plots (pp. 18–20)

A box-and-whisker plot shows how data are distributed by dividing the data into 4 groups. Each group contains about 25% of the data items. The lower quartile is the median of the data values that occur before the median in an ordered list. The upper quartile is the median of the data values that occur after the median in an ordered list.

box-and-whisker plot

Highest Positions Reached By John Lennon's Top 40 Singles

0   3   6   9   12   15   18   21   24   27   30

lower extreme
lower quartile
median
upper quartile
upper extreme

lower extreme
upper extreme
lower quartile
upper quartile

18 Key Concepts Question Use the data displays above.

a. How many #1 singles did John Lennon have? Which data display does not give you this information?
2 #1 singles; The box-and-whisker plot.

b. Which data display(s) can you use to find the mean of the data? the median? the mode? Find each of these averages.
stem-and-leaf plot; both; stem-and-leaf plot; mean: about 9.8; median: 9, modes: 1 and 3

c. About what percent of John Lennon's Top 40 singles made it to the 16th through 30th positions on the charts? about 25%

YOU WILL NEED

For Exs. 1–2:
◆ Labsheet 2A

2. **a.** Country: mean: about 32.8 years, median: 32.5 years, mode: none; Pop: mean: about 33.3, median: 31.5, mode: 24 **b.** She was almost 20 years older than the next oldest performer and in the top 10% in age; It raises the mean. **c.** Sample Response: Country: median; Pop: median; It is the value that is close to the middle of the data set.

Use Labsheet 2A for Exercises 1 and 2.

1. See Additional Answers.

1. **a.** The labsheet shows female *Grammy Award Winners* from 1975–1996. Use the data to make two stem-and-leaf plots, one for best pop performance and one for best country performance.

   b. Compare the shapes of the two stem-and-leaf plots. What do the shapes tell you about the ages of female country and pop Grammy Award winners when they won their awards?

2. **a.** Find the mean, the median, and the mode for each data set.

   b. How does Lena Horne's age compare with the ages of the other female pop winners? How does her age affect the mean for the female pop winners?

   c. Which average from part (a) do you think best represents each data set? Explain your thinking.

The table at left shows history test scores for two classes. The same data are used in the box-and-whisker plots below. Use the table and the box-and-whisker plots for Exercises 3–6.

History Test Scores

Class A		Class B	
66	100	78	64
54	90	76	77
68	72	87	93
86	64	45	47
100	59	78	80
59	100	76	76
68	84	90	100
85	100	45	83

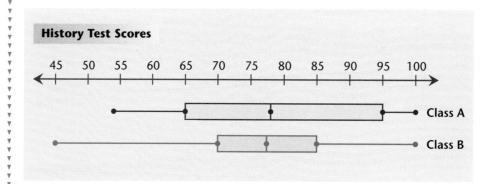

3. For each box-and-whisker plot, find the values below.

   a. the lower extreme
   Class A: 54; Class B: 45

   b. the upper extreme
   Class A: 100; Class B: 100

   c. the lower quartile
   Class A: 65; Class B: 70

   d. the upper quartile
   Class A: 95; Class B: 85

4. **a.** Sample Response: Find the median for each plot. The one that is drawn further right is greater.

4. **a.** **Writing** Explain how to use the box-and-whisker plots to compare the median test scores for the two classes.

   b. Find the mean test score for each class. Which class had at least 50% of its test scores greater than its mean?
   Class A: about 78.4; Class B: about 74.7; Class B

5. **Challenge** Diana says that you can tell from looking at the box-and-whisker plots that the mean test score for class A is higher than the mean test score for class B. Do you agree? Explain.

6. About what percent of each class's test scores are included in the box portion of each box-and-whisker plot? What do the sizes of the box portions tell you about the test scores for each class?

7. **Interpreting Data** Only one of the box-and-whisker plots below correctly displays data about the profits made by the top 40 movies of 1995. The statements below are all true of these movies. Use the statements to choose the correct box-and-whisker plot. Explain your choice.

- ◆ At least 50% of the top 40 movies brought in 66 million dollars or more.

- ◆ The least amount made by a top 40 movie was 36 million dollars.

- ◆ About 25% of the top 40 movies made between 81 and 184 million dollars.

- ◆ No top 40 movie made more than 184 million dollars.
  Plot C; lower extreme is 36, upper quartile is 81, upper extreme is 184.

5. Sample Response: No; Box-and-whisker plots do not show the mean because they do not show all the numbers in the data set or how many times each number occurs.

6. 50%; The size of the box portion shows the range of the middle 50% of the data.

Top 40 Movie Profits, 1995

| 30 | 40 | 50 | 60 | 70 | 80 | 90 | 100 | 110 | 120 | 130 | 140 | 150 | 160 | 170 | 180 | 190 |

Plot A

Plot B

Plot C

8. **Challenge** The Beatles had 50 singles that made the Top 40 charts. Of these hit singles, 20 made it to the #1 position. How does this fact explain that there is no lower whisker on the box-and-whisker plot below? The lower extreme and the lower quartile are the same.

Highest Position Reached by The Beatles' Top 40 Singles

| 0 | 5 | 10 | 15 | 20 | 25 | 30 | 35 | 40 |

Discussion

Exercise 9 checks that you can interpret stem-and-leaf plots and box-and-whisker plots.

Reflecting ◀▶ on the Section

Be prepared to discuss Exercise 9 in class.

9. Aretha Franklin is another amazing musician. During a career that spans four decades, she has won more than ten Grammy Awards. She is known as the "Queen of Soul." The stem-and-leaf plot below shows data about her Top 40 singles.

Highest Positions Reached by Aretha Franklin's Hits on the Top 40 Charts

0	1 1 2 2 3 3 4 5 5 6 6 7 7 8 9 9
1	0 1 3 3 4 6 6 7 8 9 9 9
2	0 1 2 3 4 6 6 8 8 8
3	1 3 7 7

3 | 1 represents position number 31 on *Billboard's* Top 40 chart.

a. Suppose a box-and-whisker plot was constructed from the data above. What value would be the lower extreme? the upper extreme? the median?
1, 37, 15

b. Where would the data value 11 be on the box-and-whisker plot? For example, would it be on the lower whisker?
It would be in the lower box.

c. Which whisker would be longer, the upper whisker or the lower whisker? Explain. **upper whisker; The range for the lower whisker is 1 to 6 and the range for the upper whisker is 23 to 37.**

Spiral ◀▶ Review

Copy and complete each equation. (Module 1, p. 8; Table of Measures, p. 610)

10. 4.8 m/min = __?__ m/h **288**

11. 55 mi/h = __?__ mi/min **about 0.92**

12. 8 lb/ft^2 = __?__ lb/in.^{2}
about 0.06

13. $.75 per day = __?__ per week **$5.25**

Test each number for divisibility by 2, 3, and 5. (Toolbox, p. 595)

14. 615
3 and 5 only

15. 2189
none

16. 41,852
2 only

17. 111
3 only

Replace each __?__ with > or < . (Toolbox, p. 601)

18. −6 __?__ −10 **>**

19. 3 __?__ −4 **>**

20. −12 __?__ −22 **>**

Career Counselor: Kelley Martino

A career counselor like Kelley Martino may use a box-and-whisker plot to help you understand your score on a standardized test. One type of standardized test used by colleges is the Scholastic Assessment Test, or SAT.

▲
Kelley Martino, center, helps her students research career choices.

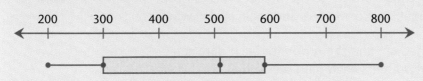

1997 SAT Mathematics Test Scores

21. In which group (lower whisker, lower box, upper box, upper whisker) would you be if your score was 400? 600? **lower box; upper whisker**

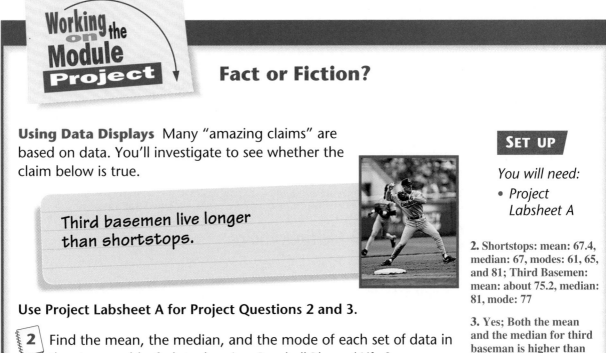

Working on the Module Project

Fact or Fiction?

Using Data Displays Many "amazing claims" are based on data. You'll investigate to see whether the claim below is true.

> Third basemen live longer than shortstops.

Use Project Labsheet A for Project Questions 2 and 3.

2. Find the mean, the median, and the mode of each set of data in the stem-and-leaf plots showing *Baseball Players' Life Spans.*

3. Tell whether you think the claim above is true. Use the data and the displays to support your answer.

SET UP

You will need:
• *Project Labsheet A*

2. Shortstops: mean: 67.4, median: 67, modes: 61, 65, and 81; Third Basemen: mean: about 75.2, median: 81, mode: 77

3. Yes; Both the mean and the median for third baseman is higher than those for shortstops. Also, the mode for third basemen is higher than two of the modes for shortstops.

Section 2

Extra Skill Practice

Use the data in the table for Exercises 1 and 2.

Ages of Academy Award Winners, 1976–1995	
Best Actor ages	60, 30, 40, 42, 37, 76, 39, 52, 45, 35, 61, 43, 51, 32, 42, 54, 52, 37, 38, 30
Best Actress ages	35, 31, 41, 33, 31, 72, 33, 49, 38, 76, 21, 41, 26, 80, 42, 29, 33, 34, 45, 49

1. Make two stem-and-leaf plots, one for Best Actor and one for Best Actress. What do the shapes of the stem-and-leaf plots tell you about the ages of female award winners and male award winners? **See Additional Answers.**

2. Find the mean, the median, and the mode for each data set. Which average best represents each data set? Why? **See Additional Answers.**

3. The box-and-whisker plots represent the data in the table. For each box-and-whisker plot, find the values below. **Best Actor: a) 30, b) 76, c) 37, d) 52; Best Actress: a) 21, b) 80, c) 32, d) 47**

   a. the lower extreme   b. the upper extreme

   c. the lower quartile   d. the upper quartile

Ages of Academy Award Winners, 1976–1995

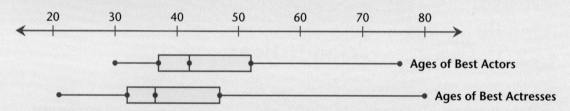

4. Jessica Tandy was 80 years old when she received the Best Actress Award. How unusual is it for an 80-year-old actress to receive this award? Explain. **Sample Response: Very unusual; She is the only person (actor or actress) in her eighties in 20 years to receive an academy award, and only 1 of 3 actresses over the age of 49.**

Standardized Testing ◀▶ Multiple Choice

1. Tell which values *cannot* be found using a box-and-whisker plot. **C and D**

   Ⓐ range   Ⓑ median   Ⓒ mean   Ⓓ mode

2. Tell which values *can* be found using a stem-and-leaf plot. **A, B, C, and D**

   Ⓐ range   Ⓑ median   Ⓒ mean   Ⓓ mode

Section ③ Scatter Plots

IN THIS SECTION

EXPLORATION 1
◆ Making a Scatter Plot

EXPLORATION 2
◆ Fitting a Line

Athletic
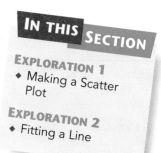
Triumphs

Setting the Stage ▶▶▶▶▶▶▶▶▶▶▶▶▶▶▶▶▶▶▶▶▶▶

The achievements of many athletes seem even more amazing when you think about the difficulties they have overcome.

WARM-UP EXERCISES

Use the table to write each pair of numbers as an ordered pair.

x	y	(x, y)
0	1	(0, 1)
1	4	(1, 4)
2	7	(2, 7)
3	10	(3, 10)
4	13	(4, 13)
5	16	(5, 16)

▲
Marla Runyan has been legally blind since the age of 9. She trains for the Olympics and won a bronze medal in the 1995 Olympic Festival. She also led the U.S. Heptathlon team to victory against Canada.

▲
At 5 ft 7 in., Anthony "Spud" Webb is much shorter than most National Basketball Association players. Yet, he won the Slam-Dunk Competition at the 1986 NBA All-Star game.

▲
Jackie Joyner-Kersee suffers from asthma, which causes breathing problems. She won gold medals in the 1988 and 1992 Olympic heptathlons. The heptathlon includes seven demanding events.

Think About It

1 With a running start, Spud Webb can jump $3\frac{1}{2}$ ft off the floor. Estimate how high Spud Webb's hand can reach when he jumps. How did you make your estimate?

2 A basketball rim is 10 ft high. About how high would you have to jump off the ground to dunk a basketball? Answers will vary.

1. Sample Response: 10 ft 2 in.; I measured my arm, added 5 ft 7 in., subtracted the distance from my shoulder to the top of my head, then added 3.5 ft.

Making a Scatter Plot

SET UP *Work in a group of six. You will need:* • *masking tape* • *tape measure or yardstick* • *ruler* • *graph paper*

▶ Spud Webb's jumping ability is amazing, even for a professional athlete. How high would someone your age need to jump to be an amazing jumper? One way to find out is to gather data and use it to predict how high a 5 ft 7 in. eighth grade student might be expected to jump.

Jumping Data		
Student	Height (in.)	Jump height (in.)
Sarah	63	89
Milo	61	85

3. Answers will vary. Check students' work.

3 a. Make a table like the one shown. Measure and record the height of each person in your group to the nearest inch.

b. Follow the directions given to measure each student's jump height to the nearest inch. Record the jump heights in your table.

First

Jump near a wall. Make two standing jumps, placing a piece of masking tape as high on the wall as possible.

Then

Record your jump height. Your jump height is the distance from the floor to your higher piece of masking tape.

4. Answers will vary. Check students' work.

4 **a.** Write an *ordered pair* like the one shown for each person in your group.

b. Write the ordered pairs on the board so each student can record the results of the entire class.

student jump
height height
(63, 89)

▶ Sometimes it is easier to see how data are related by graphing the data. On a graph, the numbers written along the axis are its **scale**. The numbers on the scale can increase by ones, but when the data are spread over a large range it may be better to choose a scale that increases by twos, fives, tens, or some other number.

5 **Try This as a Class** The questions below will help you plan how to graph your class's jumping data.

Answers will vary. Check students' work.

a. The horizontal axis of the graph will show student heights (in inches). What is the greatest student height? the least? Use these values to decide what range of heights to show on the horizontal axis. Explain your thinking.

b. Use the range for the student heights to decide how many intervals you can fit along the horizontal axis. Explain your thinking.

c. Use your answers to parts (a) and (b) to choose a scale for the horizontal axis. Explain your decision.

d. The vertical axis will show jump height (in inches). Decide what values will be shown and choose a scale for the vertical axis. Explain how you made your choices.

If your scale does not start at 0, show that with a broken line.

You may need to experiment to find a scale that works for your data.

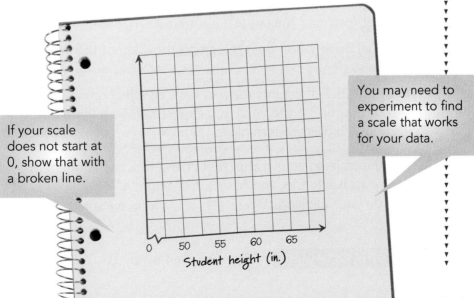

Student height (in.)

6 Use your answers to Question 5 and the class's jumping data to make your graph. **Answers will vary. Check students' work.**

   a. On graph paper draw and label the horizontal and vertical axes for your graph. Include the scale for each axis and a title for the graph.

   b. Plot the class's jumping data on your coordinate grid. You should have one point for each member of the class.

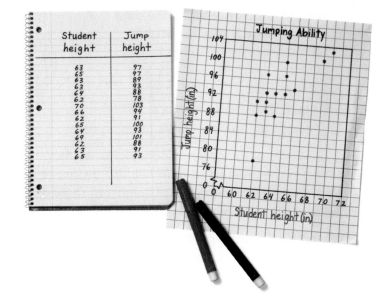

Student height	Jump height
63	97
65	97
63	89
63	93
64	88
62	78
70	103
66	94
62	91
65	100
64	93
69	101
62	88
63	91
65	93

▶ The graph you created is a *scatter plot*. A **scatter plot** can be used to compare two sets of data and look for relationships between them.

7 Discussion Use your scatter plot.

   a. Looking at the scatter plot, what can you tell about the jump heights? For example, what is the greatest height reached? the least reached? the range? **Answers will vary. Check students' work.**

   b. What information does the graph show about the heights of the students? **Sample Response: The height of the jump increases with the height of the student.**

   c. Did students' heights seem to have an effect on how high they could jump? Is this what you expected? Were there any exceptions? Explain your thinking. **Answers will vary. Check students' work.**

8 Will the scale on your scatter plot change if a new student in your class is 6 ft 1 in. and has a jump height of 9 ft 4 in.? Explain your thinking. **Answers will vary. Check students' work.**

HOMEWORK EXERCISES ▶ See Exs. 1–4 on p. 35.

Exploration 2

Fitting a L|NE

GOAL

LEARN HOW TO...
♦ use a fitted line to make predictions

AS YOU...
♦ analyze data about students' heights and their jump heights

KEY TERM
♦ fitted line

SET UP *You will need: • Labsheet 3A • ruler • your scatter plot of jumping data from Exploration 1*

▶ The scatter plot below compares performances of 26 athletes in two of the seven events in the 1992 Olympic heptathlon. Each point represents an athlete's time in the 200 meter sprint and the 100 meter hurdles.

1992 Olympic Heptathlon Performances

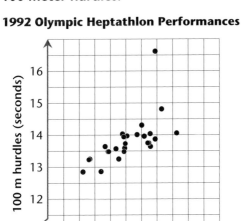

◀ Sabine Braun of Germany competes in one of the seven heptathlon events.

9 **a.** Jackie Joyner-Kersee had the fastest time in both events. Find the point on the scatter plot that represents her performance. Estimate her time in each event. **23.1 and 12.8**

b. The slowest time in the 200 m sprint was 26.13 seconds and the slowest time in the 100 m hurdles was 16.62 seconds. Did the same athlete get the slowest time in both events? Explain.
No; The person who ran the 200 in 26.13 s ran the 100 in about 14 s.

10 **Discussion** What pattern do you notice in the points on the scatter plot? **Sample Response: Athletes usually run the 100 m hurdles about twice as fast as they run the 200 m sprint.**

▶ Sometimes the data points in a scatter plot fall along a line. When this happens, a **fitted line** can be drawn to show the pattern in the data and help make predictions. An example of a fitted line is shown on the scatter plot of heptathlon performances at the top of page 32.

A fitted line is drawn so that most of the data points fall near it.

About half of the points should be above the line and about half below the line.

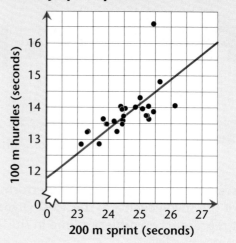

1992 Olympic Heptathlon Performances

11 **Discussion** How does the fitted line above help you see that faster sprinters were usually faster hurdlers and slower sprinters were slower hurdlers? Which points do not follow this pattern?

Sample Response: The points follow an upward trend; (26.1, 14.1) and (25.5, 16.6)

▶ The data points in a scatter plot do not always show a straight-line pattern. If you see a curved pattern or no pattern at all, it does not make sense to draw a fitted line.

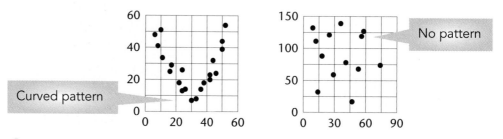

Curved pattern

No pattern

12. a. Sample Response: There is a positive relationship between how athletes do in the long jump and the 100-m hurdle. There does not seem to be a relationship in performances relating the high jump and the 200-m sprint.
b. Check students' work for fitted lines in the scatter plot comparing the long jump and the 100-m hurdles. Athletes usually do as well in the long jump as they do in the 100-m hurdle.

12 **Use Labsheet 3A.** You will look for patterns in the *Heptathlon Events* and make decisions about drawing fitted lines.

✔ **QUESTION 13**

...checks that you can draw a fitted line on a scatter plot and decide how well it represents the data.

13 ✔ **CHECKPOINT** Draw a fitted line on your scatter plot from Exploration 1. Does the line represent your data well? Explain.

Answers will vary. Check students' work.

14 **a.** How can you use your fitted line from Question 13 to decide whether your class has any "amazing jumpers"?

Sample Response: Note anyone whose jump height is markedly above the fitted line.

b. Spud Webb is 5 ft 7 in. tall. What jump height would you expect for a student as tall as Spud Webb?

Answers will vary. Check students' work.

HOMEWORK EXERCISES ▶ See Exs. 5–8 on pp. 36–37.

You can use spreadsheet software or graphing technology
to draw the scatter plots and fitted lines in this section.

Step 1   Enter your class jumping data into the spreadsheet. Enter the data
for the horizontal axis in column A. Enter the corresponding
data for the vertical axis in column B.

File	Edit	Format	Calculate	Options	View			
				STUDENT JUMPING DATA				

B5	×	√	93				
	A	**B**	**C**	**D**	**E**	**F**
1	Student Height (in.)	Jump Height (in.)				
2	67	97				
3	65	97				
4	63	89				
5	63	93				

Step 2   To create a graph, highlight the data you entered and choose
the option that makes a chart. Then select the type of graph
you want to make.

Options
Make Chart...
Protect Cells
Unprotect Cells
Add Page Break
Remove Page Break
Lock Title Position
Print Range...
Go To Cell...

Chart Options

Modify
- Axis
- Series
- Labels
- General

Gallery
- Bar
- Line
- Scatter
- Pie
- Stacked Bar
- X–Y Line
- X–Y Scatter
- Pictogram

Step 3   Experiment with the labels, grid lines, and scale until the graph
appears the way you want it to. Be sure to include a title.

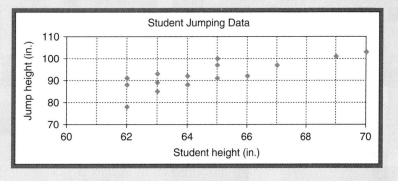

Step 4   Print out the graph and draw a fitted line through your scatter
plot as you did on page 32. Some graphing technology will
let you draw a fitted line or will draw one for you.

Section 3 Key Concepts

scatter plot

scale

fitted line

Scatter Plots (pp. 28–32)

You can use a scatter plot to compare two sets of data and look for relationships between them. The range of each data set determines the scale of each axis of the scatter plot. Sometimes the data points fall along a line. When they do, you can draw a fitted line to show a pattern and help make predictions.

Example The scatter plot below compares free throws made with free throws attempted by players on a basketball team. Because the data points tend to fall along a line, you can draw a fitted line.

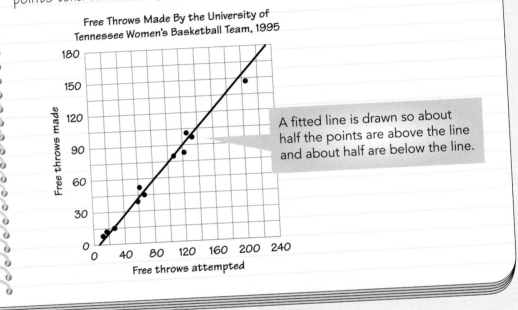

Free Throws Made By the University of Tennessee Women's Basketball Team, 1995

A fitted line is drawn so about half the points are above the line and about half are below the line.

CLOSURE QUESTION

Describe how you can tell from a scatter plot if a fitted line could be used to represent a set of data. Then describe how to draw a fitted line.

Sample Response: If the data points appear to lie on or near a line, then a fitted line could be used. Draw a fitted line through the data points so that about half of the points are above the line and half of the points are below the line.

15. a. The number of free throws made improves as the number of free throws attempted increases.

15 Key Concepts Question Use the scatter plot above.

a. Describe a relationship between the number of free throws attempted and the number made.

b. Predict the number of free throws you would expect a player to make in 100 attempts. **about 75; about 75%**

c. Would your prediction in part (b) be accurate for someone who has never played basketball before? Explain.
Sample Response: Probably not since basketball is a skill sport.

d. University of Tennessee player Dana Johnson attempted 205 free throws. About how many did she make? How does her performance compare with the other players'?
about 145; It is about 4% lower than the average.

Section 3
Practice & Application Exercises

YOU WILL NEED

For Exs. 4 and 6:
- graph paper
- two colored pencils

For Ex. 7:
- small ball
- yardstick or meter stick
- graph paper

Use Labsheet 3B. The scatterplot for Exercises 1–3 shows *World Record Marathon Times* for men and women of different ages.

1. What is the approximate age and record time of the oldest female marathon runner? of the oldest male marathon runner? **88 years: 480 min; 92 years: 564 min**

2. In what 10-year age range are the record times for men fastest? Does the fastest individual male time fall in this age range?
22 years to 32 years; Yes.

3. **Writing** Describe the pattern of the data points. Explain what it shows about the marathon runners and their times.

4. Some friends planned to travel at a rate of 12 km/h on a 20 km bike trip. Several times during the trip they recorded the total distance traveled and the time elapsed. They also recorded the time it would have taken them at their planned rate of 12 km/h. Their data are shown in the table below.
See Additional Answers.

   a. Make a scatter plot that compares distance and actual time. Put distance on the horizontal axis.

   b. On the same graph, use a different color to plot ordered pairs (distance, planned time). Use these new points to make a *line graph.* (In a line graph, a segment is drawn to connect each point to the next point.)

   c. How does the planned time compare with the actual time?

   d. During what stage of the trip were people traveling the fastest? Explain how you found your answer.

◄ Malgorzata Sorbanska of Poland leads a group of runners in a London marathon.

3. Sample Response: Marathon runners start at a relatively fast pace, peak in their 20s and 30s, then their times gradually increase over the next 30 years. Their times increase more rapidly after the age of 60.

Distance	Planned time	Actual time
0 km	0 min	0 min
2 km	10 min	6 min
4 km	20 min	22 min
6 km	30 min	32 min
10 km	50 min	45 min
14 km	70 min	58 min
15 km	75 min	60 min
17 km	85 min	77 min
20 km	100 min	90 min

5. Scatter Plot A has a straight line pattern, Scatter Plot B has a curved pattern.

5. Tell whether each scatter plot appears to have a *straight-line pattern*, a *curved pattern*, or *no pattern*.

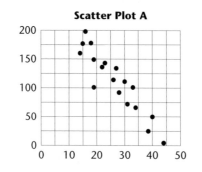

Scatter Plot A

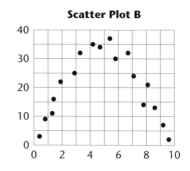

Scatter Plot B

Employment Status of Civilian Population, in millions (1960–1995)				
	Total Female Population		**Total Male Population**	
Year	**Aged 16 and over**	**Employed**	**Aged 16 and over**	**Employed**
1960	62	22	58	44
1965	67	25	62	46
1970	73	30	67	49
1975	80	34	73	51
1980	87	41	80	56
1985	94	47	84	60
1990	99	54	90	65
1995	103	58	95	67

6. a. History Make a scatter plot of the female employment data at the left. Put *population aged 16 and over* on the horizontal axis. Add the male employment data to your scatter plot. If it makes sense, draw a fitted line for each set of data points. **See Additional Answers.**

b. Open-ended Write a question that could be answered using the scatter plot. Tell how you could use the scatter plot to answer the question. **See Additional Answers.**

7. Home Involvement Use a tennis ball, racquetball, or other small ball to compare drop height and bounce height. Have a friend or family member help you.
Answers will vary. Check students' work.

a. Drop the ball from five different heights. For each drop, measure the height the ball was dropped from and the height it reached on its first bounce. Record your data.

b. Use your data to make a scatter plot. Put drop height on the horizontal axis and bounce height on the vertical axis. Draw a fitted line if it makes sense.

c. Based on your scatter plot, do you think there is a relationship between drop height and bounce height? Explain.

Reflecting on the Section

8. Explain how scatter plots could be used in a science class. Describe an actual problem or experiment where a scatter plot was used. You may want to interview a science teacher or a student in your school to see how they use scatter plots. **Answers will vary.**

RESEARCH

Exercise 8 checks that you know how to use a scatter plot.

Spiral Review

9. **Football** The heaviest football players are usually defensive linemen, linebackers, and offensive linemen. The box-and-whisker plots compare the weights of these players on an NFL team. Use the box-and-whisker plots to tell whether each statement below is *true* or *false*. Explain your thinking. (Module 1, p. 21)

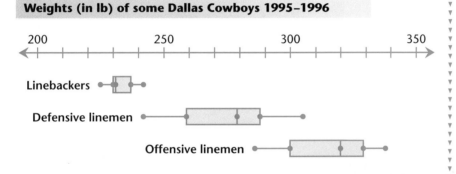

Weights (in lb) of some Dallas Cowboys 1995–1996

a. All of the linebackers weigh less than 250 lb.

b. About half of the offensive linemen weigh less than the heaviest defensive lineman.

c. At least one offensive lineman weighs less than all of the linebackers.

d. About 25% of the defensive linemen weigh less than 260 lb.

9. a. True; The upper extreme for linebackers is less than 250 lb.
b. False; The median weight for offensive linemen is more than 10 lb heavier than the heaviest defensive lineman.
c. False; The upper extreme for linebackers is about 245 lb and the lower extreme for offensive linemen is about 285 lb.
d. True; The lower quartile for defensive linemen is less than 260 lb.

Find each answer. (Toolbox, p. 592)

10. 4^2 16   11. 2^4 16   12. $3 \cdot 2^3$ 24   13. $3.14 \cdot 2.5$ 7.85

Find the area of each figure. (Toolbox, p. 605)

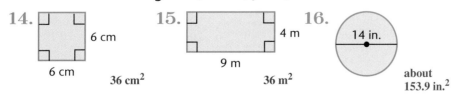

14. 6 cm, 6 cm   **36 cm²**

15. 4 m, 9 m   **36 m²**

16. 14 in.   **about 153.9 in.²**

You will need: • *graph paper* (Ex. 3)

Interpreting Data This scatter plot shows some altitude records for passenger balloons, airplanes, and other aircraft.

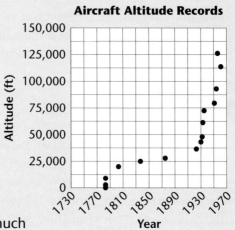

Aircraft Altitude Records

1. About how high is the highest altitude record? In about what year was that record set? about 125,000 ft; about 1955

2. Explain whether it makes sense to draw a fitted line for the scatter plot.
   Sample Response: It doesn't make sense because the data is in the shape of a curve.

3. A snack shop owner is trying to decide how much hot cocoa to make each day. The owner records the high temperatures and cocoa sales each day for two weeks. See Additional Answers.

High temperature	77	72	75	70	71	68	69	65	64	60	55	58	54	51
Cups of cocoa sold	6	6	4	7	5	9	11	14	15	18	25	21	28	31

   a. Make a scatter plot of the data. Put high temperature on the horizontal axis. Choose a scale for each axis. Explain your choices.

   b. If it makes sense to draw a fitted line, draw one.

   c. Suppose one pot makes 10 cups of cocoa. How many pots should the owner make when the high temperature is 50°? 40°?

Standardized Testing ◀▶ Free Response

Sprint times for contestants in a race at a weekend picnic are shown in the scatter plot. The contestants' ages are also shown.

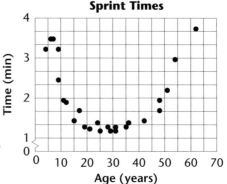

Sprint Times

1. For what ages do the times appear to be decreasing? increasing? approximately 7 through 22; approximately 35 through 52

2. Do the data appear to have a straight-line pattern or a curved pattern? Explain.
   curved pattern; Sample Response: The data decreases, then levels off, then increases. This creates a curve.

Section 4 Circumference and Volume

IN THIS SECTION

EXPLORATION 1
♦ Finding Circumference

EXPLORATION 2
♦ Finding Volume

Amazing Appetites

WARM-UP EXERCISES

Write each expression in words.

1. $3m - 8$ 8 less than the product of 3 and m.

2. $\frac{d}{15} + 11$ 11 more than the quotient of d and 15.

3. State the diameter and radius.

   8.5 in.

   diameter = 8.5 in.;
   radius = 4.25 in.

Setting the Stage ▸▸▸▸▸▸▸▸▸▸▸▸▸▸▸▸▸▸▸▸▸▸▸▸▸▸▸▸▸▸

Amazing fiction has a way of wandering into tall tales. The legend of Paul Bunyan, a giant lumberjack, came out of the logging camps of the northern United States in the 1800s. The story below tells of some amazing appetites.

> The lumber crews liked pancakes best, but they would gobble up and slurp down the pancakes so fast that the camp cooks couldn't keep up with them, even when the cooks got up twenty-six hours before daylight. The main problem was that the griddles the cooks used for frying the pancakes were too small. . . .
>
> [Paul Bunyan] went down to the plow works at Moline, Illinois, and said, "I want you fellows here to make me a griddle so big I won't be able to see across it on a foggy day."
>
> The men set to work. When they were finished, they had built a griddle so huge there was no train or wagon large enough to carry it.
>
> "Let me think what to do," said Paul. "We'll have to turn the griddle up on end, like a silver dollar, and roll it up to Michigan." He hitched [Babe] the Blue Ox to the upturned griddle, and away they went. . . . A few miles from the Big Onion lumber camp, Paul unhitched Babe and let the griddle roll on by itself.
>
> ***American Tall Tales,*** Adrien Stoutenberg

4. State the length, width, and height.

   2 cm
   11 cm
   6 cm

   length = 11 cm;
   width = 6 cm;
   height = 2 cm

Think About It

1 What amazing "facts" in the story let you know that it is a tall tale?

2 Paul Bunyan's pancake griddle was circular. According to one version of the story, its diameter was 236 ft.

    a. Sketch a circle and draw a diameter. Is this the only diameter the circle has? Explain. **No, A circle has an infinite number of diameters.**

    b. Would Paul Bunyan's griddle fit in any room in your school?
       No; A room would have to be more than 236 ft on a side for the griddle to fit inside.

GOAL

LEARN HOW TO...
- find circumference
- write and evaluate expressions

AS YOU...
- investigate a claim made in a tall tale

KEY TERMS
- circumference
- variable
- expression
- evaluate

Exploration 1

Finding Circumference

SET UP *You will need: • metric ruler • coin • calculator*

▶ One version of the story says that 3 miles from camp Paul gave the griddle a push and it rolled to the spot where he wanted it. Is this an amazing feat? One measurement that can help you answer this question is the griddle's circumference. The **circumference** of a circle is the distance around it.

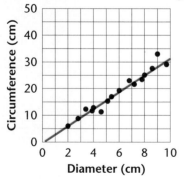

Measurements of Circular Objects

3 Some students measured the diameter and the circumference of several circular objects. Then they made a scatter plot and drew a fitted line. Does the line seem to fit the data? Explain. **Yes, All of the points lie close to the line and about half the data is above the line and the other half is below the line.**

4 a. Copy the table. Then use the fitted line on page 40 to estimate the circumferences of circles with the given diameters. See table.

Diameter (cm)	Circumference (cm)	Circumference diameter
11	? 34	? 3.1
1	? 3	? 3.0
8	? 25	? 3.1
14	? 43	? 3.1
4.5	? 14	? 3.1

b. Calculate the ratio of the *circumference* to the *diameter*. Round to the nearest tenth.
See table.

c. Discussion The circumference of a circle appears to be about how many times its diameter? about 3.1

5 Estimate the circumference of Paul Bunyan's pancake griddle. Explain how you made your estimate. Sample Response: about 732 ft; I multiplied 236 by 3.1.

▶ **Using Variables** In mathematics, symbols are often used instead of words to express relationships. A **variable** is a symbol used to represent a quantity that is unknown or that can change.

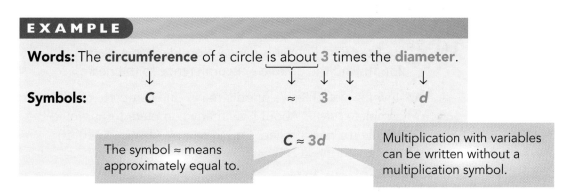

E X A M P L E

Words: The **circumference** of a circle is about 3 times the **diameter**.

Symbols: C ≈ 3 · d

$C \approx 3d$

The symbol ≈ means approximately equal to.

Multiplication with variables can be written without a multiplication symbol.

▶ C and 3d are *expressions*. An **expression** is a mathematical phrase that can contain numbers, variables, and operation symbols. Other examples of expressions are 8, *lw*, 5 + n, $9x^2$, and $\frac{a}{2}$.

6 Discussion The exact relationship between the circumference and the diameter of a circle is given below. Read π as *pi*.

$$\frac{C}{d} = \pi, \text{ or } C = \pi d$$

a. Calculator Press the π key on a calculator. What number appears? 3.141592654

b. π is actually a letter from the Greek alphabet. Does this mean that it is a variable? Explain.

c. Which is a closer approximation for π, 3.14 or $\frac{22}{7}$? Explain.

b. No; A variable is a symbol used to represent a quantity that is unknown or that can change and π is known and does not change.

c. Sample Response: $\frac{22}{7}$; The difference between $\frac{22}{7}$ and π is about 0.001264489 and the difference between π and 3.14 is about 0.001592653.

To find the circumference of a circle with a diameter of 20 cm, *evaluate* the expression πd when $d = 20$.

$$C = \pi d$$

$$= \pi(20)$$

Substitute 20 for **d**. Use parentheses to show multiplication.

$$\approx (3.14)(20)$$

$$\approx 62.8$$

Use 3.14 to approximate π.

The circumference is about 62.8 cm.

8. Sample Response: The only way to give an exact value for a circumference when only the diameter of a circle is given is to write it in terms of π.

✔ QUESTION 9

...checks that you can evaluate an expression.

7 What does it mean to evaluate an expression?
Sample Response: Find its value for given values of the variables.

8 You can also give the circumference in the Example in terms of π. Explain why the circumference is *exactly* 20π.

9 ✔ CHECKPOINT Evaluate each expression. Use 3.14 for π.

a. $2\pi r$ when $r = 6$ **b.** $3 + x$ when $x = 6$ **c.** $\dfrac{4y}{3}$ when $y = 6$
        37.68   9   8

10 a. Suppose Paul Bunyan's pancake griddle had a diameter of 236 ft. Find the griddle's circumference to the nearest foot.   741 ft

b. How far would Paul's griddle roll in one complete turn? in ten complete turns? About how many complete turns would the griddle make if it rolled 3 mi to camp? (1 mi = 5280 ft.)
741 ft; 7410 ft; about 21 complete turns

11 a. Measure the diameter of a coin to the nearest tenth of a centimeter. Then find the circumference of the coin.
See Additional Answers.

b. About how far would your coin roll in one complete turn? in ten complete turns?
See Additional Answers.

12 a. Try to match Paul Bunyan's roll. Mark a starting line on the floor and roll your coin. Then measure how far it travels.
Sample Response: 226 cm

b. How many complete turns did the coin make? How do you know?   See left.

c. Was the griddle's roll an amazing feat? Explain your thinking.   Sample Response: Yes; It would be hard to roll something that large and even harder to maintain a continuous roll.

12. b. quarter 30 turns; dime: 42 turns; nickel: 34 turns; penny: 40 turns Sample Response: Divide the distance by the circumference of the coin.

HOMEWORK EXERCISES ▶   See Exs. 1–13 on pp. 47–48.

Exploration 2

Finding VOLUME

GOAL

LEARN HOW TO...
- find the volume of rectangular prisms and circular cylinders

AS YOU...
- investigate eating records

KEY TERMS
- prism
- cylinder
- exponent

▶ **DO NOT TRY THESE AT HOME!** Have you ever watched old movies where the actors try to set a record swallowing goldfish? or eating pies? Setting eating records is dangerous to your health, but studying eating records can help you understand another Paul Bunyan legend.

- Paul Hughes ate 39 jelly sandwiches in 60 min.

- Peter Dowdeswell ate 62 pancakes with butter and syrup in 6 min 58.5 seconds.

13 On average, what fraction of a sandwich did Paul Hughes consume per minute? Do you think this is an amazing feat?
$\frac{13}{20}$; Sample Response: Yes; It means that he can eat more than a whole sandwich every two minutes and continue to do that for 60 min.

▶ Another way to decide whether Hughes's feat was amazing is to estimate the volume of what he ate. A stack of 39 jelly sandwiches would be shaped like a **prism** with a rectangular base.

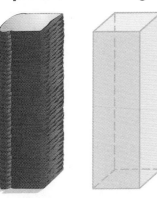

Volume of a Rectangular Prism
Volume = Area of the base × height
$V = Bh$

14 Each sandwich Paul Hughes ate measured 5 in. by 3 in. and was $\frac{1}{2}$ in. thick.

a. Estimate the height of a stack of 39 sandwiches.   about 20 in.

b. Find the actual height.   19.5 in.

c. Find the area of the base of the stack of sandwiches.   15 in.^{2}

d. Find the volume of the sandwiches Paul Hughes ate. 292.5 in.^{3}

FOR ▶ HELP

with *area* and *volume*, see
TOOLBOX, p. 605

▶ How does Peter Dowdeswell's record compare with Paul Hughes's record? To see, imagine a stack of 62 pancakes. The stack would be shaped like a **cylinder**. A circular cylinder has two circular bases.

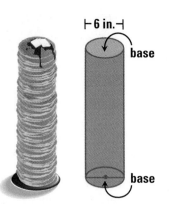

├ 6 in. ┤

base

base

15 Each pancake was $\frac{3}{8}$ in. thick and had a 6 in. diameter.

a. Show with your hands the approximate height of the stack of 62 pancakes. Compare your estimate with others in your class. **Answers will vary. Check students' work.**

b. Find the actual height of the stack of 62 pancakes. **23.25 in.**

c. Discussion Suppose you estimate the volume of the stack as the volume of a rectangular prism that contains the cylinder. Will your estimate be too large or too small? Explain.
Too large; The curved edges of a cylinder would leave gaps inside the walls of a rectangular prism.

▶ You can use the formula for the volume of a prism to find the volume of a cylinder: Volume = area of base × height or *V = Bh*. In this book, all the cylinders are circular cylinders, so you can use the formula for the area of a circle to find *B*.

FOR▶HELP

with *exponents,* see

TOOLBOX, p. 600

EXAMPLE

Find the volume of a cylinder with a height of 10 in. and a diameter of 8 in.

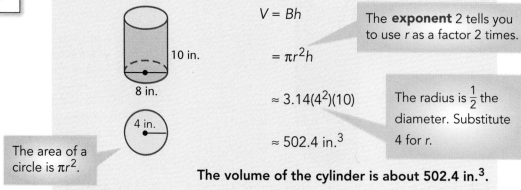

10 in.

8 in.

4 in.

The area of a circle is πr^2.

$V = Bh$

$= \pi r^2 h$

$\approx 3.14(4^2)(10)$

≈ 502.4 in.^{3}

The **exponent** 2 tells you to use *r* as a factor 2 times.

The radius is $\frac{1}{2}$ the diameter. Substitute 4 for *r*.

The volume of the cylinder is about 502.4 in.^{3}.

16 a. Discussion In the Example, why is the volume of the cylinder *about* 502.4 in.^{3}? **Sample Response: The value of π used is approximate.**

b. The volume of the cylinder in the Example is *exactly* 160π in.^{3} Explain why this is true.
Sample Response: The exact value of π cannot be expressed as a decimal, so an exact answer must be expressed in terms of π.

17 **a.** Use the information in Question 15 to find the volume of the stack of pancakes eaten by Peter Dowdeswell. **about 657.045 in.³**

 b. Who ate a greater volume of food, Dowdeswell or Hughes?

Peter Dowdeswell

▶ **Paul Bunyan may have been the most amazing eater of all, as described in the tale below.**

 . . . Paul sat down to have himself a little meal. He ate thirty-three pounds of beef, one whole venison, six hams, two bushels of fried eggs, twelve four-pound loaves of bread, twelve dozen eggs, and 678 flapjacks topped off with six gallons of maple syrup.

 Big Men, Big Country, Paul Robert Walker

18 Suppose the 678 flapjacks Paul Bunyan ate were the same size and shape as the ones eaten by Peter Dowdeswell, $\frac{3}{8}$ in. thick and 6 in. in diameter. Find the volume of a stack of 678 pancakes. **about 7185.105 in.³**

19 Paul Bunyan's pancake griddle was 236 ft in diameter.

 a. Find the radius of his griddle in inches. **1416 in.**

 b. Suppose a pancake $\frac{3}{8}$ in. thick was made to cover the entire griddle. Find the volume of the pancake in cubic inches. **about 2,360,953.44 in.³**

 c. How does the volume of one giant pancake made on Paul's griddle compare with the volume of the 62 pancakes Dowdeswell ate? (See Question 17.)
 Sample Response: It is about 3600 times as great.

 d. About how many giant pancakes would it take to equal the volume of the 678 pancakes in Question 18? **Sample Response: about $\frac{1}{300}$**

20 Who do you think is the most amazing eater, Paul Hughes, Peter Dowdeswell, or Paul Bunyan? Why? **Answers will vary.**

21 ✔ **CHECKPOINT** Find the volume of each figure.

 a. rectangular prism:
 l = 5 ft, *w* = 8 ft, *h* = 9 ft
 360 ft³

 b. cylinder:
 r = 5 cm, *h* = 3 cm
 235.5 cm³

✔ **QUESTION 21**

...checks that you can find the volumes of rectangular prisms and cylinders.

HOMEWORK EXERCISES ▶ See Exs. 14–28 on pp. 48–50.

Key Terms

variable

expression

evaluate

exponent

circumference

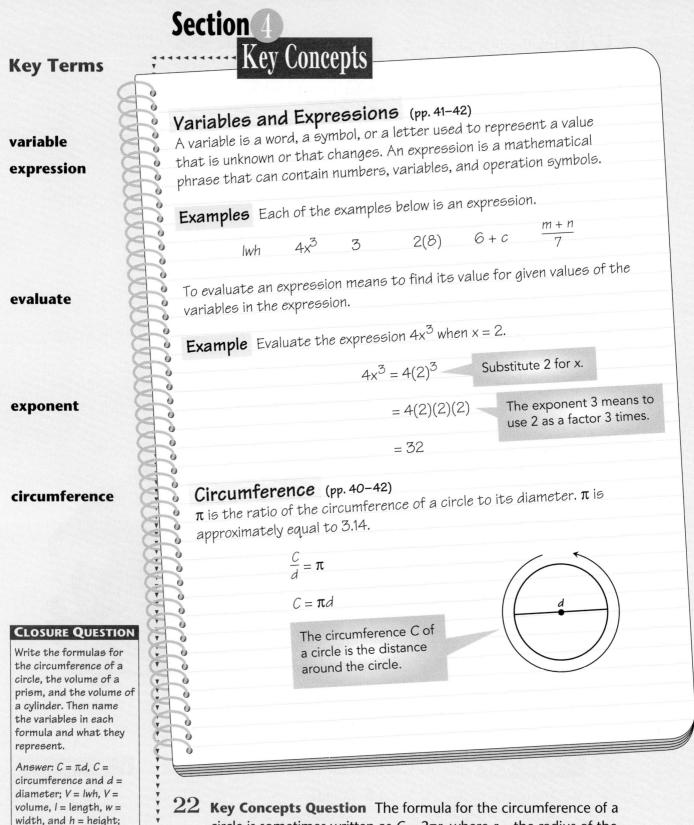

Variables and Expressions (pp. 41–42)

A variable is a word, a symbol, or a letter used to represent a value that is unknown or that changes. An expression is a mathematical phrase that can contain numbers, variables, and operation symbols.

Examples Each of the examples below is an expression.

$$lwh \qquad 4x^3 \qquad 3 \qquad 2(8) \qquad 6 + c \qquad \frac{m + n}{7}$$

To evaluate an expression means to find its value for given values of the variables in the expression.

Example Evaluate the expression $4x^3$ when $x = 2$.

$$4x^3 = 4(2)^3 \qquad \text{Substitute 2 for x.}$$

$$= 4(2)(2)(2) \qquad \text{The exponent 3 means to use 2 as a factor 3 times.}$$

$$= 32$$

Circumference (pp. 40–42)

π is the ratio of the circumference of a circle to its diameter. π is approximately equal to 3.14.

$$\frac{C}{d} = \pi$$

$$C = \pi d$$

The circumference C of a circle is the distance around the circle.

CLOSURE QUESTION

Write the formulas for the circumference of a circle, the volume of a prism, and the volume of a cylinder. Then name the variables in each formula and what they represent.

Answer: $C = \pi d$, C = circumference and d = diameter; $V = lwh$, V = volume, l = length, w = width, and h = height; $V = \pi r^2 h$, V = volume, r = radius of the base and h = height

22 Key Concepts Question The formula for the circumference of a circle is sometimes written as $C = 2\pi r$, where r = the radius of the circle. Explain how this formula is related to the formula $C = \pi d$. Then find the circumference of a circle with radius 5 cm.

Sample Response: $2r$ is equivalent to d; about 31.4 cm

Section 4

Key Concepts

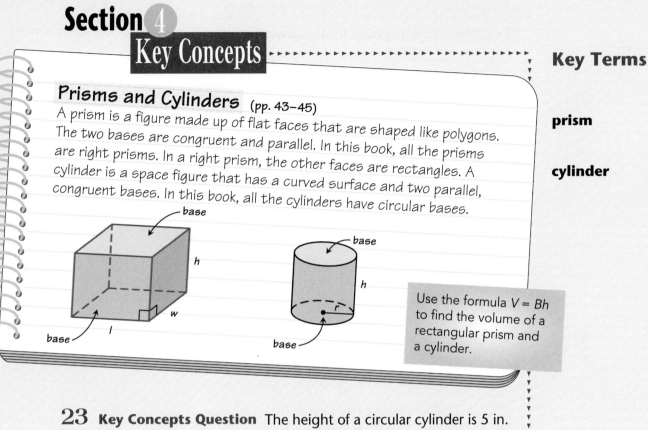

Prisms and Cylinders (pp. 43–45)

A prism is a figure made up of flat faces that are shaped like polygons. The two bases are congruent and parallel. In this book, all the prisms are right prisms. In a right prism, the other faces are rectangles. A cylinder is a space figure that has a curved surface and two parallel, congruent bases. In this book, all the cylinders have circular bases.

base

h

base

l   w

base

h

r

base

Use the formula $V = Bh$ to find the volume of a rectangular prism and a cylinder.

Key Terms

prism

cylinder

23 Key Concepts Question The height of a circular cylinder is 5 in. The diameter of its base is 4 in. Find its volume. about 62.8 in.³

Section 4

Practice & Application Exercises

YOU WILL NEED

For Exs. 38 and 39:
- scissors
- tape
- strip of paper
- colored pencils or markers

1. The world's smallest bicycle ever ridden had wheels with a diameter of 0.76 in. The world's largest bicycle had wheels with a diameter of 10 ft.

   a. Find the circumference of a wheel on each bicycle.
   smallest bicycle: about 2.39 in.; largest bicycle: about 31.4 ft

   b. How far would each bicycle travel in one complete turn of its wheels? smallest bicycle: about 2.39 in.; largest bicycle: about 31.4 ft

   c. The world's smallest bicycle was ridden a distance of 13 ft $5\frac{1}{2}$ in. About how many turns did the wheels make? about 68

   d. Suppose the wheels on the world's largest bicycle made as many turns as your answer to part (c). How far would it travel?
   2135.2 ft

Evaluate each expression for the given values of the variables.

2. $2\pi r$ when $r = 5$ about 31.4

3. $8 + x$ when $x = 92$ 100

4. $3 - m$ when $m = 0.2$ 2.8

5. $\frac{14}{y}$ when $y = 7$ 2

6. $5n^2$ when $n = 0$ 0

7. lw when $l = 6$, $w = 3$ 18

Use symbols to write an expression for each word phrase.

8. four more than six $6 + 4$

9. four less than a number $n - 4$

10. a number divided by 15 $\frac{n}{15}$

11. ten times a number $10n$

12. nine more than the product of a number and three $3n + 9$

13. Challenge Suppose two identical circles just touch each other. Then a rectangle is drawn as shown. The distance d is the diameter of the circle.

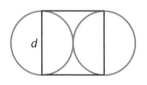

a. Write an expression for the perimeter of the rectangle. $4d$

b. Evaluate your expression when $d = 2$. 8

Find the volume of each figure.

14.

8 cm

6 cm

5 cm

240 cm³

15.

3 in.

6 in.

about 42.39 in.³

16.

8 cm

20 cm

about 1004.8 cm³

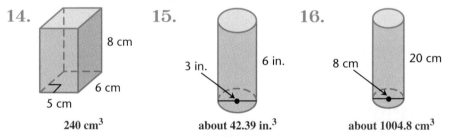

Find the volume of a cylinder with the given dimensions.

17. $r = 2$ cm
$h = 10$ cm
about 125.6 cm³

18. $r = 6.3$ cm
$h = 6.3$ cm
about 785.1 cm³

19. $r = 13$ cm
$h = 10$ cm
about 5306.6 cm³

Find the volume of a rectangular prism with the given dimensions.

20. $l = 26$ cm
$w = 26$ cm
$h = 10$ cm
6760 cm³

21. $l = 13$ cm
$w = 14$ cm
$h = 7$ cm
1274 cm³

22. $l = 4$ cm
$w = 5$ cm
$h = 12$ cm
240 cm³

23. Challenge The cylinder in Exercise 18 can fit into two of the rectangular prisms in Exercises 20–22. Which two prisms can it fit into? The prism in Exercise 21 can fit into one of the cylinders in Exercises 17–19. Which cylinder can it fit into? 18 can fit into 20 and 21; 21 can fit into 19.

24. Costume Design The Goodspeed Opera House in East Haddam, Connecticut, was a difficult place to perform the play *Bloomer Girl*. The hoop skirts in the women's 1860s costumes were too large for the narrow halls, stairways, and doors. Hoop skirts have a hoop around the hem of the skirt. This hoop can be made of steel.

a. The wardrobe master of the play said, "The real super hoops were about 11 ft in diameter, but if we had one in the show, it would cover about half our stage." Find the approximate area the super hoop would cover. about 95 ft^2

b. According to the wardrobe master's comment, about what size (in square feet) is the opera house stage? about 190 ft^2

c. Find the length of steel needed to make a super hoop. about 34.54 ft

d. The women acting in *Bloomer Girl* ended up wearing hoop skirts that were 6 ft in diameter. Determine the length of steel needed to make each hoop. about 18.84 ft

e. About what fraction of the stage did a 6 ft diameter hoop cover? about $\frac{1}{6}$

25. Music Sarah Hopkins, an Australian composer and performer, has experimented with the musical sounds of cylindrical instruments called "whirlies." Whirlies are played by whirling them through the air at different speeds. Differences in length and diameter affect the pitch and sound of each instrument.

Whirlies are flexible cylindrical hoses of various lengths and diameters.

	High Voiced Whirly	Deep Whirly
Diameter (mm)	25	32
Length (m)	1	1.75
Length (mm)	? 1000	? 1750
Volume (mm^3)	?	?

490,625   1,406,720

a. Copy and complete the table. See table.

b. Sarah Hopkins also made a whirly that is exactly twice as long as a Deep Whirly. Its diameter is the same as the Deep Whirly's. How does doubling the length of a Deep Whirly affect its volume? It doubles the volume.

Journal

Exercise 28 checks that you can find and compare the volumes of two different containers.

Beauclerc Elementary School in Jacksonville, Florida, made the largest popcorn box on record. The box was a rectangular prism 39 ft 11$\frac{1}{2}$ in. long, 20 ft 8$\frac{1}{2}$ in. wide, and 8 ft high.

26. Estimate the volume of the popcorn box. Calculate the actual volume of the popcorn box, rounding to the nearest cubic ft.
about 6400 ft³, about 6620 ft³

27. a. Suppose a regular-size popcorn box measures 3$\frac{1}{2}$ in. wide, 7$\frac{1}{2}$ in. long, and 10$\frac{1}{2}$ in. high. What is the volume of the box?

   b. About how many regular-sized boxes of popped popcorn would be needed to fill the large popcorn box? Explain.

Reflecting on the Section

Write your response to Exercise 28 in your journal.

28. Rosa takes a carton of milk out of the refrigerator and empties it into the glass shown. Amazingly, the milk fills the glass so it is perfectly even with the rim. Was the milk carton full when Rosa began filling her glass? Explain your reasoning.

No; The volume of the carton is greater than the volume of the cylinder.

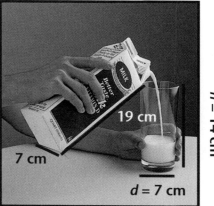
19 cm
7 cm
h = 14 cm
d = 7 cm

Spiral Review

29. The table shows sales of CDs at a record store. Make a scatter plot using the data. Put hours of operation on the horizontal axis. If it makes sense to draw a fitted line, do so. (Module 1, p. 34)
See Additional Answers.

Hours of operation	54	48	60	65	40	60	48	56
CDs sold	710	530	850	940	520	740	630	750

Find each quotient. (Toolbox, p. 594)

30. 0.141 ÷ 12
0.01175
31. 6.2 ÷ 3.1 2
32. 150.62 ÷ 18
8.367̄
33. 12.4 ÷ 12 1.03̄

Find each answer. (Toolbox, p. 600)

34. 4(2 + 3²) 44
35. 5 • 6 – 3 27
36. 16 – 8 + $\frac{42}{6}$
15
37. 11(6) ÷ 2 33

Making a Mobius Strip

There is another tale about Paul Bunyan and a conveyor belt that brought ore from a uranium mine. The belt was made with a half-twist so it would wear evenly on both sides.

38. **a.** Make a model of the conveyor belt as shown. Check students' work.

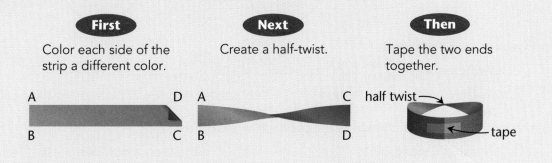

First
Color each side of the strip a different color.

Next
Create a half-twist.

Then
Tape the two ends together.

A ————————— D A ———————————— C half twist
B ————————— C B ———————————— D tape

b. Trace your finger around the belt once. How many sides does the belt actually have? one

The belt you made is called a Möbius strip.

39. When a belt twice as long and half as wide was needed, Paul said to cut the belt in two lengthwise. Was he right? Try it and see! Yes.

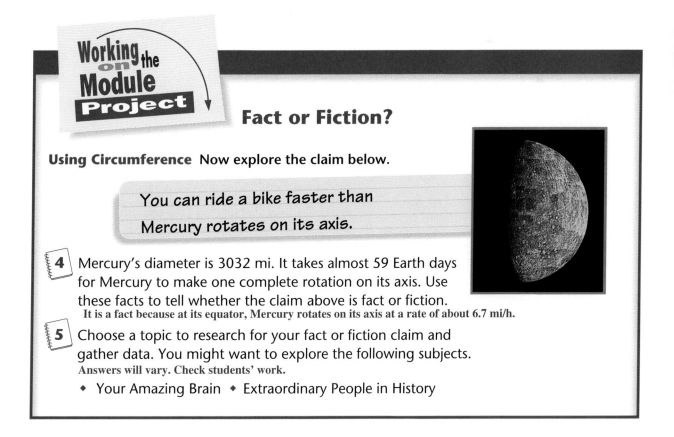

Working on the Module Project

Fact or Fiction?

Using Circumference Now explore the claim below.

> You can ride a bike faster than Mercury rotates on its axis.

4 Mercury's diameter is 3032 mi. It takes almost 59 Earth days for Mercury to make one complete rotation on its axis. Use these facts to tell whether the claim above is fact or fiction.
It is a fact because at its equator, Mercury rotates on its axis at a rate of about 6.7 mi/h.

5 Choose a topic to research for your fact or fiction claim and gather data. You might want to explore the following subjects.
Answers will vary. Check students' work.

  ◆ Your Amazing Brain ◆ Extraordinary People in History

Section 4

Extra Skill Practice

Find the circumference of each circle.

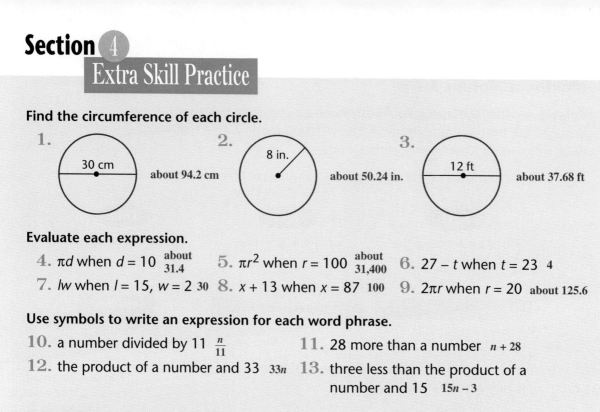

1. 30 cm   about 94.2 cm

2. 8 in.   about 50.24 in.

3. 12 ft   about 37.68 ft

Evaluate each expression.

4. πd when $d = 10$ about 31.4

5. πr^2 when $r = 100$ about 31,400

6. $27 - t$ when $t = 23$ 4

7. lw when $l = 15$, $w = 2$ 30

8. $x + 13$ when $x = 87$ 100

9. $2\pi r$ when $r = 20$ about 125.6

Use symbols to write an expression for each word phrase.

10. a number divided by 11 $\frac{n}{11}$

11. 28 more than a number $n + 28$

12. the product of a number and 33 $33n$

13. three less than the product of a number and 15 $15n - 3$

Find the volume of each figure.

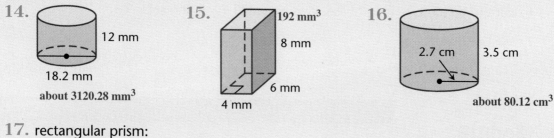

14. 12 mm, 18.2 mm   about 3120.28 mm³

15. 192 mm³, 8 mm, 6 mm, 4 mm

16. 2.7 cm, 3.5 cm   about 80.12 cm³

17. rectangular prism:

   a. $l = 4$ ft, $w = 2\frac{1}{2}$ ft, $h = 5\frac{1}{2}$ ft   55 ft³

   b. $l = 6.3$ m, $w = 2.5$ m, $h = 5.9$ m   92.925 m³

18. cylinder:

   a. $d = 10\frac{1}{2}$ in., $h = 17$ in.   about 1471.29 in.³

   b. $d = 0.5$ mm, $h = 1.2$ mm   about 0.24 mm³

1. Sample Response: Both use the formula $V = Bh$, or volume equals area of the base times the height. The base of a prism is a polygon, so the formula for the area of its base, B, varies. The base of a cylinder is a circle, so the formula for the area of its base, B, is always $B = \pi r^2$.

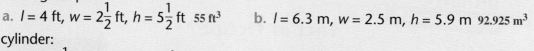

Standardized Testing ◀▶ Open-ended

1. How are the formulas for finding the volume of a prism and a cylinder alike? How are they different?   See above.

2. Write a word problem that involves finding the volume of a prism or a cylinder found in your home. Sample Response: A cereal box has a length of 10 in., a width of 3 in., and a height of 14 in. What is the volume of the cereal box? Answer: 420 in.³

EXTENDED **E2** EXPLORATION

FOR ASSESSMENT AND PORTFOLIOS

Wet Paint

The Situation See the Resource Book for a detailed discussion of this Extended Exploration.

While riding your bike, you accidentally rode across some wet paint.

The Problem

Suppose the paint spill was 4 in. wide where you rode across it. If you continue to ride in a straight line, what will the track left by the bike's tires look like? Your bike tire has a diameter of 26 in. (You can ignore the pattern of the tire tread.) The track will look like a dashed line.; 4 in.; Sample Responses are given: The paint will smudge; Use a model or draw a picture; Try a similar experiment with a coin and food coloring.

Something to Think About

◆ How much of the bike's tires will be covered with paint?

◆ What are some assumptions you can make about wet paint on a moving object?

◆ Which problem solving strategies can you use to help solve this problem?

◆ How can you test your conclusions?

Present Your Results

Describe what you did to solve the problem. Show any problem solving strategies you used. Explain why you think your answer is correct.

For help with assessing your work on this and other Extended Explorations (E²), see the Toolbox, pages 607–608.

4 in.

Section 5 Equations and Expressions

IN THIS SECTION

EXPLORATION 1
◆ Writing Equations

EXPLORATION 2
◆ Solving Equations

EXPLORATION 3
◆ Simplifying Expressions

Extraordinary Rules of Thumb

◄◄◄ Setting the Stage

Rules of thumb have been passed from one generation to the next for hundreds of years. These rules help people estimate things like the temperature outdoors. Many rules are about ordinary events, but they seem extraordinary because someone noticed patterns and connections.

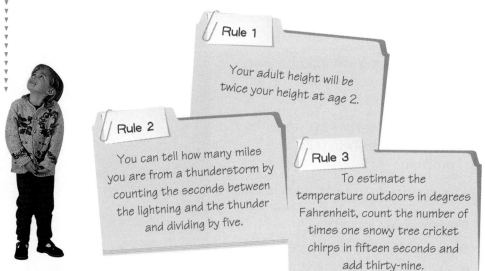

Rule 1

Your adult height will be twice your height at age 2.

Rule 2

You can tell how many miles you are from a thunderstorm by counting the seconds between the lightning and the thunder and dividing by five.

Rule 3

To estimate the temperature outdoors in degrees Fahrenheit, count the number of times one snowy tree cricket chirps in fifteen seconds and add thirty-nine.

Think About It

1 Suppose your height at age 2 years was 2 ft 10 in. How tall should you be as an adult? **5 ft 8 in.**

2 How many miles are you from a thunderstorm if you count 35 seconds between the lightning and the thunder? **7 mi**

3 Pick one rule of thumb given above. How could you test the rule to see if it is accurate? **Answers will vary.**

Writing E=quations

▶ Many rules of thumb can be written as mathematical formulas or equations. For example, the rule of thumb for finding your adult height from your height at age 2 can be represented as an equation.

> **First**   Choose a variable to represent each of the quantities that are unknown or may change.
>
> Let c = height at age 2.   Let a = adult height.
>
> **Then**   Represent the word relationships with symbols and variables.
>
> Your adult height is equal to twice your height at age 2.
>   ↓   ↓   ↓   ↓
> a =   2 · c
> $a = 2c$

4   One rule of thumb says you can estimate the temperature outdoors in degrees Fahrenheit by counting the number of times one snowy tree cricket chirps in 15 seconds and adding 39.

   a. What quantities are unknown or may change?
              temperature and the number of cricket chirps
   b. Choose a variable to represent each unknown. Then write an equation for estimating the temperature based on the number of cricket chirps.   **Sample Response: Let t = temperature and c = the number of cricket chirps in 15 s; $t = c + 39$**

5 Discussion   Another rule of thumb states that the first year of a dog's life is equivalent to 15 years of a human's life. For dogs 2 years or older, you can find the equivalent human age by multiplying the dog's age by 4 and adding 15. Which of the equations below can you use to represent this rule of thumb? Explain your choice and what h and d represent.

   A. $h = 15 + 4 + d$ **B.** $h = 15 + 4d$

   C. $h = 15 · 4d$ **D.** $h = 15d + 4$

   B; the equation describes the rule given by the words; d = dog's age, h = equivalent human age

✔ QUESTION 6

...checks that you can translate a word sentence into an equation.

6. a. Let d = distance from the thunderstorm in miles and s = the number of seconds between the lightning and thunder; $d = \frac{s}{5}$

6 ✔ **CHECKPOINT** Write an equation for each rule of thumb. Be sure to tell what each variable represents.

a. To estimate the number of miles you are from a thunderstorm, count the number of seconds between the lightning and the thunder and divide by 5.

b. To quickly convert Celsius to Fahrenheit, double the Celsius temperature and add 30. Let F = temperature in Fahrenheit and C = temperature in Celsius; $F = 2C + 30$

▶ If you know the value of one of the variables, you can evaluate one side of an equation to find the value of the other side.

EXAMPLE

Trinja was 2 ft 9 in. tall at age 2. Estimate her adult height using the rule of thumb on page 55.

SAMPLE RESPONSE

$a = 2c$ ← Write the rule of thumb as an equation.

$= 2(2.75)$

$= 5.5$ ← 2 ft 9 in. = 2.75 ft. Substitute 2.75 for the variable c.

Trinja's adult height would be 5.5 ft, or 5 ft 6 in.

FOR ▶ HELP

with *order of operations*, see

TOOLBOX, p. 600

7 a. To find the equivalent human age for a 6-year-old dog, substitute 6 for d in the equation $h = 15 + 4d$. $h = 15 + 4 \cdot 6$

b. To evaluate $15 + 4d$ when $d = 6$, which operation is performed first, addition or multiplication? Why? multiplication; Multiplication is before addition in the order of operations.

c. What is the equivalent human age for a 6-year-old dog? for an 11-year-old dog? 39 years; 59 years

✔ QUESTION 8

...checks that you can evaluate an expression.

8 ✔ **CHECKPOINT** Use an equation from Question 6 to find each quantity.

a. Estimate the distance from a thunderstorm when there are 22 seconds between the lightning and the thunder. 4.4 mi

b. Find the approximate Fahrenheit temperature for 15° Celsius. 60°F

HOMEWORK EXERCISES ▶ See Exs. 1–6 on p. 63.

Solving **E**=quations

GOAL

LEARN HOW TO...
◆ solve equations

AS YOU...
◆ work with algebra tiles and a rule of thumb about temperature

KEY TERMS
◆ solve an equation
◆ solution
◆ inverse operations

SET UP *Work with a partner. You will need algebra tiles.*

▸ A student collected temperature data for where she lives and wrote this rule of thumb. To predict the day's high temperature, add 18° to the Fahrenheit temperature at 6:00 A.M. This rule of thumb can be described by the equation below.

Let **h** = the daily high temperature (in °F).

$$h = t + 18$$

Let **t** = the temperature at 6:00 A.M. (in °F).

9 Discussion Suppose the high temperature was 23°F. How might the rule of thumb help you find the temperature at 6:00 A.M.?
Subtract 18°F from the high temperature of 23°F to get 5°F.

▸ When you answered Question 9, you *solved the equation* 23 = t + 18. To **solve an equation** means to find the **solution** of the equation, or the value of the variable that makes the equation true.

10 Try This as a Class Each folder contains a pair of equations.

1	2	3	4
$6 + n = 15$	$2w = 7$	$y - 7 = 21$	$\dfrac{a}{3} = 6$
$n = 15 - 6$	$w = \dfrac{7}{2}$	$y = 28$	$a = 18$

a. Do the equations in each pair have the same solution? How do you know? Yes; When the solution of the second equation on each card is substituted in the first equation, it makes the equation true.

b. Which operation (addition, subtraction, multiplication, or division) is used in the first equation in each box?
1: addition, 2: multiplication, 3: subtraction, 4: division

c. Which operation can you use to get from the first equation to the second equation in each box? 1: subtraction, 2: division, 3: addition, 4: multiplication

11 a. Addition is the *inverse operation* of subtraction. **Inverse operations** are operations that undo each other. What is the inverse operation of multiplication? division

b. How were inverse operations used in Question 10?
Sample Response: They were used to rewrite the equation in terms of the variable.

▶ **Using Algebra Tiles** You can model equations with algebra tiles. The ▢ tile represents the unknown quantity (the variable). The variable *t* can be represented by ▢. The number 1 is represented by one unit tile ▢. The equation you solved in Question 9 is modeled below with algebra tiles and a balance scale.

$$23 = t + 18$$

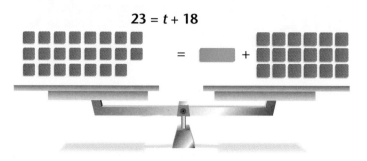

▶ When you solve an equation, the expressions on both sides of the equals sign must remain equal. The scale must remain balanced.

12. See Additional Answers.

12 a. Try This as a Class Create a model of the equation $15 = 6 + n$ with your algebra tiles.

b. Recall the inverse operation used to solve this equation in Question 10. Model this by moving some of your tiles. Be sure you keep the "scale" balanced. Write the new equation represented by the tiles.

▶ The Example below shows how to use math symbols and inverse operations to solve the equation $23 = t + 18$.

EXAMPLE

Using a Model

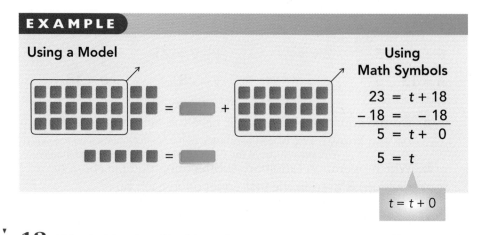

Using
Math Symbols

$$23 = t + 18$$
$$-18 = \quad -18$$
$$5 = t + 0$$
$$5 = t$$

$t = t + 0$

13 Why is 18 subtracted from both sides of the equation?
Sample Response: To put the variable by itself on one side of the equation.

14 Use your algebra tiles to model and solve each equation. Show your work using math symbols.

a. $9 + x = 11$ 2   **b.** $7 = y + 4$ 3

▶ **Two-step Equations** Some equations use more than one operation. For example, $2h + 7 = 15$ uses both multiplication and addition. You can model the equation with algebra tiles.

EXAMPLE

Solve $2h + 7 = 15$. Let ▭ represent h.

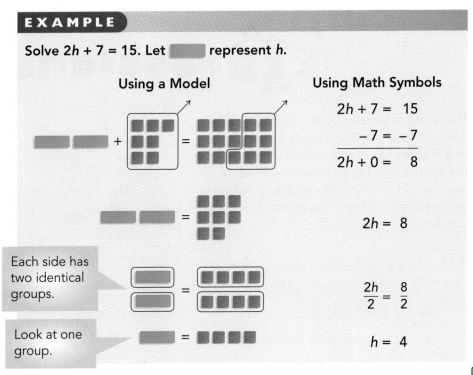

Using a Model   **Using Math Symbols**

$$2h + 7 = 15$$
$$\underline{-7 = -7}$$
$$2h + 0 = 8$$

$$2h = 8$$

Each side has two identical groups.

$$\frac{2h}{2} = \frac{8}{2}$$

Look at one group.

$$h = 4$$

15 **a. Try This As A Class** Use algebra tiles to model $2y + 9 = 13$. What inverse operation will you use first? Write the new equation represented by the algebra tiles.

   b. What inverse operation will you use next? What does y equal?   division; 2

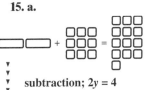

15. a.

subtraction; $2y = 4$

16 Check your solution from Question 15 by substituting your value for y into the original equation $2y + 9 = 13$. $2(2) + 9 = 4 + 9 = 13$

17 Use algebra tiles to solve each equation. Check each solution.

   a. $5 + 2m = 7$ 1   **b.** $4p = 12$ 3   **c.** $10 = 3x + 1$ 3

18 ✔ **CHECKPOINT** Solve each equation. Show your work and check your solutions.

   a. $8y + 16 = 24$ 1   **b.** $2p - 7 = 15$ 11   **c.** $4a = 10$ 2.5

   d. $\frac{n}{2} = 9$ 18   **e.** $\frac{x}{2} + 3 = 11$ 16   **f.** $\frac{r}{5} - 1 = 6$ 35

✔ **QUESTION 18**

...checks that you can use inverse operations to solve equations.

HOMEWORK EXERCISES ▶ See Exs. 7–13 on pp. 63–64.

GOAL

LEARN HOW TO...
- simplify expressions

AS YOU...
- work with a rule of thumb about laundry

KEY TERMS
- terms
- like terms
- coefficient

Simplifying EXpressions

"MAYBE WE SHOULDN'T HAVE LET THE LAUNDRY PILE UP FOR A YEAR."

▶ The average person in the United States does an amazing 8493 loads of laundry in a lifetime! A rule of thumb states that the typical adult generates one load of laundry per week, while athletes, outdoor workers, and children generate two loads per week.

19 Write an expression that represents the number of loads of laundry generated in x weeks.

   a. by one child $2x$ **b.** by one typical adult x

   c. by the child and the adult together $3x$

20 Evaluate your expression in Question 19(c) when $x = 4$.   12

▶ Consider a family with one child and two adults where one of the adults is an outdoor worker. An expression for the number of loads of laundry generated by the family in x weeks is shown below.

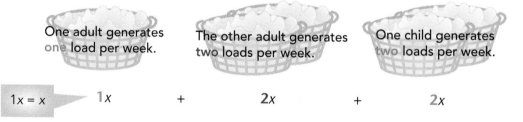

One adult generates one load per week.

The other adult generates two loads per week.

One child generates two loads per week.

$1x = x$ $1x$ $+$ $2x$ $+$ $2x$

▶ The parts of the expression that are added together are called **terms**. Each of the three terms contains the variable x. You can use algebra tiles to model an equivalent expression.

$$1x + 2x + 2x = 5x$$

There are 5 tiles in all.

21. 390 loads of laundry; Sample Response: 5x because it is easier to multiply once than to multiply 3 times and then add the products together.

21 How many loads of laundry will this family generate in $1\frac{1}{2}$ years, or 78 weeks? Did you use $1x + 2x + 2x$ or $5x$? Why?

▶ The terms 1*x*, 2*x*, and 2*x* are *like terms*. **Like terms** can be combined by adding or subtracting *coefficients*. The **coefficient** is the numeral part of the term.

22 Discussion Use the table.

a. Explain why the terms in the left column are *like* terms and the terms in the right column are *unlike* terms.

b. Describe what it means for terms to be like terms. **Sample Response: Like terms have exactly the same variables raised to the same powers.**

Like terms	Unlike terms
1, 13	4, 13*x*
2*y*, 8*y*	2*y*, 8*y*²
3*rs*, 4*rs*	3*r*, 4*rs*
$\frac{1}{4}m^2$, 7*m*²	$\frac{1}{4}m^2$, 7*p*²

22. a. Sample Response: The pairs of terms in the left column either have no variable, the same variables, or the same variable with the same exponent. The pairs of terms in the right column do not.

▶ You can add like terms to make one term, but you cannot add unlike terms. The algebra tiles below model like and unlike terms.

2*x* + *x* does equal 3*x*.   2*x* + 1 does *not* equal 3*x*.

23 Try This as a Class

a. Choose a value for *x* and substitute it in the expressions 2*x* + *x*, 3*x*, and 2*x* + 1. **Answers will vary. Check students' work.**

b. For which values of *x* does 2*x* + *x* = 3*x*? **all values of *x***

c. Are there values of *x* for which 2*x* + 1 = 3*x*? If so, which ones? **Yes; 1**

24 ✔ CHECKPOINT Combine like terms to simplify each expression.

a. 2*w* + 2*w* **4*w***   b. 4*x* − *x* **3*x***   c. 3*y* + 7*y* − 6 **10*y* − 6**   d. 2*b*² + *b*² **3*b*²**

✔ QUESTION 24

...checks that you can combine like terms.

▶ Sometimes you can combine like terms to simplify an equation.

EXAMPLE

Group and combine like terms.

$$6x + 3 - x = 18$$
$$(6x - x) + 3 = 18$$
$$5x + 3 = 18$$

25 Try This as a Class Solve the equation 5*x* + 3 = 18 in the Example. Does your solution work for the original equation 6*x* + 3 − *x* = 18 as well as for the equation 5*x* + 3 = 18? Explain.

3; Yes; Sample Response: Combining terms does not change the value of an expression.

| **HOMEWORK EXERCISES** ▶ See Exs. 14–27 on pp. 64–66.

Key Terms

solve an
equation

solution

inverse
operations

26. 1; Sample
Response: When the
expressions on both
sides of the equation
equal the same number,
the solution is correct.

terms

like terms

coefficient

Writing Equations for Word Sentences (pp. 55–56)

To write an equation, choose a variable to represent each of the quantities that are unknown or that may change. Use mathematical expressions to represent the word relationships between the quantities.

Solving Equations (pp. 57–59)

To solve an equation, you must find the solution, or the value for the variable that makes the equation true. You can do this by using inverse operations and keeping the equation balanced.

Example

$$\frac{y}{3} + 6 = 30$$

$$-6 = -6$$

The inverse of adding is subtracting.

$$\frac{y}{3} = 24$$

The inverse of dividing is multiplying.

$$\frac{y}{3} \cdot 3 = 24 \cdot 3$$

$$y = 72$$

Check Substitute 72 for y.

$$\frac{y}{3} + 6 = 30$$

$$\frac{72}{3} + 6 \stackrel{?}{=} 30$$

$$24 + 6 \stackrel{?}{=} 30$$

$$30 = 30$$

Simplifying Expressions (pp. 60–61)

Terms with identical variable parts are called like terms.
To simplify some expressions and to solve some equations you can combine like terms by adding or subtracting coefficients.

Example

$$41 = 4x - 3x - 1$$

4x and 3x are like terms.
$$4x - 3x = 1x$$

$$41 = 1x - 1$$

$$+1 = +1$$

1 and 1x are unlike terms.

$$42 = x$$

Check Substitute 42 for x.

$$41 = 4x - 3x - 1$$

$$41 \stackrel{?}{=} 4 \cdot 42 - 3 \cdot 42 - 1$$

$$41 \stackrel{?}{=} 168 - 126 - 1$$

$$41 = 41$$

CLOSURE QUESTION

What is the goal in solving equations involving a variable? What is meant by the phrase "combine like terms?"

Sample Response: To find a value for the variable that makes the equation true. "Combine like terms" means to add or subtract terms that contain identical variable parts.

26 Key Concepts Question Solve the equation $\frac{x}{6} + \frac{7}{6} = \frac{4}{3}$. Check your solution. How do you know your solution is correct? See above.

Section 5

Practice & Application Exercises

YOU WILL NEED

For Ex. 26:
◆ graph paper

1. Leona makes a flower arrangement so the flowers are about one and a half times the width of the container. Which equation represents this rule of thumb? Let a = the width of the arrangement and c = the width of the container. A

   A. $1\frac{1}{2}c = a$ B. $1\frac{1}{2}a = c$ C. $c + 1\frac{1}{2} = a$

4.5 in.

3 in.

For Exercises 2–5, change each word sentence into a mathematical equation. Tell what each variable represents.

2. The total cost of tickets for a group of children at an amusement park is $29 per child times the number of children.
   Let n = the number of children and c = the total cost; $c = 29n$

3. The total distance of a bike trip divided by 50 gives the approximate number of days the trip will take.
   Let d = distance and n = the number of days; $\frac{d}{50} = n$

4. To estimate a yearly salary from an hourly wage, double the hourly wage and multiply by 1000.
   Let s = yearly salary and w = hourly wage; $s = 2000w$

5. To estimate the length of each cord needed in macramé, multiply the length of the finished product by 8. Let f = the length of the finished product and l = the length of each cord; $l = 8f$

6. Your mass in kilograms multiplied by 0.08 is approximately equal to the volume of your blood in liters.

   a. Write an equation for this rule of thumb. Tell what each variable represents. Let m = mass in kilograms and v = volume of blood in liters; $v = 0.08m$

   b. According to this rule of thumb, how many liters of blood does a 50-kilogram person have? 4 L

7. Use the rule of thumb and the formula to convert 0°C, 15°C, and 100°C to Fahrenheit temperatures. Let C = the temperature in degrees Celsius and F = the temperature in degrees Fahrenheit. For which Celsius temperature does the rule of thumb give the best estimate of the Fahrenheit temperature you found using the formula?

7. 1) 30°F, 2) 32°F;
1) 60°F, 2) 59°F;
1) 230°F, 2) 212°F; The rule of thumb gives the best estimate for 15°C.

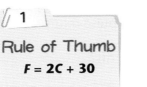

1

Rule of Thumb
$F = 2C + 30$

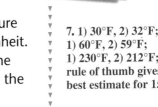

2

Formula
$F = \frac{9}{5}C + 32$

8. Use variables and symbols to write each equation modeled with the algebra tiles.

a. 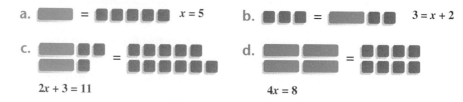 $x = 5$

b. $3 = x + 2$

c. $2x + 3 = 11$

d. $4x = 8$

9. Solve each equation in Exercise 8. a. 5; b. 1; c. 4; d. 2

10. Use inverse operations to solve each equation. Check your solutions.

a. $6 + x = 31$ 25

b. $\dfrac{x}{12} = 105$ 1260

c. $6t = 21$ $\dfrac{21}{6}$

d. $30 = 7y - 5$ 5

e. $\dfrac{y}{4} + 1 = 7$ 24

f. $3y + 5 = 11$ 2

11. **Create Your Own** Write your own rule of thumb for something you estimate and then write it as an equation. Use your equation in two examples. **Answers will vary. Check students' work.**

◀ This computer-generated image of the ocean floor was made using sonar.

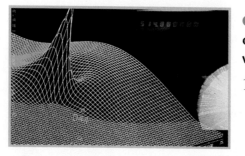

Oceanography **Ships use the speed of sound in water to help find the water's depth.**

12. a. The speed of sound in water is about five times the speed of sound in air. Write an equation for this rule of thumb.

12. a. Let w = the speed of sound in water and a = the speed of sound in air; $w = 5a$
b. 294 m/s

b. The speed of sound in ocean water with a temperature of 6°C is 1470 m/s. At about what speed does sound travel in air?

13. **Challenge** A sonar pulse from a ship is sent to the bottom of the ocean. To find the distance the pulse has traveled, multiply the speed of sound in water by the amount of time it takes for the pulse to travel from the ship to the ocean floor and back to the ship. Assume that the speed of sound in water is 1470 m/s.

13. a. The sound has traveled the distance between the ship and the ocean floor twice, so the ocean depth is half the distance traveled.

a. Suppose the sonar pulse returns in 2 seconds. Explain why the ocean depth is 1470 m rather than 2940 m. (*Hint:* Draw a diagram of the path the sound travels.)

b. Write a formula for finding ocean depth. Use your formula to find the ocean depth if the sonar pulse returns in 2.5 seconds.

$d = \dfrac{1}{2} \cdot 1470 \cdot t$; 1837.5 m

14. Which of the terms below are like terms?

x^2 $\dfrac{1}{2}x^2$ xy x^2y $2x^2$ xy^2 $x^2, \dfrac{1}{2}x^2,$ and $2x^2$

If possible, combine like terms to simplify each expression.

15. $17x + 4 - 3$ *17x + 1* 16. $8rs - 6r$ *no like terms* 17. $16w + 3 - w$ *15w + 3*

18. $3t - 2t + 9t$ *10t* 19. $19n - 19n^2$ *no like terms* 20. $4x + 4xy - 4x$ *4xy*

21. $12y^2 + 6x + 3y^2 + x$ *15y² + 7x* 22. $f^2 + 3f + 4f - 6$ *f² + 7f − 6*

23. **Geometry Connection** The perimeter of a rectangle can be represented by the equation $P = l + l + w + w$, where P = the perimeter, l = the length, and w = the width.

   a. Simplify the equation by combining like terms. *P = 2l + 2w*

   b. If $l = 10$ in. and $w = 3$ in., what is the perimeter of the rectangle? *26 in.*

   c. Solve for w when $P = 50$ cm and $l = 18$ cm. *7 cm*

   d. Solve for l when $P = 15$ m and $w = 3$ m. *4.5 m*

24. **Geometry Connection** Write an equation for finding the perimeter of each figure. Tell what each variable represents. Combine like terms when possible. *Let l = length of a side and P = perimeter.*

   a. equilateral triangle *P = 3l*

   b. square *P = 4l*

25. Find the length of one side of each figure in Exercise 24 when the perimeter is 36 yd. *equilateral triangle: 12 yd; square: 9 yd*

26. **Research** One rule of thumb from someone living in New York City states that to predict the day's high temperature, add 18 degrees to the temperature at 6:00 A.M.
   See above.

   a. Do you think this is a good rule of thumb? Explain how you can use the scatter plot to convince someone that you are right.

   b. Does it make sense to fit a line to the data in the scatter plot? Explain your reasoning.

   c. For one week, record the temperature at 6:00 A.M. and the daily high temperature for your area. Make a scatter plot of your data like the one shown. If it makes sense, draw a fitted line for your scatter plot.

   d. Write a rule of thumb for predicting the high temperature for your area based on your temperature data. If a rule cannot be written, explain why not.

26. a. Sample Response: No; the temperatures found by adding 18° to the temperatures at 6 A.M. are almost always greater than the corresponding high temperatures in the scatter plot. **b.** Yes; As the temperatures at 6 A.M. increase, the daily high temperatures also increase and seem to cluster near a line. **c–d.** Check students' work.

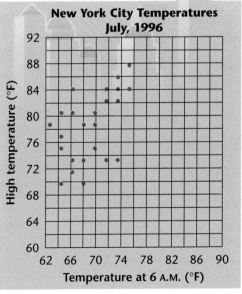

New York City Temperatures July, 1996

27. **a.** 1 cylinder and 2 pencils can be substituted for 1 cube on Balance Scale B.
b. 1 pencil; After substituting 1 cylinder and 2 pencils for a cube, Balance Scale B has 4 cylinders and 7 pencils balancing 11 pencils. Subtracting 7 pencils from each side leaves 4 pencils balancing 4 cylinders, which means 1 pencil would balance 1 cylinder. This is like solving an equation because you are doing the same thing to both sides to keep the scale balanced.

Reflecting ◀▶ on the Section

27. The balance scales below are each balanced.

    a. What objects from Balance Scale A could be substituted for a cube on Balance Scale B?

    b. Use your answer to part (a) to find how many pencils it will take to balance one cylinder. Explain how you solved this problem. How is solving it like solving an equation?

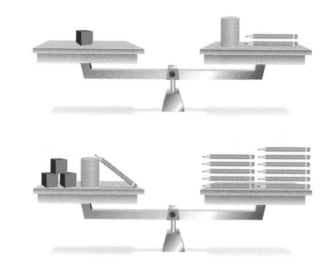

Balance Scale A

Balance Scale B

Spiral ◀▶ Review

28. Use $C = \pi d$ to find the diameter of a circle with a circumference of 78.5 cm. Use 3.14 for π. (Module 1, p. 46) **25 cm**

29. The volume of a rectangular prism is 264 in.^{3} The area of the base is 24 in.^{2}. What is the height of the prism? (Module 1, p. 47) **11 in.**

30. The equation for finding the area of a triangle is $A = \frac{1}{2}bh$, where A is the area of the triangle, b is the length of the base of the triangle, and h is the height of the triangle. Find the area of each triangle below. (Toolbox, p. 605)

    a. **24 in.^{2}**

    b. **26 m^2**

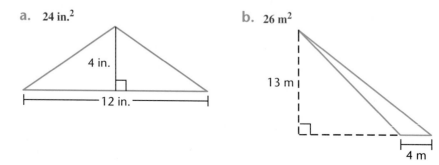

4 in.

12 in.

13 m

4 m

Extra Skill Practice

Change each statement into a mathematical equation. Tell what each variable represents.

1. The camp cooks agree that the amount of hamburger they need to purchase for a trip is $\frac{1}{4}$ lb of hamburger for each camper and an extra 5 lb. Let t = total amount of hamburger used in lb and c = the number of campers; $t = 0.25c + 5$

2. The total bus fare for a family is \$.60 for each adult and \$.10 for each child. Let f = total bus fare, a = the number of adults and c = the number of children; $f = 0.6a + 0.1c$

3. To estimate the monthly rent of an apartment in her city, Jenny multiplies the area in square feet of the apartment by \$.90. Let r = rent and a = area of the apartment; $r = 0.9a$

4. A mattress alone costs about \$25 plus half the price of the box spring and mattress together. Let c = cost of the mattress alone and p = the price of the mattress and box spring together; $c = \frac{p}{2} + 25$

Use inverse operations to solve each equation. Check your solutions.

5. $3j + 2 = 95$ 31

6. $5w = 30$ 6

7. $\frac{m}{52} = 4$ 208

8. $8 + 4z = 12$ 1

9. $r - 131 = 17$ 148

10. $27 = 14 + 2y$ 6.5

If possible, combine like terms to simplify each expression.

11. $1y + 6y - 2y$ 5y

12. $5 + 11rz - 3z$ no like terms

13. $t + 9t - 4$ $10t - 4$

14. $5p + 4p - 18pr$ $9p - 18pr$

15. $18r - 18rd + 18r$ $36r - 18rd$

16. $2h^3 + 4h$ no like terms

17. $10v + 5k^3 - v + 20k^3$ $9v + 25k^3$

18. $\frac{1}{2}xy + \frac{1}{4}x$ no like terms

19. $7 + 5w - 4w + w^2$ $7 + w + w^2$

Standardized Testing ◀▶ Multiple Choice

1. If $\frac{x}{3} - 23 = 4$, what does $2x$ equal?   D

   Ⓐ 114   Ⓑ 70   Ⓒ 54   Ⓓ 162

2. Combine like terms to simplify the expression $3x^2 + 10xy + x^2 - 7xy$. Which expression is correct?   A

   Ⓐ $4x^2 + 3xy$ Ⓑ $3x^2 + 3xy$ Ⓒ $4x^4 + 3x^2y^2$ Ⓓ $6x^6y^2$

WARM-UP EXERCISES

Find the area and perimeter or circumference of each figure.

1. rectangle with length 4 in. and width 7 in.
   $A = 28$ in.^{2};
   $P = 22$ in.

2. circle with radius 6 cm
   $A \approx 113.04$ cm^2;
   $P \approx 37.68$ cm

3. square with sides of 3.1 ft
   $A = 9.61$ ft^2;
   $P = 12.4$ ft

4. circle with diameter 17.2 yd
   $A \approx 232.2344$ yd^2;
   $P \approx 54.008$ yd

An AMAZING Lake

Setting the Stage

SET UP *You will need:* • *Labsheet 6A* • *string* • *ruler*

In this module, you have learned about amazing accomplishments of many people. In this section, you'll learn about a lake with some surprising features.

MISSOURI

Lake of the Ozarks

Lake of the Ozarks

★ A lake constructed by 20,500 workers in about 2 years

★ 61,000 acres (93 mi^2) of water surface

★ 87 billion cubic feet of water

★ A shoreline almost as long as the border of the entire state of Missouri

★ Located around the lake: 11 miniature golf courses, 6 go-cart tracks, 4 underground caves, and much more...

Think About It

1 Which claims on the travel brochure seem amazing?
Possible answers: Any of the claims may be listed.

2 **Use Labsheet 6A.** On the *Map of Missouri and the Lake of the Ozarks* a rectangle has been drawn around the lake. Use the rectangle and the map scale to see if the claim on the travel brochure about the length of the lake's shoreline could be true.
Sample Response: The only way that the claim could be true is if there are many inlets in the lake which would make the shoreline much longer than it appears to be.

Exploration 1

Exploring **Area** and **Perimeter**

SET UP *Work with a partner. You will need graph paper.*

▶ **How can the Lake of the Ozarks have a perimeter almost as long as the border of Missouri? To explore this question, you can look at a simpler problem that involves** *polygons.*

A **polygon** is a closed plane figure formed by three or more segments that do not cross each other. A **regular polygon** is a polygon with all sides of equal length and all angles of equal measure.

a polygon

not a polygon
(not closed)

not a polygon
(crosses itself)

not a polygon
(not formed
by segments)

3 Which of these figures are polygons? Which appears to be a regular polygon? Explain your thinking.

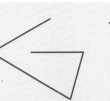

A.   B.   C.   D.

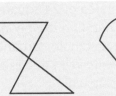

GOAL

LEARN HOW TO...
- ◆ model the relationship between the area and the perimeter of various polygons
- ◆ use tables, graphs, and equations to model relationships

AS YOU...
- ◆ learn about the Lake of the Ozarks

KEY TERMS
- ◆ polygon
- ◆ regular polygon

3. B and D; B; It appears to have all sides of equal length and all angles of equal measure.

4. b. Sample Response:

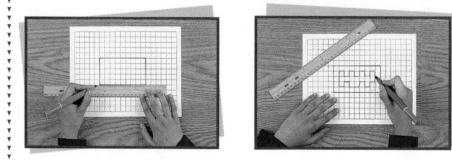

4. c. Sample Response:
perimeter: 30 units,
area: 14 units²

4 a. Draw a 5-unit by 9-unit rectangle on graph paper. Find the perimeter and the area of the rectangle. **perimeter: 28 units, area: 45 units²**

b. Draw a polygon inside the rectangle that has a perimeter greater than the perimeter of the rectangle. Use only lines on the graph paper for the sides of the polygon.

c. Find the perimeter and the area of your polygon.

5 Discussion Explain how the Lake of the Ozarks could have a shoreline almost as long as the border of Missouri, even though the area of the lake is much smaller than the area of the state. **The shoreline could be almost as long if the lake has many inlets.**

▶ **You have discovered that one polygon can have a smaller area than another but a greater perimeter. This helped explain the brochure's claim about the lake's shoreline. But how long could the lake's shoreline be and still enclose 61,000 acres? To answer this question, start by looking at a simpler problem.**

6 On graph paper, draw 8 different rectangles that have an area of 24 square units. Then find the perimeter of each rectangle. Organize your results in a table like the one shown.
See Additional Answers.

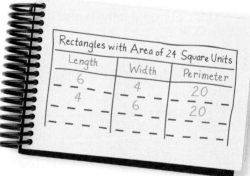

Rectangles with Area of 24 Square Units

Length	Width	Perimeter
6	4	20
4	6	20

7 Use the data in your table to plot points for the width and the perimeter of each rectangle. Put width on the horizontal axis and perimeter on the vertical axis. **See Additional Answers.**

8 Try This as a Class Use your graph from Question 7.

a. Does your graph show the perimeter of a rectangle with a width of 10 units? Explain. **No; There is no point for width = 10.**

b. Does your graph show the width of the rectangle with the least possible perimeter? Explain. **No; There are two rectangles with a perimeter of 20, so there is probably one with a smaller perimeter.**

9 a. Draw a curved line to connect the points on the graph.

b. Use your graph to estimate the perimeter of a rectangle with a width of 10 units.

c. Use your graph to estimate the width and the length of a rectangle with the least possible perimeter. Draw the rectangle.

10 a. How can you find the length of a rectangle with an area of 24 square units and a width of 16 units? What is the length?   **Divide 24 by 16; 1.5 units**

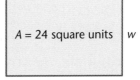

A = 24 square units w

l

b. Write an equation that tells how to find the length of a rectangle with an area of 24 square units when you know the width. Use the variables l and w for the length and width. $l = \frac{24}{w}$

c. Write an equation for the perimeter P of *any* rectangle when you know the length l and the width w. $P = 2l + 2w$

d. Use the equations from parts (b) and (c) to find the perimeter of a rectangle with an area of 24 square units and a width of 16 units.   **35 units**

▶ **Mathematical Models** Tables, graphs, and equations can be used as models to study mathematical relationships. You used them to explore relationships among the length, the width, and the perimeter of a rectangle.

11 ✔ **CHECKPOINT** Look back at the table, graph, and equation you made in Questions 6–10.   **Sample Responses are given.**

a. Suppose you want to quickly estimate the perimeter of a rectangle with an area of 24 square units and a width of 15 units. Which model would you use? Explain.
I would use the graph because it is a faster way to find an estimate.

b. Suppose a rectangle with an area of 24 square units has a width of $\frac{1}{6}$ unit. Which model would you use to find its exact length? Explain.   I would use the equation because an exact answer is needed and I could only estimate from the graph.

c. Is there a greatest possible perimeter for a rectangle with an area of 24 square units? Which model best shows this?

12 Do you think there is a greatest perimeter the Lake of the Ozarks could have and still enclose an area of 61,000 acres? Explain.

✔ **QUESTION 11**

...checks that you can use a mathematical model to study perimeter and area.

11. c. No; The graph shows that the length of one side would approach 0 and the length of the other side would become extremely large.

12. Sample Response: No; Based on my answers to Questions 6–11, it appears that there can be a least perimeter but not a greatest perimeter for a given area.

HOMEWORK EXERCISES ▶ See Exs. 1–6 on pp. 73–75.

Section 6 Key Concepts

Area and Perimeter of Polygons (pp. 69–71)

A polygon is a closed plane figure with three or more segments that do not cross. A regular polygon is a polygon with all sides congruent and all angles congruent. A polygon with a greater area than another polygon does not necessarily have a greater perimeter.

Example The area of triangle ABC is greater than the area of triangle DEF, but the perimeter of triangle ABC is less than the perimeter of triangle DEF.

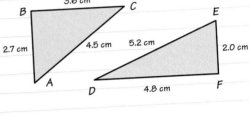

Mathematical Models (p. 71)

Tables, equations, and graphs can be used as mathematical models to study mathematical relationships.

Example Three ways to model a relationship between the circumference and the area of a circle are shown below.

Equations

$C = 2\pi r$
$A = \pi r^2$

Table

Circumference C	Area A
3.142	0.785
6.283	3.142
9.425	7.069
12.566	12.566

Graph

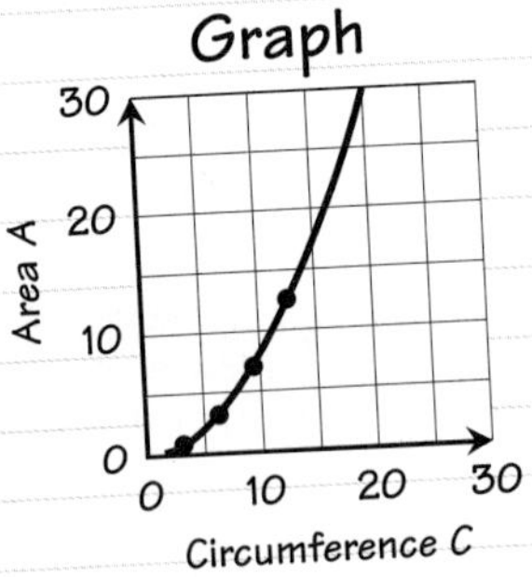

When data points fall in a curved pattern, a smooth curve can be drawn through the points as shown above.

CLOSURE QUESTION

What does the area of a polygon represent? What does the perimeter of a polygon represent?

Sample Response: The total amount of space inside the polygon.; The total length of the sides of the polygon.

13 Key Concepts Question Draw two right triangles. One triangle should have a larger area but a smaller perimeter than the second triangle. **Sample Responses are given using the triangles in the Example. perimeter: 10.8 units, area: 4.86 units² ; perimeter: 12 units, area: 4.8 units²**

Section 6

Practice & Application Exercises ▶▶▶▶▶▶▶▶

YOU WILL NEED

For Exs. 2 and 4:
♦ graph paper

For Ex. 6:
♦ square tiles

1. **Social Studies** Lake Baikal, located in southern Siberia, is the deepest lake in the world. At its deepest point its depth is 5712 ft. Lake Baikal is 386 mi long and varies in width from 9 mi to 50 mi.

   1. c. It is about in the middle; Sample Response: Yes; I would expect the average width to be about 30 mi which would make the area of this lake about 12,000 mi^2.

   a. Find the area and the perimeter of a rectangle that is 386 mi long and 9 mi wide. **perimeter: 790 mi, area: 3474 mi^2**

   b. Find the area and the perimeter of a rectangle that is 386 mi long and 50 mi wide. **perimeter: 872 mi, area: 19,300 mi^2**

   c. The area covered by Lake Baikal is 12,150 mi^2. How does this compare with the areas you found in parts (a) and (b)? Is this what you would expect? Explain your thinking.

   d. The lake has 1220 mi of shoreline. How does this compare with the perimeters you found in parts (a) and (b)? What does this tell you about the shape of the shoreline? **It is greater; There are many inlets.**

   2. See Additional Answers.
2. a. Make a table of values for the lengths, the widths, and the perimeters of 8 different rectangles. The area of each rectangle should be 30 square units.

   b. On a graph, plot points for the width and the perimeter of the rectangles. Put width on the horizontal axis. Then draw a smooth curve through the points.

   Bratsk Reservoir

   RUSSIA

   Lake Baikal

   Irkutsk •

   • Ulan-Ude

   Hovsgol Lake   MONGOLIA

   c. Estimate the width of the rectangle with the least perimeter. Estimate the length. How do the width and the length compare?

   d. Find the exact length of a rectangle with an area of 30 square units and a width of $\frac{1}{6}$ unit. Which model (*table*, *graph*, or *equation*) did you use? Why?

   e. Estimate the perimeter of a rectangle with an area of 30 square units and a width of 4 units. Which model did you use? Why?

   f. **Writing** Is there a greatest possible perimeter for a rectangle with an area of 30 square units? Explain.

3. The area of the base of a cylindrical swimming pool is 314 ft².

When finding the volume of water, use the height of the water actually in the pool.

See Additional Answers.
a. Write an equation for the volume of any cylinder.

b. **Open-ended** Make a table of values giving the volume of water in the swimming pool for different water heights. Use the equation you wrote in part (a).

c. Use your table to make a graph that compares the volume of water in the pool with the height of the water.

d. Suppose the pool has 2000 ft³ of water in it. How high is the water level? Which model (*table*, *graph*, or *equation*) did you use to find the water level? Explain your choice.

4. Challenge Suppose the perimeter of a rectangle is 28 units.
See Additional Answers.
a. Make a table showing the widths, the lengths, and the areas of rectangles with 28-unit perimeters. The rectangles should have widths between 0 and 14 units.

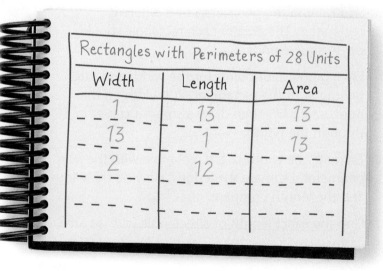

Rectangles with Perimeters of 28 Units

Width	Length	Area
1	13	13
13	1	13
2	12	

b. Use the data in your table to plot points for the width and the area of each rectangle. Put width on the horizontal axis.

c. Determine the width and the length of a rectangle with a 28-unit perimeter and the greatest area.

5. A polygon can be named by the number of sides it has. For example, a polygon with 3 sides is a triangle. Sketch an example of each type of polygon. Make one of your polygons a regular polygon. **Check students' drawings.**

a. pentagon (5 sides)

b. hexagon (6 sides)

c. heptagon (7 sides)

d. octagon (8 sides)

e. nonagon (9 sides)

f. decagon (10 sides)

Reflecting ◀▶ on the Section

6. The polygons shown were made by placing square tiles side by side so each tile shares at least one full side with another tile. Each tile measures 1 unit by 1 unit.

a. Find the perimeter of each polygon shown. **16 units; 16 units**

b. Use 9 squares to make a polygon with a 14-unit perimeter. Sketch your result. **Check students' drawings.**

c. What is the least possible perimeter for a polygon made with 9 squares? **12 units**

d. What is the greatest possible perimeter for a polygon made with 9 squares? **20 units**

Spiral ◀▶ Review

Simplify each expression. (Module 1, p. 62)

7. $2n + 4n$ **6n**

8. $6r - 5r - 1$ **r − 1**

9. $7x^2 - 2x^2 + 9x$ **$5x^2 + 9x$**

Multiply and write each answer in lowest terms. (Toolbox, p. 598)

10. $\frac{4}{9} \cdot \frac{9}{16}$ **$\frac{1}{4}$**

11. $1\frac{5}{8} \cdot \frac{2}{3}$ **$1\frac{1}{12}$**

12. $\frac{11}{12} \cdot 108$ **99**

13. $\frac{7}{8} \cdot \frac{64}{101}$ **$\frac{56}{101}$**

14. $4\frac{1}{3} \cdot 3\frac{2}{9}$ **$13\frac{26}{27}$**

15. $\frac{2}{17} \cdot \frac{51}{56}$ **$\frac{3}{28}$**

Write each fraction as a decimal and as a percent. Round to the nearest hundredth. (Toolbox, p. 599)

16. $\frac{3}{4}$ **0.75; 75%**

17. $\frac{15}{25}$ **0.6; 60%**

18. $\frac{4}{6}$ **$0.6\overline{6}$; $66\frac{2}{3}\%$**

19. $\frac{1}{3}$ **$0.3\overline{3}$; $33\frac{1}{3}\%$**

20. $\frac{9}{17}$ **0.53; 53%**

21. $\frac{5}{6}$ **$0.8\overline{3}$; 83%**

22. $\frac{4}{11}$ **$0.\overline{36}$; 36%**

23. $\frac{6}{7}$ **0.86; 86%**

You will need: • *graph paper* (Exs. 1 and 3)

Sheila was hired to organize a karate demonstration for a sports club's grand opening. She will use a space with an area of 48 square units.

1. On graph paper, draw 10 different rectangles that have an area of 48 square units. **Check students drawings. They should have 2 of each of the rectangles that are 1 by 48, 2 by 24, 3 by 16, 4 by 12, and 6 by 8.**

2. Make a table for the lengths, widths, and perimeters of your 10 rectangles. **See Additional Answers.**

3. On a graph, plot the points for the width and perimeter of each rectangle. Put width on the horizontal axis and perimeter on the vertical axis. Draw a smooth curved line to connect the points. **See Additional Answers.**

Write an equation or use the table or graph you made in Exercises 2 and 3 to complete Exercises 4 and 5.

4. Estimate the width and length of a rectangle with the least perimeter. Explain how you found your answer. **7 units; Sample Response: I used the graph to find the least perimeter.**

5. What is the exact width of a rectangle with a perimeter of 48 units and a length of 5 units? Explain how you found your answer. **19 units; Sample Response: I used the equation $p = 2l + 2w$ and substituted the values given for the variables p and l to find w.**

 Standardized Testing ▶ **Performance Task**

You will need: • *Labsheet 6B*

Use Labsheet 6B. *Pick's Formula* is a formula for finding the area of a polygon drawn on dot paper. You'll use the steps for Pick's formula below to find the area of polygons you draw on the *Polygon Dot Paper*.

 Step 1 Count the number of dots on the perimeter of the polygon and divide that number by 2. **9 ÷ 2 = 4.5**

 Step 2 Add the number of dots inside the polygon to your answer from Step 1. **4.5 + 2 = 6.5**

Step 3 To find the area of any polygon, you always subtract a certain number from your answer in Step 2. **The area of the polygon is 5.5, so subtract 1.**

Completing the Module Project

Fact or Fiction?

Throughout this module you have used mathematics to prove and disprove some amazing claims. You have also written your own amazing claims and gathered data to show whether they are true or false. Now it is time to present your amazing claims to the world!

SET UP

Work with a partner. You will need:
- *poster board*
- *markers*

6 With a partner, create a poster showing your amazing claims. Think about interesting ways to illustrate your claims and the data you have gathered. Include enough information on the poster so that anyone reading it will be able to decide whether the claims are true or false.   **Answers will vary. Check students' work.**

7 Write the solutions for your amazing claims. Show how to determine whether your claims are true or false. You may include the solutions on your poster or keep them separate.   **Answers will vary. Check students' work.**

8 Tell where you found your information. For example, if you used a book, include the title, the author, and the page number. If you used information from a computer source, include the name of the program or web site, and the name of the person or organization that created it.
Answers will vary. Check students' work.

> "Cats: Nature's Masterwork"
> by Stephen J. O'Brien
> National Geographic, June, 1997
>
> Information found:

You will need: • *graph paper* (Ex. 10)

Periodical cicadas hatch at regular intervals. In Connecticut, they hatched in 1962, 1979, and 1996. (Sec. 1, Explors. 1 and 2)

1. The year 1996 was a leap year. Leap years generally occur every four years. When will the next hatching occur in a leap year? **2064**

2. Male cicadas make a buzzing noise by using muscles to vibrate a membrane. When making this noise, the muscles move 3 times each second. How many times do the muscles move in one hour? **10,800**

Suppose two package delivery companies each have 18 airplanes. The ages of the airplanes are shown in the table. Use the table for Exercises 3 and 4. (Sec. 2, Explors. 1 and 2)

Company A	2, 3, 5, 6, 9, 15, 15, 12, 13, 17, 17, 17, 19, 18, 20, 20, 21, 26
Company B	1, 2, 3, 3, 5, 8, 7, 7, 6, 9, 12, 14, 16, 16, 25, 20, 19, 16

3. **See Additional Answers.**
3. a. Use the data to make two stem-and-leaf plots, one for each delivery company.

   b. What do the shapes of the plots tell you about the ages of the airplanes in the two companies?

   c. Find the mean, the median, and the mode of each data set.

4. **See Additional Answers.**
4. a. The box-and-whisker plots below display the data from the table. For each box-and-whisker plot, find the lower extreme, the upper extreme, the lower quartile, and the upper quartile.

   b. Use the box-and-whisker plots to compare the median ages of airplanes for the two companies.

Airplane Ages (years)

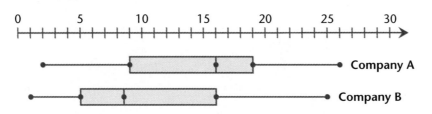

5. Which has greater volume: a box 12 in. long, 11 in. wide, and 9 in. high or 6 jars that are 14 in. tall and 4 in. in diameter? **the box** (Sec. 4, Explor. 2)

6. The Ferris wheel at the 1893 World's Columbian Exposition in Chicago had a diameter of 250 ft. Its 36 passenger cabs could hold a total of 2160 people. Suppose the cabs were evenly spaced. About how far apart would they have been?
   (Sec. 4, Explor. 1) **21.82 ft**

7. a. Admission to the Exposition was $.50 for people over age 12 and $.25 for children aged 6–12. Children under 6 were free. Write an equation that represents the cost of tickets for any group.
      $t = 0.50a + 0.25c$
   b. How much would it have cost for your family to go to the Exposition? (Sec. 5, Explor. 1) **Answers will vary.**

8. If possible, combine like terms to simplify each expression.
   (Sec. 5, Explor. 3)

   a. $rs + s + r$ b. $3y + 6y - y$ **8y**   c. $2t - t + 4$ **t + 4**   d. $x + 9xy - 2xy$
      no like terms   **x + 7xy**

9. Use inverse operations to solve each equation. (Sec. 5, Explor. 2)

   a. $6y = 32$ **$5\frac{1}{3}$**   b. $2 + 3x = 23$ **7**   c. $3s - 16 = 11$ **9**   d. $13t - \dfrac{16}{4} = 9$ **1**

10. Cassandra drew 9 right triangles. The perimeter of each triangle was 32 cm. She measured the base and the height of each triangle. Then she found the area.
    (Sec. 3, Explors. 1 and 2; Sec. 6, Explor. 1)
    See Additional Answers.
    a. Make a scatter plot of the data in the table. Put base length on the horizontal axis and area on the vertical axis. Use a straight line or a smooth curve to connect the points. Which did you use?

    b. Use your graph to estimate the length of the base of the triangle with the greatest area.

Base (cm)	Height (cm)	Area (cm²)
1.5	15.2	11.4
2.9	14.4	20.9
5.9	12.4	36.6
7.9	10.6	41.9
9.3	9.3	43.2
11.9	6.6	39.3

Reflecting ◀▶ **on the Module**

11. **Writing** Describe a problem you solved outside of math class which involved using rates, circumference, volume, perimeter, or area. Explain how you solved the problem. **Answers will vary. Check students' work.**

AT THE MALL

MODULE
2 SECTION OVERVIEW
· ·

1 Using Proportions and Percents

As you study the use of surveys:

- ◆ Estimate percents using "nice" fractions or multiples of 10%
- ◆ Find percents using equations

2 Working with Percents

As you explore shopping in malls:

- ◆ Estimate percents
- ◆ Find percents of change

3 Exploring Probability

As you find the chances of winning in a contest:

- ◆ Find theoretical probability
- ◆ Find experimental probability by repeating an experiment
- ◆ Construct tree diagrams

4 Operations with Integers

As you discover how video games are created:

- ◆ Add and subtract integers
- ◆ Multiply and divide integers

5 Operations with Fractions

As you explore a mall:

- ◆ Add and subtract positive and negative fractions

6 Inequalities and Box-and-Whisker Plots

As you read about T-shirt sales:

- ◆ Write and graph inequalities
- ◆ Construct box-and-whisker plots

The Module Project

Designing a Game

There are many games that imitate life. But who makes up these games and how much of life do they imitate? In this module you'll use mathematics to create your own board game about shopping in a mall. Then you'll play your game, refine it, and share it with your class.

More on the Module Project
See pp. 94, 104, 134, and 157.

INTERNET
To learn more about the theme:
http://www.mlmath.com

Section ① Using Proportions and Percents

IN THIS SECTION

EXPLORATION 1
◆ Proportions and Percent

EXPLORATION 2
◆ Samples and Percent

Your **OPINION COUNTS!**

1. Write 26% as a fraction and as a decimal.
$\frac{13}{50}$, 0.26

2. Write $1\frac{2}{25}$ as a percent and as a decimal.
108%, 1.08

3. Write 0.09 as a percent and as a fraction.
9%, $\frac{9}{100}$

Solve each proportion.

4. $\frac{x}{15} = \frac{16}{25}$ ⠀⠀⠀ 9.6

5. $\frac{14}{6} = \frac{y}{9}$ ⠀⠀⠀ 21

▸▸▸ *Setting the Stage*

"Of the nearly one thousand polled, 48%, said, 'Totally,' 35% said, 'Whatever,' while only 17% said, 'Well, duh!'"

TEEN SURVEY

How often do you visit malls?

How do you get there?

What kinds of stores do you like?

SET UP ⠀ *Work in a group of four. You will need Labsheet 1A.*

Where can you go if you want to meet your friends, buy a stereo, experience virtual reality, enter a spaghetti-eating contest, or ride a roller coaster? A mall, of course!

According to a national report, nearly nine in ten teens go to the mall with the intention of shopping. Because teens spend an average of $32.68 per visit, store owners want to attract them to malls. They use surveys to answer questions like the ones at the left. To see how surveys can provide information, your group will conduct a survey.

Think About It ▸

Use Labsheet 1A for Questions 1–3.

1 Answer the survey questions below. Record your group's results in
the second column of each of the *Group Survey Results* tables.
Answers will vary. Check students' work.

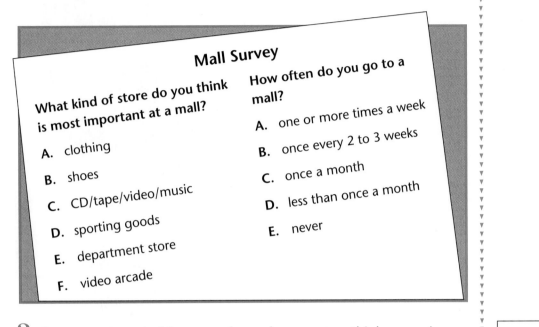

Mall Survey

**What kind of store do you think
is most important at a mall?**

A. clothing

B. shoes

C. CD/tape/video/music

D. sporting goods

E. department store

F. video arcade

**How often do you go to a
mall?**

A. one or more times a week

B. once every 2 to 3 weeks

C. once a month

D. less than once a month

E. never

2 Suppose one out of four members of your group thinks a music
store is most important at a mall. You can write this fact as a ratio
in fraction form $\left(\frac{1}{4}\right)$, decimal form (0.25), or percent form (25%).

a. Use the *Group Survey Results* tables to record each of your
group's ratios as a fraction, as a decimal, and as a percent.
Answers will vary. Check students' work.

b. Explain how you changed from the fraction form of the ratios
to the decimal form. Divided the numerator by the denominator.

c. How are the percent form and the decimal form of each ratio
related? Possible answers: The digits are the same or they are both parts
of a hundred.

d. Which form(s) of the ratio would you use to compare your
group's results to those of another group? Why?

3 Based on your group's results, do you think you can make an
accurate prediction of the number of students in your class who
rank clothing stores as the most important? Explain.

▸ **Malls have become an important part of life for many people. In this
module, you'll explore how mathematics is used at malls. You may
find that math shows up when you least expect it.**

FOR ▸ HELP

with *fractions,
decimals,* and
percents, see
TOOLBOX, p. 599

2. d. Sample Response:
decimals or percents;
They are easier to
compare than are
fractions.

3. Sample Response: No;
The number of people in
the group is too small.

GOAL

LEARN HOW TO...
- ◆ use proportional reasoning to estimate the percent of a number
- ◆ solve a proportion to find the percent of a number

AS YOU...
- ◆ make predictions based on a sample

KEY TERMS
- ◆ population
- ◆ sample
- ◆ proportion
- ◆ cross products

Exploration 1

Proportions and PERCENT

Some store owners at a mall think their sales will improve if more teenagers visit the mall. They know that about 39.9% of teenagers nationwide ride to malls with a parent or relative. They think a free shuttle service one Saturday each month might make it easier for the 4000 teenagers in the area to get to their mall. They survey 250 local teenagers (students in grades 8–11) to see whether they would use a shuttle.

▶ A survey is used to gather information about a group called a **population**. It may not be practical to contact every member of the population, so a smaller group called a **sample** is surveyed. The survey results are used to make predictions about the entire population.

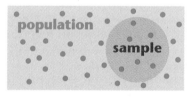

▶ For Questions 4 and 5, use the information about the mall given above.

4 Discussion What is the population that the store owners are trying to get information about? What is the sample?
4000 area teenagers; 250 local teenagers

5 Discussion Suppose 85 of the 250 students surveyed say they would use the shuttle.

a. Write the ratio of the number of students who would ride the shuttle to the number of students in the sample as a percent. 34%

b. Based on the results of the survey, do you think 2000 of the 4000 teenagers in the area will ride the shuttle? More than 2000 teenagers? Fewer than 2000 teenagers? Explain.

5. b. No; No; Yes; Sample Response: 34% of the sample say they would use the shuttle so probably about 34% of the population would use it. 2000 is half of the population and 34% is less than half.

► **Estimating with Percents** You can use the percent you found in Question 5 to estimate the total number of teenagers in the area who might ride the shuttle.

EXAMPLE

To estimate 34% of 4000, you can use the following methods.

Method 1 You can estimate 34% of 4000 by using the nearest "nice" fraction. 34% is close to $33\frac{1}{3}\%$, which equals the "nice" fraction $\frac{1}{3}$.

Method 2 You can also estimate 34% of 4000 using multiples of 10%. A percent bar model shows how this method works.

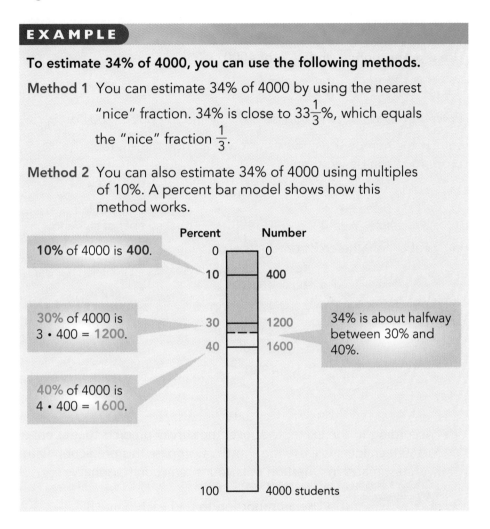

10% of 4000 is **400**.

30% of 4000 is
$3 \cdot 400 = 1200$.

40% of 4000 is
$4 \cdot 400 = 1600$.

34% is about halfway between 30% and 40%.

Percent	Number
0	0
10	400
30	1200
40	1600
100	4000 students

6 **a.** Refer to Method 1 in the Example. Estimate $\frac{1}{3}$ of 4000.   *about 1300*

b. Refer to Method 2. Use the fact that 34% is about halfway between 30% and 40% to estimate 34% of 4000.   *about 1400*

c. **Discussion** Which of your estimates from parts (a) and (b) would you use to predict how many teenagers in the area might use a shuttle to get to the mall? Explain.

7 **✔ CHECKPOINT** Estimate to find each percent.

a. 26% of 600 *about 150*

b. 68% of 50 *about 35*

c. 74% of 3000 *about 2250*

d. 21% of 150 *about 30*

6. c. Sample Response: I would use both and say that between 1300 and 1400 teenagers would use the shuttle.

✔ QUESTION 7

...checks that you can estimate a percent of a number.

▶ **Using a Proportion** Another way to predict the number of students who would ride the shuttle is to write and solve a *proportion*. A **proportion** is a statement that two ratios are equal.

EXAMPLE

Use a proportion to find 34% of 4000.

SAMPLE RESPONSE

Percent means "out of 100," so 34% means "34 out of 100" or $\frac{34}{100}$.

Let x = the number of students who would ride the shuttle. The proportion can be written:

Percent   **Number**

part ⟶ $\dfrac{34}{100}$ = $\dfrac{x}{4000}$ ⟵ number who would ride
whole ⟶ ⟵ total number of students

In a proportion, the *cross products* are equal.

$$\frac{34}{100} = \frac{x}{4000}$$

$$100 \cdot x = 34 \cdot 4000 \quad \blacktriangleleft \text{ cross products}$$

$$x = \frac{34 \cdot 4000}{100}$$

$$x = 1360$$

8 According to the Example above, the survey predicts that about 1360 teenagers will use the shuttle. Compare this prediction with your estimates in Question 6. Is your prediction reasonable?
Sample Response: Yes, 1360 is between the two estimates of 1300 and 1400.

9 ✔ **CHECKPOINT** Use a proportion to find each percent.

a. 37% of 1200 444

b. 93% of 250 232.5

10 **Try This as a Class** Suppose the survey convinced the store owners at the mall to run the shuttle. The first month 800 students ride it.

a. The second month the number of riders is 125% of the number of riders in the first month. How many riders are there in the second month? 1000 riders

b. The third month the number of riders is 0.9% more than the number the second month. How many additional riders is this? How many students ride the shuttle the third month?
9 riders; 1009 students

✔ QUESTION 9

...checks that you can find the percent of a number.

| **HOMEWORK EXERCISES** ▶ See Exs. 1–12 on pp. 91–92.

Exploration 2

Samples and PERCENT

GOAL

LEARN HOW TO...
- ◆ write equations to solve percent problems
- ◆ find a representative sample

AS YOU...
- ◆ analyze the results of the Mall Survey

KEY TERM
- ◆ representative sample

SET UP *You will need:* • *completed Labsheet 1A* • *Labsheet 1B*

11 For your survey on page 83, the population was the entire class. What was the sample? **the four group members**

▶ **Finding a Part** **You can use your group survey results to make predictions about the whole class.**

EXAMPLE

Suppose 75% of the members of a group go to the mall once a month. There are 31 students in the class. You can use this information to predict how many students in the class go to the mall once a month.

First Describe what you want to find.

75% of 31 **is** what number?

Next Write your sentence as an equation.

$0.75 \cdot 31 = x$

Use the fraction or **decimal equivalent** of 75%.

Then Solve the equation.

$23.25 = x$

About 23 students in the class go to the mall once a month.

---

12 **Use Labsheet 1A.** Count the students in your class. Then use your *Group Survey Results* data to predict each number below.

  a. the number of students in your class who visit the mall one or more times a week   **Answers will vary. Check students' work.**

  b. the number of students in your class who rank clothing stores as the most important stores at the mall
  Answers will vary. Check students' work.

  c. the number of students in your class who rank video arcades as the most important **Answers will vary. Check students' work.**

▶ To make accurate predictions based on a sample, the sample must be a **representative sample** of the total population.

13 Try This as a Class Think about the groups who answered the survey for the *Group Survey Results* tables on Labsheet 1A.

13. a. Sample Response: The sample has the same characteristics as the whole population.

    a. What do you think it means for a small group (the sample) to be representative of a larger group (the population)?

    b. Do you think your group is representative of the whole class? Why or why not? **Answers will vary. Check students' work.**

14 Use Labsheets 1A and 1B. Use the *Combined Group Survey Results* table to combine your group's survey data from Labsheet 1A with the data from two other groups. Try to choose two groups that will make the combined group as representative of the whole class as possible.
Answers will vary. Check students' work.

▶ **Finding a Percent** You can use an equation to find the percent of students in your combined groups who gave each response on the Mall Survey.

EXAMPLE

Suppose 4 out of 12 students in a group go to the mall once a month. To find what percent of the group goes to the mall once a month, you can write an equation.

First Describe what you want to find.

4 is **what percent** of 12?

Then Write your sentence as an equation.

$4 = \qquad x \qquad \cdot 12$

$4 = 12x$

15 Try This as a Class Solve the equation in the Example. Is your solution a *fraction*, a *decimal*, or a *percent*? If necessary, rewrite the solution to answer the question: What percent of the group goes to the mall once a month? $\frac{1}{3}$; a fraction; $33\frac{1}{3}\%$

Use completed Labsheet 1B for Questions 16–19.

✔ **QUESTION 16**

...checks that you can write and solve an equation to find a percent.

16 ✔ **CHECKPOINT** In Question 14, you combined your group's data with the data from two other groups. Use an equation to find the percent of the students in your combined groups who gave each of the responses described in Question 12.
Answers will vary. Check students' work.

17 Use the percents from Question 16 to predict the number of students in your class who gave each of the survey responses described in Question 12. **Answers will vary. Check students' work.**

18 Try This as a Class Find the actual number of students in your class who gave each of the responses described in Question 12.

   a. Compare your predictions in Questions 12 and 17 with the actual class results. Which predictions are more accurate?

   b. Do you think your *original group* or your *combined group* was more representative of the class? Explain.

18. a. Sample Response: the predictions from Question 17
b. Sample Response: combined group; The sample size was larger.

19 Suppose each group below answered the mall survey questions on page 83. Explain whether you think your combined class results from Question 18 can be used to predict their responses.

   a. another class of students your age   Yes.

   b. a class of fifth grade students   No.

   c. the teachers at your school   No.

▶ **Finding the Total** You can use an equation to find the total when you know a part and the corresponding percent.

EXAMPLE

In one class, 2 students said they never went to a mall. These students made up 8% of the class. To find the total number of students in the class, you can write and solve an equation.

First Describe what you want to find.

   2   is   **8%**   of   what number?

Then Write your sentence as an equation.

$$2 = 0.08 \cdot x$$
$$2 = 0.08x$$

---

20 Solve the equation in the Example. How many students were in the class? **25 students**

21 ✔ **CHECKPOINT** Write and solve an equation to find each number.

   a. 36 is 45% of what number?
   $36 = 0.45 \cdot x$; 80

   b. 7% of what number is 28?
   $0.07 \cdot x = 28$; 400

✔ **QUESTION 21**

...checks that you can find a number when a percent of it is known.

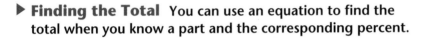

HOMEWORK EXERCISES ▶ See Exs. 13–26 on pp. 92–93.

Section 1
Key Concepts

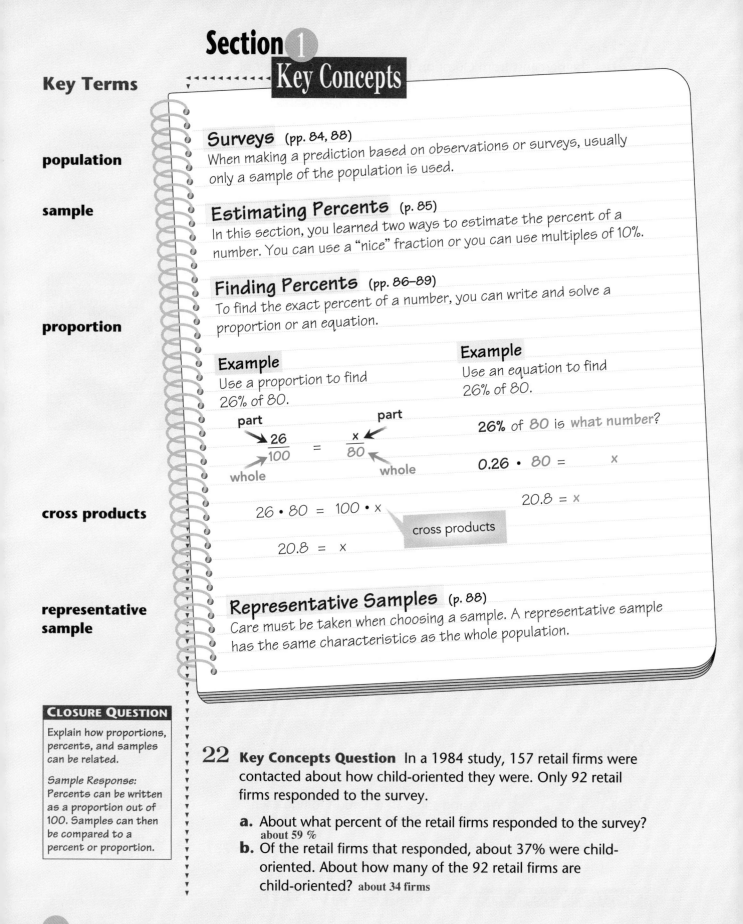

Key Terms

population

sample

proportion

cross products

representative
sample

Surveys (pp. 84, 88)
When making a prediction based on observations or surveys, usually only a sample of the population is used.

Estimating Percents (p. 85)
In this section, you learned two ways to estimate the percent of a number. You can use a "nice" fraction or you can use multiples of 10%.

Finding Percents (pp. 86–89)
To find the exact percent of a number, you can write and solve a proportion or an equation.

Example
Use a proportion to find 26% of 80.

part

part

$$\dfrac{26}{100} = \dfrac{x}{80}$$

whole   whole

$26 \cdot 80 = 100 \cdot x$

cross products

$20.8 = x$

Example
Use an equation to find 26% of 80.

26% of 80 is what number?

$0.26 \cdot 80 = x$

$20.8 = x$

Representative Samples (p. 88)
Care must be taken when choosing a sample. A representative sample has the same characteristics as the whole population.

CLOSURE QUESTION

Explain how proportions, percents, and samples can be related.

Sample Response:
Percents can be written as a proportion out of 100. Samples can then be compared to a percent or proportion.

22 Key Concepts Question In a 1984 study, 157 retail firms were contacted about how child-oriented they were. Only 92 retail firms responded to the survey.

  a. About what percent of the retail firms responded to the survey?
  about 59 %
  b. Of the retail firms that responded, about 37% were child-oriented. About how many of the 92 retail firms are child-oriented? about 34 firms

Section 1

Practice & Application Exercises

Estimate each percent. Tell which method you used. See below.

1. 76% of 200   2. 67% of $99   3. 55% of 64

Marketing Use the information at the right for Exercises 4 and 5. Round decimal answers to the nearest unit.

> In a survey of 1200 teens:
>
> **45.1%** thought that women's clothing was the most important store at the mall
>
> **15%** thought men's clothing was most important
>
> **30.9%** of the teens said they go to the mall once a month with their parents

4. a. Estimate how many of the teens thought women's clothing was the most important type of store. Then find the actual number. about 540 teens; 541 teens

   b. Estimate how many of the teens thought men's clothing was the most important type of store. Then find the actual number. about 180 teens; 180 teens

5. a. Estimate how many of the 1200 teens said they go to the mall once a month with their parents.
   about 400 teens

   b. **Alternative Method** Two methods for solving proportions are shown below. Use each method to find the number of teens surveyed who visit the mall once a month with their parents.
   about 371 teens

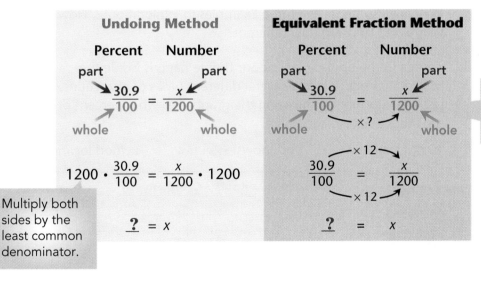

Undoing Method

Percent   Number

part   part

$$\frac{30.9}{100} = \frac{x}{1200}$$

whole   whole

$$1200 \cdot \frac{30.9}{100} = \frac{x}{1200} \cdot 1200$$

Multiply both sides by the least common denominator.

$$\underline{\quad?\quad} = x$$

Equivalent Fraction Method

Percent   Number

part   part

$$\frac{30.9}{100} = \frac{x}{1200}$$

whole   ×?   whole

$$\frac{30.9}{100} \underset{\times 12}{\overset{\times 12}{=}} \frac{x}{1200}$$

$$\underline{\quad?\quad} = x$$

What number must you multiply 100 by to get 1200?

1. Possible answers: about 150, nice fraction or using multiples of 10%

2. Possible answers: about $66, nice fraction; about $64, using multiples of 10%

3. Possible answers: about 32, nice fraction; about 35, using multiples of 10%

   c. Based on your estimate in part (a), do your answers in part (b) seem reasonable? Yes.

   d. Which method in part (b) do you like best? Why?
   Answers will vary. Check students' work.

Use a proportion to find each percent.

6. 16% of 210 33.6   7. 150% of 88 132   8. 42.2% of 500 211

9. 37.5% of 336 126 10. 105% of 20 21   11. 0.8% of 9000 72

12. Woodfield Mall: about 64%; The Galleria: about 50%; Tysons Corner Center: about 45%

12. In 1992, the Mall of America opened in Bloomington, Minnesota. Its area is about 4.2 million square feet. The table shows some of the largest malls in the United States before 1992. Use a percent to compare the area of each mall to the area of the Mall of America.

Mall	Area (square feet)
Woodfield Mall, Illinois	2,700,000
The Galleria, Texas	2,100,000
Tysons Corner Center, Virginia	1,906,000

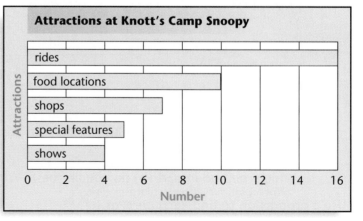

Use an equation to find each number or percent.

13. What is 40% of 80? 32

14. 0.5% of 90 is what number? 0.45

15. 30 is what percent of 125? 24%

16. 2 is what percent of 200? 1%

17. 65 is what percent of 50? 130%

18. 17% of what number is 34? 200

19. 7.2 is 12% of what number? 60

20. 30 is 150% of what number? 20

21. Sample Response: They all involve writing equations to solve percent problems; Example 1 finds the percent of a number, Example 2 finds what percent one number is of another, and Example 3 finds a number when a percent of it is known.

21. Writing Compare the three Examples in Exploration 2. How are they alike? How are they different?

22. Knott's Camp Snoopy, an indoor theme park, is inside the Mall of America. It offers several different types of attractions. Use the information shown in the graph. Tell what percent of the attractions are each type.

    a. rides about 38%   **b.** shows about 10%   **c.** food locations about 24%

Attractions at Knott's Camp Snoopy

23. Challenge 20% of a number is 24 less than the number. What is the number? 30

24. Suppose a middle school survey is given to find out if eighth graders should graduate a week before other students get out of school. The survey is given only to sixth graders.

24. b. No; Sample Response: To be representative, seventh and eighth grade students would need to be included in the sample.

   a. What is the population? What is the sample?
      middle school students; sixth graders
   b. Is this a representative sample? Why or why not?

25. The typical Monday night attendance at a movie theater in a mall is about 70 people. To increase attendance, the manager advertises that the first 45 customers on Monday nights will receive a movie poster. On the next Monday night, the first 45 customers were 60% of the total audience.

   a. Use an equation to find the total audience size that night.
      $45 = 0.6x$, 75 people
   b. Do you think the poster giveaway helped increase attendance? Why or why not? Sample Response: No; The increase was only 5 people.

   c. Suppose the posters cost the manager $2 each and the price of a ticket is $6. Was the promotion a good idea? Why?
      Sample Response: No; On an average night the theater takes in $420. After the cost of the posters they only took in $360 on the night of the promotion.

Reflecting ◀▶ on the Section

Write your response to Exercise 26 in your journal.

26. Suppose you want to predict how many students in your school are wearing sneakers. You find that 23 of the 29 students in your class are wearing sneakers. There are 583 students in your school.

   a. What is the population? What is the sample?
      583 students in school; 29 students in class
   b. Suppose your sample is representative of the students in your school. Predict how many students are wearing sneakers.
      about 462
   c. Could you use this sample to predict how many teachers are wearing sneakers? Explain. No; The sample is only students.

> **Journal**
>
> Exercise 26 checks that you can use proportions and percents to analyze survey data.

Spiral ◀▶ Review

27. What is the least possible perimeter of a rectangle whose area is 36 m^2? (Module 1, p. 72) 24 m

Divide. Round each answer to the nearest tenth. (Toolbox, p. 594)

28. 50 ÷ 2.6 **19.2**   **29.** 680 ÷ 1.8 **377.8**   **30.** 9 ÷ 3.7 **2.4**

Find each product. (Toolbox, p. 592)

31. 0.18 · 10   **32.** 6.2 · 0.01   **33.** 0.3 · 100   **34.** 0.15 · 1000
     1.8   **0.062**   **30**   **150**

Beginning the Module Project

Designing a Game

Many board games try to imitate what goes on in real life. As you work through this module, your group will create a game that imitates shopping in a mall. At the end of the module, you'll play the completed game and refine it. Then your group will present the game to the class.

Getting Started You'll start with a game board showing a map of a mall and an inventory list with prices. You'll create rules, game pieces, game cards, and anything else needed to play the game. Your game will include math topics you will learn about in this module, such as percents, proportions, and coordinate graphing.

SET UP

Work in a group.

You will need:

- *Project Labsheets A and B*

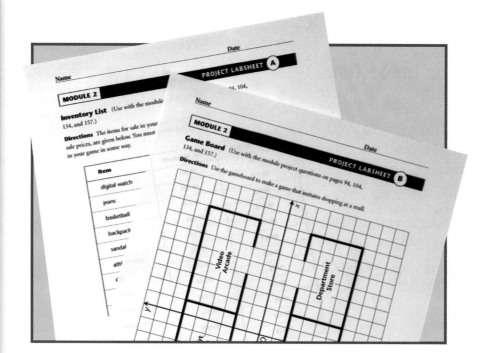

Use Project Labsheets A and B.

1. Your game must use the *Game Board* and the *Inventory List*. Describe a possible goal for your game. In other words, how can someone win?   Answers will vary. Check students' work.

2. With your group, discuss possible rules for your game.
   Answers will vary. Check students' work.

Estimate to find each percent.

1. 78% of 900   about 675
2. 86% of 1500   about 1350
3. 15% of $22   about $3.30
4. 23% of 440   about 110
5. 48% of 37,000   about 18,500
6. 14% of 1500   about 225
7. 33% of $78   about $26
8. 11% of 82   about 8.2
9. 65% of 850   about 567

Use a proportion to find each percent.

10. 53% of 820   434.6
11. 12.5% of 48   6
12. 200% of 63   126
13. 28.7% of 4700   1348.9
14. 62% of 3480   2157.6
15. 0.1% of 50,000   50
16. 120% of 55   66
17. 25% of 76   19
18. 86.9% of 10,000   8690

Use an equation to find each number or percent.

19. What is 80% of 165?   132
20. 15% of what number is 6?   40
21. 34 is what percent of 85?   40%
22. What is 20% of 8?   1.6
23. 50% of what number is 931?   1862
24. 190 is what percent of 304?   62.5%
25. What is 32% of 6350?   2032
26. 49 is what percent of 100?   49%

Study Skills ▶ Recalling Useful Facts

Sometimes it is helpful to be able to quickly recall a mathematical fact without looking it up in a book or performing calculations. One technique that can help you memorize useful facts is to repeat them aloud until you can say them without hesitating.

1. In this section you learned methods for finding percents. Memorize the fraction equivalent of each common percent below by repeating it aloud.

$$50\% = \frac{1}{2} \qquad 25\% = \frac{1}{4} \qquad 20\% = \frac{1}{5}$$

2. For each percent in Exercise 1, describe a situation in which it would be useful to recall the fraction equivalent quickly.   Answers will vary. Check students' work.

3. Name some other kinds of mathematical facts that you need to be able to recall quickly. Describe a situation in which quick recall of each fact can be helpful.   Answers will vary. Check students' work.

Section 2 Working with Percents

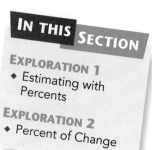

IN THIS SECTION

EXPLORATION 1
• Estimating with Percents

EXPLORATION 2
• Percent of Change

The PRICE i$ RIGHT, Isn't It?

◄◄◄ *Setting the Stage*

For most people, shopping is the main attraction at the mall. Some people like to "shop 'til they drop," always looking for the best deals, while others buy on impulse. How about you? Do you compare prices to get the best deal?

One shopper tries to save money by comparing prices at two different stores.

Item	Higher Price	Lower Price
Top-selling CD	$15.99	$12.94
Brand-name jeans	$39.99	$34.99
Video game	$79.99	$49.48
Wristwatch	$39.99	$30.07
CD player	$179.99	$159.99

Think About It

1 Estimate the total amount of money the shopper can save by comparison shopping. **about $68**

2. a. Top-selling CD: $1.60; Brand-name jeans: $4; Video game: $8; Wristwatch: $4; CD player: $18

2 **a.** Find 10% of the higher price of each item shown above. Round your answers to the nearest cent.

b. For which items is the amount saved by comparison shopping greater than 10% of the higher price of the item? **all of the items**

c. For which items can the shopper save more than 20% of the higher price? **video game and wristwatch**

 Exploration 1 ▸▸▸▸▸▸▸▸▸▸▸▸▸▸▸▸▸▸▸▸▸▸▸▸▸▸▸▸▸▸▸▸

Estimating with PERCENTS

SET UP | *Work in a group of four or five. Your group will need one card from Labsheet 2A.*

▶ Mental math and estimation are important skills for comparison shopping. In *Bargain Basement*, your team will compete to find or estimate sale prices using mental math.

Bargain Basement Game

- ◆ Each team receives a card listing four prices for the same item at four different stores. The teams have one minute to decide which price is the lowest.

- ◆ A team gets 20 points for each correct choice. If one team asks another team how they found their best buy, then the answering team gets 10 bonus points if they answer correctly.

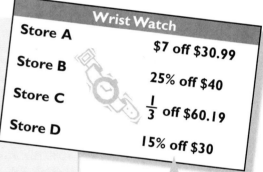

Wrist Watch

Store A $7 off $30.99

Store B   25% off $40

Store C $\frac{1}{3}$ off $60.19

Store D   15% off $30

"15% off $30" means $30 − (15% of $30).

3 a. Discussion To find the amount of the discount at Store D, use mental math to find 15% of 30. Explain your thinking.

b. Find the sale price of the watch at Store D. $25.50

4 Discussion Explain how you can use estimation or mental math to find the sale price of the watch at the other stores. Which store offers the best buy?

5 a. Cheryl calculated the sale price for the watch at Store B by finding 75% of $40. Explain why Cheryl's method works.

b. Use Cheryl's method to find the sale price of the watch at Store C.
$60.19 · $\frac{2}{3}$ ≈ $40

6 Use Labsheet 2A. Play a round of *Bargain Basement*. Be prepared to discuss the strategies your team used to determine the best buy.
Answers will vary. Check students' work.

3. a. Possible answers: Find 10% of 30, find half of that, then add both together; Find 10%, then 20%, then find the number halfway between them.

4. Sample Response: Store A: Subtract 7 from 31; Store B: Find 50% of 40, find half of that, then subtract the result from 40; Store C: Divide 3 into 60, then subtract the quotient from 60; Store A

5. a. 75% of 40 is the same as 40 − 25% of 40.

HOMEWORK EXERCISES ▸ See Exs. 1–7 on p. 101.

GOAL

LEARN HOW TO...
◆ estimate percents of change

AS YOU...
◆ analyze sale prices

KEY TERMS
◆ percent of decrease
◆ percent of increase
◆ percent of change

Exploration 2

PERCENT of CHANGE

SET UP *Work in a group of three or more.*

▶ In Exploration 1, you saw how a percent discount is sometimes taken off the price of an item. A percent discount is an example of a *percent of decrease*. If you know the original value and the amount of the decrease, you can find the *percent of decrease*.

$$\text{Percent of decrease} = \frac{\text{amount of decrease}}{\text{original amount}}$$

EXAMPLE

A store advertises that all items are on sale for 40% off. A shopper sees this price tag on a denim jacket. Is the price of the jacket 40% off?

SAMPLE RESPONSE

First Find the amount of the decrease by subtracting the sale price from the original price.

$$\text{Original price} - \text{sale price} = \text{amount of decrease}$$
$$\$60 \quad - \quad \$38 \quad = \quad \$22$$

Then Compare the amount of the decrease to the original amount.

$$x = \frac{22}{60}$$

$$x \cdot 60 = 22$$

> What percent of 60 is 22?

$$x \approx 0.37$$

The denim jacket has been discounted by about 37%, not 40%.

---

7 Try This as a Class Set up and solve a proportion to find the actual amount of decrease for a 40% discount on a $60 jacket.

$\frac{40}{100} = \frac{x}{60}$; $24

▶ **Percent of decrease can be used to describe a variety of situations.**

8 ✔ **CHECKPOINT** The average person in the United States visited a mall about 37 times in 1980 and about 24 times in 1990.

  a. Estimate the percent of decrease in the number of times a year the average person in the United States visited malls from 1980 to 1990. Explain your method of estimation.

  b. Find the actual percent of decrease. How does it compare with your estimate? about 35%; It was close to my estimate.

✔ **QUESTION 8**

…checks that you can find a percent of decrease.

8. a. $33\frac{1}{3}\%$; $\frac{37-24}{37}=\frac{13}{37}$ $\approx\frac{13}{39}=\frac{1}{3}=33\frac{1}{3}\%$

▶ A *percent of increase* can be used to describe many types of increases.

$$\text{Percent of increase} = \frac{\text{amount of increase}}{\text{original amount}}$$

9 **Discussion** A store buys a book for $12 and marks up the price to sell for $20.

  a. What was the amount of the markup? $8

  b. Find the percent of increase after the markup. $66\frac{2}{3}\%$

▶ **Notice that the new price in Question 9 is more than 100% of the original price.**

10 In Question 9, the marked-up price of $20 is what percent of the original price of $12? How did you get your answer?

$166\frac{2}{3}\%$; Possible answers: Use a proportion or use an equation.

▶ **Percent of increase and percent of decrease are examples of percent of change.**

11 From 1970 to 1990, the number of people aged 14–17 in the United States changed from about 15.9 million to 13.3 million. Find the percent of change. about 16.4% decrease

12. a. 62.5% increase; about 67.5% increase; about 3.1% increase

12 ✔ **CHECKPOINT** The average hourly wage in the United States in 1979 was $6.16. In 1990, it was $10.01. In 1991, it was $10.32.

  a. What is the percent of change from 1979 to 1990? from 1979 to 1991? from 1990 to 1991?

  b. The 1991 hourly wage is what percent of the 1979 hourly wage? about 168%

✔ **QUESTION 12**

…checks that you can estimate and find a percent of change.

HOMEWORK EXERCISES ▶ See Exs. 8–14 on pp. 102–103.

Section 2
Key Concepts

percent of
change

percent of
decrease

percent of
increase

Estimating Percents (p. 97)

You can use estimation or mental math to find a percent of a number.

Percent of Change (pp. 98–99)

Percent of decrease and percent of increase are examples of percent of change.

Example

A shirt that normally sells for $50 is on sale for $40. What is the percent of decrease in the price?

Example

The original price of a toy was $18. It is marked up to sell for $20. What is the percent of increase in the price?

$$\frac{\text{Original}}{\text{price}} - \frac{\text{sale}}{\text{price}} = \frac{\text{price}}{\text{decrease}} \qquad \frac{\text{Increased}}{\text{price}} - \frac{\text{original}}{\text{price}} = \text{markup}$$

$$\$50 - \$40 = \$10 \qquad\qquad \$20 - \$18 = \$2$$

Since 10 is $\frac{1}{5}$ of 50 and $\frac{1}{5} = 20\%$, the $10 discount is 20% of $50. The percent of decrease is 20%.

Since $2 is $\frac{1}{9}$ of $18, the percent of increase is about 11%.

CLOSURE QUESTION

Explain what is meant by percent of change. What value do you compare the increase or decrease to when finding the percent of change?

Sample Response: the percent that an amount increased or decreased; You always compare to the original value.

13 Key Concepts Question Suppose a store's sales decreased 9% from April to May and 9% from May to June.

a. Sales were $9811 in April. Estimate the sales in May. **about $8830**

b. Use your answer to part (a) to estimate the sales in June. **about $7947**

c. Find the actual sales in May. Then use your answer to find the actual sales in June. Compare the answers with your estimates in parts (a) and (b). **$8928.01; $8124.49; The actual sales and the estimates were close.**

d. Uma thinks that since sales decreased 9% in May and 9% in June, they decreased the same number of dollars each month. Is she correct? Explain why or why not. **No; The decrease in June was 9% of the sales in May which were 9% less than the sales in April.**

Practice & Application Exercises

1. Describe two different ways to estimate 69% of $59.98.

For Exercises 2–5, estimate the answer. Then find the exact answer.

2. 35% of 90
about 30; 31.5

3. 22% of 240
about 48; 52.8

4. 80% of 52
about 40; 41.6

5. 9% of 1195
about 119.5; 107.55

6. A store advertises that all items are 30–40% off. The original price is crossed out on each price tag, and the sale price is written below it. Use estimation or mental math to check that each markdown is within the advertised range. Tell which tags are marked incorrectly and explain how you know.

a. $~~$50~~ $37

b. $~~$130~~ $100

c. $~~$80~~ $55

d. $~~$29~~ $18

e. $~~$350~~ $240

f. $~~$240~~ $180

7. In a survey, 2051 teens in the United States were asked how they earned their spending money. Estimate the number of teens who made each of the responses below. Then find the actual number and compare it with your estimate.

About 47% said their parents gave them money when they needed it.

About 32% received a regular allowance.

About 45% did odd jobs.

About 26% worked part-time.

About 11% worked full time.

---

1. Sample Response: Change 69% to the "nice" fraction $\frac{2}{3}$, then find $\frac{2}{3}$ of 60; Find 10% of 60, then multiply by 7.

6. a. incorrectly marked; The minimum markdown is $15.
b. incorrectly marked; The minimum markdown is $39.
c. correctly marked; The minimum markdown is $24.
d. correctly marked; The minimum markdown is $8.70.
e. correctly marked; The minimum markdown is $105.
f. incorrectly marked; The minimum markdown is $72.

7. about 1000, 964; about 650, 656; about 900, 923; about 500, 533; about 200, 226

---

8. In 1991, the total income of 12- to 19-year-olds in the United States was $95 billion. In 1993, it was $86 billion.

8. a. about 10%; $\frac{95-86}{95} = \frac{9}{95} \approx \frac{9}{90} = \frac{1}{10} = 10\%$

a. Estimate the percent of change in total teenage income from 1991 to 1993. Explain your method of estimating.

b. Find the actual percent of change in total teenage income from 1991 to 1993. How does it compare with your estimate?

about 9.5%; It was close to my estimate.

Bicycles Sold in the United States

Millions of bicycles

■ Imported   ■ Domestic

1991: 4.4, 7.3
1992: 4.3, 7.4
1993: 5.0, 8.0

Year

For Exercises 9 and 10, use the double bar graph.

9. Describe the percent of change in bicycle sales from 1992 to 1993. Give an answer for imported, for domestic, and for the total number of bicycles.
See below.

10. Writing Explain why the percent of change in the total number of bicycles bought in the United States from 1991 to 1992 is zero.
The sales figures did not change.

11. In 1994, there were 40,368 shopping centers in the United States. In 1995, the total number of shopping centers increased by about 2.1%. Find the total number of shopping centers in 1995.
about 41,216 shopping centers

9. imports: about 16% increase; domestics: about 8% increase; total: about 11%

12. a. The regular price of a necklace is $10 at two stores. At which store do you think the final sale price will be less? Why?
Answers will vary. Check students' work.

Store A

Originally $10
SALE: 25% off

Now an additional 10% off the sale price

Store B

Take 25% off the sale price   Price Slash!

Was $10 Now 10% off

b. Find the final sale price of the necklace at each store. Was your prediction from part (a) correct? Explain.
$6.75 at both stores; Answers will vary.

12. c. No; Sample Response: The second discount is taken on an already discounted price.

c. Do you get the correct sale price if you add the two percent discounts together and then discount the price by that sum? Explain.

Item	Price then	Price now	Percent of change
movie	?	?	?
house	?	?	?
car	?	?	?

13. Home Involvement Interview an adult born before 1960 to find the prices of three items in the past. Compare each price with its equivalent today. In each case, what is the percent of change?
Answers will vary. Check students' work.

Reflecting on the Section

14. Find three sale ads in a newspaper or magazine that use percent discounts. Use estimation or mental math to determine the items on which you would save the greatest amount and the least amount. Do you always save the most with the greatest percent discount? Explain. **Answers will vary. Check students' work.**

RESEARCH

Exercise 14 checks that you can apply percent of change.

Spiral Review

Use a proportion to find each percent. (Module 2, p. 90)

15. 28% of 5200 **1456**
16. 2% of 485 **9.7**
17. 77% of 830 **639.1**
18. 100% of 61 **61**
19. 3.8% of 7900 **300.2**
20. 95% of 350 **332.5**

Find the greatest common factor and the least common multiple for each pair of numbers. (Toolbox, p. 596)

21. 10, 15 **GCF 5, LCM 30**
22. 12, 16 **GCF 4, LCM 48**
23. 9, 30 **GCF 3, LCM 90**
24. 21, 49 **GCF 7, LCM 147**

Replace each ? with >, <, or =. (Toolbox, p. 597)

25. $\frac{1}{4}$? $\frac{1}{3}$ **<**
26. $\frac{3}{8}$? $\frac{1}{2}$ **<**
27. $\frac{2}{3}$? $\frac{12}{18}$ **=**
28. $\frac{7}{8}$? $\frac{5}{6}$ **>**

Extension

Percent of Profit

Buyers are usually interested in the percent of decrease or increase in the cost of a product. Sellers are interested in how much profit has changed. Profit is based on the selling price, *s*, of an item and the cost, *c*, of making an item. Two ways to calculate the percent of profit are shown at the right.

Percent of profit on cost = $\frac{s-c}{c}$

Percent of profit on selling price = $\frac{s-c}{s}$

29. Suppose a candy bar costs 35¢ to make, and sells for 50¢. What is the percent of profit on cost? What is the percent of profit on selling price? **about 43%; 30%**

30. Which percent of profit in Exercise 29 was larger? Do you think this will always be true? Explain your thinking. **on cost; Yes; Unless an item is sold at a loss, $s > c$, so $\frac{s-c}{c} > \frac{s-c}{s}$**

Store Manager: Christopher Dyson

As manager, Christopher Dyson monitors yearly sales. The store's annual goal is to achieve 10% more sales than the previous year. Each store department has the same goal.

31. Suppose that last year the store had $30 million in total sales. If sales increase by $300,000 this year, has the store's goal of 10% growth in sales been met? No.

32. Suppose housewares sales went from $59,000 last year to $73,000 this year. Appliance sales went from $901,000 to $945,000. Which department experienced greater growth? Explain.

Sample Response: housewares; sales in housewares increased about 24%, while sales in appliances increased only about 5%.

Working on the Module Project

Designing a Game

SET UP

Constructing Game Pieces Your group has discussed how to play and win your game. Now you'll make game pieces and game cards.

Use Project Labsheets A and B for Project Questions 3 and 4.

Answers will vary. Check students' work.

3 In your game, you'll move from grid intersection to grid intersection on the *Game Board*. For each player, construct game pieces small enough to fit easily on the board.

4 Think about what might happen as a player visits the various stores on the game board. Construct cards like the ones below. You may also want to create game money to spend at the stores.

Work in a group.

You will need:
- *Project Labsheets A and B*
- *items for game pieces*
- *cardstock*
- *scissors*

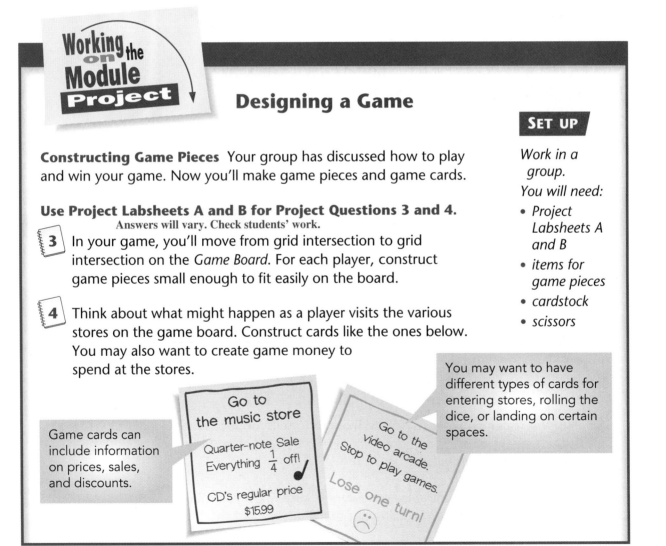

Game cards can include information on prices, sales, and discounts.

Go to the music store

Quarter-note Sale Everything $\frac{1}{4}$ off!

CD's regular price $15.99

Go to the video arcade. Stop to play games. Lose one turn!

You may want to have different types of cards for entering stores, rolling the dice, or landing on certain spaces.

Section 2

Extra Skill Practice

For Exercises 1–6, estimate the answer. Then find the exact answer.

1. 55% of 340 about 170; 187 2. 65% of 44 about 29; 28.6 3. 7% of 48 about 4.8; 3.36

4. 12% of 75 about 7.5; 9 5. 38% of 160 about 64; 60.8 6. 30% of 45 about 15; 13.5

Use the bar graph for Exercises 7–9.

7. Find the percent of decrease in the price of unleaded gas from 1992 to 1994. about 2.7%

8. Find the percent of increase in the price of unleaded gas from 1992 to 1996. about 8.8%

9. Find the percent of increase in the price of unleaded gas from 1994 to 1996. about 11.8%

10. A bicycle shop buys a new bike for $350 and sells it for $455.

    a. What is the amount of the markup? $105

    b. What is the percent of increase after the markup? 30%

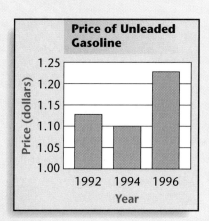

Use the table for Exercises 11–13.

11. Find the percent of decrease in the number of bald eagles from 1800 to 1974. about 99.4%

12. Find the percent of increase in the number of bald eagles from 1974 to 1994. about 342.5%

13. Find the percent of change in the number of bald eagles from 1800 to 1994. 97.2% decrease

Bald Eagle Population in the Continental United States	
Year	Number of adult eagles
1800	250,000
1974	1,582
1994	7,000

Standardized Testing ▶ Performance Task

For a Social Studies project, Diane and Rosa are ranking the 50 states based on the percent of increase in their population from 1990 to 1995. Diane says Alabama's population increase was greater and should be ranked before Alaska. Rosa says Alaska should be ranked before Alabama. Who is right? Explain.

State	1990	1995
Alabama	4,040,000	4,253,000
Alaska	550,000	604,000

Sample Response: Rosa is right. Alaska had about a 10% increase in population. Alabama had about a 5% increase.

The MALL of FAME

The Situation See the Resource Book for a detailed discussion of this Extended Exploration.

As of 1997, the Mall of America in Bloomington, Minnesota, was the largest mall in the United States. Its area is about 4.2 million square feet. The August 16, 1994, edition of *Sports Illustrated* gave the following descriptions of the mall's size.

"…could comfortably contain all the gardens of Buckingham Palace …"

"…twice the steel of the Eiffel Tower.…"

The Problem

Write your own descriptions of the size of the Mall of America. Compare the mall with sites or landmarks in your community, or with structures or objects familiar to other students. Answers will vary. Check students' work.

Sample Response: No, the descriptions refer to various aspects of the Mall of America such as floor space and the amount of steel used in construction. Possible answers: in., ft, yd, mi, cm, m, km; length, width, height, area, surface area, volume, exponents, about

Something to Think About

◆ Can each of the descriptions shown here be used to estimate the size of the Mall of America?

◆ What measurements can be used to describe size? What mathematical language and symbols are used with the measurements?

Present Your Results

Create a poster comparing the Mall of America to the sites you chose. On the back of your poster, list data to support your comparisons.

IN THIS SECTION

EXPLORATION 1
◆ Theoretical Probability

EXPLORATION 2
◆ Experimental Probability

EXPLORATION 3
◆ Tree Diagrams

WARM-UP EXERCISES

Write each rate as a fraction.

1. 3 out of 7 $\frac{3}{7}$

2. 12 : 20 $\frac{12}{20}$

Write each fraction in lowest terms.

3. $\frac{55}{30}$ $\frac{11}{6}$

4. $\frac{9}{117}$ $\frac{1}{13}$

5. $\frac{16}{27}$ $\frac{16}{27}$

Setting the Stage ▶▶▶▶▶▶▶▶▶▶▶▶▶▶▶▶▶▶▶▶▶▶▶▶▶▶▶

One way to attract shoppers to a mall is to hold a prize giveaway. Suppose four finalists for a "Grand Giveaway" are randomly selected each week from participating customers at a mall gift store. Each Saturday the four finalists line up at a box containing four giant beans, two of which are marked with stars. Each finalist draws a bean and keeps it. The two finalists who draw the marked beans win prizes.

Nancy and Becky are finalists in the giveaway. Nancy is second in the line. The first person draws a bean marked with a star.

Think About It

1 Which of Nancy's and Becky's statements do you agree with? How can you decide which comments are correct?

1. Sample Response: I agree with Nancy that the first person was lucky, and I agree with all Becky's statements. One way to decide which comments are correct is to model the contest by drawing beans from a cup.

GOAL

LEARN HOW TO...
- find theoretical probabilities
- recognize dependent and independent events

AS YOU...
- examine a promotional drawing

KEY TERMS
- experiment
- outcome
- equally likely
- event
- probability
- theoretical probability
- dependent events
- independent events
- impossible event
- certain event

THEORETICAL PROBABILITY

SET UP *Work in a group of four. You will need:* • *Labsheet 3A* • *cup* • *two white beans* • *two red beans* • *marker*

▶ **Should Nancy move to the back of the line? To help understand her problem, you'll use beans to analyze the Grand Giveaway.**

2 The red beans are the winning ones. Label them 1 and 2. The white beans represent losing draws. Label them 1 and 2 also. Put the beans in the cup and shake it to mix up the beans. **Check students' work.**

winning beans   losing beans

▶ **Drawing a bean from the cup is an example of an experiment. The result of an experiment is an outcome.**

3 Suppose a single bean is drawn from the cup.

    a. Drawing red bean number 2 is one outcome of the experiment. List the other possible outcomes. How many outcomes are there altogether? **Drawing red bean 1, drawing white bean 1, drawing white bean 2; 4**

    b. Two outcomes are **equally likely** if they have the same chance of happening. Are the outcomes of drawing each bean equally likely? Explain. **Yes; Sample Response: The beans are the same size and shape and cannot be seen, so all four outcomes are equally likely.**

    c. Suppose the red beans and the white beans were different sizes. Would the outcomes of drawing each bean be equally likely? Explain. **No; Sample Response: The person choosing the bean could tell by touch which bean they were picking up and that could change the outcome.**

▶ **Drawing a winning bean from the cup on the first draw is an example of an *event*. An event is a set of outcomes of an experiment.**

4 What outcomes make up the event of drawing a winning bean from the cup on the first draw? **drawing red bean 1 or 2**

▶ To decide whether she should move to the back of the line, Nancy can find the *probability* of drawing a winning bean. A **probability** is a number from 0 to 1 that tells how likely it is that an event will happen.

> If all of the outcomes of an experiment are equally likely, you can use this ratio to find the *theoretical probability* of an event:
>
> $$\text{Theoretical probability} = \frac{\text{number of outcomes that make up the event}}{\text{total number of possible outcomes}}$$

5 What is the theoretical probability of drawing a winning bean from the cup on the first draw? $\frac{1}{2}$

6 **✔ CHECKPOINT** Suppose the cup contains 8 red beans and 12 white beans. What is the theoretical probability of drawing a red bean on the first draw? $\frac{2}{5}$

✔ QUESTION 6

…checks that you can find theoretical probabilities.

▶ When it is Nancy's turn to draw, one bean has already been drawn from the cup. You can model her situation with your group's beans.

7 Use the four beans in your cup.

   a. Take a red bean out of the cup to represent the first draw. Do not put the bean back into the cup. What is the theoretical probability of getting a red bean on the second draw? (Put the bean back into the cup after you have answered the question.) $\frac{1}{3}$

   b. Take a white bean out of the cup to represent a different first draw. Now what is the theoretical probability of getting a red bean on the second draw? $\frac{2}{3}$

   c. Compare your answers to parts (a) and (b). Does the outcome of the first draw affect the theoretical probability of winning on the second draw? Explain.   Sample Response: Yes; If a red bean is drawn first, the probability of winning on the second draw decreases and if a white bean is drawn first, the probability of winning on the second draw increases.

▶ If the probability that one event occurs is affected by whether or not another event occurs, the events are called **dependent events**. If the probability of an event is not affected by whether or not another event occurs, the events are **independent events**.

8 Look back at your answers to Question 7. Is drawing a winning bean on the second draw independent of the first draw? Explain.
   No; The first draw affects the second draw.

9 Suppose you flip a nickel and get heads. Then you flip a penny and get tails. Are these events *independent* or *dependent*?   independent

10 ✔ **CHECKPOINT** There are two red beans and two white beans in the cup. In each situation below, the first bean drawn is put back into the cup before the second draw.

a. If you get a red bean on the first draw, what is the theoretical probability of getting a white bean on the second draw? $\frac{1}{2}$

b. If you get a white bean on the first draw, what is the theoretical probability of getting a white bean on the second draw? $\frac{1}{2}$

c. In this situation, is getting a white bean on the second draw dependent on the result of the first draw? Explain.
No; The first bean drawn is put back into the cup so it does not affect the second draw.

Use Labsheet 3A for Questions 11 and 12.

11 To see how probabilities can change in a series of events, follow the instructions on the labsheet to complete three trials of the *Group Drawings*. Start with two red beans and two white beans in the cup. **Check students' work.**

12 Use your results from the *Group Drawings*.

a. Are the numbers in the "Probability of winning" column the same in each trial? Why or why not? **Answers will vary. Check students' work.**

b. Is each draw *independent* of or *dependent* on the one before it? Explain. **dependent; The first draw affects the second draw by increasing or decreasing the probability of winning.**

13. a. Possible answers: first and second draw—red bean, third draw—white bean; first draw—red bean 1, second draw—white bean, third draw—red bean; or first draw—white bean, second and third draws—red bean; 0
b. Possible answers: first draw—white bean, second draw—red bean, third draw—white bean; first and second draws—white beans, third draw—red bean; first draw—red bean, second and third draws—white beans; 1

13 Consider the original situation of two red beans and two white beans in the cup.

a. Describe a sequence of draws in which the last person to draw cannot win. In this case, winning on the last draw is called an **impossible event**. What is the theoretical probability of this impossible event?

b. Describe a sequence of draws in which the last person to draw is sure to win. In this case, winning on the last draw is called a **certain event**. What is the theoretical probability of this certain event?

14 **Discussion** Nancy said it was "lucky" for the first contestant to draw a winning bean. Do you agree with Nancy? Why or why not? **Sample Response: The contestant won, but the probability of winning was $\frac{1}{2}$, so it didn't require much luck.**

HOMEWORK EXERCISES ▶ See Exs. 1–9 on pp. 116–117.

Exploration 2

EXPERIMENTAL PROBABILITY

GOAL

LEARN HOW TO...
- find experimental probabilities

AS YOU...
- model a promotional drawing

KEY TERM
- experimental probability

SET UP *Work in a group of three. You will need:* • *Labsheet 3B* • *cup* • *two red beans, labeled 1 and 2* • *two white beans, labeled 1 and 2*

▶ **You can use an experiment to estimate Nancy's probability of winning the Grand Giveaway.**

15 Nancy was second in line for the Grand Giveaway drawing when the first person drew a winning bean.

  a. What is the probability that the first person will draw a winning bean? (Remember, there are four beans in the box and two winning beans are marked with a star.) $\frac{1}{2}$

  b. After the first contestant draws a winning bean, what is the probability that Nancy will draw a winning bean if she draws next? $\frac{1}{3}$

Use Labsheet 3B for Questions 16–18. You'll model the *Grand Giveaway Experiment*.

16 Will moving to the back of the line improve Nancy's chance of winning? To find out, follow the directions on Labsheet 3B and complete the *Trials* table. Answers will vary. Check students' work.

17. Answers will vary. Check students' work.

17 a. Use the data in the *Trials* table. Find the number of winning beans drawn on the second draw in the 12 trials. Record it in the *Group Results* table.

b. You can use a ratio to find the *experimental probability* of winning on any draw:

Experimental probability = $\dfrac{\text{number of times an event occurs}}{\text{number of times the experiment is done}}$

Use the data in the *Trials* table to find the experimental probability of winning on the second, third, and fourth draws. Record the probabilities in the *Group Results* table.

c. Compare the experimental probabilities for winning on the second, third, and fourth draws. Do you think that you are more likely to win on any particular draw? Explain.

18 Try This as a Class To see how increasing the number of trials can affect an experimental probability, combine your group results with those of the other groups in the class.

Answers will vary. Check students' work.

a. Find the total number of times a winning bean was drawn on the second draw and the total number of trials for the entire class. Record them in the *Class Results* table.

b. Find the experimental probability of winning if you draw second. Record the probability in the *Class Results* table.

c. Use the data for the whole class to complete the *Class Results* table for the third and fourth draws.

d. Describe how the experimental probabilities for your group compare with the probabilities for the whole class.

e. Suppose 1000 trials were completed. Predict the probability of winning on each draw. Explain your thinking.

19 Discussion On page 107, is Becky correct when she says moving to the back of the line will not make a difference? Explain.

20 ✔ **CHECKPOINT** A number cube has sides numbered 1 through 6. In 20 rolls of two number cubes, a sum of 7 is rolled 4 times.

a. Find the experimental probability of rolling a sum of 7. $\frac{1}{5}$

b. Do you think that your answer to part (a) is the theoretical probability of rolling a sum of 7? Explain.

19. Sample Response: No; There is always a possibility of winning in the first or second draws but the probability of winning on the third or fourth draw could be 0.

20. b. Sample Response: No; There are 36 possible outcomes when two dice are rolled, 6 of which have a sum of 7, so the theoretical probability is $\frac{6}{36}$, or $\frac{1}{6}$.

✔ **QUESTION 20**

...checks that you can find experimental probabilities.

HOMEWORK EXERCISES ▶ See Exs. 10–12 on pp. 117–118.

Exploration 3

 **TR<EE DIAGRAMS**

GOAL

LEARN HOW TO...
◆ use a tree diagram to model and find theoretical probabilities

AS YOU...
◆ analyze a promotional drawing

KEY TERM
◆ tree diagram

 SET UP *You will need Labsheet 3C.*

▶ Using an experiment to find a probability can require many trials and take a long time. It is usually more efficient to find the theoretical probability. You can use a *tree diagram* to help you.

EXAMPLE

Two white beans labeled 1 and 2 and a red bean labeled 1 are placed in a cup. Three people each draw one bean from the cup without replacing it. The **tree diagram** shows all the possible outcomes for this experiment.

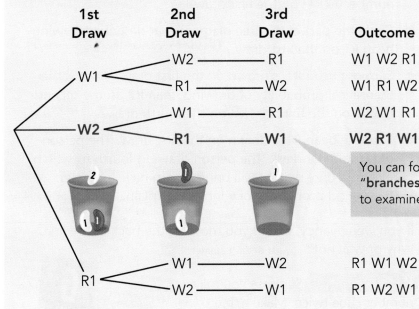

1st Draw	2nd Draw	3rd Draw	Outcome
W1	W2	R1	W1 W2 R1
	R1	W2	W1 R1 W2
W2	W1	R1	W2 W1 R1
	R1	W1	**W2 R1 W1**
R1	W1	W2	R1 W1 W2
	W2	W1	R1 W2 W1

You can follow a path along the "**branches**" of the tree diagram to examine a specific **outcome**.

Use the tree diagram in the Example for Questions 21 and 22.

21 a. What does the outcome **W2 R1 W1** mean? The first draw is white bean 2, the second draw is red bean 1 and the third draw is white bean 1.

  b. How many outcomes are shown in the tree diagram? 6

  c. Are the outcomes equally likely? Why or why not?
    Yes; All outcomes have the same chance of happening.

22 a. Using the ratio $\dfrac{\text{number of outcomes that makes the event happen}}{\text{total number of possible outcomes}}$,

what is the theoretical probability of winning (drawing a red bean) on the first draw? on the second draw? on the third draw? $\frac{1}{3}; \frac{1}{3}; \frac{1}{3}$

b. Compare the probabilities in part (a). Are you more likely to win on any particular draw? Explain. No; The probabilities are the same.

c. Describe how your answers in part (a) compare with the class experimental probabilities you found in parts (b) and (c) of Question 18 in Exploration 2. Answers will vary. Check students' work.

Use Labsheet 3C for Questions 23 and 24.

23 a. Complete the *Tree Diagram for the Grand Giveaway Experiment*. See Additional Answers.

b. How many possible outcomes are there? 24 possible outcomes

c. Find the theoretical probability of winning on each draw. $\frac{1}{2}$

24 Use the *Tree Diagram for the Grand Giveaway Experiment*.

a. What is the theoretical probability of drawing red bean number 1 (R1) on the first draw? $\frac{1}{4}$

b. Circle the part of the tree diagram that describes drawing bean R1 on the first draw. The third section of the diagram should be circled.

c. Suppose bean R1 is drawn on the first draw. What is the theoretical probability of drawing bean R2 on the second draw? on the third draw? on the fourth draw? $\frac{1}{3}; \frac{1}{3}; \frac{1}{3}$

d. Suppose bean R1 is drawn on the first draw. The person drawing second asks the person drawing fourth to switch places. If they switch, will one of them have a greater theoretical probability of winning? Explain. No; The probability does not change.

25 If you were Nancy, would you move to the back of the line? Why or why not? No; It doesn't change the probability that she will win.

✔ **QUESTION 26**

...checks that you can make and use tree diagrams.

26 ✔ **CHECKPOINT** Suppose you roll a number cube twice. Make a tree diagram that shows all the possible outcomes. Find the theoretical probability of rolling a 1 on the first roll and an odd number on the second roll. See Additional Answers.

▲ The six sides are numbered 1 through 6.

HOMEWORK EXERCISES ▶ See Exs. 13–20 on pp. 118–119.

Section 3
Key Concepts ▸▸▸▸▸▸▸▸▸▸▸▸▸▸▸▸▸▸▸▸

Key Terms

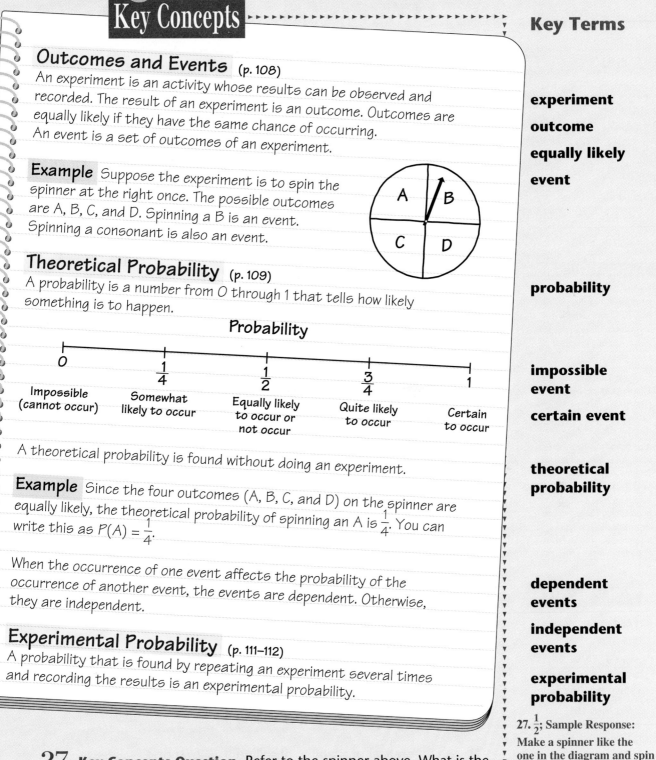

Outcomes and Events (p. 108)

An experiment is an activity whose results can be observed and recorded. The result of an experiment is an outcome. Outcomes are equally likely if they have the same chance of occurring. An event is a set of outcomes of an experiment.

Example Suppose the experiment is to spin the spinner at the right once. The possible outcomes are A, B, C, and D. Spinning a B is an event. Spinning a consonant is also an event.

Theoretical Probability (p. 109)

A probability is a number from 0 through 1 that tells how likely something is to happen.

Probability

0	$\frac{1}{4}$	$\frac{1}{2}$	$\frac{3}{4}$	1
Impossible (cannot occur)	Somewhat likely to occur	Equally likely to occur or not occur	Quite likely to occur	Certain to occur

A theoretical probability is found without doing an experiment.

Example Since the four outcomes (A, B, C, and D) on the spinner are equally likely, the theoretical probability of spinning an A is $\frac{1}{4}$. You can write this as $P(A) = \frac{1}{4}$.

When the occurrence of one event affects the probability of the occurrence of another event, the events are dependent. Otherwise, they are independent.

Experimental Probability (p. 111–112)

A probability that is found by repeating an experiment several times and recording the results is an experimental probability.

experiment

outcome

equally likely

event

probability

impossible event

certain event

theoretical probability

dependent events

independent events

experimental probability

27. $\frac{1}{2}$; Sample Response: Make a spinner like the one in the diagram and spin it a certain number of times, recording the results of each spin. Then write the fraction $\frac{\text{number of times A or C was spun}}{\text{total number of spins}}$

27 **Key Concepts Question** Refer to the spinner above. What is the theoretical probability of spinning either an A or a C? How can you find the experimental probability of this event?

Continued on next page

Section 3 Exploring Probability 115

Section 3

Key Terms

tree diagram

◀◀◀◀◀◀ Key Concepts

Tree Diagrams (p. 113–114)

A tree diagram can be used to show all the possible outcomes of an experiment.

Example The tree diagram at the right shows the possible outcomes of two flips of a coin.

First flip	Second flip	Outcome
H	H	H H
H	T	H T
T	H	T H
T	T	T T

CLOSURE QUESTION

Define theoretical probability and explain how it is different from experimental probability. What is the range for all probabilities?

Sample Response:
Theoretical probability is the ratio

number of successful outcomes
───────────────────────────
    total number of outcomes

and tells how likely it is that an event will happen. Theoretical probability is calculated probability, while experimental probability is probability based on an experiment. The range for all probabilities is from 0 to 1.

28 Key Concepts Question

a. Make a tree diagram that shows all of the possible outcomes of spinning the spinner on page 115 twice. **See Additional Answers.**

b. How many possible outcomes are shown on your diagram?
16 outcomes

c. What is the theoretical probability of spinning an A and then spinning a B? $\frac{1}{16}$

Section 3

◀◀◀◀◀◀ Practice & Application Exercises

YOU WILL NEED

For Ex. 11:
♦ a coin

For Ex. 12:
♦ six beans or two dice (optional)

For Exercises 1–3, a number cube with sides numbered 1 through 6 is rolled. Find each probability and plot it on a number line as on page 115. Label each point.

1. the theoretical probability of rolling a 7 0;

2. the theoretical probability of rolling a 1, 2, 3, or 4 $\frac{2}{3}$;

3. the theoretical probability of rolling a number less than 7
1;

4. Which events in Exercises 1–3 are certain? Which are impossible?
rolling a number less than 7; rolling a 7

116 **Module 2** At the Mall

For Exercises 5–7, tell whether the outcomes of the events described are equally likely.

5. rolling an even number on a number cube with sides numbered 1 through 6 and rolling an odd number on the same number cube
   equally likely

6. rolling a number less than 2 on a number cube with sides numbered 1 through 6 and rolling a number greater than 3 on the same number cube **not equally likely**

7. spinning an A on this spinner and spinning a B on this spinner **not equally likely**

8. **Open-ended** Describe an experiment that has three outcomes whose probabilities are $\frac{1}{2}$, $\frac{1}{3}$, and $\frac{1}{6}$. **Answers will vary. Check students' work.**

9. In a bag with 20 marbles, 4 marbles are blue.

   a. One marble is drawn from the bag. What is the probability that it is a blue marble? that it is not a blue marble? $\frac{1}{5}$; $\frac{4}{5}$

   b. Suppose a blue marble is drawn on the first draw and not replaced. What is the probability of drawing a blue marble on the second draw? $\frac{3}{19}$

   c. Suppose another color (not blue) is drawn on the first draw and not replaced. What is the probability of drawing a blue marble on the second draw? $\frac{4}{19}$

   d. Is drawing a blue marble on the second draw *dependent* on or *independent* of the first draw? Explain your answer.
      dependent; One event affects the probability of the other event.

10. **Interpreting Data** The table shows the batting records for members of a baseball team. Use the table to find each experimental probability.

    a. the probability that Erik Forgaard gets a hit $\frac{5}{8}$

    b. the probability that Larry Bryant does not get a hit $\frac{9}{33}$

Player	Number of hits	Times at bat
Ed Hightower	14	21
Erik Forgaard	5	8
Larry Bryant	24	33
Chaz Arthur	6	20

11. a. Suppose a coin is flipped once. What is the theoretical probability that it will show heads? $\frac{1}{2}$

    b. Flip a coin 20 times and record the results. Use the results to find the experimental probability that the coin shows heads.
       Answers will vary. Check students' work.

    c. Explain any differences in your answers from parts (a) and (b).

11. c. Sample Response: The experimental probability will vary depending on the outcomes. The theoretical probability is always $\frac{1}{2}$.

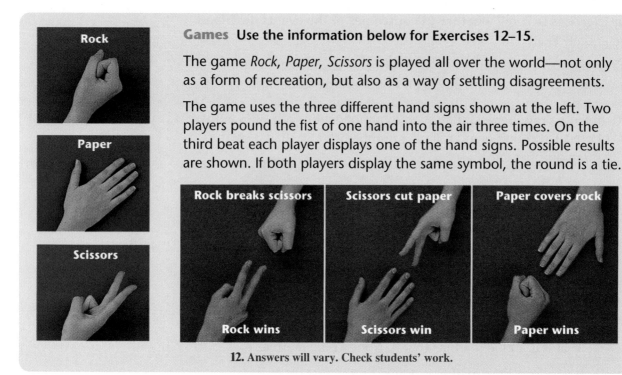

Rock

Paper

Scissors

Games Use the information below for Exercises 12–15.

The game *Rock, Paper, Scissors* is played all over the world—not only as a form of recreation, but also as a way of settling disagreements.

The game uses the three different hand signs shown at the left. Two players pound the fist of one hand into the air three times. On the third beat each player displays one of the hand signs. Possible results are shown. If both players display the same symbol, the round is a tie.

Rock breaks scissors

Rock wins

Scissors cut paper

Scissors win

Paper covers rock

Paper wins

12. Answers will vary. Check students' work.

12. a. Play 20 rounds of *Rock, Paper, Scissors* with a partner. After each round, record each player's choice (use *R* for rock, *P* for paper, and *S* for scissors) and the result in a table like this one. (*Note:* Use six beans or two dice if a partner is not available.)

Round number	Player 1	Player 2	Result
1	R	P	Player 2 wins
2	S	S	tie

b. Based on the results of your 20 rounds, what is the experimental probability of Player 1 winning? of Player 2 winning? of a tie?

c. Did Player 1 or Player 2 win most often? How can you tell using the experimental probabilities in part (b)?

d. **Writing** Do you think playing *Rock, Paper, Scissors* is a fair way to settle a disagreement? Explain.

Player 1	Player 2	Result
	R	Tie
R		
P		

13. a. Copy and complete the tree diagram shown at the left for the game *Rock, Paper, Scissors*. See Additional Answers.

b. How many outcomes are there? **9**

c. What outcomes make up the event "Player 1 does not win"?
RR, RP, PP, PS, SR, SS

d. How is the event "Player 1 does not win" different from the event "Player 1 loses"? "Player 1 does not win" includes ties and "Player 1 loses" does not.

14. **Writing** In a *fair game*, each player has an equal chance of winning. Is *Rock, Paper, Scissors* a fair game? Explain.
    Yes; The probability of winning is $\frac{1}{3}$ for each player.

15. **Challenge** Suppose you notice that your partner never uses scissors.

    a. Draw a tree diagram to show the possible outcomes if one player never uses scissors. **See Additional Answers.**

    b. How would this affect your playing strategy?

16. a. Draw a tree diagram to show all the possible outcomes when a coin is flipped three times. **See Additional Answers.**

    b. How many outcomes are there? Do you think the outcomes are all equally likely? Explain.

Use your tree diagram from Exercise 16 to find each theoretical probability.

17. no heads $\frac{1}{8}$ 18. exactly one head $\frac{3}{8}$ 19. a head on the first flip $\frac{1}{2}$

15. b. Sample Response: I would never use rock because I could only tie or lose if I did.

16. b. 8 outcomes; Yes; The outcomes on each flip are equally likely.

R e f l e c t i n g ◀▶ on the Section

Write your response to Exercise 20 in your journal.

20. Describe two dependent events and two independent events.
    Answers will vary. Check students' work.

Journal

Exercise 20 checks that you can apply ideas about probability.

S p i r a l ◀▶ Review

Use the table for Exercises 21 and 22. (Module 2, p. 100)

21. Estimate the percent of change in CD shipments from 1984 to 1990.
    about 3400% increase

22. Estimate the percent of change in record shipments from 1984 to 1990.
    about 94% decrease

Manufacturers' Shipments of Recordings (in millions of dollars)		
Recording Type	**1984**	**1990**
Vinyl records	1549	87
CDs	103	3452

Tell whether each angle is *acute, right, obtuse*, or *straight*. (Toolbox, p. 603)

23. 85° acute   24. 140° obtuse   25. 180° straight 26. 95° obtuse

Write each group of integers in order from least to greatest.
(Toolbox, p. 601)

27. –7, –10, –2
    –10, –7, –2

28. –1, –2, 3
    –2, –1, 3

29. –18, 17, 13
    –18, 13, 17

Section ③
Extra Skill Practice

Suppose you roll the object shown. It has eight sides, numbered 1 through 8. All eight outcomes are equally likely. Find the theoretical probability of each event in Exercises 1–4.

1. rolling a 2 $\frac{1}{8}$

2. rolling a 7 or 8 $\frac{1}{4}$

3. rolling a number greater than 3 $\frac{5}{8}$

4. rolling a 2, 4, 6, or 8 $\frac{1}{2}$

5. In a sack of 25 apples, 8 are red, 10 are golden, and the rest are green.

   a. One apple is taken from the sack. What is the probability that it is golden? that it is green? that it is not green? $\frac{2}{5}$, $\frac{7}{25}$, $\frac{18}{25}$

   b. If 2 red apples have been taken from the sack, what is the probability that the next apple taken will be red? will be green? $\frac{6}{23}$; $\frac{7}{23}$

   c. Are the events below *dependent* or *independent*? Explain.
      Event 1: The first apple taken is golden.
      Event 2: The second apple taken is green.

      The events are independent if the first apple is replaced before the second apple is taken. If the first apple is not replaced, the events are dependent.

The table shows the results from sixty flips of two coins. Use the table for Exercises 6–7.

Two Heads	Heads/Tails	Two Tails
14	28	18

6. What is the experimental probability of getting one heads and one tails? $\frac{7}{15}$

7. What is the experimental probability of getting two tails? $\frac{3}{10}$

8. José made a packing list for a weekend trip.

   a. Draw a tree diagram to show all the possible ways José could dress if he wears a pair of socks, a pair of pants, and a shirt.
   See Additional Answers.

   b. What is the theoretical probability that José wears the T-shirt with jeans and black socks? $\frac{1}{12}$

black socks
white socks
jeans
khaki pants
denim shirt
sweatshirt
T-shirt

Standardized Testing ◄► Free Response

1. A spinner is divided into 6 segments, each labeled with a different positive integer. The theoretical probability of spinning a number less than 8 is 1. The theoretical probability of spinning a multiple of 3 is $\frac{1}{3}$, a multiple of 4 is $\frac{1}{6}$, and an odd number is $\frac{2}{3}$. Draw the spinner.

2. What is the theoretical probability of getting all heads or all tails when a coin is flipped 3 times? 4 times? 5 times? 50 times? $\frac{1}{4}$; $\frac{1}{8}$; $\frac{1}{16}$; $\frac{1}{2^{49}}$

Section **4** Operations with Integers

IN THIS SECTION

EXPLORATION 1
♦ Adding Integers

EXPLORATION 2
♦ Subtracting Integers

EXPLORATION 3
♦ Multiplying and Dividing Integers

Setting the Stage ▸▸▸▸▸▸▸▸▸▸▸▸▸▸▸▸▸▸▸▸▸▸▸▸▸▸▸▸▸▸

Because so many people enjoy playing video games, many malls contain video arcades. Some video games depend on a player's ability to maneuver a car along a simulated race course using accelerators, steering wheels, or joy sticks.

The programmers who create video games use coordinates to make the figures move on the screen. They define a figure's location on the screen by its coordinates, and describe a move from one place to another by the change in the value of each coordinate.

WARM-UP EXERCISES

Simplify.
1. $57 + 19$ 76
2. $57 - 19$ 38
3. $57 \cdot 19$ 1083
4. $57 \div 19$ 3
5. If $6 + 11 = 17$, then $17 - 6 = \underline{\quad}$.   11
6. If $3 \cdot 18 = 54$, then $54 \div 18 = \underline{\quad}$.   3

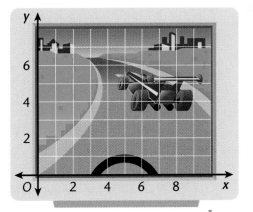

Think About It

1 Describe two different ways that the image of the red race car on the screen might change during the game. **Sample Response: The race car could turn towards the right or it could turn completely sideways.**

2 Give the coordinates of three points that are covered by the red race car. **Sample Response: (6, 4), (7, 5), (8, 5)**

LEARN HOW TO...
- ◆ add integers
- ◆ find the opposite of an integer
- ◆ find absolute values

AS YOU...
- ◆ simulate a video game

KEY TERMS
- ◆ integers
- ◆ opposite
- ◆ absolute value

 Exploration 1

Adding INTEGERS

SET UP *Work with a partner. You will need Labsheets 4A and 4B.*

▶ To get a programmer's view of how to move figures on a coordinate plane, you and your partner will compete in a race at the Integer Speedway. During the race, you'll use integers to describe your car's position and how it will move. The **integers** are the numbers ... –3, –2, –1, 0, 1, 2, 3, ...

FOR ▶ HELP

with *integers*, see **TOOLBOX, p. 601**

Use Labsheets 4A and 4B for Questions 3 and 4.

3 **Try This as a Class** Read Labsheet 4A, *Integer Speedway Rules.* You'll play the game using the *Integer Speedway* on Labsheet 4B. Part of the game board is shown here.

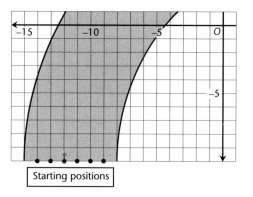

a. Suppose Player A starts at position (**–12, –10**) and moves **up 1** unit. What is the new position of Player A's car? *(–12, –9)*

b. Suppose you are at (–12, –9) after a move of 0, 1. List all the possible moves you can make. *0, 1; 1, 1; 0, 2; –1, 1*

c. After a move of 0, 2, is a move of 1, 1 allowed? Explain.

3. c. No; A player can move either horizontally or vertically but not in both directions.

4 Play a game of *Integer Speedway.* Then answer these questions.

a. Suppose your race car is at (12, –3). If the next move is –1, –3, what is the new position of your car? *(11, –6)*

b. The expression 12 + (–1) gives the new horizontal position after the move described in part (a). Write an addition expression for the new vertical position. *–3 + (–3)*

c. What move would you make next? What would the new position of your car be? *Possible answers: –1, –3(10, –9); –2, –3(9, –9); –1, –4(10, –10); 0, –3(11, –9); –1, –2(10, 8)*

▶ **Try This as a Class** For Questions 5–8, assume that a race car is at (–3, 4), as shown.

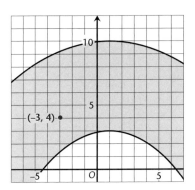

5 a. What type of integers, *positive* or *negative,* can you add to the horizontal coordinate to move the car to the left?
negative

b. Is the sum of two negative integers *positive* or *negative*? How can you find the sum of two negative integers?
negative; Add the whole-number parts of the integers and make the sum negative.

6 a. What integers can you add to the horizontal coordinate to move the car to the right without crossing the vertical axis?
1 and 2

b. When does adding a positive integer and a negative integer give a negative sum? How do you find the sum in this case?

7 a. Suppose you want to move the car so it is on the vertical axis. What integer must you add to the horizontal coordinate? Complete this addition equation to show the change in the horizontal coordinate: $-3 + \underline{\ ?\ } = \underline{\ ?\ }$. 3; 3, 0

b. When does adding a positive integer and a negative integer give a sum of 0?

8 a. Suppose you want to move the car across the vertical axis. Give an example of an integer you could add to the horizontal coordinate, and describe the final position of the car.
Sample Response: 4; (1,4)

b. When does adding a positive integer and a negative integer give a positive sum? How do you find the sum in this case?

6. b. Sample Response: when the positive integer is less than the opposite of the negative integer; subtract the positive integer from the opposite of the negative integer and make the result negative.

7. b. Sample Response: when the positive integer is the opposite of the negative integer

8. b. Sample Response: when the positive integer is greater than the opposite of the negative integer; Subtract the opposite of the negative integer from the positive integer.

▶ In Questions 5–8, you modeled the addition of integers on a coordinate plane. You can also use a number line.

EXAMPLE

To find the sum –11 + 3, start at **–11** and move **to the right 3** spaces.

Move to the right to add +3.

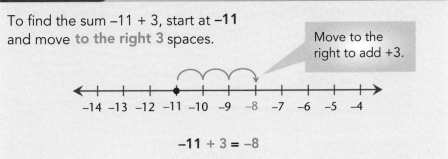

–11 + 3 = –8

9 Suppose that the sum in the Example was –11 + (–3). How would the answer be different? Sample Response: The sum, –14, would be found by moving 3 spaces to the left.

10 ✔ **CHECKPOINT** Find each sum.

  a. –8 + (–7) –15 **b.** 12 + (–7) 5 **c.** 2 + (–6) –4 **d.** –7 + 7 0

11 The numbers –3 and 3 are **opposites**. So are 7 and –7. What is true about the sum of two opposites? The sum is 0.

12 Find the opposite of each integer.

  a. –17 17   **b.** 31 –31   **c.** –215 215   **d.** 0 0

13 Suppose your car is located at (–5, 1) on the *Integer Speedway*. How far is the car from the vertical axis? from the horizontal axis? 5 units; 1 unit

▶ When you found the distance from the point (–5, 1) to the vertical axis, you found the *absolute value* of –5, or |–5|. The **absolute value** of a number is its distance from 0 on a number line.

EXAMPLE

The distance from –5 to 0 is 5 units.

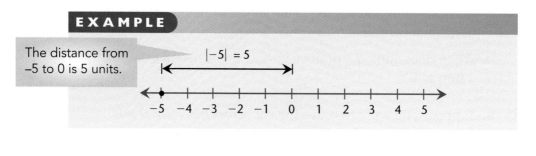

|–5| = 5

14 What other number has an absolute value of 5? 5

15 What two numbers have an absolute value of 15? –15, 15

16 Find each absolute value.

  a. |–3| 3   **b.** |0| 0   **c.** |12| 12   **d.** |–17| 17

17 **Try This as a Class** Suppose you do not know the position of a car on the *Integer Speedway*. You have these two clues about the car's coordinates (h, v). Where could the car be? Possible answers: (3, –2) or (3, 2)

Read –h as "the opposite of h."

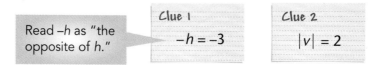

Clue 1
–h = –3

Clue 2
|v| = 2

✔ QUESTION 18

...checks that you can solve equations with opposite and absolute values.

18 ✔ **CHECKPOINT** Solve each equation.

  a. |x| = 2 –2, 2 **b.** –y = –3 3 **c.** |a| = 7 –7, 7 **d.** –b = 12 –12

HOMEWORK EXERCISES ▶ See Exs. 1–20 on pp. 131–132.

Exploration 2

Subtracting INTEGERS

GOAL

LEARN HOW TO...
◆ subtract integers

AS YOU...
◆ explore translations on a coordinate grid

KEY TERMS
◆ translation
◆ image

SET UP *You will need:* • *Labsheet 4C* • *tracing paper*

▶ When you played *Integer Speedway*, you used addition or subtraction to change the coordinates of your car. This type of move is a *translation*. A **translation**, or slide, moves each point of a figure the same distance in the same direction.

19 **Use Labsheet 4C.** The labsheet shows a translation on a coordinate grid. Points *A′*, *B′*, and *C′* (read as "*A*-prime, *B*-prime, and *C*-prime") are the **images** of points *A*, *B*, and *C* after the translation. Follow the instructions for *Exploring Translations* to learn more about translations.

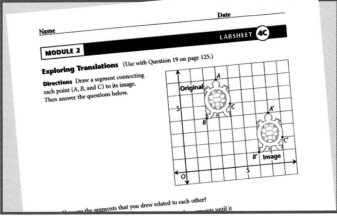

19. a. They are parallel to each other.
b. No.
c. They are the same.
d. (2, 4), (4, 5), (7, 4), (6, 1), (8, 2)
e. $x + 4$
f. $y - 3$

20 This table shows the coordinates of several points and their images after a translation.

Coordinates of the point	(3, 2)	(5, –7)	(0, –3)	(–5, 6)	(x, y)
Coordinates of the image	(2, 5)	(4, –4)	(–1, 0)	(–6, 9)	?

a. Describe the translation using the form (*x* + ___?___ , *y* + ___?___).
                                                                    –1; 3

b. Suppose the same translation is used on the point (–45, –105). What are the coordinates of the image? (–46, –102)

21 **Try This as a Class** Suppose you are programming a video game in which a jester is located at point (x, y).

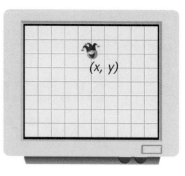

a. Write a translation in the form $(x + \underline{\ ?\ }, y + \underline{\ ?\ })$ that will move the jester to the right 2 units and up 1 unit.   **2; 1**

b. Use the form $(x - \underline{\ ?\ }, y - \underline{\ ?\ })$ to write a translation that will move the jester to the left 3 units and down 5 units.   **3; 5**

c. Rewrite the translation in part (b) in the form $(x + \underline{\ ?\ }, y + \underline{\ ?\ })$.   **–3; –5**

d. Explain how any subtraction expression can be written as addition.   **Sample Response: Add the opposite.**

22 Suppose the translation $(x - (-3), y - 4)$ is used on the jester shown in Question 21.

a. Write $1 - (-3)$ as an addition expression.   **1 + 3**

b. Suppose the jester is at point $(1, 1)$. What is its new position after the translation $(x - (-3), y - 4)$?   **(4, –3)**

c. Describe this translation in words.   **Move right 3 units and down 4 units.**

▶ **Subtracting Integers** As you saw in Questions 21 and 22, you can write any subtraction problem as an addition problem.

EXAMPLE

Find the difference: $-8 - (-7)$

SAMPLE RESPONSE

$$-8 - (-7) = -8 + 7$$

◀ Rewrite subtraction as addition.

$$= -1$$

✔ **QUESTION 23**

…checks that you can subtract integers.

23 ✔ **CHECKPOINT** Find each difference.

a. $23 - (-15)$ **38**   b. $12 - (-12)$ **24**   c. $-80 - 22$ **–102**   d. $-65 - (-43)$ **–22**

HOMEWORK EXERCISES ▶ See Exs. 21–30 on p. 132.

Exploration 3 ▸

Multiplying and Dividing INTEGERS

SET UP *You will need:* • *Labsheet 4D* • *ruler*

▶ **Programmers can move figures on a video screen by adding values to the coordinates of points. But if they multiply each coordinate by a number, a totally different visual effect is created.**

Use Labsheet 4D for Questions 24 and 25.

24 Plot points *A*, *B*, *C*, and *D* on the *Exploring Multiplication* coordinate plane. Connect the points to create a polygon.
See Additional Answers.

25 **Try This as a Class** Use your polygon from Question 24.

   a. To find the coordinates of points *A′*, *B′*, and *C′*, multiply each coordinate of each point by 3. Plot points *A′*, *B′* and *C′*.
See Additional Answers.

   b. How are the positions of points *A′*, *B′*, and *C′* related to the positions of points *A*, *B*, and *C*?

   c. The coordinates of point *D′* are 3 times the coordinates of point *D*. Use your answer to part (b) to plot the point where you think *D′* is located in the coordinate plane. *D′* is at (–3, –12).

25. b. Draw $\overline{OA'}$, $\overline{OB'}$, and $\overline{OC'}$. $\overline{OA}$ is on $\overline{OA'}$ and $OA' = 3 \cdot OA$. $\overline{OB}$ is on $\overline{OB'}$ and $OB' = 3 \cdot OB$. $\overline{OC}$ is on $\overline{OC'}$ and $OC' = 3 \cdot OC$.

▶ **Multiplying Integers** To find the vertical coordinate of point *D'* in Question 25(c), you must multiply –4 by 3. You can use repeated addition to find the product.

EXAMPLE

Use repeated addition to find 3 • (–4).

SAMPLE RESPONSE

$$3 \cdot (-4) = (-4) + (-4) + (-4)$$
$$= -12$$

Use Labsheet 4D for Question 26.

26 a. Find the horizontal coordinate of point *D'* by multiplying the horizontal coordinate of *D* by 3. –3

b. Graph point *D'* in the coordinate plane. Is the point located where you plotted it in Question 25(c)? If not, explain which is the correct point, and why. **Answers will vary. Check students' work.**

c. Draw segments to form polygon *A'B'C'D'*. Compare polygons *ABCD* and *A'B'C'D'*. How are they alike? How are they different? **The polygons are similar but they are not congruent.**

26. d. Sample Response: The figure is stretched horizontally and vertically by the same amount.

d. Discussion Describe the visual effect created by multiplying each coordinate of a set of points by a positive integer.

27 Try This as a Class Use your results from Question 26(a).

a. Is the product of a positive integer and a negative integer *positive* or *negative*? **negative**

b. Describe how to find the product of a positive integer and a negative integer. **Sample Response: Multiply the whole-number parts of the integers and make the product negative.**

28 a. Copy the table below and complete the products you know.
See table.

b. Look for patterns in the table to find the remaining products.
See table.

4(–3) = 4 • –3
Use parentheses to avoid confusion with 4 – 3.

4(–3)	3(–3)	2(–3)	1(–3)	0(–3)	–1(–3)	–2(–3)	–3(–3)	–4(–3)
–12	–9	? –6	? –3	? 0	? 3	? 6	? 9	? 12

29 Try This as a Class Use your results from Question 28.

a. Is the product of two negative integers *positive* or *negative*? **positive**

b. How can you find the product of two negative integers? **Sample Response: Multiply the whole-number part of the integers.**

30 ✔ **CHECKPOINT** Find each product.

  a. 3(–7) –21   **b.** (–8)(–13) 104 **c.** (–1)(–1) 1   **d.** 7(–9)(8) –504

✔ **QUESTION 30**

…checks that you know how to multiply integers.

▶ **Dividing Integers** In Exploration 2, you discovered that for every subtraction problem, there is a related addition problem. This is also true for multiplication and division. For every division problem, there is a related multiplication problem.

> **The multiplication equation related to**
> **30 ÷ 5 = 6 is 5 · 6 = 30.**

31 Write the multiplication equation related to 28 ÷ 7 = 4. 7 · 4 = 28

32 a. Write the multiplication equation related to –32 ÷ 8 = x. 8x = –32

  b. What number must x be to make the multiplication equation that you wrote for part (a) true? –4

  c. What is the quotient –32 ÷ 8? –4

33 Write and solve the related multiplication equation to find each quotient.

  a. 72 ÷ (–9) = x –9x = 72; –8   **b.** –16 ÷ 8 = x 8x = –16; –2

  c. –9 ÷ (–3) = x –3x = –9; 3   **d.** –24 ÷ (–6) = x –6x = –24; 4

34 Try This as a Class You can now find quotients without using multiplication.

  a. Is the quotient –264 ÷ 12 *positive* or *negative*? How do you know? negative; Sample Response: The product of a negative integer and a positive integer is negative.

  b. Write your own rules for dividing integers.

34. b. Sample Response: When you divide, if the signs are the same the quotient is positive. If the signs are different, the quotient is negative.

35 ✔ **CHECKPOINT** Find each quotient.

  a. –18 ÷ (–3) 6 **b.** $\frac{35}{-7}$ –5   **c.** –150 ÷ 5 –30 **d.** $\frac{-48}{-6}$ 8

✔ **QUESTION 35**

…checks that you know how to divide integers.

36 Discussion Suppose you connect three points on a coordinate grid to form a triangle. What visual effect do you think would be created by dividing each coordinate of each vertex by a positive integer? Test your conjecture for a triangle whose vertices are A(0, 0), B(2, 4), and C(6, –2). Is the result what you expected? Sample Response: The triangle would be shrunk both horizontally and vertically by the same amount.

HOMEWORK EXERCISES ▷ See Exs. 31–46 on pp. 132–133.

Key Concepts

Key Terms

integer

absolute value

opposite

translation

image

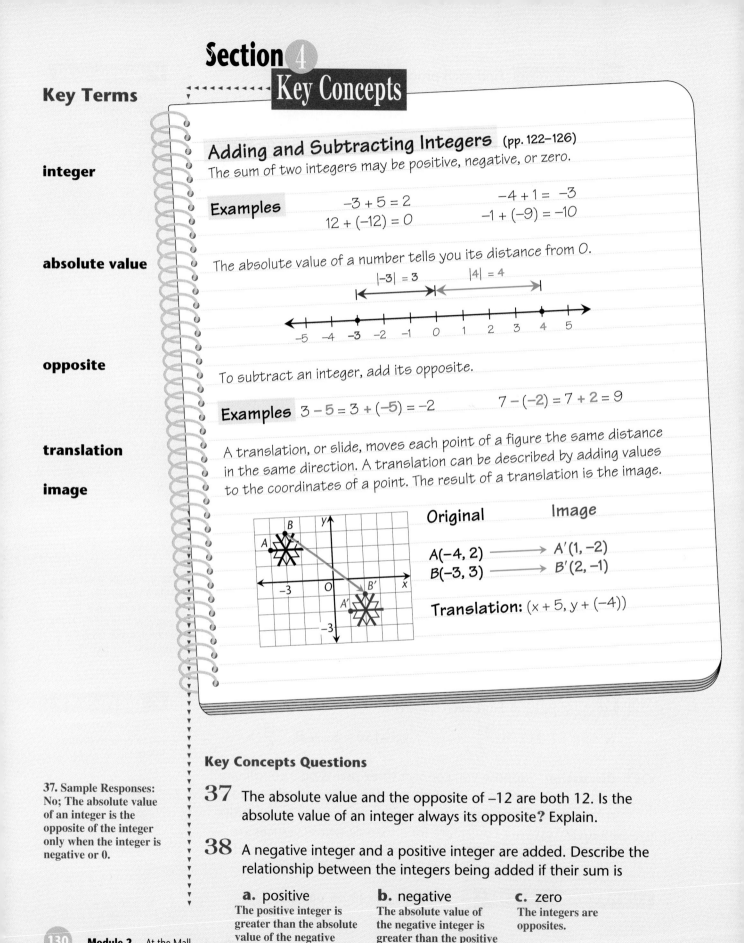

Adding and Subtracting Integers (pp. 122–126)

The sum of two integers may be positive, negative, or zero.

Examples
$$-3 + 5 = 2$$
$$12 + (-12) = 0$$
$$-4 + 1 = -3$$
$$-1 + (-9) = -10$$

The absolute value of a number tells you its distance from 0.

$|-3| = 3$ $|4| = 4$

To subtract an integer, add its opposite.

Examples $3 - 5 = 3 + (-5) = -2$ $7 - (-2) = 7 + 2 = 9$

A translation, or slide, moves each point of a figure the same distance in the same direction. A translation can be described by adding values to the coordinates of a point. The result of a translation is the image.

Original		Image
A(–4, 2)	⟶	A′(1, –2)
B(–3, 3)	⟶	B′(2, –1)

Translation: $(x + 5, y + (-4))$

Key Concepts Questions

37 The absolute value and the opposite of –12 are both 12. Is the absolute value of an integer always its opposite? Explain.

38 A negative integer and a positive integer are added. Describe the relationship between the integers being added if their sum is

a. positive
The positive integer is greater than the absolute value of the negative integer.

b. negative
The absolute value of the negative integer is greater than the positive integer.

c. zero
The integers are opposites.

37. Sample Responses: No; The absolute value of an integer is the opposite of the integer only when the integer is negative or 0.

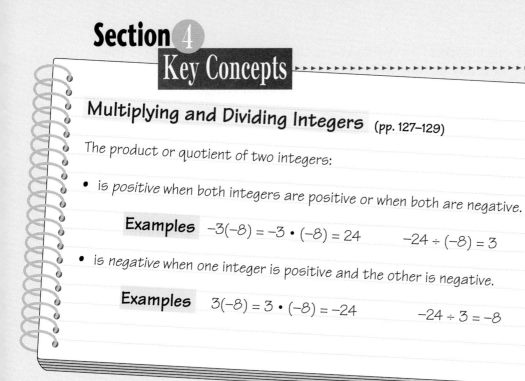

Key Concepts

Multiplying and Dividing Integers (pp. 127–129)

The product or quotient of two integers:

- is positive when both integers are positive or when both are negative.

  Examples $-3(-8) = -3 \cdot (-8) = 24$ $-24 \div (-8) = 3$

- is negative when one integer is positive and the other is negative.

  Examples $3(-8) = 3 \cdot (-8) = -24$ $-24 \div 3 = -8$

39 Key Concepts Question When is the product of three integers positive? When is it negative? When is it zero? Explain.

When one or three out of three integers is positive the product is positive; When one or three out of three integers is negative the product is negative; $(+)(-)(-) = +$, $(+)(+)(+) = +$, $(-)(+)(+) = -$, $(-)(-)(-) = -$.

Section ④

Practice & Application Exercises

YOU WILL NEED

For Ex. 30:
- graph paper

Find each sum.

1. $-23 + (-8)$ -31 2. $91 + (-10)$ 81 3. $-15 + 7$ -8

4. $12 + (-12)$ 0 5. $-88 + (-12)$ -100 6. $4 + (-10) + 7$ 1

Find the opposite of each integer.

7. -15 15 8. 101 -101 9. 74 -74 10. -62 62

Find each absolute value.

11. $|-47|$ 47 12. $|53|$ 53 13. $\left|8\frac{1}{2}\right|$ $8\frac{1}{2}$ 14. $|-0.42|$ 0.42

15. Find two different integers with an absolute value of 7. $7, -7$

Solve each equation.

16. $|y| = 12$ 17. $-w = 2$ -2 18. $|z| = 0$ 0 19. $-x = -5$ 5
    $12, -12$

20. Joe earned $15 mowing lawns, then bought a radio for $11. The next day he earned $5. He spent $3 on arcade games. Write an addition expression for his income and expenses.
15 + (–11) + 5 + (–3) or 20 + (–14)

Find each difference.

21. 5 – 9 –4   **22.** 18 – (–13) 31   **23.** 2 – (–11) 13

24. –3 – (–3) 0   **25.** –10 – 4 –14   **26.** –7 – (–19) 12

27. **Weather** Suppose the temperature was –18°F at 6:00 A.M. and 23°F at 2:00 P.M. What is the difference in the temperatures? 41°F

28. The translation (x + 2, y + (–3)) is applied to figure PQRST.

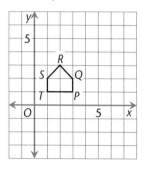

  a. Give the coordinates of the image points P', Q', R', S', and T'.
  P'(5, –2), Q'(5, –1), R'(4, 0), S'(3, –1), T'(3, –2)
  b. **Writing** Describe in words a translation that moves PQRST to the opposite side of the vertical axis.
  Sample Response: Add –4 to x and any integer to y.

29. After the translation (x + 5, y + 2), the image of a point is (12, 16). What are the coordinates of the original point? (7, 14)

30. For each pair of coordinates, describe the translation in two ways, one using only addition and one using only subtraction. Then show each translation on a graph. **See Additional Answers.**

	Original	Image	Translations	
a.	L(2, 4)	L'(1, 5)	(x + _?_ , y + _?_) or (x – _?_ , y – _?_)	–1; 1 1; –1
b.	M(0, –7)	M'(2, –1)	(x + _?_ , y + _?_) or (x – _?_ , y – _?_)	2; 6 –2; –6
c.	N(–6, 3)	N'(–10, –3)	(x + _?_ , y + _?_) or (x – _?_ , y – _?_)	–4; –6 4; 6

Find each product or quotient.

31. 8(–9) –72   **32.** –16 • 20   **33.** –2(–7)(–4)   **34.** –3(–8)(2) 48
                             –320   –56

35. –27 ÷ 9 –3   **36.** $\frac{-56}{-8}$ 7   **37.** –48 ÷ (–6) 8 **38.** $\frac{72}{-3}$ –24

Algebra Connection Evaluate each expression when a = –16, b = –4, and c = 48.

39. ab 64   **40.** bc –192   **41.** c ÷ a –3   **42.** $\frac{a}{b}$ 4

43. Football On each of three
consecutive plays, a football
team loses 5 yd. Suppose lost
yardage is represented by a
negative integer. Write a
multiplication expression
that describes the total
change in yardage and find
the total number of yards lost.
3(–5); 15 yards lost

**Use this information for Exercises 44 and 45: On a test, each correct
answer scores 5 points, each incorrect answer scores –2 points, and
each question left unanswered scores 0 points.**

44. Suppose a student answers 15 questions on the test correctly, 4
incorrectly, and does not answer 1 question. Write an expression
for the student's score and find the score. 15(5) + 4(–2) + 1(0); 67

45. Challenge Suppose you answer all 20 questions on the test.
What is the greatest number of questions you can answer
incorrectly and still get a positive score? Explain your reasoning.
14 questions; Sample Response: 14(–2) + 6(5) = –28 + 30 = 2 and 15(–2) + 5(5) =
–30 + 25 = –5.

Reflecting ◀▶ on the Section

46. Suppose you multiply each coordinate of each point of a figure
by –1. Describe the visual effect created by this operation.
Sample Response: The figure will appear to have been reflected over both the
vertical and horizontal axes.

Exercise 46 checks
your understanding
of opposites.

Spiral ◀▶ Review

**A backpack contains 4 black pens, 2 blue pens, and a red pen. Find the
theoretical probability of each event.** (Module 2, p. 115)

47. pulling out a blue pen on the first try $\frac{2}{7}$

48. *not* pulling out a black pen on the first try $\frac{3}{7}$

49. pulling out a red pen after two black pens have been removed $\frac{1}{5}$

Find each quotient. Write each answer in lowest terms. (Toolbox, p. 598)

50. $\frac{3}{8} \div \frac{1}{4}$ $1\frac{1}{2}$ **51.** $\frac{7}{12} \div \frac{5}{6}$ $\frac{7}{10}$ **52.** $\frac{33}{39} \div \frac{11}{13}$ 1   **53.** $\frac{10}{21} \div \frac{7}{9}$ $\frac{30}{49}$

**Replace each ? with the number that will make the fractions
equivalent.** (Toolbox, p. 597)

54. $\frac{1}{5} = \frac{?}{30}$ 6   **55.** $\frac{1}{3} = \frac{?}{24}$ 8   **56.** $\frac{5}{8} = \frac{35}{?}$ 56

57. $\frac{3}{10} = \frac{?}{110}$ 33   **58.** $\frac{3}{4} = \frac{21}{?}$ 28   **59.** $\frac{9}{16} = \frac{54}{?}$ 96

Absolute Value Equations

The equation $|x + 1| = 3$ includes a variable inside the absolute value bars. You can use what you know about absolute value to find the values of x that make the equation true.

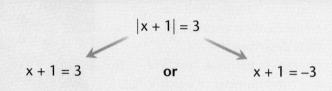

$|x + 1| = 3$

$x + 1 = 3$ **or** $x + 1 = -3$

60. Solve each equation above to find the values of x that make $|x + 1| = 3$ true. 2, –4

Solve each equation.

61. $|y + 2| = 8$ 6, –10 **62.** $|w - 5| = 10$ 15, –5 **63.** $|-2z| = 4$ –2, 2

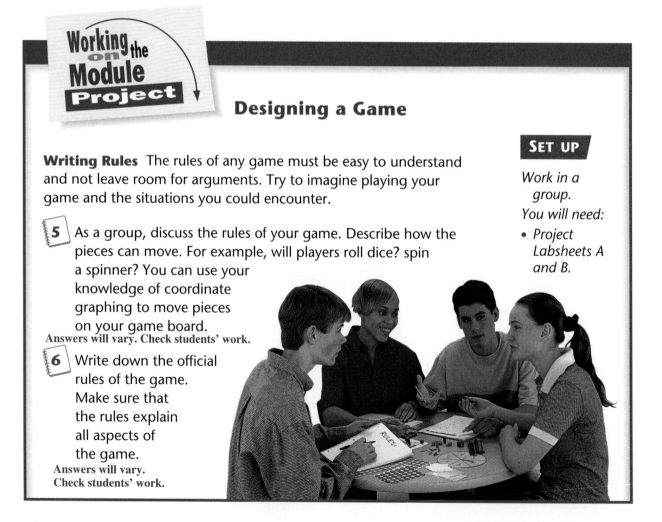

Working on the Module Project

Designing a Game

Writing Rules The rules of any game must be easy to understand and not leave room for arguments. Try to imagine playing your game and the situations you could encounter.

SET UP

Work in a group.
You will need:
- *Project Labsheets A and B.*

5 As a group, discuss the rules of your game. Describe how the pieces can move. For example, will players roll dice? spin a spinner? You can use your knowledge of coordinate graphing to move pieces on your game board.
Answers will vary. Check students' work.

6 Write down the official rules of the game. Make sure that the rules explain all aspects of the game.
Answers will vary. Check students' work.

Section 4

Find each sum.

1. $-12 + 16$ ₄
2. $27 + (-49)$ ₋₂₂
3. $-78 + 25 + (-4)$
   ₋₅₇
4. $-130 + (-65)$ ₋₁₉₅

Find the opposite of each integer.

5. 512 ₋₅₁₂
6. -43 ₄₃
7. -1 ₁
8. 38 ₋₃₈

Find each absolute value.

9. $|29|$ ₂₉
10. $|-83|$ ₈₃
11. $\left|-3\frac{3}{4}\right|$ $3\frac{3}{4}$
12. $|-1.45|$ ₁.₄₅

Find each difference.

13. $-32 - 45$ ₋₇₇
14. $26 - (-13)$ ₃₉
15. $-16 - (-22)$ ₆
16. $55 - (-55)$ ₁₁₀

Find each product.

17. $-25(-10)$ ₂₅₀
18. $4(-15)$ ₋₆₀
19. $-7 \cdot 6$ ₋₄₂
20. $-12(-5)$ ₆₀

Find each quotient.

21. $42 \div (-7)$ ₋₆
22. $-88 \div 22$ ₋₄
23. $\frac{-54}{-3}$ ₁₈
24. $\frac{95}{-5}$ ₋₁₉

Simplify each expression.

25. $-14(-3)$ ₄₂
26. $27 + (-33)$ ₋₆
27. $-24 \div (-6)$ ₄
28. $52 - (-16)$ ₆₈
29. $\frac{-76}{19}$ ₋₄
30. $-41 + (-11)$ ₋₅₂
31. $64 \div (-4)$ ₋₁₆
32. $9 \cdot (-7)$ ₋₆₃
33. $-13 - 13$ ₋₂₆

Standardized Testing ◀▶ Open-ended

1. Give an example of two numbers that fit each description below.
   If no numbers fit the description, explain why.

   a. Both the sum and the product of 2 numbers are negative.
      Sample Response: –7 and 5
   b. The sum of 2 numbers is 0 and the product is positive.
      none; Two numbers with a sum of 0 are opposites. The product of opposites is always less than or
   c. The sum of 2 numbers is positive and the quotient is negative.   **equal to zero.**
      Sample Response: 10 and –5
2. The vertical sides of rectangle *ABCD* intersect the *x*-axis, and the
   horizontal sides intersect the *y*-axis. Give a set of possible
   coordinates for *A*, *B*, *C*, and *D*. Then write the coordinates of
   A′, *B′*, *C′*, and *D′* after the translation $(x - 4, y + 6)$. **Sample Response: *A*(3, 2), *B*(3, –2),**
   ***C*(–3, –2), *D*(3, 2); *A′*(–1, 8),**
   ***B′*(–1, 4), *C′*(–7, 4), *D′*(–7, 8)**

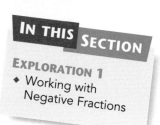

A WORLD CLASS W⊘NDER

Add or subtract.

1. $\dfrac{5}{4} - \dfrac{2}{4}$ $\dfrac{3}{4}$

2. $\dfrac{10}{12} + \dfrac{1}{6}$ 1

3. $\dfrac{7}{15} + \dfrac{13}{20}$ $1\dfrac{7}{60}$

4. $\dfrac{16}{21} - \dfrac{16}{35}$ $\dfrac{32}{105}$

5. $1\dfrac{5}{9} + 2\dfrac{2}{3}$ $4\dfrac{2}{9}$

Setting the Stage

The West Edmonton Mall in Alberta, Canada, has over 800 stores and covers the equivalent of 48 city blocks. This mall contains 55 shoe shops alone! It is also the home of *Galaxyland*, the world's largest indoor amusement park. *Galaxyland* contains 25 rides, including the *Mindbender* roller coaster and the daring *Drop of Doom*. With all of this under one roof, it is easy to see why some people have called the West Edmonton Mall the eighth wonder of the world!

▲
The first descent on the *Mindbender* is 14 stories high.

Think About It

1 One story of a building is about 10 ft. Estimate the height of the *Mindbender*. **about 140 ft**

2 On the *Drop of Doom*, the passengers' speed increases by about 22 mi/h for each second they "fall." Assume their speed at the top is 0 mi/h. What is their speed after falling for 2.5 seconds? **about 55 mi/h**

▶ In this exploration, you'll play *Fraction Drop*, a game in which numbers and symbols "fall" instead of people.

Exploration 1

Working with NEGATIVE FRACTIONS

GOAL

LEARN HOW TO...
- add and subtract positive and negative fractions

AS YOU...
- play a game with fractions

SET UP Work with a partner. You will need: • Labsheet 5A
• 14 index cards

▶ Follow the directions below to prepare to play *Fraction Drop.* You'll try to create the greatest sum or difference using numbers and symbols in a fraction expression.

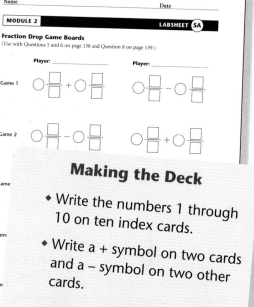

Fraction Drop Game

Playing the Game

- Labsheet 5A has 5 game boards for each player as shown. A game is completed when each player fills in one game board.

- Shuffle the deck of 14 cards, place it face down on the desk, and turn over the top card.

- If a number is turned over, each player must write it in one of his or her four squares on the game board. If a symbol is turned over, each player must write it in one of his or her two circles.

- Turn over cards from the top of the deck and record each number or symbol until you have filled your game board. Ignore any extra numbers or symbols you turn over.

- Once all the squares and circles are filled, find each player's sum or difference. The player with the greatest number wins.

Making the Deck

- Write the numbers 1 through 10 on ten index cards.

- Write a + symbol on two cards and a – symbol on two other cards.

▶ To add or subtract positive fractions and negative fractions, use the same rules as for adding or subtracting integers. Before adding or subtracting, you may have to rewrite the fractions so the denominators are the same.

3 Look at the *Fraction Drop* game board below. Find the sum and difference to determine which expression has the greatest value.

Player B

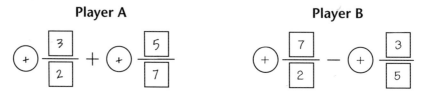

Player A   **Player B**

4 **Try This as a Class** Leeza and Rhea are playing *Fraction Drop*. Their game board shows that they have turned over the 8, 2, +, and 3 cards. The next card is a 6.

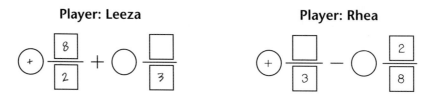

Player: Leeza   **Player: Rhea**

a. Can you tell who will win? Explain why or why not.

b. On the next draw, which symbol would be best for Rhea? Explain.

4. a. No; It depends on the next symbol turned over. If it is +, Leeza wins. If it is –, Rhea wins.
b. (–); Sample Response: She would win with a score of $2\frac{1}{4}$ over Leeza's score of 2.

Use Labsheet 5A for Questions 5 and 6.

5 Play two games of *Fraction Drop* with your partner. **Check students' work.**

6 a. Use a new game board. Play another game of *Fraction Drop*, but this time the player with the least number wins. **Check students' work.**

b. **Discussion** Which part of the board do you think is best to use for this version of the game, the part with the subtraction expression or the part with the addition expression? Explain. **Answers will vary. Check students' work.**

7 ✔ **CHECKPOINT** Find each sum or difference.

a. $-\dfrac{1}{2}+\left(-\dfrac{3}{4}\right)$ $-1\dfrac{1}{4}$ **b.** $\dfrac{5}{6}-\left(-\dfrac{4}{3}\right)$ $2\dfrac{1}{6}$ **c.** $-\dfrac{6}{10}+\dfrac{7}{8}$ $\dfrac{11}{40}$

8 **Use Labsheet 5A.** Use the remaining gameboards. Choose the symbols and numbers from the deck that give the least number. Then choose symbols and numbers that give the least positive number.

$-\dfrac{9}{2}-\dfrac{10}{1};\dfrac{9}{10}-\dfrac{7}{8}$

■ **HOMEWORK EXERCISES** ▶ See Exs. 1–32 on pp. 140–142.

✔ **QUESTION 7**

…checks that you can add and subtract positive and negative fractions.

Section 5
Key Concepts ▶▶▶▶▶▶▶▶▶▶▶▶▶▶▶▶▶▶▶▶▶▶

Adding and Subtracting Positive and Negative Fractions (p. 138)

To add and subtract positive and negative fractions, use the same rules as for adding and subtracting integers. Make sure that the denominators of the fractions are the same before adding or subtracting.

Example

$-\dfrac{5}{12}-\left(-\dfrac{1}{8}\right)=-\dfrac{5}{12}+\dfrac{1}{8}$

> Subtracting is the same as adding the opposite.

$=-\dfrac{10}{24}+\dfrac{3}{24}$

> Rewrite using the least common denominator.

$=-\dfrac{7}{24}$

Key Concepts Question

9 a. Use the numbers 1, 4, 5, and 10, the symbols + and −, and the part of the game board shown to create the greatest number you can.

b. How would your answer to part (a) be different if both of the symbols were −? $-\dfrac{4}{5}-\left(-\dfrac{10}{1}\right)=9\dfrac{1}{5}$

$+\dfrac{10}{1}-\left(-\dfrac{5}{4}\right)=11\dfrac{1}{4}$

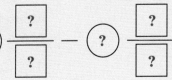

CLOSURE QUESTION

Describe the possible ways to add or subtract positive and negative fractions.

Sample Response: Addition: If both fractions are positive, add them and the result is positive. If both fractions are negative, add the absolute value of the fractions and the result is negative. If one fraction is positive and the other is negative, subtract the absolute values of the fractions and give the result the sign of the fraction with the larger absolute value. To subtract positive or negative fractions, rewrite the expression using addition and follow the given rules.

Section 5

Find each sum or difference.

1. $-\dfrac{8}{12} + \left(-\dfrac{4}{12}\right)$ –1

2. $\dfrac{4}{11} - \dfrac{10}{11}$ $-\dfrac{6}{11}$

3. $-\dfrac{8}{5} + \dfrac{2}{5}$ $-1\dfrac{1}{5}$

4. $-\dfrac{7}{16} - \left(-\dfrac{3}{8}\right)$ $-\dfrac{1}{16}$

5. $\dfrac{3}{14} + \left(-\dfrac{6}{7}\right)$ $-\dfrac{9}{14}$

6. $\dfrac{3}{4} + \left(-\dfrac{5}{12}\right)$ $\dfrac{1}{3}$

7. $-\dfrac{3}{7} - \left(-\dfrac{1}{6}\right)$ $-\dfrac{11}{42}$

8. $-\dfrac{2}{3} - \dfrac{3}{5}$ $-1\dfrac{4}{15}$

9. $-\dfrac{8}{15} - \dfrac{7}{20}$ $-\dfrac{53}{60}$

10. **Sewing** A fabric store has the three pieces of scrap material shown below. An art teacher needs four pieces of material that are each $\dfrac{3}{8}$ yd long and 1 yd wide.

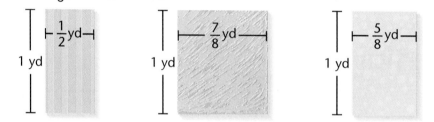

a. Is there enough fabric for the teacher? Yes.

10. b. Use one piece from the $\frac{1}{2}$ yd remnant, two pieces from the $\frac{7}{8}$ yd remnant, and one piece from the $\frac{5}{8}$ yd remnant; $\frac{1}{8}$ yd; $\frac{1}{8}$ yd; $\frac{2}{8}$ yd

b. How should the teacher cut the material? How much material will be left over from each original piece?

11. **Writing** Suppose your friend missed today's class. Write a letter to the friend describing how to add and subtract positive and negative fractions. Include several examples.
   Answers will vary. Check students' work.

12. **Patterns** The expressions below are part of a pattern.

$$\dfrac{1}{2} - \dfrac{1}{4} \qquad \dfrac{1}{2} - \dfrac{1}{4} + \dfrac{1}{8} \qquad \dfrac{1}{2} - \dfrac{1}{4} + \dfrac{1}{8} - \dfrac{1}{16}$$

12. a. $\frac{1}{2} - \frac{1}{4} + \frac{1}{8} - \frac{1}{16} + \frac{1}{32}$, $\frac{1}{2} - \frac{1}{4} + \frac{1}{8} - \frac{1}{16} + \frac{1}{32} - \frac{1}{64}$

a. Write the next two expressions in the pattern.

b. Evaluate each expression above and the two that you wrote for part (a). $\dfrac{1}{4}$ $\dfrac{3}{8}$ $\dfrac{5}{16}$ $\dfrac{11}{32}$ $\dfrac{21}{64}$

c. Sample Response: positive; The fraction to be subtracted will be smaller than the value of the twenty-ninth expression.

c. Suppose you evaluated the thirtieth expression in the pattern. Do you think the result would be *positive* or *negative*? Explain.

Mental Math Find each sum or difference without using paper and pencil.

13. $-2\dfrac{3}{5} + \left(-4\dfrac{2}{5}\right)$ –7

14. $4\dfrac{5}{6} + \left(-2\dfrac{5}{6}\right)$ 2

15. $1\dfrac{3}{8} - \left(-1\dfrac{5}{8}\right)$ 3

Stock Market The table shows how the price of a company's stock changed during one day in 1995.

16. What was the change in the stock price from 9:00 A.M. to 11:00 A.M.? $\frac{3}{8}$

17. How much did the stock change from 12:00 P.M. to 3:00 P.M.? $\frac{3}{8}$

18. 🖩 Fraction Calculator Suppose the price of the stock was $\$36\frac{1}{4}$ at 9:00 A.M. Use a fraction calculator to find the price at 5 P.M. Is the total change from the beginning of the day to the end of the day *positive* or *negative*? $\$37\frac{5}{8}$; positive

Time	Stock change
9:00 A.M.	none
10:00 A.M.	$+\frac{1}{2}$
11:00 A.M.	$-\frac{1}{8}$
12:00 P.M.	$-\frac{9}{16}$
1:00 P.M.	$+\frac{1}{2}$
2:00 P.M.	$-\frac{3}{8}$
3:00 P.M.	$+\frac{1}{4}$
4:00 P.M.	$-\frac{1}{16}$
5:00 P.M.	$+1\frac{1}{4}$

Find each sum or difference.

19. $3\frac{2}{3} - 4\frac{1}{3}$ $-\frac{2}{3}$ 20. $-1\frac{4}{5} - 6\frac{1}{5}$ -8 21. $-3\frac{1}{2} + \left(-1\frac{1}{4}\right)$ $-4\frac{3}{4}$

22. $8\frac{1}{4} + \left(-1\frac{7}{8}\right)$ $6\frac{3}{8}$ 23. $-4\frac{2}{3} - \left(-7\frac{1}{6}\right)$ $2\frac{1}{2}$ 24. $2\frac{5}{9} - \left(-3\frac{1}{3}\right)$ $5\frac{8}{9}$

25. A carpenter is making a picture frame. The width of each piece is $3\frac{5}{8}$ in. The top and bottom pieces are $15\frac{3}{4}$ in. long and the two side pieces are $23\frac{3}{8}$ in. long. When the carpenter puts it together as shown, what will the outer dimensions of the picture frame be?
$19\frac{3}{8}$ in. by 27 in.

For Exercises 26–28, find the fraction described by each set of clues.

26. The fraction is between 0 and 1. If you add $\frac{2}{8}$ to it, the result is equivalent to $\frac{10}{16}$. $\frac{3}{8}$

27. The fraction is between –1 and 0. If you subtract $\frac{2}{4}$ from it, the result is $-1\frac{1}{4}$. $-\frac{3}{4}$

28. **Challenge** The absolute value of a fraction is between 1 and 2. If you add $\frac{1}{8}$ to half the fraction, the absolute value of the result is equivalent to $\frac{1}{2}$. What is the fraction? $-\frac{5}{4}$, or $-1\frac{1}{4}$

Probability Connection The spinner below is spun twice. The score is the sum of the numbers in the sectors that the spinner lands on.

29. What is the probability of landing on red, then blue? What is your score? Do you get the same score if you land on blue, then red?

$\frac{1}{9}; -1\frac{1}{2};$ Yes.

30. Find the probability of getting a score greater than or equal to one. $\frac{1}{3}$

31. **Open-ended** Sketch a spinner that will, following the rules above, give scores of $-\frac{5}{6}, \frac{1}{6}$, and 0. (*Hint:* There may be other scores possible.)

Sample Response: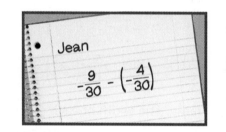

Reflecting on the Section

Be prepared to discuss your response to Exercise 32 in class.

32. Two students each started to evaluate $-\frac{3}{10} - \left(-\frac{2}{15}\right)$ as shown.

a. Describe what each student has done so far. Then write the next step for each student. Will their answers be the same?

b. Which method do you prefer? Explain your choice. **Answers will vary.**

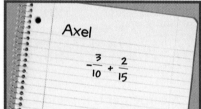

Spiral Review

Simplify each expression. (Module 2, pp. 130–131)

33. $28 + (-41)$ 34. $-12 \cdot (-8)$ 35. $72 \div (-8)$ 36. $-56 - 56$
          -13 96 -9 -112

37. The box-and-whisker plot models survey data from 16 countries. Find the lower extreme, the upper extreme, and the median of the data. (Module 1, p. 21) **10; 45; 20**

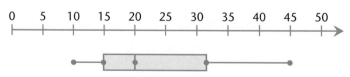

Percent of People Who Would Like to Move to Another Country

Extra Skill Practice

Find each sum or difference.

1. $\frac{3}{5} - \frac{7}{2}$ $-2\frac{9}{10}$

2. $-\frac{1}{3} - \frac{2}{7}$ $-\frac{13}{21}$

3. $\frac{4}{2} + \left(-\frac{7}{8}\right)$ $1\frac{1}{8}$

4. $4\frac{1}{9} + \frac{7}{8}$ $4\frac{71}{72}$

5. $\frac{2}{3} + \left(-1\frac{1}{3}\right)$ $-\frac{2}{3}$

6. $-\frac{4}{9} - \left(-\frac{2}{7}\right)$ $-\frac{10}{63}$

7. $-\frac{3}{10} + 2\frac{2}{5}$ $2\frac{1}{10}$

8. $\frac{5}{8} + 2\frac{1}{2}$ $3\frac{1}{8}$

9. $-1\frac{7}{9} - 1\frac{2}{6}$ $-3\frac{1}{9}$

10. $6\frac{7}{9} - \left(-\frac{5}{8}\right)$ $7\frac{29}{72}$

11. $-\frac{3}{11} + \frac{2}{3} - \frac{9}{11}$ $-\frac{14}{33}$

12. $-\frac{4}{9} - \left(-\frac{2}{3}\right) + 1\frac{1}{6}$ $1\frac{7}{18}$

13. Johanna has decided to make her own party invitations. She has already bought the envelopes which are 5 in. long and 7 in. wide.

   a. She wants to have an extra $\frac{1}{6}$ in. of clearance around each edge of an invitation when it is placed in the envelope. What size should the invitations be? $4\frac{2}{3}$ in. by $6\frac{2}{3}$ in.

   b. What size should the paper for each invitation be? Assume she folds the paper in half to make each invitation.
   Possible answers: $4\frac{2}{3}$ in. by $13\frac{1}{3}$ in. or $9\frac{1}{3}$ in. by $6\frac{2}{3}$ in.

Standardized Testing ◀▶ Multiple Choice

1. Find $-7\frac{2}{3} + 5\frac{1}{5}$. D

   Ⓐ $-12\frac{13}{15}$ 　　Ⓑ $-2\frac{13}{15}$ 　　Ⓒ $-2\frac{3}{8}$ 　　Ⓓ $-2\frac{7}{15}$

2. The expression $-5\frac{7}{16} - 3\frac{5}{8}$ has the same value as what other expression? A

   Ⓐ $-3\frac{5}{8} - 5\frac{7}{16}$ 　　Ⓑ $5\frac{7}{16} + 3\frac{5}{8}$ 　　Ⓒ $5\frac{7}{16} + \left(-3\frac{5}{8}\right)$ 　　Ⓓ $-5\frac{7}{16} + 3\frac{5}{8}$

3. Which expression has a value that is less than $-\frac{2}{3}$? A

   Ⓐ $-\frac{3}{8} - \frac{2}{3}$ 　　Ⓑ $-\frac{3}{8} + \frac{2}{3}$ 　　Ⓒ $\frac{3}{8} + \left(-\frac{2}{3}\right)$ 　　Ⓓ $\frac{3}{8} - \frac{2}{3}$

Section ⑥ Inequalities and Box-and-Whisker Plots

WARM-UP EXERCISES

Use the data to answer the questions.

7, 6, 4, 6, 9, 5, 8, 10, 8, 3, 9

1. Order the numbers from least to greatest.
3, 4, 5, 6, 6, 7, 8, 8, 9, 9, 10

2. Find the median of the set of data.   7

(Continued below.)

Nice T SHIRT!

◄ – – – **Setting the Stage**

Nearly every mall has a store that sells T-shirts. In 1996, any store that sold T-shirts was likely to sell one celebrating the Olympic Games held in Atlanta. But some Olympic T-shirts could not be found in any store. They were sold only at a charity auction.

Every day for 500 days before the start of the Olympics, a T-shirt manufacturer auctioned off a "one-of-a-kind, individually numbered" T-shirt. How much would you bid for such a T-shirt? The 500 winning bids are displayed in the box-and-whisker plot below.

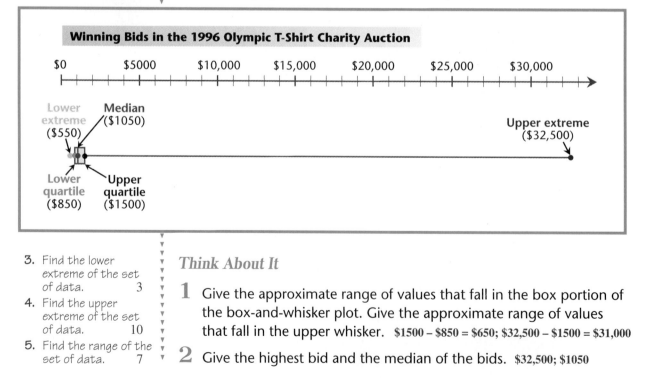

Winning Bids in the 1996 Olympic T-Shirt Charity Auction

$0 $5000 $10,000 $15,000 $20,000 $25,000 $30,000

Lower extreme ($550)
Median ($1050)
Upper extreme ($32,500)
Lower quartile ($850)
Upper quartile ($1500)

3. Find the lower extreme of the set of data.   3

4. Find the upper extreme of the set of data.   10

5. Find the range of the set of data.   7

Think About It

1 Give the approximate range of values that fall in the box portion of the box-and-whisker plot. Give the approximate range of values that fall in the upper whisker. $1500 – $850 = $650; $32,500 – $1500 = $31,000

2 Give the highest bid and the median of the bids. $32,500; $1050

3 The total proceeds from the sale of the 500 T-shirts were about $850,000. Estimate the mean of the winning bids. Compare the mean with the median. **about $1700; It is greater by about $650.**

4 What does a box-and-whisker plot show you about the data that an average such as the mean or the median does not?

Exploration 1

Graphing
INEQUALITIES

▶ In the box-and-whisker plot on page 144, you can see that most of the winning T-shirt bids were between $550 and $1500. The highest bid, $32,500, was much greater than most of the other bids. A data value that is significantly different from other values in a data set is called an **outlier**.

5 **Discussion** Use the box-and-whisker plot on page 144.

a. Can you use the plot to tell if there are any outliers other than $32,500? Explain your reasoning.

b. Ten of the 125 winning bids in the upper whisker are shown below. Which of the bids do you think are outliers?

$3250	**$8500**	**$2000**	**$27,000**	**$1650**
$20,000	**$2100**	**$2500**	**$2400**	**$5100**

c. Do you think there are any outliers in the lower whisker? Why or why not?

▶ The **interquartile range** (or **IQR**) is used to tell whether a value in a data set is an outlier. The IQR is the range of the values in the box of the box-and-whisker plot.

IQR = Upper Quartile – Lower Quartile

6 Use the data shown in the box-and-whisker plot on page 144 to find the IQR for the winning bids. **$650**

7 Try This as a Class
Follow the steps below to identify the outliers for the winning bids.

a. Multiply the IQR by 1.5.   975

b. To check for outliers in the *upper* whisker:
Add the product you found in part (a) to the upper quartile.
Data values *greater than* this sum are outliers.   2475

c. To check for outliers in the *lower* whisker:
Subtract 1.5 · IQR from the lower quartile.
Data values *less than* this difference are outliers.   –125

8
a. Which of the winning bids in Question 5(b) are outliers?

b. Discussion How can you tell by looking at the box-and-whisker plot that there are no outliers in the lower whisker?

▶ You can use an *inequality* to describe the winning bids. An **inequality** is a mathematical sentence that compares two quantities using the symbols >, <, ≥, or ≤.

EXAMPLE

All the winning bids for the Olympic T-shirts are greater than $500. Write and graph an inequality to describe this fact.

SAMPLE RESPONSE

b > 500, where *b* is the amount of the bid in dollars.

The open circle shows that 500 is not on the graph.

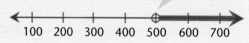

---

9 Discussion
Use the inequality above.

a. In the inequality *b* > 500, what does the symbol > mean?
is greater than

b. How do you know that the graph does not include 500? How do you know that it includes values greater than 700?

c. Write an inequality to show that the least winning bid is $550. Use the symbol ≥ (read as *is greater than or equal to*).   *b* ≥ 550

d. The graph of the inequality from part (c) is shown below. Why is the circle filled in? The solution includes 550.

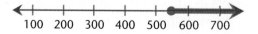

---

8. a. $3250; $8500;
$27,000; $20,000; $2500;
$5100
b. The lower extreme is greater than –125

9. b. Sample Response:
There is an open circle above 500; The heavy line and solid arrow show that the solution includes 700 and all the numbers greater than 700.

10 About 25% of the winning bids in the 1996 Olympic T-shirt charity auction are less than or equal to $850. Use the symbol ≤ (read as *is less than or equal to*) to write an inequality to show this fact. Then graph the inequality.

$b \leq 850$

▶ **The inequalities in Questions 9(c) and 10 can be combined to form one inequality.**

EXAMPLE

About 25% of the winning bids are greater than or equal to $550 and less than or equal to $850. Write and graph these inequalities.

SAMPLE RESPONSE

The inequalities $b \geq 550$ and $b \leq 850$ can be written as $550 \leq b \leq 850$, where b is the amount of the bid in dollars. You read $550 \leq b \leq 850$ as "550 is less than or equal to b and b is less than or equal to 850."

11 How is the fact that 25% of the bids are greater than or equal to $550 and less than or equal to $850 shown in the box-and-whisker plot on page 144? **It is shown by the values between the lower quartile and the lower extreme.**

12 **Try This as a Class** The winning bids in dollars lie on and between the endpoints of the graph below.

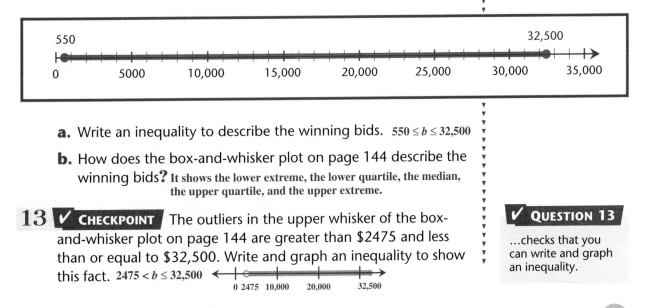

550   32,500

0   5000   10,000   15,000   20,000   25,000   30,000   35,000

   a. Write an inequality to describe the winning bids. $550 \leq b \leq 32{,}500$

   b. How does the box-and-whisker plot on page 144 describe the winning bids? **It shows the lower extreme, the lower quartile, the median, the upper quartile, and the upper extreme.**

13 ✔ **CHECKPOINT** The outliers in the upper whisker of the box-and-whisker plot on page 144 are greater than $2475 and less than or equal to $32,500. Write and graph an inequality to show this fact. $2475 < b \leq 32{,}500$

0 2475 10,000   20,000   32,500

✔ **QUESTION 13**

...checks that you can write and graph an inequality.

▶ There are 63 outliers in the winning bids. An outlier is shown on a box-and-whisker plot with an asterisk (∗) and the whisker is redrawn so that it ends at the last data point that is not an outlier.

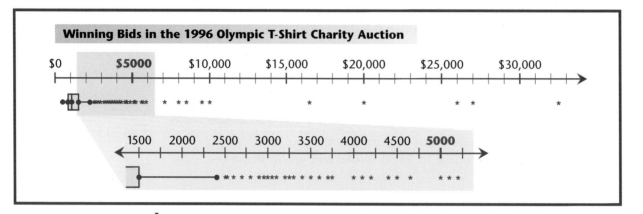

Winning Bids in the 1996 Olympic T-Shirt Charity Auction

14 a. Estimate the greatest winning bid that is not an outlier. **about $2400**

b. Estimate the least winning bid that is an outlier. **about $2500**

c. There are 46 outliers in the portion of the box-and-whisker plot that has been enlarged. Why do you think only 27 asterisks are shown? **Sample Response: Some of the bids are duplicates or so close that they are respresented by the same asterisk on the plot.**

HOMEWORK EXERCISES ▶ See Exs. 1–8 on pp. 153–154.

See Exs. 1–8 on pp. 153–154.

GOAL

LEARN HOW TO...
- make a box-and-whisker plot
- use box-and-whisker plots to make comparisons

AS YOU...
- compare T-shirt prices from different sources

Exploration 2

Making BOX-and-WHISKER PLOTS

SET UP *You will need Labsheet 6A.*

▶ You do not have to go to a mall to buy a T-shirt. The Internet can bring the mall to you! In this exploration, you will use box-and-whisker plots to compare the prices of T-shirts you can buy on the Internet with the prices of T-shirts at a mall.

▶ The steps for constructing a box-and-whisker plot are given below. In Questions 15–21, you'll explore how these steps are used to create a box-and-whisker plot.

Step 1 Put the data in order from least to greatest.

Step 2 Find the upper and lower extremes of the data.

Step 3 Find the median.

Step 4 Find the lower quartile and the upper quartile.

Step 5 Plot the lower extreme, lower quartile, median, and upper quartile, and upper extreme below a number line. Use these values to draw the box and the whiskers.

▶ **Try This as a Class** The 51 T-shirt prices in the table are from 18 different Internet sites. All prices are rounded to the nearest quarter. Use the table for Questions 15–20.

T-shirt prices on the Internet							
$11.00	$11.00	$12.00	$13.00	$15.00	$16.00	$16.00	$16.00
$16.00	$17.00	$17.00	$17.00	$17.00	$17.00	$17.00	$17.50
$18.00	$18.00	$18.00	$18.00	$18.00	$18.00	$18.00	$18.00
$18.00	$19.00	$19.00	$19.00	$20.00	$20.00	$20.00	$20.00
$20.00	$20.00	$20.00	$21.00	$22.00	$23.00	$24.00	$24.00
$24.00	$25.00	$25.00	$25.00	$26.00	$26.00	$26.00	$27.00
$28.00	$29.00	$30.00					

15 Are the T-shirt data above listed in order? Yes.

16 What are the lower and the upper extremes of the data?
lower extreme: $11.00; upper extreme: $30.00

17 Find the median of the data. Explain how you found it.
$19.00; Sample Response: There are 51 prices. The middle price is the 26th, $19.00.

18 Recall that the lower quartile is the median of the data values that occur before the median in an ordered list. (These are the values in red in the table above.) Find the lower quartile. $17.00

19 Find the upper quartile. $24.00

20 Your next step in creating a box-and-whisker plot is to draw a number line. How can you use your answers to Questions 15–19 to decide on a scale for the number line?

20. Sample Response: The number line must include both extremes. It is helpful to use units that will make it simple to locate the quartiles and the median as well.

The box-and-whisker plot below models the data in the table on page 149. Use the box-and-whisker plot for Questions 21–24.

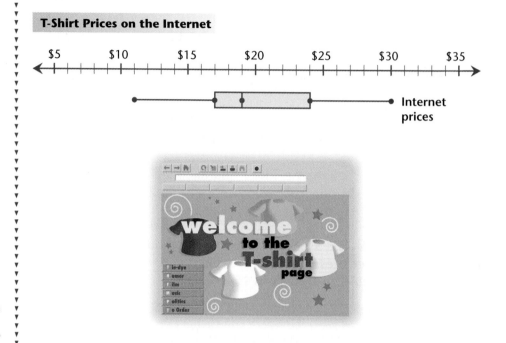

T-Shirt Prices on the Internet

Internet prices

21. Sample Response: The lower whisker extends from the lower extreme to the lower quartile. The box is drawn from the lower quartile to the upper quartile, with a vertical line indicating the median. The upper whisker is drawn from the upper quartile to the upper extreme.

23.

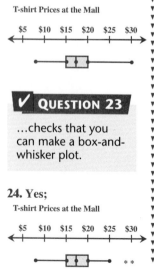

T-shirt Prices at the Mall

$5 $10 $15 $20 $25 $30

✔ **QUESTION 23**

…checks that you can make a box-and-whisker plot.

24. Yes;

T-shirt Prices at the Mall

$5 $10 $15 $20 $25 $30

21 **Discussion** Explain how the values that you found in Questions 15–19 were used to make the lower whisker, the box, and the upper whisker of the box-and-whisker plot above.

22 **a.** About what percent of the T-shirt prices are greater than or equal to $17? about 75%

b. About what percent of the prices are between the lower quartile and the upper quartile? about 50%

c. About what percent of the prices are less than or equal to $19? about 50%

Use Labsheet 6A for Questions 23–25.

23 ✔ **CHECKPOINT** Follow the instructions on the labsheet for completing the *T-shirt Box-and-Whisker Plots.*

24 Does either set of T-shirt price data contain outliers? If so, redraw the box-and-whisker plot. Use asterisks to show the outliers.

25 **Discussion** Can you get a better buy on T-shirts *on the Internet* or *at a mall*? Use your box-and-whisker plots to justify your choice. Sample Response: mall; 50% of the mall shirts cost $17 or less. 75% of the Internet shirts cost $17 or more.

HOMEWORK EXERCISES ▶ See Exs. 9–12 on pp. 154–155.

You can use a graphing calculator to make and analyze the
box-and-whisker plots from Labsheet 6A.

Step 1 To graph a box-and-whisker plot you must first enter the data by
editing the statistical lists within the STAT menu. To graph two plots,
enter the values for the first plot in List 1 and the values for the second
plot in List 2.

Step 2 Choose the type of graph to make with the STAT PLOT menu. Turn on
both Plot 1 and Plot 2 and choose the box-and-whisker type plot.
Choose List 1 for Plot 1, and List 2 for Plot 2.

Step 3 To set the *viewing window* for your graph, choose an appropriate scale
for the x-axis. Enter the minimum, maximum, and scale values for X.
Then graph.

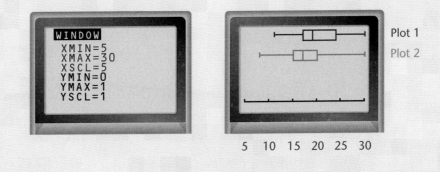

Section 6

Key Concepts

Key Terms

Key Terms

inequality

interquartile range (IQR)

outlier

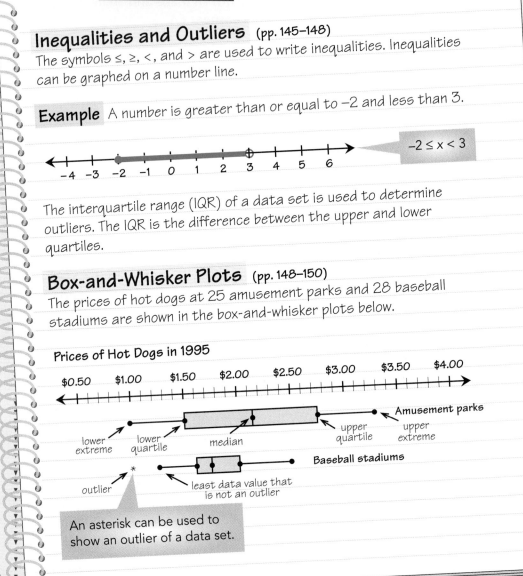

Inequalities and Outliers (pp. 145–148)

The symbols ≤, ≥, <, and > are used to write inequalities. Inequalities can be graphed on a number line.

Example A number is greater than or equal to –2 and less than 3.

$-2 \leq x < 3$

The interquartile range (IQR) of a data set is used to determine outliers. The IQR is the difference between the upper and lower quartiles.

Box-and-Whisker Plots (pp. 148–150)

The prices of hot dogs at 25 amusement parks and 28 baseball stadiums are shown in the box-and-whisker plots below.

Prices of Hot Dogs in 1995

$0.50 $1.00 $1.50 $2.00 $2.50 $3.00 $3.50 $4.00

lower extreme   lower quartile   median   upper quartile   upper extreme   **Amusement parks**

outlier   least data value that is not an outlier   **Baseball stadiums**

An asterisk can be used to show an outlier of a data set.

CLOSURE QUESTION

What is an inequality? How can an inequality be used to describe data in a box-and-whisker plot?

Sample Response: An inequality is a mathematical sentence that compares two quantities using the symbols <, >, ≤, and ≥. Inequalities can be used to compare ranges of data within a box-and-whisker plot.

---

26 Key Concepts Question Use the box-and-whisker plots above.

a. Estimate the IQR for the price of hot dogs at the baseball stadiums. about $.40

b. What is the least price for a hot dog at one of the amusement parks? at one of the baseball stadiums? $1.00; $1.00

c. About what percent of the hot dog prices are less than $2.75 at amusement parks? at baseball stadiums? about 75%; 100%

Section 6

Practice & Application Exercises

YOU WILL NEED

For Exs. 8–9:
♦ graph paper

For Ex. 11:
♦ graphing calculator

Write an inequality to describe each situation. Then graph each inequality on a number line.

1. The price of the ticket for a concert was more than $25.

2. The temperature today ranged from –10°F to 3°F.

1. $p > 25$

2. $-10 \le t \le 3$

3. The elevation of the house was less than 50 ft above sea level.

4. At a theater, people 55 years old and older pay a reduced admission price.

3. $e < 50$

4. $p \ge 55$

6. Sample Response: Let n = the number of shopping centers; $196 \le n \le 967$

Use the box-and-whisker plot and table below for Exercises 5 and 6.

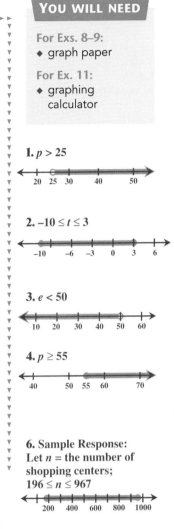

Number of Shopping Centers in Each State in the United States in 1994

51   196   588   967   ←5350

5. The upper whisker contains at least one outlier. Use the box-and-whisker plot and the data in the table to determine which states in the table are outliers.
Texas, Florida, and California

6. **Open-ended** Write and graph an inequality that shows the number of shopping centers in about 50% of the states.   See above.

7. **Challenge** Explain why there can never be more outliers than non-outliers in a box-and-whisker plot.
The whiskers would have to include more than 50% of the data.

State	Number of shopping centers
Pennsylvania	1521
Ohio	1559
New York	1598
Illinois	1961
Texas	2824
Florida	3086
California	5350

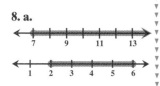
8. Geometry Connection The graph of the inequality $a \geq 7$ is a *ray*, because it is a part of a line with one endpoint. The graph of the inequality $2 \leq b \leq 6$ is a *segment*, because it is a part of a line with two endpoints.

 a. Graph each of the inequalities above on a number line and label the endpoints.

 b. A segment has endpoints at −3 and 1. Write the inequality that has this segment as its graph. $-3 \leq s \leq 1$

 c. A ray has an endpoint at 10 and points to the left. Write the inequality that has this ray as its graph. $r \leq 10$

9. The price of a T-shirt at 25 amusement parks in the United States in 1995 and 1996 is given below. **See Additional Answers.**

1995 T-shirt prices (dollars)				
5	6	6	6	7
7	7	7	8	8
8	8	8.50	9	9
10	10	10	10	10
10	11	12	12	13

1996 T-shirt prices (dollars)				
5	6	6	7	8
8	8	8	8	8
9	9	9	9	9
10	10	10	10	10
10	11	11	13	13

 a. Make a box-and-whisker plot for the 1995 prices and one for the 1996 prices below the same number line. Label each box-and-whisker plot.

 b. Does either set of data contain outliers? If so redraw the box-and-whisker plot using asterisks to show the outliers.

 c. Do the box-and-whisker plots show that the price of T-shirts at amusement parks changed significantly from 1995 to 1996? Explain.

10. Choosing a Data Display Dana keeps track of the catalogs her family receives in the mail. Each week for 26 weeks, she records the number of catalogs. She uses the data to make a line plot and a box-and-whisker plot. **Sample Responses are given.**

 a. For 3 of the 26 weeks, Dana counted 6 catalogs. How is that shown in the line plot? Does the box-and-whisker plot give this information as well? Explain. **See above.**

 b. What does the box-and-whisker plot show that the line plot does not? **the quartiles and the median**

 c. **Open-ended** Which data display do you think shows more information? Explain your choice. **Answers will vary. Check students' work.**

Number of Catalogs

11. The cost for a family of four to attend a National League baseball game at 14 different baseball stadiums in 1994 and 1995 is given. Each cost includes the items shown at the right.

| COST AT 14 STADIUMS | |
1994	1995
$79.31	$81.31
$83.34	$82.98
$82.89	$86.03
$92.18	$86.10
$86.64	$87.64
$90.73	$90.73
$91.00	$91.00
$91.06	$91.06
$91.72	$91.72
$93.40	$93.90
$82.08	$99.42
$100.80	$105.80
$108.97	$112.67
$112.98	$112.98

Each cost includes:

game programs

hot dogs

drinks

parking

a. Graphing Calculator Make a box-and-whisker plot for each set of data. **Check students' work.**

b. Does either set of data contain outliers? Explain. **See below.**

c. How does the cost for a family of four to attend a National League game in 1995 compare with the cost in 1994? Is this what you would expect? Explain.
The costs are about the same; Answers will vary. Check students' work.

baseball caps

tickets

Reflecting ◀▶ on the Section

12. Use an encyclopedia, an almanac, or another source to find a data set that has at least 30 items (for example, the population of each of the 50 states). Make a box-and-whisker plot of the data. Identify any outliers. **Answers will vary. Check students' work.**

Spiral ◀▶ Review

Find each sum or difference. (Module 2, p. 139)

13. $-\frac{1}{5} + \left(-\frac{7}{15}\right)$ **14.** $\frac{5}{8} + \left(-4\frac{1}{2}\right)$ **15.** $4\frac{1}{3} - \left(-\frac{9}{10}\right)$ **16.** $-5\frac{11}{12} - \frac{3}{4}$

Combine like terms to simplify each expression. (Module 1, p. 62)

17. $12x - 10x + 1$ **18.** $n^2 - mn + mn$ **19.** $2s + 4st + 6s$
$2x + 1$ n^2 $8s + 4st$

20. Writing A rectangular plot of land and a square plot of land each have an area of 9500 ft^2. Explain why the perimeters of the two plots are not necessarily the same. (Module 1, p. 72)

Sample Response: There are many different pairs of numbers with a product of 9500.

RESEARCH

Exercise 12 checks that you understand how to make a box-and-whisker plot.

11. b. Yes; The 1994 data contains 2 outliers, $108.97 and $112.98.

13. $-\frac{2}{3}$

14. $-3\frac{7}{8}$

15. $5\frac{7}{30}$

16. $-6\frac{2}{3}$

Section 6

Extra Skill Practice

Write an inequality to describe each situation. Then graph each inequality on a number line.

1. The woman was at least 20 years old, but not yet 25. $20 \leq g < 25$

2. The number of fish in the tank is always less than 10. $f < 10$

3. The price is $10 or above. $p \geq 10$

4. The number is greater than or equal to 2 and less than 7. $2 \leq n < 7$

5. Juan and Sarah play musical instruments. Their practice times for an eight-week period are shown below.

Number of hours practiced each week							
Juan	8.5	6	7.5	9	8	8	6.5	10
Sarah	8	9.5	5	10.5	9	7	6	7.5

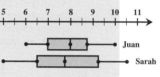

a. Make a box-and-whisker plot for Juan's practice times and one for Sarah's practice times below the same number line. Label each box-and-whisker plot.

b. Which student practices more consistently? How can you tell? **Juan**

c. Does either set of practice times contain outliers? If so, redraw the box-and-whisker plot. Use asterisks to show the outliers. **No.**

Standardized Testing ◀▶ Multiple Choice

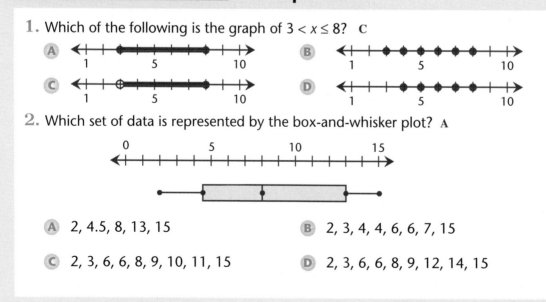

1. Which of the following is the graph of $3 < x \leq 8$? **C**

2. Which set of data is represented by the box-and-whisker plot? **A**

Ⓐ 2, 4.5, 8, 13, 15

Ⓑ 2, 3, 4, 4, 6, 6, 7, 15

Ⓒ 2, 3, 6, 6, 8, 9, 10, 11, 15

Ⓓ 2, 3, 6, 6, 8, 9, 12, 14, 15

Completing the Module Project

Designing a Game

Playing the Game During this module you have explored mathematics as it applies to shopping malls. You have designed a game and made game cards, game pieces, and rules for the game. In order to make sure your game runs smoothly, you'll now play the game.

7 With your group, assemble the game and game pieces. Review the rules.

8 Play the game.

9 After you have played the game, discuss each question below in your group.

   a. What math skills did you use while playing the game?

   b. What worked well in your game?

   c. What could you improve?

10 Make any changes necessary to improve your game. You may need to add or change rules.

11 As a group, prepare a presentation to give to the class. Each member of the group can present a part of the game. Include in your presentation the goal of the game, the rules, the mathematics used, the playing pieces, the cards, and your own experience playing the game.

You will need • *Review and Assessment Labsheet* (Exs. 23 and 32)

1. In a survey of 13- to 17-year-olds, 51% of the females and 83% of the males said sneakers were their favorite type of shoe. (Sec. 1, Explor. 1)

   a. Suppose 1030 females were surveyed. About how many of the females said sneakers were their favorite type of shoe? **about 525**

   b. Suppose 639 males answered that sneakers were their favorite type of shoe. How many males were surveyed? **about 770**

2. Of 500 New England youths surveyed, 90% said they visit a supermarket on a weekly basis. (Sec. 1, Explor. 2)

   a. What was the sample? Do you think the sample was representative of all young people in the United States? Explain.

   b. Use mental math to find how many of the 500 youths surveyed visit a supermarket on a weekly basis. **450 youths**

   2. a. 500 New England teenagers; Sample Response: No; the sample is too small and only from one region of the country.

Estimation For Exercises 3 and 4, estimate each answer. Explain how you found your estimate. (Sec. 2, Explor. 1)

3. An appliance store buys a television for $322 and marks up the price to $475 for resale. Estimate the percent of the markup. **3. about 50%; markup is $153 and $\frac{153}{322} \approx 50\%$.**

4. A $66.50 item is discounted 30%. Estimate the sale price.
   about $44.50; 30% $\approx \frac{1}{3}$ and $\frac{1}{3}$ of $66.50 $\approx$ $22. $66.50 – $22 = $44.50

5. The table shows the average amount of money four-through-twelve-year-olds received, spent, and saved each week in 1984 and 1989. Determine the percent increase in each category from 1984 to 1989. Round your answers to the nearest whole percent.

	1984	1989
Amount of income	$3.03	$4.42
Amount spent	$2.72	$3.07
Amount saved	$0.31	$1.35

   (Sec. 2, Explor. 2)   amount of income: 46%; amount spent: 13%; amount saved: 335%

For Exercises 6–9, suppose a 25¢ toy machine is usually filled with colored bouncing balls, but most of the balls have been sold and only 1 blue, 1 yellow, and 2 red balls are left. You have two quarters to spend on balls. (Sec. 3, Explors. 1, 2, and 3)

6. Are the events below *dependent* or *independent*? Explain.
   Event 1: the first ball you get is blue
   Event 2: the second ball you get is yellow **Sample Response: dependent; The outcome of Event 1 affects the probability of Event 2.**

7. What is the theoretical probability of getting two red balls? $\frac{1}{6}$

8. Draw a tree diagram showing all the possible outcomes.
   See Additional Answers.

9. Suppose you design an experiment to model the color of the first ball you buy from the machine. In each trial, you pull a ball from a bag, record the color, then replace it. The results are shown in the table. What is the experimental probability of getting a red ball? $\frac{13}{25}$

50 Trials		
Blue	Yellow	Red
14	10	26

Evaluate each expression. (Sec. 4, Explors. 1, 2, and 3)

10. 123 + (–53) 70   11. 3 + (–18) –15   12. 5 – (–12) 17   13. –2 – 35 –37

14. –6 • 15 –90   15. (–24)(–8) 192   16. –72 ÷ 8 –9   17. –108 ÷ (–9) 12

18. 6(–7)(–4) ÷ (–12) –14   19. –26 + 6 – (–20) 0   20. –36 + (–6) + (–8) –50

21. What two numbers have an absolute value of 5? (Sec. 4, Explor. 1) –5 and 5

22. Explain what is meant by the *opposite* of a number. Give three examples. (Sec. 4, Explor. 1) Sample Response: The opposite of a number is the integer you add to get a sum of 0; –2 and 2, –7 and 7, –0.34 and 0.34.

23. **Use the Review and Assessment Labsheet.** In the game *Cyber Spaceship,* a player guides a spaceship around moving obstacles. Follow the directions on the labsheet to draw the triangular obstacle after a translation. (Sec. 4, Explor. 2)

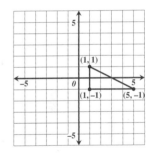

Find each sum or difference. (Sec. 5, Explor. 1)

24. $-\frac{5}{6} + \frac{3}{8}$ $-\frac{11}{24}$ 25. $-\frac{4}{5} + \left(-\frac{2}{3}\right)$ $-1\frac{7}{15}$ 26. $\frac{2}{3} - \left(-\frac{1}{6}\right)$ $\frac{5}{6}$ 27. $-\frac{4}{5} - \frac{2}{3}$ $-1\frac{7}{15}$

Graph each inequality on a number line. (Sec. 6, Explor. 1) See Additional Answers.

28. $w > -10$ 29. $1 < z \le 4$ 30. $-2 < y \le 0$ 31. $-3 \le v$

32. **Use the Review and Assessment Labsheet.** Refer to the box-and-whisker plot *Clothing Stores at 22 Malls* on the labsheet. Follow the directions on the labsheet to answer the questions and construct another box-and-whisker plot for the number of men's clothing stores. (Sec. 6, Explor. 2)

a. 28 stores
b. 60 stores; It is an outlier.
c. about 50%
d.

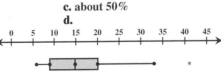

Sample Response: There are fewer men's stores than women's stores.

R e f l e c t i n g ◀▶**on the Module**

33. **Writing** Describe the mathematics you learned in this module. Discuss how you can use what you learned to be a better shopper.
   Answers will vary. Check students' work.

The Mystery of Blacktail Canyon

MATHEMATICS
The & Theme

MODULE 3 SECTION OVERVIEW

1 Square Roots and Measurement

As you learn about Anasazi ruins:
- Find and estimate square roots
- Describe patterns related to length, area, and volume

2 Equations and Graphs

As you investigate a car accident:
- Evaluate expressions with square roots and fractions bars
- Graph equations

3 Slope and Equations

As you search for a missing driver:
- Find the slope of a line
- Use an equation to make a prediction

4 Similar Figures and Constructions

As you estimate a cliff's height:
- Tell whether triangles are similar and make indirect measurements
- Find a perpendicular bisector of a chord

5 Scientific Notation and Decimal Equations

As you learn about carbon dating:
- Write very large numbers in scientific notation
- Solve equations involving decimals

6 Logical Thinking

As you solve the mystery:
- Use Venn diagrams to interpret statements with *and*, *or*, and *not*

The Module Project ↓ Solving a Mystery

Do you like a good mystery story? You'll read *The Mystery of Blacktail Canyon* and learn to use mathematics to solve mysteries. You'll gather clues to identify a thief and write the conclusion to the mystery.

More on the Module Project
See pp. 187, 198, 222, 231, and 233.

INTERNET
To learn more about the theme:
http://www.mlmath.com

161

Section ① Square Roots and Measurement

IN THIS SECTION

EXPLORATION 1
◆ Finding Square Roots

EXPLORATION 2
◆ Length, Area, and Volume

Ancient Sites of Mystery

WARM-UP EXERCISES

Use mental math to find each value.

1. 5^2 25
2. 12^2 144
3. $(-3)^2$ 9
4. $\left(\frac{1}{2}\right)^2$ $\frac{1}{4}$
5. 4^3 64

‹‹‹ Setting the Stage

In *The Mystery of Blacktail Canyon*, a crime is committed. In this module you'll read the story and solve the mystery. With the help of story characters who use their mathematical knowledge to solve mysteries, you'll collect evidence and name the criminal. Along the way, you'll learn about the people who developed a culture in the North American desert.

The Plot The story takes place in the Four Corners region of the United States. Four Corners includes parts of Utah, Arizona, Colorado, and New Mexico.

Jim Nakai, one of the main characters, is an eighth grade Navajo student in Escavada, New Mexico. He is fascinated with mysteries, both ancient and modern. His new friend Nageela Ashilaka lives in Kenya, but travels everywhere with her father, Dr. B. B. Ashilaka, an expert on prehistoric dwellings. In spite of being confined to a wheelchair due to a disabling fall, Dr. Ashilaka continues his research with the help of his daughter.

◄ Cliff Palace was built beneath a large overhang in Mesa Verde National Park, Colorado.

Where the Mystery Takes Place

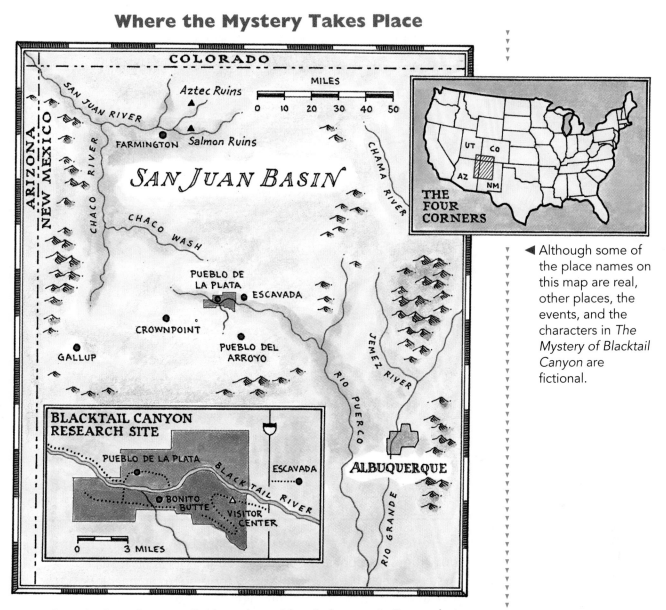

◀ Although some of the place names on this map are real, other places, the events, and the characters in *The Mystery of Blacktail Canyon* are fictional.

Historical Background Nageela and her father are in Escavada to study a people long known to archaeologists as the *Anasazi* and known to some as the *Ancestral Puebloans*. For centuries these people lived in the rugged, desert landscape of Four Corners. Many of them lived in communities built on mesas. (A *mesa* is a flat-topped area with a cliff on one or more sides.) Yet perhaps their most impressive villages were perched in caves or on ledges high above canyon floors. Many of these villages housed fewer than 100 people. They are the cliff dwellings of the Anasazi.

The Anasazi hauled stones, wood, and mud bricks over difficult terrain to build their cliff dwellings. The entrances to some of these dwellings are more than nine meters above the ground. Often the people could only reach their homes by using handholds and toeholds carved into smooth sandstone rocks.

MAP OF BALCONY HOUSE
A Cliff Dwelling in Mesa Verde National Park, Colorado

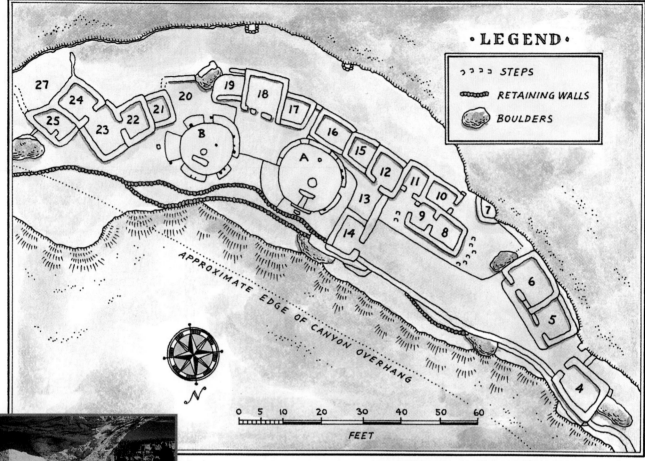

· LEGEND ·

ↄ ↄ ↄ ↄ STEPS

⬭⬭⬭⬭ RETAINING WALLS

BOULDERS

APPROXIMATE EDGE OF CANYON OVERHANG

N

0 5 10   20   30   40   50   60

FEET

▲
Anasazi people began building Balcony House in the early 1200s. They lived there for less than 100 years.

Mysteries Old and New Why the Anasazi chose to leave the tops of mesas to build communities on the cliff walls is still a mystery. They left no written history for modern archaeologists. Had an enemy driven them into hiding, or was this just an amazing way to survive in the desert?

The Anasazi lived in their cliff dwellings for only a few generations. By A.D. 1300, the cliff dwellings had been abandoned. Most of what is known about this vanished civilization comes from clues found in the ruins, including striking black-on-white pottery.

Such treasures are valuable not only to archaeologists seeking knowledge, but also to thieves who are interested only in money. In *The Mystery of Blacktail Canyon*, Dr. Ashilaka suspects there is an untouched cliff dwelling somewhere near the town of Escavada. Dr. Ashilaka's research, like a real archaeologist's work, can be destroyed when criminals damage or remove evidence from ancient sites.

You'll work along with the story characters to find a thief who damages an ancient site in Blacktail Canyon.

Use the map of Balcony House on page 164 for Questions 1 and 2.

1 **a.** Copy the map scale onto the edge of a piece of paper.   **Check students' work.**

   b. Place your copy of the map scale on the map and use it to estimate the distance from the entrance of Room 4 to the northernmost corner of Room 25.   **about 140 ft**

   c. About how long would it take you to walk from Room 4 to Room 25?   **Answers will vary.**

2 **a.** What is the approximate shape of Room 18?   **square**

   b. Estimate the area of Room 18. How does the area compare with the area of your classroom?   **about 56 ft^2; Answers will vary. Check students' work.**

Exploration 1 ▸▸▸▸▸▸▸▸▸▸▸▸▸▸▸▸▸▸▸▸▸▸▸▸▸▸▸▸▸

Finding $\sqrt{}$ Square Roots

SET UP   *Work with a partner. You will need a calculator.*

GOAL

LEARN HOW TO...
◆ find and estimate square roots

AS YOU...
◆ find dimensions of a room at an archaeological site

KEY TERMS
◆ square root
◆ principal square root
◆ perfect square

▶ In *The Mystery of Blacktail Canyon*, archaeologist Dr. B. B. Ashilaka and his daughter, Nageela, are studying ancient ruins. Their work involves finding the dimensions of archaeological sites.

3 **Discussion** The sketch shows a room at a site.

   a. What is the approximate shape of the room?   **a square**

   b. Estimate the length of one side of the room. How did you make your estimate?

   c. Let s = the length of one side of the room. Write an equation relating the area A of the room to s. $A = s^2$

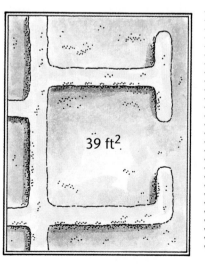

39 ft^2

3. b. about 6 ft; Sample Response: The area of a square with sides 6 ft long is 36 ft^2, which is close to 39 ft^2.

$A = s \cdot s$

$A = s^2$

s

s

▶ The area of a square can be found by multiplying the length of one of the sides by itself, or by squaring the length of a side. The equation $A = s^2$ can also be used to find the length of a side of a square with a given area.

EXAMPLE

If a side of a square is 4 cm long, then $A = 4^2$, or 16. The area is 16 cm².

If the area of a square is 25 cm², then $s^2 = 25$, so $s = 5$. The length of a side is 5 cm.

4 In the Example, the number 5 is a solution of the equation $s^2 = 25$ and is called a *square root* of 25. What is another square root of 25?

−5

▶ If $A = s^2$, then s is a **square root** of A. Since $4^2 = 16$ and $(-4)^2 = 16$, both 4 and −4 are square roots of 16. The positive solution of $s^2 = 16$ is called the **principal square root** of 16 and is indicated by $\sqrt{16}$.

$$\sqrt{16} = 4$$ The principal square root of 16 is 4.

The same symbol with a minus sign, $-\sqrt{16}$, indicates the negative square root.

$$-\sqrt{16} = -4$$ The negative square root of 16 is −4.

5 Use mental math to find each value.

a. $\sqrt{81}$ 9   **b.** $\sqrt{49}$ 7   **c.** $\sqrt{1}$ 1

d. $-\sqrt{9}$ −3   **e.** $-\sqrt{64}$ −8   **f.** $-\sqrt{144}$ −12

▶ The numbers 1, 4, 9, 16, and 25 are *perfect squares*. A **perfect square** is a number whose principal square root is a whole number.

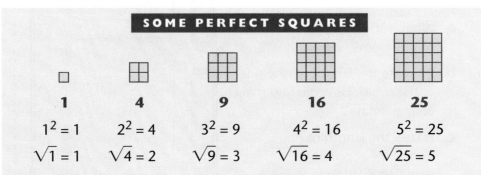

SOME PERFECT SQUARES

1	4	9	16	25
$1^2 = 1$	$2^2 = 4$	$3^2 = 9$	$4^2 = 16$	$5^2 = 25$
$\sqrt{1} = 1$	$\sqrt{4} = 2$	$\sqrt{9} = 3$	$\sqrt{16} = 4$	$\sqrt{25} = 5$

6 List the next five perfect squares after 25. Then list some numbers that are not perfect squares. *36, 49, 64, 81, 100; Sample Response: 3, 40, 65*

▶ **Estimating Square Roots** In Question 3 you estimated $\sqrt{39}$. You need to estimate many square roots.

7 🖩 Calculator Use the $\boxed{\sqrt{\ }}$ key to estimate $\sqrt{39}$. Compare this estimate with your estimate from Question 3. *about 6.24*

8 **Try This as a Class**

   a. Follow these steps to make a table.

   Step 1 List the first 25 consecutive whole numbers in the first column.

   Step 2 Find and record the principal square root of each perfect square.

   Step 3 Use a calculator to estimate the principal square roots of the other numbers.

n	$\sqrt{n}$
1	1
2	1.41
3	1.73
4	2
5	?
6	?
7	?
8	?

   b. Look at the whole numbers between 4 and 9. Compare their square roots with $\sqrt{4}$ and $\sqrt{9}$. *The square roots are between $\sqrt{4}$ and $\sqrt{9}$.*

   c. Make some predictions about the square roots of the whole numbers between 25 and 36. Check your predictions. *Sample Response: They will be between 5 and 6.*

9 **a.** Since 45 is not a perfect square, its principal square root is not a whole number. Is $\sqrt{45}$ closer to 6 or to 7? *7*

   b. Estimate $\sqrt{45}$ to the nearest tenth. Do not use your calculator.

   c. Square your estimate in part (b) to check for accuracy.

   d. Use your result in part (c) to improve your estimate.

   e. Use the $\boxed{\sqrt{\ }}$ key on your calculator to find $\sqrt{45}$ to the nearest thousandth. *6.708*

   f. When can you use mental math instead of your calculator to estimate square roots?

10 ✔ **CHECKPOINT** Use mental math to estimate each square root. Then use a calculator to find each square root to the nearest tenth.

   a. $\sqrt{55}$ **b.** $\sqrt{37}$ **c.** $\sqrt{62}$ **d.** $\sqrt{103}$
   about 7.5; 7.4 *about 6.1; 6.1* *about 7.8; 7.9* *about 10.1; 10.1*

8. a.

n	$\sqrt{n}$
1	1
2	1.41
3	1.73
4	2
5	2.24
6	2.45
7	2.65
8	2.83
9	3
10	3.16
11	3.32
12	3.46
13	3.61
14	3.74
15	3.87
16	4
17	4.12
18	4.24
19	4.36
20	4.47
21	4.58
22	4.69
23	4.80
24	4.90
25	5

9. b. Sample Response: about 6.7

c. Sample Response: 44.89

d. Sample Response: about 6.71

f. Sample Response: when the squares are close to perfect squares

✔ **QUESTION 10**

…checks that you can estimate square roots.

HOMEWORK EXERCISES ▶ See Exs. 1–23 on pp. 171–172.

LEARN HOW TO...
- describe patterns related to length, area, and volume

AS YOU...
- compare dimensions of rooms at an archaeological site

KEY TERMS
- cube
- edge
- face

Exploration 2

Length,
AREA, and volume

SET UP *Work with a partner. You will need 30 centimeter cubes.*

The Story So Far...

▶ Dr. Ashilaka and his group of amateur archaeologists take a field trip to Blacktail Canyon. While there, a sudden cloudburst forces everyone into the ruins of one of the dwellings. Jim asks about the size of a smaller room behind the room they are in, and Dr. Ashilaka asks him to estimate the size of the larger and smaller rooms.

"I know that my height and my arm span are about 5 feet. The big room is about twice my reach across the floor in both directions, and about twice my height. So, I guess it's about 10 by 10 by 10 feet. I can barely stand up in the center of the small room, and can just touch two walls. It must be about 5 by 5 by 5 feet." Jim looked puzzled. "I guess the big room is twice the size of the small one. But the funny thing is, it seems so much larger."

Dr. Ashilaka laughed and called Jim over. Nageela groaned and shook her head. She knew what was coming. She had heard the length, area, and volume lecture many times before.

11. b. Sample Response: The length, width, and height are twice the dimensions of the other room; No; 10 × 10 × 10 is 1000 and 5 × 5 × 5 is 125 so the larger room has 8 times the space of the smaller room.

11 **a.** Describe the shape of each room in the story. Sample Response: Each room is a cube.

b. Why does Jim say the big room is twice the size of the smaller room? Do you agree? Explain.

▶ Jim made a very rough estimate of the sizes of the rooms. You can use *cubes* to learn more about how the sizes of the rooms compare. A **cube** is a rectangular prism with six square faces.

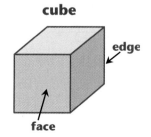

cube

edge

face

12 Build cubes with edges whose lengths are twice and three times those of a centimeter cube. Copy and complete the table.

Cube Measurements			
Length of an edge	1 cm	2 cm	3 cm
Perimeter of a face	4 cm	**?** 8 cm	**?** 12 cm
Area of a face	1 cm^2	**?** 4 cm^2	**?** 9 cm^2
Volume of the cube	1 cm^3	**?** 8 cm^3	**?** 27 cm^3

13 Let s = the length of an edge of a cube. Write expressions for the perimeter of a face, the area of a face, and the volume of the cube. $4s, s^2, s^3$

▶ When you compare objects of different sizes, you need to know whether you are comparing lengths, areas, or volumes.

14 **Try This as a Class** Study your answers in Question 12. Look for patterns for how the length, the area, and the volume of the cubes are related.

   a. When the length of a cube is multiplied by a number n, what is the perimeter of a face multiplied by**?** n

   b. When the length of a cube is multiplied by a number n, what is the area of a face multiplied by**?** n^2

   c. When the length of a cube is multiplied by a number n, what is the volume of the cube multiplied by**?** n^3

15 Without building a cube, predict the area of a single face and the volume of a cube whose dimensions are four times those of a centimeter cube. Explain your thinking.

15. 16 cm^2, 64 cm^3; The length was multiplied by 4 so the area is multiplied by 4^2 and the volume by 4^3.

16 ✔ **CHECKPOINT** Jim Nakai made good estimates of the length, width, and height of each room, but he jumped to the wrong conclusion when comparing the volumes of the rooms. Explain Jim's mistake in the story on page 168. Use mathematics to support your answer.

✔ **QUESTION 16**

…checks that you understand length, area, and volume relationships.

He was only comparing lengths. $10 \times 10 \times 10$ is 1000 and $5 \times 5 \times 5$ is 125 so the larger room has 8 times the volume of the smaller room.

HOMEWORK EXERCISES ▶ See Exs. 24–29 on pp. 172–173.

Section 1

Key Concepts

◀◀◀◀◀◀◀◀◀◀◀▼

Key Terms

square root

principal
square root

perfect square

Squares and Square Roots (pp. 165–166)

Suppose $s^2 = n$. Then s is a square root of n. Every positive number has both a positive and a negative square root. The principal square root, indicated by $\sqrt{}$, is the positive square root.

Example $5^2 = 25$ and $(-5)^2 = 25$, so both 5 and −5 are square roots of 25. The principal square root of 25 is written $\sqrt{25}$, or 5. 25 is a perfect square since $\sqrt{25}$ is a whole number.

Estimating Square Roots (p. 167)

You can use various methods to estimate a square root.

Example
Method 1 Use a calculator: $\sqrt{5} \approx 2.24$

Method 2 Estimate between two integers by looking for the closest perfect squares less than and greater than a number: $\sqrt{4} < \sqrt{5} < \sqrt{9}$, so $2 < \sqrt{5} < 3$.

cube

edge

face

Changing Dimensions (pp. 168–169)

When you compare sizes of objects, you need to know whether you are comparing lengths, areas, or volumes.

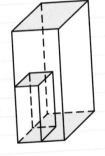

Example Suppose the length, width, and height of a prism are multiplied by 2 to create a larger prism. The areas of the faces of the longer prism are 4 times those of the smaller prism. The volume of the larger prism is 8 times the volume of the smaller prism.

CLOSURE QUESTION

Suppose that you know the area of one face of a cube. Describe how to find the dimensions of the cube and its volume.

Sample Response: Find the square root of the area of the face to find the length of each side of the cube. Cube this length to find the volume.

17 Key Concepts Question

a. Find the side length of a square whose area is 289 cm².   **17 cm**

b. Suppose each side of the square in part (a) is multiplied by 5. What is the effect on the area of the square?
The area is multiplied by 25.

Section 1

Practice & Application Exercises

Mental Math Use mental math to find each value.

1. $\sqrt{100}$ 10

2. $-\sqrt{144}$ –12

3. $\sqrt{3600}$ 60

4. $\sqrt{0.49}$ 0.7

5. $\sqrt{\dfrac{16}{100}}$ $\dfrac{2}{5}$

6. $-\sqrt{9,000,000}$ –3000

7. The dimensions of a typical sheet of notebook paper are $8\frac{1}{2}$ in. by 11 in.

   a. What is the area of the paper? **93.5 in.²**

   b. Suppose a square piece of paper has the same area. Estimate the dimensions of the square piece of paper to the nearest $\frac{1}{2}$ in.

   about $9\frac{1}{2}$ in.

8. **Estimation** Use the sketch of a floor plan.

   a. Estimate the width of the bathroom. **about 2.3 m**

   b. Estimate the perimeter of the living room. **about 18.4 m**

   c. Estimate the area of the kitchen. **about 16.5 m²**

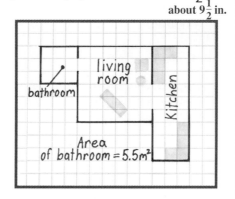

living room

bathroom

Kitchen

Area of bathroom = 5.5m²

Estimation **Estimate each square root to the nearest tenth.**

9. $\sqrt{39}$
about 6.2

10. $\sqrt{55}$
about 7.4

11. $\sqrt{12}$
about 3.5

12. $\sqrt{125}$
about 11.2

13. **Challenge** The lunar crater Copernicus covers a circular area of about 6793 km². Estimate the diameter of the crater. **about 93 km**

14. **Algebra Connection** What whole numbers can you substitute for n to make the statement $6 < \sqrt{n} < 7$ true?

    37, 38, 39, 40, 41, 42, 43, 44, 45, 46, 47, 48

15. **Probability Connection** Suppose a spinner is equally likely to land on any integer from 1 through 100. Find the probability that it lands on a perfect square. $\frac{1}{10}$

16. Rae says that every positive number is greater than or equal to its square root. Find examples to support her statement. Can you find a counterexample?

    Sample Response: $\sqrt{4}$ is 2 and 4 > 2, $\sqrt{25}$ is 5 and 25 > 5;

    $\sqrt{\dfrac{1}{4}} = \dfrac{1}{2}$ and $\dfrac{1}{4}$ is not greater than or equal to $\dfrac{1}{2}$.

Copernicus, at the far left, is an impact crater believed to be less than 1 billion years old.

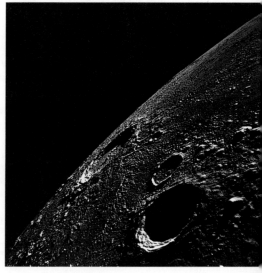

24. No; The area of the bedroom is 225 ft² and the area of the closet is 25 ft² so the cost of the closet carpet would be one-ninth the cost of the bedroom carpet.

26. a.
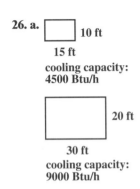
10 ft
15 ft
cooling capacity:
4500 Btu/h

20 ft
30 ft
cooling capacity:
9000 Btu/h

27. a.
18 ft
24 ft
cooling capacity:
7320 Btu/h

18 ft
12 ft
cooling capacity:
5160 Btu/h

Choosing a Method Find each value. Tell whether your answer is exact or an estimate.

17. $-\sqrt{810,000}$
−900; exact

18. $\sqrt{810}$
about 28.5; estimate

19. $-\sqrt{33}$
about −5.7; estimate

20. $\sqrt{0.25}$
0.5; exact

21. $\sqrt{1000}$
about 31.6; estimate

22. $\sqrt{0.0064}$
0.08; exact

23. Estimation The area of a square plot of land is about 9500 yd². Estimate the length of a side and the perimeter of the plot of land.
length about 97 yd, perimeter about 388 yd

24. Writing A homeowner figures that the cost of carpet for the walk-in closet will be one-third the cost of carpet for the bedroom. The carpet chosen is sold by the square foot. Do you agree with the homeowner? Explain. **See above.**

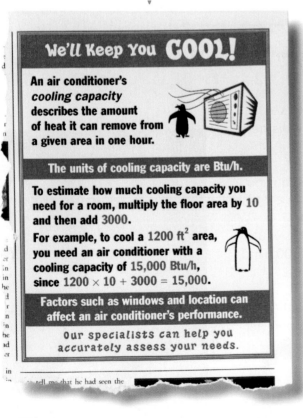

15 ft
15 ft bedroom 5 ft
5 ft
closet

Air Conditioning For Exercises 25–27, use the ad below.

25. Algebra Connection Write an equation that you can use to estimate how much cooling capacity is needed for a room with a given floor area. $c = 10a + 3000$ where c represents cooling capacity and a represents area

26. A room in Bob Lang's house is 10 ft × 15 ft. Another room is 20 ft × 30 ft. Bob estimates that he needs an air conditioner with twice as much cooling capacity for the larger room as for the smaller room.

   a. Sketch each room. Label the dimensions. Then find the cooling capacity needed for each room. **See above.**

   b. Do you think Bob is correct? Explain.
   Yes; Sample Response: 9000 is 2 · 4500.

27. One room in Maria Franco's house is 18 ft × 12 ft. Another room is 18 ft × 24 ft. Maria estimates that she needs an air conditioner with twice as much cooling capacity for the larger room as for the smaller room.

   a. Sketch each room. Label the dimensions. **See above.**

   b. Do you think Maria is correct? Explain.
   No; Sample Response: The cooling capacity needed for the larger room is about 1.5 times greater than the capacity needed for the smaller room.

We'll Keep You **COOL!**

An air conditioner's *cooling capacity* describes the amount of heat it can remove from a given area in one hour.

The units of cooling capacity are Btu/h.

To estimate how much cooling capacity you need for a room, multiply the floor area by 10 and then add 3000.

For example, to cool a 1200 ft² area, you need an air conditioner with a cooling capacity of 15,000 Btu/h, since 1200 × 10 + 3000 = 15,000.

Factors such as windows and location can affect an air conditioner's performance.

Our specialists can help you accurately assess your needs.

28. Challenge A company makes and sells small and large boxes. The same materials are used to make each size.

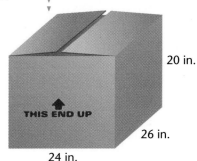

20 in.

a. Compare the amount of cardboard needed to make each box. About how many times as much cardboard is needed for the large box? **4 times**

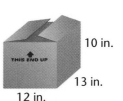

10 in.

26 in.

b. The volume of the large box is about how many times the volume of the small box? **8 times**

13 in.

12 in.

24 in.

c. **Writing** The company plans to charge $1.50 for a small box. How much do you think the company should charge for a large box? **Possible answer: $6.00 if they charge according to the amount of material used or $12.00 if they charge by volume**

Reflecting ◀▶ on the Section

Be prepared to report on the following topic in class.

29. In *The Mystery of Blacktail Canyon*, Dr. Ashilaka asks Jim to estimate the size of two rooms in a dwelling. When Jim is done, Dr. Ashilaka gives him a lecture about the relationships among length, area, and volume. Pretend you are Dr. Ashilaka and write what you would say to Jim. Then present your lecture to the class. **Answers will vary. Check students' work.**

Oral Report

Exercise 29 checks that you can compare length, area, and volume relationships.

Spiral ◀▶ Review

30. Use the data to create a box-and-whisker plot. Identify any outliers. (Module 2, p. 152) **See Additional Answers.**

Amounts Raised by Students at a Charity Dance Marathon (dollars)
55, 60, 65, 70, 80, 80, 80, 90, 100, 110, 115, 150, 170, 175, 175, 450

Solve each equation. (Module 2, p. 130)

31. $|x| = 4$
−4, 4

32. $|n| = 11$
−11, 11

33. $-y = 19$ **−19**

34. $-r = -6$ **6**

Use the figure shown. (Module 2, p. 130)

35. a. Give the coordinates of points *A, B, C,* and *D.* $A(-2, -2), B(-2, 1),$ $C(1, 1), D(2, -1)$

b. Give the coordinates of the image points *A′, B′, C′,* and *D′* after a translation of $(x + 2, y)$.
$A′(0, -2), B′(0, 1), C′(3, 1), D′(4, -1)$

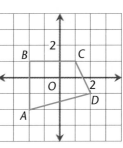

Mental Math Use mental math to find each value.

1. $\sqrt{490,000}$ 700   2. $-\sqrt{16}$ –4   3. $\sqrt{\dfrac{1}{100}}$ $\dfrac{1}{10}$ 4. $\sqrt{0.01}$ 0.1

5. $\sqrt{0.0036}$ 0.06   6. $-\sqrt{2500}$ –50   7. $\sqrt{0.0004}$ 0.02   8. $\sqrt{\dfrac{4}{25}}$ $\dfrac{2}{5}$

Estimation Estimate each square root to the nearest tenth.

9. $\sqrt{50}$
about 7.1

10. $\sqrt{22}$
about 4.7

11. $\sqrt{136}$
about 11.7

12. $\sqrt{67}$
about 8.2

13. $\sqrt{43}$
about 6.6

14. $\sqrt{94}$
about 9.7

15. $\sqrt{32}$
about 5.7

16. $\sqrt{85}$
about 9.2

Choosing a Method Find each square root. Tell whether your
answer is exact or an estimate.   18. about –7.9; estimate

17. $\sqrt{28.4}$
about 5.3; estimate

18. $-\sqrt{63}$

19. $\sqrt{6.25}$
2.5; exact

20. $-\sqrt{9000}$
about –94.9; estimate

21. $\sqrt{4.81}$
about 2.2; estimate

22. $\sqrt{\dfrac{1}{36}}$ $\dfrac{1}{6}$; exact

23. $\sqrt{0.64}$
0.8; exact

24. $\sqrt{0.064}$
about 0.3; estimate

25. The volume of a cube is 64 cm^3. What will be its volume if its
edge length is halved? **The volume will be divided by 8.**

Study Skills ▶ Preparing for Assessment

Planning ahead is important when you prepare for a test. Try to
study every day instead of waiting until the night before a test.
Also, be sure to practice what you have learned. Some people
find it helpful to make review cards for important ideas, rules,
and formulas.   Answers will vary. Check students' work.

Suppose you have 3 days to prepare for a test on this section.

1. Make a list of the important ideas in the section.

2. Develop a plan for dividing up the section so that you can study
part of it each day.

3. Write and solve some practice problems for the topics you plan to
study each day.

4. Make review cards of important ideas, rules, and formulas in
the section.

Section 2 Equations and Graphs

IN THIS SECTION

EXPLORATION 1
◆ Order of Operations

EXPLORATION 2
◆ Graphing Equations

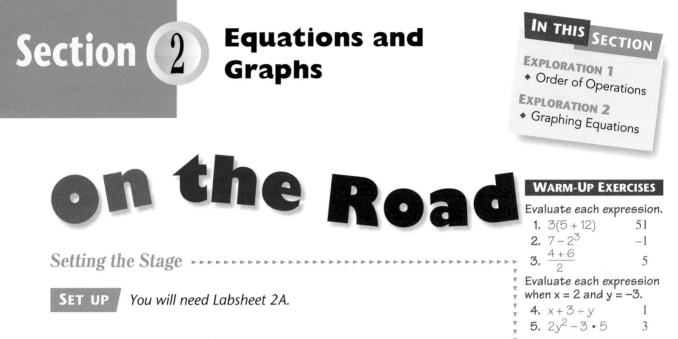

WARM-UP EXERCISES

Evaluate each expression.
1. $3(5 + 12)$ 51
2. $7 - 2^3$ -1
3. $\dfrac{4 + 6}{2}$ 5

Evaluate each expression when $x = 2$ and $y = -3$.
4. $x + 3 \div y$ 1
5. $2y^2 - 3 \cdot 5$ 3

Setting the Stage ▸▸▸▸▸▸▸▸▸▸▸▸▸▸▸▸▸▸▸▸▸▸▸▸▸▸▸▸▸▸▸▸▸▸▸

SET UP   *You will need Labsheet 2A.*

The Story So Far...

▶ On the drive back from Blacktail Canyon, Jim and Nageela find Highway Patrol Officer Ferrel Yellow Robe investigating a single-car accident. The officer explains how he knows that the missing driver of the car was going too fast on the wet curve.

"When I investigate an accident, I check the road conditions, the length of the skid, and the condition of the tire tread. There's a chart that we use to figure the speed the car was going when the driver hit the brakes, or we can plug the numbers into a formula. Just routine."

To estimate the car's speed, Ferrel needs to know the distance the car skidded and a number called the *coefficient of friction*. This number is a measure of the friction between the car's tires and the road surface.

Think About It

1   *Friction* is the force that resists the motion of objects in contact with each other. Try pushing a notebook quickly, then slowly, across two different surfaces, such as carpet and wood. Describe the amount of friction present in each instance. **Sample Response: There is more friction on a rough surface, like a carpet, than a smooth surface, like wood.**

2   Suppose you ride a bike across dirt, ice, dry asphalt, and wet asphalt. Which surface do you think is the least safe? the safest?
ice; dry asphalt

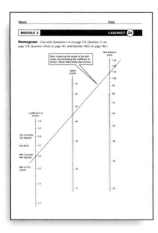

Use Labsheet 2A for Questions 3–6. In the story on page 175, Officer Yellow Robe mentions a chart. This chart is called a *Nomogram*.

3 Officer Yellow Robe measures the skidding distance and estimates the coefficient of friction at the crash site. He then uses the data to draw a line as shown on the labsheet.

   a. Describe the road conditions. What is the coefficient of friction? **wet concrete or asphalt; 0.6**

   b. How long were the skid marks? **110 ft**

   c. Estimate the car's speed when the driver hit the brakes. **about 45 mi/h**

4 An officer measures 45 ft skid marks on wet asphalt at a crash site. Use the *Nomogram* to estimate the car's speed. **about 29 mi/h**

5 A driver is traveling at 35 mi/h on dry asphalt. Estimate how far the car will skid if the driver hits the brakes. **about 51 ft**

6 Can two cars traveling at the same speed leave different skid mark lengths? Explain. **Yes; Sample Response: The condition of the road is a factor in the length of the skid mark.**

GOAL

LEARN HOW TO...
◆ evaluate expressions with square roots and fraction bars

AS YOU...
◆ estimate speeds of cars involved in accidents

Exploration 1

Order of Operations

SET UP *You will need: • Labsheet 2A • calculator*

▶ Nomograms are only one way to estimate speed from skid marks. Most of the time, accident investigators use two formulas to find the speed.

The formula shown at the right is used first to find a coefficient of friction for the road where the accident happened. An officer drives a patrol car at a certain speed and then hits the brakes to find a skid distance.

Coefficient of friction

Car's speed in miles per hour before braking

$$f = \frac{s^2}{30d}$$

Distance in feet the car skidded before stopping

EXAMPLE

Officer Patricia Hayes conducts a skid test at an accident site. She uses the formula $f = \dfrac{s^2}{30d}$ to find the coefficient of friction.

FOR ▶ HELP
with the *order of operations*, see
TOOLBOX, p. 600

REPORTING OFFICER	LOCATION OF ACCIDENT		
Hayes, Patricia	Mile 6, Adobe Road		

DATE OF ACCIDENT			TIME OF ACCIDENT		AM	PM
Mo	Day	Yr	Hour	Min.		
05	19	98	3	41	☐	☒

Result of Skid Test

Speed before brakes were applied: 32 mi/h

Skid distance: 50 ft

$f = \dfrac{s^2}{30d}$

$f = \dfrac{32^2}{30 \cdot 50}$

$f = \dfrac{1024}{1500} \approx 0.68$

The fraction bar is a grouping symbol. Simplify the power in the numerator first.

The coefficient of friction is about 0.68.

▶ **For Questions 7 and 8, use the Example above.**

7 **Try This as a Class** Explain each step of Officer Hayes's work. How did she use the order of operations?

8 ✔ **CHECKPOINT** To make sure her results are accurate, Officer Hayes conducts two skid tests. She finds the coefficient of friction for each test, and then finds an average.

    a. In her second skid test, Officer Hayes's speed is 34 mi/h and her skid distance is 60 ft. Find the coefficient of friction. about 0.64

    b. Use your answer to part (a) and the coefficient of friction from the Example to find the mean coefficient of friction. about 0.66

7. Step 1: Copy the formula; Step 2: Substitute 32 for speed (*s*) and 50 for distance (*d*); Step 3: Evaluate the expression; Step 4: Simplify.

✔ **QUESTION 8**

…checks that you understand how to evaluate an expression with a fraction bar.

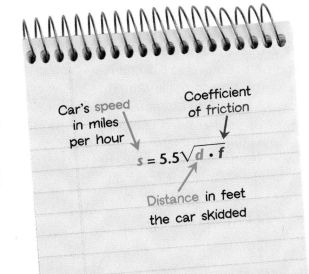

Car's speed in miles per hour

Coefficient of friction

$s = 5.5\sqrt{d \cdot f}$

Distance in feet the car skidded

▶ **Another Grouping Symbol**
When a patrol officer knows the coefficient of friction, he or she can use the formula shown at the left to estimate a car's speed when the brakes were applied. The $\sqrt{}$ symbol in the formula is a grouping symbol.

EXAMPLE

A car skids 49 ft in an accident. The investigating officer finds that the coefficient of friction is 0.75. Estimate the car's speed.

SAMPLE RESPONSE

Evaluate the formula $s = 5.5\sqrt{d \cdot f}$ for $d = 49$ and $f = 0.75$.

$s = 5.5\sqrt{49(0.75)}$ — Perform the operations under the $\sqrt{}$ symbol first.

$s = 5.5\sqrt{36.75}$

$s \approx 5.5(6.06)$ — Then find the square root of 36.75.

$s \approx 33$ mi/h

The car's speed was approximately 33 mi/h.

✓ QUESTION 9

…checks that you can find the value of an expression with grouping symbols.

9 ✓ CHECKPOINT Find each value.

a. $1.65\sqrt{32 \cdot 2}$ 13.2   **b.** $\dfrac{5 - 13}{2^3}$ –1   **c.** $\dfrac{3 - 21}{-2(3)}$ 3

d. $\sqrt{\dfrac{19 + 8}{3}}$ 3   **e.** $12\sqrt{\dfrac{12}{56 - 8}}$ 6   **f.** $8 + 2\sqrt{9 \cdot 4}$ 20

10 📟 **Calculator** You can use a calculator to simplify expressions with grouping symbols. For example, one way to simplify $5.5\sqrt{49(0.75)}$ is to enter a key sequence that uses parentheses to group operations under the $\sqrt{}$ symbol:

(49 × 0.75) √ × 5.5 =

Does this key sequence work on your calculator? If not, describe another key sequence you could use.

Sample Response: On a graphing calculator, $5.5 \times \sqrt{}$ (49 × .75) ENTER

11 **Use Labsheet 2A.** Suppose a car leaves 60 ft skid marks on dry gravel in a 30 mi/h speed zone. Use the *Nomogram* and then the formula $s = 5.5\sqrt{d \cdot f}$ to estimate the car's speed. How do your answers compare? Was the driver speeding?

The results are about 30 mi/h using the nomogram and about 30.1 mi/h using the formula; The driver was not speeding.

HOMEWORK EXERCISES ▷ See Exs. 1–20 on pp. 184–185.

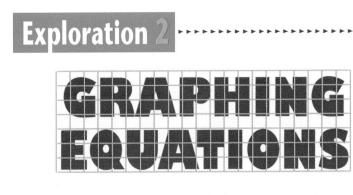

GRAPHING EQUATIONS

GOAL

LEARN HOW TO...
◆ graph equations

AS YOU...
◆ investigate highway safety issues

KEY TERMS
◆ solution of the equation
◆ linear
◆ nonlinear

SET UP You will need: • Labsheet 2A • graph paper
• graphing calculator (optional)

▶ To prevent highway collisions, it is important to leave enough "following distance" between your car and the car ahead of you. The table models a relationship between speed and recommended following distance that drivers have used for years. Some new guidelines call for even greater following distances.

Recommended Following Distances	
Speed of a car (mi/h)	Following distance (ft)
10	15
20	30
30	45
40	60
50	75

Use the table for Questions 12–14. You'll use an equation and a graph to model the relationship between a car's speed and the recommended following distance.

12 **a.** Use the table to complete this equation:

Following distance = __?__ × speed
1.5

b. Follow these steps to graph the equation from part (a).

12. b.

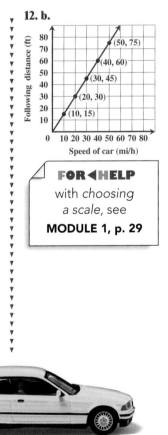

First Make a coordinate grid. You want to show how following distance depends on speed, so put following distance on the vertical axis. In general, when one quantity depends on another, put the dependent quantity on the vertical axis.

Next Write the data in the table as ordered pairs: (Speed, Following distance).

Then Plot the ordered pairs. Draw a smooth curve through the points or connect the points in order with segments.

FOR◀HELP
with *choosing a scale*, see
MODULE 1, p. 29

c. A driver is traveling at 45 mi/h. Use your graph and the equation to recommend a following distance to the driver. 67.5 ft

d. Which model in part (c) did you find easier to use? Which gave the most accurate answer?
Sample Response: the graph; the equation

13 Let *s* = the speed of a car in miles per hour. Let *d* = the recommended following distance in feet. Model the relationship in Question 12(a) with an equation using the variables *s* and *d*.

$$d = 1.5s$$

14 Discussion Some drivers estimate the distance between their car and the one ahead using a car length as a benchmark. At 50 mi/h, how many car lengths would you recommend as a minimum following distance between two cars? Explain your thinking.

5 car lengths; Sample Response: I used the equation to find the traveling distance of 75 ft, then divided 75 by 15 to get the number of car lengths.

I car length ≈ 15 ft

Your Car

Car in Front

▶ The equation you wrote in Question 13 has two variables. An ordered pair of numbers that make an equation with two variables true is a **solution of the equation**. The graph of an equation includes all possible solutions of the equation.

> ### EXAMPLE
>
> Follow these steps to graph the equation *y* = 2*x* + 1.
>
> **First** Make a table of values. Include several values so you can see the pattern in the points you plot. Include both positive and negative values for *x*.
>
> **Then** Plot the ordered pairs on a coordinate grid. Draw a curve or a line to show the pattern. Use arrowheads to show that the graph extends.
>
> | *x* | *y* | (*x*, *y*) |
> |-----|-----|------------|
> | –2 | –3 | (–2, –3) |
> | –1 | –1 | (–1, –1) |
> | 0 | 1 | (0, 1) |
> | 1 | 3 | (1, 3) |
> | 2 | 5 | (2, 5) |
>
>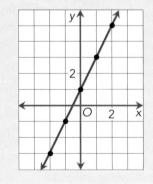

15. a. Yes.
b. No.
c. No.
d. Yes.
Sample Response: Substitute the values given for *x* and *y* or extend the graph.

15 Try This as a Class Tell whether each ordered pair is a solution of the equation in the Example. Explain your thinking.

 a. (–5, –9)   **b.** (–4, 9)   **c.** (3, 1)   **d.** (9, 19)

16 ✓ **CHECKPOINT** Graph each equation.

a. $y = x$　　　　　**b.** $y = x - 4$　　　　　**c.** $y = -2x$

▶ **Linear and Nonlinear Graphs** When the graph of an equation is a straight line, the graph and the equation are called **linear**. Now you will look at a relationship whose graph is **nonlinear**.

17 Copy and complete the table. Use the formula $s = 5.5\sqrt{d \cdot f}$ from page 177. (The coefficient of friction for dry concrete is 0.81.) Round all values to the nearest unit.

48, (95, 48); 56, (129, 56); 61, (154, 61)

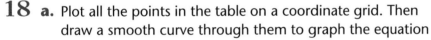

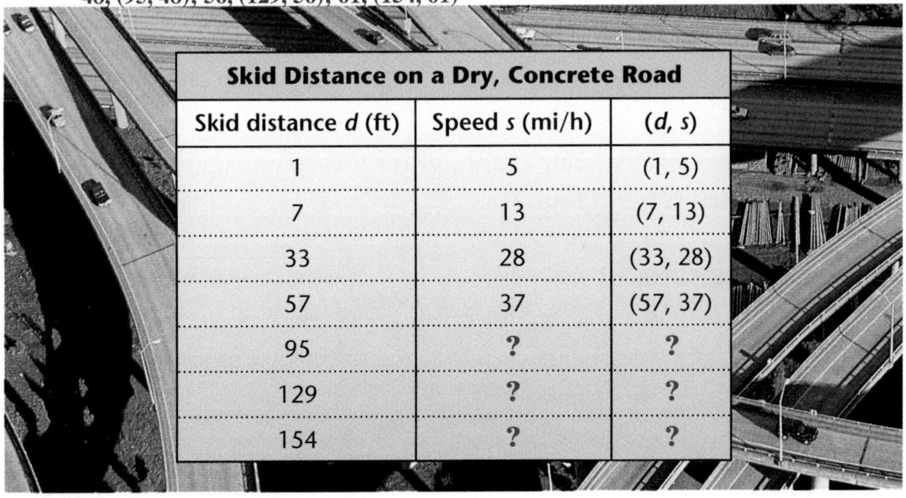

Skid Distance on a Dry, Concrete Road		
Skid distance d (ft)	Speed s (mi/h)	(d, s)
1	5	(1, 5)
7	13	(7, 13)
33	28	(33, 28)
57	37	(57, 37)
95	?	?
129	?	?
154	?	?

18 a. Plot all the points in the table on a coordinate grid. Then draw a smooth curve through them to graph the equation $s = 5.5\sqrt{d \cdot f}$. **See Additional Answers.**

b. Use your graph to estimate the speed of a car that leaves 19 ft skid marks on a road with a coefficient of friction of 0.81. **about 20 mi/h**

c. Use your graph to estimate how far a car traveling at 55 mi/h on a dry, concrete road will skid when the driver slams on the brakes. **about 120 ft**

d. Use Labsheet 2A. Use the *Nomogram* to estimate how far a car traveling at 55 mi/h on a dry, concrete road will skid. How does this estimate compare with your estimate from part (c)? **about 125 ft; Sample Response: It is slightly greater.**

19 📐 Graphing Calculator Graph each equation. Tell whether the graph is *linear* or *nonlinear*. **Check students' graphs.**

a. $y = x + 20$ **linear**　**b.** $y = \sqrt{x}$ **nonlinear**　**c.** $y = 1 + \sqrt{x}$ **nonlinear**

HOMEWORK EXERCISES ▶ See Exs. 21–34 on pp. 185–186.

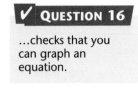

✓ **QUESTION 16**

…checks that you can graph an equation.

16. a.

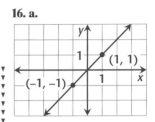

b.

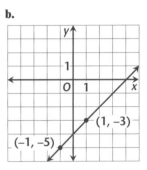

c.

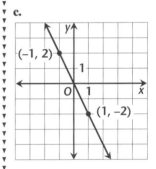

You can use a graphing calculator or graphing software to graph the equation from Question 12 on page 179.

Step 1 Enter the equation to graph using the Y= feature.

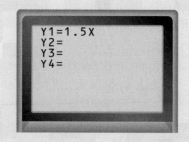

Step 2 To set the *viewing window* for your graph, enter the values you want shown along each axis. Then graph.

Enter the minimum, maximum, and scale values for X and Y.

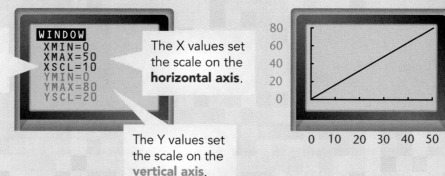

The X values set the scale on the **horizontal axis**.

The Y values set the scale on the **vertical axis**.

Step 3 Use the TRACE feature to estimate values on the graph in Question 12(c), or use the TABLE feature to find exact values.

See coordinates of points by using the arrow keys to trace along the line.

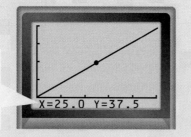

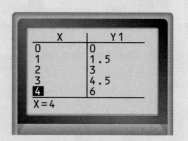

Section 2
Key Concepts

Order of Operations (pp. 176–178)

The order of operations is a set of rules for evaluating an expression so that the expression has only one value.

First Perform all calculations inside grouping symbols. Grouping symbols include parentheses, fraction bars, and square root symbols.

Next Perform multiplications and divisions in order from left to right. Simplify exponents before other multiplications.

Then Perform additions and subtractions in order from left to right.

Example $2\sqrt{6 + 3} = 2\sqrt{9} = 2(3) = 6$

> Do the addition inside the square root symbol first.

Graphing Equations (pp. 179–181)

The graph of an equation includes all possible solutions of the equation. Some graphs are linear. Some are nonlinear.

solution of the equation

Examples

Linear graph	Nonlinear graph
$y = x + 4$	$y = 2\sqrt{x - 1}$

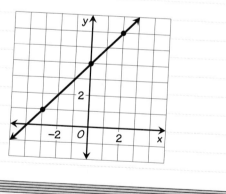

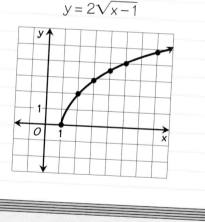

linear

nonlinear

CLOSURE QUESTION

Why might you need to be concerned about the order of operations when graphing an equation?

Sample Response: To graph the equation, you first find a table of values. The order of operations may be needed when evaluating the equation for different values of the first variable in the table.

---

20 **Key Concepts Question** Use the equations graphed in the Examples above. For which equation is (10, 6) a solution? How do you know? $y = 2\sqrt{x - 1}$; **Sample Response: Use the graph or use substitution.**

Section 2

YOU WILL NEED

For Exs. 22–27 and 33:
♦ graph paper

For Exs. 30–32:
♦ graph paper or graphing calculator (optional)

For Ex. 34(b):
♦ Labsheet 2A

Evaluate each expression. Round decimals to the nearest hundredth.

1. $\dfrac{3 \cdot 10}{5 - 3}$ 15

2. $\dfrac{2(8 - 3)}{5}$ 2

3. $\dfrac{(-3)^2}{8 + 1 - 2(3)}$ 3

4. $9\sqrt{2 \cdot 3}$ 22.05

5. $-\sqrt{8 \cdot 2} + 7$ 3

6. $\dfrac{\sqrt{16 - 4}}{6}$ 0.58

Exercises 7–10 show the incorrect answers a student gave on a quiz. Describe the mistakes the student made.

7. $12 + 6 \div 3 = 6$

8. $3 \times 8 - 4 \times 5 = 100$

9. $\dfrac{3 + 5}{5} = 4$

10. $\sqrt{4 + 9} = 5$

7. The addition was done before the division.

8. The subtraction was done before the second multiplication.

9. The 5 in the numerator was divided by 5 but the 3 was not.

10. $\sqrt{4}$ was added to $\sqrt{9}$ instead of finding $\sqrt{13}$.

Biology Scientists use the expression below to measure how circular a lake is. The closer the value of the expression is to 1, the more circular the lake. Use the expression for Exercises 11–13.

L = the length of the shoreline

$$\dfrac{L}{2\sqrt{\pi A}}$$

A = the surface area of the lake

11. The length of Crater Lake's shoreline is about 26 mi, and its surface area is about 21 mi². Evaluate the expression above for Crater Lake.   1.6

12. a. Suppose a lake is perfectly circular and has a 2 mi diameter. Evaluate the expression for this lake.   1

   b. Evaluate the expression for two other perfectly circular lakes. (You choose the diameters.) What pattern do you see?
   The value of the expression is always 1.

13. a. Evaluate the expression for the Lake of the Ozarks. The length of its shoreline is about 1350 mi, and its surface area is about 93 mi².   about 39

   b. You learned about the Lake of the Ozarks on page 68. Would you have expected a value close to 1 for this lake? Explain.
   Sample Response: No; The length of the shoreline is very large compared to the surface area.

Evaluate each expression when $b = 5$ and $c = -2$. Round decimal answers to the nearest hundredth.

14. $3\sqrt{b + c}$ 5.20

15. $\dfrac{8b + 7}{c}$ −23.5

16. $\dfrac{c^3}{bc}$ 0.8

17. $\dfrac{b^2 + 8c}{9bc}$ −0.1

18. $\dfrac{30b}{5 \cdot 3} - c$ 12

19. $\dfrac{\sqrt{b^2 \cdot 36}}{c^2}$ 7.5

▲ Crater Lake lies in the "bowl" of an extinct volcano in Oregon.

20. Challenge Write a numerical expression that equals 5. Your expression should include a fraction bar, a $\sqrt{}$ symbol, and at least three different numerical operations. **Sample Response:** $\dfrac{\sqrt{100}}{6 - 4(-2 + 3)}$

21. History The article below first appeared in a November 1896 issue of *Scientific American*.

"An immense crowd assembled near the Hotel Metropole, London, November 14, to witness the departure of the motor carriages for their race to Brighton, 47 miles. The occasion of the race was the going into effect of the new law which opens up the highways to the use of the motor carriages. . . . under the old law self-propelled vehicles were not allowed to go faster than six miles an hour and had to be preceded by a horseman waving a red flag. . . . the race was won by the American Duryea motor wagon. The distance was covered in four hours."

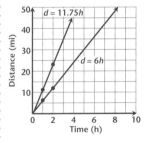

◀ The annual run from London to Brighton is a test of endurance, not speed. Most of the cars were built before 1918.

a. Find the average speed of the winning car. Write an equation for the distance *d* it could travel in *h* hours at this speed.
11.75 mi/h; $d = 11.75h$

b. According to the article, what was the speed limit before the new law went into effect? Write an equation for the distance *d* a vehicle could travel in *h* hours at this speed. **6 mi/h; $d = 6h$**

c. Graph the equations from parts (a) and (b) on the same pair of axes. Use the graph to estimate how long it would take to finish the race if you traveled at the old speed limit. **about 8 h**

21. c.

(graph showing Distance (mi) on vertical axis from 0 to 50, Time (h) on horizontal axis from 0 to 10, with lines $d = 11.75h$ and $d = 6h$)

Graph each equation. **See Additional Answers.**

22. $y = 2x - 3$ **23.** $y = -3x$ **24.** $y = -3x + 2$

25. $y = 4$ **26.** $y = 90 + x$ **27.** $y = 100 - x$

28. For which equations in Exercises 22–27 is (5, 95) a solution?
$y = 90 + x, y = 100 - x$

29. For which equation in Exercises 22–27 is (2.5, 4) a solution? $y = 4$

Graphing Calculator **Graph each equation. Tell whether the graph is *linear* or *nonlinear*.** **Check students' graphs.**

30. $y = x + \sqrt{5}$ **31.** $y = 2\sqrt{x}$ **32.** $y = 0.5x^2$
linear   **nonlinear**   **nonlinear**

Radius r (cm)	Volume V (cm³)
1	? 4
2	? 34
3	? 113
5	? 524
10	? 4189
20	? 33,510

33. Geometry Connection A table, an equation, and a graph can all model the relationship between the radius r of a sphere and the volume V.

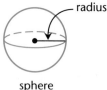

radius

sphere

a. Copy and complete the table. Use the formula for the volume of a sphere, $V = \frac{4}{3}\pi r^3$. Round your answers to the nearest whole number. **See table.**

b. Graph the data in the table. Is the graph *linear* or *nonlinear*?
See Additional Answers for graph; nonlinear

c. The radius of a tennis ball is about 6.5 cm. Use the graph and the equation to estimate its volume. **about 1150 cm³**

Reflecting ◀▶ on the Section

Write your response to Exercise 34 in your journal.

34. In this section, you used both a formula and a nomogram to estimate the speed of a car based on skid mark length. Another formula you can use is $2\sqrt{5d}$. This formula does not include friction as a variable.

Length of skid (ft)	Approximate speed of car (mi/h)
1	$2\sqrt{5(1)} \approx 4.5$
5	? 10
15	? 17.3
35	? 26.5
55	? 33.2
75	? 38.7
100	? 44.7
150	? 54.8

a. Copy and complete the table using the formula $s = 2\sqrt{5d}$ to estimate the speed s for each skid length d. **See table.**

b. **Use Labsheet 2A.** For what road conditions does the formula $s = 2\sqrt{5d}$ give a good estimate of a car's speed?
dry brick

c. If you want to quickly estimate a car's speed based on skid length, which method would you use? Why? Sample Response: I would use the nomogram. You can quickly read the speed estimate.

Spiral ◀▶ Review

Estimate each value. (Module 3, p. 170)

35. $-\sqrt{8}$
about −2.8

36. $\sqrt{11}$
about 3.3

37. $-\sqrt{15}$
about −3.9

38. $\sqrt{0.144}$
about 0.4

39. Use the coordinate plane shown. List the ordered pairs for the points labeled on line j and line k. (Module 1, p. 29)
$A\,(-2, -3)$, $B\,(0, -1)$, $C\,(1, 0)$, $M\,(-2, 2)$, $N\,(1, -1)$

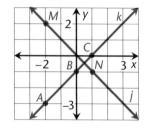

For each rate, write a unit rate (Module 1, p. 9)

40. $1.69 for 12 oz
$.14/oz

41. 5.2 mi in 18 h
0.3 mi/h

42. $280 for 3.75 h
$74.67/h

Journal

Exercise 34 checks that you can use and interpret formulas and graphs.

Working with Formulas

43. a. A car involved in a crash leaves 150 ft skid marks (d). The coefficient of friction (f) for the road surface is 0.8. Show how to use the formula $f = \dfrac{s^2}{30d}$ to estimate the speed (s) of the car.

Substitute 0.8 for f and 150 for d. Multiply both sides of the equation by 4500, then find the square root of each side. The speed is about 60 mi/h.

b. Use the formula $s = 5.5\sqrt{d \cdot f}$ to estimate the speed of the car. Compare this estimate with the one from part (a).

about 60.2; They are about the same.

1. Dr. Ashilaka is an expert on cliff dwellings and is giving a lecture and tour of Anasazi cliff dwellings. His daughter, Nageela, helps her paralzyed father by being his "eyes and legs."; They hope to find a previously undiscovered Anasazi site where a local boy found pottery.

3. Uncle LeVerle, science teacher, who seemed quite interested in the topic; Gloria Blanco, art teacher; Teresa Seowtewa, social studies teacher; Ms. Weatherwax, principal, who doesn't really know anything about Anasazi pottery; Perry Martinez, mathematics teacher

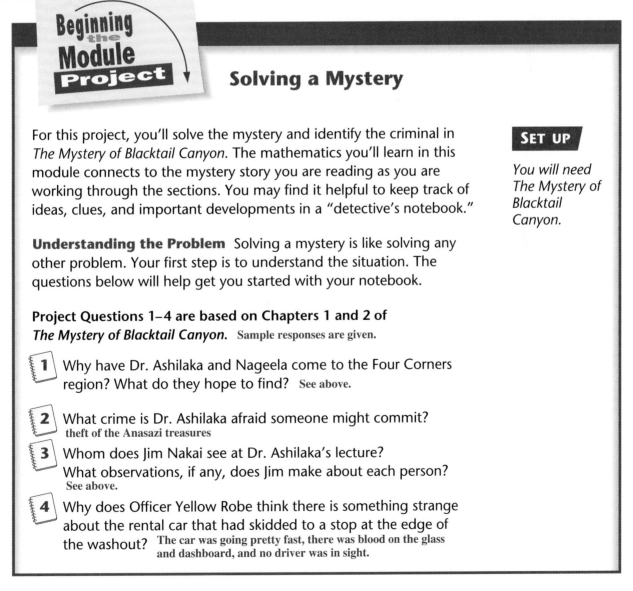

Beginning the **Module** **Project**

Solving a Mystery

For this project, you'll solve the mystery and identify the criminal in *The Mystery of Blacktail Canyon*. The mathematics you'll learn in this module connects to the mystery story you are reading as you are working through the sections. You may find it helpful to keep track of ideas, clues, and important developments in a "detective's notebook."

SET UP

You will need The Mystery of Blacktail Canyon.

Understanding the Problem Solving a mystery is like solving any other problem. Your first step is to understand the situation. The questions below will help get you started with your notebook.

Project Questions 1–4 are based on Chapters 1 and 2 of *The Mystery of Blacktail Canyon*. Sample responses are given.

1 Why have Dr. Ashilaka and Nageela come to the Four Corners region? What do they hope to find? See above.

2 What crime is Dr. Ashilaka afraid someone might commit?
theft of the Anasazi treasures

3 Whom does Jim Nakai see at Dr. Ashilaka's lecture? What observations, if any, does Jim make about each person? See above.

4 Why does Officer Yellow Robe think there is something strange about the rental car that had skidded to a stop at the edge of the washout? The car was going pretty fast, there was blood on the glass and dashboard, and no driver was in sight.

Section 2

Extra Skill Practice

You will need: • *graph paper* (Exs. 10–15 and 18–20)

Evaluate each expression. Round decimal answers to the nearest hundredth.

1. $\dfrac{8 \cdot 3}{5 + 9 - 2(4)}$ 4

2. $8 + 6\sqrt{7 \cdot 4}$ 39.75

3. $\dfrac{\sqrt{13 + 5}}{9}$ 0.47

4. $(5 + 3)\sqrt{4(12)}$ 55.43

5. $\dfrac{37 + 2(-5)}{3^3}$ 1

6. $\sqrt{\dfrac{7}{11 - 3}}$ 0.94

Evaluate each expression for $f = -3$ and $g = 4$. Round decimal answers to the nearest hundredth.

7. $\dfrac{2 - 6f}{g}$ 5

8. $\dfrac{\sqrt{f^2 - 2g}}{g - f}$ 0.14

9. $\dfrac{-2f}{8 + g} - g$ –3.5

Graph each equation.   See Additional Answers.

10. $y = 4x$

11. $y = 2x + 6$

12. $y = -2x + 12$

13. $y = 3x - 8$

14. $y = x - 9$

15. $y = 0.5x + 2$

16. For which equations in Exercises 10–15 is (7, –2) a solution? $y = -2x + 12, y = x - 9$

17. For which equations in Exercises 10–15 is (4, 4) a solution? $y = -2x + 12, y = 3x - 8,$ $y = 0.5x + 2$

Graph each equation. Tell whether the graph is *linear* or *nonlinear*.   See Additional Answers.

18. $y = \sqrt{4x}$

19. $y = x^3 - 1$

20. $y = 1.5x + 2.5$

Standardized Testing ◀▶ Multiple Choice

1. Evaluate $\dfrac{\sqrt{7 + 2 \cdot 3^2}}{3 + 6 \div 3}$.   A

   Ⓐ 1   Ⓑ 3   Ⓒ 9   Ⓓ 2.6

2. Which point lies on the graph of $y = 3x - 2$?   C

   Ⓐ (0, 2)   Ⓑ (5, 17)   Ⓒ (6, 16)   Ⓓ (4, 2)

3. Which ordered pair is *not* a solution of $y = 3 - 8x$?   B

   Ⓐ (0, 3)   Ⓑ (3, 21)   Ⓒ (–1, 11)   Ⓓ (–3, 27)

Section **3** **Slope and Equations**

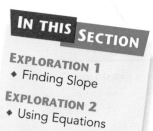

IN THIS SECTION

EXPLORATION 1
◆ Finding Slope

EXPLORATION 2
◆ Using Equations

bIG foot

Setting the Stage ▶▶▶▶▶▶▶▶▶▶▶▶▶▶▶▶▶▶▶▶▶▶▶▶▶▶▶▶▶▶

WARM-UP EXERCISES

Decide whether the point (−2, 3) lies on each line.
1. $y = 5x + 7$ no
2. $y = -x + 1$ yes
3. $y = 2x - 8$ no

Find the values of y when x = −1, 0, and 2.
4. $y = 15x$ −15, 0, 30
5. $y = 4x - 11$
           −15, −11, −3

The Story So Far…

▶ Jim, Nageela, and Officers Ferrel Yellow Robe and Charlotte Lopez search for the missing driver of an abandoned car. When Jim finds some footprints, the officers think they can make some deductions about the person who left them.

"Do you think these are the driver's footprints?" Nageela asked.

"They must be," said Ferrel. "Otherwise, the rain would have washed them away. Now we can tell how tall the driver is."

"How will you do that?" asked Jim. "All I can tell is which way the tracks are going."

"It's all right here in the sand," said Charlotte. "All you have to do is look. By the looks of the stride, this person could cover quite a bit of ground if he or she was in a hurry. If he got to the top of the canyon, he'd be back to the main road easily by now."

Think About It

1 How do you think a person's height can be determined by examining his or her footprints?
Answers will vary.

2 What can you tell about the person who made the footprints in the photo on this page? Explain your thinking.
Sample Responses: size of person's feet, person's footwear, length of person's stride

LEARN HOW TO...
◆ find the slope of a line
◆ use equations and graphs to model situations

AS YOU...
◆ compare walking rates

KEY TERMS
◆ slope
◆ rise
◆ run

 Exploration 1

Finding SLOPE

SET UP *Work with a partner.*

▶ In this exploration, you'll use graphs to explore rates. The mathematics you'll learn will help you find the height of the missing driver in Exploration 2.

3. Sample Response: Stride is the length between a person's feet when he or she walks; It takes everyone about the same amount of time to complete one stride but the length of the stride varies depending on the length of the person's legs. The length of the stride determines how quickly a person can cover a distance.

3 Look back at the story on page 189. What does Charlotte mean by the word *stride*? How does your stride affect the distance you can cover in a given amount of time?

4 **Discussion** The red and blue lines on the coordinate plane below show distances two different people can walk over time. You and your partner each choose one of the lines.

a. Work on your own. Choose at least three different travel times. For each time find the distance traveled. Record your results in a table like the one shown.

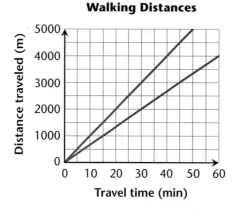

Walking Distances

Time (min)	Distance (m)	Rate (m/min)
?	?	?
?	?	?
?	?	?
?	?	?

Sample Responses: 15, 1500 or 15, 1000; 30, 3000 or 30, 2000; 45, 4500 or 45, 3000

b. Compare your tables. Which person is walking at a faster rate? The person represented by the upper line.

c. How do the graphs show who is walking at a faster rate? The graph of the faster rate is steeper.

d. Suppose the missing driver in *The Mystery of Blacktail Canyon* has a faster walking rate than the rates you found. How would a line graph of the driver's distance walked over time compare with the graphs shown? It would be steeper.

▶ **Finding Slope** The **slope** of a line is a ratio that measures the line's steepness.

EXAMPLE

Slope = $\dfrac{\text{rise}}{\text{run}}$

Slope = $\dfrac{3}{2}$

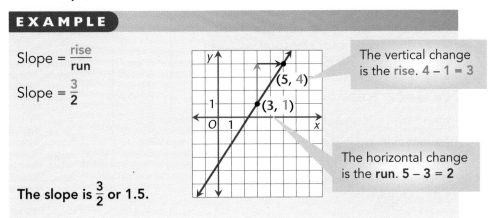

The vertical change is the **rise.** $4 - 1 = 3$

The horizontal change is the **run.** $5 - 3 = 2$

The slope is $\dfrac{3}{2}$ or 1.5.

5 **Try This as a Class** Try using a different pair of points to find the slope of the line in the Example. Do you think it matters which points you choose? No.

6 ✔ **CHECKPOINT** Find the slope of each line.

a. 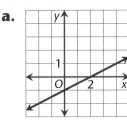 $\dfrac{1}{2}$

b. 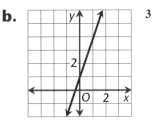 3

✔ **QUESTION 6**

...checks that you can find the slope of a line.

7 Look back at the graph in Question 4. Find the slope of each line. How does the slope compare with the person's walking rate?

$100, 66\frac{2}{3}$; Greater slope means faster walking rate.

▶ **Writing an Equation** You can use an equation to model the distance a person walking at a steady rate can cover in a given amount of time.

Distance = rate × time
$$d = rt$$

8 Use the rates you found in Question 4. Write an equation that can be used to estimate the distance d each person can walk in t minutes. How is the slope you found in Question 7 related to your equation? $d = 100t$; $d = 66\frac{2}{3}t$; slope $= r$

▶ The slope of a line often gives you information about a situation. Sometimes you can use that information to write an equation.

Use the graph to find the daily rate Crownpoint Car Rental charges. Then write an equation for the total cost of renting a car for a given number of days.

SAMPLE RESPONSE

First Find the daily rate. To find the daily rate, find the slope of the line. The slope is 20, so the rate is $20 per day.

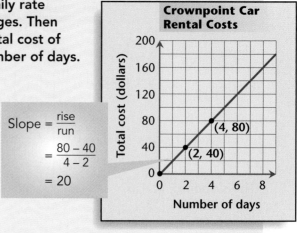

Crownpoint Car Rental Costs

Slope = $\frac{\text{rise}}{\text{run}}$

$= \frac{80 - 40}{4 - 2}$

$= 20$

Next Write an equation. Let C = total cost and d = the number of days.

Total cost = daily rate × number of days

$$C = 20d$$

Then Check your work. Choose at least two points from the graph. Check that their coordinates are solutions of the equation $C = 20d$.

Choose (3, 60). 60 = 20(3) ✔

Choose (4, 80). 80 = 20(4) ✔

9 Try This as a Class How does the graph in the Example show what the units of the daily rate are? Sample Response: The rise is given in dollars and the run in days, so $\frac{\text{rise}}{\text{run}} = \frac{\text{dollars}}{\text{days}}$.

10 Try This as a Class Suppose Crownpoint Car Rental's rate becomes $25 per day. How will the graph of rental costs be different? How will the equation be different? The slope will be steeper; $C = 25d$

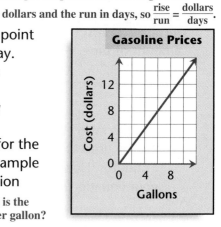

Gasoline Prices

...checks that you can apply the idea of slope to model a situation with an equation.

11 ✔ CHECKPOINT Write an equation for the graph shown at the right. Give an example of a problem you can use your equation to solve. $C = 1.33g$; Sample Response: What is the cost of 10 gal of gasoline at $1.33 per gallon?

HOMEWORK EXERCISES ▶ See Exs. 1–7 on p. 196.

Using Equ+ati=ons

SET UP ▸ *Work in a group of four. You will need: • Labsheet 3A • meter stick • masking tape • marker • graph paper*

▶ In *The Mystery of Blacktail Canyon,* **Officer Yellow Robe says that he can use the footprints Jim found to estimate the height of the missing driver. In this Exploration, you'll use an equation to estimate heights from foot lengths.**

12–14. Answers will vary. Check students' work.
Use Labsheet 3A for Questions 12–14.

12 Follow the directions on the labsheet for collecting and recording data in the *Foot Length and Height Table.* You'll use the data to make a scatter plot and a fitted line.

13 The footprint of the missing driver in *The Mystery of Blacktail Canyon* is 29 cm long. Use your fitted line to predict the person's height.

14 Suppose you guess that an equation for your fitted line from Question 12 follows the pattern you saw in Exploration 1. It would be in this form:

Height = slope × foot length

a. Find the slope of your fitted line. (You may need to estimate the coordinates of the points you use to find the slope.)

b. Let f = foot length and let h = height. Write an equation for your fitted line, based on the pattern described above.

c. Choose two points from your fitted line to see whether their coordinates make the equation true. Do you think your equation is correct? Explain.

▶ In Question 14, you probably found that the pattern from Exploration 1 did not work for your fitted line. In Question 15, you'll explore how to adjust the pattern to write an equation for your fitted line.

15 a. Copy and complete the table below. As shown, use two different methods to predict height. **Answers will vary. Check students' work.**

First Use your fitted line to make a prediction.

Next Use your equation from Question 14 to make a prediction.

Then Find the difference between the two predictions.

Foot length (cm)	Height (cm) (Fitted line prediction)	Height (cm) (Equation prediction)	Difference
24 cm	?	?	?
26 cm	?	?	?
28 cm	?	?	?
30 cm	?	?	?

b. How do your predictions compare? **Answers will vary. Check students' work.**

c. Discussion How would you revise the equation you wrote in Question 14? Explain your thinking.

16 Use your revised equation from Question 15 to predict the height of the missing driver. Compare your prediction with the one you made in Question 13. **Sample Response: about 174 cm**

15. c. Answers will vary. Sample Response: The equation prediction is always too low by about the same amount, so I need to add that amount to the height = slope × foot length equation.

✔ **QUESTION 17**

…checks that you can use an equation of a fitted line to make predictions.

17. a. $h = 4a - 13$; Sample Response: I tested the coordinates of a point on the fitted line in both equations. I chose the point (48, 180). When the arm length is 48 cm, the equation $h = 4a - 13$ gives a height closer to 180 cm than the equation $h = 4a$ does.

17 ✔ **CHECKPOINT** Use the scatter plot.

a. Which equation can you use to predict a person's height if you know his or her lower arm length: $h = 4a$ or $h = 4a - 13$? Explain your choice.

b. Use the equation you chose to predict the height of someone whose lower arm length is 45 cm. **167 cm**

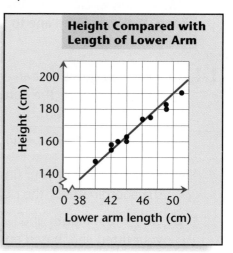

Height Compared with Length of Lower Arm

Height (cm) — vertical axis: 140, 160, 180, 200

Lower arm length (cm) — horizontal axis: 0 38 42 46 50

HOMEWORK EXERCISES ▶ See Exs. 8–14 on p. 197.

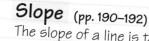

Section 3
Key Concepts

> > > > > > > > > > > > > > > > > > >

Key Terms

Slope (pp. 190–192)

The slope of a line is the ratio of its rise to its run. Sometimes the slope of a line gives you information about an everyday situation.

slope

rise

run

Example Water is added to a tub at a steady rate. The graph shows the amount of water in the tub over time. The slope of the line is a rate.

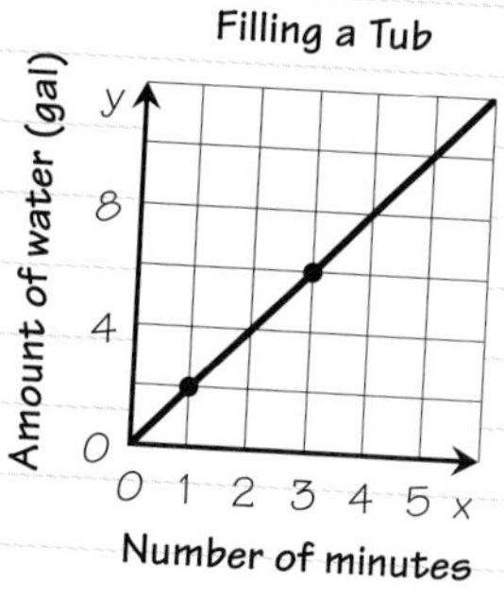

Filling a Tub

Amount of water (gal)

Number of minutes

$$\text{Slope} = \frac{\text{rise}}{\text{run}} = \frac{6-2}{3-1} = \frac{4}{2} = 2$$

Water is added to the tub at a rate of 2 gal/min.

Equations for Predictions (pp. 193–194)

You can use an equation of a fitted line to make predictions.

Example An equation of the fitted line shown is

$$w = 5.4h - 202,$$

where w = weight in pounds, and h = height in inches. You can predict that a 78 in. tall player will weigh about 219 lb.

$$w = 5.4(78) - 202$$

$$w \approx 219$$

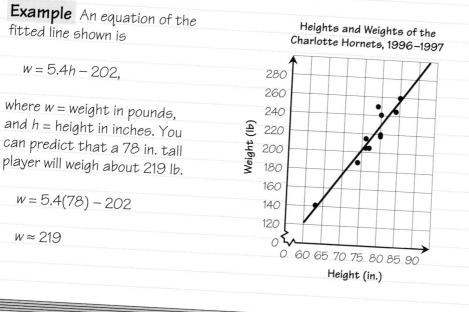

Heights and Weights of the Charlotte Hornets, 1996–1997

Weight (lb)

Height (in.)

CLOSURE QUESTION

Describe how to use a line to make predictions when given a set of data involving two variables.

Sample Response: Set the data in ordered pairs and graph them on a scatter plot. Draw a fitted line for the plot. You can then use the line to predict the value of one variable when given the other, or you can find the equation of the line and then use the equation to make predictions.

---

18 **Key Concepts Question** Explain how you can check to make sure that that the equation for the fitted line in the second Example is the correct equation. **Sample Response: Choose points on the line to substitute values in each equation or to write an equation.**

Section ③ Practice & Application Exercises

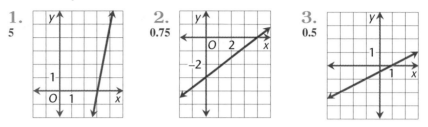

Find the slope of each line.

1. 5

2. 0.75

3. 0.5

4. Darryl says that the slope of the line in Exercise 3 is 2. Is he correct? Explain. **Sample Response: No; he calculated the run over the rise.**

5. **Race Walking** The first official world record in the 20 km race walk was set in 1918 by Niels Petersen of Denmark. As of 1996, Bernardo Segura of Mexico held the world record. The graph shows the average walking rates of these two athletes.

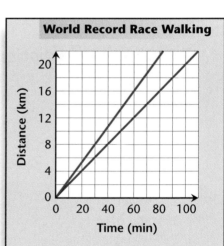

World Record Race Walking

a. Which line shows Segura's walking rate? How do you know? **the upper line; The slope is steeper so the rate is greater.**

b. Find each athlete's average rate. **Segura: about 0.27 km/min; Peterson: 0.2 km/min**

c. Write equations you can use to find the average distance each athlete walks in a given amount of time. **Segura: $d = 0.27t$; Peterson: $d = 0.2t$ where d = distance (km) and t = time (min)**

6. d.

Sarah Kane's Earnings

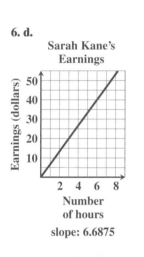

slope: 6.6875

6. The graph models the relationship between the number of hours Sarah Kane works and the amount she gets paid.

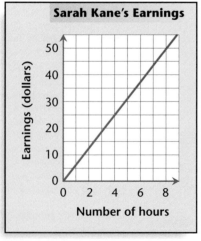

Sarah Kane's Earnings

a. How much does Sarah get paid per hour? **$6.25**

b. Write an equation for the amount she makes based on the number of hours she works. **$s = 6.25h$ where s = salary ($) and h = number of hours**

c. Suppose Sarah gets a 7% raise in her hourly wage. Write a new equation to model the amount she makes. **$s = 6.6875h$**

d. Graph the new equation. Find the slope of the graph. **See above.**

7. **Challenge** Find the slope of a line that passes through the points (−2, 4) and (3, 4). **0**

Match each equation with one of the lines. Explain your thinking.

8. $y = 0.75x$

B; slope is 0.75, (0, 0) is on the line.

9. $y = 0.75x - 10$

A; slope is 0.75, (0, –10) is on the line.

10. $y = 0.75x + 10$

C; slope is 0.75, (0, 10) is on the line.

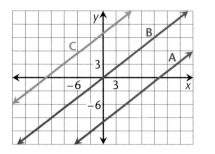

Nutrition Leafy green vegetables are great sources of vitamin C whether raw or cooked. Use the table for Exercises 11–13.

11. **Interpreting Data** On average, what percent of vitamin C is lost when you cook a typical leafy green vegetable? Explain your answer.
See above.

12. a. Use the data to make a scatter plot. Use the horizontal axis for the raw vegetable data v and the vertical axis for the cooked vegetable data c. See Additional Answers.

b. Draw a fitted line. Then find its slope. 0.5

c. Suppose you guess that an equation for your fitted line follows this pattern:

Amount in cooked = slope × amount in raw.

Write an equation for your fitted line based on this pattern. $c = 0.5v$

d. As you did in Exploration 2, use two different methods to predict values for c. Answers will vary. Check students' work.

e. How would you revise the equation you wrote in part (c)? Explain your thinking. Sample Response: I would adjust the slope based on my new predictions.

13. Use your equation from Exercise 12(e) to predict the amount of vitamin C in 1 lb of cooked mustard spinach. (1 lb of raw mustard spinach has about 590 milligrams of vitamin C.) 295 mg

11. about 50%; Sample Response: Subtract the amount of Vitamin C in the cooked vegetables from the amount in the raw vegetables and divide by the amount in the raw vegetables.

Approximate Amounts of Vitamin C in Leafy Green Vegetables (in milligrams)		
Vegetable	1 lb Raw	1 lb Cooked*
Bok choy	113	68
Collards	417	209
Kale	844	422
Mustard greens	440	218
Spinach	231	127
Swiss chard	145	73
Turnip greens	631	313
* Amounts can vary depending on cooking time and amount of water used.		

14. Sample Response: No, the sample is too small to let me reasonably predict the height of anyone in the world.

Discussion

Exercise 14 checks that you understand how reasonable it is to make a prediction from a scatter plot.

Reflecting ◀▶ on the Section

Be prepared to discuss your response to Exercise 14 in class.

14. In Exploration 2 you predicted height from foot length using data collected from a sample of people. Do you think the sample will enable you to reasonably predict the height of anyone in the world from the person's foot length? Explain. See above.

Evaluate each expression. (Module 3, p. 183)

15. $\dfrac{8(-4)}{-7+4}$ $10\frac{2}{3}$ 16. $3\sqrt{8-(-8)}$ 12   17. $\dfrac{\sqrt{12\cdot 3}}{8}$ $\frac{3}{4}$ 18. $\dfrac{(-12)^2}{11+1}$ 12

19. Tell what inverse operation you would use to solve $\frac{x}{8} = 17$. Then solve the equation. (Module 1, p. 62) **multiplication; 136**

Use a proportion to find each percent. (Module 2, p. 90)

20. 15% of 90 13.5   21. 22.5% of 118 26.55   22. 0.4% of 17 0.068

Working on the Module Project

Solving a Mystery

Making Predictions In Chapter 3 of *The Mystery of Blacktail Canyon*, Officer Charlotte Lopez examines the footprints and the length of the stride of the person they are tracking. You used Charlotte's measurement of foot length to predict the missing driver's height in Exploration 2 on pages 193–194. You can also use her clue about the missing driver's stride length to get more information.

SET UP

You will need The Mystery of Blacktail Canyon.

CLUE Measurements taken by Officer Lopez:
- foot length: 29 cm
- stride length: 155 cm

5 The scatter plot is based on stride length and height data collected from 10 adults. Which equation best matches the fitted line? C

   A. $y = 0.6x - 84$

   B. $y = 0.6x$

   C. $y = 0.6x + 84$

6 a. Use the equation you chose in Project Question 5 to predict the height of the driver from the stride length measurement. **177 cm**

   b. Use this prediction and the one from Exploration 2 to give a reasonable range of heights for the driver. **Sample Response: from 174 to 177 cm**

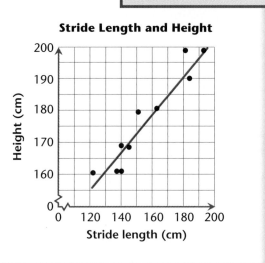

Stride Length and Height

Section 3
Extra Skill Practice

Find the slope of each line.

1.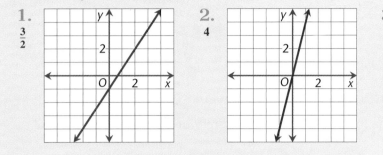
$\dfrac{3}{2}$

2.
4

3.
$\dfrac{1}{3}$

The scatterplot shows the number of pounds of ice used each day at a school lunch center based on the outdoor temperature. Use the scatterplot for Exercises 4–6.

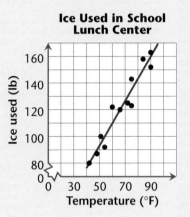

Ice Used in School Lunch Center

4. Predict the amount of ice used if the temperature is 70°F. about 125 lb

5. Find the slope of the fitted line. $\dfrac{5}{3}$

6. Let t = the temperature in °F. Let p = the number of pounds of ice used. Which equation can you use to predict the number of pounds of ice used if you know the outdoor temperature? D

   A. $p = \dfrac{5}{3}t$ B. $p = \dfrac{3}{5}t + 10$ C. $p = \dfrac{3}{5}t - 10$ D. $p = \dfrac{5}{3}t + 10$

Standardized Testing ▶ Open-ended

Make up a story that explains the graph below. Write a title and appropriate labels and scales on the graph. Be sure to explain how the situation shown by the red line is different from the situation shown by the green line. Answers will vary. Check students' work.

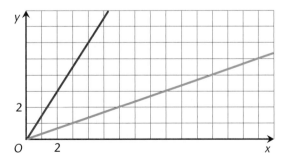

FOR ASSESSMENT AND PORTFOLIOS

Mystery State

The Situation See the Resource Book for a detailed discussion of this Extended Exploration.

Try the following puzzle. Is mystery or mathematics at work?

* Pick an integer between 1 and 10.
* Multiply your number by 6.
* Add 12.
* Divide by 3.
* Subtract 4.
* Divide by your original number.
* Add 4.
* Match the number with the corresponding letter of the alphabet (1 = A, 2 = B, *etc.*).
* Think of a state in the United States that begins with that letter.
* Look at the third letter of the name of the state. Think of a fruit that begins with that letter and grows in that state.
* Turn your book upside-down and look at the bottom of the page to complete the mystery.

See Additional Answers.
The Problem

Find out why the mystery puzzle works. Then create one of your own.

Something to Think About

* How might examining a mystery puzzle with fewer steps help you?
* Does this puzzle work for any positive integer? Would it work for negative integers? decimals? fractions?

Present Your Results

Write your puzzle on a sheet of paper. Include the solution on the back. Explain why the puzzle above works, and why your mystery puzzle works.

You thought of oranges in Florida.

Section ④ Similar Figures and Constructions

IN THIS SECTION

EXPLORATION 1
◆ Similar Figures

EXPLORATION 2
◆ Bisecting Chords

CLIFF DWELLERS

WARM-UP EXERCISES

Solve each proportion.
Round decimal answers
to the nearest tenth.

1. $\frac{2}{3} = \frac{x}{9}$ 6

2. $\frac{20}{16} = \frac{5}{x}$ 4

3. $\frac{45}{126} = \frac{x}{51}$ 18.2

4. $\frac{4.3}{x} = \frac{9.7}{21.4}$ 9.5

5. What are
perpendicular lines?

Lines that intersect in
a right angle.

Setting the Stage ▸▸▸▸▸▸▸▸▸▸▸▸▸▸▸▸▸▸▸▸▸▸▸▸▸▸▸▸▸▸

The Story So Far...

▶ **The missing driver's tracks lead to a previously undiscovered cliff
dwelling. Nageela wonders if her 40 m rope will reach the site.
Charlotte Lopez has a method for estimating the cliff height.**

She used her pocket knife to pry the ink cartridge out of the plastic
body of the pen.

. . . Charlotte marked a spot on the ground, then paced off the
distance to the foot of the cliff. Next, she had Jim stand between her
marked spot and the cliff. Finally, she lay down with her head on the
ground and sighted the top of Jim's head through the hollow pen.

"Take two steps back, Jim," she said.
"Good! Now, how tall are you?"

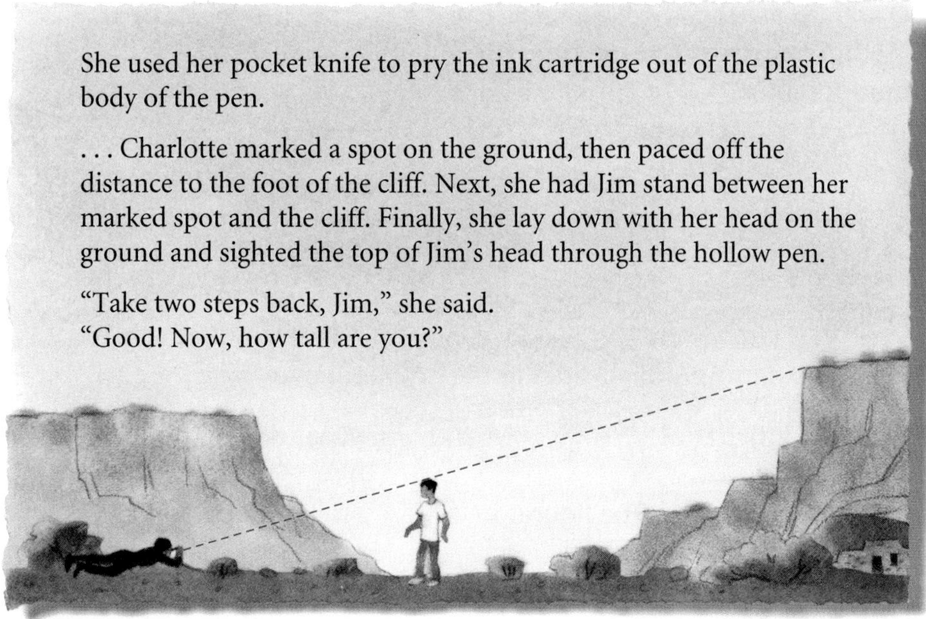

Drawing not to scale

Think About It

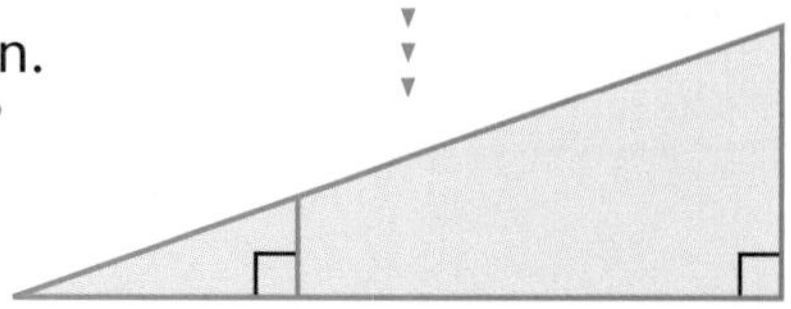

1 The diagram models the situation in the story selection.
Which line represents Jim? Which represents the cliff?
the shorter perpendicular line; the longer perpendicular line

2 What kind of triangles do you see in the diagram?
right triangles

GOAL

LEARN HOW TO...
- tell whether triangles are similar
- make indirect measurements

AS YOU...
- estimate the height of a cliff

KEY TERMS
- similar
- corresponding angles
- corresponding sides

 Exploration 1

Similar Figures
Similar Figures

Similar Figures

SET UP *You will need:* • *Labsheet 4A* • *ruler* • *protractor*

▶ As you'll see in this exploration, Charlotte Lopez uses *similar* figures to estimate the cliff height. Two figures are **similar** if they have the same shape, but not necessarily the same size. The figures below are similar.

∠P and ∠T are *corresponding angles.*
Corresponding angles have the same measure.

$m\angle P = m\angle T$

> Read $m\angle T$ as "the measure of angle *T*."

$\overline{PQ}$ and $\overline{TU}$ are *corresponding sides.* The lengths of **corresponding sides** are in proportion.

$$\frac{PQ}{TU} = \frac{QR}{UV}.$$

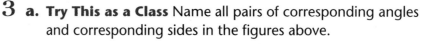

> Read $\overline{TU}$ as "segment *TU*." Read *TU* as "the length of segment *TU*."

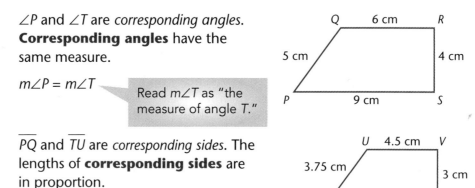

3. a. ∠*P*, ∠*T*; ∠*Q*, ∠*U*; ∠*R*, ∠*V*; ∠*S*, ∠*W*; $\overline{PQ}$, $\overline{TU}$; $\overline{QR}$, $\overline{UV}$; $\overline{RS}$, $\overline{VW}$; $\overline{PS}$, $\overline{TW}$
b. All four ratios are 4:3; The ratios are equal.

3 a. Try This as a Class Name all pairs of corresponding angles and corresponding sides in the figures above.

b. Find the ratios $\frac{PQ}{TU}$, $\frac{QR}{UV}$, $\frac{RS}{VW}$, and $\frac{PS}{TW}$. What do you notice?

✔ QUESTION 4

...checks your understanding of the definition of similar figures.

4 ✔ CHECKPOINT The figures below are similar. Copy and complete each statement.

a. $m\angle C = m$ __?__ $\angle G$

b. $\frac{BC}{FG} = \frac{?}{GH}$ *CD*

c. $\frac{?}{AD} = \frac{EF}{?}$ *EH; AB*

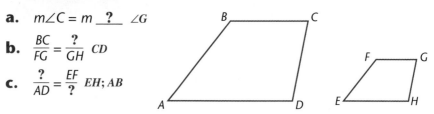

▶ **Naming Similar Figures** The symbol ~ means "is similar to." When you name similar figures, be sure to put their corresponding angles in the same order.

5 **Try this as a Class** The triangles at the right are similar. Which of the statements below are written correctly? Explain your thinking.

A. △ABC ~ △CDE

B. △ABC ~ △EDC

C. △BAC ~ △DEC

D. △ACB ~ △ECD

B, C, D; The corresponding angles are listed in the same order.

> Symbols are used to show which angles have the same measure.

> A vertex is a point where sides of a figure come together.

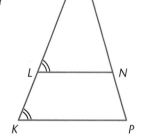

6 **Use Labsheet 4A.** You'll use a protractor and a ruler to determine whether the *Two Right Triangles* are similar. See above.

▶ To tell whether figures are similar, you need to check corresponding angle measures and the ratios of corresponding side lengths. For similar *triangles*, you only need to check the angle measures.

7 **a.** Name two triangles in the diagram at the right that appear to be similar. △MLN and △MKP

b. Which angle do the triangles share? ∠M

c. Which pair of corresponding angles have the same measure? ∠L and ∠K

d. Discussion The sum of the angles of any triangle is 180°. Explain why you do not need a protractor to tell whether these triangles are similar.

▶ **A Test for Similar Triangles** Two triangles are similar if two angles of one triangle have the same measures as two angles of the other triangle.

8 **Try This as a Class** Explain why the test for similar triangles works for all triangles. Do you think it would work for other similar figures? Would it work for the triangles on page 201? Explain.

▶ **Indirect Measurement** In *The Mystery of Blacktail Canyon*, Charlotte cannot directly measure the height of the cliff. She can use similar figures to make an indirect measurement.

6. a. $AB = 4.8$ cm, $BC = 2.4$ cm, $AC = 4.3$ cm; $AD = 1.8$ cm, $DE = 0.9$ cm, $AE = 1.6$ cm; All ratios are about 2.7

b. $m\angle A = 30°$, $m\angle B = 60°$, $m\angle C = 90°$, $m\angle A = 30°$, $m\angle D = 60°$, $m\angle E = 90°$

c. Sample Response: ∠C and ∠E are marked as right angles so I knew their measures were 90°. I measured ∠A and got 30° and then used the fact that the sum of the angles of a triangle is 180° to get measures of 60° for ∠B and ∠D.

d. All the corresponding angles have the same measure and all the corresponding sides are in the same proportion.

7. d. The sum of the angle measures is the same for both triangles. Since $m\angle M = m\angle M$ and $m\angle L = m\angle K$, $m\angle N = m\angle P$

8. Sample Response: The sum of the measures of the angles of any triangle is 180° so when you know the measure of two angles you can find the measure of the third, 180 less the sum of the two known measures. So if two triangles have two angles with the same measure, the measure of third angle in each triangle would have to be the same; No; Yes; It works for all triangles.

To estimate the cliff height, Charlotte uses what she knows about similar triangles to write and solve a proportion.

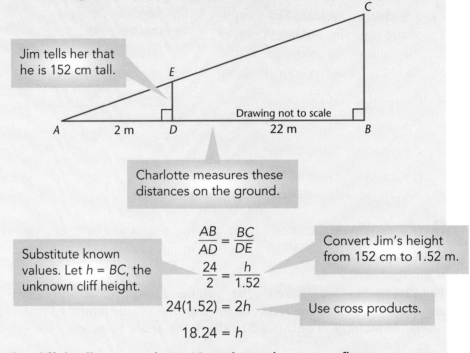

Jim tells her that he is 152 cm tall.

Drawing not to scale

A   2 m   D   22 m   B

Charlotte measures these distances on the ground.

Substitute known values. Let $h = BC$, the unknown cliff height.

$$\frac{AB}{AD} = \frac{BC}{DE}$$

$$\frac{24}{2} = \frac{h}{1.52}$$

$$24(1.52) = 2h$$

$$18.24 = h$$

Convert Jim's height from 152 cm to 1.52 m.

Use cross products.

The cliff dwellings are about 18 m above the canyon floor.

▶ **Try This as a Class** For Questions 9–11, use the Example.

9 Suppose you do not convert Jim's height to meters. What answer do you get? **1824 cm**

10 Can Charlotte use the proportion $\frac{DE}{BC} = \frac{DA}{BA}$ to find the distance to the cliff dwellings? Explain. **Yes; She can use any proportion involving corresponding sides that has the same crossproducts as in the Example.**

11 In *The Mystery of Blacktail Canyon*, Nageela's climbing rope is 40 m long. She needs "as much going down as going up." Is her rope long enough to reach the cliff dwellings? **Yes.**

...checks that you can use a proportion to find an unknown side length.

12 ✔ **CHECKPOINT** △RST ~ △UVW.
Tell which side length you can find. Then find it.
UV; about 6.7 in.

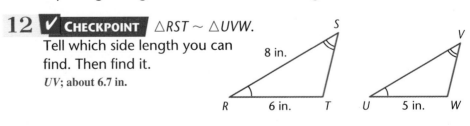

8 in.

R   6 in.   T   U   5 in.   W

HOMEWORK EXERCISES ▶ See Exs. 1–14 on pp. 208–209.

Exploration 2

BISECTING Chords

SET UP *Work with a partner. You will need:* • *Labsheets 4B and 4C*
• *scissors* • *compass* • *ruler*

GOAL

LEARN HOW TO...
♦ find a
   perpendicular
   bisector of a
   chord

AS YOU...
♦ estimate
   dimensions of
   artifacts

KEY TERMS
♦ circle
♦ chord
♦ diameter
♦ radius
♦ perpendicular
   bisector

The Story So Far...

▶ After using the rope to climb up the cliff, Nageela discovers broken
pottery pieces in a dwelling. Jim is surprised that Nageela can
estimate the original size of the pottery.

"You mean you can tell the diameter of a platter just
by tracing a little broken part? How do you do it?"

".... It's easy, really." Nageela knelt and drew a circle
with her finger. "But first you have to know a few
things about circles."

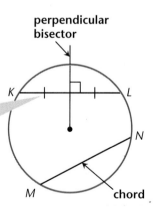

13 **Use Labsheet 4B.**

   a. Cut out *Circle 1*. Fold the circle in half and draw a segment on
   the crease. Then rotate the circle and repeat with a new crease.

   b. What is another name for the segments you drew? Where
   do they intersect? Would other segments constructed in the
   same way intersect at the same point?

   13. b. diameters; at the
   center of the circle; Yes.

   c. Cut out *Circle 2* and fold it so points *K* and *L* meet. Draw a
   segment on the crease. Refold so points *M* and *N* meet. Draw
   a segment on the crease. Where do the segments intersect?
   at the center of the circle

14 **Try This as a Class** $\overline{KL}$ and $\overline{MN}$ are called
chords. A **chord** is a segment that joins
two points on a circle. The segment you
drew through each chord is a
perpendicular bisector. Why is this a
good name for these segments?
Sample Response: It is a perpendicular
line that divides the chord in half.

Symbols are
used to show
that the two
halves of $\overline{KL}$ are
equal in length.

perpendicular
bisector

chord

Circles

A **circle** is the set of all points in a plane that are a given distance from a point called the center of the circle.

A **chord** is a segment that has both endpoints on the circle.

A **diameter** is a chord that passes through the center of the circle.

center

A **radius** is a segment that connects a point on the circle to the center.

Constructing a Circle

First Choose a radius.

Then Draw the circle.

---

15 Discussion Use your compass to make a circle. Draw two chords. Then fold the circle to find the perpendicular bisector of each chord. What do you observe about the perpendicular bisectors of two chords drawn in the same circle?

They intersect at the center of the circle.

▶ **Nageela found a pottery fragment that was originally part of a platter. Her first steps in estimating the platter's size are shown.**

First Nageela traced the pottery fragment's outline in the sand.

Then She drew two chords.

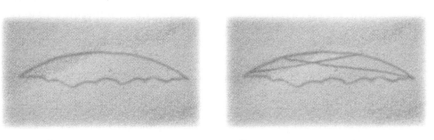

16. Sample Response: She will find the perpendicular bisectors of the chords, then draw a circle with its center at the intersection of the perpendicular bisectors. Then she'll know the radius.

16 Discussion What do you think Nageela's next steps are?

17  **CHECKPOINT** **Use Labsheet 4C.** You'll use perpendicular bisectors to estimate the original diameter of a *Circular Platter*.

about 16.5 cm

✔ **QUESTION 17**

...checks your understanding of perpendicular bisectors and chords.

HOMEWORK EXERCISES ▶ See Exs. 15–19 on p. 210.

Section 4
Key Concepts

Similar Figures (pp. 202–203)

Two figures are similar if they have the same shape, but not necessarily the same size. The measures of their corresponding angles are equal, and the ratios of their corresponding side lengths are in proportion.

Example △MNL ~ △PQR

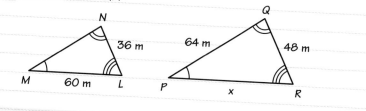

Similar Triangles and Indirect Measurement
(pp. 203–204)

Two triangles are similar if two angles of one triangle have the same measure as two angles of the other. You can use similar triangles to make indirect measurements and find missing side lengths.

Example Find the length of $\overline{PR}$ in the diagram above.

Let x = PR. Solve for x.

$$\frac{ML}{PR} = \frac{NL}{QR}$$

$$\frac{60}{x} = \frac{36}{48}$$

$$x = 80 \text{ m}$$

Circles and Chords (pp. 205–206)

The perpendicular bisectors of any two chords on a circle intersect at the center of the circle.

The perpendicular bisector forms a right angle with the chord. It divides the chord in half.

similar

corresponding angles

corresponding sides

circle

chord

diameter

radius

perpendicular bisector

19. Sample Response: Label the endpoints and fold the paper so that they meet. Label the midpoint of the line, then fold the paper again so that the midpoint meets one of the endpoints.

Key Concepts Questions

18 Use the triangles above. Find the length of $\overline{MN}$. 48 m

19 Draw a line segment on a piece of paper. Describe a method for dividing the segment into four equal parts.

YOU WILL NEED

For Ex. 11:
♦ ruler

For Exs. 20–21:
♦ graph paper

For Exs. 18, 33:
♦ compass

For Ex. 34:
♦ protractor

For Exercises 1–3, use similar figures *ABCD* and *MNQP*.

1. Find the ratio of the corresponding side lengths. $\frac{5}{3.3}$

2. Copy and complete each statement.

   a. $m\angle A = m\ \underline{\ ?\ }\ \angle M$

   b. $\frac{BA}{NM} = \frac{BC}{?}\ NQ$

   c. $\frac{QP}{CD} = \frac{?}{AD}\ MP$

3. Find each measure.

   a. $m\angle M$ **65°**   b. *NM* **7.26 cm**   c. *CD* **7.58 cm**

For each pair of figures, write a mathematical statement saying the figures are similar.   **4–7. Sample Responses are given.**

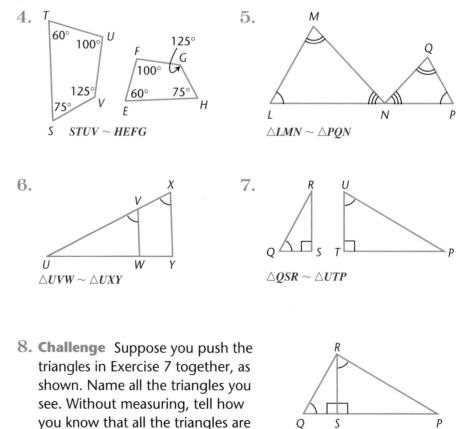

4.
   STUV ~ HEFG

5.
   △*LMN* ~ △*PQN*

6.
   △*UVW* ~ △*UXY*

7.
   △*QSR* ~ △*UTP*

8. △*QSR*, △*QRP*, △*RSP*;
$m\angle Q = m\angle PRS = m\angle Q$
and, since $m\angle QRS = 90° - m\angle Q$, $m\angle PRQ = m\angle PRS + m\angle QRS = m\angle Q + 90° - m\angle Q = 90°$.
Then two angles of each triangle have the same measures as two angles of each other triangle.

8. **Challenge** Suppose you push the triangles in Exercise 7 together, as shown. Name all the triangles you see. Without measuring, tell how you know that all the triangles are similar.

For Exercises 9–11, use the trapezoids _MNQR_ and _NLPQ_.

9. Byron assumes that the trapezoids are similar. Why do you think he might make that assumption?

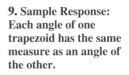

9. Sample Response: Each angle of one trapezoid has the same measure as an angle of the other.

10. Suppose the trapezoids are similar. Which of these statements would be true? **B**

   A. $\dfrac{PQ}{QR} = \dfrac{MN}{NL}$

   B. $\dfrac{PQ}{QR} = \dfrac{LP}{NQ}$

11. Use a ruler to check whether the statement you chose in Exercise 10 is true. Are the trapezoids similar? **No.**

12. **Open-ended** Explain why you need to check more than the angle measures to tell whether the figures described below are similar. Sketch some examples to support your answers.

   a. 2 rectangles   b. 2 trapezoids   c. 2 parallelograms

   The sides may not be in proportion. Check students' drawings.

13. **Challenge** Kasey can see the top of a 788 ft tall skyscraper over the top of a 15 ft flag pole at her school. She estimates that she is about 300 ft away from the flagpole. About how many miles is she from the skyscraper? (*Note:* 1 mi = 5280 ft) **about 3 mi**

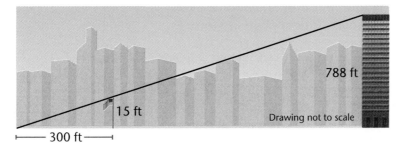

788 ft

15 ft

Drawing not to scale

—— 300 ft ——

14. As shown by the diagram, you can think of rays of light from the sun as hitting the ground at the same angle.

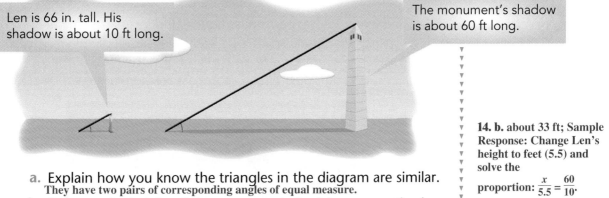

Len is 66 in. tall. His shadow is about 10 ft long.

The monument's shadow is about 60 ft long.

14. b. about 33 ft; Sample Response: Change Len's height to feet (5.5) and solve the proportion: $\dfrac{x}{5.5} = \dfrac{60}{10}$.

   a. Explain how you know the triangles in the diagram are similar.
   They have two pairs of corresponding angles of equal measure.
   b. Estimate the height of the monument. Explain your method.

15. Yes; If you fold along one diagonal you'll see the top and right sides are the same length. Fold along the other and you'll see the top and left sides as well as the bottom and right sides are the same length.

16. a.

b. Yes; Measure the lengths of the sides to find out if they are in proportion.

17.

Yes.

15. Visual Thinking Troy drew a rectangle. He noticed that one diagonal was the perpendicular bisector of the other diagonal. He decided that the rectangle must be a square. Do you agree with his decision? Explain. Use sketches to support your answer.

16. a. Draw a rectangle and a diagonal. Then draw a smaller rectangle inside the first rectangle, as shown.

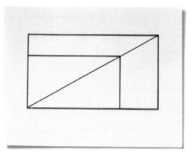

 b. Do the rectangles appear to be similar? What do you need to check to make sure?

 c. Repeat part (a) several times. Use different sizes of rectangles each time. Do all the rectangle pairs appear to be similar? Yes.

17. Use the method in Exercise 16 to make two parallelograms that are not rectangles. Does this method appear to produce similar parallelograms? Use examples to support your answer.

18. a. Draw a circle. Then draw two chords. The chords can be any length, but they should intersect. Connect the endpoints to form two triangles, as shown.
 Answers will vary. Check students' drawings.

 b. Repeat part (a) at least three times, using different chords.
 Answers will vary. Check students' drawings.

 c. What do you notice about the triangles in each circle?
 They are similar.

Reflecting ◀▶ on the Section

19. The design below uses similar figures and segments that are perpendicular bisectors. Create your own design. Explain which figures in your design are similar, and give the ratio of the corresponding sides. Which segments are perpendicular bisectors?
 Answers will vary. Check students' work.

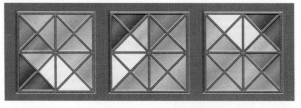

S p i r a l ▶Review

Plot each pair of points on a coordinate plane and draw a line through them. Find the slope of the line. (Module 3, p. 195)

20. (1, 1) and (–3, 3) **21.** (0, –5) and (2, 3)

Find each percent of change. (Module 2, p. 100)

22. A $45.00 book sells for $30.00. $33\frac{1}{3}\%$ **decrease**

23. A tree grows from 4 ft to 5 ft 6 in. **37.5% increase**

24. In 1850, New Mexico's population was about 93,516. In 1860, it was about 61,547. **about 34% decrease**

Find each product. (Toolbox, p. 600)

25. $3.6 \cdot 10^2$ **26.** $0.4 \cdot 10^1$ **27.** $249 \cdot 10^3$ **28.** $0.007 \cdot 10^2$
   360   **4**   **249,000**   **0.7**

29. $75.3 \cdot 10^4$ **30.** $9.87 \cdot 10^5$ **31.** $0.16 \cdot 10^2$ **32.** $10.18 \cdot 10^6$
   753,000   **987,000**   **16**   **10,180,000**

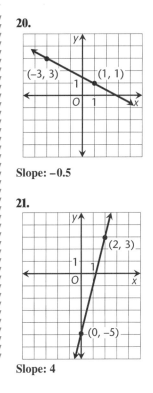

20.

Slope: –0.5

21.

Slope: 4

Extension ▶ ▶

Making a Conjecture

33. Draw five circles with the same radius. For each circle, follow these steps:

First Draw a diameter.

Then Choose a point on the circle and draw a triangle. The diameter should form one side of the triangle. Be sure to choose a different point for each circle.

Answers will vary. Check students' drawings.

All three vertices of the triangle should be on the circle.

One side of the triangle should be the diameter of the circle.

34. Compare the angle measures of the triangles. Then make a conjecture about triangles drawn this way. Did the observations of other students support your conjecture? **They are all right triangles: Yes.**

Section 4

Extra Skill Practice

For Exercises 1–3, use the triangles shown. The triangles are similar.

1. Find the ratio of the corresponding side lengths. $\frac{3}{8}$

2. Copy and complete each statement.

   a. $\frac{WV}{WY} = \frac{?}{XY}$ UV

   b. $\frac{UV}{?} = \frac{?}{YW}$ XY; VW

   c. $\triangle UVW \sim$ __?__ $\triangle XYW$

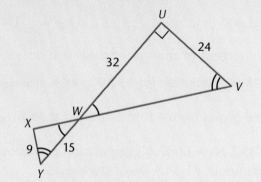

3. Find each measure.

   a. $m\angle X$ 90°   b. XW 12   c. VW 40

You are standing on shore at point A. A raft is anchored in a bay at point B. Your friends Cathy, Damien and Ellen are standing at points C, D, and E.

4. Which triangles are similar? How do you know? $\triangle CDE \sim \triangle CAB$; $\angle C$ is in both triangles and $m\angle D = m\angle A = 90°$

5. Explain how your friends can help you find the distance from you to the raft by using similar triangles. Is there any information on the drawing that you will *not* need? See above.

5. Use the proportion $\frac{20}{40} = \frac{15}{x}$ then solve for x; The length of $\overline{CE}$ is not needed.

6. Find the distance from point A to point B.   30 m

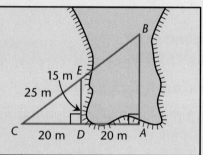

Standardized Testing ◀▶ Free Response

1. $\overline{AB}$ is the perpendicular bisector of $\overline{CD}$. Name two segments in the diagram that have the same measure and two angles that have the same measure. $\overline{CP}, \overline{PD}$; any two of $\angle CPA, \angle CPB, \angle BPD$, and $\angle DPA$

2. Suppose the measures of the corresponding sides of two similar rectangles are in the ratio 2 : 1. Give possible dimensions of the rectangles. Include a sketch of the rectangles with their dimensions labeled. Sample Response: 14 cm by 6 cm and 7 cm by 3 cm; Check student's drawings.

Section 5 Scientific Notation and Decimal Equations

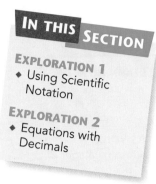

Forgotten BONES

Setting the Stage ▸▸▸▸▸▸▸▸▸▸▸▸▸▸▸▸▸▸▸▸▸▸▸▸▸▸▸▸▸▸▸▸▸▸▸▸▸

SET UP   *You will need Labsheet 5A.*

The Story So Far...

▸ Nageela visits Dr. Beatrice Leschensky, a scientist who is analyzing the bones found at the site. Dr. Leschensky explains how she uses *carbon dating* to estimate the age of the bones.

"Every living creature contains a certain amount of a radioactive substance known as *carbon-14*. After a plant or an animal dies, the carbon-14 decays, so that there is less and less carbon-14 over time. After about 5730 years, only half the carbon-14 remains. After another 5730 years or so, only one fourth the carbon-14 remains. After each additional 5730 years, only half the previous amount of carbon-14 remains. By measuring the amount of carbon-14 in these bones, I was able to estimate their age. That's all there is to it."

Think About It

1 Scientists say that carbon-14 has a half-life of 5730 years. Why is *half-life* a good term to use? **Sample Response: because half of the carbon-14 remains**

2 What fraction of carbon-14 is left in an 11,460-year-old bone? in a 17,190-year-old bone? How do you know? **one-fourth; one-eighth;** $\frac{1}{2} \cdot \frac{1}{2} = \frac{1}{4}$ **and** $\frac{1}{2} \cdot \frac{1}{4} = \frac{1}{8}$

3 **Use Labsheet 5A.** Use a table and a graph to model the *Half-Life of Carbon-14*. **See Additional Answers.**

▸ In this section, you'll use mathematics to find out more about the bones found in the cliff dwelling in *The Mystery of Blacktail Canyon*.

LEARN HOW TO...
◆ write very large numbers in scientific notation

AS YOU...
◆ estimate ages of bones

KEY TERMS
◆ scientific notation
◆ decimal notation

 Exploration 1

Using **Scientific** Notation

SET UP *You will need:* • *Labsheet 5A* • *calculator*

▶ Here is a summary of Dr. Leschensky's report on the bones found in the cliff dwelling. Use the report for Questions 4–6.

Carbon-14 Dating of Bone Samples

Bone sample	Gender	Bone type	Diameter (cm)	Length (cm)	Estimated age (years)
1	male	femur	3.3	38.9	$1.7 \cdot 10^2$
2	female	femur	3.1	35.6	$1.18 \cdot 10^3$

$$10^3 = 10 \cdot 10 \cdot 10$$

FOR ▶ HELP
with *powers*, see
TOOLBOX, p. 600

4. Sample 1: 170 years, Sample 2: 1180 years; Sample 1: 1828, Sample 2: 818

4 About how many years old was each bone sample? To what year does each bone date back? (Assume *The Mystery of Blacktail Canyon* takes place in 1998.)

▶ **Writing Very Large Numbers** The ages in Dr. Leschensky's report are written in *scientific notation*. Scientists use this notation as shorthand for writing some numbers.

Decimal notation		Scientific notation
5,900,000,000	=	$5.9 \cdot 10^9$

A number greater than or equal to 1 and less than 10

A power of 10

5. a. No; 11.8 is greater than 10.
b. Yes; 6.9 is greater than or equal to 1 and less than 10 and it's multiplied by a power of 10.
c. No; 0.7 is less than 1.
d. No; 5^3 is not a power of 10.

5 **Try This as a Class** Tell whether each number is in scientific notation. Explain your answers.

   a. $11.8 \cdot 10^7$ **b.** $6.9 \cdot 10^5$ **c.** $0.7 \cdot 10^{18}$ **d.** $1.2 \cdot 5^3$

6 Write each product as a number in decimal notation.

   a. $9.3 \cdot 10^4$ **b.** $4.5 \cdot 10^5$ **c.** $3.8 \cdot 10^6$ **d.** $2.3 \cdot 10^1$ 23
   93,000   450,000   3,800,000

The age of the oldest fossils found on Earth is about 3,500,000,000. Write this age in scientific notation.

SAMPLE RESPONSE

First Move the decimal point to get a number greater than or equal to 1 and less than 10.

3,500,000,000

Then Count how many places the decimal point moves to decide on the power of 10.

$3.5 \cdot 10^9$

Decimal point moved 9 places to the left.

The fossils are about $3.5 \cdot 10^9$ years old.

---

7 Try This as a Class Jackie got a different answer for the Example above. Explain her mistake.

$3,500,000,000 = 35 \cdot 10,000,000 = 35 \cdot 10^8$

Her answer is not in scientific notation; 35 > 10.

8 Discussion Describe how you can reverse the process in the Example to write $3.5 \cdot 10^9$ in decimal notation.

8. Sample Response: Write the decimal with enough zeros to move the decimal point the number of places indicated by the power of 10.

9 Calculator Many calculators use scientific notation to display very large numbers.

a. Use the key sequence below.

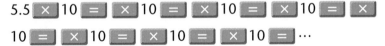

$5.5 \boxed{\times} 10 \boxed{=} \boxed{\times} 10 \boxed{=} \boxed{\times} 10 \boxed{=} \boxed{\times} 10 \boxed{=} \boxed{\times}$
$10 \boxed{=} \boxed{\times} 10 \boxed{=} \boxed{\times} 10 \boxed{=} \boxed{\times} 10 \boxed{=} \cdots$

Continue multiplying each product by 10 until your calculator switches to scientific notation. How is the number of times you pressed the $\boxed{=}$ key related to the power of 10 on the display?

It is the same.

b. Your calculator may have a special key for entering numbers in scientific notation. For example, to enter $3.2 \cdot 10^{14}$, you might use one of these key sequences:

$3.2 \boxed{\text{EXP}} 14$ $\qquad$ $3.2 \boxed{\text{EE}} 14$

Find out the key sequence that your calculator uses. Then practice by entering $5.88 \cdot 10^{12}$. How does the number appear on the display? Check students' calculators.

Sample Response: 5.88 12

10 ✔ **CHECKPOINT** Write each number in scientific notation.

a. 2390 $2.39 \cdot 10^3$ $\qquad$ **b.** 4,500,000 $\qquad$ **c.** 365,000,000,000

$4.5 \cdot 10^6$ $\qquad$ $3.65 \cdot 10^{11}$

✔ **QUESTION 10**

...checks that you can write very large numbers in scientific notation.

11 **Use Labsheet 5A.** Look back at Dr. Leschensky's report on page 214. Bone sample 2 contains about $\frac{7}{8}$ of the original amount of carbon-14. Use your graph from Question 3 to estimate its age. How does this estimate compare with Dr. Leschensky's? **about 1200 years; Sample Response: It is close.**

HOMEWORK EXERCISES ▶ See Exs. 1–10 on pp. 219–220.

See Exs. 1–10 on pp. 219–220.

Look back at Dr. Leschensky's report on page 214.

GOAL

LEARN HOW TO...
◆ solve equations involving decimals

AS YOU...
◆ estimate heights

◄ **Exploration 2**

Equations with D.e.c.i.m.a.l.s

The Story So Far...

▶ Dr. Leschensky believes that the bones found in the cliff dwelling came from two skeletons, one male and one female. She explains how she can use the bones to learn more about these skeletons.

"We have a number of equations that help us predict the heights of people based on different bones of the body.... Since we have the measurements of two femurs, we will use these equations." She erased the chalkboard and wrote two formulas on it.

Male height from femur length | Female height from femur length

$$h = 61.41 + 2.38f \qquad h = 49.74 + 2.59f$$

"You see, h represents height and f is femur length in centimeters.... When we use the formulas, we get close to the real height, but the answer may not be exact."

12. Sample 1: 154 cm; Sample 2: 142 cm; Sample Response: Parts of the bone may have disintegrated enough to change the length.

12 Look back at Dr. Leschensky's data from page 214 to estimate the height of each skeleton to the nearest centimeter. Explain why it may not be reasonable to make a closer estimate.

13 Dr. Leschensky is 172 cm tall. Write an equation you could use to estimate her femur length. $172 = 49.74 + 2.59f$ where f represents femur length

14. Step 1: Substitute 152 for h in the formula; Step 2: Subtract 61.41 from both sides of the equation to undo the addition; Step 3: Simplify; Step 4: Divide both sides of the equation by 2.38 to undo the multiplication; Step 5: Simplify.

16. a. $100(152) = 100(61.41 + 2.38f)$
$$15{,}200 = 6141 + 238f$$
$$15{,}200 - 6141 = 6141 + 238f - 6141$$
$$9059 = 238f$$
$$\frac{9059}{238} = \frac{238f}{238}$$
$$38.06 = f$$

b. Sample Responses are given.
$10(9.7) = 10(3 + 2.7x)$; 1; There is one digit to the right of the decimal point.

EXAMPLE

Jim's height is 152 cm. Nageela uses the formula $h = 61.41 + 2.38f$ to estimate his femur length to the nearest centimeter.

Substitute 152 for h in the formula. Then solve using inverse operations.

$$152 = 61.41 + 2.38f$$
$$152 - 61.41 = 61.41 + 2.38f - 61.41$$
$$90.59 = 2.38f$$
$$\frac{90.59}{2.38} = \frac{2.38f}{2.38}$$
$$38.06 \approx f$$

Jim's femur is about 38 cm long.

14 **Try This as a Class** Describe the steps in the Example above. Tell which inverse operations were used. **See above.**

15 **Discussion** As shown at the right, Nageela checks her solution from the Example. She wonders if she is wrong. What do you think? Explain. **The answers are different because the decimal has been rounded to the nearest hundredth.**

$$152 \stackrel{?}{=} 61.41 + 2.38(38.06)$$
$$152 \neq 151.99$$

16 **Discussion** You can first multiply both sides of the equation shown in the Example by a power of ten to avoid working with decimals. **See above.**

$$100(152) = 100(61.41 + 2.38f)$$

a. Copy this first step. Then finish solving the equation.

b. Show how you would use this method to solve $9.7 = 3 + 2.7x$. What power of ten did you use? Why?

17 ✔ **CHECKPOINT** Solve each equation. Round decimal solutions to the nearest hundredth.

a. $18 = 3.7x - 5.3$ **6.30** **b.** $4.1 + 0.5n = 4.1$ **0** **c.** $\frac{x}{9.8} + 1 = 10$ **88.20**

d. $0.57r - 3 = 8.2$ **19.65** **e.** $\frac{m}{5.5} - 120 = -2.5$ **646.25** **f.** $\frac{t}{4.5} - 13 = -12$ **4.5**

✔ **QUESTION 17**

...checks that you can solve an equation involving decimals.

18 Estimate Dr. Leschensky's femur to the nearest centimeter by solving the equation you wrote in Question 13. **about 47 cm**

HOMEWORK EXERCISES ▶ See Exs. 11–26 on pp. 220–221.

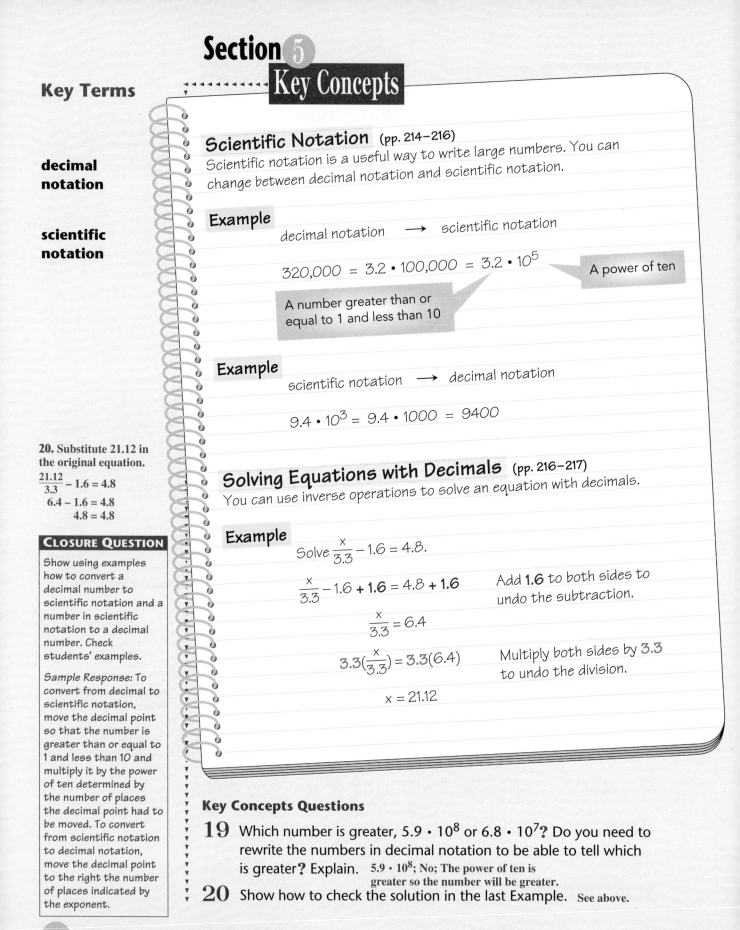

Section 5
Key Concepts

Key Terms

decimal
notation

scientific
notation

Scientific Notation (pp. 214–216)

Scientific notation is a useful way to write large numbers. You can change between decimal notation and scientific notation.

Example

decimal notation $\longrightarrow$ scientific notation

$$320{,}000 = 3.2 \cdot 100{,}000 = 3.2 \cdot 10^5$$

A power of ten

A number greater than or equal to 1 and less than 10

Example

scientific notation $\longrightarrow$ decimal notation

$$9.4 \cdot 10^3 = 9.4 \cdot 1000 = 9400$$

Solving Equations with Decimals (pp. 216–217)

You can use inverse operations to solve an equation with decimals.

Example

Solve $\dfrac{x}{3.3} - 1.6 = 4.8$.

$$\frac{x}{3.3} - 1.6 + \mathbf{1.6} = 4.8 + \mathbf{1.6}$$

Add **1.6** to both sides to undo the subtraction.

$$\frac{x}{3.3} = 6.4$$

$$\mathbf{3.3}\left(\frac{x}{3.3}\right) = \mathbf{3.3}(6.4)$$

Multiply both sides by **3.3** to undo the division.

$$x = 21.12$$

20. Substitute 21.12 in the original equation.

$$\frac{21.12}{3.3} - 1.6 = 4.8$$
$$6.4 - 1.6 = 4.8$$
$$4.8 = 4.8$$

CLOSURE QUESTION

Show using examples how to convert a decimal number to scientific notation and a number in scientific notation to a decimal number. Check students' examples.

Sample Response: To convert from decimal to scientific notation, move the decimal point so that the number is greater than or equal to 1 and less than 10 and multiply it by the power of ten determined by the number of places the decimal point had to be moved. To convert from scientific notation to decimal notation, move the decimal point to the right the number of places indicated by the exponent.

Key Concepts Questions

19 Which number is greater, $5.9 \cdot 10^8$ or $6.8 \cdot 10^7$? Do you need to rewrite the numbers in decimal notation to be able to tell which is greater? Explain. $5.9 \cdot 10^8$; No; The power of ten is greater so the number will be greater.

20 Show how to check the solution in the last Example. See above.

Section 5

Practice & Application Exercises ▶▶▶▶▶▶▶

YOU WILL NEED

For Ex. 7:
♦ calculator

For Exercises 1–4, write each number in decimal notation.

1. Approximate age of Earth: at least $4.5 \cdot 10^9$ years 4,500,000,000

2. The distance from Earth to the sun: about $9.3 \cdot 10^7$ mi 93,000,000

3. Speed of light: about $1.86 \cdot 10^5$ mi/s 186,000

4. Distance light travels in a year: about $5.88 \cdot 10^{12}$ mi 5,880,000,000,000

5. Which numbers below are written in scientific notation? Explain.

   A. $7.987 \cdot 10^2$ B. $3.57 \cdot 10^{99}$ C. $82.1 \cdot 10^3$ D. $5.13 \cdot 2^{10}$

5. A and B; The numbers are written as the product of a number greater than or equal to 1 and less than 10 and a power of ten. In C, 82.1 is greater than 10; in D, 2^{10} is not a power of 10.

Astronomy A *light-year* is the distance that light travels in a vacuum in one year. One light year ≈ $5.88 \cdot 10^{12}$ miles. Use this fact and the bar graph below for Exercises 6–8.

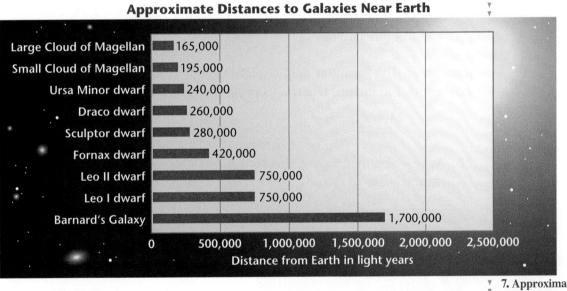

Approximate Distances to Galaxies Near Earth

Galaxy	Distance
Large Cloud of Magellan	165,000
Small Cloud of Magellan	195,000
Ursa Minor dwarf	240,000
Draco dwarf	260,000
Sculptor dwarf	280,000
Fornax dwarf	420,000
Leo II dwarf	750,000
Leo I dwarf	750,000
Barnard's Galaxy	1,700,000

Distance from Earth in light years
0   500,000   1,000,000   1,500,000   2,000,000   2,500,000

6. Which galaxy is a little more than 10 times as far from Earth as the Large Cloud of Magellan? **Barnard's Galaxy**

7. 🖩 Calculator Find the distance to each galaxy in miles. Write your answers in scientific notation. Round the decimal part of each number to the nearest tenth.

8. **Challenge** Suppose a fictional space ship travels from Earth to the Large Cloud of Magellan in 3 weeks. Estimate its speed in miles per hour. about $1.925 \cdot 10^{15}$ mi/h

7. Approximate distances
Large Cloud of Magellan: $9.7 \cdot 10^{17}$ mi;

Small Cloud of Magellan: $1.1 \cdot 10^{18}$ mi;

Ursa Minor dwarf: $1.4 \cdot 10^{18}$ mi;

Draco dwarf: $1.5 \cdot 10^{18}$ mi;

Sculptor dwarf: $1.6 \cdot 10^{18}$ mi;

Fornax dwarf: $2.5 \cdot 10^{18}$ mi;

Leo II dwarf: $4.4 \cdot 10^{18}$ mi;

Leo I dwarf: $4.4 \cdot 10^{18}$ mi;

Barnard's Galaxy: $1.0 \cdot 10^{19}$ mi

FOR ▶ HELP
with the *metric
system*, see
TOOLBOX, p. 593

9. **Oceanography** On average, the ocean is about $3.795 \cdot 10^3$ m deep. Its deepest point is $11.033 \cdot 10^3$ m.

a. Which of these measurements is in scientific notation? **the average depth**

b. Give each measurement in kilometers. Use decimal notation.
average depth: 3795 km; deepest point: 11,033 km

10. **Population Growth** In 1650, the world population was about 470 million. In 1990, it was about 5.292 billion.

a. Write each population in scientific notation and in decimal notation. $4.7 \cdot 10^8$ or 470,000,000; $5.292 \cdot 10^9$ or 5,292,000,000

b. **Estimation** Compare the 1650 and 1990 populations. About how many times greater is the 1990 world population?
about 11 times greater

Solve each equation. Round decimal answers to the nearest hundredth.

11. $12.5 = 2.5x$ **5**   12. $0.7x - 2 = 19$ **30**   13. $\frac{m}{0.3} = 8$ **2.4**

14. $7 = 0.5p - 2.5$ **19**   15. $12.4 = \frac{w}{2.4} + 2.4$ **24**   16. $\frac{n}{0.33} - 9 = 12.99$ **7.26**

17. $-8.3 + 0.7n = -8.3$ **0**   18. $0.15p - 12.95 = -12.75$ **1.33**

19. $4.1x + 5.8 = 10$ **1.02**   20. $-0.36 - 1.05x = 9.2$ **−9.10**

Shoe Sizes The formulas below relate United States shoe size *s* to foot length *f* in inches. Use the formulas for Exercises 21–24.

Men's shoes	Women's shoes
$s = 3f - 22$	$s = 3f - 20.7$

21. Barry wears men's shoe size 10. Estimate his foot length to the nearest inch. **11 in.**

22. Tia wears women's shoe size 8. Estimate her foot length to the nearest inch. **10 in.**

23. Edie usually wears a women's size 10 shoe. She wants to try on a pair of men's running shoes. Running shoes come in whole and half sizes. What size should she try on? **size $8\frac{1}{2}$ or 9**

24. According to these formulas and your foot length measurement in inches, what size shoe should you wear?
Answers will vary. Check students' work.

25. Open-ended If you buy shoes from another country, you may need to know your European shoe size. The formulas below relate European size *e* to United States size *u*. Write a word problem that can be solved by using one or both of the formulas.

Men's shoes	Women's shoes
$e = 1.29u + 30.8$	$e = 1.24u + 28.7$

25. Sample Response: In United States sizes, Ismail wears a men's size $9\frac{1}{2}$ and Tracy wears a woman's size $7\frac{1}{2}$. Find their European shoe sizes. (43, 38)

Reflecting ◀▶ on the Section

26. Find three large numbers in a newspaper or encyclopedia. Write them in scientific notation and add labels that explain what the numbers mean. **Answers will vary. Check students' work.**

RESEARCH

Exercise 26 checks that you know how scientific notation is applied.

Spiral ◀▶ Review

27. △*ABC* ~ △*ADE*.
Find the length of $\overline{DE}$.
(Module 3, p. 207)
about 3 m

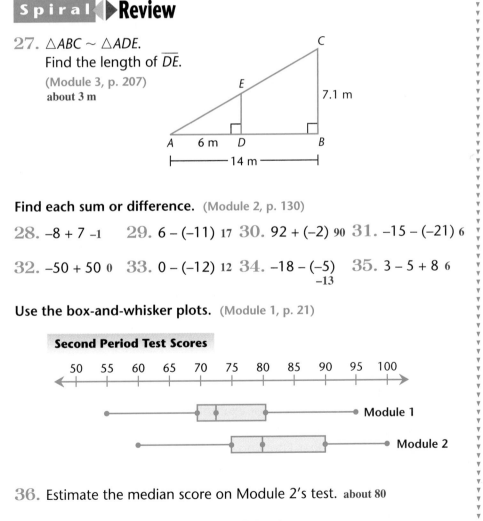

Find each sum or difference. (Module 2, p. 130)

28. –8 + 7 **–1**   **29.** 6 – (–11) **17**   **30.** 92 + (–2) **90**   **31.** –15 – (–21) **6**

32. –50 + 50 **0**   **33.** 0 – (–12) **12**   **34.** –18 – (–5) **–13**   **35.** 3 – 5 + 8 **6**

Use the box-and-whisker plots. (Module 1, p. 21)

Second Period Test Scores

50 55 60 65 70 75 80 85 90 95 100

Module 1

Module 2

36. Estimate the median score on Module 2's test. **about 80**

37. Estimate the high score on Module 1's test. **about 95**

Working on the Module Project

Solving a Mystery

Gathering and Reviewing Evidence To answer the questions below, you need to read Chapter 7 of *The Mystery of Blacktail Canyon.* You'll use some of the skills you have learned to estimate the heights of two suspects, Ms. Weatherwax and Mr. Martinez.

SET UP

You will need The Mystery of Blacktail Canyon.

7 How can knowing the heights of Ms. Weatherwax and Mr. Martinez help Jim and Nageela find the thief?

7. They already know the blood type and that both people have bumps on their heads so knowing their heights and matching them with the footprints will identify the thief.

In Chapter 7 Jim measures Ms. Weatherwax's stride length. Her stride is about 22 hand-widths long. After leaving the school, Jim and Nageela find that Jim's hand is 7 cm wide.

8 How many centimeters long is Ms. Weatherwax's stride? **154 cm**

9 Look back at Project Questions 5 and 6 on page 198. Use the information to estimate Ms. Weatherwax's height. Describe your method. **about 176.4 cm; I used the equation for the fitted line on the scatter plot.**

In the story, Jim measures Mr. Martinez's shadow length. At the same time, he also measures Nageela's height and shadow length. Use the diagrams below for Project Questions 10 and 11.

10 Are the triangles in the diagram similar? How do you know?
Yes; The angle measures are the same.

11 Find Mr. Martinez's height. Describe your method.
174.9 cm; Set up a proportion using the lengths of corresponding sides.

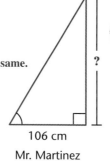 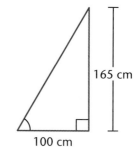

? 106 cm — Mr. Martinez

165 cm — 100 cm — Nageela

12 Summarize the clues you have gathered. Make sure you list everything you know or suspect about the thief. For example, what do you know about the person's appearance? Do you know the person's height and foot size? How does knowing that the thief was injured help you? Did the suspect attend Dr. Ashilaka's lecture? the field trip? How do you know? Is the thief a stranger or someone who knows the area? Explain your reasoning. **Answers will vary. Check students' work.**

Section 5

Extra Skill Practice

Write each number in scientific notation.

1. 5,180,000 $5.18 \cdot 10^6$
2. 870 $8.7 \cdot 10^2$
3. 28,900,000 $2.89 \cdot 10^7$
4. 3,120 $3.12 \cdot 10^3$
5. 362,900,000,000
   $3.629 \cdot 10^{11}$
6. 15,000 $1.5 \cdot 10^4$

Write each number in decimal notation.

7. $3.5 \cdot 10^8$ 350,000,000
8. $5.23 \cdot 10^3$ 5230
9. $8.1 \cdot 10^5$ 810,000
10. $6.91 \cdot 10^1$ 69.1
11. $4.8 \cdot 10^{14}$
    480,000,000,000,000
12. $2.25 \cdot 10^2$ 225
13. $4.76 \cdot 10^4$ 47,600
14. $1.853 \cdot 10^7$ 18,530,000
15. $6 \cdot 10^{10}$ 60,000,000,000

Solve each equation. Round decimal answers to the nearest hundredth.

16. $5.3 = 2.2k - 6.4$ 5.32
17. $\frac{t}{8.1} - 13.5 = 2.9$ 132.84
18. $0.39w + 4.5 = 8.4$ 10
19. $24.6 + \frac{q}{0.2} = 30.1$ 1.1
20. $5.08z - 6.17 = 4.13$ 2.03
21. $7.25 = \frac{m}{3.34} - 12.83$ 67.07
22. $15.6 = 1.6v + 7.36$ 5.15
23. $38.62 = \frac{r}{6.49} + 27.53$ 71.97
24. $1.2g + 110.9 = 121.7$ 9
25. $0.02x - 0.13 = 5.9$ 301.5
26. $\frac{c}{0.17} + 6.9 = 11.3$ 0.75
27. $3.62n - 0.23 = 4.6$ 1.33
28. $76.8y - 5.31 = 2.37$ 0.1
29. $6.387 + 2.8p = 15.349$ 3.20

Standardized Testing ◆▶ Multiple Choice

1. The area of the Pacific Ocean is about 166,000,000 km². How is this measure expressed in scientific notation? D

   A 1.66 million km²
   B $16.6 \cdot 10^7$ km²
   C 1.668 km²
   D $1.66 \cdot 10^8$ km²

2. What is the value of y in the equation $16.8 = \frac{y}{1.2} + 4.8$? B

   A 144
   B 14.4
   C 1.44
   D 0.144

Whodunit?

◀◀◀ **Setting the Stage**

The Story So Far…

▶ The police know that the thief has blood type A. They also know that he or she did not go on Dr. Ashilaka's field trip. Jim and Nageela use a computer database at the police station to see which of the 22 suspects match up with these clues. But Jim thinks they have made a mistake.

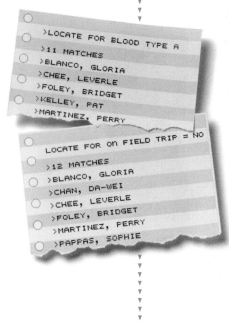

>LOCATE FOR BLOOD TYPE A
>11 MATCHES
>BLANCO, GLORIA
>CHEE, LEVERLE
>FOLEY, BRIDGET
>KELLEY, PAT
>MARTINEZ, PERRY

LOCATE FOR ON FIELD TRIP = NO
>12 MATCHES
>BLANCO, GLORIA
>CHAN, DA-WEI
>CHEE, LEVERLE
>FOLEY, BRIDGET
>MARTINEZ, PERRY
>PAPPAS, SOPHIE

"My first step was to search for suspects with blood type A. The computer found 11 people who match up. But then I ran a new search to find suspects who did not go on the field trip. Now look! Twelve people! That makes a total of 23 suspects, but there are only 22 suspects in the database! And I haven't even searched for suspects with the right height or hair color yet."

"Oh no," moaned Nageela. "You're right! We've done something wrong!"

Think About It

1 What did Jim tell the computer to search for?
suspects with blood type A, then suspects who did not go on the field trip

2 Do you think Jim and Nageela did something wrong? Use the printout from Jim's computer search to help explain your thinking. Sample Response: No; Some suspects are on both search lists.

Exploration 1

▶▶▶▶▶▶▶▶▶▶▶▶▶▶▶▶▶▶▶▶▶▶▶▶▶▶▶▶▶▶▶▶▶▶

Using AND, OR, NOT

SET UP *Work as a class. You will need:* • *Labsheet 6A* • *tape*

▶ **You'll use a diagram to search for suspects who have blood type A
and were absent from the field trip to Blacktail Canyon.**

3 **Use Labsheet 6A.** The *Suspect List* gives information about each of
the 22 suspects in *The Mystery of Blacktail Canyon.* Your class should
follow these steps: **See Additional Answers.**

- ◆ Your teacher will assign a suspect name to each student in the
  class. Write your suspect's name on a small slip of paper.

- ◆ Your teacher will draw a large diagram on the chalkboard. Tape
  your suspect's name in the correct part of the diagram.

GOAL

LEARN HOW TO...
- ◆ interpret
  statements with
  and, or, and *not*
- ◆ organize
  information in a
  Venn diagram

AS YOU...
- ◆ analyze clues in
  a mystery

KEY TERMS
- ◆ Venn diagram
- ◆ and
- ◆ or
- ◆ not

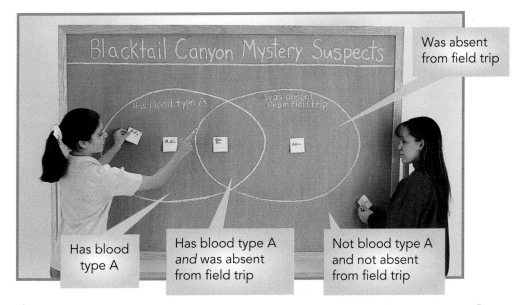

Was absent
from field trip

Has blood
type A

Has blood type A
and was absent
from field trip

Not blood type A
and not absent
from field trip

4 Look back at the story on page 224. How could your class diagram
help Nageela and Jim understand their mistake? **Sample Response:**
It shows the suspects who have blood type A and who were not on the field trip.

▶ **The diagram your class made is called a *Venn diagram*. Venn diagrams
are used to model relationships between groups. They can help you
interpret statements using the words *and, or,* and *not*.**

This Venn diagram organizes information about eight pieces of pottery Nageela found on one shelf of a cliff dwelling. She used the letters A–H to label the pieces.

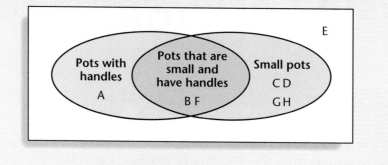

▶ The diagrams below show groupings that use the words *and, or,* and *not.* Notice that the word *or* has special meaning in mathematics. It means *one or the other or both.*

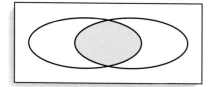

2 pots are small **and** have handles.

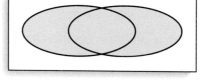

7 pots are small **or** have handles (or both).

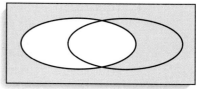

5 pots do **not** have handles.

CLOSURE QUESTION

Think of three different school sports. How would you make a Venn diagram to show the number of people in your class who play each sport?

Sample Response: Make three overlapping ovals. Label each oval with one of the sports. Put the names of the people who play all three sports in the center overlap, then put the names of the people who play two sports in the overlap of just those two ovals. Put the names of the people who play one of the sports in its oval but not in the overlapping section. Finally, put the names of those people who play none of the sports outside all of the ovals.

5 Try This as a Class Use the Venn diagram from the Example.

a. How many pots are small? How many pots are *not* small? 6 pots; 2 pots

b. How many pots are *not* small *and* do *not* have handles? 1 pot

c. To count the number of small pots or pots with handles, Angela says you should add the number of small pots and the number with handles to get 5. Do you agree? Explain.
No; She is not including the small pots that have handles.

6 Try This as a Class Use the Venn diagram of suspects your class created.

a. How many suspects do *not* have blood type A? 11 suspects

b. How many have blood type A *or* were absent from the field trip? 14 suspects

c. How many do *not* have blood type A *and* were not absent from the field trip? 8 suspects

d. In what group will Jim and Nageela find the thief? the suspects who have type A and were absent from the field trip

7 **CHECKPOINT** Six friends were talking about whether they had been to Canada and Mexico. Paolo, Maria, Dan, and Jim have been to Mexico. Paolo, Maria, and Stacey have been to Canada. Rob has never visited either country. Use this information to make a Venn diagram. Shade the diagram to show which friends have been to Canada or Mexico. **See Additional Answers.**

HOMEWORK EXERCISES ▶ See Exs. 1–14 on pp. 228–230.

✔ **QUESTION 7**

...checks that you can use a Venn diagram to interpret statements with *and*, *or*, and *not*.

Section 6
Key Concepts

Key Terms

Venn Diagram (pp. 225–227)

A Venn diagram models relationships among groups. It can help you interpret statements that use the words *and*, *or*, and *not*.

Venn diagram

Example Joshua kept track of how many days in August were sunny and how many days were over 90°. He made the Venn diagram below.

and

or

Weather Patterns for 31 Days in August

Sunny days 21 — Sunny days over 90° 5 — Days over 90° 3 — 2

not

Number of sunny days:
21 + 5 = 26

Number of days that were sunny or over 90°: 21 + 5 + 3 = 29

Number of days that were not sunny and not over 90°: 2

8 **Key Concepts Question** Use the Venn diagram above. How many days in August were not over 90°? About what percent of the days in August were not over 90°? Give your answer to the nearest percent. Show how you got your answer.

8. 23 days; Sample Response: about 74%; Add 23 + 8 (number of days over 90°). Use the proportion $\frac{23}{31} = \frac{x}{100}$ and solve for x.

YOU WILL NEED

For Exs. 22–24:
◆ compass
◆ metric ruler

Language Arts In everyday English, the word *or* can be *exclusive* or *inclusive,* as shown below.

Exclusive *Or*
Nao drives or takes a bus to work. Nao either drives or takes a bus, not both. She cannot do both at the same time.

Inclusive *Or*
Nao eats lunch or reads at noon. Nao can eat lunch, read, or do both activities at once.

For Exercises 1 and 2, tell whether the *inclusive* or the *exclusive or* is used. (*Note*: All other exercises in this book use the inclusive *or.*)

1. Brad has saved enough money to buy either a touring bike *or* a mountain bike. He can afford only one bike. **exclusive**

2. On cold days, Maria wears a sweater *or* a jacket or both. **inclusive**

Track For Exercises 3–6, use the Venn diagram below.

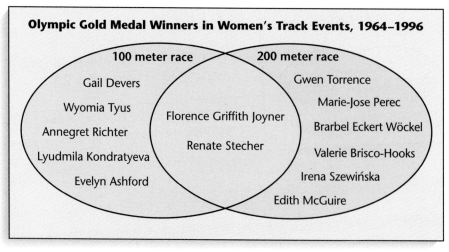

Olympic Gold Medal Winners in Women's Track Events, 1964–1996

100 meter race

Gail Devers
Wyomia Tyus
Annegret Richter
Lyudmila Kondratyeva
Evelyn Ashford

Florence Griffith Joyner
Renate Stecher

200 meter race

Gwen Torrence
Marie-Jose Perec
Brarbel Eckert Wöckel
Valerie Brisco-Hooks
Irena Szewińska
Edith McGuire

3. Which runners have won the 100 m race and the 200 m race?
Florence Griffith Joyner, Renate Stecher

4. How many runners have won the 100 m race? **7**

5. How many runners have won the 100 m race or the 200 m race? **13**

6. In the 1996 Olympics, Svetlana Masterkova won the gold medal in the 800 m race, but she has not won the gold medal in an Olympic 100 m or 200 m race. Describe where to put her name in the diagram on page 228. **inside the rectangle and outside both ovals**

For Exercises 7–10, use the Venn diagram at the right.

7. How many students acted in *Hello Dolly* or in *A Midsummer Night's Dream?* **42 students**

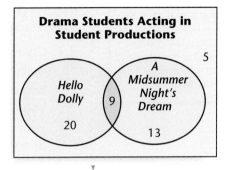

Drama Students Acting in Student Productions

8. How many drama students acted in both plays? How many drama students did not act in both plays?
9 students; 38 students

9. The drama teacher estimates that about 60% of the students acted in *Hello Dolly.* How close is this estimate? **She is off by about 2%.**

10. Challenge Suppose some students act in *The Marriage Proposal,* a short play with only three characters. Two of these students also act in both *Hello Dolly* and *A Midsummer Night's Dream.* The third student does not appear in either of these plays. Revise the Venn diagram to include this information. **See Additional Answers.**

Geography **For Exercises 11 and 12, use the map below.**

11. Make a Venn diagram that includes all 50 states. Use these categories: **See Additional Answers.**

  ◆ States that border another country or a Great Lake
  ◆ States that border an ocean

12. Use your Venn diagram to answer each question.

  a. How many states border another country or a Great Lake? **20 states**

  b. How many states border an ocean? **23 states**

  c. How many states border an ocean or a country or a Great Lake? **36 states**

  d. How many states do not border an ocean? **27 states**

  e. What percent of the states border an ocean and border a country or a Great Lake? **14%**

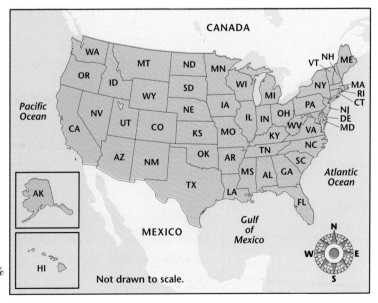

13. **Open-ended** Write a word problem that can be solved using a Venn diagram. Then solve the problem. Explain your solution using the words *and, or,* and *not.* **Answers will vary. Check students' work.**

RESEARCH

Exercise 14 checks that you can create and interpret a Venn diagram.

Reflecting ◀▶on the Section

14. Collect data from friends and family members and use the data to make a Venn diagram. For example, you may want to ask people two questions, such as, "Do you like to watch soccer?" and "Do you like to watch figure skating?" Share your Venn diagram with your class. Explain how you collected your data.
Answers will vary. Check students' work.

Spiral ◀▶Review

Solve each equation. Round decimal answers to the nearest hundredth. (Module 3, p. 218)

15. $30.9 = 0.3x + 6$ 83   16. $\frac{p}{0.12} = 5$ 0.6   17. $-13.2 = 24 + 0.7n$ –53.14

18. The eighth grade class is asked to choose two students to help plan an event for the school's field day. Mary, John, Sue, and José all volunteer. The class decides to choose names out of a hat to decide who will help. (Module 2, p. 116)

18. a.
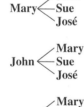

John
Mary ⟨ Sue
José

Mary
John ⟨ Sue
José

Mary
Sue ⟨ John
José

Mary
José ⟨ John
Sue

a. Copy and complete the tree diagram showing the possible pairs of students who can be chosen.

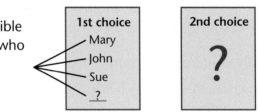

1st choice

Mary
John
Sue
?

2nd choice

?

b. Find the probablility that José and Sue will help plan the trip. $\frac{1}{6}$

Tell whether each triangle is *isosceles, equilateral,* or *scalene.* (Toolbox, p. 604)

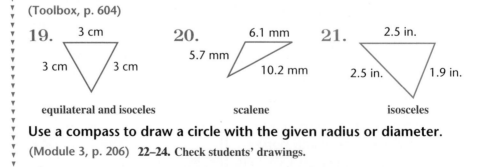

19.   3 cm

3 cm   3 cm

equilateral and isoceles

20.   6.1 mm

5.7 mm

10.2 mm

scalene

21.   2.5 in.

2.5 in.   1.9 in.

isosceles

Use a compass to draw a circle with the given radius or diameter. (Module 3, p. 206) **22–24. Check students' drawings.**

22. $r = 1.5$ cm   23. $d = 5$ cm   24. $r = 6$ cm

Internet Forum Manager and Host: Georgia Griffith

Georgia Griffith is the host of seven internet discussion groups. To settle debates, she researches subjects on the internet by using key subject words and the words AND, OR, and NOT.

25. Replace each _?_ with AND, OR, or NOT to find someone from Hawaii or California who is interested in surfing but not windsurfing.

▲ Georgia Griffith uses a special braille device to read her computer screen.

Hawaii __?__ California __?__ surfing __?__ windsurfing
OR; AND; NOT

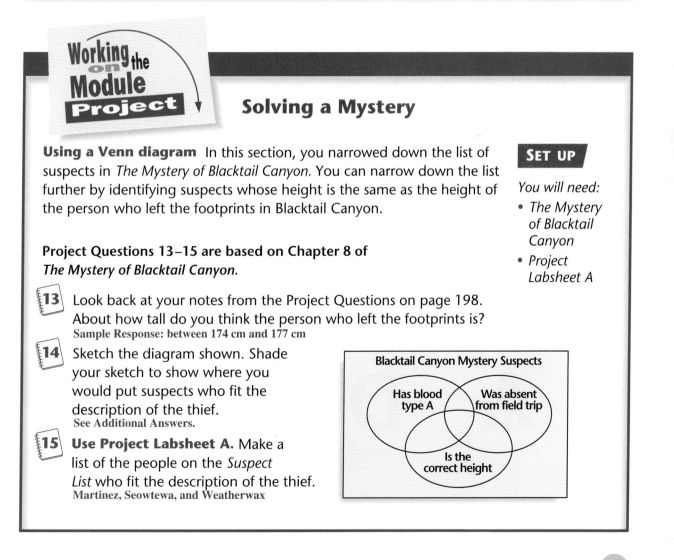

Working on **the** **Module** **Project**

Solving a Mystery

Using a Venn diagram In this section, you narrowed down the list of suspects in *The Mystery of Blacktail Canyon.* You can narrow down the list further by identifying suspects whose height is the same as the height of the person who left the footprints in Blacktail Canyon.

Project Questions 13–15 are based on Chapter 8 of *The Mystery of Blacktail Canyon.*

13 Look back at your notes from the Project Questions on page 198. About how tall do you think the person who left the footprints is?
Sample Response: between 174 cm and 177 cm

14 Sketch the diagram shown. Shade your sketch to show where you would put suspects who fit the description of the thief.
See Additional Answers.

15 **Use Project Labsheet A.** Make a list of the people on the *Suspect List* who fit the description of the thief.
Martinez, Seowtewa, and Weatherwax

SET UP

You will need:
• *The Mystery of Blacktail Canyon*
• *Project Labsheet A*

Blacktail Canyon Mystery Suspects

Has blood type A

Was absent from field trip

Is the correct height

For Exercises 1–5, use the Venn diagram below. It shows the animals that a class chose for their research reports.

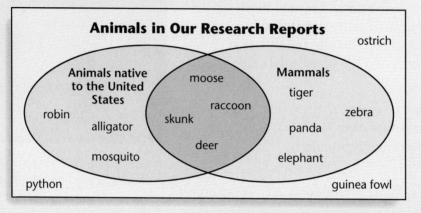

Animals in Our Research Reports

ostrich

Animals native to the United States

robin
alligator
mosquito

moose
raccoon
skunk
deer

Mammals

tiger
zebra
panda
elephant

python

guinea fowl

1. Which animals are mammals in the United States? **moose, raccoon, skunk, deer**

2. Which animals are not mammals and not in the United States? **ostrich, python, guinea fowl**

3. How many animals are from the United States? **7 animals**

4. The mosquito belongs to which category or categories? **animals native to the United States**

5. A llama is a mammal found in South America. Describe where you would put a llama in the Venn diagram. **in the blue part of the oval labeled "Mammals"**

6. Make a Venn diagram of the days of the week. In one category put all the days you are at school. In another category put all the days that contain the letter *n*. **See Additional Answers.**

Standardized Testing ◀▶ Performance Task

Many letters of the alphabet show line symmetry. Some have a vertical line of symmetry, some have a horizontal line of symmetry, and some have both. Make a Venn diagram that organizes all 26 capital letters by the types of line symmetry they show. **See Additional Answers.**

vertical line
of symmetry

horizontal line
of symmetry

vertical and horizontal
lines of symmetry

Completing the Module Project

Solving a Mystery

Drawing Conclusions Throughout this module, you have used mathematics to help identify a thief. You have discovered some characteristics of the guilty person, and you have narrowed a list of 22 possible suspects to three. Now you'll receive more information from your teacher that will help you narrow the list even further.

SET UP

Work in a group of four. You will need:
- *Your "detective's notebook" or journal*
- *Clues and transcripts chosen by your teacher*

16 Some information gathered during an investigation is useful. Some is not. Review the clue cards. Discuss the clues with your group. Write down the names of people you believe may have committed the crime. Explain why you feel these people and no others are guilty. **See Additional Answers.**

17 Review the interview transcripts from the police investigation. Who do you now believe committed the crime? Is your final suspect one of the people you chose in Project Question 16? Explain why you feel this person and no one else is guilty.

See Additional Answers.

18 Have your teacher check your answers to Project Questions 16 and 17. If you made an error, review your evidence and revise your solution. Record your new conclusion, explaining your errors as well as your new answer. **Answers will vary. Check students' work.**

Like you, Nageela and Jim think they know the identity of the thief. Ferrel, Jack, and Charlotte agree with their conclusion. At the end of Chapter 10, the five sleuths leave the station to catch the suspect.

19 What happens after the police, Nageela, and Jim leave the station? Write an ending to *The Mystery of Blacktail Canyon* in your journal.
Answers will vary. Check students' work.

Review and Assessment

You will need • *graph paper* (Exs. 9–12) • *compass, ruler, and Review and Assessment Labsheet* (Ex. 18)

Find each value. Describe your method. Tell whether your answer is exact or an estimate. (Sec. 1, Explor. 1)

Methods will vary.
Sample Responses are given.

1. $\sqrt{0.09}$ 0.3; mental math; exact

2. $\sqrt{16,000}$ about 126.5; calculator; estimate

3. $-\sqrt{96}$ about –9.8; calculator; estimate

4. $\sqrt{\dfrac{4}{81}}$ $\dfrac{2}{9}$; mental math; exact

5. Keith Loughlin estimates that the large can will hold twice as much as the small can. Explain his mistake. (Sec. 1, Explor. 2) **See Additional Answers.**

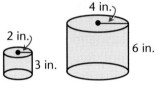

Find each value. (Sec. 2, Explor. 1)

6. $\dfrac{3(4) + 21}{\sqrt{102 + 19}}$ 3

7. $\sqrt{\dfrac{8(3) + 2(-4)}{36}}$ $\dfrac{2}{3}$

8. $\dfrac{5^2}{4(-3) + 87}$ $\dfrac{1}{3}$

Graph each equation. Tell whether the graph is *linear* or *nonlinear*.
(Sec. 2, Explor. 2) **9–12. See Additional Answers for graphs.**

9. $y = 4x - 3$ linear

10. $y = -2x + 1$ linear

11. $y = x^2 + 1$ nonlinear

12. $y = 3x - 6$ linear

Find the slope of each line. (Sec. 3, Explor. 1)

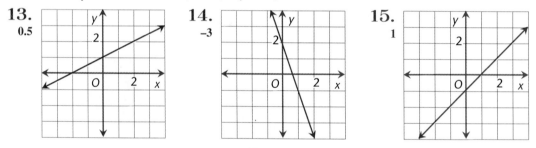

13. 0.5

14. –3

15. 1

16. The scatter plot shows the change in population in a number of counties in Texas between 1990 and 1996. The 1990 population is on the horizontal axis and the 1996 population is on the vertical axis. (Sec. 3, Explor. 2)

a. Which equation best fits the fitted line on the scatter plot? **I**
   I. $y = 1.2x - 660$
   II. $y = 1.2x$
   III. $y = 1.2x + 660$

b. Use the equation you chose in part (a) to predict the 1996 population for a county that had a population of 6200 in 1990. **6780**

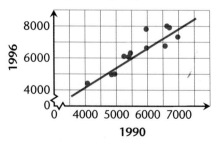

County Populations

17. Estimate the height of the building if the person shown is about 6 ft tall.

(Sec. 4, Explor. 1) about 30 ft

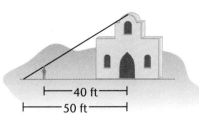

├─────40 ft─────┤
├───────50 ft───────┤

23. Sample Response: Substitute 180 for h in the formula and solve for t to get $t \approx 40$ cm. If the bone is from the same skeleton, it should be about 40 cm long.

18. Use the Review and Assessment Labsheet.
Follow the directions to find the diameter of the tree trunk. Mark a radius and a chord. (Sec. 4, Explor. 2) about 22 cm or about $8\frac{3}{4}$ in.; Check students' drawings.

Write each number in scientific notation. (Sec. 5, Explor. 1)

19. About 52,500,000 pet dogs lived in the United States in 1991.
$5.25 \cdot 10^7$

20. The area of Mexico is about 762 thousand square miles.
$7.62 \cdot 10^5$

For Exercises 21 and 22, write each product in decimal notation.
(Sec. 5, Explor. 1)

21. The entrance to Mesa Verde Park is $6.95 \cdot 10^3$ ft above sea level. 6950

22. The mesa dwellings were abandoned about $7 \cdot 10^2$ years ago. 700

23. Writing Jill Wu is an anthropologist. She finds the incomplete skeleton of a 180 cm tall male at a site. She thinks another bone (a tibia) found nearby is part of the same skeleton. Explain how she can use the formula $h = 78.62 + 2.52t$, where h = the height of the skeleton and t = the length of the tibia in centimeters, to see whether she is correct. (Sec. 5, Explor. 2) See above.

Means of Transportation
airplane
bicycle
bus
car
helicopter
skateboard
skis
speedboat
train
truck

Make a Venn diagram that includes the means of transportation listed. Use the categories *Has Engine* and *Travels Only On Ground*.
(Sec. 6, Explor. 1)

24. Which means of transportation have an engine? airplane, bus, car, helicopter, speedboat, train, truck

25. Which means of transportation have an engine and travel only on the ground? bus, car, train, truck

26. Add two more means of transportation to the Venn diagram.
Sample Response: raft (neither), motorcycle (both)

Reflecting ◀▶ **on the Module**

27. Writing Explain how mathematics is important to the work of a police officer. What kinds of mathematics are used in investigations? Answers will vary. Check students' work.

PATTERNS
and
DISCOVERIES

MODULE 4   SECTION OVERVIEW

The Module Project

Creating a Pattern

The world is filled with natural and human-made patterns. In this module, you'll examine and recreate some of these patterns. Then you'll create a work of art based on a mathematical pattern.

More on the Module Project
See pp. 253, 266, 300, and 313

INTERNET
To learn more about the theme:
http://www.mlmath.com

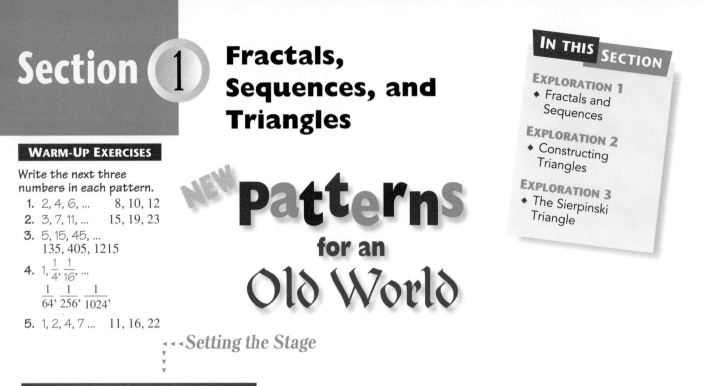

IN THIS SECTION

EXPLORATION 1
♦ Fractals and Sequences

EXPLORATION 2
♦ Constructing Triangles

EXPLORATION 3
♦ The Sierpinski Triangle

WARM-UP EXERCISES

Write the next three numbers in each pattern.

1. 2, 4, 6, ...   8, 10, 12
2. 3, 7, 11, ...   15, 19, 23
3. 5, 15, 45, ...
   135, 405, 1215
4. $1, \frac{1}{4}, \frac{1}{16}, ...$
   $\frac{1}{64}, \frac{1}{256}, \frac{1}{1024},$
5. 1, 2, 4, 7 ...   11, 16, 22

NEW Patterns for an Old World

◂◂◂ *Setting the Stage*

[Standard geometry cannot] describe the shape of a cloud, a mountain, a coastline, or a tree. Clouds are not spheres, mountains are not cones, coastlines are not circles, and bark is not smooth, nor does lightning travel in a straight line.

The Fractal Geometry of Nature by Benoit Mandelbrot

▲ Filmakers use computer-generated fractals to create life-like images, such as this scene from *Star Wars*.

Since ancient times, people have tried to use common geometric shapes to describe the world. In 1975, Benoit Mandelbrot first used the word *fractal* to describe geometric patterns like those found in nature. An object that contains smaller and smaller copies of the whole object is a **fractal**.

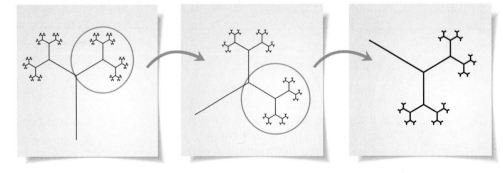

The right branch looks like a smaller version of the whole tree, rotated to the right.

The smaller branches look like miniature copies of larger ones, and of the whole tree.

Think About It ▸

Use the fractal at the bottom of page 238 to answer Questions 1 and 2. Sample Responses are given.

1 Describe how the circled parts in the fractal tree are similar to the whole tree. Does the tree contain other parts that are similar to the whole tree? Explain your thinking.

2 Describe something you might see in nature that looks like a fractal. Explain why you think it looks like one.
broccoli; Each floweret branch is a smaller version of the main stem.

▸ In this module you'll explore fractal patterns and other patterns in the world around you. You'll use mathematics to describe those patterns.

1. The circled branches are smaller versions of the tree trunk itself; Yes; Each time the branches split off into other branches the pattern is the same as the pattern of the original split.

Exploration 1 ▸▸▸▸▸▸▸▸▸▸▸▸▸▸▸▸▸▸▸▸▸▸▸▸▸▸▸▸▸

Fractals & Sequences

SET UP *You will need:* • *Labsheet 1A* • *ruler* • *4 different-colored pencils*

GOAL

LEARN HOW TO...
◆ write rules for sequences

AS YOU...
◆ explore fractals

KEY TERMS
◆ fractal
◆ sequence
◆ term
◆ self-similar

Use Labsheet 1A for Questions 3–5.

3 Follow the steps below to draw a *Fractal Tree*. Fill in the table on the labsheet through Step 3.

3. Steps 1–5

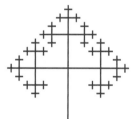

Table, Steps 3–7:

$9, \frac{1}{2}, 3\frac{1}{2}, 4\frac{1}{2}, 9\frac{1}{2},$

$27, \frac{1}{4}, 3\frac{3}{4}, 6\frac{3}{4}, 16\frac{1}{4},$

$81, \frac{1}{8}, 3\frac{7}{8}, 10\frac{1}{8}, 26\frac{3}{8},$

$243, \frac{1}{16}, 3\frac{15}{16}, 15\frac{3}{16}, 41\frac{9}{16},$

$729, \frac{1}{32}, 3\frac{31}{32}, 22\frac{25}{32}, 64\frac{11}{32}$

Step 1

The first branch of the tree has been drawn for you on the labsheet.

Step 2

Add three branches to the first branch. Make each of them 1 in. long.

Step 3

Add three branches, each $\frac{1}{2}$ in. long, to each branch added in Step 2.

4. The lengths of the branches added in Step 2 are one half the length of the trunk; The lengths of the branches added in Step 3 are one half the length of the branches added in Step 2.

4 Compare the length of the branch in Step 1 and the length of a branch added in Step 2. How are they related? How is the length of each branch added in Step 3 related to the length of a branch added in Step 2?

5 Add the new branches for Steps 4 and 5 to your fractal tree. Then fill in the table on the labsheet for these steps. See page 239.

▶ **Describing Sequences** You may have noticed some number patterns in the table on Labsheet 1A. These patterns are called *sequences*. A **sequence** is an ordered list of numbers or objects called **terms**. You can write rules to describe some sequences.

7. Column 1: To find the number of new branches multiply the previous number of new branches by 3.
Column 2: To find the length of each new branch multiply the length of each previous new branch by $\frac{1}{2}$.
Column 3: To find the height of the tree add the previous height of the tree to the length of one new branch.
Column 4: To find the total length of new branches multiply the length of one new branch by the number of new branches.
Column 5: To find the total length of all branches add the previous total length of all branches to the total length of new branches.

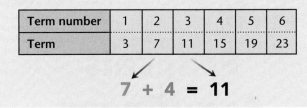

EXAMPLE

Rule: To find a term of the sequence below, add 4 to the previous term.

Term number	1	2	3	4	5	6
Term	3	7	11	15	19	23

7 + 4 = 11

6 Suppose the first term in a sequence is 3, and the rule for finding a term is to multiply the previous term by 4. Give the first 6 terms of this sequence. **3, 12, 48, 192, 768, 3072**

7 **Use Labsheet 1A.** Write a rule for the sequence in each column on the labsheet. Then use your rules to complete Steps 6 and 7 on the labsheet.

✔ **QUESTION 8**

…checks that you can write a rule for a sequence.

8 ✔ **CHECKPOINT** Write a rule for finding a term of each sequence. Then give the next three terms of the sequence.

a. 2, 4, 8, 16, …

b. $3x$, $3x^2$, $3x^3$, $3x^4$, …

c. 0.3, 0.03, 0.003, …

d. 400, 299, 198, …

8. Sample Responses are given.
a. Multiply the previous term by 2; 32, 64, 128
b. Multiply the previous term by x; $3x^5$, $3x^6$, $3x^7$
c. Divide the previous term by 10; 0.0003, 0.00003, 0.000003
d. Subtract 101 from the previous term; 97, −4, −105

▶ A fractal is **self-similar** if it is made of smaller pieces that are similar to the whole figure. The self-similar figure you created on Labsheet 1A is not a complete fractal. The fractal is the figure you would get if the sequence was carried out forever. The human eye could never see all the parts of a fractal.

9 Discussion Suppose you could continue adding branches to your fractal tree forever. **See below.**

a. How tall would the final fractal tree be? How wide would it be? Would the tree ever be too large to fit on your paper? Explain your thinking.

b. Can you find the total length of all the branches in the final fractal tree? Explain.

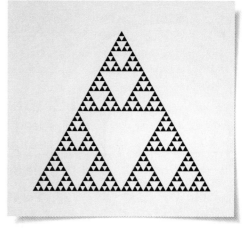

HOMEWORK EXERCISES ▶ See Exs. 1–10 on pp. 248–249.

9. a. about 4 in.; about 4 in.; No; The height and width of the tree increases by smaller and smaller fractions so they will never get much wider than at the stage shown in the figure.
b. No; Since the sum increases by greater and greater amounts, the total length increases without limit.

Exploration 2 ▶▶▶▶▶▶▶▶▶▶▶▶▶▶▶▶▶▶▶▶▶▶▶▶▶▶

Constructing TRIANGLES

SET UP *Work in a group of three. You will need:* • compass • ruler • plain white paper • protractor

GOAL

LEARN HOW TO...
◆ name congruent figures
◆ apply the triangle inequality

AS YOU...
◆ construct triangles

KEY TERMS
◆ congruent
◆ arc
◆ triangle inequality

▶ In 1916, almost 60 years before Mandelbrot used the word *fractal*, a Polish mathematician named Waclaw Sierpinski created a figure that is called the *Sierpinski triangle*.

10 In Exploration 1, you looked at self-similar fractals. How is the Sierpinski triangle self-similar?
All of the smaller pieces are similar to the whole figure.

11 Two figures are **congruent** if they are the same shape and size. Are there any congruent figures in the Sierpinski triangle? Explain your answer.
All of the triangles produced in a given step are congruent.

▶ In this exploration, you'll learn about congruent triangles. You'll also learn how to construct a triangle using a compass and a ruler.

Constructing a Triangle

You can construct a triangle if you know its side lengths. The figures below show the steps for constructing a triangle that has side lengths of 4 in., $3\frac{1}{2}$ in., and 3 in.

Step 1 Draw a line segment 4 in. long. Label the endpoints *A* and *B*.

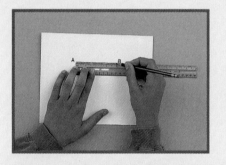

Step 2 Adjust the compass to a radius of $3\frac{1}{2}$ in. Put the compass point on *A* and draw an arc.

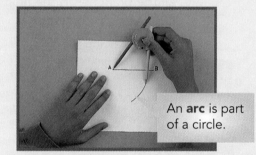

An **arc** is part of a circle.

Step 3 Adjust the compass to a radius of 3 in. Put the compass point on *B*. Draw another arc that intersects the first arc.

Step 4 Label the point where the arcs intersect *C*. Draw segments from *A* to *C* and from *B* to *C*.

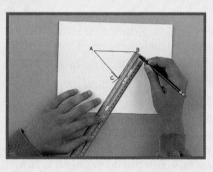

12 Each member of your group will construct a triangle with side lengths of 5 in., 4 in., and 3 in., starting with a different side length. (Use the Student Resource above.) **Check students' drawings.**

Person 1: Draw the 5 in. line segment first.

Person 2: Draw the 4 in. line segment first.

Person 3: Draw the 3 in. line segment first.

Compare your results. How are all three triangles alike?
They are congruent.

▶ **In the diagram below, △ABC is congruent to △DEF. This is written △ABC ≅ △DEF. Corresponding angles of congruent triangles have the same measure, and corresponding sides are the same length.**

13 Are your triangles from Question 12 congruent? Explain how you know.

14 Try This as a Class How can you tell from the statement △ABC ≅ △DEF which angles are corresponding angles?
Corresponding angles are named in the same order when the triangle is labeled.

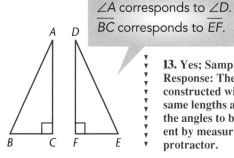

∠A corresponds to ∠D.
$\overline{BC}$ corresponds to $\overline{EF}$.

13. Yes; Sample Response: The sides were constructed with the same lengths and I found the angles to be congruent by measuring with a protractor.

▶ **One way to know if triangles are congruent is to measure their side lengths. If the sides of one triangle have the same lengths as the sides of another triangle, the triangles are congruent. This is called the *Side–Side–Side* rule.**

15 Label the vertices of each of the triangles your group made in Question 12. (Use different letters for each triangle.) Write statements like the one in Question 14 telling that the triangles are congruent. Be sure to list the corresponding vertices in the same order. **Sample Response: △ABC ≅ △TUV**

16 ✔ **CHECKPOINT** Sketch and label two congruent triangles. Explain how you know the triangles are congruent.
Check students' drawings; Sample Response: the Side-Side-Side rule.

17 Try to construct triangles with the given side lengths. Describe any problems you have.

a. 2 in., 3 in., 2 in.
Check students' drawings.
c. 1 in., 1 in., 1 in.
Check students' drawings.

b. 1 in., 2 in., 3 in. impossible
d. $1\frac{1}{2}$ in., $1\frac{1}{2}$ in., 4 in. impossible

18 Try This as a Class Look at your work in Question 17.

a. How can you predict whether three side lengths can be used to construct a triangle?

b. Test your answer to part (a) by making up three side lengths that can be used to construct a triangle. Give another three lengths that *cannot* be used to construct a triangle. Tell what happens when you try to construct each triangle.
Sample Response: 3 in., 3 in., 3 in.; 4 in., 2 in., 1 in; A triangle is formed; The segments do not connect.

▶ **The relationship among the side lengths of a triangle that you described in Question 18 is called the triangle inequality.**

✔ **QUESTION 16**

…checks that you can identify congruent triangles.

18. a. The sum of the lengths of any two sides must be greater than the length of the third side.

✔ QUESTION 19

...checks that you understand the relationship among the side lengths of any triangle.

19 ✔ **CHECKPOINT** Tell whether it is possible to construct a triangle with the given side lengths.

a. 2 cm, 4 cm, 6 cm No.   **b.** 3 cm, 9 cm, 8 cm Yes.

c. $\frac{1}{2}$ in., $\frac{1}{4}$ in., $\frac{3}{8}$ in. Yes.   **d.** 1.5 m, 4.9 m, 3.4 m No.

HOMEWORK EXERCISES ▷ See Exs. 11–21 on pp. 249–250.

GOAL

LEARN HOW TO...
◆ use a compass and ruler to construct a perpendicular bisector

AS YOU...
◆ make a Sierpinski triangle

KEY TERM
◆ midpoint

Exploration 3

The Sierpinski ▲▲▲▲ TRIANGLE

SET UP *You will need:* • *Labsheet 1B* • *compass* • *protractor* • *ruler* • *plain white paper* • *black paper* • *marker*

▶ You'll use a compass and the straight edge of a ruler to explore patterns in a Sierpinski triangle.

20 Follow these steps to begin creating a Sierpinski triangle.

Check students' work.

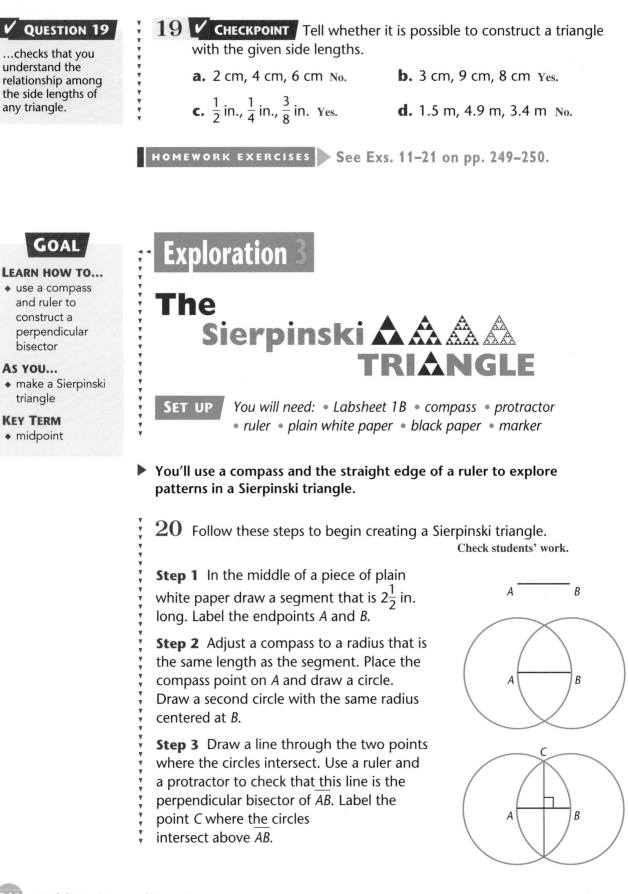

Step 1 In the middle of a piece of plain white paper draw a segment that is $2\frac{1}{2}$ in. long. Label the endpoints A and B.

Step 2 Adjust a compass to a radius that is the same length as the segment. Place the compass point on A and draw a circle. Draw a second circle with the same radius centered at B.

Step 3 Draw a line through the two points where the circles intersect. Use a ruler and a protractor to check that this line is the perpendicular bisector of $\overline{AB}$. Label the point C where the circles intersect above $\overline{AB}$.

▶ **In Question 20 you used a perpendicular bisector to find the** *midpoint* **of the segment. The midpoint of a segment divides it into two congruent segments.**

21 Follow the steps below to continue creating your Sierpinski triangle. **Check students' work.**

Step 4 Draw segments from *A* to *C* and from *B* to *C*. Use a marker to trace the triangle.

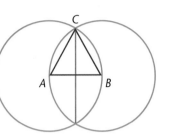

Step 5 Place the compass point on *C* and draw a third circle the same size as the first two. Locate the midpoints of $\overline{AC}$ and $\overline{BC}$ as you did in Step 3 of Question 20. Mark the midpoints but do not draw a line.

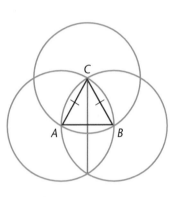

Step 6 Connect the midpoints by drawing segments inside the triangle. You now have one large triangle divided into four smaller triangles. Shade the middle triangle.

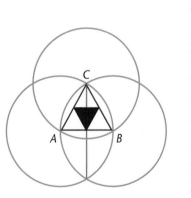

22 What type of triangles have you constructed? How is the area of each small triangle related to the area of the large triangle?

23 **a.** Measure with a ruler to find the midpoints of the sides of each of the three unshaded triangles. Connect the midpoints to form new triangles. Shade the middle triangle in each group.
Check students' drawings.

b. How is the area of each of these smaller shaded triangles related to the area of the largest triangle? It is $\frac{1}{16}$ of the area of the large triangle.

22. equilateral triangles; The areas of the small triangles are equal and each is $\frac{1}{4}$ the area of the larger triangle.

▶ You could continue the process of shading smaller and smaller triangles, but your original triangle is too small to show what a Sierpinski triangle would look like.

24 Work with two other students. Cut out the triangle you constructed in Questions 21 and 23. Place it on black paper with two other triangles, as shown. Check students' work.

25 **Use Labsheet 1B.** Each time you shade a part of your Sierpinski triangle, it is as if you are putting a "hole" in the figure.

a. To see what would happen if you kept putting smaller and smaller holes in the figure, complete the *Sierpinski Triangle Table*.

b. Discussion How does the total area of the shaded triangles change as the step numbers increase? It gets closer and closer to 1.

c. Discussion Remember that a fractal is the result of carrying out steps forever. Will there be any unshaded areas left in the Sierpinski triangle if you could continue the process of making smaller and smaller holes forever? Explain. Yes, but they will be too small to see with the naked eye.

25. a. $9, \frac{1}{16} \approx 0.063, \frac{9}{16} \approx 0.56;$

$27, \frac{1}{64} \approx 0.016, \frac{27}{64} \approx 0.42;$

$81, \frac{1}{256} \approx 0.004, \frac{81}{256} \approx 0.32;$

$243, \frac{1}{1024} \approx 0.001,$

$\frac{243}{1024} \approx 0.24;$

$729, \frac{1}{4096} \approx 0.0002,$

$\frac{729}{4096} \approx 0.18$

✔ QUESTION 26

...checks that you can construct a perpendicular bisector.

26 ✔ **CHECKPOINT** Copy each triangle onto a separate sheet of paper. For each triangle construct the perpendicular bisectors of each side. Check students' drawings.

a. **b.**

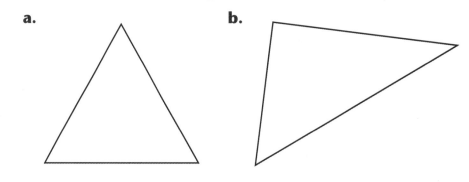

27 What do you notice about the perpendicular bisectors of each of the triangles in Question 26? Do you think this will always be true? Explain. They intersect at a single point; Yes. I tried other triangles and the perpendicular bisectors always intersected at a single point.

HOMEWORK EXERCISES ▶ See Exs. 22–25 on p. 250–251.

Section ① Key Concepts

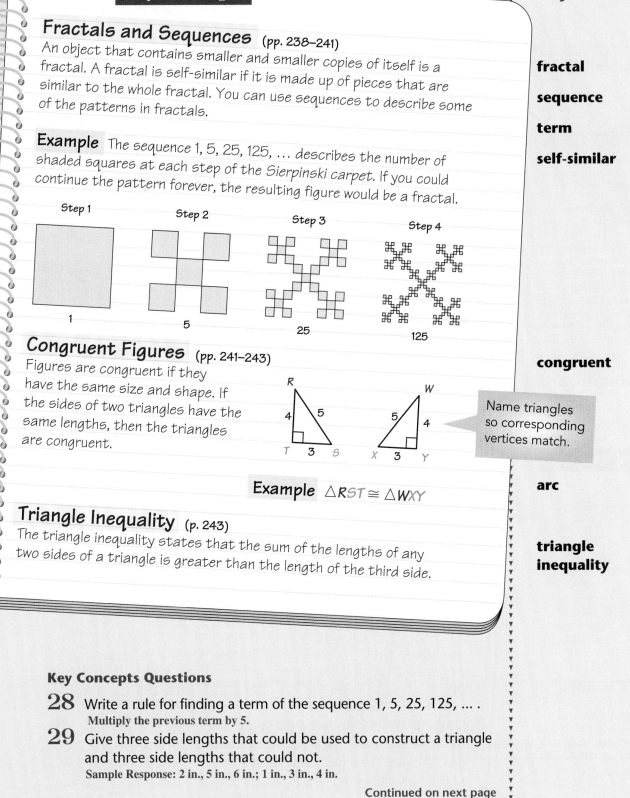

Fractals and Sequences (pp. 238–241)

An object that contains smaller and smaller copies of itself is a fractal. A fractal is self-similar if it is made up of pieces that are similar to the whole fractal. You can use sequences to describe some of the patterns in fractals.

Example The sequence 1, 5, 25, 125, ... describes the number of shaded squares at each step of the Sierpinski carpet. If you could continue the pattern forever, the resulting figure would be a fractal.

Step 1   Step 2   Step 3   Step 4

1   5   25   125

fractal

sequence

term

self-similar

Congruent Figures (pp. 241–243)

Figures are congruent if they have the same size and shape. If the sides of two triangles have the same lengths, then the triangles are congruent.

Name triangles so corresponding vertices match.

Example △RST ≅ △WXY

congruent

arc

Triangle Inequality (p. 243)

The triangle inequality states that the sum of the lengths of any two sides of a triangle is greater than the length of the third side.

triangle inequality

Key Concepts Questions

28 Write a rule for finding a term of the sequence 1, 5, 25, 125, ...
   Multiply the previous term by 5.

29 Give three side lengths that could be used to construct a triangle and three side lengths that could not.
   Sample Response: 2 in., 5 in., 6 in.; 1 in., 3 in., 4 in.

Continued on next page

Section ①

Key Concepts

Perpendicular Bisectors (pp. 244–246)

The midpoint of a segment divides it into two congruent parts. You can find the midpoint of a segment by constructing the perpendicular bisector of the segment.

First Set your compass to a radius that is greater than half the length of the segment.

Next Place the compass point on each endpoint of the segment and draw faint arcs that intersect above and below the segment.

Then Use a ruler to draw the perpendicular bisector through the points where the arcs intersect.

CLOSURE QUESTION

How can sequences be used to describe fractals?

Sample Response: Sequences can be used to describe various attributes of each step of the fractal. For example, with the Sierpinski triangle, sequences were used to describe the number of unshaded triangles, and the total area of the unshaded triangles. These sequences can help you understand the steps of the fractal beyond those that can be physically drawn.

30 Key Concept Question Find the midpoint of a line segment that is 3.7 cm long by constructing its perpendicular bisector.
Check students' drawings, to see that the midpoint is 1.85 cm from either end.

Section ①

Practice & Application Exercises

YOU WILL NEED

For Ex. 1:
♦ Labsheet 1C

For Exs. 15–20 and Ex. 22:
♦ compass
♦ ruler

Exs. 33–34:
♦ grid paper
♦ green, red, and blue pencils

1. Use Labsheet 1C. You'll look for patterns and describe a sequence related to the *Star Fractal*. **See below.**

Write a rule for finding a term of each sequence. Then find the next three terms of the sequence. 2–7. Sample Responses are given.

1. a. Check students' lab-sheets.
b. They are the total number of points of the stars at each step; $t_n = 6t_{n-1}$; 1296: 7776; 46,656; 279,936; 1,679,616

2. $\frac{1}{2}, \frac{1}{4}, \frac{1}{8}, \ldots$ **Multiply the previous term by $\frac{1}{2}$; $\frac{1}{16}, \frac{1}{32}, \frac{1}{64}$**

3. 94, 47, 23.5, ... **Divide the previous term by 2; 11.75, 5.875, 2.9375**

4. $10x, 20x^2, 40x^3, \ldots$ **Multiply the previous term by $2x$; $80x^4, 160x^5, 320x^6$**

5. 128, 32, 8, 2, ... **Divide the previous term by 4; 0.5, 0.125, 0.03125**

6. 0.8, 1.3, 1.8, ... **Add 0.5 to the previous term; 2.3, 2.8, 3.3**

7. –7, 21, –63, 189, ... **Multiply the previous term by –3; –567, 1701, –5103**

8. Kanesha wrote a sequence using the rule *multiply the previous term by 2 and subtract 3*. What is the fifth term of the sequence if the first term is 6? Will each new term always be an odd number? Explain your thinking. **51; Yes; Sample Response: Multiplying by 2 will give you an even number and subtracting 3 will make that number odd.**

9. Use the sequences below.

Sequence I

Term number	1	2	3	4	5	...	n
Term	2	4	6	8	10	...	?

Sequence II

Term number	1	2	3	4	5	...	n
Term	3	5	7	9	11	...	?

a. For each sequence, write a rule. Find the nth term if you know its term number n.

b. How are the rules you wrote in part (a) different from the rules you wrote in Exercises 2–7?

9. a. I: Multiply the term number by 2; $2n$; II: Multiply the term number by 2 and add 1; $2n + 1$
b. Sample Response: They are based on the term number instead of the previous term.

10. **Challenge** The table below shows a sequence related to the zigzag pattern at the right.

a. What feature of the pattern do the numbers describe? **the lengths of the segments**

b. Find the next three terms of the sequence. Explain how you found them. **0.625, 0.5, 0.3125;**
Sample Response: Let t_n be the nth term. For $n > 2$, $t_n = \frac{1}{2}t_{n-2}$

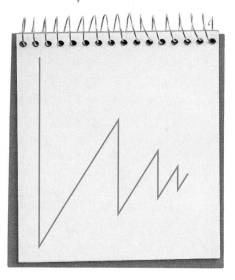

Term number	1	2	3	4	5	6
Term	5	4	2.5	2	1.25	1

Visual Thinking Without measuring or making any drawings, decide whether each set of line segments could form the sides of a triangle. Explain your thinking.

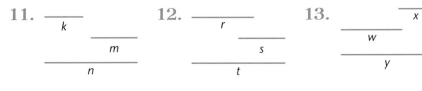

11. $\dfrac{}{k}$ 12. $\dfrac{}{r}$ 13. $\dfrac{}{x}$

11. No; $k + m < n$

12. Yes; $r + s > t$

13. Yes; $x + w > y$

14. **Algebra Connection** A triangle has side lengths 3, 8, and x. Use inequalities to describe all the possible values of x. $5 < x < 11$

Tell whether it is possible to construct a triangle with the given side lengths. If it is possible, construct the triangle. Check students' drawings.

15. 3 in., 2 in., 2 in. Yes.

16. 4 in., 1 in., 2 in. No.

17. 3 in., 3 in., 3 in. Yes.

18. 5 in., 2 in., 3 in. No.

19. 3 in., 2 in., $2\frac{1}{2}$ in. Yes.

20. $1\frac{3}{4}$ in., $1\frac{5}{8}$ in., $3\frac{3}{4}$ in. No.

21. △s 1 and 3, △s 2 and 5, △s 4, 6, and 7; △s 2 and 5; △s 4 and 6; For similiar △s check the shape, for congruent △s use the side-side-side rule. △GHK ≅ △EFD, △STV ≅ △QPR

21. Compare the triangles below. Which appear to be similar? Which appear to be congruent? Explain how you can check. Then write mathematical statements like the one in the Example on page 247 telling which triangles are congruent.

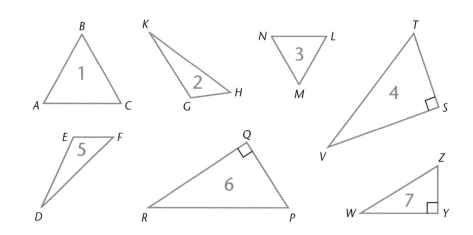

22. You can create a version of the Sierpinski triangle that is not based on an equilateral triangle.

 a. Construct a triangle with side lengths of 4 in., 5 in., and 6 in.
Check students' drawings.

 b. Find the midpoints of the sides of the triangle by constructing perpendicular bisectors. Connect the midpoints to form a middle triangle. Shade this triangle. Check students' drawings.

 c. How does the area of the shaded triangle compare to the area of the original triangle? How does the area of the shaded triangle compare to the areas of the three unshaded triangles?
It is one fourth of the area; The four have the same area.

 d. Measure with a ruler to find the midpoints of the sides of each unshaded triangle. Connect the midpoints to form a middle triangle. Shade each new middle triangle. Check students' drawings.

 e. Suppose you could continue creating smaller and smaller shaded triangles forever. How would the resulting fractal compare to the Sierpinski triangle you made in Exploration 3?
Sample Response: The number of unshaded triangles and the ratio of the area of unshaded triangles to shaded triangles would be the same.

23. Writing In Module 3, you learned a method for bisecting a line segment that used paper folding. Compare this method with the one you learned in Exploration 3 of this section. Which method do you think is more useful? Sample Response: Paper folding may not be convenient, especially when finding the midpoint of more than one segment.

24. Visual Thinking Draw any four-sided polygon. Find the midpoint of each of the four sides. Then connect the midpoints to form another four-sided polygon. What type of figure is this new polygon? a parallelogram

Reflecting ▶ on the Section

Write your answer to Exercise 25 in your journal.

25. Read the retelling of the beginning of Hans Christian Andersen's story "The Emperor's New Clothes." Then create an ending to the story that tells how the tailors could use a process like the one you used to make a Sierpinski triangle to make their cloth. Include a mathematical sequence in your story ending.
Answers will vary. Check students' work.

Journal

Exercise 25 checks that you can identify and describe a sequence.

The Emperor's New Clothes

Many years ago there lived an Emperor who was so tremendously fond of fine new clothes that he spent all his money on being elegantly dressed. He took no interest in his army or the theatre or in driving through the country, unless it was to show off his new clothes. He had different clothes for every hour of the day and, just as you might say of a King that he was in the council-chamber, so it was always said of the Emperor, "He is in his wardrobe."

There was plenty of fun going on in the city where the Emperor lived. Strangers were continually arriving, and one day there came two swindlers. They made out they were weavers and could weave the very finest stuff imaginable. Not only were colours and design unusually attractive, but the clothes made from their material had the peculiarity of being invisible to anyone who wasn't fit for his post or who was hopelessly stupid.

Hans Christian Andersen: Eighty Fairy Tales, translated by R.P. Keigwin

▲ Hans Christian Andersen, a story-teller from Denmark, wrote "The Ugly Duckling" and "The Little Mermaid."

Use the Venn diagram for Exercises 26–28. (Module 3, p. 227)

26. How many students had a fruit topping? **26 students**

27. How many students had a granola topping? **28 students**

28. How many students did not have a topping? **3 students**

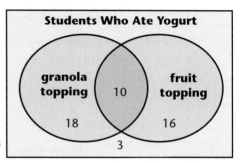

Students Who Ate Yogurt

granola topping   10   fruit topping

18   16

3

Copy and complete each equation. (Module 1, p. 9)

29. 25 mi/h = __?__ mi/min
about 0.42

30. \$0.17 per oz = \$__?__ per lb   **\$2.72**

31. 3.4 m/s = __?__ m/min   **204**

32. \$5.35 per hour = \$__?__ per min
about \$0.09

Digital Artist: Junpei Sekino

When Junpei Sekino was 10 years old he won first prize for the junior division in a national printmaking contest in Japan. He now combines art and mathematics to create fractal art.

33. Computers are often used to generate fractals and other patterns. Follow the steps below to get an idea of how computers are used to create patterns.
See Additional Answers.

First Draw a coordinate grid. Label the x-axis and the y-axis from 0 to 10.

Next Evaluate the expression xy using the coordinates for each point on the grid. For example, the coordinates (2, 3) would give a value of 2 · 3, or 6.

Then Plot and color the point for each coordinate on your grid using the following rules.

- If xy is a multiple of 10, color the point green.
- If xy is an odd number, color the point blue.
- If xy is neither of these, color the point red.

34. What patterns do you see on your grid? What do you think would be the result if the numbers on the grid went to 100? **See Additional Answers.**

▲
Junpei Sekino uses fractals to show the beautiful patterns in mathematics, as in his digital art, *Snail*, below.

Creating a Pattern

Patterns are all around you. How many can you find? In this module you'll explore natural and human-made patterns. You'll use mathematics to describe patterns. You'll also create a work of art that is based on a mathematical pattern.

Using Sequences Use the sculpture pictured at the right for Project Questions 1 and 2.

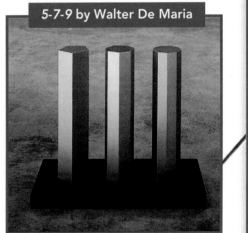

5-7-9 by Walter De Maria

1 Walter De Maria's sculpture shows a pattern that you can describe mathematically. Look at the number of sides for each column and write a rule for the sequence. **Add 2 to the previous term.**

2 Suppose the sculpture is continued with three more columns. How many sides will each column have? **11, 13, 15**

3 Using items from your classroom or from home, create your own art using a sequence. Write a rule for the sequence. **Answers will vary. Check students' work.**

You will need: • *compass and ruler (Ex. 8)*

Write a rule for finding a term of each sequence. Then find the next three terms.

1–4. Sample Responses are given.

1. $1 + x$, $2 + x$, $3 + x$, ... Add 1 to the previous term. $4 + x, 5 + x, 6 + x$

2. 64, 16, 4, 1, ... Divide the previous term by 4. $\frac{1}{4}, \frac{1}{16}, \frac{1}{64}$

3. 51, 17, $5\frac{2}{3}$, ... Divide the previous term by 3. $1\frac{8}{9}, \frac{17}{27}, \frac{17}{81}$

4. –1, 70, –4900, 343,000, ... Multiply the previous term by –70. –24,010,000; 1,680,700,000; –117,649,000,000

Tell whether it is possible to construct a triangle with the given side lengths.

5. 5 cm, 4 cm, 10 cm No.

6. $2\frac{5}{16}$ in., 4 in., $1\frac{5}{8}$ in. No.

7. 8 cm, 24 cm, 24 cm Yes.

8. Suppose △ABC has side lengths of 4 cm, 5 cm, and 6 cm.

   a. Construct a triangle that is congruent to △ABC. Label the vertices of this new triangle. Then write a mathematical statement saying that the triangle is congruent to △ABC. Check students' drawings.

   b. Find the midpoint of each side of the triangle you constructed in part (a). (Use the method of constructing a perpendicular bisector that you learned in Exploration 3 of this section.) Connect the midpoints to form a new triangle. Check students' drawings.

   c. Does the new triangle appear to be similar to the original triangle? Describe how you could check to make sure.

      Yes; Possible answers: The triangles are similiar if the measures of the two pairs of corresponding angles are equal or if the lengths of corresponding sides are in proportion.

Study Skills ▶ Test-Taking Strategies

There are many different types of test questions, including multiple choice, free response, open-ended, and performance task. The Standardized Testing feature in this book provides practice with these types of questions.

1. When you answer a multiple choice question, it is important to read all the choices before you decide which one is correct. Look back at the multiple choice questions in the Standardized Testing feature on page 223. For each question, explain why each choice is either correct or incorrect. See Additional Answers.

2. When you complete a performance task, it is important to show all your work. Look back at the performance task in the Standardized Testing feature on page 232. Describe the steps that you should show in your solution. See Additional Answers.

Changing SHAPE

The Situation   See the Resource Book for a detailed discussion of this Extended Exploration.

Some fractals can be constructed in surprising ways. Here are the first six steps for constructing a Sierpinski triangle using circles.

The Problem   Count the circles in the first four steps and then find the sequence used. Step 7 would have 1095 circles, Step 8 would have 3282 circles, and Step 9 would have 9843 circles

Find a method for finding the number of circles in each step.

Then find the number of circles that would be needed for Steps 7–9.

Something to Think About

* How is the fractal described above self-similar?   See below.

* How were the figures for each step created?
  Sample Response: by multiplying the number of circles in the last step by 3 and subtracting 3

Present Your Results   Answers will vary. Check students' work.

Explain how you solved the problem and why your method worked.

Use tables and drawings to support your explanation.

Sample response: Each figure is formed by reducing the size of the previous triangle and putting three of the reduced copies together so that one vertex of each triangle overlaps a vertex of each of the other triangles that form the figure.

IN THIS SECTION

EXPLORATION 1
◆ Rotational Symmetry

EXPLORATION 2
◆ Rational and Irrational Numbers

Nature's Sequences

WARM-UP EXERCISES

Rewrite each fraction with a denominator that is a power of 10.

1. $\frac{4}{5}$ $\frac{8}{10}$

2. $\frac{3}{25}$ $\frac{12}{100}$

3. $\frac{3}{4}$ $\frac{75}{100}$

Find each square root.

4. $\sqrt{9}$ 3

5. $\sqrt{64}$ 8

▲ Roman and Arabic numerals

◄◄◄ *Setting the Stage*

SET UP   *Work with a partner.*

His neighbors called him *Bigollone*, which means "the blockhead." His real name was Leonardo Fibonacci, and he was not a blockhead at all. He was a mathematician. He was born in Italy around 1170, but grew up in the city of Bougie on the Barbary Coast of North Africa.

Fibonacci learned the Arabic number system in Africa. He realized that Arabic numerals were much easier to use than the Roman numerals then used in Europe. In 1202 Fibonacci published a book that introduced Arabic numerals to the European world. In his book he presented a mathematical problem that has fascinated people for centuries.

Suppose two newborn rabbits, male and female, are put in a cage. How many pairs of rabbits will there be at the end of one year if this pair of rabbits produces another pair every month, and every new pair of rabbits produces another new pair every month? All rabbits must be two months old before they can produce more rabbits.

Here is what happens in the first three months after the first pair of newborn rabbits are put in the cage:

Start   Start with **1st pair** of newborn rabbits.
Month 1   **1st pair** are growing.
Month 2   **1st pair** are adults. They produce **2nd pair** of rabbits.
Month 3   **1st pair** produce a **3rd pair** of rabbits.
              2nd pair are growing.

Think About It ▶▶▶▶▶▶▶▶▶▶▶▶▶▶▶▶▶▶▶▶▶▶▶▶▶▶▶▶▶▶

1 Solve Fibonacci's rabbit problem. Start by creating a model or diagram that shows the total number of rabbit pairs over the first six months of the year. Find a way to show new-born, growing, and adult rabbits. Use your model to help complete a table like the one shown. **See Additional Answers.**

Month	Number of rabbit pairs			Total number of rabbit pairs
	Newborn	Growing	Adult	
Start	1	0	0	1
1	0	1	?	?
2	?	?	?	?

2 The number pattern in the last column of the table you made in Question 1 is known as the *Fibonacci sequence*. The numbers in the sequence are sometimes called Fibonacci numbers.

Fibonacci sequence				
1	1	2	3	5...
↓	↓	↓		
1st term	2nd term	3rd term		

a. How are any two consecutive terms of the Fibonacci sequence used to find the next term in the sequence? **Each term after the second is the sum of the two previous consecutive terms.**

b. What is the answer to Fibonacci's rabbit problem? Explain how you got your answer.

2. b. 233 rabbits; The total number of pairs are terms of the Fibonacci sequence. The thirteenth term, which corresponds to the twelfth month, or one year, is 233.

▶ Fibonacci's rabbit problem is not a realistic model of how rabbits reproduce. Nevertheless, in this section you'll see that the Fibonacci sequence has a strange way of showing up in nature.

GOAL

LEARN HOW TO...
◆ describe rotational symmetry

AS YOU...
◆ discover patterns in nature

KEY TERMS
◆ rotational symmetry
◆ minimum rotational symmetry

Exploration 1

Rotational Symmetry

SET UP You will need: • Labsheet 2A • protractor

▶ Botanists use numbers to describe the growth patterns of plants. A plant's *phyllotaxis* is a ratio that describes the arrangement of leaves on a stem. The plant shown has a phyllotaxis of $\frac{2}{5}$. Each new leaf is produced after $\frac{2}{5}$ of a revolution around the stem.

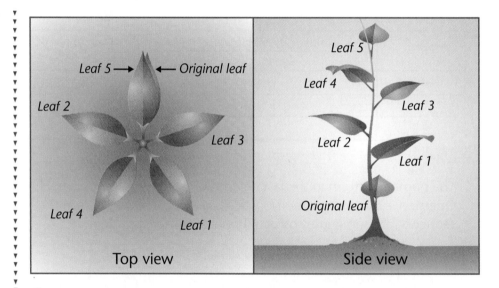

Top view   Side view

3. Table: $\frac{6}{5}, \frac{8}{5}, \frac{10}{5}$
a. Leaf 5
b. It is directly above it.
c. more; A full revolution is 1 and $\frac{6}{5}$ is greater than 1.

3 Use Labsheet 2A. You'll use the plant diagram and look for a pattern to learn more about the *Plant's Phyllotaxis.*

4 The plant's phyllotaxis, $\frac{2}{5}$, is a ratio written as a fraction. The numerator, 2, tells you the number of revolutions around the stem before a leaf appears directly above the original leaf. What do you think the denominator tells you? Sample Response: The number of leaves that are produced before a leaf appears directly above the original leaf.

▶ The two-dimensional drawing above on the left shows what the leaves look like when viewed from above. This drawing of leaves 1 through 5 has *rotational symmetry*. A figure has **rotational symmetry** if it fits exactly on itself after being rotated less than 360° around a center point.

EXAMPLE

The plant on page 258 has rotational symmetries of 72°, 144°, 216°, and 288°. The **minimum rotational symmetry** is 72°. To find the minimum rotational symmetry, you can use either method shown.

Method 1
Use a protractor to measure the angle between the leaves.

Method 2
There are 360° in a circle. Divide 360° by the number of congruent angles in the plant.

5 **Try This as a Class** Objects in nature may seem symmetrical, though they do not have perfect symmetry. Tell which figures appear to have rotational symmetry. For those that do, give the minimum rotational symmetry. Tell what other rotational symmetries they appear to have.

a. minimum: 60°; 120°, 180°, 240°, 300°.

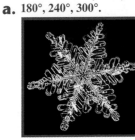

b. no rotational symmetry

c. minimum: 120°; 240°.

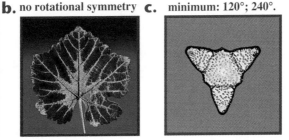

6. Sample Response:

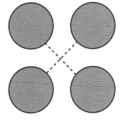

6 ✔ **CHECKPOINT** Sketch a shape that has rotational symmetries of 90°, 180°, and 270°.

✔ **QUESTION 6**

...checks that you can use rotational symmetry to create shapes.

7 **Discussion** Botanists have found plants with phyllotaxes of $\frac{1}{2}$, $\frac{1}{3}$, $\frac{2}{5}$, $\frac{3}{8}$, $\frac{5}{13}$, and $\frac{8}{21}$. What pattern do you notice in the numerators and denominators of these fractions? The numerators are the first 6 terms of the Fibonacci sequence and the denominators are terms 3–8.

HOMEWORK EXERCISES ▶ See Exs. 1–5 on pp. 263–264.

GOAL

LEARN HOW TO...
- recognize rational and irrational numbers
- use notation for repeating decimals

AS YOU...
- explore ratios

KEY TERMS
- rational number
- terminating decimal
- repeating decimal
- irrational number

Exploration 2

Rational and Irrational Numbers

▶ The fractions used to describe the phyllotaxes of plants are examples of *rational numbers*. A **rational number** is a number that can be written in the form $\frac{a}{b}$, where a and b are integers and $b \neq 0$.

EXAMPLE

0.3 is a rational number because it can be written as $\frac{3}{10}$.

3.8 is a rational number because it can be written as $\frac{38}{10}$.

9 is a rational number because it can be written as $\frac{9}{1}$.

$-2\frac{1}{3}$ is a rational number because it can be written as $\frac{-7}{3}$.

8 Use your calculator to write each rational number as a decimal. Give the decimal displayed on the calculator. Do not round.

a. $\frac{1}{2}$ 0.5   **b.** $\frac{1}{3}$ 0.333333333 **c.** $\frac{4}{25}$ 0.16   **d.** $\frac{3}{8}$ 0.375

9 Try to write each fraction so the denominator is a power of 10.
Sample Responses are given.
a. $\frac{1}{2}$ $\frac{5}{10}$ **b.** $\frac{1}{3}$ not possible **c.** $\frac{4}{25}$ $\frac{16}{100}$ **d.** $\frac{3}{8}$ $\frac{375}{1000}$

10 **Discussion** In Question 9, were you able to write $\frac{1}{3}$ as a fraction with a denominator that is a power of 10? Why or why not?

▶ The fractions $\frac{1}{2}$, $\frac{2}{5}$, and $\frac{3}{8}$ can be written as *terminating decimals*.
A **terminating decimal** contains a limited number of digits.
Some fractions, such as $\frac{1}{3}$, can be written as *repeating decimals*.
A **repeating decimal** contains a number or group of numbers that repeats forever.

11 **Try This as a Class** Any rational number can be written as a terminating or repeating decimal. Explain how you can tell whether a particular fraction will be a *terminating* or a *repeating* decimal.

FOR ▶ HELP
with *equivalent fractions*, see
TOOLBOX, p. 597

10. It was impossible; There is no multiple of 3 that is a power of 10.

11. Find out if the denominator can be written as a power of 10. The fraction will be a terminating decimal if it can and it may be repeating if it cannot.

12 Without using your calculator, divide 7 by 11 and find the answer to eight decimal places. Explain how you know the decimal will continue to repeat beyond the place where you stopped dividing.

0.63636363; The division pattern repeats.

▶ You can use an overbar to show which digits in a decimal repeat.

> **EXAMPLE**
>
> $$\frac{7}{11} = 0.636363\ldots = 0.\overline{63} \text{ so}$$
>
> $\frac{7}{11}$ is exactly equal to $0.\overline{63}$ and $-\frac{7}{11}$ is exactly equal to $-0.\overline{63}$.

13 In the decimal $0.6\overline{3}$, only the digit 3 repeats. Write each decimal below using six decimal places, as shown in the Example. Then write the decimals in order from least to greatest.

 a. $0.8\overline{2}$ $0.\overline{828}$ $0.8\overline{2}$ 0.822

 b. $-0.8\overline{28}$ $-0.\overline{8}$ -0.8 $-0.82\overline{8}$

13. **a.** 0.822222, 0.828828, 0.828282, 0.822000; 0.822, 0.8$\overline{2}$ 0.8$\overline{2}$, 0.$\overline{828}$
b. −0.828282, −0.888888, −0.800000, −0.828888; −0.$\overline{8}$, −0.8$\overline{28}$, −0.82$\overline{8}$, −0.8

14 Write each rational number as a repeating or a terminating decimal. Then write the numbers in order from least to greatest.

 a. $\frac{5}{11}$ $0.\overline{45}$ **b.** $-3\frac{1}{4}$ -3.25 **c.** 6 6 **d.** $-\frac{14}{6}$ $-2.\overline{3}$

14. $-3\frac{1}{4}, -\frac{14}{6}, \frac{5}{11}, 6$ or $-3.25, -2.\overline{3}, 0.\overline{45}, 6$

▶ An **irrational number** cannot be written as the quotient of two integers. When written as a decimal, an irrational number does not terminate or repeat. Both π and $\sqrt{10}$ are examples of irrational numbers. The square root of any integer that is not a perfect square is an irrational number.

15 Tell whether each square root is a *rational* or an *irrational* number.

 a. $\sqrt{81}$ **b.** $\sqrt{18}$ **c.** $-\sqrt{8}$ **d.** $\sqrt{25}$

   rational   irrational   irrational   rational

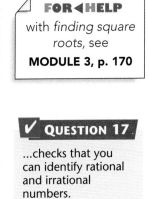

FOR◄HELP

with *finding square roots*, see
MODULE 3, p. 170

16 For each expression in Question 15, find the exact square root or estimate the square root to the nearest tenth.

      a. 9;   **b.** 4.2;   **c.** −2.8;   **d.** 5

17 ✔ **CHECKPOINT** Tell whether each number is a *rational* or an *irrational* number.

 a. $\sqrt{2}$ irrational   **b.** -0.8 rational   **c.** $\frac{9}{17}$ rational

 d. $2\frac{4}{7}$ rational   **e.** $7.\overline{45}$ rational   **f.** $\sqrt{49}$ rational

✔ **QUESTION 17**

...checks that you can identify rational and irrational numbers.

HOMEWORK EXERCISES ▷ See Exs. 6–14 on pp. 264–265.

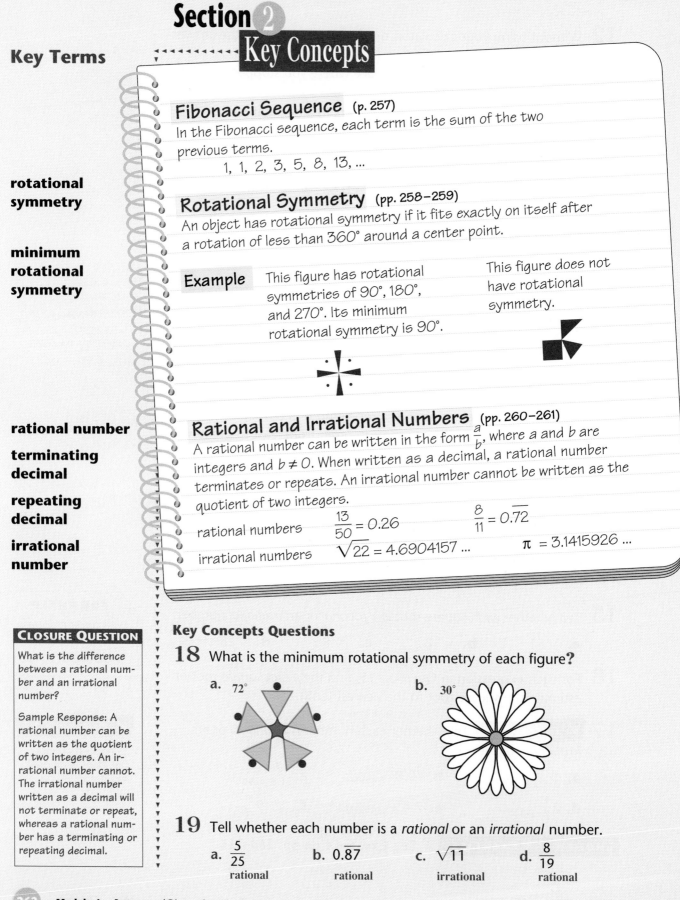

Key Terms

Key Concepts

Fibonacci Sequence (p. 257)

In the Fibonacci sequence, each term is the sum of the two previous terms.

1, 1, 2, 3, 5, 8, 13, ...

rotational symmetry

Rotational Symmetry (pp. 258–259)

An object has rotational symmetry if it fits exactly on itself after a rotation of less than 360° around a center point.

minimum rotational symmetry

Example   This figure has rotational symmetries of 90°, 180°, and 270°. Its minimum rotational symmetry is 90°.

This figure does not have rotational symmetry.

rational number

terminating decimal

repeating decimal

irrational number

Rational and Irrational Numbers (pp. 260–261)

A rational number can be written in the form $\frac{a}{b}$, where a and b are integers and $b \neq 0$. When written as a decimal, a rational number terminates or repeats. An irrational number cannot be written as the quotient of two integers.

rational numbers $\frac{13}{50} = 0.26$ $\frac{8}{11} = 0.\overline{72}$

irrational numbers $\sqrt{22} = 4.6904157 ...$ $\pi = 3.1415926 ...$

CLOSURE QUESTION

What is the difference between a rational number and an irrational number?

Sample Response: A rational number can be written as the quotient of two integers. An irrational number cannot. The irrational number written as a decimal will not terminate or repeat, whereas a rational number has a terminating or repeating decimal.

Key Concepts Questions

18 What is the minimum rotational symmetry of each figure?

a. 72°

b. 30°

19 Tell whether each number is a *rational* or an *irrational* number.

a. $\frac{5}{25}$
rational

b. $0.\overline{87}$
rational

c. $\sqrt{11}$
irrational

d. $\frac{8}{19}$
rational

Section ② Practice & Application Exercises

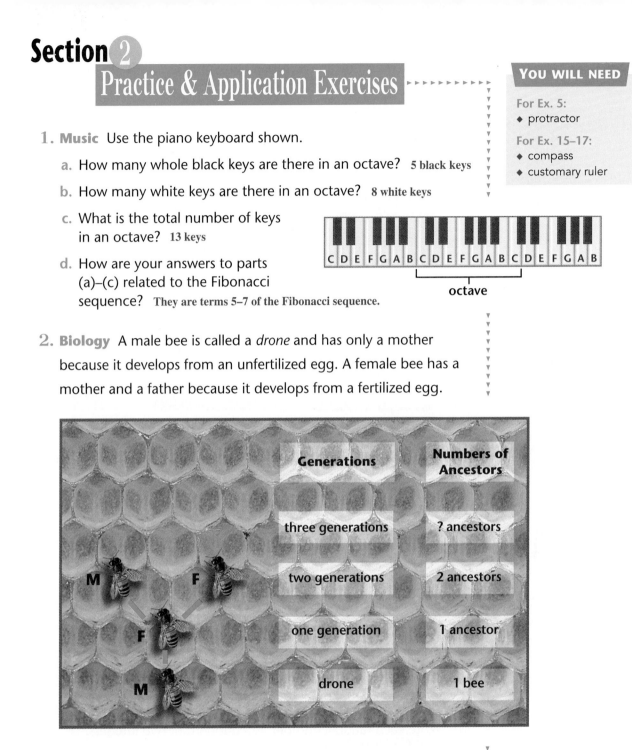

YOU WILL NEED

For Ex. 5:
♦ protractor

For Ex. 15–17:
♦ compass
♦ customary ruler

1. **Music** Use the piano keyboard shown.

   a. How many whole black keys are there in an octave? **5 black keys**

   b. How many white keys are there in an octave? **8 white keys**

   c. What is the total number of keys in an octave? **13 keys**

   d. How are your answers to parts (a)–(c) related to the Fibonacci sequence? **They are terms 5–7 of the Fibonacci sequence.**

2. **Biology** A male bee is called a *drone* and has only a mother because it develops from an unfertilized egg. A female bee has a mother and a father because it develops from a fertilized egg.

Generations	Numbers of Ancestors
three generations	? ancestors
two generations	2 ancestors
one generation	1 ancestor
drone	1 bee

   a. Copy and continue the "family tree" for a drone bee. Extend the family tree 6 generations back. **See Additional Answers.**

   b. Use your family tree to find the total number of bees at each generation. What pattern do you see? **1, 1, 2, 3, 5, 8, 13; the Fibonacci sequence**

   c. Without extending the diagram, find the total number of ancestors the drone would have eight generations back. Explain how you got your answer.
   34 ancestors are in the 8th generation back; Possible answer: Find the next two numbers in the Fibonacci sequence.

3. A figure has a minimum rotational symmetry of 30°. What other rotational symmetries does the figure have?
60°, 90°, 120°, 150°, 180°, 210°, 240°, 270°, 300°, 330°

4. Use the objects shown.

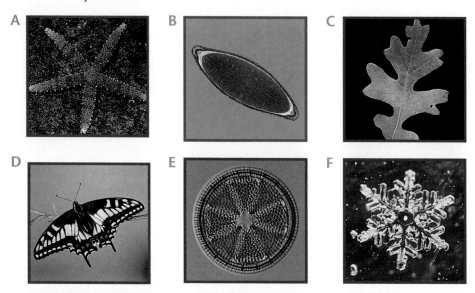

A   B   C

D   E   F

4. a. A, 72°, Divide 360 by 5; B, 180°, Divide 360 by 2; E, 45°, Divide 360 by 8; F, 60°, Divide 360 by 6.

a. Tell which objects appear to have rotational symmetry. For each of these, find the minimum rotational symmetry and explain how you found your answer.

b. A figure has *line symmetry* if one half of the figure is the mirror image of the other half. Tell which objects appear to have line symmetry. **A, B, D, E, and F**

c.

```
| line       |  rotational | rotational  |
| symmetry   |  & line     | symmetry    |
|            |  symmetry   |             |
|    D       |  A, B, E, F |          C  |
```

c. Make a Venn diagram that organizes the objects into these categories: objects that have line symmetry, objects that have rotational symmetry, objects that have both types of symmetry, and objects that have neither type of symmetry.

5. **Create Your Own** Create 3 different designs that involve rotational symmetry. Use a different minimum rotational symmetry for each design. List all the rotational symmetries for each design.
Check students' drawings.

6. Write each rational number as a quotient of two integers.
Sample Responses are given.
a. −4 $\frac{-4}{1}$ b. $\sqrt{16}$ $\frac{4}{1}$ c. 0.25 $\frac{1}{4}$ d. $2\frac{3}{7}$ $\frac{17}{7}$

7. Write each rational number as a repeating or terminating decimal.

a. $2\frac{3}{5}$ 2.6   b. $\frac{9}{11}$ $0.\overline{81}$ c. $\frac{8}{27}$ $0.\overline{296}$ d. $\frac{7}{20}$ 0.35

8. **Writing** Explain why 0.666667 is not exactly equal to $\frac{2}{3}$.
Sample Response: 0.666667 is a terminating decimal, while the decimal form of $\frac{2}{3}$ is not.

9. Write the repeating decimals below in order from least to greatest. Explain your thinking. **0.12̄, 0.1̄2̄5̄, 0.125̄, 0.1̄25; I wrote the repeating forms and compared them.**

    0.1̄25   0.125̄   0.12   0.125

10. Jodie uses her calculator to find a decimal value for $\frac{8}{23}$. Her calculator displays 0.3478260, so she decides $\frac{8}{23}$ is an irrational number. Do you agree with her? Why or why not? **No; $\frac{8}{23}$ is the quotient of two integers.**

11. a. Suppose the decimal 0.12112111211112... continues to follow the same pattern forever. Write the next six digits. **111112**

    b. Why is 0.1̄2̄ a rational number and 0.12112111211112... irrational, even though they both continue forever? **0.1̄2̄ is a repeating decimal and 0.12112111211112111112... is not.**

12. Tell whether each number is a *rational* or an *irrational* number. Then write the numbers in order from least to greatest.

    a. $\sqrt{17}$ **irrational** b. $\frac{16}{3}$ **rational**   c. $-14.\overline{14}$ **rational** d. -1 **rational**

    e. $5\frac{4}{9}$ **rational**   f. -14.1 **rational**   g. 5.33 **rational**   h. $-\sqrt{4}$ **rational**

    $-14.\overline{14}, -14.1, -\sqrt{4}, -1, \sqrt{17}, 5.33, \frac{16}{3}, 5\frac{4}{9}$

13. The number π is irrational. However, the rational numbers $\frac{22}{7}$ and 3.14 are often used to approximate π. Why do you think rational numbers are sometimes used in place of irrational numbers? **Sample Response: It is easier to calculate and compare rational numbers.**

Reflecting ◀▶ **on the Section**

14. Make a list of five objects in your home that have rotational symmetry and five objects that do not. Make a sketch of the objects that have rotational symmetry. Then find the minimum rotational symmetry for each object you sketched. **Answers will vary. Check students' work.**

Spiral ◀▶ **Review**

Tell whether it is possible to construct a triangle with the given side lengths. If it is possible, construct the triangle. (Module 4, p. 247)

15. 6 in., 7 in., 8 in.   16. 2 in., 2 in., 5 in.   17. 4 in., 9 in., 6 in.
Yes; Check students' drawings.   **No.**   **Yes; Check students' drawings.**

Find each sum or difference. (Module 2, p. 139)

18. $-2\frac{1}{5} - \frac{3}{5}$ $-2\frac{4}{5}$ 19. $-3\frac{1}{2} + \left(-3\frac{1}{8}\right)$ $-6\frac{5}{8}$ 20. $-6\frac{2}{3} - \left(-3\frac{1}{4}\right)$ $-3\frac{5}{12}$

21. In the diagram $\triangle ABC \sim \triangle XYZ$. Find the length of $\overline{AC}$.
    (Module 3, p. 207) **21 mm**

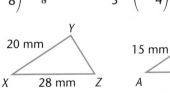

Repeating Decimals

The decimal 0.25 can be written as the fraction $\frac{25}{100}$, or $\frac{1}{4}$. A repeating decimal such as $0.\overline{36}$ can also be written as a fraction.

Step 1 Write an equation. $x = 0.\overline{36}$

Step 2 Multiply both sides by 100 since $0.\overline{36}$ $100x = 100(0.\overline{36})$
has two numbers that repeat. $100x = 36.\overline{36}$

Step 3 Subtract $x = 0.\overline{36}$ from the resulting $- \quad x = - 0.\overline{36}$
equation. $99x = 36$

Step 4 Solve for x and write in lowest terms. $x = \frac{36}{99} = \frac{4}{11}$

Write each repeating decimal as a fraction in lowest terms.

22. $0.\overline{48}$ $\frac{16}{33}$ 23. $0.\overline{2}$ $\frac{2}{9}$ 24. $0.\overline{123}$ $\frac{41}{333}$

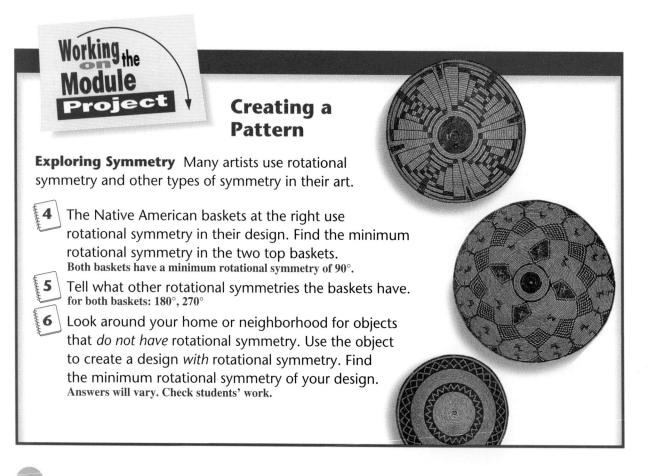

Working on the Module Project

Creating a Pattern

Exploring Symmetry Many artists use rotational symmetry and other types of symmetry in their art.

4 The Native American baskets at the right use rotational symmetry in their design. Find the minimum rotational symmetry in the two top baskets.
Both baskets have a minimum rotational symmetry of 90°.

5 Tell what other rotational symmetries the baskets have.
for both baskets: 180°, 270°

6 Look around your home or neighborhood for objects that *do not have* rotational symmetry. Use the object to create a design *with* rotational symmetry. Find the minimum rotational symmetry of your design.
Answers will vary. Check students' work.

Section 2

Extra Skill Practice

Tell whether each figure appears to have rotational symmetry. If the figure has rotational symmetry, give the minimum rotational symmetry and tell what other rotational symmetries it has.

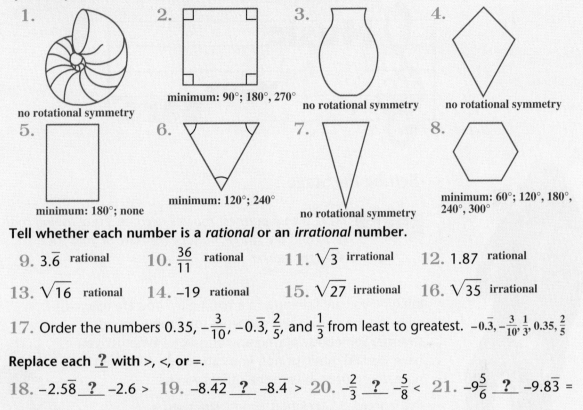

1. no rotational symmetry

2. minimum: 90°; 180°, 270°

3. no rotational symmetry

4. no rotational symmetry

5. minimum: 180°; none

6. minimum: 120°; 240°

7. no rotational symmetry

8. minimum: 60°; 120°, 180°, 240°, 300°

Tell whether each number is a *rational* or an *irrational* number.

9. $3.\overline{6}$ rational

10. $\frac{36}{11}$ rational

11. $\sqrt{3}$ irrational

12. 1.87 rational

13. $\sqrt{16}$ rational

14. -19 rational

15. $\sqrt{27}$ irrational

16. $\sqrt{35}$ irrational

17. Order the numbers 0.35, $-\frac{3}{10}$, $-0.\overline{3}$, $\frac{2}{5}$, and $\frac{1}{3}$ from least to greatest. $-0.\overline{3}, -\frac{3}{10}, \frac{1}{3}, 0.35, \frac{2}{5}$

Replace each ? with >, <, or =.

18. $-2.5\overline{8}$ __?__ -2.6 >

19. $-8.\overline{42}$ __?__ $-8.\overline{4}$ >

20. $-\frac{2}{3}$ __?__ $-\frac{5}{8}$ <

21. $-9\frac{5}{6}$ __?__ $-9.8\overline{3}$ =

1. Which figure does not have rotational symmetry? C

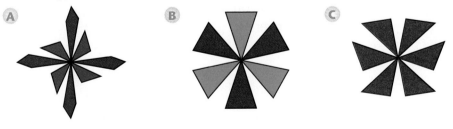

A   B   C

2. Which of the following numbers is an irrational number? B

Ⓐ 40   Ⓑ $\sqrt{108}$ Ⓒ $\frac{29}{28}$ Ⓓ $3.\overline{51}$

Section 3 Equations with Fractions and Quadrilaterals

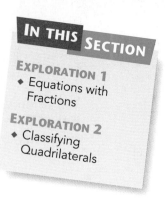

WARM-UP EXERCISES

Divide.

1. $18 \div \frac{1}{3}$ 54

2. $\frac{3}{5} \div \frac{1}{5}$ 3

3. $9 \div 1\frac{1}{2}$ 6

Solve.

4. $2x = 12$ 6

5. $x - 6 = 11$ 17

6. $3x + 4 = 10$ 2

Music to Your Ears

Setting the Stage

SET UP Work with a partner. You will need: • 3 ft of fishing cord or plastic kite string • a tape measure or yard stick • a dark marker

Imagine you are listening to a band play. You are relaxed, enjoying the music, and suddenly something sounds strange. Somebody played a wrong note! Whether you have studied music or not, you can usually tell when a note does not fit in with the others you hear.

Pythagoras, a Greek mathematician, used a monochord to find pairs of musical notes that sounded nice when played together. His discoveries about mathematical relationships related to these pairs of notes are still studied by musicians today. The following experiment will help you understand Pythagoras's discoveries.

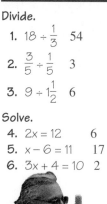

▲ This washtub base is a type of monochord used by musicians today.

◀ A monochord is a musical instrument with one string.

Think About It ▸▸▸▸▸▸▸▸▸▸▸▸▸▸▸▸▸▸

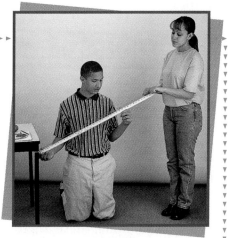

1 Follow the steps to make a simple model of a monochord.

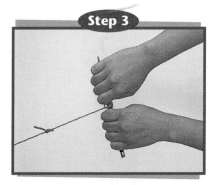

Step 1

Tie one end of your string to a stationary object such as a desk or chair. Measure and mark the string 24 in. from the knot.

Check students' work.

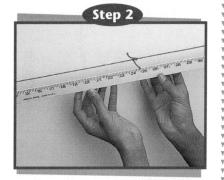

Step 2

Find the length that is $\frac{3}{4}$ of 24 in. Measure and mark that length from the knot. Measure from the knot and mark the lengths that are $\frac{1}{2}$ and $\frac{1}{3}$ of the 24 in. string.

$\frac{3}{4}(24) = 18$; 18 in.; 12 in., 8 in.

Step 3

Tie the loose end of the string around a pencil and roll the string tightly around the pencil until you reach the 24 in. mark.

Check students' work.

Step 4

Pluck the string and listen closely to the sound it makes. Repeat Step 3 for each mark on the string. Tell whether each sound has a higher or lower pitch (sounds higher or lower) than the one before.

Check students' work.

2 List the four string lengths in order from the lowest sound to the highest sound. What pattern do you see?

24 in., 18 in., 12 in., 8 in.; The longer the string is, the lower the sound will be.

GOAL

LEARN HOW TO...

♦ solve equations with fractional coefficients

AS YOU...

♦ discover patterns in music

KEY TERM

♦ reciprocal

Equations
With
Fractions

▶ One pair of notes that sound nice together are the notes C and F. In the C major scale, these are the first and fourth notes of the scale. Musicians call the difference in pitch of these notes a *fourth*. The difference in pitch between G and C is also a fourth.

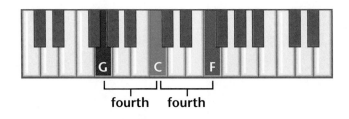

▶ Pythagoras discovered that if string lengths have a ratio of 1 to $\frac{3}{4}$, the strings produce notes that are a fourth apart.

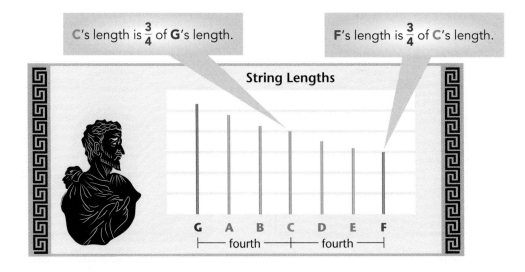

C's length is $\frac{3}{4}$ of G's length.

F's length is $\frac{3}{4}$ of C's length.

String Lengths

G A B C D E F
├── fourth ──┼── fourth ──┤

3 Try This as a Class Use the diagram above.

   a. Write an equation showing how the length *f* of the string for F is related to the length *c* of the string for C. $f = \frac{3}{4}c$

   b. Suppose the string for C is 12 in. long. Find the length of the string for F. **9 in.**

4 Try This as a Class Use the diagram on page 270.

    a. Write an equation showing how the length c of the string for C is related to the length g of the string for G. $c = \frac{3}{4}g$

    b. Suppose the string for C is 12 in. long. Rewrite your equation from part (a) using this information. $12 = \frac{3}{4}g$

▶ **In your equation from Question 4, the variable is multiplied by a fraction. To solve for the variable, you can undo the multiplication by dividing by the fraction. To divide by a fraction, multiply by its *reciprocal*. Two numbers are *reciprocals* if their product is 1.**

EXAMPLE

To solve $8 = \frac{4}{5}x$, you can undo the multiplication by dividing both sides of the equation by $\frac{4}{5}$.

$$8 = \frac{4}{5}x$$

$$8 \div \frac{4}{5} = \frac{4}{5}x \div \frac{4}{5}$$

To divide by $\frac{4}{5}$, multiply by its reciprocal, $\frac{5}{4}$.

$$8 \cdot \frac{5}{4} = \frac{4}{5}x \cdot \frac{5}{4}$$

$$10 = x$$

FOR ▶ HELP

with *dividing fractions*, see

TOOLBOX, p. 598

---

5 Discussion The second step of the Example shows $\frac{4}{5}x \div \frac{4}{5}$. Explain why this could be rewritten as x. $\frac{4}{5}x \div \frac{4}{5} = 1 \cdot x = x$

6 Suppose the string for C is 12 in. long. Solve your equation from Question 4(b) to find how long the string should be for G. 16 in.

7 Try This as a Class Describe the steps you would use to solve each equation.

    a. $4\frac{1}{2}x = 180$ **b.** $5 + \frac{2}{3}x = 11$

8 ✔ **CHECKPOINT** Solve each equation.

    a. $\frac{1}{3}t = 21$ 63   **b.** $\frac{1}{6}y = 20$ 120   **c.** $2\frac{2}{3}n = 8$ 3

    d. $12 + \frac{1}{2}r = 20$ 16   **e.** $\frac{1}{7} = \frac{5}{7}x$ $\frac{1}{5}$ **f.** $1\frac{1}{2}s - 6 = 22$ $18\frac{2}{3}$

7. **a.** Divide both sides of the equation by $4\frac{1}{2}$.

b. Step 1: Subtract 5 from both sides of the equation; **Step 2:** Multiply both sides of the equation by $\frac{3}{2}$ to find x.

✔ **QUESTION 8**

...checks that you can solve equations with fractional coefficients.

HOMEWORK EXERCISES ▶ See Exs. 1–9 on p. 276.

GOAL

LEARN HOW TO...
◆ classify
  quadrilaterals

AS YOU...
◆ look at different
  musical
  instruments

KEY TERMS
◆ quadrilateral
◆ rectangle
◆ parallelogram
◆ rhombus
◆ trapezoid
◆ square

Classifying Quadrilaterals

SET UP *Work with a partner. You will need:* • *Labsheet 3A*
• *protractor* • *ruler*

▶ **Musical instruments can be classified by how they produce sounds. For example, a monochord and a violin are classified as *stringed instruments*. A piano and a drum are classified as *percussion instruments*.**

9–10. Sample Responses are given. See below.

9 **Discussion** How are a monochord and a violin alike? How are they different?

10 **Discussion** Why do you think a piano is classified as a percussion instrument? How else could you classify a piano? Explain.

▶ *Quadrilaterals* **can be classified by their properties. A quadrilateral is a polygon with four sides.**

▲
The musical group Sweet Honey in the Rock uses traditional percussion instruments.

9. Both are stringed instruments; a monochord has one string, a violin has more than one.

10. Sound is made by striking a string; stringed; sound is produced by strings.

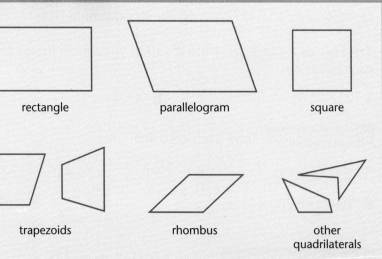

rectangle   parallelogram   square

trapezoids   rhombus   other quadrilaterals

11 Although you can not see all four sides, the polygon partially hidden behind the screen is a quadrilateral. The hidden quadrilateral could be a trapezoid or some other quadrilateral.

trapezoid   quadrilateral

a. How are the trapezoid and the quadrilateral shown different from each other?

b. Can the hidden quadrilateral be any of the other types of quadrilaterals shown on page 272? Explain why or why not.
No; It has no right angles and no parallel sides.

12 Discussion Tell what types of quadrilaterals could be hidden behind each screen. Explain your reasoning.

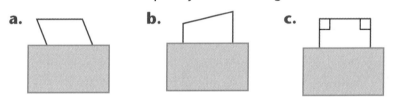

a.   **b.**   **c.**

13 Sketch a partially hidden quadrilateral. Tell what types of quadrilaterals it could be. Sample Response: ⬓; parallelogram, trapezoid

▶ **Characteristics of Quadrilaterals** You can use the notation below to identify certain characteristics of quadrilaterals. Symbols are used to indicate right angles, sides that are equal in length, and sides that are parallel.

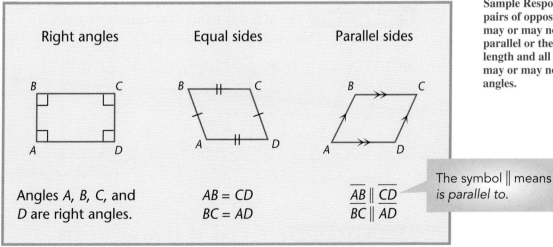

Right angles   Equal sides   Parallel sides

Angles *A, B, C,* and *D* are right angles.

$AB = CD$
$BC = AD$

$\overline{AB} \parallel \overline{CD}$
$\overline{BC} \parallel \overline{AD}$

The symbol ‖ means *is parallel to.*

11. a. The quadrilateral has no parallel sides and the trapezoid has one pair of parallel sides.

12. a. parallelogram, trapezoid, rhombus; Sample Response: Both pairs of opposite sides may or may not be parallel or the same length. It cannot be a square or a rectangle because the angles are not right angles.

b. parallelogram, trapezoid, rhombus; Sample Response: Both pairs of opposite sides may or may not be parallel or the same length. It cannot be a square or a rectangle because the angles are not right angles.

c. rectangle, parallelogram, square, trapezoid, or rhombus; Sample Response: Both pairs of opposite sides may or may not be parallel or the same length and all the angles may or may not be right angles.

Use Labsheet 3A for Questions 14–16.

14 Follow the instructions on the labsheet for identifying *Characteristics of Quadrilaterals.* You'll use a protractor and ruler to make measurements. Then you'll use the notation on page 273 to mark angles and sides. **See Additional Answers.**

▶ Quadrilaterals can be classified according to their properties. Because different quadrilaterals can have the same properties, the quadrilaterals on Labsheet 3A may have more than one name.

15 a. A **parallelogram** is a quadrilateral that has two pairs of parallel sides. Identify all the parallelograms on the labsheet.

W, X, Y, Z

b. A **rectangle** is a quadrilateral that has four right angles. Identify all the rectangles on the labsheet. **W, Y**

c. A **rhombus** is a quadrilateral that has four sides of equal length. Identify all the rhombuses on the labsheet. **W, X**

d. A **trapezoid** is a quadrilateral that has exactly one pair of parallel sides. Identify all the trapezoids on the labsheet. **V**

e. Use your results from parts (a)–(c) to give a definition for a **square**. Then identify all the squares that are on the labsheet.

16 Try This as a Class Follow the directions below for completing the Venn diagram on Labsheet 3A.

a. Decide on a category label for each oval. Then write the letters of the five quadrilaterals in the Venn diagram.

b. Where did you put the trapezoid? Why did you put it there?

c. Which quadrilateral on the labsheet has the greatest number of names? **the square**

15. e. Sample Response:
A square is a parallelogram that is both a rectangle and a rhombus. W

16. a. Sample Response:

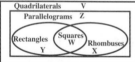

b. In the quadrilateral section but outside the parallelogram section; It is a quadrilateral and not a parallelogram.

✔ **QUESTION 17**

...checks that you can classify quadrilaterals.

17 ✔ **CHECKPOINT** List as many names as possible for each quadrilateral. Which name is most precise?

a.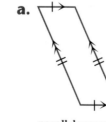

parallelogram

b.

trapezoid

c.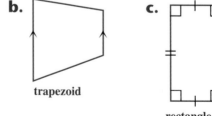

rectangle, parallelogram; rectangle

HOMEWORK EXERCISES ▶ See Exs. 10–17 on pp. 276–278.

Section ③
Key Concepts

Reciprocals and Equations (pp. 270–271)

You can use inverse operations to solve an equation with a fraction for a coefficient. To solve $\frac{7}{8}x = 4$, divide both sides of the equation by $\frac{7}{8}$. To divide by a fraction you can multiply by its reciprocal, $\frac{8}{7}$. Two numbers are reciprocals if their product is 1.

Example

To divide by $\frac{7}{8}$, multiply by its reciprocal, $\frac{8}{7}$.

$$\frac{7}{8}x = 4$$

$$\frac{7}{8}x \div \frac{7}{8} = 4 \div \frac{7}{8}$$

$$\frac{7}{8}x \cdot \frac{8}{7} = 4 \cdot \frac{8}{7}$$

$$x = 4\frac{4}{7}$$

Classifying Quadrilaterals (pp. 272–274)

A quadrilateral is a polygon with four sides. Quadrilaterals are classified by their angle measures, parallel sides, and side lengths. Each quadrilateral in the diagram below has the characteristics of the quadrilateral(s) linked to it above.

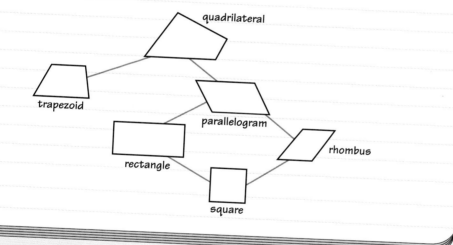

- quadrilateral
- trapezoid
- parallelogram
- rhombus
- rectangle
- square

quadrilateral

rectangle

parallelogram

rhombus

trapezoid

square

Key Concepts Questions

18 Solve the equation $20 = \frac{2}{3}y - 7$. Explain the steps you use.

19 **Use Labsheet 3A** Compare the "quadrilateral tree" shown above with the Venn diagram on the labsheet. How are they alike? How are they different? For example, how does each model show that a rhombus is a parallelogram? Sample Response: Both show how quadrilaterals are related; In the Venn diagram relationships are modeled by overlapping regions. In the tree, relationships are modeled by connecting lines.

18. $40\frac{1}{2}$; Step 1: Add 7 to both sides of the equation; Step 2: Multiply both sides of the equation by $\frac{3}{2}$ to solve for y.

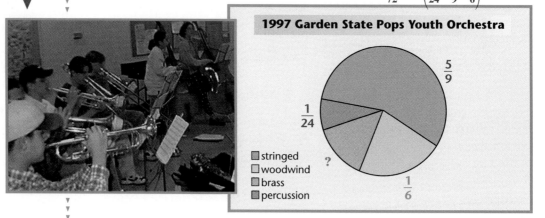

Practice & Application Exercises

YOU WILL NEED

For Ex. 13:
♦ Labsheet 3B

Members of the 1997 Garden State Pops Youth Orchestra during a rehearsal.

1. **Music** The 1997 Garden State Pops Youth Orchestra had four sections. The circle graph shows what fraction of the orchestra played in three of the sections.

    a. Forty orchestra members played stringed instruments. How many members were in the entire orchestra? **72 members**

    b. What fraction of the orchestra members played brass instruments? How did you find your answer? $\frac{17}{72}; 1 - \left(\frac{1}{24} + \frac{5}{9} + \frac{1}{6}\right)$

1997 Garden State Pops Youth Orchestra

$\frac{5}{9}$

$\frac{1}{24}$

□ stringed
□ woodwind
□ brass
□ percussion

?

$\frac{1}{6}$

2. **Challenge** Soft drinks come in four sizes at a local convenience store: small, medium, large, and jumbo. The small is $\frac{1}{9}$ the size of the jumbo. The jumbo is 2 times the size of the large and the medium is $\frac{1}{3}$ the size of the large. If the medium is 12 ounces, find the size of the jumbo, the large, and the small. **jumbo: 72 oz; large: 36 oz; small: 8 oz**

Solve each equation.

3. $\frac{3}{5}n = 15$ **25**   4. $10 = \frac{3}{2}x$ $\frac{20}{3}$ 5. $1\frac{2}{3}r = 120$ **72**

6. $\frac{5}{6}b + 14 = 15$ $\frac{6}{5}$ 7. $45 = \frac{3}{4}h - 12$ **76**   8. $2\frac{1}{4}s - 7 = 20$ **12**

9. **Geometry Connection** The area of the triangle is 209 ft². Find the length of the base of the triangle. **22 ft**

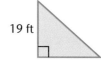

19 ft

22 ft

Tell whether each statement is *True* or *False*. Explain your answer.

10. A square is *always* a rectangle. **True; A square has four right angles.**

11. A quadrilateral is *always* a trapezoid. **False; A quadrilateral can have two pairs of parallel sides, or no parallel sides.**

12. A rectangle is *sometimes* a rhombus.
    True; A rectangle that is a square is a rhombus.

13. Use Labsheet 3B. List as many names as possible for each of the *Quadrilaterals*. Circle the name for each figure that is most precise.

14. Use the descriptions to draw and label each quadrilateral. Then give the most specific name for the quadrilateral that you sketched. **Check students' drawings.**

    a. A quadrilateral with two pairs of parallel sides, four sides of equal length, and no 90° angles. **rhombus**

    b. A quadrilateral with exactly one pair of parallel sides and exactly two 90° angles. **trapezoid**

    c. A quadrilateral with two pairs of congruent sides and four right angles that is not a rhombus. **rectangle**

Architecture **Architects often use geometric figures when designing buildings.**

15. Identify the type of quadrilaterals outlined on each building. Explain your answers.

13. A: parallelogram, rectangle (most precise); B: parallelogram, rhombus (most precise); C: trapezoid; D: quadrilateral; E: quadrilateral; F: parallelogram, rectangle, rhombus, square (most precise); G: trapezoid; H: quadrilateral; I: trapezoid

Julia Morgan was one of the first women architects in the United States ▼

a.

▲ Karla Kowalski designed this addition to Grosslobming Castle in Austria.
a. trapezoid, parallelogram, trapezoid

b.

▲ Julia Morgan was one of the architects for Phoebe Hearst's castle in California.
b. square, trapezoid, rectangle

16. Challenge The 62-story John Hancock Tower in Boston has an 8-story base and a 54-story tower. The figures below show an overhead view of the building.

    a. What type of quadrilateral is used for the base of the building? for the roof of the tower? **trapezoid; parallelogram**

    b. How would you find the area of the base of the building? How would you find the area of the roof of the tower?

Use the formula for the area of a trapezoid; use the formula for the area of a parallelogram, or use the formula for the area of a triangle and subtract the area of the right triangle from the area of the trapezoid.

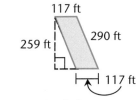

117 ft
259 ft   290 ft
246 ft
Base of building

117 ft
259 ft   290 ft
117 ft
Roof of tower

Reflecting ◀▷ on the Section

17. A piece of paper, a door, and a cassette tape box are all examples of rectangles. Find real-world examples of other types of quadrilaterals. Make sketches of what you find.
    Answers will vary. Check students' work.

Spiral ◀▷ Review

Tell whether each number is a *rational* or an *irrational* number. (Module 4, p. 260)

18. $\frac{18}{1}$ rational

19. 15.5217 rational

20. $\sqrt{15}$ irrational

21. $\sqrt{289}$ rational

Tell whether each ordered pair is a solution of the equation $y = -x + 2$. (Module 3, p. 183)

22. (0, 2) Yes.

23. (–1, –1) No.

24. (–2, 0) No.

25. (2, 4) No.

Solve each equation. Round decimal solutions to the nearest hundredth. (Module 3, p. 218)

26. $19 = 2.5x - 3.1$ 8.84

27. $\frac{n}{4.4} - 39 = -52.6$ –59.84

28. $3.7 + 0.6z = 11$ 12.17

29. $\frac{r}{2} + 31.1 = 21$ –20.2

Extension ▶▶

Other Equations with Fractions

Sometimes equations are written so that the variable is part of a fraction. In Exercises 30–32 you'll explore different methods for solving an equation like $\frac{3x}{5} = 10$.

30. One method for solving the equation $\frac{3x}{5} = 10$ is to first rewrite it as $\frac{3}{5}x = 10$. Solve $\frac{3}{5}x = 10$. Check that your answer is also the solution of $\frac{3x}{5} = 10$. $16\frac{2}{3}; \frac{3x}{5} = \frac{3 \cdot 16\frac{2}{3}}{5} = \frac{50}{5} = 10$

31. Another way to solve $\frac{3x}{5} = 10$ is to first multiply both sides of the equation by 5. Why is it helpful to use this as a first step? Finish solving the equation. to eliminate fractions; $3x = 50$, $x = 16\frac{2}{3}$

32. **Choosing a Method** Solve each equation.
    a. $\frac{5y}{6} = 18$ $21\frac{3}{5}$
    b. $21 = \frac{3n}{10}$ 70
    c. $\frac{p}{8} + 10 = 20$ 80

Solve each equation.

1. $\frac{1}{8}x = -3$ –24

2. $5 = 3 + \frac{2}{3}y$ 3

3. $4 = \frac{7}{3}m$ $\frac{12}{7}$

4. $\frac{1}{2} = \frac{3}{4}x + \frac{1}{2}$ 0

5. $\frac{2}{5}m - \frac{1}{10} = \frac{3}{10}$ 1

6. $\frac{2}{9} + \frac{1}{3}b = \frac{7}{9}$ $\frac{15}{9}$, or $\frac{5}{3}$

7. $\frac{3}{2}t + 15 = 30$ 10

8. $4 = 2 + \frac{1}{4}s$ 8

9. $6 = \frac{4}{9}x - \frac{1}{9}$ $\frac{55}{4}$

List as many names as possible for each figure.

10. 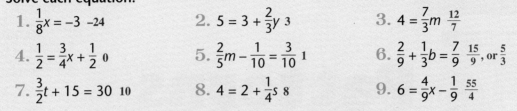   quadrilateral, parallelogram

11.   quadrilateral, parallelogram

12. 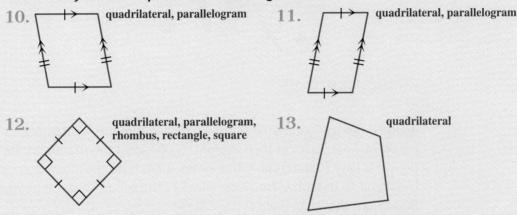   quadrilateral, parallelogram, rhombus, rectangle, square

13.   quadrilateral

Tell whether each statement is _True_ or _False_. Explain your answer.

14. A rhombus is *always* a parallelogram.   True; A rhombus has two pairs of parallel sides.

15. A trapezoid is *never* a square.   True; A trapezoid has exactly one pair of parallel sides and a square has two pairs of parallel sides.

16. A parallelogram is *always* a trapezoid.
    False; A parallelogram has two pairs of parallel sides and a trapezoid has exactly one pair of parallel sides.

Standardized Testing ◀▶ Open-ended

1. Write a real-world problem that can be modeled by each equation. **Sample Responses are given.**

   a. $\frac{3}{5}y = 30$

   b. $\frac{1}{2}n + 12 = 40$

   1. a. Kelly saves $\frac{3}{5}$ of every dollar she earns. How much must she earn to put $30 in her savings account?

   b. Moses paid $40 for a full-price CD at $12 and a half-priced boxed set. Find the regular price of the boxed set.

2. Name a type of quadrilateral that always has the given characteristic. What other characteristics does it have? **Possible answers are given.**

   a. at least one pair of parallel sides   trapezoid, parallelogram, rhombus, rectangle, square

   b. at least one right angle   rectangle, square

   c. at least two sides of equal length   parallelogram, rhombus, rectangle, square

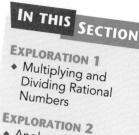

WARM-UP EXERCISES

Solve.
1. $3x + 4 = -2$ -2
2. $5 - x = -11$ 16
3. $15 = 4x - 3$ 4.5
4. $-3x + 7 = 10$ -1
5. $-13 = 5x - 3$ -2

Patterns in Art

◄◄◄ Setting the Stage

Artists often use geometric figures such as segments, rectangles, triangles, and circles in their designs. Sometimes the pattern in the design is easy to describe. Other times there is no definite pattern or it is difficult to describe. Two examples of abstract art that use geometric figures are shown below.

Electric Prisms by Sonia Delaunay

Untitled by Richard Anusziewicz

Think About It

1 Describe the patterns you see in the paintings. **Answers will vary.**

2 How does Richard Anusziewicz show depth in his art? **Answers will vary.**

▶ In this section, you'll explore mathematical patterns in abstract art and create your own artwork based on a pattern.

GOAL

LEARN HOW TO...
♦ solve equations containing rational numbers

AS YOU...
♦ create an abstract art design

Multiplying and Di|vi|ding Rational Numbers

SET UP *You will need:* • *unlined paper* • *ruler* • *colored pencils*

▸ Sometimes the patterns, colors, or shapes in a work of art can be described with numbers or mathematical symbols. The painting *Untitled* on page 280 is a series of squares laid one upon another. The side length of each square can be represented by a number and the change in color by positive and negative signs.

3 **Try This as a Class** The sequence 5, –2.5, 2, and –0.7 was used to create the design at the right.

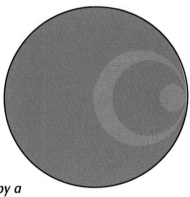

a. How do you think the numbers 5, 2.5, 2, and 0.7 were used to create the design? **They are the diameters of the circles.**

b. What do the signs of the numbers represent in the design? **positive: green; negative: yellow**

▸ Each term of the sequence in Question 3 was generated using the same rule. The rule for finding a term is *multiply the previous term by a number n, and add 0.5.* To find the value of *n*, you can solve any of the equations below.

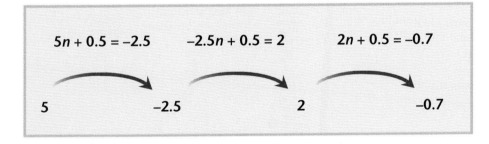

$5n + 0.5 = -2.5$ $-2.5n + 0.5 = 2$ $2n + 0.5 = -0.7$

5   –2.5   2   –0.7

4 Will *n* be negative or positive? How do you know?

5 a. What would be your first step in solving $2n + 0.5 = -0.7$? **Subtract 0.5 from both sides of the equation.**

b. What would be your second step? **Divide both sides of the equation by 2 to solve for *n*.**

4. negative; $5n + 0.5$ is negative so $5n$ is negative and *n* is negative.

▶ To solve the equation in Question 5 you need to divide –1.2 by 2. The rules for multiplying and dividing negative rational numbers are the same as for integers.

6 **a.** Solve $2n + 0.5 = -0.7$. What is the value of n? –0.6

   b. Try solving one of the other equations on page 281. Do you get the same value for n? Yes.

7 **Try This as a Class** Only multiplication was used to create the sequences below. Find the next term in each sequence.

   a. $\frac{4}{25}$, $-\frac{4}{5}$, 4, ... –20   **b.** 6.75, –4.5, 3, ... –2

...checks that you can solve equations containing rational numbers.

8 ✔ **CHECKPOINT** Solve each equation.

   a. $-1.1 = -0.5a - 1.2$ **b.** $2.9 - 0.2x = 1.2$ **c.** $-\frac{2}{3}y - \frac{1}{2} = 4$ $-\frac{27}{4}$
   -0.2 8.5

9 Follow the steps below to create your own abstract art design.
   Answers will vary. Check students' work.

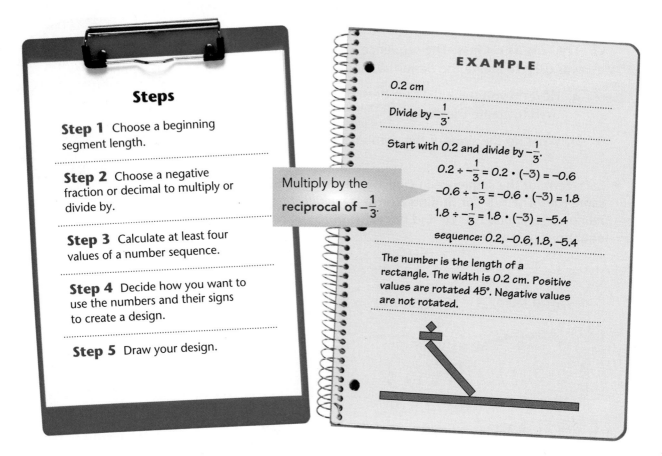

Steps

Step 1 Choose a beginning segment length.

Step 2 Choose a negative fraction or decimal to multiply or divide by.

Step 3 Calculate at least four values of a number sequence.

Step 4 Decide how you want to use the numbers and their signs to create a design.

Step 5 Draw your design.

EXAMPLE

0.2 cm

Divide by $-\frac{1}{3}$.

Start with 0.2 and divide by $-\frac{1}{3}$.

$0.2 \div -\frac{1}{3} = 0.2 \cdot (-3) = -0.6$

$-0.6 \div -\frac{1}{3} = -0.6 \cdot (-3) = 1.8$

$1.8 \div -\frac{1}{3} = 1.8 \cdot (-3) = -5.4$

sequence: 0.2, –0.6, 1.8, –5.4

The number is the length of a rectangle. The width is 0.2 cm. Positive values are rotated 45°. Negative values are not rotated.

Multiply by the reciprocal of $-\frac{1}{3}$.

HOMEWORK EXERCISES ▶ See Exs. 1–11 on p. 286.

Angles of POLYGONS

SET UP *Work with a partner. You will need:* • *Labsheets 4A and 4B* • *ruler* • *scissors* • *plain white paper*

10 Discussion In Theo van Doesburg's painting *Composition*, the rectangles fit together with no overlaps or gaps.

a. Why do rectangles fit together so well**?** Suppose van Doesburg used congruent rectangles. Could he choose congruent rectangles that fit together with no overlaps or gaps**?** Explain. **See below.**

b. Suppose van Doesburg used the polygons shown below. Do you think copies of either polygon would fit together without overlaps or gaps**?** **pentagon: No; hexagon: Yes.**

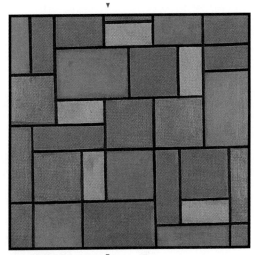

Composition by Theo Van Doesburg

10. a. Sample Response: All the corners are square; Yes; Think of covering a walk with bricks; The brick faces are congruent rectangles.

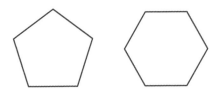

c. Use Labsheet 4A. Work with a partner to create two designs using *Pentagons and Hexagons*. **Answers will vary.** **Check students' work; The hexagon will cover without overlaps or gaps.**

11. Sample figure for a, b, d, f:

a. 180° **c.** 2 △s, 360° **e.** 3 △s, 540° **g.** 4 △s 720° **h.** It is two less than the number of sides. **i.** Multiply two less than the number of sides of the polygon by 180°.

concave polygon

▶ The pentagons and hexagons you used to create your designs are examples of *convex* polygons. A polygon is convex if all its diagonals lie inside the polygon. A polygon that is not convex is *concave*. To decide whether copies of a convex polygon will fit together without gaps or overlaps, it helps to think about the *interior angles* of the polygon.

11 Use Labsheet 4B. Follow the directions on the labsheet for finding *Patterns in Polygons*. You'll explore the relationship between the number of sides of a convex polygon and the measure of its interior angles.

✔ **QUESTION 12**

...checks that you can find the sum of the measures of the interior angles of a polygon.

14. The sum of the angle measures at a vertex must be 360°. Pentagons don't work because 108° angles can't be combined to total 360°. Hexagons work because joining three hexagons at a vertex results in an angle measure sum of 360°.

12 ✔ **CHECKPOINT** Find the sum of the measures of the interior angles of each convex polygon.

a. heptagon
(7-sided polygon)
900°

b. nonagon
(9-sided polygon)
1260°

c. decagon
(10-sided polygon)
1440°

13 The interior angles of a *regular polygon* are congruent. What is the measure of one interior angle of a regular hexagon? 120°

14 **Use Labsheet 4A.** Use what you know about interior angles of convex polygons to explain what you observed about pentagons and hexagons. (*Hint:* Find the sum of the angle measures where the vertices of more than one polygon touch.)

HOMEWORK EXERCISES ▶ See Exs. 12–24 on pp. 287–288.

⬛ **TECHNOLOGY** | **Using Computer Drawing Software**

You can use computer drawing software to create polygons that fit together without gaps or overlaps.

Step 1 Use the polygon tool to draw a regular polygon. Choose a polygon that can be duplicated to fit together without any gaps or overlaps.

Step 2 Duplicate the polygon you made. Move the copy so that one of its sides coincides with a side of the original polygon. Continue to do this until a pattern is formed.

Step 3 Group the pattern together. You can now duplicate and move the pattern to cover your entire screen without any gaps or overlaps.

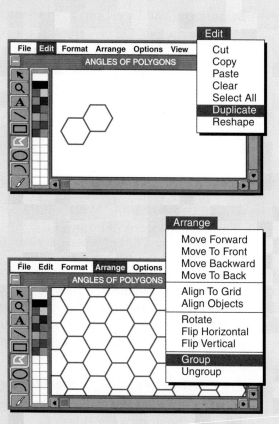

Section 4
Key Concepts

Multiplying and Dividing Rational Numbers (pp. 281–282)

You can solve equations that contain rational numbers. The rules for multiplying and dividing negative rational numbers are the same as the rules for multiplying and dividing integers.

Example

$$-\frac{3}{4}x + 5 = 10$$

$$-\frac{3}{4}x + 5 - 5 = 10 - 5$$

> Subtract 5 from both sides.

$$-\frac{3}{4}x = 5$$

$$-\frac{3}{4}x \div \left(-\frac{3}{4}\right) = 5 \div \left(-\frac{3}{4}\right)$$

> Divide both sides by $-\frac{3}{4}$.

$$-\frac{3}{4}x \cdot \left(-\frac{4}{3}\right) = 5 \cdot \left(-\frac{4}{3}\right)$$

> Multiply by the reciprocal of $-\frac{3}{4}$.

$$x = -\frac{20}{3} = -6\frac{2}{3}$$

Interior Angles of Polygons (pp. 283–284)

The sum of the measures of the interior angles of a convex polygon depends on the number of sides. The equation $s = 180°(n - 2)$ gives the sum s of the measures of the interior angles of a polygon with n sides.

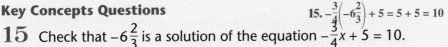

CLOSURE QUESTION

Explain how to find the sum of the measures of the interior angles of a polygon. Give a formula that you can use.

Sample Response: The sum of the measures of the interior angles of a polygon can be found by multiplying two less than the number of sides of the polygon by 180°. The formula is $s = 180(n - 2)$, where s is the sum of the measures of the interior angles and n is the number of sides.

Key Concepts Questions

15. $-\frac{3}{4}\left(-6\frac{2}{3}\right) + 5 = 5 + 5 = 10$

15 Check that $-6\frac{2}{3}$ is a solution of the equation $-\frac{3}{4}x + 5 = 10$.

16 What is the sum of the measures of the interior angles of each polygon above? 900°; 1800°

YOU WILL NEED

For Ex. 22:
◆ protractor

For Ex. 23:
◆ cardboard or thick paper
◆ scissors
◆ ruler

1. For which of the sequences below can you use the rule *divide the previous number by* $-\frac{1}{2}$ *and then subtract* $\frac{3}{4}$ to find a term? **A, C, and D**

   A. $10\frac{1}{2}, -21\frac{3}{4}, 42\frac{3}{4}, \ldots$

   B. $10\frac{1}{2}, -32\frac{1}{4}, 96, \ldots$

   C. $0, -\frac{3}{4}, \frac{3}{4}, \ldots$

   D. $2\frac{7}{16}, -5\frac{5}{8}, 10\frac{1}{2}, \ldots$

2. Write a sequence of at least three numbers using the rule in Exercise 1. Use 1 for the first term in the sequence.
   1, –2.75, 4.75, –10.25

Solve each equation.

3. $3x + 6 = 21$ **5**

4. $-0.75x - 1.25 = 6.75$ **$-10\frac{2}{3}$**

5. $-\frac{3}{4}x = -\frac{11}{12}$ **$\frac{11}{9}$**

6. $-\frac{4}{5}x + \frac{3}{5} = \frac{13}{25}$ **$\frac{1}{10}$**

7. $6.25x + 3 = -4.5$ **–1.2**

8. $\frac{2}{3}x + 6 = \frac{4}{9}$ **$-\frac{25}{3}$**

9. While planning a hiking trip through Europe, Jill needed to convert miles to kilometers. To do this, she multiplied the number of miles by 1.6.

   9. a. Let k = the number of kilometers and m = the number of miles; $k = 1.6m$

   a. Write an equation to estimate miles from kilometers.

   b. About how many kilometers is 55 mi? **88 km**

   c. About how many miles is 120 km? **75 mi**

10. The equation $C = \frac{5}{9}F - 17\frac{7}{9}$ can be used to convert degrees Fahrenheit (F) to degrees Celsius (C).

    a. What is the Celsius temperature for 212°F? **100°C**

    b. What is the Fahrenheit temperature for –20°C? **–4°F**

11. a. Suppose you drive at an average speed of 40 mi/h for 2.5 h. How many miles will you travel? **100 mi**

    b. Write an equation for finding the distance traveled if you know the speed and time. **Let d = distance, r = rate of speed, and t = time; $d = rt$**

    c. Suppose you drive for $3\frac{1}{2}$ h and travel 130 mi. What will be your average speed? **about 37 mi/h**

Find the sum of the measures of the interior angles of each polygon.

12. 1080°

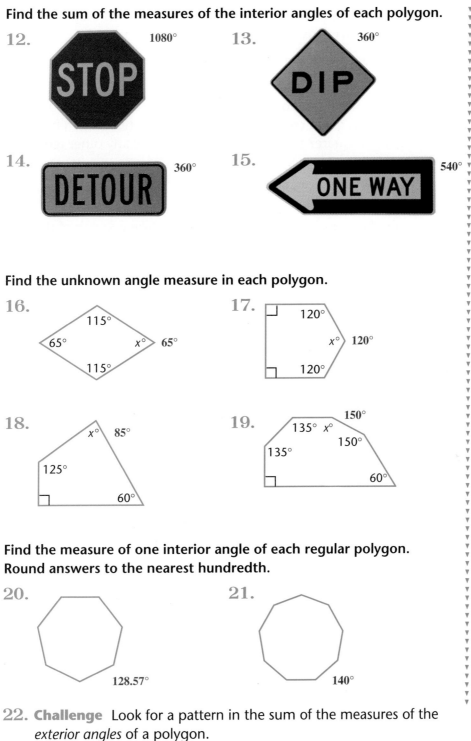

13. 360°

14. 360°

15. 540°

Find the unknown angle measure in each polygon.

16.

115°

65° $x°$ 65°

115°

17.

120°

$x°$ 120°

120°

18.

$x°$ 85°

125°

60°

19.

150°

135° $x°$

135°   150°

60°

**Find the measure of one interior angle of each regular polygon.
Round answers to the nearest hundredth.**

20.

128.57°

21.

140°

22. Challenge Look for a pattern in the sum of the measures of the *exterior angles* of a polygon.

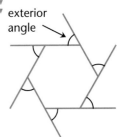

exterior angle

  a. Draw several polygons with different numbers of sides.
     Draw one exterior angle at each vertex.   Check students' drawings.

  b. Find the measures of the exterior angles you sketched. Record
     your results in a table. What pattern do you see?
     Sample Response: triangle, quadrilateral, pentagon, hexagon, heptagon; all 360°

23. A *tessellation* is a covering of a plane with polygons that has no gaps or overlaps.

   a. Draw and cut out a triangle or a quadrilateral. Trace around it several times to create a tessellation. **Answers will vary. Check students' work.**

   b. On Labsheet 4A, you discovered that only one of the regular polygons could create a tessellation. Can a tessellation be made using a square? an equilateral triangle? Will any other regular polygons work? Explain your thinking. **Yes; Yes; Yes, a regular hexagon; Their interior angle measures are factors of 360.**

   c. The tessellation below uses regular hexagons and equilateral triangles. List two other combinations of regular polygons that could be used to create a tessellation. Make a sketch of these new combinations of polygons. **Sample Response: octagons and squares, triangles and squares; Check students' drawings.**

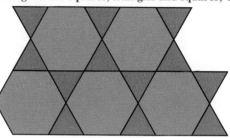

Journal

Exercise 24 checks that you can use a formula to find the sum of the measures of interior angles of a polygon.

Reflecting ◀▶ on the Section

Write your response to Exercise 24 in your journal.

24. Use the equation $s = 180°(n - 2)$ to explain why it is impossible to have an *n*-sided polygon for which the sums of the measures of the interior angles is 600°. **Sample Response: If $600° = 180°(n - 2)$, then $n = 5\frac{1}{3}$ and *n* must be a whole number.**

Spiral ◀▶ Review

Solve each equation. (Module 4, p. 275)

25. $\frac{2}{3}x = 20$ **30**   **26.** $40 = \frac{1}{2}r - 6$ **92**   **27.** $16 = \frac{3}{8}z + \frac{1}{8}z$ **32**

Find the unknown angle measure of each triangle. Tell whether each triangle is *acute*, *right*, or *obtuse*. (Toolbox, p. 604)

28. 39°, 45° **96°; obtuse** **29.** 16°, 92° **72°; obtuse** **30.** 55°, 63° **62°; acute**

Evaluate each expression. Round decimal answers to the nearest hundredth. (Module 3, p. 183)

31. $\frac{12 + 13}{7}$ **3.57**   **32.** $\frac{9}{2}\sqrt{6 + 5}$ **14.92**   **33.** $\frac{8}{12 - 3}$ **0.89**

Section 4

Only multiplication was used to create each sequence below. Find the next number in each sequence.

1. 4.6, –13.8, 41.4, ... **–124.2**

2. $8\frac{2}{3}, -2\frac{8}{9}, \frac{26}{27}, \ldots$ **$-\frac{26}{81}$**

3. For which of the sequences below can you use the rule *multiply the previous term by –0.3 and then add 1.1* to find the next term? **A and C**

   A 1, 0.8, 0.86　　　B 5, –1.25, 0.3125　　　C 7.2, –1.06, 1.418

Solve each equation.

4. $3.2x - 2.7 = -8.4$ **–1.78125**　5. $-2.5x + 3 = 5.75$ **–1.1**　6. $2.6 = 2.7 + 2.5x$ **–0.04**

7. $\frac{2}{3}x + 1 = \frac{1}{6}$ **$-\frac{5}{4}$**　　8. $\frac{3}{5} - \frac{2}{5}x = \frac{21}{25}$ **$-\frac{3}{5}$**　　9. $6\frac{1}{4} = -\frac{5}{12}x$ **–15**

Find the sum of the measures of the interior angles of each convex polygon.

10. a 100-sided polygon
    17,640°

11. an 11-sided polygon
    1620°

12. an 18-sided polygon
    2880°

Find the unknown angle measure in each polygon.

13.

14.

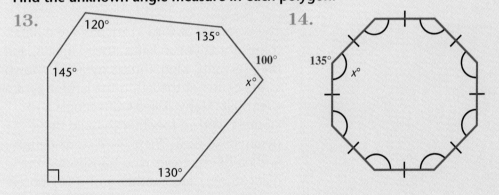

---

1. The first term in a sequence is –5. The rule for finding a term in the sequence is *divide the previous term by $\frac{2}{3}$ and then add $\frac{3}{4}$.* What is the fourth term in the sequence?　**$-13\frac{5}{16}$**

2. Each measure below is the sum of the measures of the interior angles of a convex polygon. How many sides does each polygon have?

   a. 360° **4 sides**　　　b. 1800° **12 sides**　　　c. 5940° **35 sides**

Can the three given lengths form a triangle?

1. 4 cm, 6 cm, 2 cm
   No.

2. 3.9 mm, 4.2 mm, 7.9 mm   Yes.

3. How do you know if a triangle is obtuse, right, or acute? If it has a right angle it is right. If one angle is greater than 90°, it is obtuse, and if all the angles are less than 90°, it is acute.

Evaluate. Round your answer to the nearest hundredth.

4. $\sqrt{15}$ 3.87
5. $\sqrt{34}$ 5.83

Right ON!

<◄◄ *Setting the Stage*

SET UP *Work in a group of three or four. You will need:*
• centimeter grid paper • tape or glue • construction paper
• scissors

The pyramids at Giza in Egypt were built as tombs for Egyptian kings, their families, and their servants. King Khufu's pyramid, shown in the center at the left, is the largest pyramid ever built. Many skilled craftspeople and laborers worked together to build the pyramids at Giza. There were stone cutters and polishers, crews who transported the giant stones, and another group of laborers called *rope stretchers*.

The rope stretchers tied equally spaced knots in a piece of rope. They knew they could form a right triangle with side lengths of 3, 4, and 5 units by arranging the rope as shown. The rope triangle was then used at a construction site to measure distances and to form 90° angles at the corners of a pyramid.

4 units

5 units

3 units

Think About It ▸

1 **a.** Cut three squares from centimeter grid paper. One square should have side lengths of 3 units, one should have side lengths of 4 units, and one should have side lengths of 5 units. **Check students' work.**

b. Describe two ways to find the area of one of the squares. Then label each square with its area and the length of one side.

c. Use your three squares to form a triangle. Tape the arrangement into place on construction paper. Label the two shorter sides *a* and *b* and the longest side *c*. Is the triangle a right triangle? Explain how you can check. **Yes; Measure the angle that appears to be a right angle with a protractor.**

d. What is the relationship between the areas of the two smaller squares and the area of the largest square?

e. Do you think this relationship will work for other triangles? How can you find out? **No; Try other triangles that are not right triangles.**

1. b. Possible answers: Count the individual units in each square, multiply the length times the width, or square the length of one side; 3 units, 9 square units; 4 units, 16 square units; 5 units, 25 square units

d. The sum of the areas of the two smaller squares is equal to the area of the largest square.

▸ **Your discovery about the 3-4-5 triangle is part of a larger pattern. In this section, you'll learn more about the relationship among side lengths of triangles.**

GOAL

LEARN HOW TO...
◆ identify different
types of triangles
by looking at their
side lengths

AS YOU...
◆ work with paper
squares

 **Exploration 1**

TRI△NGLE Side **Length** Relationships

SET UP *Work in a group of three or four. You will need:*
• Labsheet 5A • centimeter grid paper • scissors
• construction paper • tape or glue • protractor

2 Follow the steps below with your group. **Check students' work.**

First Cut out 10 squares from the grid paper with side lengths ranging from 6 cm to 15 cm. No two squares should be the same size.

Next Spread out the squares. Have one group member close his or her eyes and choose a square. Set this square aside.

Then Work together to try to form 3 triangles with the remaining 9 squares. (The triangles do not have to be right triangles.)

3 a. Are there some sets of squares that will not form a triangle? If so, explain why.

b. Tape or glue each triangle to construction paper. **Check students' work.**

Use Labsheet 5A for Questions 4 and 5.

4 Follow the directions on the labsheet to complete the *Triangle Table* and classify the triangles made by your group. **Answers will vary. Check students' work.**

3. a. If the lengths of any two sides is not greater than the third side, a triangle cannot be formed.

FOR▶HELP
with *classifying triangles,* see
TOOLBOX, p. 604

5 **Try This as a Class** Share your group's triangles and data from the *Triangle Table* with the other groups in your class.

   a. Use the extra spaces in the *Triangle Table* to record the data from other groups for any triangles that your group did not make.   **Answers will vary. Check students' work.**

   b. How many different triangles did your class find altogether? Do you think that these are all the possible arrangements? How could you find out?   **Answers will vary. Check students' work.**

   c. Look at the last two columns in the *Triangle Table*. What do you notice about the relationship between the sum of the areas of the smaller squares and the area of the largest square for an acute triangle? a right triangle? an obtuse triangle?
   greater than; equal; less than

▶ **If you know the side lengths of a triangle, you can tell what type of triangle it is.**

EXAMPLE

For a right triangle, the sum of the squares of the lengths of the shorter sides equals the square of the length of the longest side. Tell whether the triangle shown is a right triangle.

SAMPLE RESPONSE

$(12)^2 + (16)^2 \stackrel{?}{=} (21)^2$

$144 + 256 \neq 441$

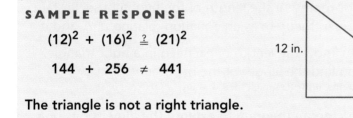

The triangle is not a right triangle.

---

6 What type of triangle is shown in the Example? Explain.
   Sample Response: obtuse; $12^2 + 16^2 < 21^2$

7 ✔ **CHECKPOINT** Tell whether a triangle with the given side lengths is *acute*, *right*, or *obtuse*.

   a. 11 cm, 13 cm, 20 cm obtuse   **b.** 16 mm, 18 mm, 10 mm acute

   c. 17 in., 15 in., 8 in. right   **d.** 6.5 cm, 4.2 cm, 7.9 cm obtuse

8 Give the side lengths of a triangle (other than a 3-4-5 triangle) that the Egyptian rope stretchers could have used to form a right angle. Sketch a picture of a rope triangle with these new side lengths.

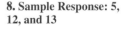

...checks that you can use the lengths of the sides of a triangle to determine what type of triangle it is.

8. Sample Response: 5, 12, and 13

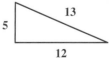

HOMEWORK EXERCISES ▶ See Exs. 1–7 on p. 298.

◆ use the Pythagorean theorem to find an unknown side length of a right triangle

AS YOU...

◆ explore the dimensions of the I.M. Pei Pyramid

KEY TERMS

◆ Pythagorean theorem
◆ hypotenuse
◆ leg

 **Exploration 2**

The PYTHAGOREAN Theorem

▶ Throughout history, people from many lands have made interesting discoveries about right triangles. One of the most important discoveries is named after the Greek mathematician Pythagoras.

The **Pythagorean theorem** says that in a right triangle the square of the length of the *hypotenuse* is equal to the sum of the squares of the lengths of the *legs*. The **hypotenuse** is the side opposite the right angle. The **legs** are the sides adjacent to the right angle.

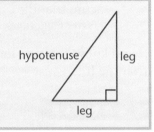
hypotenuse | leg
leg

9 **Try This as a Class** Use the diagram above.

a. Let a and b represent the lengths of the legs of the right triangle. Let c represent the length of the hypotenuse. Restate the Pythagorean theorem as an equation relating a, b, and c.
$$a^2 + b^2 = c^2$$

b. Suppose you know the length of each leg in a right triangle. How can you find the length of the hypotenuse?
Square the lengths of the legs, add, then find the square root of the sum.

▶ You'll use the Pythagorean theorem to explore the dimensions of a pyramid designed by architect I.M. Pei. The pyramid, shown below, is part of the Louvre Museum in Paris, France.

▶ **The Louvre pyramid has a square base and four triangular faces. The** *slant height* **of the pyramid is the height of one of the triangular faces.**

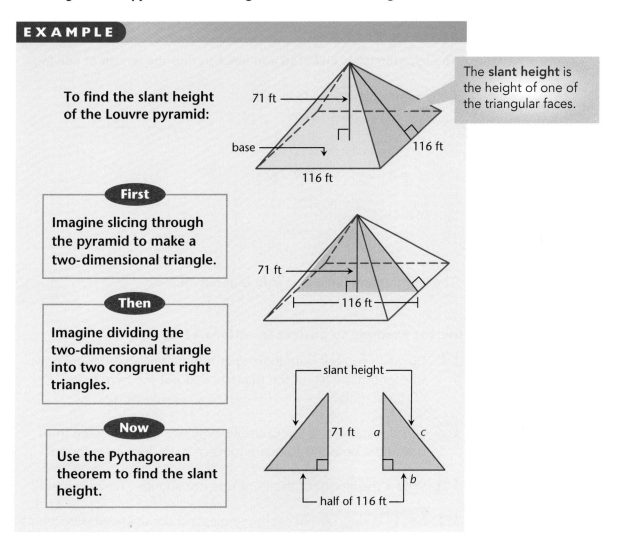

EXAMPLE

To find the slant height of the Louvre pyramid:

71 ft

base

116 ft

116 ft

The **slant height** is the height of one of the triangular faces.

First

Imagine slicing through the pyramid to make a two-dimensional triangle.

71 ft

116 ft

Then

Imagine dividing the two-dimensional triangle into two congruent right triangles.

slant height

71 ft a c

b

half of 116 ft

Now

Use the Pythagorean theorem to find the slant height.

10 Try This as a Class Use the Example above.

a. Use your equation from Question 9(a) to find the length of the hypotenuse of one of the congruent right triangles. $\sqrt{8405}$

b. What is the slant height of the Louvre pyramid? Give your answer to the nearest foot. **about 92 ft**

c. Now that you know the slant height, explain how you can find the area of one triangular face of the pyramid.
Find $\frac{1}{2}bh$ where $b = 116$ and $h = 92$.

▶ **You can use the Pythagorean theorem to find the length of one side of a right triangle if you know the lengths of the other two sides. This is shown in the Example on the next page.**

How can you use the lengths of the sides of a triangle to find out if the triangle is acute, right, or obtuse? When can you use the Pythagorean theorem and what does it tell you?

Sample Response: Look at the sum of the squares of the lengths of the shorter sides of the triangle. If this sum is less than the square of the length of the longer side, the triangle is obtuse. If the sum and the square of the length of the longer side are equal, the triangle is a right triangle. If the sum is greater than the square of the length of the longer side, the triangle is acute. If a triangle is a right triangle, you can use the Pythagorean Theorem to find the length of one of the sides if you know the lengths of the other two sides.

✔ QUESTION 14

...checks that you can use the Pythagorean theorem to find an unknown side length.

EXAMPLE

Use the Pythagorean theorem to find the unknown side length of the triangle below.

SAMPLE RESPONSE

The hypotenuse is given, so you need to find the length of one leg.

Let a = the unknown side length.

$$a^2 + 9^2 = 17^2$$
$$a^2 + 81 = 289$$
$$a^2 + 81 - 81 = 289 - 81$$
$$a^2 = 208$$
$$\sqrt{a^2} = \sqrt{208}$$
$$a \approx 14.42$$

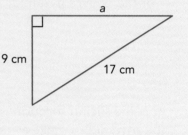

The length of the unknown side is about 14.4 cm.

Use the Example to answer Questions 11–13.

11 How can you tell from looking at the triangle that the unknown side length is a leg of the triangle, and not the hypotenuse of the triangle? **Sample Response: It is not opposite the right angle.**

12 In the equations in the Example, why was 81 subtracted from both sides before the square roots of both sides were found? **to isolate the variable on one side of the equation**

13 Why is the length of the third side not an exact measurement? **The sum, 208, is not a perfect square.**

14 **✔ CHECKPOINT** For each triangle, find the unknown side length.

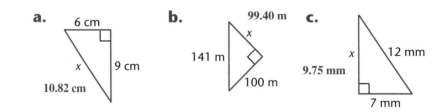

a. 6 cm, 9 cm, 10.82 cm, x

b. 99.40 m, x, 141 m, 100 m

c. 12 mm, x, 9.75 mm, 7 mm

15 Suppose the length of the longest side of a right triangle is $\sqrt{90}$. The other two side lengths are equal. Give the lengths of the shorter sides. Round your answer to the nearest tenth. **6.7**

HOMEWORK EXERCISES ▶ See Exs. 8–18 on pp. 298–299.

Key Concepts

Key Terms

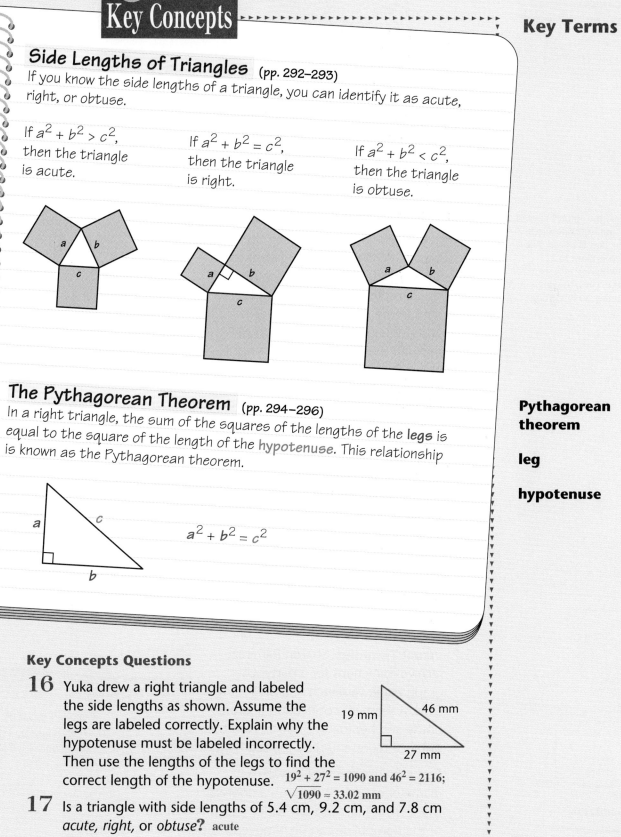

Side Lengths of Triangles (pp. 292–293)

If you know the side lengths of a triangle, you can identify it as acute, right, or obtuse.

If $a^2 + b^2 > c^2$, then the triangle is acute.

If $a^2 + b^2 = c^2$, then the triangle is right.

If $a^2 + b^2 < c^2$, then the triangle is obtuse.

The Pythagorean Theorem (pp. 294–296)

In a right triangle, the sum of the squares of the lengths of the **legs** is equal to the square of the length of the **hypotenuse**. This relationship is known as the Pythagorean theorem.

$$a^2 + b^2 = c^2$$

Pythagorean theorem

leg

hypotenuse

Key Concepts Questions

16 Yuka drew a right triangle and labeled the side lengths as shown. Assume the legs are labeled correctly. Explain why the hypotenuse must be labeled incorrectly. Then use the lengths of the legs to find the correct length of the hypotenuse. $19^2 + 27^2 = 1090$ and $46^2 = 2116$; $\sqrt{1090} \approx 33.02$ mm

19 mm   46 mm   27 mm

17 Is a triangle with side lengths of 5.4 cm, 9.2 cm, and 7.8 cm *acute, right,* or *obtuse*? acute

Section 5

YOU WILL NEED

For Ex. 14:
◆ graph paper

Tell whether a triangle with the given side lengths is *acute*, *right*, or *obtuse*.

1. 5 cm, 12 cm, 13 cm right

2. 5 mm, 9 mm, 7 mm obtuse

3. 8 in., 10 in., 9 in. acute

4. 11.5 m, 6.2 m, 7 m obtuse

5. 16 cm, 20 cm, 17 cm acute

6. 15 mm, 12 mm, 9 mm right

7. Yes; the square root of the sum of the squares of the legs is about 20.81, which is close to 21. Allowing for measurement errors, the angle is probably a right angle.

7. **Carpentry** Carpenters can use a method like the one used by the rope stretchers of ancient Egypt to check whether a corner is "square." For example, a carpenter took the measurements shown to check a right angle on a table. Is the angle opposite the 21 in. diagonal a right angle? Explain your thinking.

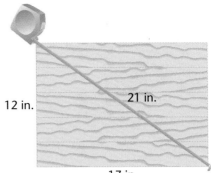

12 in. 21 in. 17 in.

For each triangle, find the unknown side length. Give each answer to the nearest tenth.

8.
7 in. x
10 in.
12.2 in.

9.
3 mm
15 mm x
14.7 mm

10.
14 ft 13 ft
x
5.2 ft

11.
15 cm
17 cm x
8 cm

12.
9.8 in. x
10.2 in.
14.1 in.

13.
20 mm
x 16 mm
12 mm

14.

Route 14

N
W   E
S

Highway 7

Route 16 ▬ = 10 mi

Highway 9

Start

about 121 mi

14. **Visual Thinking** Sharon Ramirez receives directions for a party. Use graph paper to sketch Sharon's route. Draw a segment connecting Sharon's house and her friend's house. Find the distance represented by the segment.

Hey Sharon!
Here are the directions to the party! Hope you can make it!

First, drive 70 mi north on Highway 9.
Then drive 80 mi west on Route 16.
Then drive 40 mi north on Highway 7.
Then drive 30 mi east on Route 14.

15. Can a circular trampoline with a diameter of 16 ft fit through a doorway that is 10 ft high and 8 ft wide? (Assume that the legs of the trampoline can be removed.) Explain your answer.
No; The diagonal is only about 12.8 ft.

16. **Architecture** Many building codes specify that the ratio of the *rise* of a stair to its *tread* cannot exceed the ratio 3:4.

   a. Find the ratio of the rise to the tread on the staircase shown. Does the staircase shown follow the building code described above?
   3:4; Yes.

   b. What is the length of the green trim on the staircase shown? 75 in.

   c. **Research** Measure the rise and the tread of a stair in your home or school. Find the ratio of the rise to the tread. Does the staircase follow the building code described above?
   Answers will vary. Check students' work.

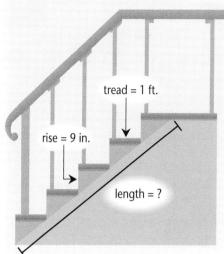

tread = 1 ft.

rise = 9 in.

length = ?

17. **Challenge** Find the next 3 terms in the sequence 3, 4, 5, 6, 8, 10, 9, 12, 15, ... Explain how you got your answer.
12, 16, 20; The pattern is $1 \times 3, 1 \times 4, 1 \times 5, 2 \times 3, 2 \times 4, 2 \times 5, ..., 4 \times 3, 4 \times 4, 4 \times 5$.

Reflecting ◀▷ on the Section

Be prepared to report on the following topic in class.

18. Imagine you just discovered the relationship among the side lengths of a right triangle. Unfortunately, no one believes your discovery is very important. Write a persuasive speech explaining how useful your discovery is. Make visual aids to use with your speech.
Answers will vary. Check students' work.

Oral *Report*

Exercise 18 checks that you can explain how to use the Pythagorean theorem.

Spiral ◀▷ Review

Find the unknown angle measure for each polygon. (Module 4, p. 285)

19.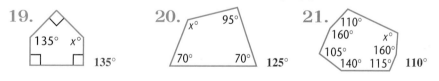
135° x°
135°

20.
x° 95°
70° 70° 125°

21.
110°
160° x°
105° 160°
140° 115° 110°

22. Find the volume of a rectangular prism when the length is 7.2 cm, the width is 15.8 cm, and the height is 6.5 cm. (Module 1, p. 47)
739.44 cm^3

There are 7 red apples and 5 green apples in a paper bag.
(Module 2, p. 115)

23. What is the probability of drawing a red apple? $\frac{7}{12}$

24. Suppose a green apple is drawn first and not replaced. What is the probability of getting a green apple on a second draw? $\frac{4}{11}$

Working on the Module Project **Creating a Pattern**

Spiral Patterns Artists often use spirals in their work. Spirals also appear in nature. Did you know that many spirals are based on mathematical patterns? You can create a spiral based on right triangles.

SET UP

You will need:
- *cardboard*
- *metric ruler*
- *protractor*

7 Follow these steps to create a spiral.

Step 1 Make a cardboard square with side lengths of 3 cm. Use the square to draw a right triangle with legs that are 3 cm long. This is **Triangle 1**. See below.

Step 2 Use your cardboard square to draw **Triangle 2**. Use the hypotenuse of **Triangle 1** as one leg. Make the other leg 3 cm long.

Step 3 Draw **Triangle 3**. Use the hypotenuse of **Triangle 2** as one leg. Make the other leg 3 cm long.

Step 4 Continue the pattern you started in Steps 1–3 until you have a 10-triangle spiral.

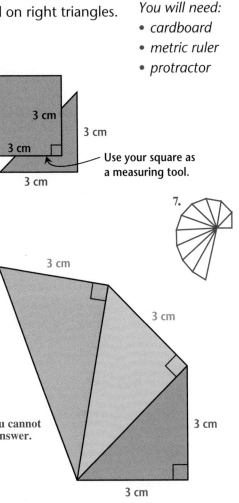

8 The exact length of the hypotenuse of **Triangle 1** is $\sqrt{18}$ cm. The approximate length of the hypotenuse is 4.24 cm. Explain why.

$\sqrt{18}$ is irrational so you cannot give an exact decimal answer.

9 Use a calculator to find the exact length and the approximate length of the hypotenuse of **Triangle 2**.

Hint: $\left(\sqrt{18}\right)^2 = 18$. $3\sqrt{3}, 5.20$

10 Find the exact lengths of the hypotenuses of the other triangles. What pattern do you see?

$3\sqrt{4}$ (or 6), $3\sqrt{5}$, $3\sqrt{6}$, $3\sqrt{7}$, $3\sqrt{8}$ (or $6\sqrt{2}$), $3\sqrt{9}$ (or 9), $3\sqrt{10}$, $3\sqrt{11}$; the length of the hypotenuse of the nth triangle is $3\sqrt{n+1}$.

Tell whether each triangle is *acute*, *right*, or *obtuse*.

1. 6 in. 12 in. 14 in.
   obtuse

2. 25 ft 21 ft 33 ft
   obtuse

3. 10 mm 12.8 mm 8 mm
   acute

4. 6.4 m 3.2 m 6.8 m
   acute

5. 6 cm 6 cm 10 cm
   obtuse

6. 7.5 m 18 m 19.5 m
   right

For each triangle, find the unknown side length. Round each answer to the nearest tenth.

7. 13 in. x 10 in.
   8.3 in.

8. 9 ft 8 ft x
   4.1 ft

9. 8 cm 6 cm x 10 cm

Tell whether the given side lengths could be the side lengths of a right triangle. Explain why or why not.

10. 4.5 cm, 6 cm, 7.5 cm
    Yes; $4.5^2 + 6^2 = 7.5^2$

11. 3 in., 3 in., 5 in.
    No; $3^2 + 3^2 \neq 5^2$

12. 2.5 m, 6 m, 6.5 m
    Yes; $2.5^2 + 6^2 = 6.5^2$

Standardized Testing ◀▶ Performance Task

1. The lengths of the two shortest sides of a triangle are given. What is a possible length of the third side if the triangle is acute? right? obtuse? **Possible answers are given.**

   a. 6 cm, 4.5 cm $6 < x < 7.5, 7.5,$
      $7.5 < x < 10.5$

   b. 2 in., $5\frac{1}{2}$ in. $5.5 < x < \sqrt{34.25}, \sqrt{34.25},$
      $\sqrt{34.25} < x < 7.5$

2. Find the combined area of all four triangular faces of the pyramid. Assume the triangular faces are congruent. **48 ft²**

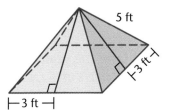

5 ft
3 ft
3 ft

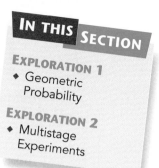

IN THIS SECTION

EXPLORATION 1
- Geometric Probability

EXPLORATION 2
- Multistage Experiments

WARM-UP EXERCISES

Find the area of each figure.

1. a circle with radius 5 cm   about 78.5 cm^2
2. a circle with diameter 12.4 in.   about 120.7 in.^{2}
3. a triangle with base 2 mm and height 14 mm   14 mm^2

Discoveries in the DEEP

Setting the Stage

Exploring the Titanic

No one ever dreamed that her first voyage would also be her last. On the night of April 14, 1912, the passenger liner *R.M.S. Titanic* struck an iceberg in the North Atlantic. Within minutes water began pouring into her lower decks. Less than three hours later her propellers started to rise out of the water. For the more than 1,500 people left on board there was little hope of escape. Soon the biggest ship the world had ever seen would plunge to the bottom of the ocean.

Robert D. Ballard

Over the years, a number of different expeditions tried to find the *Titanic*'s final resting place. One of the most challenging problems faced by searchers was locating the exact spot where the *Titanic* sank. The *Titanic* reported her position when she struck the iceberg. Another ship, the *Carpathia*, reported the location of the lifeboats it picked up some time later. Still, no one knew exactly where the *Titanic* lay.

1   A team of searchers from the United States and France predicted that the *Titanic*'s final resting place was likely to be in the region outlined with dashed lines on the map below. Estimate the area in square kilometers of this *predicted shipwreck region*. **about 320 km²**

2   In 1985, the French ship *Le Suroit* searched in the pink shaded region. Due to strong currents and other factors, *Le Suroit* could not search the entire predicted shipwreck region. Estimate how many square kilometers of the predicted shipwreck region *Le Suroit* covered in its search.   **about 240 km²**

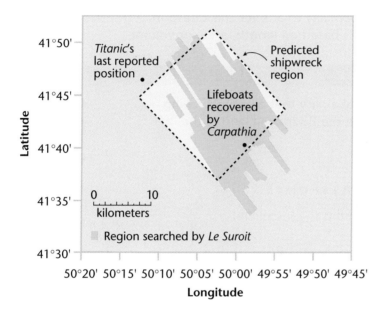

▶ **Knowledge about historical events, ocean currents, and other conditions helped the people who eventually found the *Titanic* predict where the ship might be found. In this section, you'll use mathematics to explore the probability of finding the *Titanic*.**

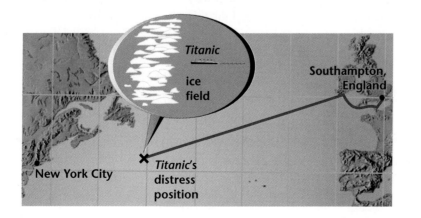

GOAL

LEARN HOW TO...
◆ find probabilities using areas

AS YOU...
◆ examine the area of a shipwreck

KEY TERM
◆ geometric probability

Exploration 1

Geometric Probability

SET UP *You will need: • Labsheet 6A • metric ruler*

▶ How likely was it that *Le Suroit* would find the *Titanic*? You can use *geometric probability* to answer this question. A **geometric probability** is based on length, area, or volume.

EXAMPLE

Find the probability that an object falling randomly on the figure will land in the blue circle.

SAMPLE RESPONSE

P(landing in the shaded circle) = $\dfrac{\text{area of circle}}{\text{area of square}} \approx \dfrac{3.14 \text{ ft}^2}{4 \text{ ft}^2} = 0.785$

The probability of landing in the shaded circle is 78.5%.

---

3 Use your answers to Questions 1 and 2 on page 303. Assume the *Titanic* lay in the predicted shipwreck region. Estimate the probability that the *Titanic* lay in the region *Le Suroit* searched.   **about 75%**

✓ QUESTION 4

...checks that you can find geometric probabilities.

4 **✓ CHECKPOINT** Find the probability that an object falling randomly on each figure will land in the blue region.

a. 37.5%

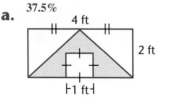

b. 62.5%

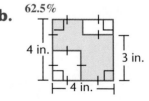

5 **Use Labsheet 6A.** Suppose you are on a ship that is *Searching for the Titanic*. Follow the directions on the labsheet to estimate the probability that the *Titanic* lies in your search region.
a. about 100 km²; **b.** about 70 km²; **c.** about 70%

HOMEWORK EXERCISES ▶ See Exs. 1–5 on p. 309.

Multistage Experiments

SET UP *You will need:* • *Labsheets 6A and 6B* • *graph paper*
• *blue and red colored pencils* • *metric ruler*

▶ The searchers knew that ocean currents could have pulled the sinking *Titanic* several kilometers from her last reported position. Although they could not pinpoint the exact location of the sunken ship, they felt fairly certain they were looking in the right region.

6 **Use Labsheet 6A.** Look back at the map on the labsheet. Suppose your crew estimates that the probability the *Titanic* is in the predicted shipwreck region is 80%. Estimate the probability that the *Titanic* is *not* in the predicted shipwreck region. How did you find the probability? 20%; 100% − 80% = 20%

▶ The events in Question 6 are called *complementary events*. Two events are **complementary events** if one or the other must occur but they cannot both occur.

7 The tree diagram shown models the probabilities of the complementary events in Question 6. What must be true about the probabilities of two events that are complementary? The sum of the probabilities must be 1.

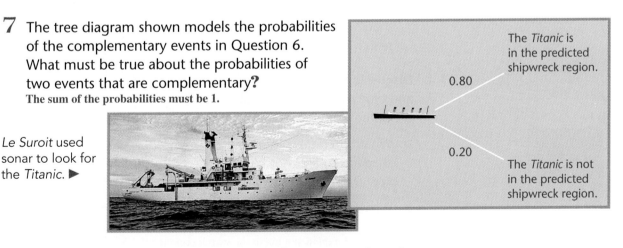

Le Suroit used sonar to look for the *Titanic*. ▶

The *Titanic* is in the predicted shipwreck region.

0.80

0.20

The *Titanic* is not in the predicted shipwreck region.

▶ In Question 5 of Exploration 1, you found that your search region covers about 70% of the predicted shipwreck region.

8 What percent of the predicted shipwreck region is not covered by your search region? about 30%

► Suppose your crew estimates an 80% probability that the *Titanic* is in the predicted shipwreck region and you search 70% of that region. You can use a tree diagram to find the probability that you find the *Titanic* during your search.

▼ **Use Labsheet 6B for Questions 9 and 11.**

9 **Try This as a Class** The *Tree Diagram* on the labsheet is based on the one shown on page 305.

a. Follow the instructions on the labsheet for completing the *Tree Diagram*.

b. What outcome does NP Y represent?
The *Titanic* is not in the predicted shipwreck region, and is in the search region.

c. Why is the probability for the branch from NP to NY equal to 1.00? If the *Titanic* is not inside the predicted shipwreck region, then it is certainly not inside the search region

9. a. 0.30; 0.20; NP Y;
Titanic is found; NP NY;
Titanic is not found.

► The situation described in Question 9 is an example of a *multistage experiment*. A **multistage experiment** involves two or more events happening.

column
↓

row →

10. a.

10. b.

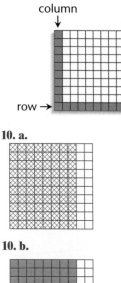

10 You can use a 10 × 10 grid like the one shown at the left to model the multistage experiment in Question 9. Start by drawing a 10 × 10 grid on graph paper.

a. Color 80% of the columns red. The red shading models the probability that the *Titanic* is in the predicted shipwreck region.

b. With a blue pencil, color in 70% of the red area. The blue shading models the probability that the *Titanic* is in your search region.

11 **Discussion** The portion of the grid that you colored both red and blue models the probability that the *Titanic* is in both the predicted shipwreck region and in your search region.

a. What outcome is modeled by the portion of the grid that is shaded red and not blue? How is this outcome shown on the *Tree Diagram* on the labsheet? The *Titanic* is in the predicted shipwreck region and is not in the search region; P NY

b. What does the uncolored portion of the grid model? How is this shown on the *Tree Diagram*? The *Titanic* is not in the predicted shipwreck region and not in the search region; NP NY

► You can use a rectangular grid to find probabilities of outcomes in multistage experiments.

12 a. In this 10 × 10 grid, the portion that is shaded red and not blue models the probability that the *Titanic* is in the predicted shipwreck region and not in your search region. Count the number of squares shaded red and not blue. **24 squares**

b. Divide your answer to part (a) by 100, the total number of grid squares. Write the result as a decimal. This is the probability that the *Titanic* is in the predicted shipwreck region and not in your search region. **0.24**

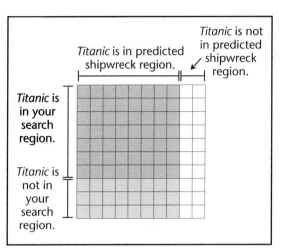

▶ **You can also use multiplication to find probabilities of outcomes in multistage experiments.**

13 Use Labsheet 6B. The value 0.8 represents the probability that the *Titanic* is in the predicted shipwreck region.

a. What does the value 0.3 represent? Where can you find 0.8 and 0.3 on the *Tree Diagram*? **the probability that the *Titanic* is not in the search region; the branches for P and NY**

b. When you multiply 0.8 by 0.3, you get the result 0.8 · 0.3 = 0.24. Compare this result with your answer to Question 12(b). What outcome has a probability of 0.24?

13. b. They are the same; The *Titanic* is in the predicted shipwreck region and is not in the search region.

c. Explain how you can compute the probability that the *Titanic* is in the predicted shipwreck region and not in your search region without using a grid. **Multiply the probabilities for P and NY in the tree diagram.**

14 ✓ **CHECKPOINT** **Use Labsheet 6B.** Use the grid model in Question 12, or use multiplication and the *Tree Diagram* from the labsheet.

✓ **QUESTION 14**

... checks that you can find the probability of an outcome of a multistage experiment.

a. What is the probability that the *Titanic* is both in the predicted shipwreck region and in your search region? **0.56**

b. You want to know the probability that you do not find the *Titanic*. Which outcomes correspond to this event? Find the probability that you do not find the *Titanic*. Explain your method. **P NY; NP Y; and NP NY; 0.44; Sample Response: Add the probabilities of the three indicated outcomes.**

15 Suppose your crew estimates an 80% probability that the *Titanic* is in the predicted shipwreck region. You want your probability of finding the *Titanic* to be at least 0.6. What percent of the predicted shipwreck region must your search region cover? **75%**

HOMEWORK EXERCISES ▶ See Exs. 6–12 on pp. 309–311.

Key Terms

geometric
probability

complementary
events

multistage
experiment

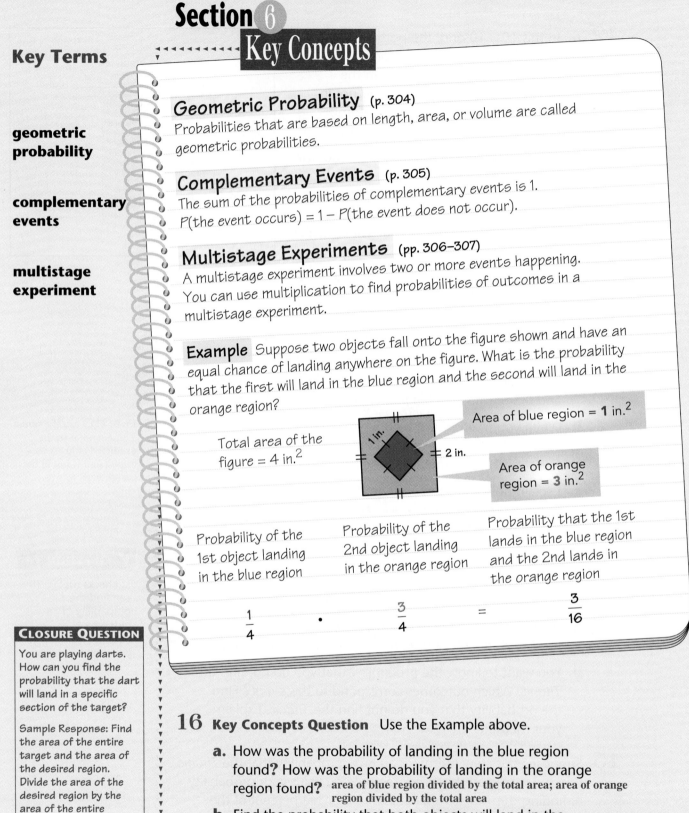

Geometric Probability (p. 304)

Probabilities that are based on length, area, or volume are called geometric probabilities.

Complementary Events (p. 305)

The sum of the probabilities of complementary events is 1.
P(the event occurs) = 1 − P(the event does not occur).

Multistage Experiments (pp. 306–307)

A multistage experiment involves two or more events happening. You can use multiplication to find probabilities of outcomes in a multistage experiment.

Example Suppose two objects fall onto the figure shown and have an equal chance of landing anywhere on the figure. What is the probability that the first will land in the blue region and the second will land in the orange region?

Total area of the figure = 4 in.^{2}

1 in.

2 in.

Area of blue region = **1** in.^{2}

Area of orange region = **3** in.^{2}

| Probability of the 1st object landing in the blue region | Probability of the 2nd object landing in the orange region | Probability that the 1st lands in the blue region and the 2nd lands in the orange region |

$$\frac{1}{4} \cdot \frac{3}{4} = \frac{3}{16}$$

CLOSURE QUESTION

You are playing darts. How can you find the probability that the dart will land in a specific section of the target?

Sample Response: Find the area of the entire target and the area of the desired region. Divide the area of the desired region by the area of the entire target.

16 Key Concepts Question Use the Example above.

a. How was the probability of landing in the blue region found? How was the probability of landing in the orange region found? area of blue region divided by the total area; area of orange region divided by the total area

b. Find the probability that both objects will land in the orange region. $\frac{9}{16}$

Section 6

Find the probability that an object falling randomly on each figure will land in the shaded area. Round answers to the nearest hundredth.

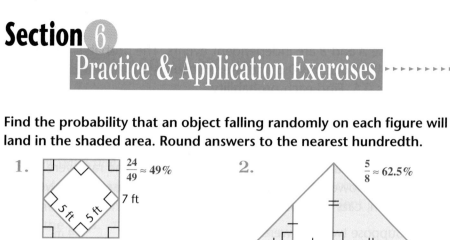

1. $\dfrac{24}{49} \approx 49\%$

7 ft
5 ft 5 ft
7 ft

2. $\dfrac{5}{8} \approx 62.5\%$

2 cm   4 cm

3. $\dfrac{1}{\pi} \approx 31.84\%$

1 in.
1 in.
1 in.

4. $1 - \dfrac{\pi}{4} \approx 21.5\%$

3 ft
6 ft

5. **Visual Thinking** A 12 in. by 14 in. rectangular cake is divided into 2 in. squares. If your piece is chosen at random, what is the probability that your piece is from the outside edge of the cake?

5. $\dfrac{11}{21} \approx 52.4\%$

6. Denise lost her ring and her house key while playing volleyball. Assume that each object is equally likely to be anywhere in the entire region shown.

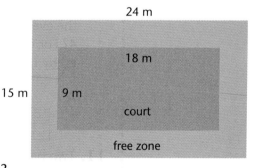

24 m

18 m

15 m   9 m

court

free zone

a. Find the probability that Denise's ring is on the court. Then find the probability that her house key is in the free zone. **45%, 55%**

b. The 10 × 10 grid at the right models the probabilities you found in part (a). What do the green columns represent?
probability that her ring is on the court

c. What outcome is represented by the portion of the grid that is colored both blue and green? What outcome is represented by the uncolored portion of the grid? **ring is on court and key in free zone; ring not on court and key not in free zone**

d. **Choosing a Method** Use the grid or a tree diagram and multiplication. Find the probability that Denise's ring is on the court and her house key is not in the free zone. How did you find your answer? **20.25%; Sample Response: I looked at the part of the grid shaded green and not blue.**

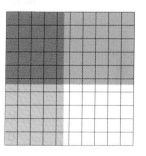

Extra Skill Practice

Suppose that during a storm, two groups of hikers get lost in the area shown. Assume each group of hikers is equally likely to be anywhere in the area.

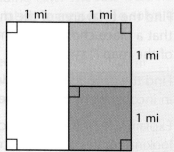

1. What is the probability that the first group is in the white region? **50%**

2. What is the probability that the first group is in the tan region? **25%**

3. What is the probability that the second group is in the red region? **25%**

4. What is the probability that the second group is in the white or the tan region? **75%**

5. What is the probability that the first group is not in the white region? **50%**

6. What is the probability that the first group is in the red region and the second group is in the white region? **12.5%**

7. What is the probability that both groups are in the tan region. **6.25%**

8. What is the probability that the first group is in the tan region and the second group is not in the white region? **12.5%**

9. What is the probability that the first group is not in the tan region and the second group is in the red region? **18.75%**

Standardized Testing ◀▶ **Multiple Choice**

1. A coin is tossed and a six-sided die is rolled. What is the probability of getting heads and a number greater than 4? **C**

   A $\frac{5}{6}$ **B** $\frac{3}{8}$ **C** $\frac{1}{6}$ **D** $\frac{5}{8}$

2. What is the probability that an object falling randomly onto the figure shown will land in the green region? **C**

   A $\frac{\pi}{3}$ **B** $\frac{1}{3}$ **C** $1 - \frac{\pi}{4}$ **D** $\frac{\pi}{4}$

Creating a Pattern

Throughout this module you have used mathematics to describe patterns that you see in art. You have made and explored patterns based on sequences, rotational symmetry, and constructions. Now you are ready to create your own work of art based on mathematical patterns.

Check students' work.

11 Before you begin your design, think about the different mathematical patterns you might want to use. You can use one type of pattern or combine several different types.

12 After deciding what types of patterns you want to use, make a rough sketch of your design. Will other students be able to recognize the patterns you are using? How can you make your design more attractive?

13 When you are satisfied with the design you have chosen, make your final art work. You can use markers, paint, construction paper, or any other materials to create your work of art. Consider how the colors and materials you choose affect the appearance of your design.

14 On a separate sheet of paper, give a mathematical description of the pattern or patterns you used in your design. Be prepared to present your art to the class and to explain the mathematics you used.

You will need: • *compass and ruler* (Exs. 5–8)

Write a rule for finding a term for each sequence. Then find the next three terms. (Sec. 1, Explor. 1) **1–4. Sample Responses are given.**

1. $\dfrac{1}{y}, \dfrac{1}{y^2}, \dfrac{1}{y^3}, \dfrac{1}{y^4}, \cdots$ See below.

2. 1, 10, 19, 28, ... **Add 9 to the previous term; 37, 46, 55**

3. 10; 100; 1000; 10,000; ... See below.

4. 1, 0.5, 0.25, 0.125, ... **Divide the previous term by 2; 0.0625, 0.03125, 0.015625**

Tell whether it is possible to construct a triangle with the given side lengths. If it is possible, construct the triangle. (Sec. 1, Explor. 2)

5. 2.5 in., 3.5 in., 5 in.
Yes; Check students' drawings.

6. 4.8 cm, 4.8 cm, 9.8 cm
No.

7. 6.5 cm, 4 cm, 6 cm
Yes; Check students' drawings.

8. Draw a line segment of any length. Then construct its perpendicular bisector. Show all of your work. (Sec. 1, Explor. 3)
Check students' drawings.

9. A carpenter designs and makes wooden tabletops. List all of the rotational symmetries for the tabletop shown. Find the minimum rotational symmetry.

(Sec. 2, Explor. 1) **60°, 120°, 180°, 240°, 300°, 360°; 60°**

Tell whether each number is a *rational* or an *irrational* number.
(Sec. 2, Explor. 2)

10. $\sqrt{75}$ **irrational**

11. $\sqrt{36}$ **rational**

12. $\sqrt{\dfrac{25}{9}}$ **rational**

13. $\sqrt{0.64}$ **rational**

14. Write the numbers in order from least to greatest. (Sec. 2, Explor. 2)

$0.\overline{72}, \dfrac{5}{7}, 0.7\overline{2}, 0.72, \dfrac{3}{4}, -0.7, -\dfrac{8}{11}, -0.72, -\dfrac{3}{4}$ $\;-\dfrac{3}{4}, -\dfrac{8}{11}, -0.72, -0.7, \dfrac{5}{7}, 0.72, 0.7\overline{2}, 0.\overline{72}, \dfrac{3}{4}$

Solve each equation. (Sec. 3, Explor. 1)

15. $5 = \dfrac{1}{3}x$ **15**

16. $4 + \dfrac{2}{3}t = 12$ **12**

17. $\dfrac{2}{3}b - 11 = 5$ **24**

18. A quadrilateral has two pairs of parallel sides and no right angles. Tell what types of quadrilaterals it could be. Include sketches with your answer. (Sec. 3, Explor. 2) **parallelogram or rhombus**

Solve each equation. (Sec. 4, Explor. 1)

19. $0.23 = -0.6a - 0.3$ **0.88$\overline{3}$**

20. $-6y - 1.5 = -21$ **3.25**

21. $\dfrac{3}{4} + 2x = \dfrac{1}{2}$ **$-\dfrac{1}{8}$**

1. Multiply the previous term by $\dfrac{1}{y}$; $\dfrac{1}{y^5}, \dfrac{1}{y^6}, \dfrac{1}{y^7}$

3. Multiply the previous term by 10; 100,000, 1,000,000, 10,000,000

22. In this module you discovered the formula for finding the sum of the angles of a polygon. Suppose you cannot remember the formula. Describe a method for finding the sum of the angles of the polygon shown. (Sec. 4, Explor. 2)

22. Possible answers: Measure all the angles with a protractor and add; Divide the polygon into $n - 2$ triangles and multiply the number of triangles by 180°.

23. Beth Loecke wants to plant a rectangular garden in her back yard. If she uses the measurements shown will her garden be rectangular? Explain why or why not. (Sec. 5, Explor. 1)

Yes. $7.5^2 + 4^2 = 8.5^2$, so both triangles are right triangles and the garden is a rectangle.

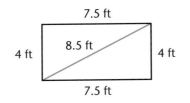

7.5 ft

4 ft   8.5 ft   4 ft

7.5 ft

For each triangle, find the unknown side length. (Sec. 5, Explor. 2)

24.

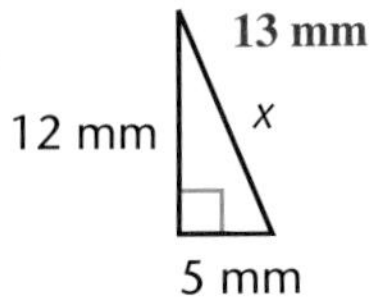

13 mm

12 mm x

5 mm

25.   6 ft

8 ft x

10 ft

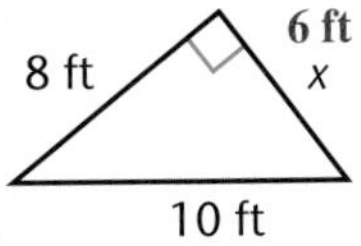

26.   1 in.

x 1 in.

$\sqrt{2} \approx 1.4$ in.

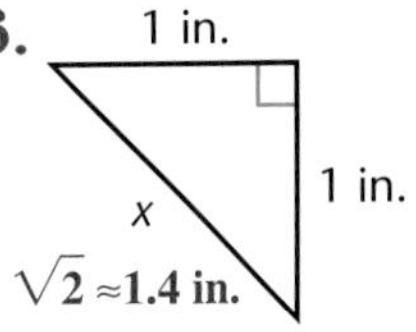

Two objects fall into the figure shown. Each object has an equal chance of landing anywhere in the figure. (Sec. 6, Explors. 1 and 2)

27. What is the probability that an object will land in the orange region? 50%

28. What is the probability that both objects will land in the orange region? 25%

29. What is the probability that the first object will land in the orange region and the second object will not land in the orange region? 25%

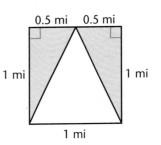

0.5 mi   0.5 mi

1 mi   1 mi

1 mi

Reflecting ◀▶ on the Module

30. Name at least three different mathematical relationships you explored in this module. What discoveries did you make about these relationships? What patterns did you see? Answers will vary. Check students' work.

MATHEMATICS
The & Theme

1 Working with Cylinders

As you read about tin cans:
- ◆ Find the surface area of a cylinder
- ◆ Find and interpret the ratio of surface area to volume

2 Slopes and Equations of Lines

As you explore TV sales:
- ◆ Identify positive, negative, zero, and undefined slopes
- ◆ Write equations of lines in slope-intercept form

3 Working with Exponents

As you read about the invention of the telescope and the microscope:
- ◆ Multiply and divide powers
- ◆ Simplify powers with zero and negative exponents

4 Complements, Supplements, and Tangents

As you learn about the astrolabe:
- ◆ Identify complementary and supplementary angles
- ◆ Find and use the tangent of an angle

5 Counting Techniques

As you learn about Braille:
- ◆ Count numbers of choices
- ◆ Find numbers of permutations
- ◆ Find numbers of combinations

6 Working with Probability

As you examine different keys for locks:
- ◆ Find probabilities of events

The Module Project ➜ Building a Ramp

The ancient Egyptians may have used ramps and cylinders to move the stone blocks that form the Pyramids of Giza. You'll use mathematics to design and build your own model ramp and cylinders that you can use to move small objects.

More on the Module Project
See pp. 328, 342, 367, and 389.

INTERNET
To learn more about the theme:
http://www.mlmath.com

Section ① Working with Cylinders

IN THIS SECTION

EXPLORATION 1
 ♦ Surface Areas of Cylinders

EXPLORATION 2
 ♦ Surface Area and Volume

Can Do!

◄ ‑ ‑ ‑ *Setting the Stage*

The French general Napoleon Bonaparte once said that "an army marches on its stomach." He was not exaggerating. Hunger and poor nutrition caused more casualties in Napoleon's armies than actual combat. In 1795, the French government offered a prize of 12,000 francs to anyone who could invent a way to preserve food for the military.

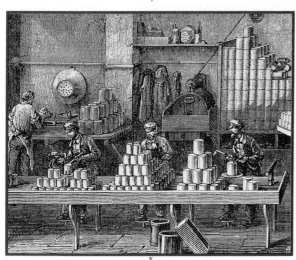

Nicolas Appert, a candy maker from Paris, won the prize in 1809. Appert found that you can preserve food for months by sealing it in glass jars and heating the jars in boiling water. Glass jars break easily, however, and soldiers needed stronger containers.

This problem was solved by Peter Durand, an English inventor. Durand patented the use of metal cans for storing food. These cans were made of *tin plate* (iron coated with tin to prevent rusting) and came to be known as "tin cans." Tin cans were first used in 1813 to supply food to the British military.

Think About It

1 What two-dimensional shapes could you cut from a sheet of tin plate to make a tin can? two circles and a rectangle

2 What factors might a manufacturer consider before designing a can? Sample Response: the cost of the material, the capacity of the container

▶ In this module, you'll learn about the history of inventions like the tin can. You'll also see how these inventions relate to mathematics.

Surface Areas of Cylinders

GOAL

LEARN HOW TO...
+ find the surface area of a cylinder

AS YOU...
+ make a paper can

KEY TERM
+ surface area

SET UP *You will need:* • *compass* • *metric ruler* • *scissors* • *tape* • $8\frac{1}{2}$ *in. by 11 in. sheet of paper*

▶ **A tin can is made by cutting two circles and a rectangle from a sheet of tin plate. The rectangle is rolled into a tube. The circles are added to the ends of the tube to form a cylinder.**

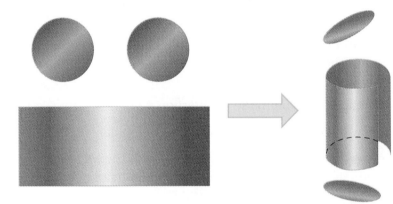

3 You can create your own can with paper. **Answers will vary. Check students' work.**

a. Think about the dimensions of cans you see in a supermarket. Then choose a realistic radius and height for your paper can. Give the radius and the height in centimeters.

b. Use a compass to draw two circles having the radius you chose in part (a). Label the radius of each circle *r* as shown.

c. Draw a rectangle that you think you can use to make your can. Label the rectangle's length *l* and its width *w* as shown. Measure *l* and *w* to the nearest tenth of a centimeter.

4 Cut out the circles and the rectangle
you drew in Question 3. Tape the edges
of the rectangle together with little or
no overlap to form a tube. Hold a circle
over the top of the tube as shown.

a. In order for the tube and the circles
to form a can, how should the
length, *l*, of the rectangle be related
to the radius, *r*, of each circle? $l = 2\pi r$

b. How should the width, *w*, of the rectangle be related to the
height you chose in Question 3(a)? **It should be the same.**

c. If necessary, make a new rectangle whose length and width
have the properties you described in parts (a) and (b). Tape the
rectangle and circles together to form a paper can.
Check students' work.

▶ **A cylinder's *surface area* is the sum of the areas of the circles and the
rectangle that form the cylinder. In general, the surface area of a
space figure is the combined area of the figure's outer surfaces.**

5 Use the paper can you made in Question 4.

a. How is the area of each circle related to the can's radius?
Area = π • (radius)²
b. How is the area of the rectangle related to the rectangle's
length and width? to the can's radius and height?
Area = length • width; Area = 2π • radius • height
c. Use your answers from parts (a) and (b) to write a formula for
the surface area, *S.A.*, of a cylinder in terms of its radius, *r*, and
height, *h*. $S.A. = 2\pi r^2 + 2\pi rh$

d. Find the surface area of your paper can. **Answers will vary.**
Check students' work.

✔ **QUESTION 6**

…checks that you
can find a cylinder's
surface area given its
radius and height.

6 ✔ **CHECKPOINT** Find the surface area of each can.
For answers given throughout, 3.14 is used. Answers may vary slightly if the π key is used.

a. 3.4 cm **about 286.12 cm²**   b. 3.9 cm **about 303.70 cm²**

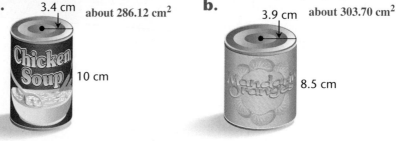

10 cm   8.5 cm

7 Which of the cans in Question 6 uses more metal? Explain.
can (b); It's surface area is greater.

HOMEWORK EXERCISES ▶ See Exs. 1–9 on p. 325.

Exploration 2

Surface Area and Volume

 SET UP *Work in a group. You will need:* • *Labsheet 1A* • *metric ruler* • *five cans with different sizes and shapes* • *calculator*

▶ An *efficient* can is one that uses a small amount of metal compared to the amount of food or drink it holds.

8 Discussion What are some advantages of efficient cans?

9 A small juice can uses about 300 cm² of metal and holds about 400 cm³ of juice. A large juice can uses about 400 cm² of metal and holds about 600 cm³ of juice.

  a. Mental Math How much metal is used per cubic centimeter of juice for the small can? for the large can? How did you get your answers? **0.75 cm²; 0.67 cm²; Sample Response: I divided the amount of metal used in each can by the amount of juice it can hold.**

  b. Which can is more efficient? Explain.
  The larger can is more efficient because it uses less metal per cubic centimeter.

▶ **Using Ratios** One measure of the efficiency of a can is the ratio $\frac{S.A.}{V}$, where *S.A.* is the can's surface area and *V* is the can's volume. Your group will use this ratio to compare the efficiency of your cans.

10 Measure the diameter and the height of each of your cans to the nearest tenth of a centimeter. For each can, find the radius, the surface area *S.A.*, the volume *V*, and the ratio $\frac{S.A.}{V}$. **Answers will vary. Check students' work.**

11 a. If the ratio $\frac{S.A.}{V}$ is greater for can A than for can B, what can you say about the efficiency of the cans? Explain. **See above.**

  b. Rank your cans from most efficient to least efficient.
  Answers will vary. Check students' work.

8. Possible answers: They cost less to produce, require less packaging by the case, and weigh less, so they are easier to carry and cost less to ship.

FOR ◀ HELP
with the *volume of a cylinder,* see **MODULE 1, p. 47**

11. a. Can B is more efficient than can A; Since can B has a smaller ratio it uses less material per unit volume.

...checks that you can find and interpret the ratio of a cylinder's surface area to its volume.

12. tomato can, tuna can, milk can; I ranked the cans from least to greatest value of $\frac{S.A.}{V}$.

12 ✔ **CHECKPOINT** Rank the cans shown from most efficient to least efficient. Explain your thinking.

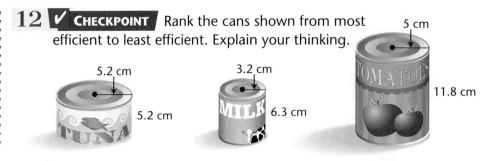

5 cm

5.2 cm

5.2 cm

3.2 cm

6.3 cm

11.8 cm

▶ **Of all cans having a given volume, which one uses the least metal? Canning companies often want to solve this problem, since using less metal reduces costs. You'll explore this problem below.**

Use Labsheet 1A for Questions 13 and 14.

13. S.A. = 106.76, V = 50.24; S.A. = 75.36, V = 50.24; S.A. = 125.6, V = 50.24; S.A. = 414.48, V = 50.24; They are the same.

13 Labsheet 1A shows four *Cylinders*. Find each cylinder's surface area and volume. What do you notice about the volumes?

14 What are the height and the radius of the cylinder with the least surface area? What is the ratio of the height to the radius?
height: 4, radius: 2; 2 to 1

15 Of all cylinders having a given volume, the cylinder whose height is twice its radius has the least surface area.

15. a. Step 1: Substitute $\pi r^2 h$ for V; Step 2: Substitute $2r$ for h.
b. The commutative property of multiplication can be used to rewrite $\pi r^2(2r)$ as $2\pi r^2 r = 2\pi r^3$. Substitute 3.14 for π and solve for r^3 in the equation $2(3.14)r^3 = 800$:

$6.28r^3 = 800$ so $r^3 = \frac{800}{6.28} \approx 127$.

c. $5^3 = 125$ and $6^3 = 216$; since $5^3 < r^3 < 6^3$, $5 < r < 6$, $r = 5.03$; about 5.03 cm

a. A snack food company plans to sell peanuts in cans with a volume of 800 cm^3. An engineer at the company found the dimensions of the can that has this volume and uses the least amount of metal. The engineer's solution starts like this:

$$V = 800$$
$$\pi r^2 h = 800$$
$$\pi r^2(2r) = 800$$

Explain each step of the solution so far.

b. Show that $\pi r^2(2r) = 800$ can be written as $r^3 \approx 127$.

c. 📱 Calculator Explain why the solution of $r^3 \approx 127$ must satisfy $5 < r < 6$. Use a calculator and a guess-and-check strategy to find r to the nearest hundredth. What is the radius of the peanut can that uses the least amount of metal?

d. Find the height of the peanut can that uses the least amount of metal. How did you get your answer? about 10.06 cm; Multiply the radius by 2.

16 Discussion Why might a food or drink manufacturer use a can that does *not* have the least surface area for its volume?
Sample Response: The manufacturer may want to use a can that is a standard size for the product.

HOMEWORK EXERCISES ▶ See Exs. 10–19 on pp. 326–327.

You can also use a spreadsheet to calculate ratios of surface area to volume as you did in Question 10 on page 321.

 Step 1 Set up a spreadsheet with the column headings shown below. Enter the contents, radius, and height of each of your group's cans.

 Step 2 In cell D2 (column D and row 2), enter the formula for the surface area of a cylinder. Every formula must begin with an equals sign. The formula uses the radius in cell B2 and the height in cell C2 to find the surface area of the can in row 2.

Type "PI()" for π and "B2^2" for $(B2)^2$.

File   Edit   Format   Calculate   Options   View

SURFACE AREA TO VOLUME RATIOS

D2 | × | √ | = 2*PI()*B2^2+2*PI()*B2*C2

	A	B	C	D	E	F
1	Contents of Can	r (cm)	h (cm)	S (cm^2)	V (cm^3)	S/V
2	Beef stew	5.4	8.6	475.01		
3	Coffee	7.8	15.9			
4	Parmesan cheese	2.2	14.2			
5	Ravioli	3.7	11.1			
6	Tuna	4.3	3.7			

 Step 3 In cell E2, enter the formula "= PI()*B2^2*C2" to calculate the volume of the can in row 2.

Step 4 In cell F2, enter the formula "= D2/E2" to calculate the ratio of surface area to volume for the can in row 2.

Step 5 Use the *fill down* command in columns D, E, and F to apply the formulas you entered in Steps 2–4 to the remaining rows.

Calculate

Move...
Fill Right
Fill Down
Sort...

Insert Cells...
Delete Cells...

Calculate Now
Auto Calc

File   Edit   Format   Calculate   Options   View

SURFACE AREA TO VOLUME RATIOS

F2 | × | √ | = D2 / E2

	A	B	C	D	E	F
1	Contents of Can	r (cm)	h (cm)	S (cm^2)	V (cm^3)	S/V
2	Beef stew	5.4	8.6	475.01	787.84	0.60
3	Coffee	7.8	15.9	1161.51	3039.04	0.38
4	Parmesan cheese	2.2	14.2	226.70	215.92	1.05
5	Ravioli	3.7	11.1	344.07	477.39	0.72
6	Tuna	4.3	3.7	216.14	214.93	1.01

Key Term

surface area

Surface Area of a Cylinder (pp. 319–320)

The surface area, S.A., of a cylinder with radius r and height h is given by the formula S.A. $= 2\pi r^2 + 2\pi rh$.

Example You can use the radius and height of the cylinder shown to find its surface area.

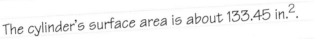

$$S.A. = 2\pi r^2 + 2\pi rh$$
$$\approx 2(3.14)(2.5)^2 + 2(3.14)(2.5)(6)$$
$$\approx 133.45$$

2.5 in.

6 in.

The cylinder's surface area is about 133.45 in.^{2}.

Comparing Surface Area to Volume (pp. 321–322)

For a container (such as a can) with surface area S.A. and volume V, the ratio $\frac{S.A.}{V}$ is a measure of the container's efficiency. The smaller this ratio, the more efficient the container.

Example

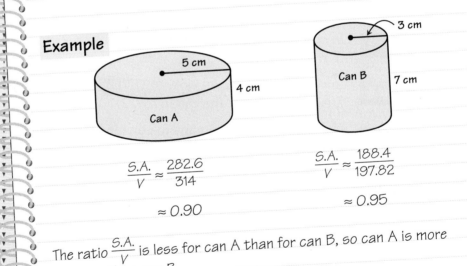

Can A — 5 cm, 4 cm

Can B — 3 cm, 7 cm

$$\frac{S.A.}{V} \approx \frac{282.6}{314}$$
$$\approx 0.90$$

$$\frac{S.A.}{V} \approx \frac{188.4}{197.82}$$
$$\approx 0.95$$

The ratio $\frac{S.A.}{V}$ is less for can A than for can B, so can A is more efficient than can B.

CLOSURE QUESTION

Explain how you can use the ratio $\frac{surface\ area}{volume}$ or $\frac{S.A.}{V}$ to find the most efficient use of materials to make a can or cylinder.

Sample Response: The lower the ratio, the more efficient the can or cylinder.

17 Key Concepts Question A coffee can has a radius of 8 cm and a height of 16 cm. A tomato sauce can has a radius of 3 cm and a height of 8 cm. Which can is more efficient? Explain.

the coffee can; The ratio of surface area to volume for the coffee can is less than the same ratio for the tomato sauce can.

Section ①
Practice & Application Exercises ▸▸▸▸▸▸▸▸

Find the surface area of the cylinder with the given radius *r* and height *h*.

1. *r* = 2 cm, *h* = 7 cm
   113.04 cm²

2. *r* = 1 m, *h* = 3 m
   25.12 cm²

3. *r* = 6 in., *h* = 6 in.
   452.16 in.²

4. *r* = 8 ft, *h* = 4 ft
   602.88 ft²

5. *r* = 1.7 m, *h* = 8 m
   about 103.56 m²

6. *r* = 2.4 in., *h* = 9.6 in.
   about 180.86 in.²

7. **Mental Math** Use mental math to estimate the surface area of a cylinder with a radius of 1 in. and a height of 4 in. Use $\pi \approx 3$.
   about 30 in.²

Science Sometimes stars explode, releasing tiny particles called *neutrinos* that may eventually reach Earth. The sun is also a source of neutrinos. To detect neutrinos, scientists built the "Super Kamiokande," a huge cylindrical tank of water located in a mine near Toyama, Japan.

◀ The top, bottom, and side of the tank are completely covered with light detectors. The tank has a radius of about 20 m and a height of about 40 m.

8. Estimate the surface area of the tank using $\pi \approx 3$. Then find the surface area to the nearest whole number.
   about 7200 m²; 7536 m²

9. The light detectors are mounted on rectangular frames like the one shown. Each frame is about 210 cm by 280 cm and holds 12 detectors.

   a. About how many frames were needed to cover the inside of the tank?
      about 1282 frames

   b. About how many light detectors were needed?
      about 15,384 light detectors

10. about 0.86

11. about 0.84

12. about 1.01

Find the ratio of surface area to volume for each can.

10. 3.8 cm / 6 cm   **11.** 4.3 cm / 5.4 cm   **12.** 3.3 cm / 5 cm

13. Use your answers for Exercises 10–12 to rank the cans shown above from most efficient to least efficient. water chestnuts, olives, chili peppers

14. Architecture A *Quonset hut* is a building shaped like a half cylinder and made of corrugated steel. Examples of a Quonset hut and of a greenhouse also shaped like a half cylinder are shown.

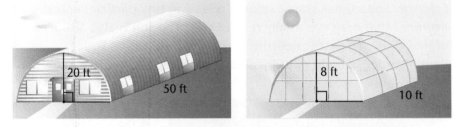

20 ft   50 ft   8 ft   10 ft

a. Find the ratio of surface area to volume for each building. Include the floors of the buildings when calculating surface area.
Quonset hut: 0.20; greenhouse: 0.61

b. Which building encloses space more efficiently? Explain.
the Quonset hut; it requires less surface area per cubic foot of volume

c. **Writing** Would the more efficient of the two buildings be the better building in all situations? Why or why not?
Answers will vary. Check students' work.

Look back at your answers to Questions 13–15 on page 322 in Exploration 2. Use what you learned to complete Exercises 15 and 16.

15. Research Go to a supermarket and look at some of the canned foods sold. Find a can that uses approximately the least amount of metal possible for its volume. Also find a can that uses a large amount of metal for its volume. Explain how you chose your cans.
Answers will vary. Check students' work.

16. Agriculture A farmer decides to roll hay into large cylindrical bales, each with a volume of 100 ft^3. (A bale this size will feed 2 horses for about a month.) To keep the bales dry, the farmer plans to seal them in plastic wrap. What should the dimensions of each bale be if the farmer wants to use the least amount of plastic wrap possible?

radius: about $2\frac{1}{2}$ ft; height: about 5 ft.

17. Challenge A log of firewood burns faster if you chop it into pieces before throwing it in a fireplace. This is because chopping a log increases the total area of wood exposed to the flames. For example, suppose you chop a log into four equal pieces as shown.

12 in.

18 in.

a. Find the surface area of the log before it was chopped up. **2260.8 in.²**

b. Find the combined surface area of the four chopped-up pieces. **3988.8 in.²**

c. Compare your answers from parts (a) and (b). By what percent does chopping up the log increase the surface area? **about 76%**

18. Algebra Connection The surface area of a cylinder is 850 cm². Find a radius and a height that this cylinder could have. (*Hint:* First choose a radius. Then use the formula $S.A. = 2\pi r^2 + 2\pi rh$ to solve for the height.) **Sample Response: radius = 5 cm, height = about 22 cm**

Reflecting ◀▶ on the Section

19. Describe how you can find a cylinder's surface area either by using a formula or by thinking about the shapes that form the cylinder. **Sample Response: Use the formula $2\pi r^2 + 2\pi rh$ or find the area of the top and bottom of the cylinder (two circles) and add the area of the rectangle that makes up the side of the cylinder.**

Spiral ◀▶ Review

20. A dart is thrown randomly at the square target shown. Find the probability that the dart hits the red region. (Module 4, p. 308) **50%**

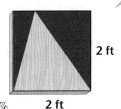

2 ft

2 ft

Estimation Estimate each percent. (Module 2, p. 90)

21. 11% of 200
about 20

22. 19% of 3500
about 700

23. 79% of 660
about 528

Plot each pair of points on a coordinate plane and draw a line through them. Find the slope of the line. (Module 3, p. 195)

24. (0, 0) and (1, 4)
See above.

25. (4, 5) and (2, 1)

26. (−6, −3) and (−2, 7)

24.

slope: 4

25.

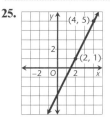

slope: 2

26.

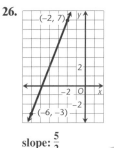

slope: $\frac{5}{2}$

Building a Ramp

The ancient Egyptians built the Pyramids of Giza using thousands of stone blocks. The Egyptians may have used ramps and logs to roll the blocks into place. The diagrams show how you can model this process using a miniature ramp, several cylinders, and a small block.

SET UP

You will need:
* *Project Labsheet A*

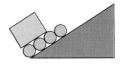 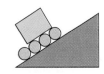 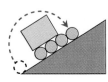

Step 1 Use one more cylinder than is needed to support the block.

Step 2 Roll the block up the ramp to the edge of the highest cylinder. The cylinders will roll some as the block rolls.

Step 3 Move the lowest cylinder to the front of the block.

Step 4 Repeat Steps 2 and 3 until the block reaches the top of the ramp.

For your module project, you'll design and build a model ramp with cylinders that you can use to move small objects.

Working with Cylinders One step in building your model is choosing the diameter of the cylinders. The diameter may affect how much the cylinders cost and how easy they are to use.

Use Project Labsheet A for Project Questions 1–4.

1 The labsheet shows four diagrams of a *Ramp and Cylinders*. Use the diagrams to complete the table at the bottom of the labsheet.
3, 84.78, 254.34; 4, 37.68, 150.72; 5, 21.195, 105.975; 7, 9.42, 65.94

2 As the diameter of the cylinders decreases, what happens to:

a. the number of cylinders you need to move the block? The number increases.

b. the volume of material needed for all of the cylinders? The volume decreases.

3 How does the diameter of the cylinders affect the number of times you must move a cylinder from the lowest position to the highest position on the ramp? The number increases as the diameter decreases.

4. Sample Response: Cylinders with smaller diameters weigh less so they would be easier to manuever, but more of them are required so they would cost more to produce.

4 What are some advantages of using cylinders with a small diameter? What are some disadvantages? Be sure to discuss how the diameter affects the cost and ease of use of the cylinders.

Section 1

Find the surface area of the cylinder with the given radius _r_ and height _h_.

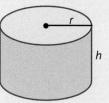

1. _r_ = 5 in., _h_ = 3 in.
   251.2 in.²

2. _r_ = 3 in., _h_ = 5 in.
   150.72 in.²

3. _r_ = 11 cm, _h_ = 40 cm
   3523.08 cm²

4. _r_ = 9.5 cm, _h_ = 9.5 cm
   1133.54 cm²

5. _r_ = 1.8 m, _h_ = 6.2 m
   about 90.43 m²

6. _r_ = 33 ft, _h_ = 100 ft
   27,562.92 ft²

Find the ratio of surface area to volume for each cylinder.

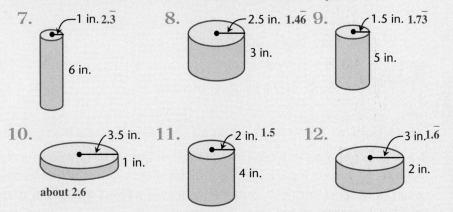

7. —1 in. 2.$\overline{3}$
   6 in.

8. 2.5 in. 1.4$\overline{6}$
   3 in.

9. 1.5 in. 1.7$\overline{3}$
   5 in.

10. 3.5 in.
    1 in.
    about 2.6

11. 2 in. 1.5
    4 in.

12. 3 in. 1.$\overline{6}$
    2 in.

13. Suppose you have six plastic storage containers with the same dimensions as the cylinders in Exercises 7–12. Which container was made most efficiently? Explain.

    The cylinder with a radius of 2.5 in. and a height of 3 in.;
    The ratio of surface area to volume is lowest.

Study Skills ◀▶ **Comparing and Contrasting**

When you compare and contrast objects or ideas, you consider how they are alike and how they are different. Comparing and contrasting can help you see how things are related and extend your understanding of what you have learned.

1. Compare and contrast the formulas for the surface area and volume of a cylinder. See above.

2. Graph _y_ = 3_x_ + 2 and _y_ = −3_x_ + 2. Compare and contrast the lines that you graphed.

3. Give an example of when comparing and contrasting helped you make decision. Answers will vary. Check students' work.

1. Sample Response: The two formulas are alike in that they both use π, _r_, and _h_. They are different in that the formula for surface area ($2\pi r^2 + 2\pi rh$) uses both multiplication and addition and has an answer in square units, while the formula for volume ($\pi r^2 h$) uses only multiplication and has an answer in cubic units.

2.

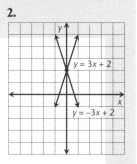

Sample Response: The lines both intersect the _y_-axis at 2 and have the same steepness. The first equation has 3_x_ and slopes up to the right, but the second equation has −3_x_ and slopes down to the right.

FOR ASSESSMENT AND PORTFOLIOS

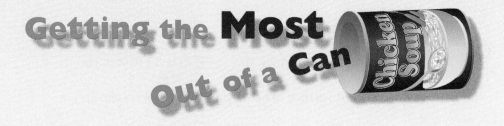

Getting the Most Out of a Can

SET UP *You will need:* • *compass* • *ruler* • *scissors* • *tape*
• *$8\frac{1}{2}$ in. by 11 in. sheet of paper*

The Situation   See the Resource Book for a detailed discussion of this Extended Exploration.

Most cans you find in a supermarket are designed to have a specific volume. However, a package manufacturer sometimes needs to design a can or other cylindrical container that uses a fixed amount of material and has the greatest volume possible.

The Problem   Answers will vary. Check students' work.

Make a "paper can" with the greatest volume possible by cutting and taping together two circles and a rectangle from an $8\frac{1}{2}$ in. by 11 in. sheet of paper. (The circles and the rectangle should all be from a single piece of paper and should not be a combination of several smaller pieces.)

Something to Think About

◆ How must the length of one side of the rectangle for your can be related to each circle's radius?   The length must be equal to 2π times the radius.

◆ Which dimension—the *radius* or the *height*—has a greater effect on the can's volume?   the radius

◆ Is it possible for you to make your can without wasting any paper?   No.

Present Your Results

Give the radius and the height of the can you made, and explain how you chose those dimensions. Explain why you think it is not possible to make a can that has a greater volume. Show any diagrams, tables, or equations you used to solve the problem.   Answers will vary. Check students' work.

Section ② Slopes and Equations of Lines

WARM-UP EXERCISES

Graph each on the same set of axes.

1. the point (−1, 4)
   See graph below.
2. the point (2, −2)
   See graph below.
3. Draw the line through these points.
   See graph below.
4. Name another point on the line.   Answers will vary. Sample Response: (3, −4)
5. Name the point where the graph crosses the x-axis.   (1, 0)
6. Name the point where the graph crosses the y-axis.   (0, 2)

Setting the Stage ▷▷▷▷▷▷▷▷▷▷▷▷▷▷▷▷▷▷▷▷▷▷▷▷▷▷▷▷▷

If you try to buy a black-and-white TV today, you may have trouble finding one. Demand for black-and-white TVs has almost disappeared. In 1995, more than 98% of all TVs sold were color TVs.

Although the first color telecast was in 1953, it was not until 1970 that color TVs began outselling black-and-white TVs. In fact, the graph shows that sales of black-and-white TVs did not start declining steadily until around 1980.

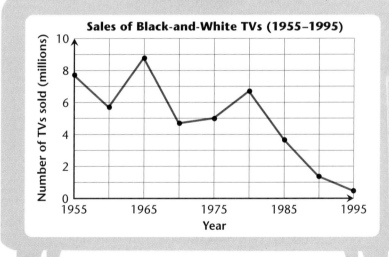

Sales of Black-and-White TVs (1955–1995)

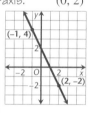

Think About It

1 About how many black-and-white TVs were sold in 1955? in 1980? in 1995?   **about 7.75 million TVs; about 6.75 million TVs; about 0.5 million TVs**

2 Why do you think people continued to buy large numbers of black-and-white TVs for so many years after color TVs became available? What may have caused the steady decline in black-and-white TV sales beginning around 1980?   **Sample Response: Not many programs in color, black-and-white TVs were less expensive; more color programs, prices of color TVs became more affordable.**

LEARN HOW TO...
- find and interpret positive and negative slopes
- identify slopes of horizontal and vertical lines

AS YOU...
- investigate TV sales

 **Exploration 1**

Exploring *Slope*

SET UP *You will need:* • Labsheet 2A • *graph paper*

Use the line graph on page 331 for Questions 3 and 4.

3. 1960–1965 and 1970–1980; 1955–1960, 1965–1970, 1980–1995; Lines going up from left to right show an increase and lines going down from left to right show a decrease.

3 Discussion During which periods did sales of black-and-white TVs increase? During which periods did they decrease? How can you tell?

4 Discussion During which five-year period do you think sales decreased the most? Explain your thinking.

1965–1970; Sample Response: The graph is steepest there.

▶ In Module 3, you learned that the *slope* of a line is a ratio that measures the steepness of the line.

FOR◀HELP
with *slope*, see
MODULE 3, p. 195

$$\text{slope} = \frac{\text{rise}}{\text{run}} = \frac{\text{vertical change}}{\text{horizontal change}}$$

In this exploration, you'll see how slope can give you other information about a line.

Use Labsheet 2A for Questions 5–9.

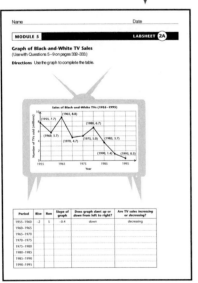

5 Try This as a Class Labsheet 2A shows the *Graph of Black-and-White TV Sales* that you saw in the Setting the Stage. Ordered pairs for certain points are included on the graph.

a. The first row of the table below the graph has been completed. Explain how the rise, run, and slope were found. See below.

b. Why is the slope negative?
The rise is negative and the run is positive, so $\frac{\text{rise}}{\text{run}}$ is negative.

6 Complete the table on the labsheet. For each five-year period: **3.1, 5, 0.62, up, increasing; –4.1, 5, –0.82, down, decreasing; 0.3, 5, 0.06, up, increasing; 1.7, 5, 0.34, up, increasing; –3, 5, –0.6, down, decreasing; –2.3, 5, –0.46,**
- Find the slope of the graph for the period. **down, decreasing; –0.9, 5, –0.18, down, decreasing**

- Tell whether the graph slants *up* or *down* from left to right.

- Tell whether TV sales were *increasing* or *decreasing*.

5. a. The rise was found by subtracting the *y*-coordinate for 1955 from the *y*-coordinate for 1960. The run was found by subtracting the *x*-coordinate for 1955 from the *x*-coordinate for 1960. The slope is the ratio of rise to run.

7 a. Look at the periods in the table where the graph's slope is positive. For these periods, does the graph slant *up* or *down* from left to right? Were sales of black-and-white TVs *increasing* or *decreasing*? up; increasing

b. Repeat part (a) for the periods in the table where the graph's slope is negative. down; decreasing

c. Based on your observations, what can you say about the slope of a line that slants up from left to right? that slants down from left to right? Slope is positive; Slope is negative.

8 Try This as a Class According to the table on the labsheet, the graph's slope for the period 1955–1960 is –0.4.

a. Explain why this number is a rate. What are the rate's units?
It compares quantities measured in different units; sales in dollars and number of years

b. What information does the rate give you about black-and-white TV sales during the period 1955–1960?
Sales decreased at a rate of $.4 million per year during those 5 years.

9 Discussion Compare the graph and the table on the labsheet.

a. How can you tell when black-and-white TV sales were increasing most rapidly by looking at the graph? by looking at the slopes in the table?

b. How can you tell when sales were decreasing most rapidly by looking at the graph? by looking at the slopes in the table?

10 ✔ **CHECKPOINT** Use the lines shown.

a. Which lines have slopes that are positive? lines *A* and *D*

b. Which lines have slopes that are negative? line *B* and *C*

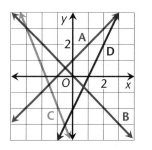

FOR◀HELP
with *rates*,
see
MODULE 1, p. 9

9. a. The steepest upward line shows the greatest increase on the graph; the greatest positive number shows the greatest increase
b. the steepest downward line shows the greatest decrease on the graph; the least negative number shows the greatest decrease

✔ **QUESTION 10**

...checks that you understand the relationship between a line's appearance and its slope.

▶ **Horizontal and Vertical Lines** You have seen that some lines have positive slopes and some have negative slopes. In Questions 11 and 12, you'll explore the slopes of horizontal and vertical lines.

11 Draw several horizontal lines on a coordinate plane. Find the slope of each line. What do you notice about the slopes?
They are all 0.

12 a. Draw several vertical lines on a coordinate plane. Then try to find the slope of each line. What do you notice?
The slope can't be calculated.

b. The slope of a vertical line is said to be *undefined*. Why do you think this is so? The run is always 0 and division by 0 is undefined.

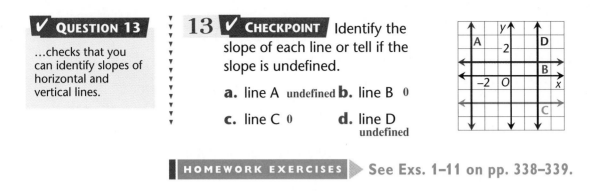

✔ **QUESTION 13**

...checks that you can identify slopes of horizontal and vertical lines.

13 ✔ **CHECKPOINT** Identify the slope of each line or tell if the slope is undefined.

a. line A undefined **b.** line B 0

c. line C 0 **d.** line D

undefined

HOMEWORK EXERCISES ▶ See Exs. 1–11 on pp. 338–339.

GOAL

LEARN HOW TO...
• identify the y-intercept of a line
• write an equation of a line in slope-intercept form

AS YOU...
• model TV sales at an electronics store

KEY TERMS
• y-intercept
• slope-intercept form

Exploration 2

Slope-Intercept Form

SET UP *Work with a partner. You will need graph paper.*

▶ **In this exploration, you and your partner will look for relationships between lines and their equations.**

14 An electronics store sold 800 color TVs and 40 black-and-white TVs in 1995. The store manager expects color TV sales to increase by about 60 TVs per year and black-and-white TV sales to decrease by about 4 TVs per year over the next five years.

a. You and your partner should each choose one of the tables below. Copy and complete your table.

14. a. Color TV sales:
800 + 60(3) = 980;
800 + 60(4) = 1040;
800 + 60(5) = 1100;
Black-and-White TV
sales: 40 − 4(3) = 28;
40 − 4(4) = 24;
40 − 4(5) = 20

Expected Color TV Sales		Expected Black-and-White TV Sales	
x = years since 1995	y = TVs sold	x = years since 1995	y = TVs sold
0	800	0	40
1	800 + 60(1) = 860	1	40 − 4(1) = 36
2	800 + 60(2) = 920	2	40 − 4(2) = 32
3	?	3	?
4	?	4	?
5	?	5	?

b. Make a scatter plot of the ordered pairs (*x, y*) in your table. What do you notice about the points in the scatter plot? See graphs at right. They lie on a straight line.

c. Draw a line through the points in your scatter plot. Find the slope of the line. Color TV sales: 60; Black-and-White TV sales: –4

d. Look for a pattern in your table. Use the pattern to write an equation relating *y* and *x*. Color TV sales: $y = 60x + 800$; Black-and-White TV sales: $y = -4x + 40$

e. Discussion Compare the equations that you and your partner wrote with the lines you both drew. How is the slope of each line related to the equation of the line? Is there any other way in which the lines and the equations are related? Explain. See below.

▶ The *y*-intercept of a line is the *y*-coordinate of the point where the line crosses the *y*-axis.

EXAMPLE

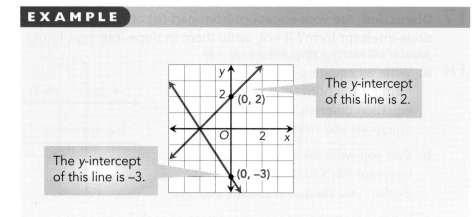

The *y*-intercept of this line is 2.

The *y*-intercept of this line is –3.

15 a. Look back at the lines you drew in Question 14. Give the *y*-intercept of each line. Color TV sales: 800; Black-and-White TV sales: 40

b. How is the *y*-intercept of each line related to the line's equation? It is the number being added (the constant).

c. What information do the *y*-intercepts give you about black-and-white and color TV sales? the number of sets sold in 1995

16 ✔ CHECKPOINT Give the *y*-intercept of each line. a. –3 b. –3 c. 1

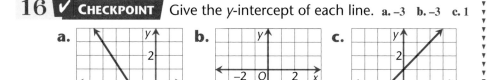

a.

b.

c.

14. b.

Expected Color TV Sales

Expected Black-and-White TV Sales

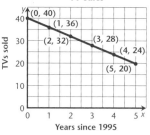

14. e. The slope is the number multiplied by *x* or the coefficient of *x*; The number being added (the constant) is the point where the line crosses the *y*-axis.

✔ QUESTION 16

...checks that you can identify the *y*-intercept of a line.

Key Terms

slope-intercept
form

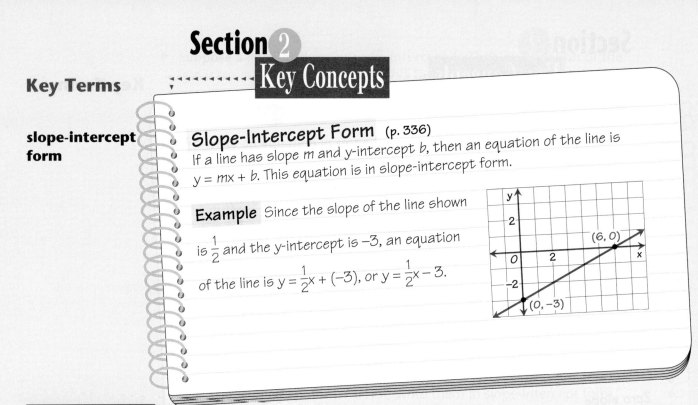

Slope-Intercept Form (p. 336)

If a line has slope m and y-intercept b, then an equation of the line is $y = mx + b$. This equation is in slope-intercept form.

Example Since the slope of the line shown is $\frac{1}{2}$ and the y-intercept is -3, an equation of the line is $y = \frac{1}{2}x + (-3)$, or $y = \frac{1}{2}x - 3$.

21 Key Concepts Question A line passes through the points $(0, 5)$ and $(2, 0)$. Is this enough information for you to write an equation of the line? If so, write an equation of the line in slope-intercept forms. If not, explain why not. Yes; $y = -\frac{5}{2}x + 5$

Section ② Practice & Application Exercises

YOU WILL NEED

For Ex. 22:
◆ graphing calculator or graph paper

For Exs. 23–28:
◆ graph paper

Find the slope of each line. 1. $-\frac{3}{5}$ 2. 0 3. $\frac{1}{3}$

1.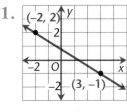

2.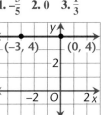

3.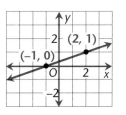

Find the slope of the line through the given points. You may find it helpful to plot the points and draw a line through them first.

4. $(2, 7)$ and $(4, 1)$ -3

5. $(3, 8)$ and $(6, 8)$ 0

6. $(-9, -4)$ and $(5, 0)$ $\frac{2}{7}$

7. $(-4, 4)$ and $(3, -5)$ $-\frac{9}{7}$

8. Use the lines shown.

a. Which line has a positive slope? line A

b. Which line has a negative slope? line C

c. Which line has a slope of zero? line B

d. Which line has a slope that is undefined?
line D

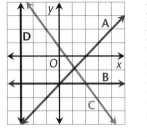

Endangered Species The Kemp's ridley sea turtle was listed as endangered by the United States government in 1970 and is still the most endangered sea turtle. Almost all remaining Kemp's ridley turtles nest on a single beach in Mexico. The graph shows how the number of nests on the beach has changed over time.

Kemp's Ridley Turtle Nests (1970–1995)

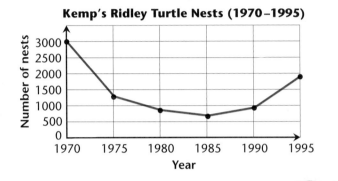

9. Estimation For each five-year period shown on the graph's horizontal axis, estimate the average annual rate of change in the number of turtle nests. Start with 1970–1975. Organize your results in a table. See Additional Answers.

10. During which five-year period from Exercise 9 did the number of turtle nests increase most rapidly? decrease most rapidly?
1990–1995; 1970–1975

11. Writing Mexico and the United States decided to work together to protect the beach where the Kemp's ridley turtle nests. About when do you think they made this decision? Explain.
Sample Response: 1985; The number of nests began to increase in 1985.

For each line, write an equation in slope-intercept form.

12. **13.** **14.**

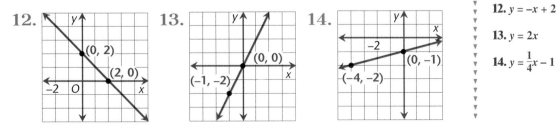

12. $y = -x + 2$

13. $y = 2x$

14. $y = \frac{1}{4}x - 1$

Write an equation in slope-intercept form for the line through the given points. You may find it helpful to plot the points and draw a line through them first.

15. (0, 7) and (1, 2) $y = -5x + 7$ 16. (0, 4) and (2, 8) $y = 2x + 4$

17. (–5, 5) and (3, –1) $y = -\frac{3}{4}x + \frac{5}{4}$ 18. (–3, –5) and (4, –5) $y = -5$

Environment Air pollution causes acid rain, which can damage the environment. From 1975 to 1978, scientists measured the acidity of rain and snow in a Colorado forest. The graph shows a fitted line that the scientists found for their data. Use the graph for Exercises 19–21.

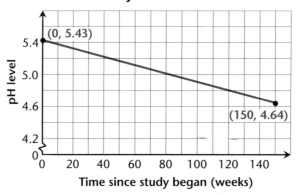

Acidity of Rain and Snow

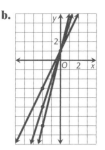

The acidity of rain or snow is given by a *pH level*. A decreasing pH level means that acidity is increasing.

22. a. slope = 1

They are parallel; Lines with the same slope are parallel to each other.

b.

They all have the same *y*-intercept; they have different slopes.

19. **Interpreting Data** Did the environmental situation in the forest get better or worse during the years 1975–1978? Explain. It got worse; The line shows a decrease in pH which means that the acidity of the rain increased.

20. **a.** Find the line's slope and *y*-intercept. What information does the slope give about the situation? What information does the *y*-intercept give about the situation? slope: about –0.005, *y*-intercept: 5.43; the rate at which the pH is decreasing per week; the pH level at the time the study began
   b. Write an equation for the line.
   $y = -0.005x + 5.43$, where *x* is the number of weeks since the study began.

21. The scientists' study ended after 150 weeks. Estimate the acidity of rain and snow in the forest 20 weeks after the study ended. Explain your thinking. about 4.58; I assumed the trend would continue, so I solved the equation for *x* = 170.

22. 📉 Graphing Calculator Use a graphing calculator or graph paper to complete parts (a) and (b).

   a. Give the slope of the lines $y = x + 2$, $y = x + 3$, and $y = x + 4$. Then graph all three lines on the same coordinate plane. What do you notice about the lines? Write a statement about lines with the same slope.

   b. Graph $y = 2x + 1$, $y = 3x + 1$, and $y = 4x + 1$ on the same coordinate plane. How are the lines alike? How are they different?

23. Alternative Method Maria uses what she knows about slope-intercept form to graph the equation $y = \frac{3}{4}x + 2$.

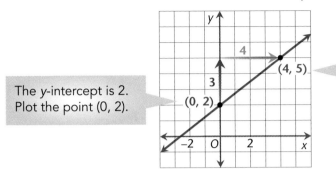

The y-intercept is 2. Plot the point (0, 2).

The slope is $\frac{3}{4}$. Count 3 units up and 4 units right. Plot a second point, then draw the line.

23. a.

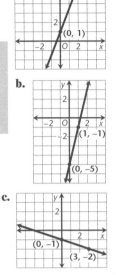

Use Maria's method to graph each equation.

a. $y = \frac{5}{2}x + 1$ b. $y = 4x - 5$ c. $y = -\frac{1}{3}x - 1$

24. Challenge Graph each pair of lines on a coordinate plane.

See Additional Answers.

a. $y = 2x, \ y = -\frac{1}{2}x$ b. $y = 3x, \ y = -\frac{1}{3}x$ c. $y = \frac{2}{3}x, \ y = -\frac{3}{2}x$

d. Describe the relationship between the lines in each pair. Write equations for two other lines that have this relationship.

Graph each equation. Give the slope of each line. See Additional Answers.

25. $y = 8$ **26.** $y = -4$ **27.** $x = 3$ **28.** $x = -1$

R e f l e c t i n g ▶ on the Section

Be prepared to discuss your response to Exercise 29 in class.

29. Given a graph of a line, what can you tell about its slope, even before you do any calculations? How can you find an equation of the line? Possible answers: It is possible to tell if the slope is positive, negative, 0, or undefined; Identify two points on the line to find the slope and determine where the line crosses the y-axis to determine the y-intercept.

Discussion

Exercise 29 checks that you understand slopes and equations of lines.

S p i r a l ▶ Review

30. Find the surface area of a cylinder that has a radius of 4 in. and a height of 10 in. (Module 5, p. 324) 351.68 in.²

Use an equation to find each percent or number. (Module 2, p. 90)

31. 33 is what percent of 60? 55% **32.** What is 15% of 30? 4.5

Write each number in scientific notation. (Module 3, p. 218)

33. 700 $7 \cdot 10^2$ **34.** 2593 $2.593 \cdot 10^3$ **35.** 101,000 $1.01 \cdot 10^5$

Working on the Module Project

Building a Ramp

Choosing a Ramp's Slope Like the slope of a line, a ramp's slope is the ratio of its rise to its run. Suppose you want to design a ramp that is 6 ft wide and reaches 8 ft above the ground. The diagrams show four ramps with different slopes that you could design.

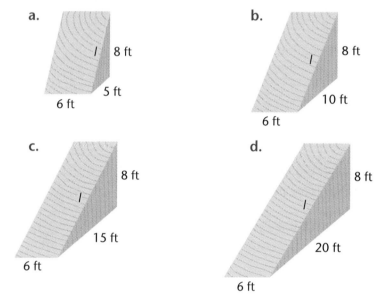

a.

8 ft

5 ft

6 ft

b.

8 ft

10 ft

6 ft

c.

8 ft

15 ft

6 ft

d.

8 ft

20 ft

6 ft

Use the diagrams to answer Project Questions 5–8.

5 Find the slope of each ramp. How does a ramp's slope affect how much effort it takes to move an object a fixed distance (say, 4 ft) up the ramp? Ramp A: $\frac{8}{5}$; Ramp B: $\frac{4}{5}$; Ramp C: $\frac{8}{15}$; Ramp D: $\frac{2}{5}$; As the slope decreases, the effort required to move an object up the ramp decreases.

6 Use the Pythagorean theorem to find the length, l, of each ramp. How does a ramp's slope affect the total distance you must move an object in order to get it to the top of the ramp? Ramp A: about 9.4 units; Ramp B: about 12.8 units; Ramp C: 17 units; Ramp D: about 21.5 units; The total distance increases as the slope decreases.

7 Suppose the ramps shown are made of solid concrete, so that the cost of making a ramp depends on the ramp's volume. How does a ramp's slope affect its volume in the diagrams shown? How does a ramp's slope affect its cost? The volume increases as the slope decreases; The cost increases as the slope decreases.

8 Based on your answers to Project Questions 5–7, what are some advantages of ramps with small slopes? What are some advantages of ramps with large slopes? Sample Response: Ramps with small slopes require less effort to move an object a fixed distance; Ramps with large slopes are shorter and less expensive to construct.

Section ②
Extra Skill Practice

Find the slope of the line through the given points. You may find it helpful to plot the points and draw a line through them first.

1. (0, 1) and (1, 4) 3
2. (4, –3) and (2, 5) –4
3. (–1, –1) and (8, –4) $-\frac{1}{3}$
4. (3, –5) and (7, 5) $\frac{5}{2}$
5. (5, –3) and (1, –3) 0
6. (6, –2) and (6, 6) undefined

Use the lines shown for Exercises 7–10.

7. Which line has a positive slope? line B

8. Which line has a negative slope? line D

9. Which line has a slope of zero? line A

10. Which line has a slope that is undefined?
    line C

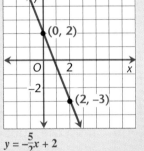

For each line, write an equation in slope-intercept form.

11.

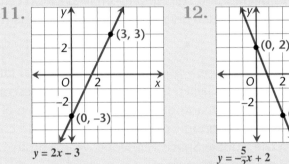

$y = 2x - 3$

12.

$y = -\frac{5}{2}x + 2$

13.

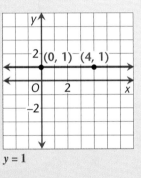

$y = 1$

Write an equation in slope-intercept form for the line through the given points. You may find it helpful to plot the points and draw a line through them first.

14. (3, 7) and (5, 7) $y = 7$
15. (0, 5) and (5, 0)
    $y = -x + 5$
16. (3, 4) and (–2, –2) $y = \frac{6}{5}x + \frac{2}{5}$

Standardized Testing ◀▶ Open-ended

Write an equation in slope-intercept form for a line that satisfies the given condition(s). Sample responses are given.

1. The line has a negative slope and a y-intercept of 4. $y = -5x + 4$

2. The line has a slope of 3 and a negative y-intercept. $y = 3x - 2$

3. The line has a slope of zero and a positive y-intercept. $y = 2$

4. The line is steeper than the line with equation $y = -2x + 7$. $y = -3x + 7$

Section ③ Working with Exponents

IN THIS SECTION

EXPLORATION 1
◆ Rules of Exponents

EXPLORATION 2
◆ Zero and Negative Exponents

Big and Small

◄◄◄ Setting the Stage

There is a lot in the universe that your eyes cannot see without help—objects as big as planets and stars and as small as blood cells and bacteria. The invention of the telescope and the microscope made these objects visible.

The first known telescope was built in 1608. One year later, the Italian scientist Galileo Galilei began using telescopes to study the moon and the planets. Today, some of the clearest astronomical images ever recorded come from the Hubble Space Telescope, which orbits Earth 380 mi above its surface.

The microscope was invented at about the same time as the telescope. There are several types of microscopes. An *optical microscope* uses lenses to make objects appear up to 3000 times larger than they actually are. An *electron microscope* is even more powerful. It can magnify objects up to 1,000,000 times.

Think About It

1 Why do you think the Hubble Space Telescope can provide clearer images of astronomical objects than telescopes located on Earth's surface? **Sample Responses: It does not need to see through the Earth's atmosphere. It is more powerful than telescopes on Earth's surface.**

2 The width of a human hair is about 0.003 in. How wide would a hair appear to be if it were magnified 3000 times? if it were magnified 1,000,000 times? **about 9 in.; about 3000 in.**

Rules of *Exponents*

GOAL

LEARN HOW TO...
- multiply and divide powers

AS YOU...
- work with astronomical distances

KEY TERMS
- product of powers rule
- quotient of powers rule

▸ In 1995, the Hubble Space Telescope sent an image of the giant star Betelgeuse to Earth. This was the first detailed image of a star other than the sun. However, the image actually showed what the star looked like hundreds of years ago! The diagram explains why.

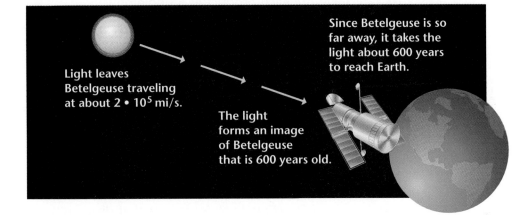

Light leaves Betelgeuse traveling at about $2 \cdot 10^5$ mi/s.

The light forms an image of Betelgeuse that is 600 years old.

Since Betelgeuse is so far away, it takes the light about 600 years to reach Earth.

▸ How many miles is it from Betelgeuse to Earth? You can use the information in the diagram to find out.

3 You first need to convert the speed of light given in the diagram from miles per second to miles per year.

a. Show that there are about $3 \cdot 10^7$ seconds in one year.

b. Explain why the speed of light in miles per year is the product of $2 \cdot 10^5$ and $3 \cdot 10^7$. Show that this product can be written as $6 \cdot (10^5 \cdot 10^7)$.

c. How many factors of 10 are there in the product $10^5 \cdot 10^7$?
12 factors

d. Use your answer from part (c) to write $6 \cdot (10^5 \cdot 10^7)$ as $6 \cdot 10^k$ for some integer k. How is the exponent in 10^k related to the exponents in $10^5 \cdot 10^7$? $6 \cdot 10^{12}$; $k = 5 + 7$

4 Try writing each product as a single power. Use a calculator to check each answer.

a. $10^2 \cdot 10^3$ 10^5 **b.** $10^5 \cdot 10^4$ 10^9 **c.** $3^6 \cdot 3^6$ 3^{12} **d.** $2^{10} \cdot 2^7$ 2^{17}

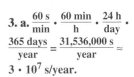

3. a. $\dfrac{60 \text{ s}}{\text{min}} \cdot \dfrac{60 \text{ min}}{\text{h}} \cdot \dfrac{24 \text{ h}}{\text{day}} \cdot \dfrac{365 \text{ days}}{\text{year}} = \dfrac{31{,}536{,}000 \text{ s}}{\text{year}} \approx 3 \cdot 10^7$ s/year.

FOR ▸ HELP

with *powers*, see

TOOLBOX, p. 600

3. b. $2 \cdot 10^5$ is the speed of light in mi/s and there are about $3 \cdot 10^7$ seconds in a year; The commutative property can be used to rearrange the factors:
$2 \cdot 10^5 \cdot 3 \cdot 10^7 =$
$2 \cdot 3 \cdot 10^5 \cdot 10^7 =$
$6 \cdot (10^5 \cdot 10^7)$.

5 Complete this rule for multiplying powers with the same base: $b^m \cdot b^n = b^?$. This is called the **product of powers rule**.
$b^m \cdot b^n = b^{m+n}$

FOR◄HELP

with *scientific notation*, see

MODULE 3, p. 218

6 It takes about 600 years for light from Betelgeuse to reach Earth.

a. Write 600 in scientific notation. $6 \cdot 10^2$

b. Use your answer from part (a), the speed of light in miles per year from Question 3, and the product of powers rule to show that Betelgeuse is about $36 \cdot 10^{14}$ mi from Earth.
$6 \cdot 10^{12} \cdot 6 \cdot 10^2 = 36 \cdot 10^{14}$

c. Explain why $36 \cdot 10^{14}$ is not in scientific notation. Then use the product of powers rule to write $36 \cdot 10^{14}$ in scientific notation. (*Hint:* $36 = 3.6 \cdot 10^1$.) 36 is greater than 10; $3.6 \cdot 10^{15}$

✔ QUESTION 7

...checks that you can use the product of powers rule to multiply powers.

7 **✔ CHECKPOINT** Write each product as a single power.

a. $10^3 \cdot 10^4$ 10^7 **b.** $5^9 \cdot 5^2$ 5^{11} **c.** $a \cdot a^7$ a^8 **d.** $b^5 \cdot b^8 \cdot b^2$ b^{15}

8 Betelgeuse is huge, even for a star. You can use a *quotient of powers* to compare the sizes of Betelgeuse and the sun.

a. The diameter of Betelgeuse is roughly 10^9 mi. The diameter of the sun is roughly 10^6 mi. Write a fraction that represents the ratio of Betelgeuse's diameter to the sun's diameter. $\frac{10^9}{10^6}$

b. Rewrite the fraction showing all of the factors of 10 in the numerator and in the denominator. Then write the fraction as a single power of 10. (*Hint:* Look for factors that divide out.) See below.

c. How is the exponent of this single power of 10 related to the exponents of the powers in the numerator and denominator of the fraction you wrote in part (a)? It is the difference between them.

d. Betelgeuse is about how many times as wide as the sun? about 10^3 or 1000 times

9 Try writing each quotient as a single power. Use a calculator to check each answer.

a. $\frac{10^6}{10^2}$ 10^4 **b.** $\frac{10^8}{10^3}$ 10^5 **c.** $\frac{6^7}{6^4}$ 6^3 **d.** $\frac{2^{13}}{2^5}$ 2^8

10 Complete this rule for dividing powers with the same base:
$\frac{b^m}{b^n} = b^?$. This is called the **quotient of powers rule**. $\frac{b^m}{b^n} = b^{m-n}$

✔ QUESTION 11

...checks that you can use the quotient of powers rule to divide powers.

11 **✔ CHECKPOINT** Write each quotient as a single power.

a. $\frac{10^5}{10^3}$ 10^2 **b.** $\frac{5^9}{5^4}$ 5^5 **c.** $\frac{a^7}{a^2}$ a^5 **d.** $\frac{c^{11}}{c \cdot c^7}$ c^3

HOMEWORK EXERCISES ► See Exs. 1–28 on pp. 351–352.

8. b. $\dfrac{10 \cdot 10 \cdot 10 \cdot 10 \cdot 10 \cdot 10 \cdot 10 \cdot 10 \cdot 10}{10 \cdot 10 \cdot 10 \cdot 10 \cdot 10 \cdot 10}$; 10^3

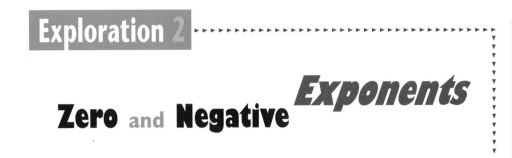

Exploration 2

Zero and Negative Exponents

GOAL

LEARN HOW TO...
- simplify powers with zero and negative exponents
- represent small numbers in scientific notation and in decimal notation

AS YOU...
- investigate dimensions of real-world objects

▶ **Look at the photographs shown. As you go from one to the next, the width of the field of view decreases by a factor of 10.**

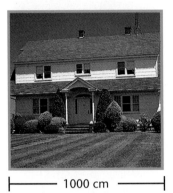

├─────── 1000 cm ───────┤

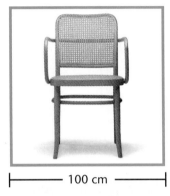

├─────── 100 cm ───────┤

├─────── 10 cm ───────┤

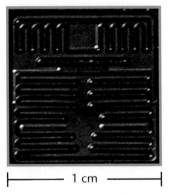

├─────── 1 cm ───────┤

12 The table gives the width of the field of view for each photograph shown above.

   a. Copy the table. Complete the first three rows. **See table.**

   b. Look for a pattern in the second column of the table. As you move down the column, what happens to the exponents in the powers of 10? **They decrease by 1.**

   c. Use the pattern you observed in part (b) to complete the last row of the table. Check your answer with a calculator. 10^0

Width of field of view (cm)	Width expressed as a power of 10
1000	? 10^3
100	? 10^2
10	? 10^1
1	?

13 Use a calculator to evaluate each power.

    a. 2^0 1   **b.** 9^0 1   **c.** 75^0 1   **d.** $(3.14)^0$ 1

14 Based on your results from Questions 12 and 13, what is the value of b^0 for any positive number b? 1

▶ **The photographs below continue the pattern started on the previous page. The width of the field of view continues to decrease by a factor of 10 from one photograph to the next.**

These photographs ▶ are of the head of a pin, a dust mite, and a red blood cell.

$\frac{1}{10}$ cm $\frac{1}{100}$ cm $\frac{1}{1000}$ cm

15 The table gives the width of the field of view for each photograph shown above.

    a. Copy the table. Use the pattern you observed in Question 12(b) to complete the table. Check your answers with a calculator.
    See table.

Width of field of view (cm)	Width expressed as a power of 10
$\frac{1}{10}$	? 10^{-1}
$\frac{1}{100}$	? 10^{-2}
$\frac{1}{1000}$	? 10^{-3}

    b. Let n be a positive integer. Complete this equation: $\frac{1}{10^n} = 10^?$. $-n$

16 Try writing each power as a fraction without exponents. Check each answer with a calculator. How did you get your answers?

    a. 7^{-2} $\frac{1}{49}$ **b.** 4^{-3} $\frac{1}{64}$ **c.** 15^{-1} $\frac{1}{15}$ **d.** 2^{-4} $\frac{1}{16}$
    Use a numerator of 1. Find the positive power of the number and use it as the denominator.

17 Suppose b is any positive number and n is any positive integer. Use your results from Questions 15 and 16 to complete this equation: $b^{-n} = \frac{1}{?}$. b^n

✔ **QUESTION 18**

...checks that you can simplify powers with zero and negative exponents.

18 ✔ **CHECKPOINT** Write each power as a whole number or a fraction without exponents.

    a. 6^0 1   **b.** 8^{-1} $\frac{1}{8}$ **c.** 3^{-4} $\frac{1}{81}$ **d.** 5^{-3} $\frac{1}{125}$

▶ **You can use negative exponents to write small numbers in scientific notation. For example, a red blood cell's diameter is $7.5 \cdot 10^{-3}$ mm.**

19 Explain why $7.5 \cdot 10^{-3}$ is in scientific notation. Use a calculator to evaluate $7.5 \cdot 10^{-3}$. Give the answer in decimal notation.
It is a number greater than 1 and less than 10 multiplied by a power of 10; 0.0075

20 Use a calculator to change each number to decimal notation.

   a. $9 \cdot 10^{-3}$ 0.009   **b.** $5.2 \cdot 10^{-1}$ 0.52   **c.** $4.26 \cdot 10^{-2}$ 0.0426

21 Look for a pattern in your answers to Questions 19 and 20. Explain how you can change a small number from scientific notation to decimal notation *without* using a calculator. See above.

22 ✔ **CHECKPOINT** Write each number in decimal notation without using a calculator.

   a. $2 \cdot 10^{-4}$ 0.0002   **b.** $8.4 \cdot 10^{-5}$
                                            0.000084   **c.** $6.31 \cdot 10^{-8}$
                                                                   0.0000000631

▶ **In the questions above, you changed small numbers from scientific notation to decimal notation. You can also reverse this procedure.**

EXAMPLE

In 1996, scientists used an electron microscope to study a meteorite from Mars. The photograph shows tiny tube-shaped forms found inside the meteorite. A typical form is about 0.00000007 m long. Write this length in scientific notation.

SAMPLE RESPONSE

Count how many places the decimal point in 0.00000007 must be moved to get a number that is at least 1 but less than 10.

$$0.0000000\underset{\text{8 places}}{7} = \frac{7}{10^8}$$ Note that $1 \le 7 < 10$.

$$= 7 \cdot \frac{1}{10^8}$$

$$= 7 \cdot 10^{-8}$$

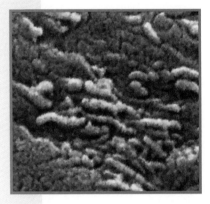

23 Describe a shortcut for writing 0.00000007 in scientific notation.
See above.

24 ✔ **CHECKPOINT** Write each number in scientific notation.

   a. 0.4 $4 \cdot 10^{-1}$ **b.** 0.0089 $8.9 \cdot 10^{-3}$ **c.** 0.00000123
                                                                              $1.23 \cdot 10^{-6}$

HOMEWORK EXERCISES ▶ See Exs. 29–54 on pp. 352–353.

---

21. Sample Response:
Move the decimal point as many places to the left as the opposite of the exponent.

23. Count the number of places from the decimal point to the right of 7. Then write the number as the product of 7 and 10 raised to the opposite of that number; $7 \cdot 10^{-8}$

✔ **QUESTION 22**

...checks that you can change small numbers from scientific notation to decimal notation.

✔ **QUESTION 24**

...checks that you can change small numbers from decimal notation to scientific notation.

Key Terms

product of powers rule

quotient of powers rule

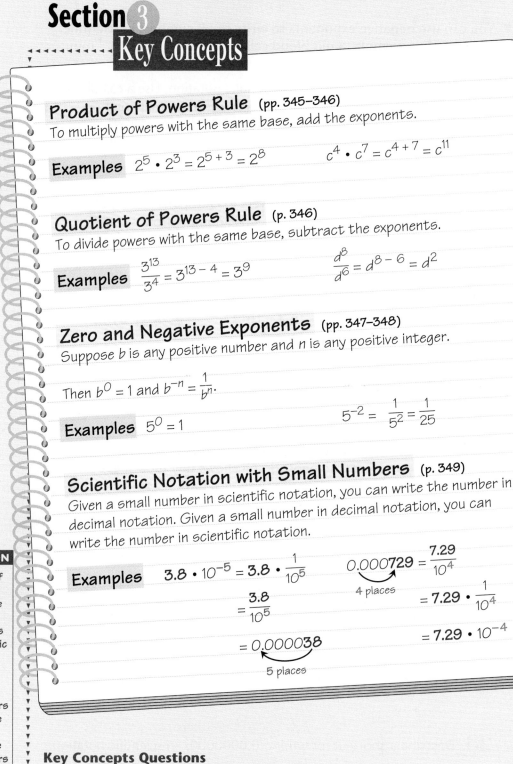

Product of Powers Rule (pp. 345–346)

To multiply powers with the same base, add the exponents.

Examples $2^5 \cdot 2^3 = 2^{5+3} = 2^8$ $c^4 \cdot c^7 = c^{4+7} = c^{11}$

Quotient of Powers Rule (p. 346)

To divide powers with the same base, subtract the exponents.

Examples $\dfrac{3^{13}}{3^4} = 3^{13-4} = 3^9$ $\dfrac{d^8}{d^6} = d^{8-6} = d^2$

Zero and Negative Exponents (pp. 347–348)

Suppose b is any positive number and n is any positive integer.

Then $b^0 = 1$ and $b^{-n} = \dfrac{1}{b^n}$.

Examples $5^0 = 1$ $5^{-2} = \dfrac{1}{5^2} = \dfrac{1}{25}$

Scientific Notation with Small Numbers (p. 349)

Given a small number in scientific notation, you can write the number in decimal notation. Given a small number in decimal notation, you can write the number in scientific notation.

Examples $3.8 \cdot 10^{-5} = 3.8 \cdot \dfrac{1}{10^5}$

$= \dfrac{3.8}{10^5}$

$= 0.000038$ (5 places)

$0.000729 = \dfrac{7.29}{10^4}$ (4 places)

$= 7.29 \cdot \dfrac{1}{10^4}$

$= 7.29 \cdot 10^{-4}$

CLOSURE QUESTION

How are the *product of powers rule* and the *quotient of powers rule* related? How are zero and negative exponents used in writing scientific notation?

Sample Response: The product of powers rule is used when two powers with the same base are being multiplied. The quotient of powers rule is used when two powers with the same base are being divided. Zero and negative exponents are sometimes used as the exponent of ten when writing numbers in scientific notation.

Key Concepts Questions

25 Write b^7 as a product of two powers. Is there only one product that you can write? Explain. **Sample Response:** $b^2 \cdot b^5$; No; There are many ways to write 7 as a sum of two numbers.

26 Negative exponents are used to write small numbers in scientific notation. What precisely is a "small number" in this situation? **Any number less than 1.**

Section 3
Practice & Application Exercises

Write each product as a single power.

1. $10^4 \cdot 10^2$ 10^6
2. $10^5 \cdot 10^8$ 10^{13}
3. $2^3 \cdot 2^6$ 2^9
4. $5^5 \cdot 5^5$ 5^{10}

5. $3^9 \cdot 3$ 3^{10}
6. $7^2 \cdot 7^6 \cdot 7^3$ 7^{11}
7. $a \cdot a^3$ a^4
8. $c^2 \cdot c^{10}$ c^{12}

9. $b^4 \cdot b^4$ b^8
10. $d^8 \cdot d^{12}$ d^{20}
11. $w^{60} \cdot w^{20}$ w^{80}
12. $t^5 \cdot t \cdot t^7$ t^{13}

Oceanography In his book *The Perfect Storm*, Sebastian Junger describes how the amount of energy in ocean waves depends on the wind speed.

Unfortunately for mariners, the total amount of wave energy in a storm doesn't [depend on the first power of] wind speed, but [on the] fourth power. The seas generated by a forty-knot wind aren't twice as violent as those from a twenty-knot wind, they're seventeen times as violent. A ship's crew watching the anemometer [an instrument that measures wind speed] climb even ten knots could well be [in great danger].

◀ As the anemometer spins in the wind, revolutions per minute are converted to miles per hour to calculate the wind speed.

13. The equation $h = 0.019s^2$ gives the height h (in feet) of waves caused by wind blowing at a speed of s knots. (One knot is slightly faster than 1 mi/h.) The equation $E = 8h^2$ gives the energy E (in foot-pounds) in each square foot of a wave with height h.

    a. Write an equation that relates E and s. (*Hint:* First write $E = 8h^2$ as $E = 8 \cdot h \cdot h$. Then use the fact that $h = 0.019s^2$ to write another equation for E.) $E = 0.002888s^4$

    b. Junger says that wave energy depends on the fourth power of wind speed. Is this true? Explain. Yes; in the equation, s is raised to the fourth power.

    c. What is the wave energy per square foot when the wind speed is 20 knots? when the wind speed is 40 knots? Is the wave energy for a 40-knot wind about 17 times the wave energy for a 20-knot wind, as Junger states?
    462.08 ft-lb; 7393.28 ft-lb; It is 16 times the wave energy.

14. **Open-ended** Junger says that even a 10-knot increase in wind speed can be very dangerous for a ship. Pick two wind speeds that differ by 10 knots, and compare the resulting wave energies.
    Sample Response: 146.205 ft-lb at 15 knots and 1128.125 ft-lb at 25 knots; The wave energy is about 8 times greater.

Write each quotient as a single power.

15. $\dfrac{10^6}{10^4}$ 10^2

16. $\dfrac{10^9}{10^3}$ 10^6

17. $\dfrac{2^5}{2}$ 2^4

18. $\dfrac{3^{10}}{3^7}$ 3^3

19. $\dfrac{7^{15}}{7^6}$ 7^9

20. $\dfrac{5^3 \cdot 5^8}{5^2}$ 5^9

21. $\dfrac{a^5}{a^2}$ a^3

22. $\dfrac{b^6}{b^5}$ b

23. $\dfrac{c^{12}}{c^6}$ c^6

24. $\dfrac{d^7}{d}$ d^6

25. $\dfrac{u^{95}}{u^{52}}$ u^{43}

26. $\dfrac{v^{18}}{v^4 \cdot v^3}$ v^{11}

27. **Challenge** Write $\dfrac{a^5 b^9}{ab^4}$ as the product of a power of a and a power of b. $a^4 b^5$

Biology The average weight w (in pounds) of an Atlantic cod aged t years can be modeled by the equation $w = 1.16(1.44)^t$.

28. a. Find the ratio of the weight of a 5-year-old cod to the weight of a 2-year-old cod. Express this ratio as a power of 1.44. 1.44^3

    b. A 5-year-old cod weighs how many times as much as a 2-year-old cod?
    about 3 times

29. According to the given equation, what is the average weight of an Atlantic cod when it is born? How did you get your answer?
    1.16 lb; I substituted 0 for t in the equation.

Write each power as a whole number or fraction without exponents.

30. 8^0 1

31. 3^{-2} $\frac{1}{9}$

32. 2^{-3} $\frac{1}{8}$

33. 5^{-1} $\frac{1}{5}$

Write each expression without using zero or negative exponents.

34. a^0 1

35. b^{-6} $\frac{1}{b^6}$

36. c^{-10} $\frac{1}{c^{10}}$

37. $4w^{-2}$ $\frac{4}{w^2}$

38. **Personal Finance** Many people invest in stocks as a way to save for retirement. Based on the history of stock prices from 1926 to 1995, the amount A you need to invest in order to have D dollars after n years can be estimated using this equation:

$$A = D(1.105)^{-n}$$

    a. How much money would you need to invest in stocks now to have $1,000,000 after 10 years? after 20 years? after 40 years?
    about $368,449; about $135,755; about $18,429

    b. **Writing** Explain why your answers from part (a) show the importance of starting to save for retirement at an early age.
    Sample Response: The earlier you begin saving, the less money you need to invest to reach a certain dollar amount.

Write each number in decimal notation.

39. $9 \cdot 10^{-1}$ 0.9

40. $3 \cdot 10^{-2}$ 0.03

41. $1.8 \cdot 10^{-4}$ 0.00018

42. $4.4 \cdot 10^{-7}$
    0.00000044

43. $2.65 \cdot 10^{-6}$
    0.00000265

44. $7.523 \cdot 10^{-8}$
    0.00000007523

Geology Rock fragments ejected through the air or water from a volcano are called *tephra*. Geologists classify tephra by size, as shown in the table. Use the table for Exercises 45 and 46.

Types of Tephra	
Name	s = size (meters)
ash	$s < 0.002$
lapilli	$0.002 \le s \le 0.064$
bombs	$0.064 \le s \le 0.256$
blocks	$s > 0.256$

45. Rewrite each inequality in the table so that the numbers in the inequality are expressed in scientific notation. $s < 2 \cdot 10^{-3}$; $2 \cdot 10^{-3} \le s \le 6.4 \cdot 10^{-2}$; $6.4 \cdot 10^{-2} \le s \le 2.56 \cdot 10^{-1}$; $s > 2.56 \cdot 10^{-1}$

46. In each of parts (a)–(c), the size of a piece of tephra is given. Classify each piece of tephra.

   a. $8 \cdot 10^{-2}$ m bomb   b. $5 \cdot 10^{-4}$ m ash   c. $7 \cdot 10^{-3}$ m lapilli

Write each number in scientific notation.

47. 0.3 $3 \cdot 10^{-1}$ 48. 0.0087 $8.7 \cdot 10^{-3}$ 49. 0.00025 $2.5 \cdot 10^{-4}$

50. 0.00001199 $1.199 \cdot 10^{-5}$ 51. 0.000000006 $6 \cdot 10^{-9}$ 52. 0.000000408 $4.08 \cdot 10^{-7}$

53. **Probability Connection** If you flip a coin n times, the theoretical probability of getting n heads is 2^{-n}.

   a. Find the probability of getting 25 heads in 25 flips. Write your answer in scientific notation. about $3 \cdot 10^{-8}$

   b. Compare your answer from part (a) with the probability of winning a common type of state lottery (about $7.15 \cdot 10^{-8}$). The probability is about 2.5 times greater that you will win the lottery than that you will get 25 heads in 25 flips.

Reflecting ◀▶ on the Section

Write your response to Exercise 54 in your journal.

54. Write a quiz that covers the mathematical topics presented in this section. Include at least two questions for each topic. Then make an answer key for your quiz.   Answers will vary. Check students' work.

Journal

Exercise 54 checks that you understand and can apply the mathematical ideas in this section.

Spiral ◀▶ Review

55. Give the slope and the y-intercept of the line with equation $y = -2x + 9$. (Module 5, p. 338) slope: –2; y-intercept: 9

56. **Estimation** Estimate $\sqrt{60}$ between two consecutive integers. (Module 3, p. 170) between 7 and 8

Solve each equation. (Module 1, p. 62)

57. $\frac{x}{3} = 4$ 12   58. $\frac{w}{13} + 2 = 7$ 65   59. $6 = \frac{t}{85}$ 510

Scientist: France Córdova

Dr. France Córdova was Chief Scientist at the National Aeronautics and Space Administration (NASA) from 1993–1996. She studies small, dense, rapidly spinning stars called *pulsars*, which result when a giant star undergoes a supernova explosion.

60. A pulsar's *mass density*—its mass per unit volume—is about 10^{11} kg/cm^3. (A handful of material from a pulsar would weigh more than all the people on Earth combined!) The volume of a typical pulsar is about 10^{19} cm^3. Find the mass of a pulsar with this volume. 10^{30} kg

61. Pulsars rotate very rapidly. The *period* of a pulsar is the time required for one rotation. The fastest-rotating pulsar known has a period of about 0.00156 s. Write this period in scientific notation. $1.56 \cdot 10^{-3}$ s

Extension ▶▶

Extending the Rules of Exponents

In this section, you applied the product and quotient of powers rules to expressions containing only positive exponents. Also, the quotient of powers rule was applied only to quotients where the exponent in the numerator was greater than the exponent in the denominator. However, both rules work for any exponents.

Examples:

$$3^{-2} \cdot 3^7 = 3^{-2 + 7} = 3^5 \qquad \frac{5^8}{5^{11}} = 5^{8 - 11} = 5^{-3}$$

62. Show that $3^{-2} \cdot 3^7 = 3^5$ and $\dfrac{5^8}{5^{11}} = 5^{-3}$ without using the product of powers and quotient of powers rules. (*Hint:* Write 3^{-2} and 5^{-3} using positive exponents.) Sample Response: $\frac{1}{3 \cdot 3} \cdot 3 \cdot 3 \cdot 3 \cdot 3 \cdot 3 \cdot 3 \cdot 3 = 3 \cdot 3 \cdot 3 \cdot 3 \cdot 3$ or 3^5; $\frac{5 \cdot 5 \cdot 5 \cdot 5 \cdot 5 \cdot 5 \cdot 5 \cdot 5}{5 \cdot 5 \cdot 5 \cdot 5 \cdot 5 \cdot 5 \cdot 5 \cdot 5 \cdot 5 \cdot 5 \cdot 5} = \frac{1}{5 \cdot 5 \cdot 5}$ or 5^{-3}

Write each product as a single power.

63. $2^{-1} \cdot 2^3$ 2^2 64. $10^9 \cdot 10^{-4}$ 10^5 65. $a^6 \cdot a^{-10}$ a^{-4} 66. $x^{-3} \cdot x^{-5}$ x^{-8}

Write each quotient as a single power.

67. $\dfrac{3^5}{3^7}$ 3^{-2} 68. $\dfrac{7^2}{7^{-12}}$ 7^{14} 69. $\dfrac{b^{-8}}{b^{-3}}$ b^{-5} 70. $\dfrac{y^{-2}}{y^{10}}$ y^{-12}

Section 3
Extra Skill Practice

Write each product as a single power.

1. $6^4 \cdot 6^3$ 6^7
2. $9^{10} \cdot 9^{17}$ 9^{27}
3. $11^{11} \cdot 11^{23}$ 11^{34}
4. $2^2 \cdot 2^{21} \cdot 2$ 2^{24}

5. $b^3 \cdot b^9$ b^{12}
6. $h^5 \cdot h^{19}$ h^{24}
7. $k^{33} \cdot k^{48}$ k^{81}
8. $n^7 \cdot n^8 \cdot n^9$ n^{24}

Write each quotient as a single power.

9. $\dfrac{10^{12}}{10^2}$ 10^{10}
10. $\dfrac{9^6}{9}$ 9^5
11. $\dfrac{8^{21}}{8^{19}}$ 8^2
12. $\dfrac{6^{15}}{6^4 \cdot 6^7}$ 6^4

13. $\dfrac{p^8}{p^5}$ p^3
14. $\dfrac{z^{57}}{z^{39}}$ z^{18}
15. $\dfrac{m^{82}}{m^{78}}$ m^4
16. $\dfrac{t^{26}}{t^7 \cdot t^{11}}$ t^8

Write each power as a number without exponents.

17. 24^0 1
18. 6^{-3} $\frac{1}{216}$
19. 11^{-2} $\frac{1}{121}$
20. 4^{-4} $\frac{1}{256}$
21. 13^{-1} $\frac{1}{13}$

Write each expression without using zero or negative exponents.

22. h^{-3} $\frac{1}{h^3}$
23. p^{-8} $\frac{1}{p^8}$
24. k^0 1
25. $3r^{-7}$ $\frac{3}{r^7}$
26. $12g^{-32}$ $\frac{12}{g^{32}}$

Write each number in decimal notation.

27. $8 \cdot 10^{-3}$
0.008
28. $3.6 \cdot 10^{-4}$
0.00036
29. $6.14 \cdot 10^{-7}$
0.000000614
30. $1.271 \cdot 10^{-8}$
0.00000001271

Write each number in scientific notation.

31. 0.06
$6 \cdot 10^{-2}$
32. 0.000412
$4.12 \cdot 10^{-4}$
33. 0.000001013
$1.013 \cdot 10^{-6}$
34. 0.000000761
$7.61 \cdot 10^{-7}$

Standardized Testing ◀▶ Multiple Choice

1. Simplify $3^4 \cdot 3^5$. A
   - Ⓐ 3^9
   - Ⓑ 3^{20}
   - Ⓒ 9^9
   - Ⓓ 9^{20}

2. Simplify $\dfrac{2^{15}}{2^3}$. C
   - Ⓐ 5
   - Ⓑ 2^5
   - Ⓒ 2^{12}
   - Ⓓ 2^{18}

3. Simplify 8^{-2}. D
   - Ⓐ $\frac{1}{4}$
   - Ⓑ $\frac{1}{8}$
   - Ⓒ $\frac{1}{16}$
   - Ⓓ $\frac{1}{64}$

4. Which number is *not* in scientific notation? D
   - Ⓐ $4.3 \cdot 10^{-5}$
   - Ⓑ $1 \cdot 10^4$
   - Ⓒ $7.01 \cdot 10^{-8}$
   - Ⓓ $12 \cdot 10^{-3}$

Section 4

Complements, Supplements, and Tangents

IN THIS SECTION

EXPLORATION 1
♦ Complementary and Supplementary Angles

EXPLORATION 2
♦ The Tangent Ratio

WARM-UP EXERCISES

Write each comparison as a rate.

1. 7 mi in 9 min $\frac{7}{9}$ mi/min

2. 12 c in 3 qt $\frac{12}{3}$ or 4 c/qt

Solve.

3. $\frac{d}{15} = \frac{12}{45}$ 4

4. $\frac{21}{40} = \frac{m}{25}$ 13.125

Use a protractor to find the measure of each angle.

5. 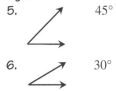 45°

6. 30°

1. Sample Response:
Use known lengths of any two corresponding sides of two similar triangles to determine a ratio, then use that ratio and the length of a known side to find the length of an unknown side.

▲
Astrolabes are used primarily for measuring the positions of stars, but they can also be used to find heights of objects.

Oh, What a Sight!

◄◄◄ *Setting the Stage*

Long ago, heights of objects were found indirectly by comparing their shadows with the shadows of objects whose heights were known. However, cloudy days and a growing interest in astrology and astronomy created a need for a new measuring instrument. One of the first instruments designed for measuring the angle between a star and the horizon was the astrolabe, which many scholars believe was invented by the Greek mathematician Hypatia.

Hypatia taught in Alexandria, Egypt. People would travel from many far away places to hear her lecture. She also wrote mathematical articles that she used to teach her students.

Most of Hypatia's works have been lost, but many of her teachings have survived and updated forms of her inventions are still used today.

Think About It

1 On page 204 you learned a method for measuring heights indirectly. Describe this method. **See above.**

2 Most of Hypatia's articles were lost. How do you think her ideas and inventions survived? **Sample Response: Her teachings may have been passed on orally by those who heard her speak and read her work.**

▶ In this section, you'll construct an astrolabe and use it to find the height of your classroom.

GOAL

LEARN HOW TO...
◆ identify special pairs of angles

AS YOU...
◆ make and use an astrolabe

KEY TERMS
◆ complementary angles
◆ complement
◆ supplementary angles
◆ supplement

Complementary and Supplementary ANGLES

SET UP ▸ *Work with a partner. You will need:* • *8 in. of string*
• *weight (such as a washer)* • *drinking straw* • *protractor*
• *tape* • *scissors*

▸ **In this exploration, you and your partner will make an astrolabe.
You'll use your astrolabe to measure an angle that will help you find
your classroom's height.**

3 Follow the steps to construct an astrolabe. **Check students' work.**

Step 1 Tie the weight to one end of the string. Tie the other end of the string to the center of the straw.

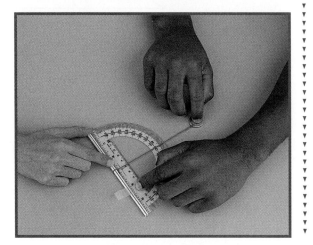

Step 2 Tape the straw along the straight edge of the protractor so that the string passes through 90°. Cut off the end portions of the straw that extend beyond the protractor.

4 Follow the steps below with your partner. You'll collect data that will be used in Exploration 2 to find your classroom's height.
Check students' work.

Step 1 Face toward a wall of your classroom. Have your partner measure your distance from the wall and the height of your eyes above the floor.

Step 2 Raise the astrolabe to one eye and look straight ahead through the straw as shown. Have your partner check that the string is centered on 90°.

Step 3 Tilt your head, keeping the straw lined up with your eye, until you can see the top of the wall through the straw.

Have your partner record the angle measure shown on the astrolabe. If the protractor has two scales, use the measure that is less than 90°.

5 The diagram below shows the situation in Step 3 of Question 4. In the diagram, ∠A is the *angle of elevation*. This is the angle between your eye level and your line of sight to the top of the wall.

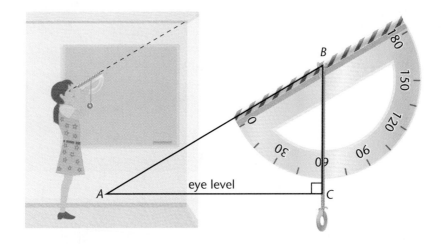

a. Which angle, ∠A, ∠B, or ∠C, is the angle whose measure is shown on the astrolabe? ∠B

b. What is the measure of ∠C? 90°

c. What is the sum of m∠A and m∠B? (*Hint:* The sum of the angle measures in any triangle is 180°.) 90°

d. Explain how you can use the astrolabe reading you took in Question 4 to find the measure of the angle of elevation. Then find this angle measure. (You'll need it for Exploration 2.)
The angle of elevation will be 90° — the astrolabe reading; Answers will vary.

▶ Two angles whose measures have a sum of 90° are **complementary angles**. Each angle is called a **complement** of the other angle.

> ### E X A M P L E
>
> A 60° angle and a 30° angle
> are complementary angles.
>
> 60° + 30° = 90°
>
> A 60° angle is a complement of a 30° angle
> and a 30° angle is a complement of a 60° angle.
>
> 60°   30°

6 Look back at the diagram in Question 5. Which two of ∠A, ∠B, and ∠C are complementary angles? ∠A and ∠B

7 ✔ **CHECKPOINT** Find the complement of each angle measure.

  a. 22° 68°   **b.** 50° 40°   **c.** 18° 72°   **d.** 84° 6°

8 a. A student incorrectly read an astrolabe measurement as 130°. What do you think the correct measurement is? Explain your thinking. 50°; 50° and 130° are at the same point. The student read the wrong scale.

  b. Suppose the student continues to make the same mistake in reading the astrolabe. Explain how to find correct readings without using the astrolabe again.
  Sample Response: Subtract the incorrect astrolabe reading from 180°.

✔ **QUESTION 7**

…checks that you can find the complement of an angle measure.

▶ Two angles whose measures have a sum of 180° are **supplementary angles**. Each angle is called a **supplement** of the other angle.

> ### E X A M P L E
>
> A 55° angle and a 125° angle
> are supplementary angles.
>
> 55° + 125° = 180°
>
> A 55° angle is a supplement of a 125° angle
> and a 125° angle is a supplement of a 55° angle.
>
> 55°   125°

9 ✔ **CHECKPOINT** Find the supplement of each angle measure.

  a. 15° 165°   **b.** 38° 142°   **c.** 110° 70°   **d.** 153° 27°

✔ **QUESTION 9**

…checks that you can find the supplement of an angle measure.

HOMEWORK EXERCISES ▶ See Exs. 1–22 on p. 364.

GOAL

LEARN HOW TO...

◆ use the tangent ratio to find unknown side lengths in right triangles

AS YOU...

◆ investigate heights of objects

KEY TERM

◆ tangent

The **Tangent Ratio**

SET UP | *Work in a group. You will need:* • *protractor* • *metric ruler* • *scissors* • *calculator*

▶ **How can an astrolabe be used to find the heights of objects? In this exploration, you'll study a ratio that will help you answer this question.**

10 Adriana uses an astrolabe to sight the top of her school. She finds that the angle of elevation (∠A in the diagram) measures 40°.

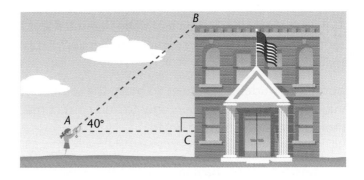

10. a. No; She needs to know her distance from the building as well.

a. If Adriana knows only that $m\angle A = 40°$, can she find the height of her school? Explain your thinking.

b. Each person in your group should complete these steps:
Answers will vary. Check students' work.

Step 1 Draw a right triangle, △ABC, such that ∠C is the right angle and $m\angle A = 40°$. The triangles your group draws should be different sizes.

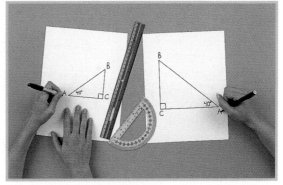

Step 2 Measure BC and AC in your triangle to the nearest tenth of a centimeter. Label $\overline{BC}$ and $\overline{AC}$ with their lengths.

11 Discussion Cut out your group's triangles, and arrange them in order from smallest to largest. A sample triangle is shown.

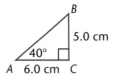

B
5.0 cm
40°
A   6.0 cm   C

a. Are all the triangles similar? How can you tell for sure? Yes; They have the same angle measures.

b. As *BC* increases from one triangle to the next, what happens to *AC*? It increases.

c. Find the ratio $\frac{BC}{AC}$ for each triangle. Write each ratio as a decimal rounded to the nearest hundredth. What do you notice? The ratios are the same, about 0.84.

d. What seems to be true for any right triangle with a 40° angle?

11. d. The ratio of the length of the side opposite the 40° angle to the length of the side adjacent to it is about 0.84.

12 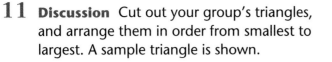 Calculator Enter this key sequence on a calculator: **4** **0** **TAN** . How does the number in the display compare with the ratios your group calculated in Question 11? Rounded to the hundredths it is the same.

▶ In a right triangle, the **tangent** of an acute angle is the ratio of the length of the side *opposite* the angle to the length of the side *adjacent* to the angle. The tangent of an angle *A* is written "tan *A*."

$$\tan A = \frac{\text{opposite}}{\text{adjacent}}$$

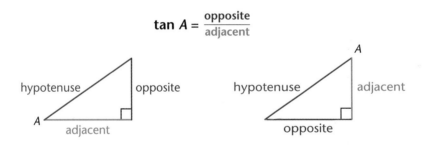

hypotenuse   opposite

A
adjacent

A
hypotenuse   adjacent

opposite

13 Use the triangle to find each tangent. Check your answers with a calculator. (*Note:* Side lengths are approximate.)

8.5 cm   55°   4.9 cm
35°
7 cm

a. tan 35°   0.7

b. tan 55°   about 1.43

14 a. Copy the table. Use a calculator to complete the table.

0.176   0.364   0.577   0.839   1.192   1.732   2.747   5.671   57.290

Angle measure	10°	20°	30°	40°	50°	60°	70°	80°	89°
Tangent	?	?	?	?	?	?	?	?	?

b. What happens to the tangent as the angle measure increases? It increases.

c. Try finding tan 90° on your calculator. What happens? Why do you think this happens? An error message is displayed; Sample Response: a right triangle cannot have two right angles.

▶ **You can use what you know about the tangent ratio to measure the heights of objects indirectly.**

15 Look back at Question 10. Suppose that, in addition to the angle of elevation, Adriana knows her distance from the school and the height of her eyes above the ground.

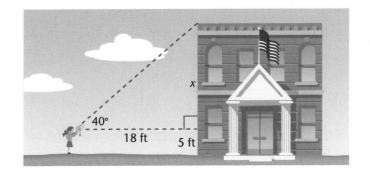

a. Write an equation that Adriana can use to find the value of x.

$$\tan 40° = \frac{x}{18}$$

b. Find tan 40°. Use your answer to solve your equation for x.

about 0.839; 15.1

c. What is the height of the school?

about 20.1 ft

16 **Try This as a Class** Use the triangle.

a. Write an equation relating tan 39° and x. $\tan 39° = \frac{9}{x}$

b. How is your equation different from the equation you wrote in Question 15? How can you solve this new type of equation?

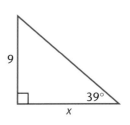

16. b. *x* is in the denominator; Sample Response: Multiply both sides of the equation by *x*, then divide both sides by tan 39°.

✔ **QUESTION 17**

...checks that you can use the tangent ratio to find unknown side lengths in right triangles.

17 ✔ **CHECKPOINT** Find the value of each variable. Answers are rounded to the nearest tenth.

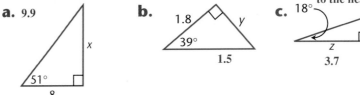

a. 9.9

b.

c.

18 Look at the measurements you found in Questions 4 and 5 on page 358 of Exploration 1. Use these measurements and the tangent ratio to find the height of your classroom. You may find it helpful to draw a diagram like the one shown in Question 15.

Answers will vary. Check students' work.

HOMEWORK EXERCISES ▶ See Exs. 23–31 on pp. 364–366.

Section 4
Key Concepts

Complementary and Supplementary Angles (pp. 357–359)

Two angles whose measures have a sum of 90° are complementary angles. Two angles whose measures have a sum of 180° are supplementary angles.

Examples

∠MKN is a complement of ∠NKP.

∠LKN is a supplement of ∠NKP.

The Tangent Ratio (pp. 360–362)

In a right triangle, the tangent of an acute angle is the ratio of the length of the side opposite the angle to the length of the side adjacent to the angle. You can use the tangent ratio to find unknown side lengths in right triangles.

Example You can use the tangent ratio to find the value of h in △ABC.

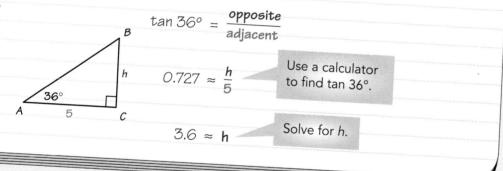

$$\tan 36° = \frac{\text{opposite}}{\text{adjacent}}$$

$$0.727 \approx \frac{h}{5}$$

Use a calculator to find tan 36°.

$$3.6 \approx h$$

Solve for h.

Key Terms

complementary angles

supplementary angles

complement

supplement

tangent

CLOSURE QUESTION

Describe the relationship between the two acute angles in a right triangle. Then define the tangent ratio using words and symbols.

Sample Response: The two acute angles are complementary. The tangent of any acute angle in a right triangle is the ratio of the length of the side opposite the angle to the length of the side adjacent to the angle. That is, $\tan \angle A = \frac{\text{opposite}}{\text{adjacent}}$.

19. c. $\tan B = \frac{5}{h}$ and $m\angle B = 54°$ so $h = \frac{5}{\tan\angle B} \approx 3.6$.

19 Key Concepts Question Use △ABC in the second Example above.

a. Which two angles in △ABC are complements? ∠A and ∠B

b. What is the measure of ∠B? 54°

c. Show how you can use the tangent of ∠B to find the value of h.

d. Can you use an equation involving the tangent ratio to find AB? Explain. No; AB is not part of the tangent ratio for ∠A or ∠B

Section 4

> ◄◄◄◄◄◄◄◄ **Practice & Application Exercises**

YOU WILL NEED

For Exs. 23–31
and 36:
♦ calculator

Mental Math Use mental math to find the complement of each angle measure.

1. 63° 27°   2. 19° 71°   3. 48° 42°   4. 81° 9°

5. 12° 78°   6. 22° 68°   7. 36° 54°   8. 74° 16°

Use the diagram.

9. Name an angle that is a supplement of ∠AEC. ∠CED

10. Name an angle that is a complement of ∠BEC. ∠CED

11. Name an angle that is a supplement of ∠BCE. ∠DCE

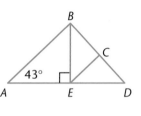

12. **Writing** Suppose m∠ABC = 90°. Find m∠EBC. Explain how you got your answer.

12. 43°; Find m∠ABE by subtraction: 180° − 90° − 43° = 47°. (The sum of the measures of a triangle is 180°.) Find m∠EBC by subtraction: 90° − 47°. (∠EBC is complementary to ∠ABE.)

Choosing a Method Use mental math or a calculator to find the supplement of each angle measure.

13. 60° 120°   14. 132° 48°   15. 90° 90°   16. 18° 162°

17. 45° 135°   18. 24° 156°   19. 120° 60°   20. 98° 82°

Algebra Connection For Exercises 21 and 22, write and solve an equation to find the value of each variable.

21. x + 35 = 180; x = 145   22. y + 45 = 90; y = 45

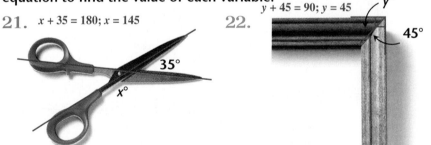

For Exercises 23–25, use the triangle to find the given tangent. Check each answer with a calculator. (*Note:* Side lengths are approximate.)

23. tan 45° 1   24. tan 65° about 2.15   25. tan 28° about 0.53

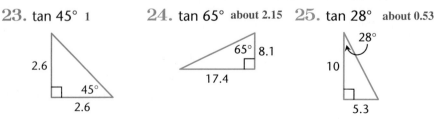

26. Architecture Mark uses an astrolabe to sight the top of the Sears Tower in Chicago.

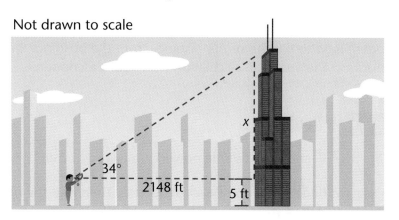

Not drawn to scale

34°
2148 ft
5 ft
x

a. About how tall is the Sears Tower? **about 1454 ft**

b. Suppose Mark changes his position so that the angle of elevation is now 32°. About how far from the Sears Tower is he standing? **about 2319 ft**

Find the value of each variable. **Answers are rounded to the nearest tenth.**

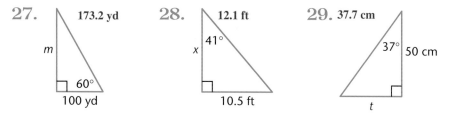

27.
173.2 yd
m
60°
100 yd

28.
12.1 ft
41°
x
10.5 ft

29. 37.7 cm
37°
50 cm
t

30. Challenge The *angle of depression* from an airplane to the outskirts of a city measures 5.8°. The airplane is flying 6 mi above the ground at a speed of 200 mi/h. How much time will elapse before the airplane begins passing over the city? **approximately 18 min**

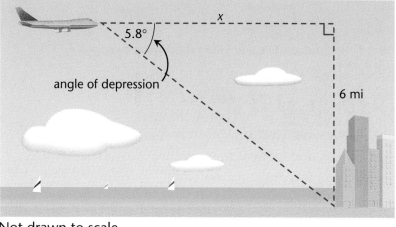

x
5.8°
angle of depression
6 mi

Not drawn to scale

Reflecting on the Section

31. Look up the height of a famous building in an encyclopedia or other source. Describe how a person could use this height and the tangent ratio to find his or her distance from the building. Include a diagram and a sample calculation with your description.
Answers will vary. Check students' work.

Spiral Review

32. Write $3^5 \cdot 3^8$ and $\dfrac{a^{22}}{a^{15}}$ as single powers. (Module 5, p. 350) $3^{13}; a^7$

Write a rule for finding a term of each sequence. Then find the next three terms. (Module 4, p. 247)

33. 11, 22, 44, ...
Multiply the previous term by 2; 88, 176, 352

34. $x + 2, 2x + 3, 3x + 4, ...$
Add $x + 1$ to the previous term; $4x + 5, 5x + 6, 6x + 7$

35. Make a tree diagram that shows all the possible outcomes when you flip a coin 3 times. (Module 2, p. 116) **See Additional Answers.**

Extension ▶▶

The Sine and Cosine Ratios

Like the tangent ratio, the *sine ratio* and the *cosine ratio* are ratios of side lengths in a right triangle. These ratios are defined below.

hypotenuse 13   5 opposite
A 12   adjacent

$$\sin A = \frac{\textbf{opposite}}{\textbf{hypotenuse}}$$

You write the sine of $\angle A$ as "sin A."

$$\cos A = \frac{\textbf{adjacent}}{\textbf{hypotenuse}}$$

You write the cosine of $\angle A$ as "cos A."

36. a. Use the triangle above. Find sin A and cos A. sin A: about 0.385; cos A: about 0.923

b. Calculator In the triangle above, $m\angle A \approx 22.6°$. On a calculator, enter [2] [2] [.] [6] [SIN] to find sin A. Then enter [2] [2] [.] [6] [COS] to find cos A. Do your answers agree (approximately) with your answers to part (a)? Yes.

37. Use the definitions of sine, cosine, and tangent to show that $\tan A = \dfrac{\sin A}{\cos A}$ for any acute $\angle A$ in a right triangle.

Sample Response:
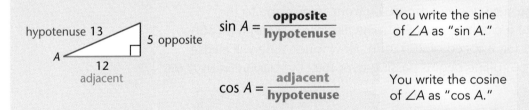

$$\tan A = \frac{\text{opposite}}{\text{adjacent}}; \frac{\sin A}{\cos A} = \frac{\text{opposite}}{\text{hypotenuse}} \div \frac{\text{adjacent}}{\text{hypotenuse}}$$
$$= \frac{\text{opposite}}{\text{hypotenuse}} \cdot \frac{\text{hypotenuse}}{\text{adjacent}}$$
$$= \frac{\text{opposite}}{\text{adjacent}}$$

Building a Ramp

Ramps and Angles An engineer designing a ramp often has to be concerned about the angle that the ramp makes with the ground. For example, the American National Standards Institute (ANSI) limits the possible angles for a wheelchair ramp like the one shown.

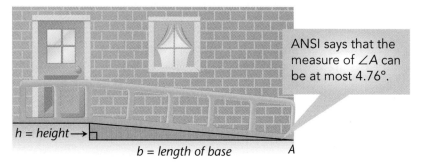

ANSI says that the measure of ∠A can be at most 4.76°.

h = height →
b = length of base   A

9 Write an equation involving tangent that relates ∠A, h, and b. $\tan A = \frac{h}{b}$

10 Michelle is designing a wheelchair ramp that is supposed to reach a door 2 ft above the ground and have an angle of 4.76°. What should the length of the ramp's base be? **about 24 ft**

11. b. It increases; Sample Response: Since the ratio of height to length (tangent) stays the same, when one dimension increases the other dimension will also increase.

11 Before designing your model ramp, you may want to know some possible angles, heights, and base lengths your ramp could have.

a. Copy the table below. Replace each **?** with the length of the base of a ramp that has the given angle and height.

Answers are rounded to the nearest inch

Base Lengths of Ramps for Different Angles and Heights				
Angle＼Height	6 in.	8 in.	10 in.	12 in.
10°	? 34	? 45	? 57	? 68
20°	? 16	? 22	? 27	? 33
30°	? 10	? 14	? 17	? 21
40°	? 7	? 10	? 12	? 14

b. If you increase the height of a ramp and keep the angle constant, what happens to the base length? Explain.
   See above.

11. c. It decreases; Sample Response: As the angle measure increases, the ratio of height to length (tangent) increases. Since the height stays the same, the length of the base decreases.

c. If you increase the angle of a ramp and keep the height constant, what happens to the base length? Explain.

Find the complement of each angle measure.

1. 32° 58°   2. 65° 25°   3. 53° 37°   4. 77° 13°

5. 8° 82°   6. 27° 63°   7. 58° 32°   8. 89° 1°

Find the supplement of each angle measure.

9. 102° 78°   10. 81° 99°   11. 152° 28°   12. 113° 67°

13. 12° 168°   14. 77° 103°   15. 109° 71°   16. 36° 144°

Use the triangle to find the given tangent. Check each answer with a calculator. (*Note:* Side lengths are approximate.) 17–19. Answers are rounded to the nearest hundredth.

17. tan 61° 1.80   18. tan 22° 0.40   19. tan 70° 2.75

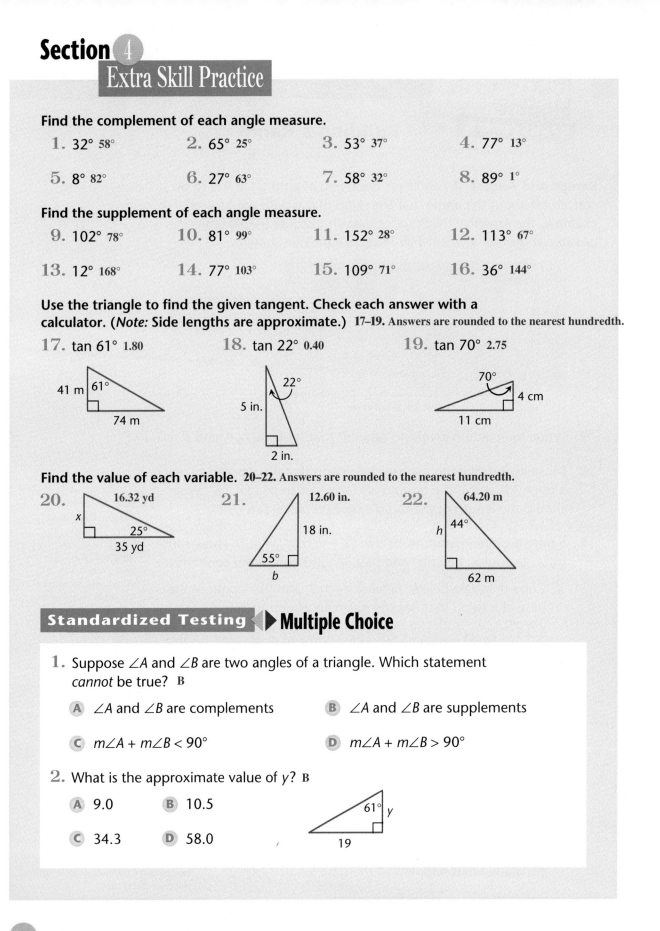

Find the value of each variable. 20–22. Answers are rounded to the nearest hundredth.

20.   21.   22.

1. Suppose $\angle A$ and $\angle B$ are two angles of a triangle. Which statement *cannot* be true? **B**

   Ⓐ $\angle A$ and $\angle B$ are complements   Ⓑ $\angle A$ and $\angle B$ are supplements

   Ⓒ $m\angle A + m\angle B < 90°$ Ⓓ $m\angle A + m\angle B > 90°$

2. What is the approximate value of y? **B**

   Ⓐ 9.0   Ⓑ 10.5

   Ⓒ 34.3   Ⓓ 58.0

Section 5 Counting Techniques

IN THIS SECTION

EXPLORATION 1
♦ Counting and Permutations

EXPLORATION 2
♦ Combinations

Reading is Believing

WARM-UP EXERCISES

Multiply.
1. $3 \cdot 4 \cdot 6 \cdot 12$ 864
2. $6 \cdot 5 \cdot 4 \cdot 3 \cdot 2 \cdot 1$ 720

State the number of possible choices for each event.
3. choosing a letter of the alphabet   26
4. choosing a one-digit number   10
5. choosing a primary color (red, blue, or yellow)   3
6. choosing one student from your class Answers will vary.

Setting the Stage ▸▸▸▸▸▸▸▸▸▸▸▸▸▸▸▸▸▸▸▸▸▸▸▸▸▸▸▸▸▸

SET UP   *You will need Labsheet 5A.*

Louis Braille (1809–1852) was blinded in an accident when he was only three years old. As a young boy, he anxiously awaited the day when he could go to school and learn to read. In her book *Seeing Fingers: The Story of Louis Braille*, Etta DeGering describes Louis's first year in school.

Seeing Fingers by Etta DeGering

Since Monsieur Becheret, the teacher, lectured one day and questioned the next, Louis did not find it too difficult to compete with his sighted classmates. After a few weeks he stood at the top of most of his classes.

In arithmetic he could often work a problem in his head as quickly as the other pupils on paper. But when it came to the reading and writing periods there was nothing for him to do. There were no books for blind boys to read and no way for them to write. This he learned the first day of school. When the primers were passed out, he held out his hand and was given one. He touched [his cousin] Jean to see how the reading was done. He held his book in the same way, but the pages told him no magic words.

"Are there no books for blind boys to read?" he asked the teacher.

When Monsieur Becheret said "None that I know of," Louis put his head down on his desk and wept.

Louis did not give up, however. Between the ages of 12 and 15, he created a code that he hoped would allow blind students to read. His code used groups of raised dots to represent letters of the alphabet. Today the code Louis created is called Braille in his honor. The Braille alphabet is shown below.

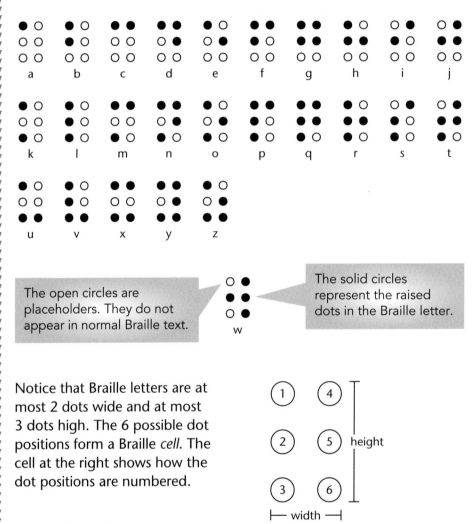

The open circles are placeholders. They do not appear in normal Braille text.

The solid circles represent the raised dots in the Braille letter.

Notice that Braille letters are at most 2 dots wide and at most 3 dots high. The 6 possible dot positions form a Braille *cell*. The cell at the right shows how the dot positions are numbered.

Think About It

1 **Use Labsheet 5A.** One day at school, Louis showed the Braille alphabet to some of his classmates. As his classmates discussed what the new alphabet would allow them to do, his friend Gabriel interrupted them excitedly. "Already I know the alphabet. I have written a sentence." Follow the directions on the labsheet to read *Gabriel's Sentence.* **I can write; I: 2, 4; C: 1, 4; A: 1; N: 1, 3, 4, 5; W: 2, 4, 5, 6; R: 1, 2, 3, 5; I: 2, 4; T: 2, 3, 4, 5; E: 1, 5.**

▶ **In this section, you'll discover why Louis Braille's decision to use 6 dot positions in a Braille cell was a very important one. You'll also explore how he constructed the Braille alphabet.**

Exploration 1

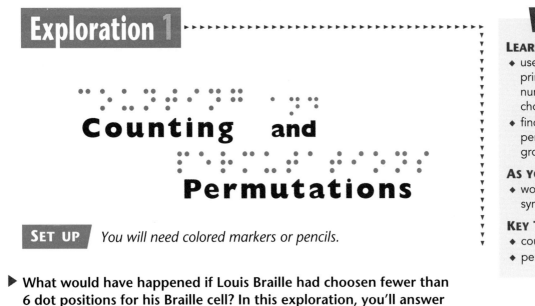

Counting and Permutations

GOAL

LEARN HOW TO...
- use the counting principle to count numbers of choices
- find the number of permutations of a group of objects

AS YOU...
- work with Braille symbols

KEY TERMS
- counting principle
- permutation

SET UP *You will need colored markers or pencils.*

▶ What would have happened if Louis Braille had chosen fewer than 6 dot positions for his Braille cell? In this exploration, you'll answer this question.

2 Suppose Louis Braille had used only 1 dot position for the Braille cell. How many different symbols could he make? (Include the symbol with no raised dot.) 2 **symbols**

▶ You can use a tree diagram to find the number of different symbols you can make with a Braille cell that has 2 dot positions.

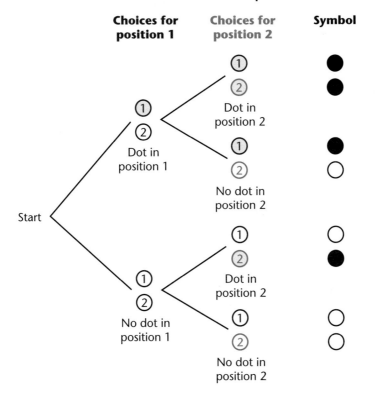

3 Use the tree diagram on page 371 for a 2-position Braille cell.

    a. How many choices are there for position 1 of the cell? For each choice for position 1, how many choices are there for position 2? **2 choices; 2 choices**

    b. How many different symbols can you make with a 2-position Braille cell? **4 choices**

    4. See Additional Answers.

4 **a.** Draw a tree diagram that lists the number of different symbols you can make with a 3-position Braille cell like the one shown. Use color to indicate the choices in your tree diagram, as was done in the diagram on page 371.

        ① ② ③

    b. How many choices are there for position 1? for position 2? for position 3?

    c. How many different symbols can you make with a 3-position Braille cell?

    d. How are your answers to parts (b) and (c) related? Is this relationship also true for parts (a) and (b) of Question 3?

▶ The relationship you described in Question 4(d) is called the **counting principle**. This principle says that the total number of ways a sequence of decisions can be made is the product of the number of choices for each decision.

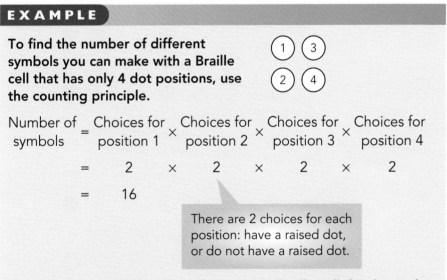

EXAMPLE

To find the number of different symbols you can make with a Braille cell that has only 4 dot positions, use the counting principle.

① ③
② ④

$$\begin{matrix} \text{Number of} \\ \text{symbols} \end{matrix} = \begin{matrix} \text{Choices for} \\ \text{position 1} \end{matrix} \times \begin{matrix} \text{Choices for} \\ \text{position 2} \end{matrix} \times \begin{matrix} \text{Choices for} \\ \text{position 3} \end{matrix} \times \begin{matrix} \text{Choices for} \\ \text{position 4} \end{matrix}$$

$$= \quad 2 \quad \times \quad 2 \quad \times \quad 2 \quad \times \quad 2$$

$$= \quad 16$$

There are 2 choices for each position: have a raised dot, or do not have a raised dot.

You can make 16 different symbols with a Braille cell that has 4 dot positions.

5 ✔ **CHECKPOINT** How many different symbols can you make with a 5-position Braille cell? with a 6-position Braille cell? Explain how you got your answers. 32 symbols; 64 symbols; Possible answers: Find 2^5 and 2^6 or multiply $2 \cdot 2 \cdot 2 \cdot 2 \cdot 2$ for 5 positions and $2 \cdot 2 \cdot 2 \cdot 2 \cdot 2 \cdot 2$ for 6 positions.

6 What is the least number of dot positions you need in order to make a symbol for each of the 26 letters in the English alphabet? Why do you think Louis Braille used more dot positions than this? 5 positions; Sample Response: to allow for punctuation and other symbols

✔ **QUESTION 5**

...checks that you can use the counting principle to count numbers of choices.

▶ **Today new technologies make it easier for blind people to work. For example, there are Braille keyboards and Braille printers. There are also electronic Braille displays that convert text on a computer screen into Braille text.**

7 Max Jones uses a Braille keyboard and a Braille display at his job. He needs to choose a password for his company's e-mail system. He decides to use an arrangement of the letters in his first name. You can find the number of passwords that Max can choose by using the counting principle.

a. How many choices are there for the first letter in an arrangement of the letters in *Max*? 3 choices

b. After the first letter of the arrangement is chosen, how many choices are there for the second letter? 2 choices

c. After the first and second letters of the arrangement are chosen, how many choices are there for the third letter? 1 choice

d. Discussion Use the counting principle to find the number of different arrangements of the letters in *Max*. How many of these arrangements can Max use as a password? Explain your reasoning. 6 arrangements; 5 arrangements; He wants to use a rearrangement of the letters.

e. Make a list, in Braille, of the passwords that Max can use. See Additional Answers.

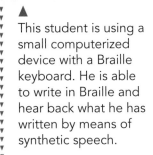

▲

This student is using a small computerized device with a Braille keyboard. He is able to write in Braille and hear back what he has written by means of synthetic speech.

▶ **An arrangement of a group of items in a definite order is called a permutation of the items. For example, AMX and MAX are permutations of the letters M, A, and X.**

8 ✔ **CHECKPOINT** Find the number of permutations of the letters in each word.

a. HAT 6   **b.** DEAL 24   **c.** SIGNAL 720

✔ **QUESTION 8**

...checks that you can find the number of permutations of a group of items.

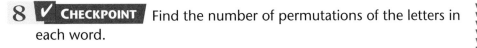

HOMEWORK EXERCISES ▶ See Exs. 1–12 on p. 378.

GOAL

LEARN HOW TO...
- find numbers of combinations

AS YOU...
- investigate the first ten letters of the Braille alphabet

KEY TERM
- combination

Exploration 2

Combinations

SET UP *You will need Labsheet 5B.*

▶ In *Seeing Fingers: The Story of Louis Braille,* Etta DeGering describes how Louis created the first ten letters of the Braille alphabet.

> The first ten letters had been the most difficult. [Louis] made them from different arrangements of the top four dots of the [Braille cell]. A was dot 1, B dots 1 and 2, C dots 1 and 4 . . . .

9. 4 symbols

○○ ○○ ○○ ○○
○○ ○○ ○○ ○○
○○ ○○ ○○ ○○

10. a.

Position of 1st dot	Position of 2nd dot	Positions chosen
4	1	4, 1
	2	4, 2
	5	4, 5
5	1	5, 1
	2	5, 2
	4	5, 4

12 paths

b. No; Sample Response: The order in which a dot is chosen does not change its position, so, for example, 1, 4 and 4, 1 represent the same letter.

c. 6 symbols

○○ ○○ ○○
○○ ○○ ○○
○○ ○○ ○○

○○ ○○ ○○
○○ ○○ ○○
○○ ○○ ○○

▶ The first ten Braille letters (a–j) occupy the first row of the Braille alphabet on page 370. As the passage above states, each letter is formed using only dots in the top 4 positions of a Braille cell.

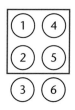

9 Draw all possible Braille symbols (including symbols that are not letters) that have exactly 1 dot in the top 4 positions and no dots in the bottom 2 positions. How many symbols did you get? **See above.**

10 **Use Labsheet 5B.** You can use the unfinished *Tree Diagram* on the labsheet to find the Braille symbols with exactly 2 dots in the top 4 positions and no dots in the bottom 2 positions. **See above.**

a. Finish drawing the tree diagram. How many paths through the tree diagram are there?

b. Does each path through the tree diagram represent a different Braille symbol? Explain.

c. How many Braille symbols are there with exactly 2 dots in the top 4 positions and no dots in the bottom 2 positions? Draw each symbol.

▶ In Question 10, you formed Braille symbols by choosing 2 of the top 4 positions in a Braille cell. The order in which you chose the positions did not matter. This kind of selection is a **combination**.

11 **a.** Try drawing all possible Braille symbols that have exactly 3 dots in the top 4 positions and no dots in the bottom 2 positions. How many symbols did you get?

11. a. 4 symbols

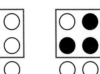

b. Look at the top 4 positions of the two Braille symbols shown at the right. How can you obtain the 3-dot symbol from the 1-dot symbol?

b. Sample Response: Reverse the pattern so that postion 1 is not used but the other 3 positions are used.

c. Explain why the number of symbols with 3 dots in the top 4 positions must equal the number of symbols with 1 dot in the top 4 positions. Use this fact and your results from Question 9 to check your answer to part (a). Sample Response: The pattern can be reversed for all 4 positions.

12 How many Braille symbols have exactly 4 dots in the top 4 positions and no dots in the bottom 2 positions? Draw the symbol(s). 1 symbol

13 **a.** Summarize your results from Questions 9–12 by copying and completing the table. 4; 6; 4; 1

Number of dots in top 4 positions	Number of Braille symbols
1	?
2	?
3	?
4	?

b. Find the sum of the numbers in the second column of the table. How many Braille symbols can you make that have from 1 to 4 dots in the top 4 positions and no dots in the bottom 2 positions? 15 symbols

c. For the letters a–j, Louis Braille used only ten of the symbols you counted in part (b). Which symbols did he *not* use?

Positions 2; 4; 5; 2, 5; and 4, 5

14 ✔ **CHECKPOINT** Find the number of Braille symbols that have exactly 2 dots if the dots can occupy any of the 6 positions in a Braille cell. 15 symbols

✔ **QUESTION 14**

...checks that you can find numbers of combinations.

15 **Discussion** Look at the Braille alphabet on page 370.
Sample responses are given.
a. How is the second row of the alphabet constructed from the first row? For each letter in the second row, a dot is added in position 3

b. How is the third row constructed from the second row?
For each letter in the third row, a dot is added in position 6

HOMEWORK EXERCISES ▶ See Exs. 13–19 on p. 379.

Key Terms

Using a Tree Diagram to Count Choices (pp. 371–372)

You can use a tree diagram to count choices in a given situation.

Example Brian is trying to choose an outfit for a party. He has a pair of **blue pants** and a pair of **gray pants**. He also has a **white shirt**, a **blue-striped shirt**, a **gray-striped shirt**, and a **plaid shirt**. The tree diagram shows that there are 8 different outfits Brian can wear.

Pants	Shirt	Outfit
blue pants	white shirt	blue pants, white shirt
	blue-striped shirt	blue pants, blue-striped shirt
	gray-striped shirt	blue pants, gray-striped shirt
	plaid shirt	blue pants, plaid shirt
gray pants	white shirt	gray pants, white shirt
	blue-striped shirt	gray pants, blue-striped shirt
	gray-striped shirt	gray pants, gray-striped shirt
	plaid shirt	gray pants, plaid shirt

counting principle

The Counting Principle (p. 372)

The total number of ways that a sequence of decisions can be made is the product of the number of choices for each decision.

Example In the Example above, Brian can choose his pants in **2** ways and his shirt in **4** ways. So Brian can choose $2 \cdot 4 = 8$ outfits.

Example Suppose a license plate can have any three letters followed by any three digits from 0 to 9. Since there are 26 possible letters and 10 possible digits, the number of possible license plates is:

$$26 \cdot 26 \cdot 26 \cdot 10 \cdot 10 \cdot 10 = 17,576,000$$

↑ Choices for 1st letter   ↑ Choices for 2nd letter   ↑ Choices for 3rd letter   ↑ Choices for 1st digit   ↑ Choices for 2nd digit   ↑ Choices for 3rd digit

16 Key Concepts Question In the license plate Example above, suppose a letter or digit can be used only once. How many plates are possible? **11,232,000 plates**

Key Concepts

Key Terms

Permutations (p. 373)

A permutation of a group of items is an arrangement of the items in a definite order.

permutation

Example A pizzeria offers 3 specialty pizzas: the Meat Combo (M), the Vegetarian (V), and the Supreme (S). Each way of arranging the pizzas on the menu is a permutation. You can find the number of permutations using the counting principle:

$$3 \cdot 2 \cdot 1 = 6$$

Choices for 1st pizza   Choices for 2nd pizza   Choices for 3rd pizza

The 6 permutations are MVS, MSV, VMS, VSM, SMV, and SVM.

Combinations (pp. 374–375)

A combination is a selection of items from a group where order is not important.

combination

Example The Shaw family wants to buy 2 of the 3 specialty pizzas listed in the Example above. Since the order in which the pizzas are chosen is not important, each possible selection is a combination. You can use a tree diagram to find the number of combinations.

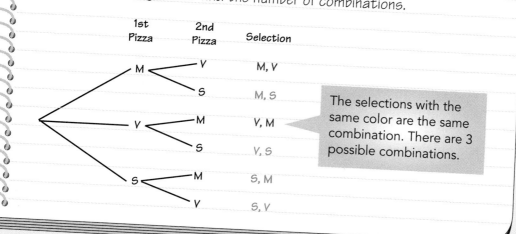

| 1st Pizza | 2nd Pizza | Selection |

The selections with the same color are the same combination. There are 3 possible combinations.

CLOSURE QUESTION

Explain how the counting principle and a tree diagram are alike. Explain how permutations and combinations are different.

Sample Response: Both are ways to count choices in certain situations. A tree diagram is a picture that represents the counting principle. When finding the number of permutations of a group of items, the order that each item is chosen matters. When finding the combinations of a group of items, the order that each item is chosen does not matter.

17 Key Concepts Question Does counting the ways to choose 3 of 8 possible toppings for a pizza involve *permutations* or *combinations*? Explain. **combinations; The order in which the toppings are chosen isn't important.**

Practice & Application Exercises

YOU WILL NEED

For Ex. 28:
♦ Labsheet 5C

1. A certain model of car is available in 6 exterior colors: white, red, navy blue, forest green, tan, and maroon. The car is also available in 2 interior colors: black and gray. **See Additional Answers.**

   a. Draw a tree diagram showing the different color choices available for the exterior and interior of the car.

   b. In how many ways can you choose an exterior color and an interior color for the car?

2. **Consumer Electronics** Rosa Hernandez wants to buy a new TV and a new VCR. A consumer magazine she reads rates 3 TVs and 5 VCRs as "best buys." If Rosa limits her choices to the "best buys," in how many ways can she choose a TV and a VCR? **15 ways**

3. At a certain restaurant, dinners include one entree, one vegetable, and one dessert from the menu shown. **See Additional Answers.**

   a. Draw a tree diagram showing the different dinners that a customer at the restaurant can order.

   b. How many different dinners can a customer order?

Entrée
spaghetti, chicken, roast beef

Vegetable
corn, squash

Dessert
apple pie, cherry pie, pecan pie

4. **Forensics** A system for facial identification, called Photo-FIT, has been used by police in the United Kingdom to identify crime suspects. The basic kit contains 195 hairlines, 99 eyes and eyebrows, 89 noses, 105 mouths, and 74 lower faces. How many different faces can be constructed? **13,349,986,650**

Find the number of permutations of the letters in each word.

5. HI 2

6. TEA 6

7. MULE 24

8. BAKERY 720

9. SPINACH 5040

10. CENTRIFUGAL 39,916,800

11. **Sports** In the Olympics, 8 swimmers participate in the final race of the women's 100-meter freestyle event. In how many different orders can the swimmers finish the race? **40,320 orders**

12. A building inspector is supposed to inspect 10 buildings for safety code violations. In how many different orders can the inspector visit the buildings? **3,628,800 orders**

13. Carol McLeish requires her students to answer 2 of the 4 essay questions on a history test. How many combinations of 2 questions can Carol's students answer? **6 combinations**

14. **Personal Finance** Ian finds 6 books in a bookstore that he would like to read, but he only has enough money to buy 4 of them. How many combinations of 4 books can Ian buy? (*Hint:* Choosing 4 books to buy is the same as choosing 2 books *not* to buy.)
    15 combinations

15. Kaya has roses, lilies, tulips, daisies, and poppies growing in her flower garden. She wants to make a bouquet for a friend. How many combinations of types of flowers can Kaya have in the bouquet if she uses:

    a. exactly 1 type of flower? **5**   b. exactly 2 types of flowers? **10**

    c. exactly 3 types of flowers? **10**   d. at least 3 types of flowers? **16**

16. 1, 3, 6, 10, 15

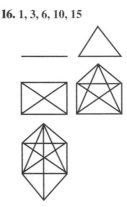

Geometry Connection A *complete graph* is a collection of points, called *vertices*, and segments, called *edges*, such that every pair of vertices is joined by an edge. One complete graph is shown below.

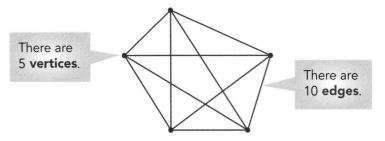

There are 5 **vertices**.

There are 10 **edges**.

19. Order is important in a permutation but not a combination; Sample Response: Choosing a president and vice president of a club involves permutations. Choosing a two-person executive committee involves combinations.

16. Copy the table. For each number of vertices in the table, draw a complete graph with that many vertices. In the table, record the number of edges each complete graph has.
    See above.

Number of vertices	Number of edges
2	?
3	?
4	?
5	?
6	?

17. **Writing** Explain how the numbers of edges in the table are related to combinations. (*Hint:* Think about the number of edges you can draw at each vertex without redrawing any of the edges.) **The number of edges is the number of combinations of 2 vertices.**

18. **Challenge** Write a formula for the number of edges, *e*, in a complete graph with *v* vertices. $e = \frac{v(v-1)}{2}$

Reflecting ▶on the Section

Be prepared to report on the following topic in class.

19. Describe how a combination differs from a permutation. Use at least two real-world examples to help illustrate the difference.
    See above.

Oral Report

Exercise 19 checks that you know the difference between a combination and a permutation.

Spiral ▶Review

Find the complement of each angle measure. (Module 5, p. 363)

20. 18° 72°   **21.** 54° 36°   **22.** 81° 9°

Find the sum of the measures of the interior angles for each polygon.
(Module 4, p. 285)

23. 720°   **24.** 540°

Find the theoretical probability of each outcome when you roll a six-sided die. (Module 2, p. 115)

25. rolling an even number $\frac{1}{2}$ **26.** rolling a number less than 5 $\frac{2}{3}$

Extension ▶▶

Pascal's Triangle

The triangle of numbers shown below is part of *Pascal's triangle*. You can use Pascal's triangle to solve problems involving combinations. To find the number of combinations of *r* objects taken from a group of *n* objects, locate the (*r* + 1)st entry in row *n*.

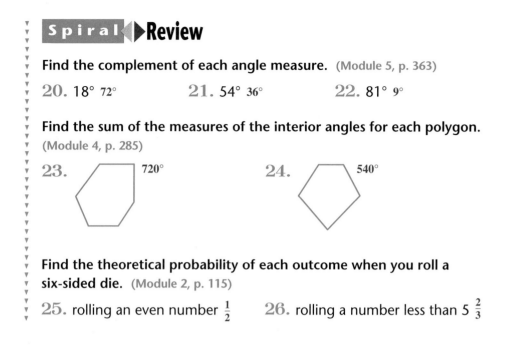

```
row 0 ──────────────→ 1
row 1 ─────────────→ 1    1
row 2 ────────────→ 1    2    1
row 3 ───────────→ 1    3    3    1
row 4 ──────────→ 1    4    6    4    1
row 5 ─────────→ 1    5   10   10    5    1
```

The number of combinations of 2 objects taken from a group of **4** objects is the 3rd entry in row **4**. There are **6** combinations.

27. Writing Look at the numbers in Pascal's triangle that are not equal to 1. Explain how each of these numbers is related to the two numbers directly above it. **It is the sum of the two numbers directly above it.**

28. Use Labsheet 5C. The labsheet shows the part of *Pascal's Triangle* given above. Use the pattern you found in Exercise 27 to complete rows 6–8 of Pascal's triangle.
1, 6, 15, 20, 15, 6, 1; 1, 7, 21, 35, 35, 21, 7, 1; 1, 8, 28, 56, 70, 56, 28, 8, 1

29. Suppose you have 8 short-sleeved shirts and want to pack 4 of these shirts to take on a vacation to Florida. Use Pascal's triangle to find the number of ways you can choose the 4 shirts. **70 ways**

1. At a video rental store, there are 6 comedies, 8 dramas, and 3 science fiction films that Maureen wants to see. In how many ways can she choose one of each type of movie to rent? **144 ways**

2. How many permutations are there of the letters in the word BOWLING? **5040 arrangements**

3. A president and a vice-president are to be selected from a 6-member student council committee. In how many ways can the selection be made? **30 ways**

4. Two of the 5 players on a basketball team are to be selected as co-captains. In how many ways can the selection be made? **10 ways**

5. In how many ways can 4 people line up for a photograph? **24 ways**

6. In a group of 4 people, each person shakes hands with everyone else once. How many handshakes are there? (*Hint:* How many combinations of 2 people are there?) **6 handshakes**

7. In how many ways can you complete a 10-question true-false test if every question must be answered? **1024 ways**

8. In how many ways can you complete a 10-question multiple choice test if there are 4 choices for each question and every question must be answered? **1,048,576 ways**

9. In how many ways can 8 books be arranged on a shelf? **40,320 ways**

10. A chicken dinner comes with any 3 of these side dishes: mashed potatoes, baked beans, corn, rice, or stuffing. How many combinations of 3 side dishes are possible? (*Hint:* Choosing 3 side dishes is the same as *not* choosing the other 2 side dishes.) **10 combinations**

Standardized Testing ▸ Performance Task

Tonya makes 3 sketches of different classmates for her art class.

1. In how many ways can Tonya select 2 of the 3 sketches to include in her final portfolio? Is this a *permutations* problem or a *combinations* problem? Explain. **3 ways; combination; The order in which she selects her sketches is not important.**

2. After her art class is over, Tonya decides to hang all 3 of the sketches she made in a row on her bedroom wall. In how many ways can she arrange the sketches? Is this a *permutations* problem or a *combinations* problem? Explain. **6 ways; permutation; The order in which she hangs her sketches is important.**

Section 6 Working with Probability

Lock It Up!

A box contains a red flag, a blue flag, a white flag, and a green flag. State the number of choices for each event.

1. In how many ways can the four flags be picked?   24

2. In how many ways can two flags be picked?   12

3. In how many ways can three flags be picked?   24

Write each fraction as a decimal to the nearest hundredth.

4. $\frac{3}{7}$ 0.43

5. $\frac{140}{253}$ 0.55

⋯Setting the Stage

Have you ever misplaced your keys? You would not be as likely to lose special keys made in ancient Rome. Occasionally large bronze keys were made that were as long as your arm and weighed over 10 lb! Modern keys are much smaller and come in a variety of forms. Finding the correct key can sometimes be difficult.

Think About It

1 Combination locks use a sequence of numbers or letters for the key. Suppose the key is a 3-digit sequence using the numbers 1, 2, 3, 4, or 5, and that each number in the key is used only once. Use the counting principle to find the number of possible 3-digit keys.   **60 keys**

2 Create your own 3-digit key. Use any of the numbers 1, 2, 3, 4, or 5, but do not use any number more than once. Keep your key a secret for now.   **Answers will vary. Check students' work.**

3 For each group described below, do you think the probability that everyone chose a different key is closer to 0, 0.25, 0.50, 0.75, or 1? Explain your thinking.   **Answers will vary.**

   a. a group of 4 students   **b.** your entire class

Exploration 1

Probability and Counting

▶ **How likely is it that everyone in your class chose a different 3-digit key in Question 2? You can find out by looking at a simpler situation and thinking about probability.**

4 Suppose a 3-digit key can be made with only the numbers 1, 2, and 3, and each number cannot be used more than once in a key.

a. How many different keys are possible? **6 keys**

b. Use the numbers 1, 2, and 3 to list all the possible keys.
123, 132, 213, 231, 312, 321

c. Suppose two people each choose one of the keys from part (b). The model at the right shows all the ways they can choose two keys. Copy and complete the model. Mark each box with a **D** if the people choose different keys or with an **S** if they choose the same key. **See table.**

		1st person's choice					
		1-2-3	1-3-2	2-1-3	? 2-3-1	? 3-1-2	? 3-2-1
2nd person's choice	1-2-3	S	? D	? D	? D	? D	? D
	1-3-2	D	? S	? D	? D	? D	? D
	2-1-3	? D	? D	? S	? D	? D	? D
	? 2-3-1	? D	? D	? D	? S	? D	? D
	? 3-1-2	? D	? D	? D	? D	? S	? D
	? 3-2-1	? D	? D	? D	? D	? D	? S

◀ The **S** shows that the 1st and 2nd persons both choose 1-2-3.
The **D** shows that the 1st person chooses 1-2-3 but the 2nd person chooses 1-3-2.

5 Use your completed model from Question 4.

a. How many ways can the two people choose the keys? How does the model show this? **36 ways; Sample Response: Each box in the table represents one way that two people can choose a key.**

b. What is the probability that both people choose the *same* key? **5. b. $\frac{1}{6}$ or about 0.17**

c. What is the probability that both people choose *different* keys?
$\frac{5}{6}$ or about 0.83

▶ **You can also use the counting principle to find the probability that the two people in Question 4 choose different keys.**

EXAMPLE

Two people each choose one of the six 3-digit keys that use each of the numbers 1, 2, and 3 exactly once. The probability that they choose different keys is given by this ratio:

$$\text{Probability} = \frac{\text{Ways to choose different keys}}{\text{Total ways to choose keys}}$$

If each person chooses a *different* key, the first person has 6 choices and the second person has 5 choices. If each person can choose *any* key, the first person has 6 choices and the second person also has 6 choices.

$$\text{Probability} = \frac{6 \cdot 5}{6 \cdot 6} \leftarrow \text{Use the counting principle.}$$

$$= \frac{5}{6}, \text{ or about } 0.83$$

FOR ◄ HELP
with *the counting principle*, see
MODULE 5, p. 376

6 Discussion In the Example, why does the second person have 5 choices rather than 6 if the keys must be different?
Sample Response: One of the 6 choices has already been taken by the first person.

7 Try This as a Class Suppose three people each choose one of the keys you listed in Question 4(b).

a. Find the total number of ways for three people to choose the keys. **216 ways**

b. How many ways can the three people all choose different keys? **120 ways**

c. What is the probability that everyone chooses a different key? $\frac{5}{9} \approx 0.56$

8 ✓ CHECKPOINT Look back at Question 4.

a. What is the probability that everyone will choose a different key if there are 4 people choosing keys? $\frac{5}{18} \approx 0.28$

b. What is the probability that everyone will choose a different key if there are 5 people choosing keys? $\frac{5}{54} \approx 0.09$

✓ QUESTION 8

...checks that you can use the counting principle to find probabilities.

9 Try This as a Class In Question 2, each person in your class chose a 3-digit key that uses the numbers 1, 2, 3, 4, or 5.

a. Find the probability that everyone in a group of four would choose a different 3-digit key. Would you expect any two people in a group of four to have the same key? $\frac{32,509}{36,000} \approx 0.90$; It is unlikely.

b. Form a group of four students. Check to see if any two people chose the same key. **Answers will vary. Check students' work.**

c. Find the probability that everyone in your class chose a different 3-digit key. Would you expect any two people in your class to have the same key? Sample Response: about 0.003 for a class of 25 students; Yes.

d. Check to see if any two people in your class chose the same key.
   Answers will vary. Check students' work.

e. How do the probabilities from parts (a) and (c) compare to your answers from Question 3 on page 382?
   Answers will vary. Check students' work.

HOMEWORK EXERCISES ▶ See Exs. 1–10 on pp. 386–387.

See Exs. 1–10 on pp. 386–387.

CLOSURE QUESTION

Define what is meant by probability. Then explain how the counting principle can be used to help solve some probability problems.

Answer: Probability =

$$\frac{\text{number of successful choices}}{\text{total number of choices}};$$

Sample Response: The counting principle can be used to find both the number of successful choices in the numerator and the total number of choices in the denominator. Then the probability can be found.

Section 6

Key Concepts

▶▶▶▶▶▶▶▶▶▶▶▶▶▶▶▶▶▶▶▶▶

Probability and Counting (pp. 383–385)

You can use the counting principle to find some probabilities.

Example Suppose three 6-sided dice are rolled. The probability that the dice show different numbers is given by this ratio:

$$\text{Probability} = \frac{\text{Ways to roll different numbers}}{\text{Total ways to roll dice}}$$

If different numbers must be rolled, there are **6** possibilities for the 1st die, **5** possibilities for the second die, and **4** possibilities for the third die. If any numbers can be rolled, there are **6** possibilities for each die.

$$\text{Probability} = \frac{6 \cdot 5 \cdot 4}{6 \cdot 6 \cdot 6}$$

$$= \frac{5}{9}, \text{ or about } 0.56$$

10 Key Concepts Question Suppose you roll three 4-sided dice. The sides of each die are numbered 1, 2, 3, and 4. What is the probability that all the dice show different numbers on the bottom? Is this probability *greater than*, *less than*, or *equal to* the probability for three 6-sided dice? Explain.

$\frac{3}{8} = 0.375$; less than; The probability for three 6-sided dice is $\frac{5}{9} \approx 0.56$.

Section 6

For Exercises 1–3, suppose three coins are tossed and the number of heads is recorded.

1. List all the possible outcomes when three coins are tossed.
   HHH, HHT, HTH, HTT, THH, THT, TTH, TTT

2. What is the probability of getting 3 heads? 2 heads? 1 head? 0 heads? $\frac{1}{8} = 0.125; \frac{3}{8} = 0.375; \frac{3}{8} = 0.375; \frac{1}{8} = 0.125$

3. What is the probability of getting at least one head? $\frac{7}{8} = 0.875$

4. **Government** Your Social Security number is a 9-digit number. Suppose the last four digits are chosen randomly from the numbers 0–9.

   a. How many sequences are possible for the last four digits?
   10,000 sequences

   b. What is the probability of getting a 5 or 0 in the last digit? $\frac{1}{5} = 0.2$

   c. What is the probability of getting two 5's in the last two digits? $\frac{1}{100} = 0.01$

5. Suppose a license plate for a car has 4 letters followed by 1 number and then 3 more letters. The letters and numbers are chosen randomly.

   a. How many license plates are possible? 80,318,101,760, or about $8 \cdot 10^{10}$ license plates

   b. Compare the probability that a license plate spells MATH4YOU with the probability that the first four letters spell MATH.

5. b. MATH4YOU: about $\frac{1}{8 \cdot 10^{10}}$; MATH as first four letters: about $\frac{1 \cdot 1 \cdot 1 \cdot 1 \cdot 10 \cdot 26^3}{8 \cdot 10^{10}}$; the latter is 175,760 times more likely.

6. **History** In a game popular in France during the seventeenth century, a player tried to roll a six-sided die four times without getting a 6. What is the probability that a player wins this game? $\frac{625}{1296} \approx 0.48$

7. **Electronics** A certain model of automatic garage door opener can be assigned one of 512 possible codes. If the openers for two garage doors have the same code, then the transmitter for one door will also open the other door.

   a. Find the probability that two neighbors who each buy this brand of garage door opener $\frac{511}{512} = 0.998$ get openers with different codes.

   b. **Writing** If you are one of the neighbors in part (a), do you want the probability you found to be high or low? Explain.
   high; It means that the probability that two neighbors get the same code is low.

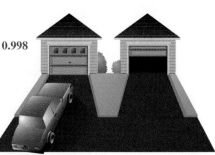

8. **Open-ended** Describe a real-world problem whose solution involves using the counting principle to find a probability.
   Answers will vary. Check students' work.

9. **Challenge** Suppose a group of *n* people is randomly selected. For each value of *n*, find the probability that everyone in the group has a different birthday. (Assume no one is born on February 29 of a leap year, so that there are 365 equally likely birthdays possible.)

   a. *n* = 5 about 0.97   b. *n* = 10 about 0.88   c. *n* = 20 about 0.59

Reflecting ◀▶ on the Section   10. See Additional Answers.

10. a. Suppose two people each choose 1 of 3 colors: red, yellow, or blue. Explain how the model shows all the ways the people can choose their colors.

    b. What is the probability that the two people choose different colors? the same color?

    c. **Create Your Own** Suppose three people each choose one of two colors. Create a model that shows all the ways they can choose their colors. What is the probability that all three people choose the same color?

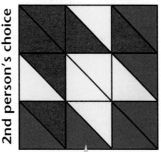

1st person's choice

2nd person's choice

The 1st person chooses yellow and the 2nd person chooses blue.

Spiral ◀▶ Review

11. Michael Kiefer needs to choose 2 of his 4 suits to take on a business trip. How many combinations of 2 suits can Michael choose? (Module 5, p. 377)   6 combinations

12. **Choosing a Data Display** Some test scores for a science class are listed below. Display the scores using either a stem-and-leaf plot or a box-and-whisker plot. (Module 1, p. 21; Module 2, p. 152)
    See Additional Answers.

    78, 61, 94, 68, 52, 81, 70, 64, 53, 86, 99, 72, 87,
    59, 81, 75, 93, 81, 66, 75, 48, 96, 85, 77, 98, 41

13. Find the surface area and the volume of a cube whose edges are 7 cm long. (Toolbox, p. 605)   surface area: 294 cm², volume: 343 cm³

Section 6

Extra Skill Practice

One model of briefcase has a lock with three dials. Each dial can show a digit from 0 to 9. The lock opens when the dials are turned to a certain three-digit key, such as 2-0-7. Suppose Jamal, Lisa, and Kim each buy this model of briefcase. Find the probability of each outcome.

1. The last two digits in Jamal's key are both 8. $\frac{1}{100} = 0.01$

2. Each digit in Lisa's key is less than 7. $\frac{343}{1000} = 0.343$

3. None of the digits in Kim's key are 0 or 5. $\frac{64}{125} = 0.512$

4. Each digit in Kim's key is either 0 or 5. $\frac{1}{125} = 0.008$

5. Jamal and Lisa have different keys. $\frac{999}{1000} = 0.999$

6. Jamal, Lisa, and Kim have different keys. $\frac{498,501}{500,000} \approx 0.997$

One popular game involves rolling 5 six-sided dice. Find the probability of each outcome when rolling the dice.

7. all 1's $\frac{1}{7776} \approx 0.00013$

8. all even numbers $\frac{1}{32} = 0.03125$

9. all different numbers $\frac{5}{54} \approx 0.093$

10. all numbers greater than 2 $\frac{32}{243} \approx 0.13$

11. no 4's $\frac{3125}{7776} \approx 0.40$

12. all perfect squares $\frac{1}{243} \approx 0.0041$

Standardized Testing ◀▶ Free Response

1. Suppose you flip a coin 4 times. What is the probability that you get all heads? $\frac{1}{16} = 0.0625$

2. A certain two-person game is played with pegs that have 6 possible colors: black, blue, green, red, white, and yellow. Player 1 forms a sequence of 4 pegs that is not shown to Player 2, such as green-black-yellow-green. (The same color may be used more than once.) Player 2 tries to guess Player 1's sequence.

   a. What is the probability that Player 2 correctly guesses Player 1's sequence on the first try? $\frac{1}{1296} \approx 0.00077$

   b. What is the probability that Player 2 guesses the wrong color for every position in Player 1's sequence on the first try? $\frac{625}{1296} \approx 0.48$

Completing the Module Project

Building a Ramp

Throughout this module, you have used mathematics to analyze different ramps and cylinders. Now you are ready to design and build your own model ramp and cylinders.

12–15. Answers will vary. Check students' work.

12 Before designing your model, think about these factors:

* the size of the object you want to move up your ramp

* the number of cylinders you want to use, as well as each cylinder's diameter d and length l

* the height h and width w you want your ramp to have

* the desired steepness of your ramp as measured by the angle A that the ramp makes with the ground or by the ramp's slope $\frac{h}{b}$ (where b is the length of the ramp's base)

Then make a sketch, similar to the one shown below, of the ramp and cylinders you plan to build. Label all dimensions with their measures.

SET UP

You will need:
* *ruler*
* *protractor*
* *material for ramp*
* *material for cylinders*
* *small object*

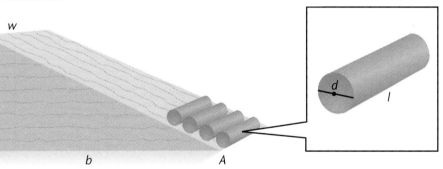

13 Choose the materials you will use to build your ramp and cylinders. For example, you may want to make your ramp out of cardboard or wood. The cylinders can be wooden dowels, markers, paper towel rolls, or other household items.

14 Construct your ramp and cylinders. Then test how well your model works by trying to move a small object (such as a book) up the ramp using the procedure described on page 328.

15 Demonstrate your ramp and cylinders to your class. Explain why you designed your model as you did.

Find the surface area of the cylinder with the given radius *r* and height *h*. (Sec. 1, Explor. 1)

1. *r* = 3 cm, *h* = 4 cm
131.88 cm²

2. *r* = 2 in., *h* = 6 in.
100.48 in.²

3. *r* = 1.5 ft, *h* = 12 ft
127.17 ft²

Find the ratio of surface area to volume for each cylinder.
(Sec. 1, Explor. 2)

4. 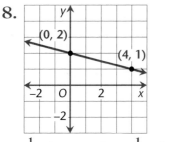 3 cm 0.8$\overline{3}$
12 cm

5. 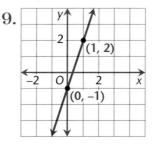 4 cm 0.7
10 cm

6. 0.8 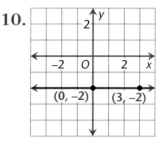 5 cm
5 cm

7. Suppose you have three cans with the same dimensions as the cylinders in Exercises 4–6. Rank the cans from most efficient to least efficient. Explain your ranking. (Sec. 1, Explor. 2)
r = 4 cm, *h* = 10 cm; *r* = 5 cm, *h* = 5 cm; *r* = 3 cm, *h* = 12 cm; The cans are ranked from lowest to highest value of $\frac{S.A.}{V}$.

For each line, find the slope and the *y*-intercept. Then write an equation of the line in slope-intercept form. (Sec. 2, Explors. 1 and 2)

8.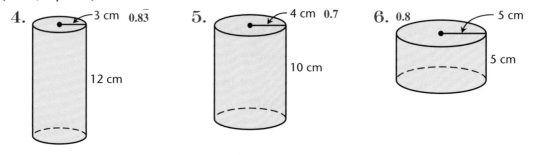

slope: $-\frac{1}{4}$; *y*-intercept: 2; $y = -\frac{1}{4}x + 2$ slope: 3; *y*-intercept: –1; $y = 3x - 1$ slope: 0; *y*-intercept: –2; $y = -2$

Write each product or quotient as a single power. (Sec. 3, Explor. 1)

11. $10^8 \cdot 10^3$ 10^{11} **12.** $a^4 \cdot a^5$ a^9 **13.** $\frac{2^{10}}{2^3}$ 2^7 **14.** $\frac{b^{23}}{b^{19}}$ b^4

Write each power as a whole number or fraction without exponents. (Sec. 3, Explor. 2)

15. 4^0 1 **16.** 11^{-2} $\frac{1}{121}$ **17.** 3^{-3} $\frac{1}{27}$ **18.** 2^{-6} $\frac{1}{64}$

Write each number in decimal notation. (Sec. 3, Explor. 2)

19. $5 \cdot 10^{-2}$ 0.05 **20.** $8.03 \cdot 10^{-4}$ 0.000803 **21.** $1.266 \cdot 10^{-7}$ 0.0000001266

Write each number in scientific notation. (Sec. 3, Explor. 2)

22. 0.0024 $2.4 \cdot 10^{-3}$ **23.** 0.0000752 $7.52 \cdot 10^{-5}$ **24.** 0.0000003061 $3.061 \cdot 10^{-7}$

Use the diagram for Exercises 25–27. (Sec. 4, Explor. 1)

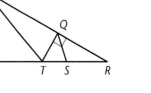

25. Which angle is a supplement of ∠UTQ? ∠QTR

26. Which angle is a complement of ∠SQR? ∠SQT

27. Suppose m∠UPT = 40°. Find m∠PTR. 130°

Find the value of each variable. (Sec. 4, Explor. 2) Answers are rounded to the nearest hundredth.

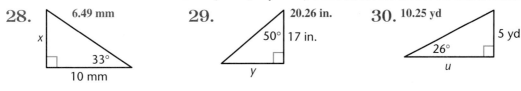

28. 6.49 mm, x, 33°, 10 mm

29. 20.26 in., 50°, 17 in., y

30. 10.25 yd, 5 yd, 26°, u

31. At a local pizza parlor, 5 employees work on Saturday nights: Armand, Cathy, Ishana, Jim, and Susan. Employees must wear uniforms consisting of tan or black pants and red, green, or black shirts. (Sec. 5, Explors. 1 and 2)

 a. How many different uniforms are possible? **6 uniforms**

 b. On one Saturday night, all 5 employees decide to line up and sing "Happy Birthday" to a customer. In how many different ways can they line up? **120 ways**

 c. Usually, 2 employees are needed to take telephone orders on Saturday nights. List all possible combinations of 2 employees who can be assigned to answer telephones.

31. c. Armand and Cathy, Armand and Ishana, Armand and Jim, Armand and Susan, Cathy and Ishana, Cathy and Jim, Cathy and Susan, Ishana and Jim, Ishana and Susan, Jim and Susan

32. A certain bank issues cards that let its customers use automatic teller machines (ATMs). Each customer is given a random 4-digit identification number that he or she must enter before using an ATM. The digits are integers from 0 to 9. (Sec. 6, Explor. 1)

 a. How many different identification numbers are possible? **10,000 numbers**

 b. What is the probability that the first and last digits in a customer's identification number are both greater than 6? $\frac{9}{100} = 0.09$

Reflecting ◀▶ **on the Module**

33. Writing Make a list of what you think are the ten most important mathematical concepts in this module. Write and solve an exercise that illustrates each concept. Answers will vary. Check students' work.

MODULE 6 · SECTION OVERVIEW

1 Geometry and Perspective

As you model buildings made with cubes:

- ◆ Explore volumes and surface areas
- ◆ Draw three-dimensional figures and flat views

2 Geometry and Constructions

As you construct space figures:

- ◆ Sketch nets for pyramids and prisms
- ◆ Construct angle bisectors
- ◆ Compare triangles for congruence

3 Surface Area and Volume

As you look at dwellings:

- ◆ Find surface areas of prisms and pyramids
- ◆ Find volumes of prisms, pyramids, and cones
- ◆ Explore composite figures

4 Angles Formed by Intersecting Lines

As you study the Chunnel:

- ◆ Find measures of angles formed by intersecting lines

5 Solving Inequalities

As you study seat design:

- ◆ Write inequalities
- ◆ Solve inequalities

6 Scale Drawings and Similar Figures

As you draw your classroom:

- ◆ Make scale drawings
- ◆ Find perimeters and areas of similar figures

The Module Project

Creating a Model Town

Have you ever thought about how you would design a house, an office, or a school? In this module, you'll learn about nets and scale models and use these tools to design and construct a model building for your class's model town.

More on the Module Project
See pp. 416, 430, 461, and 463.

INTERNET
To learn more about the theme:
http://www.mlmath.com

393

Section ① Geometry and Perspective

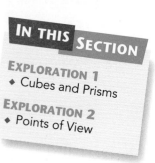

IN THIS SECTION

EXPLORATION 1
♦ Cubes and Prisms

EXPLORATION 2
♦ Points of View

Where do you Stand?

Use the figure below.

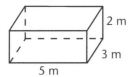

2 m

3 m

5 m

1. Find the area of the bottom and top of the prism.   15 m²

2. Find the area of the front and back of the prism.   10 m²

3. Find the area of each side of the prism.   6 m²

4. Find the total surface area of the prism.   62 m²

5. Find the volume of the prism.   30 m³

1. Not all; When viewed from the bottom, all the cross sections would look the same except   . It would look like   .

◄◄◄ Setting the Stage

This picture shows the Sears Tower in Chicago. At the time of its completion in 1974, it was the world's tallest building, with 110 stories and a height of 1454 ft.

The Sears Tower is actually a group of nine towers of various heights, with the four different cross sections shown. The tower's appearance changes when it is viewed from different sides.

When architects design buildings, they must be able to visualize the geometric figures within them and draw many different views.

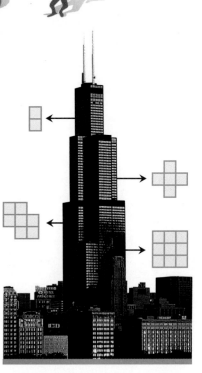

Think About It

1 The cross sections are drawn as if the viewer were looking down on the building from above. Would they look the same if the viewer could look up at the building from below? Explain.

2 Copy the 3 by 3 cross section of the Sears Tower. Then shade the squares that are directly under the highest part of the tower.

3 In the photo you can see two sides of the Sears Tower. Will it look the same when viewed from the corner formed by the two sides you *cannot* see? Explain. (*Hint:* Look at the cross sections.)
No; The building is not symmetrical.

▶ In this module you'll see how architects and engineers use mathematics to design and construct buildings and other structures.

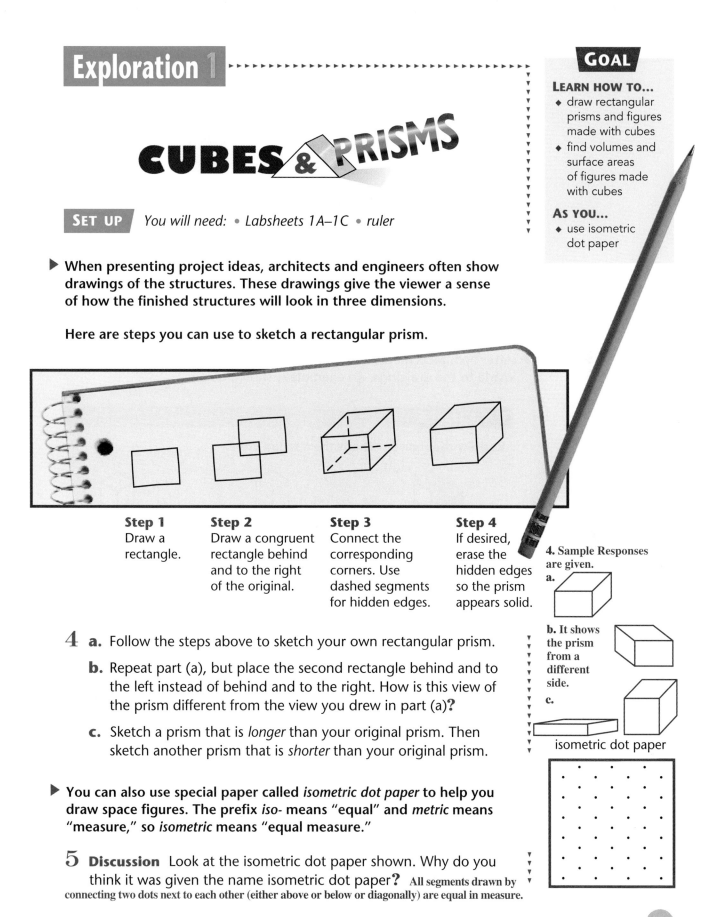

Exploration 1

CUBES & PRISMS

GOAL

LEARN HOW TO...
- draw rectangular prisms and figures made with cubes
- find volumes and surface areas of figures made with cubes

AS YOU...
- use isometric dot paper

SET UP *You will need:* • *Labsheets 1A–1C* • *ruler*

▶ When presenting project ideas, architects and engineers often show drawings of the structures. These drawings give the viewer a sense of how the finished structures will look in three dimensions.

Here are steps you can use to sketch a rectangular prism.

Step 1
Draw a rectangle.

Step 2
Draw a congruent rectangle behind and to the right of the original.

Step 3
Connect the corresponding corners. Use dashed segments for hidden edges.

Step 4
If desired, erase the hidden edges so the prism appears solid.

4. Sample Responses are given.
a.

b. It shows the prism from a different side.

c.

isometric dot paper

4 a. Follow the steps above to sketch your own rectangular prism.

b. Repeat part (a), but place the second rectangle behind and to the left instead of behind and to the right. How is this view of the prism different from the view you drew in part (a)**?**

c. Sketch a prism that is *longer* than your original prism. Then sketch another prism that is *shorter* than your original prism.

▶ You can also use special paper called *isometric dot paper* to help you draw space figures. The prefix *iso-* means "equal" and *metric* means "measure," so *isometric* means "equal measure."

5 Discussion Look at the isometric dot paper shown. Why do you think it was given the name isometric dot paper**?** All segments drawn by connecting two dots next to each other (either above or below or diagonally) are equal in measure.

▶ **Drawing Figures Made with Cubes** Here are steps you can use to draw a cube on isometric dot paper.

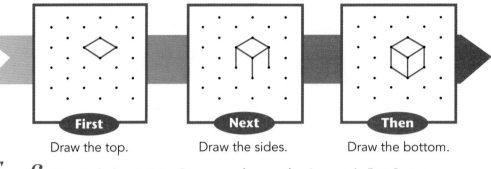

First	Next	Then
Draw the top.	Draw the sides.	Draw the bottom.

6 **Use Labsheet 1A.** Draw a cube on the *Isometric Dot Paper.*
Check students' work.

7 **Use Labsheet 1B.** Follow the directions on the labsheet to make *Isometric Drawings.*   Check students' work.

▶ After architects meet with a client, there are often adjustments to be made to the drawings. An example is shown below.

EXAMPLE

Redraw the figure without the shaded cube.

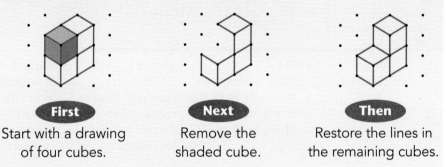

First	Next	Then
Start with a drawing of four cubes.	Remove the shaded cube.	Restore the lines in the remaining cubes.

Use Labsheet 1C for Questions 8 and 9.

8 Follow the directions on the labsheet to redraw each of the *Cube Figures.* You'll find the volume and the surface area, including the base, before and after the change. See above.

9 How did removing one block affect the volume of each of the *Cube Figures?* How did it affect the surface area?
It decreased the volume by 1 cubic unit; The effect varies.

10 ✔ **CHECKPOINT** **Use Labsheet 1A.** Draw a rectangular prism that is *not* a cube. Find its surface area and volume.

HOMEWORK EXERCISES ▶ See Exs. 1–7 on pp. 400–401.

---

8. a. 4 cubic units, 18 square units, 3 cubic units, 14 square units

b. 8 cubic units, 32 square units, 7 cubic units, 30 square units

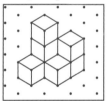

10. Sample Response: Surface area is 16 square units and volume is 4 cubic units.

✔ **QUESTION 10**

…checks that you can draw a rectangular prism and find its surface area and volume.

Exploration 2

Points of View

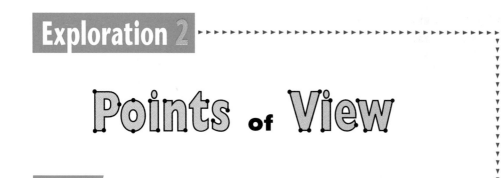

SET UP You will need: • Labsheet 1D • centimeter cubes • ruler

▶ In Exploration 1 you saw how to use isometric dot paper to draw figures made with cubes. This type of drawing can be used to help show how a real building will appear. But, as you'll see, one viewpoint does not always show you the whole building.

11 The picture at the right shows the front and left sides of a building. Use centimeter cubes to build a model of the building. How many cubes did you use? **4**

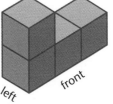

12 Three other views of the building in Question 11 are shown below. What can be seen in these three views that was not visible in the first view? **a fifth cube**

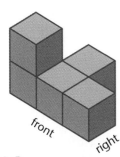
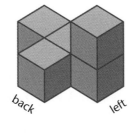
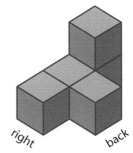

13 Why is it important to show different views of a building?
Sample Response: Parts of buildings can be hidden behind larger or taller parts.

14 ✔ **CHECKPOINT** Use Labsheet 1D.

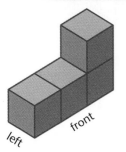

a. Suppose each cube in this building shares at least one face with another cube. Can there be more than four cubes?
See Additional Answers.

b. Labsheet 1D has isometric dots and labeled viewpoints for *Three Views of a Building*. Use them to make isometric drawings of the building. See Additional Answers.

✔ QUESTION 14

...checks that you can draw three-dimensional figures from different viewpoints.

▶ **Flat Views** The views of the buildings you have seen so far give them a three-dimensional appearance. Suppose you were to view the buildings straight on from any side. What you would see would appear flat and could be called a *flat view*.

15 Use centimeter cubes to build the four-cube building shown in the photo. Position it so that the flat view from the front of the building is as shown at the right. **Check students' work.**

front view

16 Flat views of two other sides of the building in the photo are shown. Sketch the right-side view of the building. **right**

left-side view   back view

17 a. How are the front and back views of the building in the photo related? **They are congruent, but they are mirror images of each other.**

b. How are the left- and right-side views related? **They are the same.**

▶ A flat view of the top of the building in the photo above is shown at the right. This top view shows what the building looks like from directly above and also identifies each of the sides.

back
left   right
front

18 a. The building in the photo is not the only cube building that could have the flat view of the top shown above. Explain why.
Sample Response: The top view shows only the cubes in the base. It does not show height.
b. Use flat views to draw the four side views of another building that has the same top view as shown above. **Sample Response:**

left   right   front   back

✔ **QUESTION 19**

…checks that you can draw flat views from different viewpoints.

19 ✔ **CHECKPOINT** The building at the right contains only five cubes. Draw flat views of the building from each of the following viewpoints: front, back, left, right, and top.

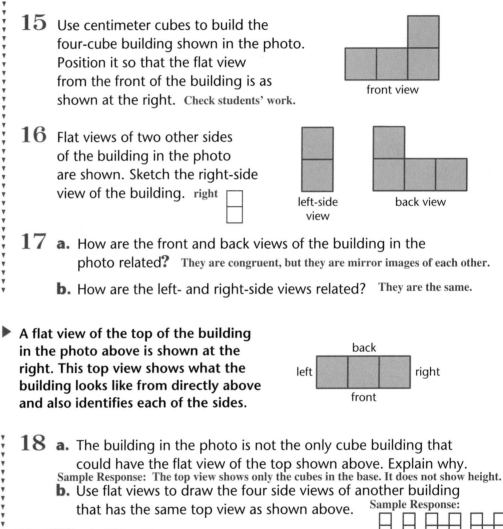

front   back   left   right   front
                                    top

back
left   right

front   right

HOMEWORK EXERCISES ▶ See Exs. 8–15 on pp. 401–402.

Section 1
Key Concepts

Isometric Drawings (pp. 395–397)

Isometric dot paper can be helpful in drawing space figures.

Example Four different views of the same figure are shown on isometric dot paper.

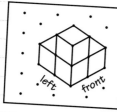 left front

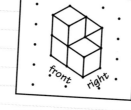 front right

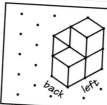 right back

back left

The volume is 4 cubic units. The surface area is 18 square units, including the base.

Flat Views (p. 398)

Flat views of a building can be used to show what the building will look like when viewed directly from the front, back, left side, or right side, or from the top (directly above).

Example These are the flat views of the building modeled above.

Side Views

front view   back view   left-side view   right-side view

Top View

back
left   right
front

Key Concepts Question

20 Use Labsheet 1A. Imagine removing the top cube from the figure above. On the *Isometric Dot Paper*, draw four different views of the new figure. Then draw five different flat views.

front   back   left   right   top

CLOSURE QUESTION

Name one way that isometric drawings and flat view drawings of space figures are alike. Name one way that they are different.

Sample Response: Both are representations of a three-dimensional figure on a two-dimensional surface; isometric drawing show all three dimensions of a space figure and flat view drawings show only two dimensions.

20.

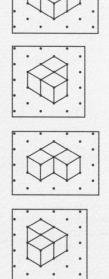

◄◄◄◄◄◄◄◄ ## Practice & Application Exercises

1. Sketch a cube using the steps on page 395 for drawing a rectangular prism.

2. **Use the *Isometric Dot Paper* on Labsheet 1A.**
   See Additional Answers.
   a. Draw a rectangular prism.

   b. Draw a rectangular prism that is twice as long as the first.

   c. Draw a rectangular prism that is three times as wide as the first.

   d. **Writing** Record the number of cubes, the surface area, and the volume of each rectangular prism you drew in parts (a)–(c). What relationships do you notice among these measurements?

3. **Use the *Isometric Dot Paper* on Labsheet 1A.** How many different rectangular prisms can you draw that are made up of 12 cubes?   4 prisms: 1 · 1 · 12; 1 · 2 · 6; 1 · 3 · 4; 2 · 2 · 3

4. Prisms are named for their bases. Steps similar to those on page 395 for drawing a rectangular prism can be used to sketch other prisms.

   a. Sketch a triangle.   **4. a–c.**

   b. Sketch a congruent triangle that is placed behind and to the right of the triangle in part (a).

   c. Connect corresponding vertices to form a triangular prism.

   d. Sketch a prism as in parts (a)–(c) with a trapezoid (instead of a triangle) for a base.

Use Labsheet 1A. On the *Isometric Dot Paper,* draw the figure that results from removing the shaded cube(s). Then give the volume and the surface area of the figure before and after removing the cube(s). Assume there are no gaps on the bottom layer. Also assume that the only hidden cubes are directly beneath the cubes on the top layer.

5.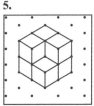

figure before removing cubes: surface area = 24 square units, volume = 8 cubic units; figure after removing cube: surface area = 24 square units, volume = 7 cubic units

6.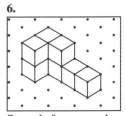

figure before removing cubes: surface area = 36 square units, volume = 12 cubic units; figure after removing cubes: surface area = 30 square units, volume = 8 cubic units

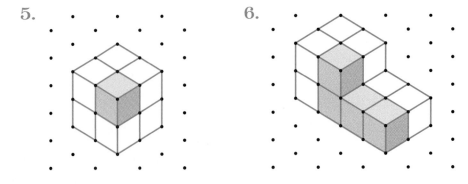

5.   6.

7. Use Labsheet 1A. A client has hired you to build an addition on the office building shown below.

a. The pink face represents the place where the client might like to have the addition attached. On the *Isometric Dot Paper*, redraw the building with the addition in place. (Add only one cube.)

b. **Open-ended** Select another location where you might ask the client to consider adding the additional office space. Redraw the building with the addition in place.

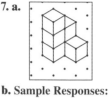

7. a.

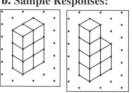

b. Sample Responses:

For Exercises 8–10, tell whether each view shows the *front view*, the *left-side view*, or the *top view* of the canister at the right. (Ignore the design on the canister.)

front

8.
top

9.
front or back

10.
left or right

11. Assume the building at the right contains five cubes. Draw flat views of the building from each of the following viewpoints: front, back, left, right, and top.

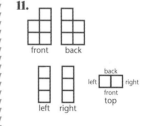

left   front

11.

front   back

back

left   right

front

top

left   right

12. **Use the *Isometric Dot Paper* on Labsheet 1A.** Draw and label front-right, right-back, and back-left views of the building in Exercise 11.

See Additional Answers.

13. **Use the *Isometric Dot Paper* on Labsheet 1A.** Suppose that the view shown in Exercise 11 is for a building containing six cubes. Think about where the hidden cube must be located if it shares at least one face with another cube. Then carry out the steps in Exercises 11 and 12 for the six-cube building. See Additional Answers.

14. There are several possible answers. Check students' work. Sample Response:

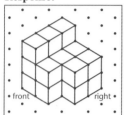
• front   right •

Vi**su**a**l**
THINKING

Exercise 15 checks that you can visualize figures made with cubes.

15. a.

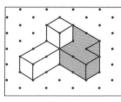

b.

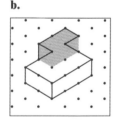

c.

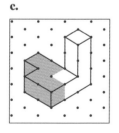

Use Labsheet 1A for Exercise 14.

14. Challenge Five flat views of a figure made with cubes are shown. On *Isometric Dot Paper,* draw a view of the figure from the front-right corner.

Side Views

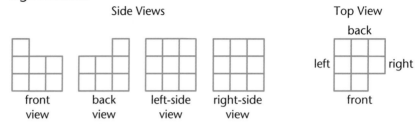

front view   back view   left-side view   right-side view

Top View
back
left   right
front

Reflecting ◀▶ **on the Section**

15. Use Labsheet 1D. A blue space figure and a green space figure were put together to form the building shown below at the right. The two colors help you see how the figures fit together. Use shading to show how the two figures fit together to form each of the *Three Buildings* on the labsheet.

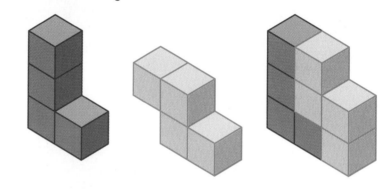

Spiral ◀▶ **Review**

16. Evetta, Luisa, and Yoko are auditioning for a part in a play. The order of their auditions will be determined by a random drawing. What is the probability that Evetta will audition first? that Yoko will *not* audition last? (Module 5, pp. 376–377)

$\frac{1}{3}$, or about 0.33; $\frac{2}{3}$, or about 0.67

Write each product or quotient as a single power. (Module 5, p. 350)

17. $(n^8)(n^5)$ n^{13} **18.** $(4a)(a^5)(2a^{-3})$ $8a^3$ **19.** $(3x^2y)(5xy^3)$ $15x^3y^4$

20. $\frac{a^8}{a^5}$ a^3 **21.** $\frac{20c^{12}}{4c^3}$ $5c^9$ **22.** $\frac{m^7n^2}{m^3n^6}$ $\left(\frac{m}{n}\right)^4$

Construct a triangle with the given side lengths. (Module 4, p. 242)

23. 2 cm, 5 cm, 6 cm    **24.** 5 cm, 12 cm, 13 cm 12 cm \ 13 cm

5 cm

Section 1
Extra Skill Practice

You will need: • *Labsheet 1A* (Exs. 3–5, 8, and 9) • *ruler* (Exs. 3–5 and 7–9)

Follow the steps on page 395 for drawing a rectangular prism.

Sample Responses are given.

1. Sketch a rectangular prism whose height is twice its width.

2. Sketch a rectangular prism whose height is one third its width.

Use the *Isometric Dot Paper* on Labsheet 1A. Draw all the different rectangular prisms that can be made from each number of cubes.

3. three cubes   4. four cubes   5. eight cubes

See Additional Answers.

6. **Writing** Record the number of cubes, the surface area, and the volume of each rectangular prism you drew in Exercise 3. What relationships do you notice among these measurements?

See Additional Answers.

7. Assume the building at the right contains five cubes. Draw flat views of the building from each of the following viewpoints: front, back, left, right, and top.

See below.

8. **Use the *Isometric Dot Paper* on Labsheet 1A.** Draw and label left-front, right-back, and back-left views of the building at the right.

See Additional Answers.

9. **Use the *Isometric Dot Paper* on Labsheet 1A.** Suppose that the view shown in Exercise 7 is for a building containing six cubes. Think about where the hidden cube must be located if it shares at least one face with another cube. Then carry out the steps in Exercises 7 and 8 for the six-cube building.

See Additional Answers.

1. 2.

3.

4.

front   *right*

7.

front   back   left   right   front top   back   left   right

Study Skills ▶ Identifying Weaknesses

When you complete a module or a section of a textbook, it can be helpful to identify anything that you do not fully understand. By writing out a list of questions to discuss with your teacher or other students, you can fill in any gaps in your understanding before moving on.

Describe a topic in this section about which you have questions. Write down your questions and try to obtain answers. Write the answers in your own words to be sure you understand them fully.

Check students' work.

Building BLOCKS

‹‹‹ Setting the Stage

Paul Spooner is a mechanical engineer of sorts. He designs and constructs moving sculptures made from paper and other simple materials. With scissors, glue, paper folding, and craftsmanship, Spooner's two-dimensional patterns can be turned into playful three-dimensional animals that you animate with the turn of a handle.

▶

Over 45 separate pieces were put together to create this anteater sculpture.

Think About It

1 What is the mathematical term for the general shape of the space figure the anteater is standing on in the photograph? **rectangular prism**

2 Describe the general shape of the anthill in the photograph. **pyramid**

3 Describe what you think happens when someone turns the handle on the model shown in the photograph. **Sample Response: the handle rotates the circle that the ant is on, allowing the ant to go into the anthill.**

▶ **In this section, you'll build space figures from two-dimensional patterns.**

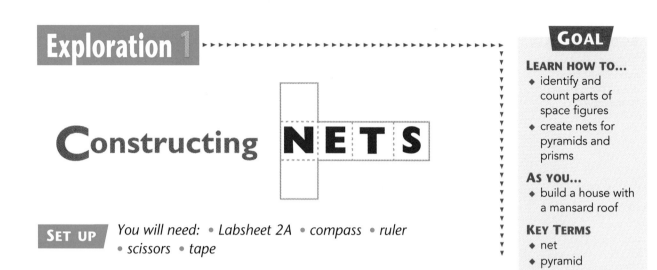

Exploration 1

Constructing **N E T S**

GOAL

LEARN HOW TO...
- identify and count parts of space figures
- create nets for pyramids and prisms

AS YOU...
- build a house with a mansard roof

KEY TERMS
- net
- pyramid
- tetrahedron
- base
- face
- edge
- vertex (plural: vertices)

SET UP | *You will need:* • *Labsheet 2A* • *compass* • *ruler* • *scissors* • *tape*

▶ You can use a compass and the straight edge of a ruler to create two-dimensional patterns for some of the space figures that Paul Spooner uses in his moving sculptures. A two-dimensional pattern that can be folded into a space figure is a **net**.

4 The ant hill in the photograph on page 404 resembles a *pyramid*. Follow the steps below to construct a net to make a simple pyramid. **Check students' work.**

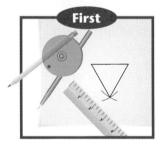
First

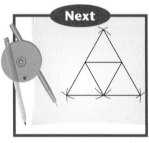
Next

Then

Use a compass and a straightedge to construct any equilateral triangle.

Construct another equilateral triangle on each side of the original triangle.

Cut out the net and fold it along the sides of the original triangle.

FOR◀HELP

with *constructing a triangle*, see **MODULE 4, p. 242**

▶ A **pyramid** is a space figure with one base that can be any polygon. The other faces are triangles that meet at a common vertex. A pyramid with four triangular faces, including the base, is a **tetrahedron**.

5 **a.** How many edges does the tetrahedron you made in Question 4 have? how many vertices? how many faces, including the base? **6 edges; 4 vertices; 4 faces**

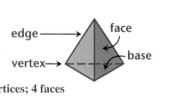
edge → face
vertex → base

b. How are the faces related? How can you tell?
They are all congruent equilateral triangles; they all fit exactly onto each other when the net is folded.

...checks that you
can identify and
count parts of a
space figure.

6 ✔ **CHECKPOINT** How many edges does a cube have?
How many vertices? How many faces, including the bases?
12 edges; 8 vertices; 6 faces;

▶ **Nets for Buildings** Architects sometimes make nets to build
cardboard models of the buildings they design. A model of a building
allows an architect to see what the real building will look like and
make changes before it is actually built.

7 The roof of the house in the sketch below is a modified mansard
roof. This type of roof creates extra space for living quarters in
an attic.

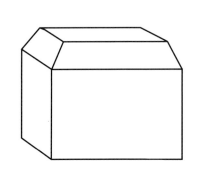

a. What polygons are used to create the modified mansard
roof? Sketch one face of the roof.
rectangles and trapezoids; ⟋▱⟍ or ▭

b. What polygons are used to create the vertical walls of the
building? Sketch one wall. rectangles; ▭

Use the _Net for a House_ on Labsheet 2A for Questions 8–10.

8 Follow the directions on the labsheet to make a model of a
house with a modified mansard roof. Check students' work.

9 How many edges does the model house have? how many
vertices? how many faces, including the top and the bottom?
20 edges; 12 vertices; 10 faces

10. Sample Response:
Remove the trapezoids
and the smallest
rectangle. Replace the
two removed polygons
from the lower right
corner with a rectangle
congruent to the one in
the lower left corner.

10 **Discussion** How could you modify the _Net for a House_ you
used in Question 8 to create a net for a rectangular prism?

✔ **QUESTION 11**

...checks that you
can sketch a net for
a prism.

11 ✔ **CHECKPOINT** Sketch a net for a rectangular prism.
Then find the number of edges, the number of vertices,
and the number of faces, including the bases.

12 edges; 8 vertices; 6 faces; Sample Response:

HOMEWORK EXERCISES ▶ See Exs. 1–6 on pp. 412–413.

Exploration 2

Angles and *Tri'angles*

SET UP Work with a partner. You will need: • plain paper • compass • ruler • scissors • protractor • tape

GOAL

LEARN HOW TO...
- bisect an angle using a compass
- compare triangles using two sides and the included angle

AS YOU...
- construct a net for a pyramid

KEY TERMS
- angle bisector
- included angle

▶ At the right is a net for the anthill in Paul Spooner's paper anteater shown on page 404. You need a protractor to draw this net, but some nets like it can be constructed by bisecting angles.

The steps below show how to bisect an angle using a compass and the straight edge of a ruler.

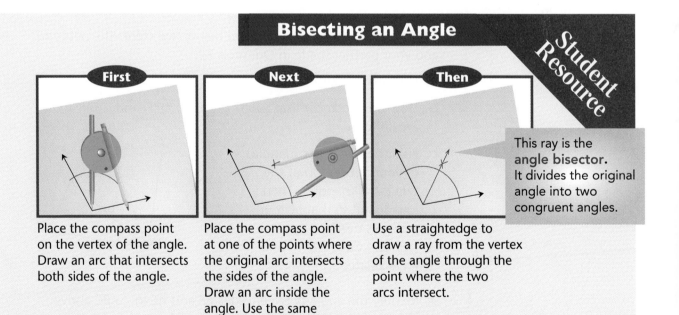

Bisecting an Angle

Student Resource

First

Place the compass point on the vertex of the angle. Draw an arc that intersects both sides of the angle.

Next

Place the compass point at one of the points where the original arc intersects the sides of the angle. Draw an arc inside the angle. Use the same compass setting to draw an arc from the other inter-section point as shown.

Then

Use a straightedge to draw a ray from the vertex of the angle through the point where the two arcs intersect.

This ray is the **angle bisector.** It divides the original angle into two congruent angles.

12 Use a compass and a ruler. Follow the instructions below with the diagrams to help you and your partner draw nets for the triangular faces of two simple pyramids.
Check students' work.

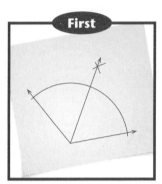

First

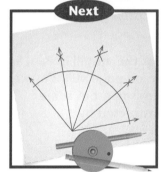

Next

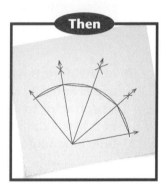

Then

Draw an obtuse angle. Then follow the steps on page 407 to bisect the angle, using a large radius for the initial arc.

Bisect each of the two new angles that you just formed. You do not have to draw the first arc again, just use the one already drawn.

Use a straightedge to connect the points where the arc intersects each ray. Cut out the net formed by the four triangles.

13. a. They are radii of the same circle.
b. They were constructed by bisecting two congruent angles.
c. They are congruent triangles.

13 **Discussion** Suppose the diagram below represents the nets you and your partner made in Question 12.

a. How do you know that $\overline{AB}$, $\overline{AC}$, $\overline{AD}$, $\overline{AE}$, and $\overline{AF}$ are congruent?

b. How do you know that $\angle BAC$, $\angle CAD$, $\angle DAE$, and $\angle EAF$ are congruent?

c. Fold the two outer triangles of your net on top of the two inner triangles. Then fold again, so that all four triangles overlap. How are $\triangle BAC$, $\triangle CAD$, $\triangle DAE$, and $\triangle EAF$ related?

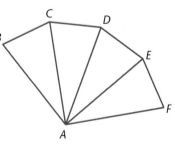

14 a. Identify the angle between sides $\overline{BA}$ and $\overline{AC}$ in $\triangle ABC$ above. This angle is referred to as the **included angle** between sides $\overline{BA}$ and $\overline{AC}$. $\angle BAC$

b. Identify the included angle between sides $\overline{AC}$ and $\overline{CB}$. $\angle ACB$

15 Use a ruler and a protractor to complete parts (a)–(e). You and your partner should each make a triangle.

   a. Draw a triangle and label the vertices *A*, *B*, and *C*.

   b. Draw a segment that is congruent to $\overline{AB}$. Label the endpoints of the new segment *P* and *Q*.

   c. Draw an angle with the same measure as ∠*ABC* that has *Q* as its vertex and $\overrightarrow{QP}$ as a side.

   d. On the side of ∠*Q* that does not contain point *P*, draw a segment with the same length as $\overline{BC}$ that has one endpoint at *Q*. Label the other endpoint *R*.

   e. Connect points *P* and *R* to form another triangle.

   f. Discussion How are △*ABC* and △*PQR* related? How do you know? **They are congruent; I measured the sides and angles.**

16 Try This as a Class Suppose two sides and the included angle of one triangle are congruent to two sides and the included angle of another triangle. Based on the results of Questions 13 and 15, what do you think is the relationship between the two triangles?

They are congruent.

17 ✔ **CHECKPOINT** How are △*ABC* and △*DEF* related? Explain your reasoning. △*ABC* ≅ △*DEF*; $\overline{AB} \cong \overline{DE}$, $\overline{BC} \cong \overline{EF}$, and the included angles ∠*ABC* and ∠*DEF* are congruent.

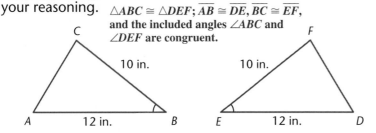

18 **a.** The net you made in Question 12 is made up of four congruent triangles. Tape two edges of the net together to form the sides of a pyramid. **Check students' work.**

   b. What shape needs to be added to the net to form the base of the pyramid? **a square**

   c. Make a sketch to show how you could change the net to include a base.

   d. Discussion Compare the net you sketched in part (c) with the net that your partner sketched. **Answers will vary.**

HOMEWORK EXERCISES ▶ See Exs. 7–16 on pp. 413–414.

See Exs. 7–16 on pp. 413–414.

15. a–e. Sample Response:

✔ **QUESTION 17**

…checks that you can compare triangles based on two sides and the included angle.

18. c. Sample Response:

You can use geometric drawing software to draw the triangles for Question 15 on page 409. You can also use the software to measure the sides and the angles so you can compare the triangles.

Step 1 Draw a triangle with vertices A, B, and C. Draw a segment that is congruent to AB. Label the endpoints of the new segment P and Q.

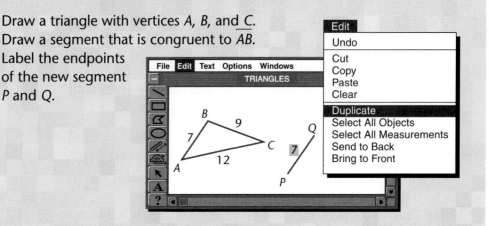

Step 2 Draw an angle with the same measure as ∠ABC that has Q as its vertex and $\overrightarrow{QP}$ as a side. On the side of ∠Q that does not contain point P, draw a segment with the same length as BC that has one endpoint at Q. Label the other endpoint R.

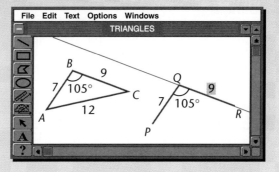

Step 3 Connect points P and R to form another triangle. Find and compare the lengths of the sides and the measures of the angles of △PQR with those of △ABC.

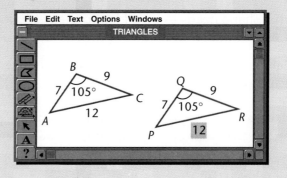

Nets for Pyramids and Prisms (pp. 405–406)

A pyramid is a space figure with one polygon-shaped base. The other faces are triangles that meet at a common vertex. Pyramids and other space figures can be built from two-dimensional nets.

pyramid

net

Examples This pyramid is a tetrahedron because all the faces, including the base, are triangles. Pairs of faces meet in segments called edges. A tetrahedron has 4 faces, 6 edges, and 4 vertices.

tetrahedron
   base
   face
   edge
   vertex

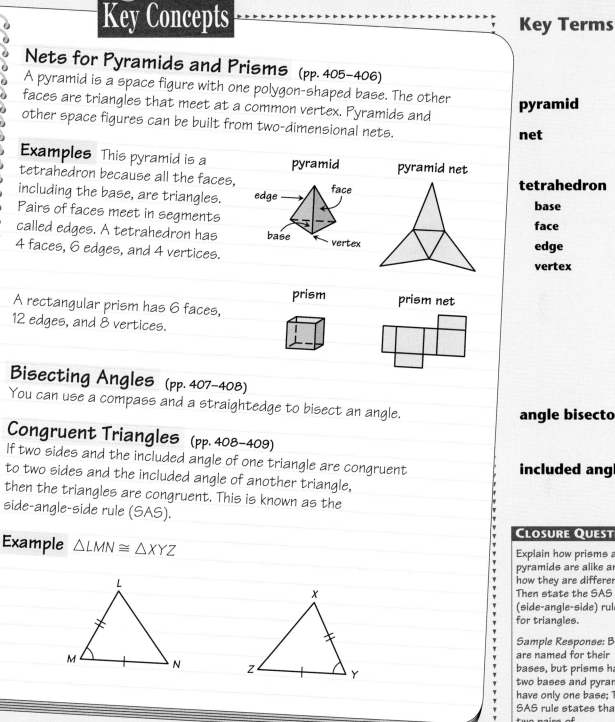

pyramid

edge → ← face

base → ← vertex

pyramid net

A rectangular prism has 6 faces, 12 edges, and 8 vertices.

prism

prism net

Bisecting Angles (pp. 407–408)

You can use a compass and a straightedge to bisect an angle.

angle bisector

Congruent Triangles (pp. 408–409)

If two sides and the included angle of one triangle are congruent to two sides and the included angle of another triangle, then the triangles are congruent. This is known as the side-angle-side rule (SAS).

included angle

Example △LMN ≅ △XYZ

L

M   N

X

Z   Y

CLOSURE QUESTION

Explain how prisms and pyramids are alike and how they are different. Then state the SAS (side-angle-side) rule for triangles.

Sample Response: Both are named for their bases, but prisms have two bases and pyramids have only one base; The SAS rule states that if two pairs of corresponding sides and the included angles of two triangles are congruent, then the triangles are congruent.

19 Key Concepts Question Sketch a net for a square pyramid. Draw the base in the center as in the pyramid net above. How many edges does the square pyramid have? how many vertices? how many faces, including the base? 8 edges; 5 vertices; 5 faces

2. Sample Response:

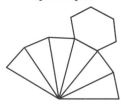

7 faces, 15 edges, 10 vertices

3. Sample Response:

7 faces, 12 edges, 7 vertices

1. A net for a hexagonal prism is shown at the right. How many faces, edges, and vertices will the prism have?
8 faces, 18 edges, and 12 vertices

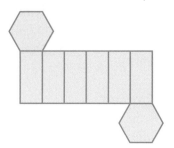

2. **Open-ended** Sketch a net for a pentagonal prism. How many faces, edges, and vertices will the prism have?

3. **Open-ended** Sketch a net for a hexagonal pyramid. How many faces, edges, and vertices will the pyramid have?

4. **Home Involvement** Find a real product whose package is a prism. Estimate the area of each face and the total area of the package. Carefully unfold the package and sketch its pattern.
Answers will vary. Check students' work.

5. The base of a building does not have to be a rectangle. For example, a hexagon can form the base of a tower, a carousel, a ticket office, or a circus tent.

a. Follow the steps below to construct a regular hexagon.

Check students' work.

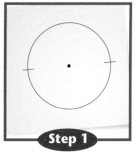

Step 1

Draw a circle with a compass. Leave the compass set to the circle's radius. Use a straightedge to mark the endpoints of a diameter.

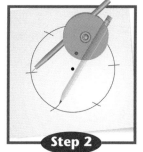

Step 2

Set the compass point on one endpoint of the diameter and mark two arcs that intersect the circle. Do the same for the other endpoint.

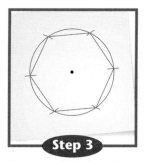

Step 3

Connect the six points to form a regular hexagon.

b. In Step 3, what other polygon can you form by connecting the six points *and* drawing a diameter? **a trapezoid**

c. What other polygon can you form by connecting every other point you drew on the circle in Step 2? **a triangle**

6. a. The base of the tent pictured below is a regular hexagon. What shapes are the other faces of the tent?

triangles and rectangles

b. Make a rough sketch of a net for the tent, including the base.

c. How many faces, edges, and vertices does the tent have?

13 faces, 24 edges, 13 vertices

d. **Challenge** Use a compass and the straight edge of a ruler to create a net for the tent. Cut it out and check that your design works. If it does not, tell what needs to be changed.

Check students' work.

7. Draw an acute angle. Use your compass and the straight edge of a ruler to bisect the angle. Do not erase your compass marks.

For Exercises 8–11, choose the letter of the space figure that matches each net.

A. triangular pyramid   B. triangular prism   C. octagonal pyramid   D. octagonal prism

8. D

9. B

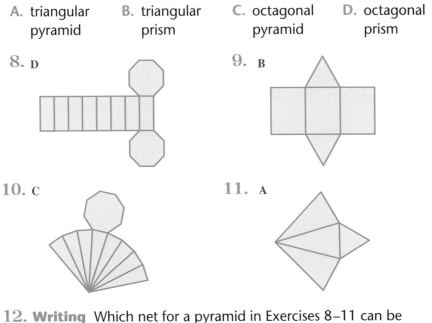

10. C

11. A

12. **Writing** Which net for a pyramid in Exercises 8–11 can be constructed using angle bisectors as on page 408? Which net for a pyramid cannot be constructed that way? Explain.

octagonal pyramid; Sample Response: An even number of congruent angles is required to construct nets using the angle bisecting method.

6. b.

7. Sample Response:

13. congruent; Two sides and the included angle of △ABC are congruent to two sides and the included angle of △DEF.

Tell whether the triangles in each pair are congruent. Explain.

13. △ABC, △DEF

A
2 cm
C 3 cm B

D
2 cm
E 3 cm F

14. △PQS, △RSQ

P 4 m Q
8 m   8 m
S 4 m R

congruent; All corresponding sides are congruent.

15. △ABC, △WXY

A 8 ft B
10 ft
C
Y
10 ft
X 8 ft W

not congruent; The corresponding sides are not congruent.

Oral Report

Exercise 16 checks that you can use constructions to draw nets.

Reflecting▶on the Section

Be prepared to report on the following topic in class.

16. Describe how you can draw a right angle by constructing an angle bisector. Then describe how to use this construction to draw a net for a cube using a compass and a straightedge.

16. Sample Response: Draw and bisect a segment to construct a right angle with vertex A. Use the compass to construct congruent segments $\overline{AB}$ and $\overline{AD}$ on the side of the right angle. With the same compass setting and centers A and B, draw intersecting arcs. Label the intersection C. Draw $\overline{BC}$ and $\overline{DC}$ to complete square ABCD. Repeat to construct 6 squares in this pattern:

17.

Spiral◀▶Review

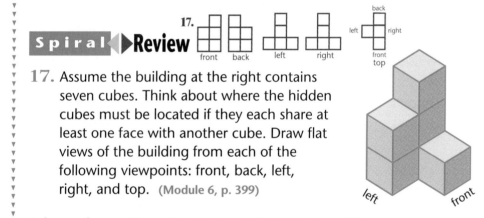

17. Assume the building at the right contains seven cubes. Think about where the hidden cubes must be located if they each share at least one face with another cube. Draw flat views of the building from each of the following viewpoints: front, back, left, right, and top. **(Module 6, p. 399)**

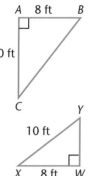

Solve each equation. **(Module 3, p. 218; Module 4, p. 275)**

18. $-2.4x = 72$ –30 **19.** $-0.9y + 1.8 = 0.9$ 1 **20.** $32 = -2.5z - 18$ –20

21. $-2.7 = 5.4m$ –0.5 **22.** $1.5n - 3.5 = -0.5$ 2 **23.** $4 + 9.6k = 0.8$ $-0.\overline{3}$

24. $\frac{3}{5}a = 27$ 45 **25.** $\frac{2}{3}b - 5 = 5$ 15 **26.** $\frac{4}{3}c + 9 = 49$ 30

For each triangle, find the unknown side length. **(Module 4, p. 297)**

27.

13 m
x
5 m
12 m

28.

6 ft
10 ft
y
8 ft

Euler and Space Figures

In the mid 1700s, a Swiss mathematician named Leonhard Euler observed a relationship among the numbers of faces, edges, and vertices of a space figure whose faces are polygons. In Exercises 29–32, you'll explore this relationship.

29. Copy and complete the chart below for at least five space figures. You can use some of the figures you constructed in this section or use objects with faces that are polygons. See chart.

Description or sketch of space figure	Number of faces	Number of vertices	Number of edges
peaked-roof house 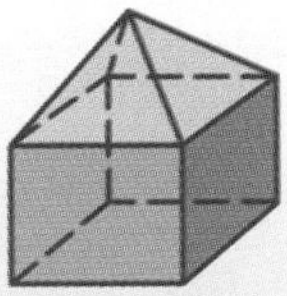	? 9	? 9	? 16
tetrahedron 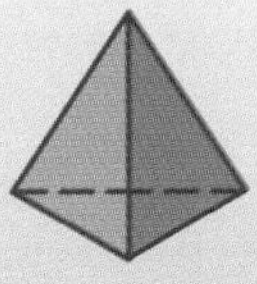	? 4	? 4	? 6
? cube	? 6	? 8	? 12
square ? pyramid	? 5	? 5	? 8
hexagonal ? prism	? 8	? 12	? 18

30. Look for a relationship among the number of faces, edges, and vertices.

  a. If you only know the number of faces and vertices, how can you determine the number of edges?
  Add the number of faces and vertices, then subtract 2 from the sum.

  b. Write an equation that shows the relationship among the number of faces, vertices, and edges. $F + V - 2 = E$ where F = the number of faces, V = the number of vertices, and E = the number of edges.

31. If a space figure has 7 faces and 10 vertices, how many edges will it have? 15 edges

32. An *icosahedron* has 20 faces (all triangles) joined by 30 edges. How many vertices does it have? 12 vertices

Creating a Model Town

When architects and urban planners design housing developments and business districts, they draw plans and build models to show people how the buildings will look. For your module project, you and your classmates will draw plans for a model town and then build it.

SET UP

Work as a class.

Sketching Nets One way to create a model for a building is to make a net that can be folded into the shape of the building.

1–3. Answers will vary. Check students' work.

1 Work as a class.

    a. Brainstorm ideas for your town. Will you make houses, offices, stores, or some combination? How many styles of buildings will there be? You may want to look at books or magazines to help generate ideas.

    b. Based on your ideas from part (a), decide which buildings will be included in your town and who will design and make each one. You will each make one building.

2 Sketch a view of your building that gives it a three-dimensional look. Then sketch a net for it. Label your sketches with the dimensions that the actual building would have. (*Hint:* Begin with dimensions of rooms or buildings you are familiar with.)

3 What polygons are used to create the floor, the walls, and the roof of your building?

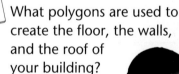

You will need: • *compass, ruler* (Exs. 3–4) • *scissors, tape* (Ex. 3)

1. Sketch a net for an octagonal prism. How many faces, edges, and vertices will the prism have?

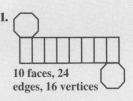

1.

10 faces, 24 edges, 16 vertices

2. Sketch a net for a pentagonal pyramid. How many faces, edges, and vertices will the pyramid have?

2.

6 faces, 10 edges, 6 vertices

3. a. Make a rough sketch of a net for a hexagonal pyramid. Then use a compass and a ruler's straight edge to create the net. (*Hint:* Follow Steps 1–3 on page 412 to draw the base.)

b. Build the pyramid. If your net does not work, explain how to fix it.   **Check students' work.**

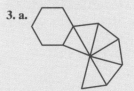

3. a.

4. Draw an obtuse angle. Use your compass and a ruler's straight edge to bisect the angle. Do not erase your compass marks.

Tell whether the triangles in each pair are congruent. Explain.

4. Sample Response:

5. △PQR, △NML

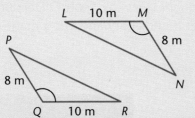

congruent; Two sides and the included angle of △PQR are congruent to two sides and the included angle of △NML.

6. △ABD, △CBD

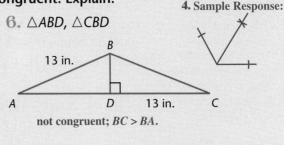

not congruent; BC > BA.

Standardized Testing ◀▶ Performance Task

Two identical pyramids can be put together with the bases matching up to form a new space figure. Copy and complete the table below. Explain the reasoning you used to complete the table.

Sample Response: The number of faces is twice the number of sides on the base, the number of edges is 3 times the number of sides on the base, and the number of vertices is 2 more than the number of sides on the base.

Number of sides on the base of each pyramid	Number of faces on the new space figure	Number of edges on the new space figure	Number of vertices on the new space figure
3	? 6	? 9	? 5
4	? 8	? 12	? 6
5	? 10	? 15	? 7
100	? 200	? 300	? 102

Section ③ Surface Area and Volume

IN THIS SECTION

EXPLORATION 1
◆ Surface Areas of Prisms and Pyramids

EXPLORATION 2
◆ Volumes of Prisms, Pyramids, and Cones

Where You Live

WARM-UP EXERCISES

Use the net given below.

1. What kind of space figures does the net represent?
   a hexagonal prism

2. How many faces does the prism have? **8**

3. How many edges does the prism have? **18**

4. How many vertices does the prism have? **12**

5. Is this a right prism? How can you tell?
   Yes; the sides are rectangles.

---Setting the Stage

People around the world build homes to keep them safe and comfortable in their environments. The design of the buildings and the materials used for construction depend on local conditions. In the passage below from *Black Star, Bright Dawn* by Scott O'Dell, Bright Dawn describes how she and her friends Katy and Oteg made an igloo.

Black Star, Bright Dawn
by Scott O'Dell

I had helped to make an igloo at school, so I showed her how to cut the blocks. I handed them to Oteg and he put them side by side in a circle. When he had one row, he trimmed off the top edges so that each of the blocks slanted in.

We worked until there was a circle three rows high. It was not yet an igloo, but it helped to shield us from the bitter wind. . . .

At dawn we began again on the igloo. One by one Oteg added rows of blocks until they met above the top. He got down on his knees, cut a round hole in the wall, and crawled out. The cracks between the blocks were filled with soft snow. The opening at the top of the dome was closed with a piece of clear ice.

Think About It ▸

1. a–b. Sample Responses are given.

1 **a.** Igloos have a dome shape that encloses a large volume for a given surface area. What does *volume* mean? What does *surface area* mean? What do they tell you about a structure?

b. Why would it be desirable to have a large volume compared to the surface area? **to provide maximum space with minimum use and cost of materials, or minimum exposure to the outside**

2 How might the shape of an igloo be helpful in a windy climate? **They provide maximum living space with minimal area exposed to the elements.**

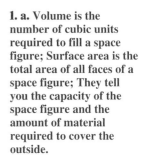

1. a. Volume is the number of cubic units required to fill a space figure; Surface area is the total area of all faces of a space figure; They tell you the capacity of the space figure and the amount of material required to cover the outside.

Exploration 1 ▸

SURFACE AREAS *of* PRISMS *and* PYRAMIDS

SET UP *You will need:* • *Labsheet 3A* • *metric ruler*

Long ago, people did not always have a choice of building materials. In the Southwest, *adobe houses* were built from baked mud bricks because mud was usually available. Rooms of an adobe house were built roughly in the shape of a rectangular prism.

GOAL

LEARN HOW TO...
◆ find surface areas of prisms and pyramids

AS YOU...
◆ explore the shape of an Adobe house

KEY TERM
◆ slant height

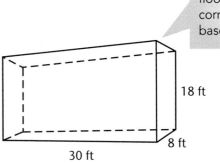

The roof and floor of the house correspond to the bases of the prism.

18 ft

30 ft

8 ft

3 **a.** Sketch a net for the rectangular prism shown above. Use the dimensions shown to label the length of each edge of the net.

b. The surface area of the prism is the total area of all six faces, including the bases. Find the area of each face of the prism. Then find the surface area of the prism. **1848 ft²**

3. a. Sample Response:

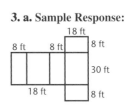

▶ You can find the surface area (*S.A.*) of any prism by adding the areas of all the faces.

EXAMPLE

To find the surface area of the trapezoidal prism shown, you need to use the formula $A = \frac{1}{2}(b_1 + b_2)h$ for the area *A* of a trapezoid with height *h* and base lengths b_1 and b_2.

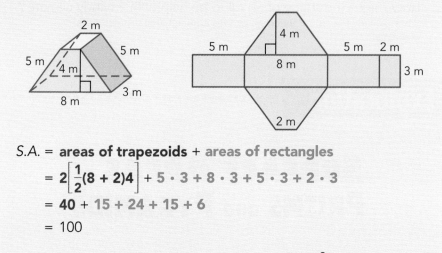

S.A. = **areas of trapezoids** + areas of rectangles

$$= 2\left[\frac{1}{2}(8 + 2)4\right] + 5 \cdot 3 + 8 \cdot 3 + 5 \cdot 3 + 2 \cdot 3$$

$$= 40 + 15 + 24 + 15 + 6$$

$$= 100$$

The surface area of the trapezoidal prism is 100 m².

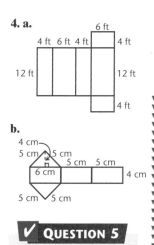

4. a.

b.

4 Sketch a net for each prism. Label the length of each edge.

a.

6 ft
4 ft
12 ft

b.

5 cm   6 cm
4 cm   5 cm
4 cm

✔ **QUESTION 5**

…checks that you can find the surface area of a prism.

5 ✔ **CHECKPOINT** Find the surface area of each prism in Question 4.

a: 288 ft²; b: 88 cm²

▶ **Surface Area of a Pyramid** You can use a method similar to the one in the Example to find the surface area of a pyramid.

6 a. Use Labsheet 3A. Cut out the *Square Pyramid Net* and fold it to make a pyramid with a square base. Check students' work.

b. Use a ruler to help you find the surface area of the pyramid. 96 cm²

c. Measure the height of the pyramid. 4 cm

d. Did you need the height of the pyramid to find its surface area? What information did you need? No; The dimensions of the faces (the length and width of the base and the base and height of each triangle.)

▶ The pyramid in Question 6 is a *regular pyramid,* because the base is a regular polygon and its other faces are congruent isosceles triangles. The **slant height** of a regular pyramid is the height of a triangular face.

7 **a.** What is the slant height of your pyramid from Question 6? 5 cm

b. What is the length of an edge of the base of the pyramid? 6 cm

c. Discussion Explain how to use your answers to parts (a) and (b) to find the height of the pyramid. Then find the height.

d. How does the height you calculated in part (c) compare with your answer in Question 6(c)? It is the same.

7. c. The slant height is the length of the hypotenuse of a right triangle. The length of one leg is half the length of the base of the pyramid and the length of the other is h, the height of the pyramid. By the Pythagorean theorem, $h^2 + 3^2 = 5^2$; 4 cm

▶ The surface area of a regular pyramid is found using its slant height.

EXAMPLE

Find the surface area of the regular pyramid.

SAMPLE RESPONSE

Use the Pythagorean theorem to find the slant height c.

$$5^2 + 12^2 = c^2$$

$$169 = c^2$$

$$13 = c$$

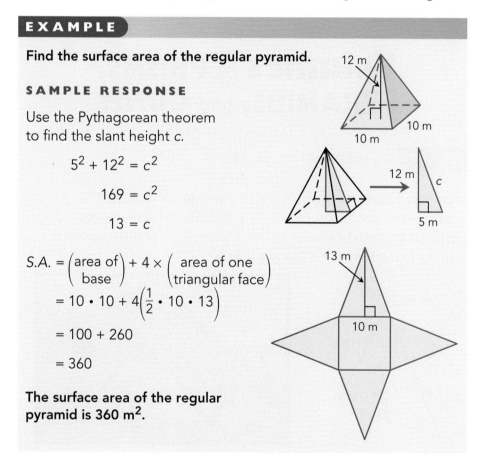

$$S.A. = \left(\begin{array}{c}\text{area of}\\\text{base}\end{array}\right) + 4 \times \left(\begin{array}{c}\text{area of one}\\\text{triangular face}\end{array}\right)$$

$$= 10 \cdot 10 + 4\left(\frac{1}{2} \cdot 10 \cdot 13\right)$$

$$= 100 + 260$$

$$= 360$$

The surface area of the regular pyramid is 360 m².

8 Why is it necessary to find the slant height in the Example above in order to calculate the surface area of the pyramid?
Sample Response: It is the height of each triangular face.

9 In the Example, a right triangle is used to find the slant height of the pyramid. The length of one leg of this triangle is the height of the pyramid. Explain why the length of the other leg is 5 m.
It is half the length of the base of the pyramid.

10 ✔ **CHECKPOINT** Find the surface area of each regular pyramid.

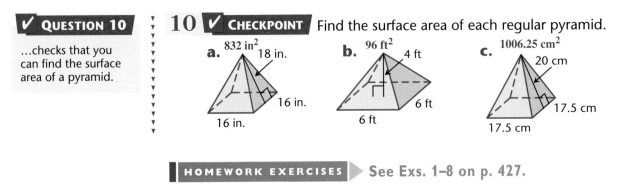

a. 832 in² 18 in. 16 in. 16 in.

b. 96 ft² 4 ft 6 ft 6 ft

c. 1006.25 cm² 20 cm 17.5 cm 17.5 cm

HOMEWORK EXERCISES ▶ See Exs. 1–8 on p. 427.

GOAL

LEARN HOW TO...
◆ find volumes of prisms, pyramids, and cones

AS YOU...
◆ look at models of block pyramids and prisms

KEY TERM
◆ cone

Exploration 2

Volumes *of* PRISMS, PYRAMIDS, *and* CONES

SET UP *You will need Labsheet 3B.*

Winter *mat houses* were once used by people living in the Plateau region of the northwestern United States. These homes were usually occupied from mid-October to mid-March. A mat house was built roughly in the shape of a triangular prism.

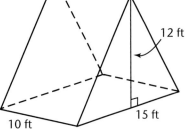

12 ft
10 ft
15 ft

11 In Module 1 you learned how to use the formula

Volume = area of base × height, or *V* = *Bh*

to find the volume of a cylinder or a rectangular prism. This formula can also be used to find volumes of prisms with other bases. How can you use this formula to find the volume of the triangular prism above? Find the area of the triangular base using $A = \frac{1}{2}bh$. Then multiply by the height of the prism.

▶ **Volume of a Pyramid** The Great Pyramid of Giza is made from blocks of stone. The sides are jagged, but they look smooth when viewed from afar, as if the block pyramid had straight edges and flat faces. Now you'll look at block pyramids and block prisms to discover the relationship between the volume of a pyramid and the volume of a prism with the same base and height.

Use Labsheet 3B for Questions 12–14.

12 Follow the directions on the labsheet to complete the *Table of Volumes*.
See Additional Answers.

13 Look at the volume ratio column of the table. What patterns do you notice in the values?
As the height increases, the ratio decreases.

14 **Discussion** If the last column of the table were continued, the ratio for the 50th entry would be 0.343 and the 100th entry would be 0.338. What "nice" fraction do the ratios appear to be approaching? $\frac{1}{3}$

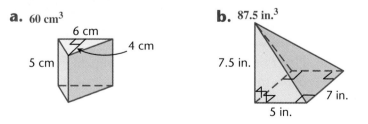

Table of Volumes (Use with Questions 12–14 on page 423.)

MODULE 6

Name

Date

LABSHEET 3B

Directions
• Find the height, the area of the base, and the volume of each block prism in the table.
• The block pyramids have the same heights and bases as the corresponding prisms. Complete the block pyramid portion of the table.
• For each row, find the ratio of the volume of the block pyramid to the volume of the prism. In the last column, write each answer in decimal form and round to the nearest thousandth.

Block Prisms					Block Pyramids			
	Height h	Area of base B	Volume of prism $V = B \cdot h$		Height h	Area of base B	Volume of block pyramid	Volume Ratio: $\frac{\text{Volume of block pyramid}}{\text{Volume of prism}}$
	1	1	1		1	1	1	$1 \div 1 = 1.000$
	2	4	8		2	4	5	$5 \div 8 = 0.625$
	6							
	7							
	8							
	9							
	10							

15 **Try This as a Class** Use your answer to Question 14.

a. The volume of a prism is about how many times the volume of a pyramid that has the same base and height? about 3 times

b. Using *V* for the volume, *B* for the area of the base, and *h* for the height, write a formula for the volume of a pyramid. $V = \frac{1}{3}Bh$

c. Use your formula from part (b) to find the volume of a pyramid that has the same base and height as the triangular prism on page 422. 300 ft³ (Be sure students use the triangular base of the prism as the base of the pyramid.)

16 ✔ **CHECKPOINT** Find the volume of each space figure. Round decimal answers to the nearest tenth.

a. 60 cm³

6 cm
4 cm
5 cm

b. 87.5 in.³

7.5 in.
7 in.
5 in.

✔ **QUESTION 16**

...checks that you can find volumes of prisms and pyramids.

▶ **Volume of a Cone** The relationship between the volume of a *cone* and the volume of a cylinder with the same base and height is the same as the relationship between the volume of a pyramid and the volume of a prism with the same base and height.

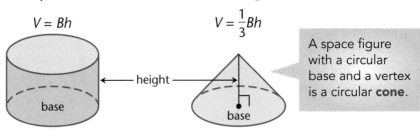

$V = Bh$ $V = \frac{1}{3}Bh$

A space figure with a circular base and a vertex is a circular **cone**.

▶ **All the cones in this book have circular bases. You can refer to them as cones rather than as *circular cones*.**

For answers given throughout, 3.14 is used. Answers may vary slightly if the π key is used.

17 Try This as a Class

a. How would you find the area of the base of a cone?
Square its radius and multiply by π.

b. Write a formula for the volume of a cone in terms of the radius of the base *r* and the height *h*. $V = \frac{1}{3}\pi r^2 \cdot h$

c. The radius of the base of a cone is 5 ft, and the height of the cone is 10 ft. Use the formula you wrote in part (b) to find the volume of the cone. Round your answer to the nearest tenth. 261.7 ft³

✔ QUESTION 18

...checks that you can find the volume of a cone.

18 ✔ CHECKPOINT The shape of tepees used by Native American peoples on the Great Plains resembles a cone. A typical tepee might have stood 18 ft high and had a diameter of 15 ft at its base. Estimate the volume of such a tepee.
about 1059.75 ft³

▶ **Most buildings are made up of a variety of space figures. The shape below is an alternate representation of a mat house. It is a triangular prism with half of a cone at either end.**

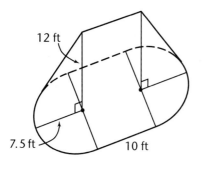

12 ft

7.5 ft   10 ft

19 Discussion Describe how you would find the volume of a mat house shaped like the figure above. Then find the volume. Round your answer to the nearest tenth. **Sample Response:**
Find the sum of the volume of the cone (since two halves make a whole) and the volume of the triangular prism; 1606.5 ft³

HOMEWORK EXERCISES ▶ See Exs. 9–21 on pp. 428–429.

Surface Areas of Prisms and Pyramids (pp. 419–422)

The surface area of a pyramid or a prism is the sum of the areas of the faces of the figure, including the base or bases. You can use a net to help you find the surface area.

Example

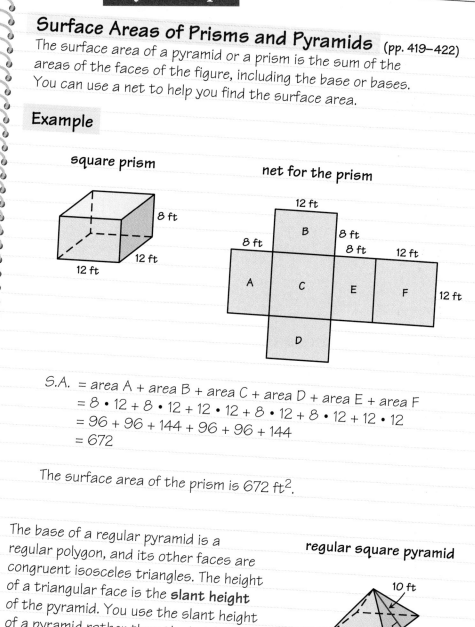

square prism

net for the prism

S.A. = area A + area B + area C + area D + area E + area F

= 8 • 12 + 8 • 12 + 12 • 12 + 8 • 12 + 8 • 12 + 12 • 12

= 96 + 96 + 144 + 96 + 96 + 144

= 672

The surface area of the prism is 672 ft².

The base of a regular pyramid is a regular polygon, and its other faces are congruent isosceles triangles. The height of a triangular face is the **slant height** of the pyramid. You use the slant height of a pyramid rather than the height of the pyramid to find its surface area.

regular square pyramid

slant height

20 Key Concepts Question Find the surface area of the pyramid above. If you stack the pyramid directly on top of the prism above, what will be the surface area of the new figure? Explain.

Continued on next page ▾

20. 384 ft²; 768 ft²; The resulting figure has one 12 × 12 square face, four 12 × 8 rectangular faces, and four triangular faces with base 12 and height 10.

Key Terms

Volumes of Prisms (p. 422)

You can use the formula Volume = area of base × height, or $V = Bh$, to find the volume of any prism. Many buildings consist of two or more space figures. To find the volume, you add the volumes of the parts.

Example

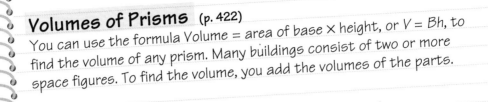

Volume of rectangular prism
$$V = Bh = (12 \cdot 25)18 = 5400$$

Volume of triangular prism
$$V = Bh = \left(\frac{1}{2} \cdot 12 \cdot 8\right)25 = 1200$$

The total volume is 6600 m³.

cone

Volumes of Pyramids and Cones (pp. 423–424)

The volume of a pyramid is one-third the volume of a prism with the same base and height. The volume of a cone is one-third the volume of a cylinder with the same base and height.

The formula Volume = $\frac{1}{3}$ × area of base × height, or $V = \frac{1}{3}Bh$, can be used to find the volume of a pyramid or a cone.

Example

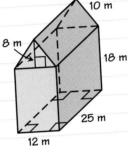

$$V = \frac{1}{3}Bh$$
$$= \frac{1}{3} \cdot \pi r^2 \cdot h$$
$$\approx \frac{1}{3} \cdot (3.14) \cdot 3^2 \cdot 5$$
$$\approx 47.1$$

The volume of the cone is about 47.1 m³.

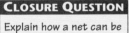

CLOSURE QUESTION

Explain how a net can be used to find the surface area of a prism or a pyramid. Then explain the relationship between the volume of a cone and the volume of a cylinder.

Sample Response: Draw the faces and the base(s) of the prism or pyramid, find the area of each face and the base(s), then add the areas to find the total surface area. The volume of a cone is $\frac{1}{3}$ the volume of a cylinder with the same base and height.

21 Key Concepts Question Find the volume of the prism and the volume of the pyramid on page 425. If you stack the pyramid directly on top of the prism, will there be a change in the total volume? Explain. prism: 1152 ft³, pyramid: 384 ft³, combined: 1536 ft³; No; The volume of a figure that consists of two or more space figures is the sum of their volumes.

Section 3
Practice & Application Exercises

YOU WILL NEED

For Exs. 30–31:
◆ Labsheets 3C and 3D
◆ scissors
◆ paper clip

Find the surface area of each rectangular or triangular prism. Round decimal answers to the nearest tenth.

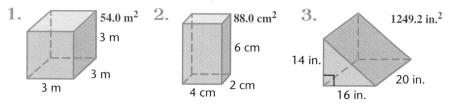

1. 54.0 m² 3 m 3 m 3 m

2. 88.0 cm² 6 cm 4 cm 2 cm

3. 1249.2 in.² 14 in. 20 in. 16 in.

Find the surface area of each regular pyramid. Round decimal answers to the nearest tenth.

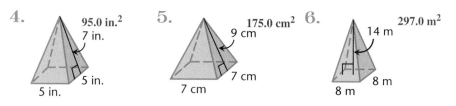

4. 95.0 in.² 7 in. 5 in. 5 in.

5. 175.0 cm² 9 cm 7 cm 7 cm

6. 297.0 m² 14 m 8 m 8 m

7. **Challenge** Many products are packaged in boxes that are the shape of a rectangular prism. In some cases, more unusual shapes are used. A net for a box designed to hold a desk lamp is shown.
   See Additional Answers.
   a. Find the surface area of the box.

   b. Sketch a view of the box that looks three-dimensional.

   c. Find the volume of the box.

8. The figure below represents a Navajo *hogan* like the one shown in the photograph. The base is a square and the edges that form the peak of the roof are each 8 ft long.

   a. What two space figures combine to form the figure shown?
   a rectangular prism and a square pyramid
   b. Sketch a net of the figure. Label the edges with their lengths.
   See above.
   c. Find the surface area of the figure to the nearest tenth.
   about 668.5 ft²

8. b.

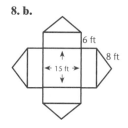
6 ft 8 ft 15 ft

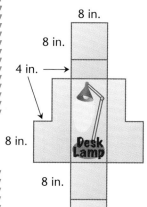
8 in. 8 in. 4 in. 8 in. Desk Lamp 8 in.

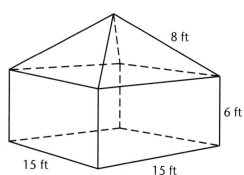
8 ft 6 ft 15 ft 15 ft

Find the volume of each pyramid or cone with the given height and base. Round decimal answers to the nearest tenth.

9. height = 3 in.
4 in.^3

2 in.

2 in.

10. height = 4 cm
5.3 cm^3

2 cm

4 cm

11. height = 2 m
4.7 m^3

2 m

2 m

5 m

12. height = 23.5 ft
2559.0 ft^3

10.2 ft

13. height = 20 mm
3014.4 mm^3

12 mm

14. height = 14 yd
1186.9 yd^3

18 yd

15. The diagram represents a *yurt*, which is a dwelling used by nomadic tribes. The walls of a yurt fold up, making it easy to put up and take down. It is also very weather resistant.

a. What two space figures combine to form the yurt?
a cylinder and a cone

b. Find the volume of the yurt in the diagram. Round your answer to the nearest tenth. 339.9 ft^3

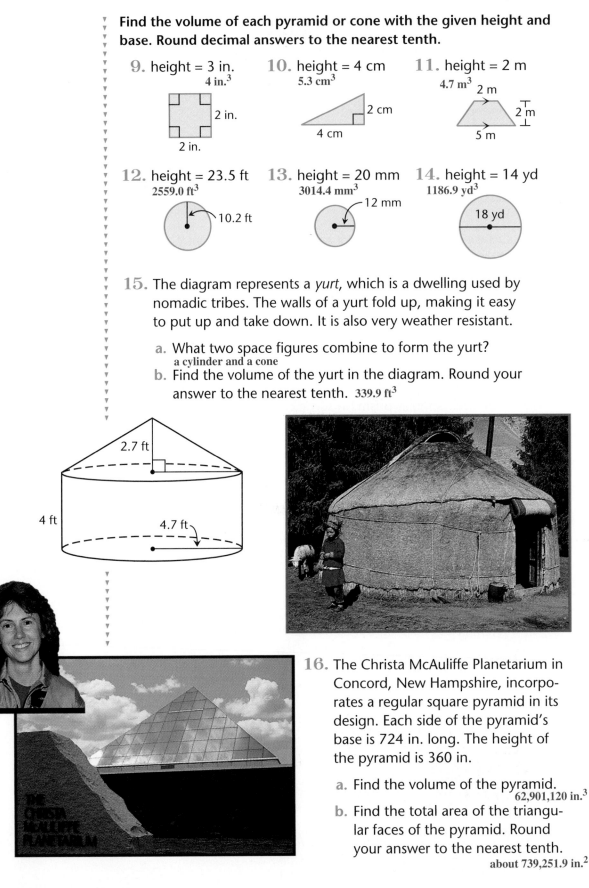

2.7 ft

4 ft

4.7 ft

16. The Christa McAuliffe Planetarium in Concord, New Hampshire, incorporates a regular square pyramid in its design. Each side of the pyramid's base is 724 in. long. The height of the pyramid is 360 in.

a. Find the volume of the pyramid.
$62,901,120 \text{ in.}^3$

b. Find the total area of the triangular faces of the pyramid. Round your answer to the nearest tenth.
about $739,251.9 \text{ in.}^2$

Find the surface area and the volume of each composite figure. Assume that the pyramid is regular.

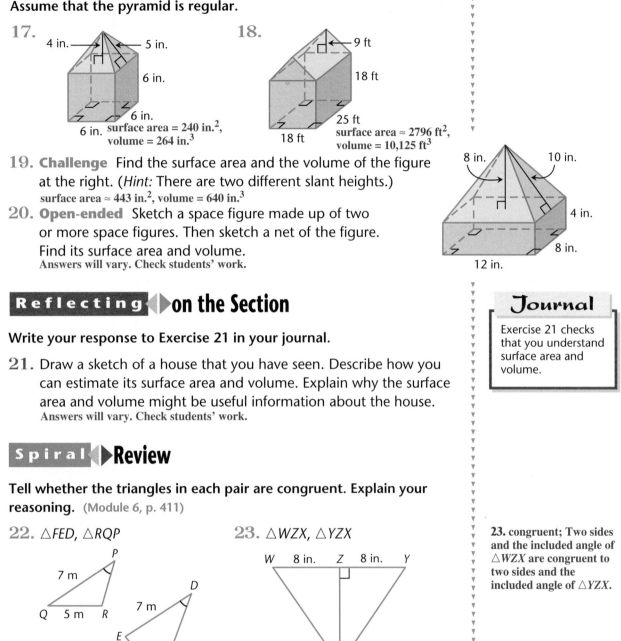

17.
4 in. — 5 in.
6 in.
6 in.
6 in. surface area = 240 in.², volume = 264 in.³

18.
9 ft
18 ft
25 ft
18 ft
surface area ≈ 2796 ft², volume = 10,125 ft³

19. **Challenge** Find the surface area and the volume of the figure at the right. (*Hint:* There are two different slant heights.)
surface area ≈ 443 in.², volume = 640 in.³

20. **Open-ended** Sketch a space figure made up of two or more space figures. Then sketch a net of the figure. Find its surface area and volume.
Answers will vary. Check students' work.

8 in.   10 in.
4 in.
8 in.
12 in.

R e f l e c t i n g ◀▶ on the Section

Write your response to Exercise 21 in your journal.

21. Draw a sketch of a house that you have seen. Describe how you can estimate its surface area and volume. Explain why the surface area and volume might be useful information about the house.
Answers will vary. Check students' work.

Journal

Exercise 21 checks that you understand surface area and volume.

S p i r a l ◀▶ Review

Tell whether the triangles in each pair are congruent. Explain your reasoning. (Module 6, p. 411)

22. △FED, △RQP

P
7 m
Q   5 m   R
D
7 m
E
5 m
F

not congruent;
Corresponding sides $\overline{PR}$ and $\overline{DF}$ are not congruent.

23. △WZX, △YZX

W   8 in.   Z   8 in.   Y
X

23. congruent; Two sides and the included angle of △WZX are congruent to two sides and the included angle of △YZX.

Write an equation in slope-intercept form of a line that has the given slope and y-intercept. (Module 5, p. 338)

24. slope = 3, y-intercept = 2
y = 3x + 2

25. slope = −4, y-intercept = 5
y = −4x + 5

Find the supplement of each angle. (Module 5, p. 363)

26. 12° 168°   27. 90° 90°   28. 116° 64°   29. 153° 27°

Surface Areas of Cones

Use Labsheets 3C and 3D for Exercises 30 and 31.

30. Follow the *Pattern for a Cone* directions on Labsheet 3C to form a cone. Then find the *Dimensions of a Cone* as you complete Labsheet 3D. **a.** $2\pi r$; **b.** the circumference of the partial circle; **c.** the radius of the partial circle

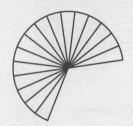

31. Suppose the partial circle from Labsheet 3C is divided into sections and they are rearranged to form a figure like a parallelogram.

   a. What is the height of the "parallelogram"? Why?
      s; Each section is a sector of a circle with radius s.
   b. What is the length of the base of the "parallelogram"? How can you tell?
      πr; Each base has length one-half the circumference of the partial circle.
   c. Use your answers from parts (a) and (b) to find an expression for the area of the "parallelogram." This expression represents the surface area of the cone, not including the base. $A = \pi r s$

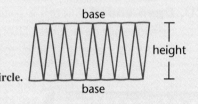

base

height

base

Working on the Module Project

Creating a Model Town

Surface Area and Volume The surface area of a building determines how much siding and roofing material is needed. The volume of a building determines what size heating and cooling systems should be installed.

Answers will vary. Check students' work.

Use your sketches from Project Question 2 on page 416.

4. Find the surface area of your building.

5. Find the volume of your building.

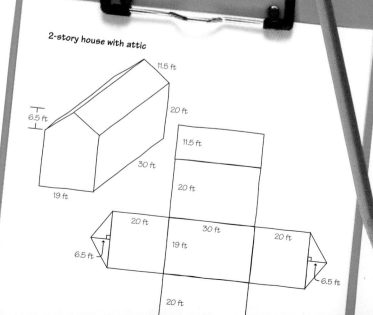

2-story house with attic

11.5 ft

6.5 ft

20 ft

11.5 ft

30 ft

20 ft

19 ft

20 ft

30 ft

20 ft

19 ft

6.5 ft

20 ft

6.5 ft

Find the surface area of each right prism or regular pyramid.

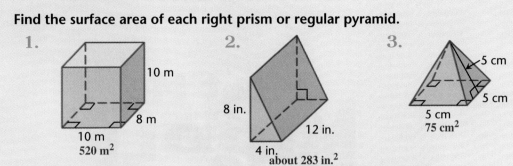

1.

10 m
8 m
10 m
520 m²

2.

8 in.
12 in.
4 in.
about 283 in.²

3.

5 cm
5 cm
5 cm
75 cm²

For Exercises 4 and 5, round decimal answers to the nearest tenth.

4. The height of a cone is 2 m and the radius of the base is 4 m. Find the volume. **33.5 m³**

5. The height of a square pyramid is 9 ft and the length of each side of the base is 0.5 ft. Find the volume. **0.75 ft³**

6. The volume of a cone is $64y^3$. Find the volume of a cylinder with the same base area and height as the cone. **$192y^3$**

Find the surface area and the volume of each figure. Assume that the pyramid is regular. Round decimal answers to the nearest tenth.

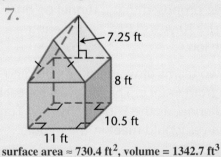

7.

7.25 ft
8 ft
10.5 ft
11 ft
surface area ≈ 730.4 ft², volume = 1342.7 ft³

8.

6 m
3 m
6 m
6 m
surface area ≈ 188.5 m², volume = 180 m³

Standardized Testing ◀▶ Open-ended

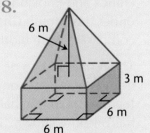

1. Sketch a square pyramid and a square prism that have the same volume. Label the heights and the dimensions of the bases.
   Sample Response:
   6
   2
   2
   2
   2
   2
   2

2. For each situation, sketch two rectangular prisms that fit the description. Label the length of each edge. **Sample responses are given.**

   2. a.

   a. The volume of one prism is three times the volume of the other.
   2
   6
   3
   2
   3
   2

   b. The volume of one prism is eight times the volume of the other.
   b.
   4
   2
   6
   2
   3
   1

   c. The surface area of one prism is twice the surface area of the other.
   c.
   3
   3
   3
   3
   3
   7.5
   3

Section ④ Angles Formed by Intersecting Lines

◄◄◄ *Setting the Stage*

> **SET UP** *Work with a partner. You will need:* • *Labsheets 4A and 4B* • *protractor* • *metric ruler*

In 1750, as part of a competition to improve trade links between France and England, an engineer proposed that a tunnel be built under the English Channel. Over 230 years later, engineering companies were bidding for the job.

The tunnel was to be built by two teams of workers: one digging from England and one digging from France. The idea was for each team to build one half of the *Chunnel*, as the English Channel Tunnel has become known. The two halves would meet in the middle.

According to Derek Wilson in his book *Breakthrough, Tunnelling the Channel*, one company submitted a very low bid to construct the Chunnel. The company was asked if it had carefully planned for the meeting of the two halves. The reply was, "Oh well, if we miss you'll get two tunnels for the price of one."

Use Labsheets 4A and 4B for Questions 1 and 2.

1 **a.** Work with a partner. One of you should complete the *Chunnel Dig from England* while the other completes the *Chunnel Dig from France.* Follow the directions on each labsheet to dig a portion of a mock Chunnel.
   Check students' work.

   b. Fold Labsheet 4A along the right edge of the box and line up the right edge of the box with the left edge of the box on Labsheet 4B.
   Check students' work.

   c. Do your two halves of the tunnel line up? If not, measure to the nearest millimeter the gap between the two ends.
   Answers will vary. Check students' work.

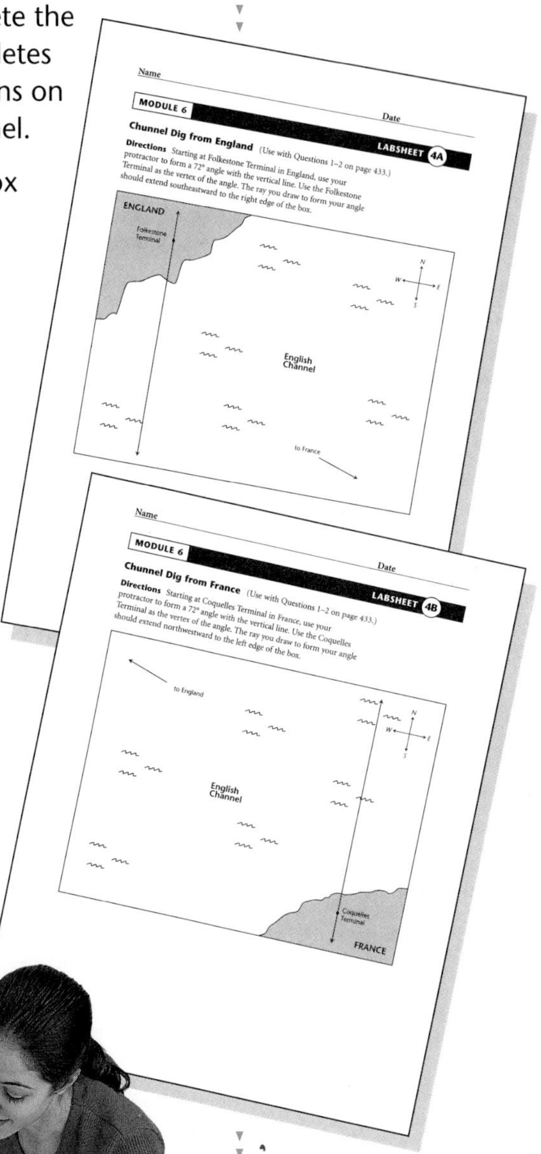

2 The distance from Folkestone to Coquelles along a straight line is about 29 mi.

   a. Estimate the actual distance represented by the value you found in Question 1(c).
   Answers will vary. Check students' work.

   b. In the drawings on your labsheets, 1 cm represents 1 mi. How many miles does 1 mm on the drawing represent? 0.1 mi

   c. Use the result from part (b) and your measurement from Question 1(c). Find the size, in miles, of the gap between the ends of your two tunnels How big is the gap in feet?

   Let *x* be the number of millimeters from 1(c); distance in miles = 0.1*x*, distance in feet = 528*x*.

GOAL

LEARN HOW TO...
* identify and find the measures of pairs of angles formed by intersecting lines

AS YOU...
* learn about the construction of the Chunnel

KEY TERMS
* transversal
* alternate interior angles
* alternate exterior angles
* vertical angles
* corresponding angles

Exploration 1

Parallel Lines AND Transversals

SET UP   *Work in a group. You will need:* • *ruler* • *protractor*

The Chunnel engineers had the assistance of lasers, satellites, and surveyors to line up the two halves of the tunnel. At times, the measures were off and had to be corrected. In the end, the final connection point was only off by a few centimeters.

▶ **In the Chunnel Dig activity you completed, you did not have precision equipment to line up the two tunnels. The following questions will help you see why the tunnels would meet if precise measurements could be made.**

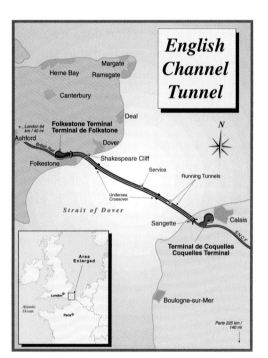

English Channel Tunnel

Angles between lines *m* and *n* are called **interior angles**.

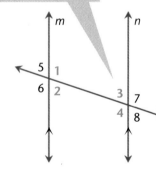

transversal

3 In the diagram above on the left, the Chunnel is represented by a segment cutting across two parallel lines. This segment lies on line *t*. Line *t* is called a **transversal**.

   a. Angles 1 and 4 are **alternate interior angles**. Angles 6 and 7 are *not* alternate interior angles. Identify another pair of alternate interior angles. angles 2 and 3

   b. Angle 6 and angle 7 are **alternate exterior angles**. How does this name describe the location of the angles? Identify another pair of alternate exterior angles. Sample Response: The angles are on opposite sides of the transversal and outside the parallel lines; angles 5 and 8

4 Discussion Use a ruler and a protractor.

    a. Draw a pair of parallel lines cut by a transversal. Measure the angles formed. What do you notice about each pair of alternate interior angles? alternate exterior angles? Compare your results with those of the other members of your group.
        The angles are congruent; the angles are congruent.

    b. Repeat part (a) with *nonparallel lines*. What do you notice?
        The angles are not congruent.

5 Try This as a Class Suppose two lines are cut by a transversal. What can you conclude about the measures of the alternate interior angles? What seems to be true about the measures of the alternate exterior angles? See above.

6 Discussion Lines *p* and *q* in the diagram are parallel.

    a. Describe what *vertical angles* are. Give three examples.

    b. Describe what *corresponding angles* are. Give three examples.

∠**4** and ∠**6** are **vertical angles**.

∠5 and ∠7 are **corresponding angles**.

7 Try This as a Class Use the diagram in Question 6.

    a. What relationship do you think exists between vertical angles formed by intersecting lines? They are congruent.

    b. What relationship do you think exists between corresponding angles formed when parallel lines are cut by a transversal? They are congruent.

▶ **Angle Measures** You can use the relationships between pairs of angles, including supplementary angles, to find measures of angles formed when parallel lines are cut by a transversal.

8 Discussion Use the diagram in Question 6. Suppose *m*∠6 is 56°. Explain how to find *m*∠5, *m*∠2, and *m*∠8.
        See Additional Answers.

9 ✔ **CHECKPOINT** Use the diagram at the right.

    a. Name all the pairs of alternate interior angles, alternate exterior angles, vertical angles, and corresponding angles.

    b. Suppose lines *p* and *n* are parallel and *m*∠1 is 60°. Find *m*∠8, *m*∠5, and *m*∠4.
        120°, 60°, 120°

HOMEWORK EXERCISES ▶ See Exs. 1–16 on pp. 437–438.

---

5. Sample Response: If the lines are parallel, the measures of the alternate interior angles are equal and the measures of the alternate exterior angles are equal. If the lines are not parallel, the measures for each pair of angles described are not equal.

6. a. the angles with the same vertex whose sides are opposite rays; Possible answers: ∠1 and ∠7, ∠2 and ∠8, ∠3 and ∠5, ∠4 and ∠6

6. b. angles in the same position with respect to two lines and a transversal; Possible answers: ∠1 and ∠3, ∠2 and ∠4, ∠5 and ∠7, ∠6 and ∠8

9. a. alternate interior angles: ∠3 and ∠7, ∠4 and ∠8; alternate exterior angles: ∠1 and ∠5, ∠2 and ∠6; vertical angles: ∠1 and ∠3, ∠2 and ∠8, ∠4 and ∠6, ∠5 and ∠7; corresponding angles: ∠1 and ∠7, ∠2 and ∠4, ∠3 and ∠5, ∠6 and ∠8

✔ **QUESTION 9**

…checks that you can identify and find the measures of pairs of angles formed by intersecting lines.

Key Concepts

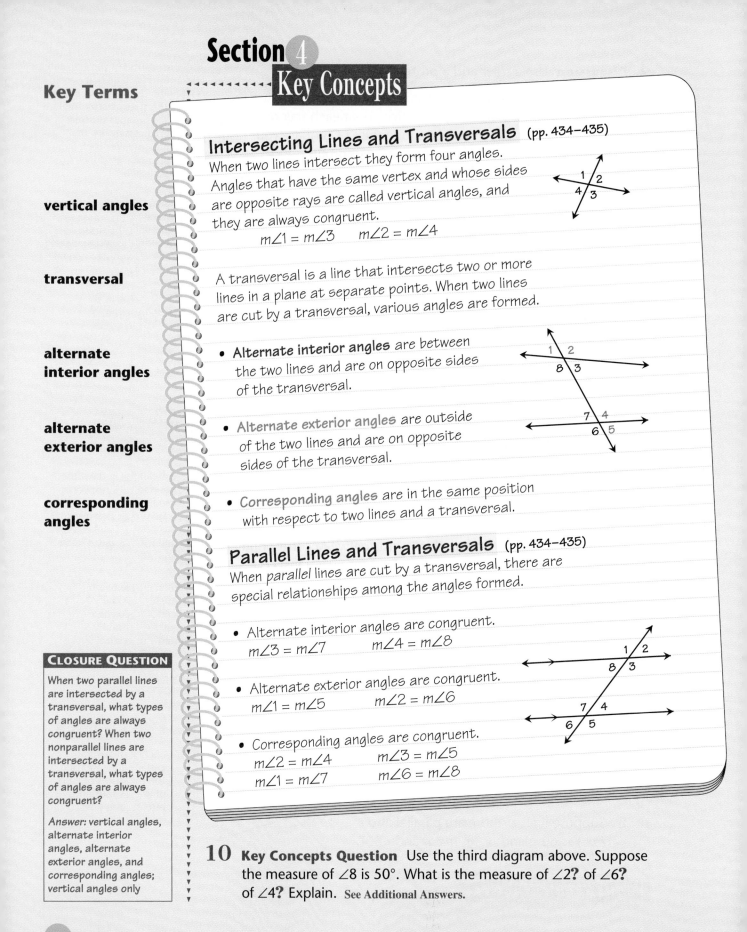

Key Terms

vertical angles

transversal

alternate interior angles

alternate exterior angles

corresponding angles

Intersecting Lines and Transversals (pp. 434–435)

When two lines intersect they form four angles. Angles that have the same vertex and whose sides are opposite rays are called vertical angles, and they are always congruent.

$$m\angle 1 = m\angle 3 \qquad m\angle 2 = m\angle 4$$

A transversal is a line that intersects two or more lines in a plane at separate points. When two lines are cut by a transversal, various angles are formed.

- **Alternate interior angles** are between the two lines and are on opposite sides of the transversal.

- **Alternate exterior angles** are outside of the two lines and are on opposite sides of the transversal.

- **Corresponding angles** are in the same position with respect to two lines and a transversal.

Parallel Lines and Transversals (pp. 434–435)

When *parallel* lines are cut by a transversal, there are special relationships among the angles formed.

- Alternate interior angles are congruent.
  $$m\angle 3 = m\angle 7 \qquad m\angle 4 = m\angle 8$$

- Alternate exterior angles are congruent.
  $$m\angle 1 = m\angle 5 \qquad m\angle 2 = m\angle 6$$

- Corresponding angles are congruent.
  $$m\angle 2 = m\angle 4 \qquad m\angle 3 = m\angle 5$$
  $$m\angle 1 = m\angle 7 \qquad m\angle 6 = m\angle 8$$

CLOSURE QUESTION

When two parallel lines are intersected by a transversal, what types of angles are always congruent? When two nonparallel lines are intersected by a transversal, what types of angles are always congruent?

Answer: vertical angles, alternate interior angles, alternate exterior angles, and corresponding angles; vertical angles only

10 **Key Concepts Question** Use the third diagram above. Suppose the measure of ∠8 is 50°. What is the measure of ∠2? of ∠6? of ∠4? Explain. See Additional Answers.

Section 4

Practice & Application Exercises ▸▸▸▸▸

The diagram shows part of the road layout of Washington, D.C. In the diagram, 12th St. is a transversal of Massachusetts Ave. and Constitution Ave. Replace each __?__ with the correct angle.

1. ∠2 and __?__ are vertical angles. ∠8

2. ∠6 and __?__ are corresponding angles. ∠8

3. ∠3 and __?__ are alternate interior angles. ∠7

4. ∠5 and __?__ are alternate exterior angles. ∠1

In the diagram, line *p* is parallel to line *q* and line *r* is parallel to line *s*. Find each angle measure.

5. m∠7 30°

6. m∠5 150°

7. m∠4 30°

8. m∠1 30°

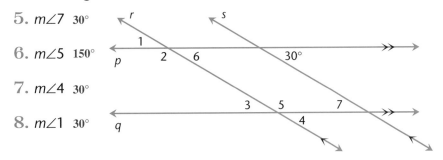

For Exercises 9–12, use the diagram. Lines *m* and *n* are parallel.

9. m∠1 = m∠3 = m∠5 = 110°, m∠2 = m∠4 = m∠6 = 70°

9. Find the measures of angles 1–6.

10. What is the sum of the measures of angles 1 and 2? 180°

11. What is the sum of the measures of angles 5 and 6? 180°

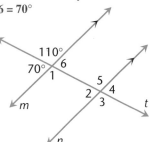

12. Angles 1 and 2 are called *same-side interior angles*.

Sample Responses are given.

a. Describe what you think this term means.
angles that are on the same side of a transversal between two lines

b. When two parallel lines are cut by a transversal, how do you think the measures of same-side interior angles are related?
The sum of the measures is 180°.

13. ∠4 and ∠5 are supplementary so $m\angle 4$ = $180° - m\angle 5$; ∠6 and ∠5 are also supplementary, so $m\angle 6 = 180° - m\angle 5$. Thus $m\angle 4 = m\angle 6$. ∠6 and ∠8 are corresponding angles so $m\angle 6 = m\angle 8$. Therefore $m\angle 4 = m\angle 8$.

14. 125°; 125°; The angles labeled $x°$ and $(3x - 250)°$ are alternate exterior angles, so their measures are equal. Solving $x = 3x - 250$ for x gives $x = 125°$. The angles labeled $x°$ and $y°$ are corresponding angles, so they have the same measure.

13. Writing Lines p and q are parallel. Use the relationships between supplementary angles and between corresponding angles to explain why $m\angle 4 = m\angle 8$.

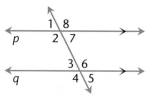

14. Algebra Connection Line m and line n are parallel. What is the value of x? What is the value of y? Explain your reasoning.

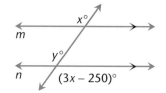

15. Challenge Around the late 3rd century B.C., Eratosthenes estimated Earth's circumference. He used the fact that sunbeams, which cause shadows, are parallel when they strike Earth. At noon on the summer solstice, he measured the shadow cast by a pole in Alexandria, north of Syene. He chose noon because he knew that then the sun would be directly over Syene and would cast no shadow there. The diagram shows an interpretation of what he found.

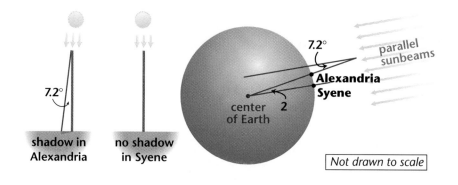

15. a. 7.2°; The rays of the sun are parallel and the line through the center of Earth and Alexandria is then a transversal. Alternate interior angles 1 and 2 are therefore congruent.

a. What is the measure of ∠2 in the diagram? Explain.

b. Eratosthenes believed the distance between Alexandria and Syene was 5000 stades, or about 575 mi. Use this distance to estimate Earth's circumference in miles. Explain your method.

about 28,750 mi; Let C = the circumference of Earth and d = the distance between Alexandria and Syene; $\dfrac{7.2°}{360°} = \dfrac{d}{C} \approx \dfrac{575 \text{ mi}}{C}$. Solve the proportion to find $C \approx 28,750$ mi.

Reflecting ◀▶ on the Section

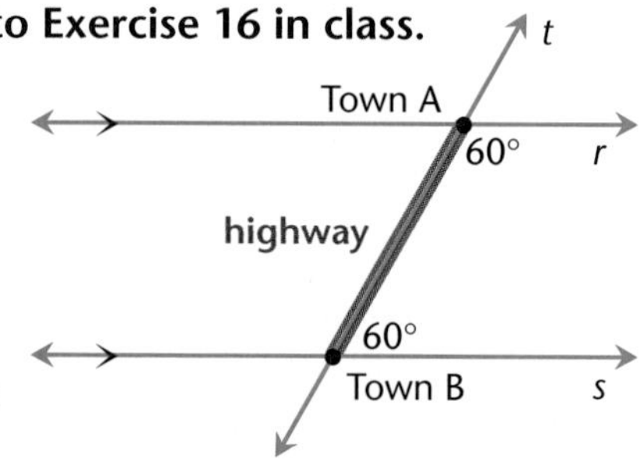

Discussion

Exercise 16 checks that you understand the relationships between pairs of angles formed by a transversal.

Be prepared to discuss your response to Exercise 16 in class.

16. A highway is to be built to join Town A and Town B. If road r is parallel to road s, are the measures of the angles correctly labeled? Explain why or why not.

No; They are same-side interior angles and should be supplementary, not congruent.

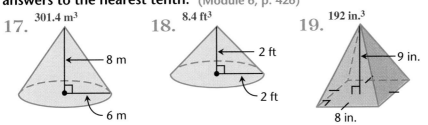 S p i r a l ▶Review

Find the volume of each cone or regular pyramid. Round decimal answers to the nearest tenth. (Module 6, p. 426)

17. 301.4 m³
8 m
6 m

18. 8.4 ft³
2 ft
2 ft

19. 192 in.³
9 in.
8 in.

20. Interpreting Data Make a scatter plot of the data. Does it make sense to fit a line to this data? Why or why not? (Module 1 p. 34)

U.S. Sports Participation (People 6 Years Old and Older, 1991 to 1996)						
Number roller skating (millions)	24.8	22.6	22.2	21.0	18.5	15.3
Number in-line skating (millions)	6.2	9.4	12.6	18.8	22.5	27.5

Graph each inequality on a number line. (Module 2, p. 152)

21. $x \geq 4$　　**22.** $m < 3$　　**23.** $n \leq 0$　　**24.** $-1 < x$

20.
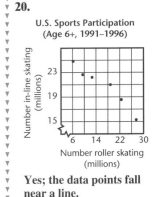
U.S. Sports Participation
(Age 6+, 1991–1996)

Yes; the data points fall near a line.

21.
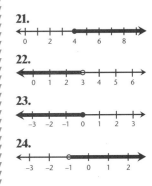

22.

23.

24.

Career ▪ Connection

Surveyor: Lonnie Bitsoi

You have learned that if two parallel lines are cut by a transversal, then alternate interior angles are equal. It is also true that if two lines are cut by a transversal and alternate interior angles are equal, then the two lines are parallel. Surveyor Lonnie Bitsoi has used this second fact while surveying boundary lines for the Navajo Reservation and for the Bureau of Land Management.

25. The diagram shows how Lonnie Bitsoi would construct angles to survey around a tree.

　a. What is the relationship between line *AB* and line *CD*? Explain your reasoning. **See below.**

　b. In order to continue line *AB* at point *E*, what must be the measure of $\angle DEF$? **60°**

　25. a. They are parallel; The alternate interior angles formed by the transversal $\overline{CB}$ are congruent.

Section 4 Angles Formed by Intersecting Lines **439**

For Exercises 1–5, use the diagram.

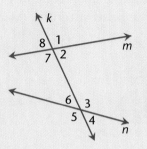

1. Which line is the transversal? Line *k*

2. Identify each pair of vertical angles.
   ∠1 and ∠7, ∠2 and ∠8, ∠3 and ∠5, ∠4 and ∠6

3. Identify each pair of corresponding angles.
   ∠1 and ∠3, ∠2 and ∠4, ∠5 and ∠7, ∠6 and ∠8

4. Identify each pair of alternate interior angles.
   ∠2 and ∠6, ∠3 and ∠7

5. Identify each pair of alternate exterior angles.
   ∠1 and ∠5, ∠4 and ∠8

In the diagram, line *k* is parallel to line *p*. Find each measure.

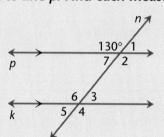

6. $m\angle 1$ 50°

7. $m\angle 7$ 50°

8. $m\angle 6$ 130°

9. $m\angle 5$ 50°

10. $m\angle 3 + m\angle 6$ 180°

Standardized Testing ◀▶ Multiple Choice

1. Line *n* is parallel to line *k*. Lines *p* and *q* are transversals that intersect at a point on line *n*. Which of the following statements is *not* true? **C**

   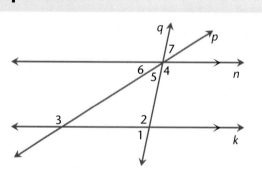

   Ⓐ $m\angle 2 = m\angle 4$

   Ⓑ $m\angle 1 = 180° - m\angle 2$

   Ⓒ $m\angle 6 = m\angle 7$

   Ⓓ $m\angle 1 = m\angle 5 + m\angle 6$

2. Line *n* is parallel to line *k* and line *q* is a transversal. If $m\angle 1 = 40°$ and $m\angle 2 = 75°$, what is $m\angle 3$? **B**

   Ⓐ 65°   Ⓑ 115°

   Ⓒ 140°   Ⓓ 75°

   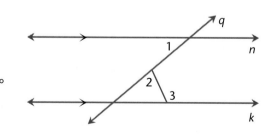

FOR ASSESSMENT AND PORTFOLIOS

Mathematical

SET UP *You will need:* • *compass* • *ruler* • $8\frac{1}{2}$ *in. by 11 in. plain paper* • *colored pencils or markers*

The Situation See the Resource Book for a detailed discussion of this Extended Exploration.

Some very beautiful artwork is based on geometric designs. The design shown was created using a compass and the straight edge of a ruler.

The Problem

Create your own design using two or three of the following constructions: *copy a segment*, *draw a perpendicular bisector*, or *draw an angle bisector*. Your design should almost cover a sheet of paper, and you should use only a compass and a straightedge.

Something to Think About

◆ Do you want your design to be symmetrical?

◆ How can you make variations on the constructions you have already learned to make more interesting designs?

◆ How else can you add to your design?

Present Your Results

Create a poster displaying your design. Add color if you wish. On a separate sheet of paper, describe how you used constructions to make your design. Also note anything special you used in your design that was not one of the three constructions mentioned above.

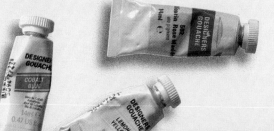

 **Section 5** **Solving Inequalities**

IN THIS SECTION

EXPLORATION 1
◆ Solving Simple Inequalities

EXPLORATION 2
◆ Multistep Inequalities

WARM-UP EXERCISES

Solve each equation.
1. $y - 6 = 14$ 20
2. $6x = 18$ 3
3. $\frac{2}{3}m = 14$ 21
4. $17 = 13 - 3r$ $-\frac{4}{3}$

Write an equation and then solve it.
5. three more than 2 times a number is 8
$2n + 3 = 8$; 2.5
6. five is 9 less than eight time a number
$5 = 8n - 9$; 1.75

The Human Factor

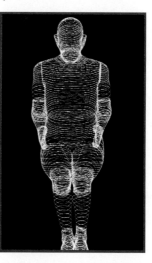

Setting the Stage

How high should the seat of a chair be so it is comfortable for most people? Is there a way to arrange the seats in a theater so everyone can see the screen? To get answers to questions like these, the person to call is a *human factors engineer*. These engineers make use of data about people—heights, weights, leg lengths, and so on. They use the information to help design buildings, furniture, tools, appliances, and cars that are comfortable for as many people as possible.

To decide how high to make the seat of a chair, for example, a human factors engineer would study the data below on *popliteal height*.

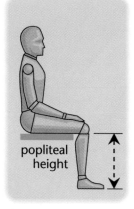

▲
Popliteal height is the distance from the floor to the underside of the knees when a person is seated.

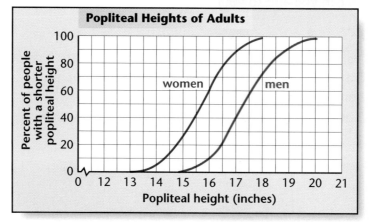

1 About what percent of adult women have a popliteal height less than 17 in.? about what percent of adult men? about 90%; about 40%

2 The popliteal height of 5% of women is less than how many inches? about 14 in.

3 Can you tell from the graph if any men have a popliteal height less than the number of inches you found in Question 2? Explain.
No; The percent is 0, but the number may not be

Exploration 1 ▸

Solving Simple Inequalities

GOAL

LEARN HOW TO...
◆ write and solve inequalities that involve one operation

AS YOU...
◆ study the seat heights of chairs

KEY TERMS
◆ solution of an inequality
◆ solve an inequality

▶ **Some human factors engineers recommend that for comfort, the height of a chair seat should be less than or equal to the popliteal height of the person sitting in it plus 1.5 in. Adding 1.5 in. adjusts for the thickness of the soles and heels of the person's shoes.**

4 **a.** Use h for the seat height and p for the popliteal height. Write an inequality for the recommended height of a chair seat.
$h \leq p + 1.5$

b. Chair seats of what height will be comfortable for a person with a popliteal height of 17 in.? heights less than or equal to 18.5 in.

c. Graph your solution from part (b) on a number line.

◀——|——|——|——●——|——|——▶
  16   17 18 18.5 19   20

5 **Try This as a Class** Suppose the seat height of a chair is 17 in.

a. Write an inequality for the popliteal heights of the people who would be comfortable in this chair by substituting 17 in. for the seat height in the inequality from Question 4(a).
$17 \leq p + 1.5$

b. A value of a variable that makes an inequality true is a **solution of the inequality**. Are 14 in. and 18 in. solutions of the inequality in part (a)? Why or why not?

c. People with what popliteal heights would be comfortable in such a chair? Explain how you found your answer.

d. Use the graph on page 442. About what percent of adult women would not be comfortable in the chair? About what percent of adult men would not be comfortable?
about 45%; about 5%

5. b. 14 is not a solution because $14 + 1.5 = 15.5$ and 15.5 is not greater than or equal to 17; 18 is a solution because $18 + 1.5 = 19.5$ and 19.5 is greater than or equal to 17.
c. people with popliteal heights greater than or equal to 15.5 in.; $15.5 + 1.5 = 17$ so any number greater than or equal to 15.5 would be a solution.

▶ In Question 5(c), you **solved the inequality** $17 \leq p + 1.5$ by finding all of the solutions of the inequality. In Questions 6–8 you will investigate some of the operations that can be used to solve inequalities.

6 Choose two different numbers (the numbers can both have the same sign, or they can have opposite signs). Write an inequality that compares the numbers. **Sample Response: 8 > –2**

7 Do each operation below to both sides of the original inequality you wrote in Question 6. Then write the correct inequality symbol between the two new numbers. **Responses based on the inequality 8 > –2 are given.**

a. add 5 **13 > 3**   **b.** subtract 5 **3 > –7**   **c.** multiply by 5 **40 > –10**

d. divide by 5 $\frac{8}{5} > -\frac{2}{5}$ **e.** add –2 **6 > –4**   **f.** subtract –2 **10 > 0**

g. multiply by –2 **–16 < 4**   **h.** divide by –2 **–4 < 1**   **i.** add $-\frac{1}{4}$ $7\frac{3}{4} > -2\frac{1}{4}$

j. subtract $-\frac{1}{4}$ $8\frac{1}{4} > -1\frac{3}{4}$ **k.** multiply by $-\frac{1}{4}$ $-2 < \frac{1}{2}$ **l.** divide by $-\frac{1}{4}$ **–32 < 8**

8 **Try This as a Class** Look back at your results from Question 7.

a. How do you think adding or subtracting the same number on both sides of an inequality affects the inequality? Why?
It does not affect the inequality; Both sides increase or decrease by the same amount.

b. How do you think multiplying or dividing both sides of an inequality by the same number affects the inequality?
If the number is positive, it does not affect the inequality. If the number is negative, it reverses the inequality.

▶ The properties found in Question 8 can be used to solve inequalities.

EXAMPLE

Adding the same number to both sides of an inequality does not affect the inequality.

$$x - 7 \leq -2$$
$$x - 7 + 7 \leq -2 + 7$$
$$x \leq 5$$

Dividing both sides of an inequality by a negative number **reverses the inequality**.

$$-6x > 18$$
$$\frac{-6x}{-6} < \frac{18}{-6}$$
$$x < -3$$

---

9 **Discussion** How would you check the solutions of the inequalities in the Example? How is this different than checking the solution of an equation? **Sample Response: Substitute any value in the solution; Only one value is substituted to check an equation.**

10 ✔ **CHECKPOINT** Solve. Check and then graph each solution.

a. $36 < x + 13$ $x > 23$

b. $\dfrac{x}{3} \geq -2$ $x \geq -6$

c. $-7x > -63$ $x < 9$

✔ **QUESTION 10**

...checks that you can solve inequalities that involve one operation.

11 Experts recommend that the seat height of a non-adjustable chair should be at least 16 in.

a. Write an inequality for the popliteal heights of the people who would be comfortable in a chair with a seat height of 16 in.
$16 \leq p + 1.5$

b. People with what popliteal heights would be comfortable in the chair? **greater than or equal to 14.5 in.**

c. Use the graph on page 442. About what percent of adult women would not be comfortable in the chair? About what percent of adult men would not be comfortable? **about 15%; 0%**

d. Why do you think this seat height is recommended instead of a greater one?
Sample Response: 85%–100% of adults would be comfortable with this seat height.

■ **HOMEWORK EXERCISES** ▶ See Exs. 1–15 on pp. 447–448.

Exploration 2 ▶▶▶▶▶▶▶▶▶▶▶▶▶▶▶▶▶▶▶▶▶▶▶▶

MULTI-STEP INEQUALITIES

GOAL

LEARN HOW TO...
- solve inequalities that have more than one operation

AS YOU...
- plan the arrangement of the seats in a theater

In this exploration, you'll use human factors engineering to design comfortable seating for a theater.

12 It has been recommended that for comfortable seating, the width of a theater seat should be from 20 to 26 in. and the depth of each row should be from 34 to 42 in.

a. What is the least area in square feet needed for a person to have a comfortable seat? What is the greatest area needed? (*Hint:* 1 ft² = 144 in.²)
about 4.7 ft²; about 7.6 ft²

b. What seat width and row depth would you recommend for each seat in a theater? Why?
Answers will vary. Check students' work.

c. Based on your recommendation, how many square feet would be needed for each seat in a theater?
Multiply seat width by row depth (in inches) and divide by 144.

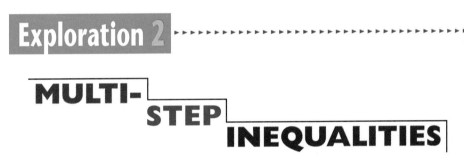

width of seat

depth of row

13 A new auditorium will be 48 ft long and 36 ft wide. Two aisles are needed, one down the center of the auditorium and one between the front row and the screen. The aisles will be 4 ft wide.

a. Make a sketch of the auditorium showing the locations and dimensions of the aisles.

b. What is the total area of the auditorium? of the aisles?
   1728 ft^2; 320 ft^2

13. a.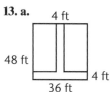
4 ft
48 ft
4 ft
36 ft

14 **Try This as a Class** The total area of the auditorium *t* must be greater than or equal to the area per seat times the number of seats *s*, plus the area of the aisles *a*. Use the area per seat that you recommended in Question 12(c).

a. Write an inequality relating *t*, *s*, and *a*. $t \geq$ (area per seat)$s + a$

b. Use your answers to Question 13(b) to write an inequality for the number of seats the auditorium can hold.
   $1728 \geq$ (area per seat)$s + 320$

c. The inequality in part (b) uses both addition and multiplication. What are their inverse operations? subtraction and division

d. In what order would you use the inverse operations to solve the inequality in part (b)? Why? Subtraction, then division; It requires fewer steps.

e. About how many seats can the auditorium hold? Answers will vary. Check students' work.

✔ **QUESTION 15**

...checks that you can solve inequalities that involve two operations.

15 ✔ **CHECKPOINT** Solve each inequality.

a. $14 < 5x - 9$
   $x > 4.6$

b. $-\frac{x}{2} - 3 \geq -2$
   $x \leq -2$

c. $-3x + 17 > -4$
   $x < 7$

16 a. Let *n* represent the number of seats in each row. Use the aisle width and the auditorium width from Question 13, and the seat width you chose in Question 12(b), to write an inequality for *n*. $36 \geq$ (seat width in feet)$n + 4$

b. Suppose that, in each row, there will be the same number of seats on either side of the aisle. How many seats can you have in each row? $n \leq \frac{32}{\text{seat width in feet}}$

c. Use the row depth you chose in Question 12(b). How many rows can you have? $r \leq \frac{44}{\text{row depth in feet}}$

d. How many seats will fit in the auditorium? How does this compare with your answer to Question 14(e)?
   $n \cdot r$; Answers will vary. Check students' work.

17 **Discussion** Human factors engineers recommend that the rows of seats be staggered as in the picture on page 445. How would this affect the number of seats you can have in the auditorium?
   It would decrease the number of seats.

HOMEWORK EXERCISES ▶ See Exs. 16–29 on pp. 448–449.

Section 5

Key Concepts

Solving Inequalities (pp. 443–446)

All the values of a variable that make an inequality true are the solution of the inequality. When you find them, you are solving the inequality.

Key Terms

solution of an inequality

solve an inequality

Example

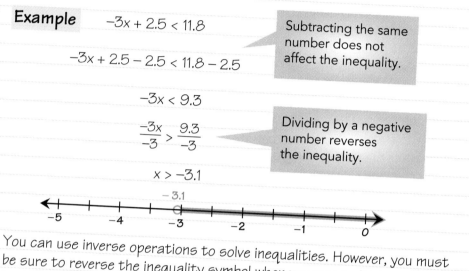

$-3x + 2.5 < 11.8$

Subtracting the same number does not affect the inequality.

$-3x + 2.5 - 2.5 < 11.8 - 2.5$

$-3x < 9.3$

$\dfrac{-3x}{-3} > \dfrac{9.3}{-3}$

Dividing by a negative number reverses the inequality.

$x > -3.1$

You can use inverse operations to solve inequalities. However, you must be sure to reverse the inequality symbol whenever you multiply or divide both sides by a negative number.

CLOSURE QUESTION

When solving inequalities, are the operations of addition and subtraction or multiplication and division normally undone first? Explain.

Sample Response: Addition and subtraction; It is easier to add or subtract to combine like terms and then multiply or divide to find a final solution.

18 **Key Concepts Question** How is the solution of $-2a - 3 \geq 5$ like the solution of $-2a - 3 = 5$? How is it different?

Both solutions include –4; The solution of the equation is –4 and the solution of the inequality is all numbers less than or equal to –4.

Section 5

Practice & Application Exercises

1. Is 6 a solution of the inequality $-8 + x < 2$? Explain.
Yes; The statement $-8 + 6 < 2$ is true.

Solve each inequality. Check and graph each solution.

2. $a + 17 < 37$ $a < 20$

3. $8 + w \geq 10$ $w \geq 2$

4. $-13 > b - 7$ $b < -6$

5. $x - (-3) \leq 8$ $x \leq 5$

6. $96 \leq 12n$ $n \geq 8$

7. $-0.5z > -6.5$ $z < 13$

8. $\dfrac{y}{2} < 2.5$ $y < 5$

9. $-7 \geq \dfrac{q}{-1.5}$ $q \geq 10.5$

10. $-\dfrac{2}{3}x < 6$ $x > -9$

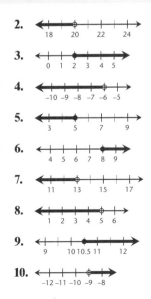

For Exercises 11–14, write and solve an inequality for each situation.

11. Seven more than a number is less than seven. $n + 7 < 7; n < 0$

12. The opposite of a number is greater than or equal to five. $-n \geq 5; n \leq -5$

13. A family needs to drive 95 miles in less than 1 hour and 45 minutes. What average speed must they drive?
$1.75s \geq 95; s \geq 54.3;$ at least 54.3 mi/h

14. **Building Codes** The Uniform Building Code requires that there be at least 20 ft^2 of space for each person in a classroom. Suppose a classroom is 28 ft long and 18 ft wide. How many people can be in the classroom? $20p \leq 504; p \leq 25.2;$ no more than 25 people

15. **Theater Design** Rows in a theater are often elevated so each person can look over the head of the person in front of him or her. Theater floors must either be sloped or have steps. Whether the floor can be sloped depends on the depth of the row d and the amount of rise r. A floor can only be sloped if $r \leq \frac{d}{8}$.

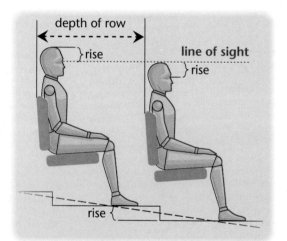

depth of row

rise

line of sight

rise

rise

a. A rise of 5 in. will give the maximum visibility for the greatest number of people. How deep can the rows be if the floor is sloped and has a rise of 5 in.? up to 40 in.

b. Many theaters have 32-inch-deep rows. What is the maximum rise for a sloped floor? 4 in.

c. A certain theater chain claims to give everyone an unobstructed view of the screen. Suppose the rise is 10.8 in. What is the minimum row depth for a sloped floor? Why do you think these theaters have stepped floors? 86.4 in.; The rows would have to be so far apart that they would lose too much seating if they used a sloped floor.

d. What are some advantages of a stepped floor? What are some advantages of a sloped floor?

15. d. More rows are possible with a stepped floor because of a higher rise and shorter row depth, but a sloped floor may be safer, since people may be less likely to trip in low light.

For Exercises 16–19, write and solve an inequality for each situation.

16. Two times a number minus 13 is less than 47. $2n - 13 < 47; n < 30$

17. Twenty-four minus half of a number is greater than or equal to 132.
$24 - 0.5n \geq 132; n \leq -216$

18. The difference when 1.57 is subtracted from 3 times a number is less than or equal to 10.62. $3n - 1.57 \leq 10.62; n \leq 4.063$

19. Suppose you can rent a snowmobile for an initial fee of $25, plus $12.50 per hour. For how many hours can you rent a snowmobile and still spend less than $90? $12.50h + 25 < 90; h < 5.2;$ less than 5.2 h

Solve each inequality. Check and graph each solution.

20. $-5b + 77 \geq 92$ $b \leq -3$

21. $-8z + 11 \geq 93$ $z \leq -10.25$

22. $-32 + (-41x) \leq -155$ $x \geq 3$

23. $1.2a - 0.97 < 2.63$ $a < 3$

24. $\frac{3}{4}y + \frac{11}{16} > \frac{19}{16}$ $y > \frac{2}{3}$

25. $\frac{8}{9} - \frac{1}{3}m < \frac{23}{27}$ $m > \frac{1}{9}$

26. $5.95 - 2.95x > -11.75$ $x < 6$

27. $49y + 249 \leq -976$ $y \leq -25$

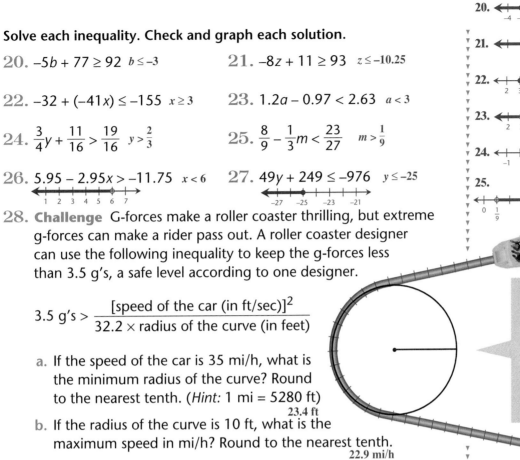

28. **Challenge** G-forces make a roller coaster thrilling, but extreme g-forces can make a rider pass out. A roller coaster designer can use the following inequality to keep the g-forces less than 3.5 g's, a safe level according to one designer.

$$3.5 \text{ g's} > \frac{[\text{speed of the car (in ft/sec)}]^2}{32.2 \times \text{radius of the curve (in feet)}}$$

a. If the speed of the car is 35 mi/h, what is the minimum radius of the curve? Round to the nearest tenth. (*Hint:* 1 mi = 5280 ft)
   23.4 ft

b. If the radius of the curve is 10 ft, what is the maximum speed in mi/h? Round to the nearest tenth.
   22.9 mi/h

c. Do you think it is reasonable to design a roller coaster to go around a curve at 100 mi/h? Explain.
   Sample Response: No; The radius must be at least 191 ft.

> The amount of g-force you feel depends on the car's speed and the curve of the track, which can be thought of as part of a circle.

Reflecting ◆ on the Section

Write your response to Exercise 29 in your journal.

29. You can solve the inequality $2 - x < 5$ by adding x to both sides. Explain why multiplying by x to solve the inequality $\frac{2}{x} < 5$ might lead to an error.

   $2 - x + x < 5 + x$
   $2 < 5 + x$
   $2 - 5 < 5 + x - 5$
   $-3 < x$

   Assuming that x is not 0, x can be either positive or negative; you don't know whether to reverse the inequality or not.

> **Journal**
> Exercise 29 checks that you understand how to solve inequalities.

Spiral ◆ Review

Use the diagram to find each angle measure. (Module 6, p. 436)

30. $m\angle 3$ **105°**

31. $m\angle 5$ **105°**

32. $m\angle 7$ **105°**

Solve each proportion. (Module 2, p. 90)

33. $\frac{x}{100} = \frac{3}{5}$ **60**

34. $\frac{9}{x} = \frac{2}{3}$ **13.5**

35. $\frac{1}{2} = \frac{x}{4.5}$ **2.25**

Section 5

Solve each inequality. Check and graph each solution.

1. $x + 4 \leq 2$

2. $-5y \geq 30$

3. $16a > 2$

4. $-2 + x < 3$

5. $a - 2 \geq 4$

6. $7x \geq 84$

7. $-0.2u < 8$

8. $60 > -4c$

9. $15 \geq \dfrac{m}{3}$

10. $x - \dfrac{4}{3} \geq 3$

11. $\dfrac{n}{-3} < 9$

12. $-\dfrac{3}{4}q < 12$

13. $\dfrac{x}{5} < -\dfrac{3}{5}$ $x < -3$

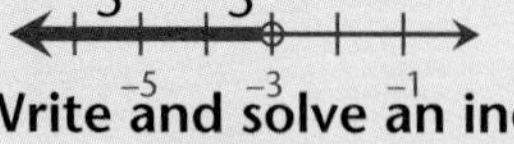

14. $\dfrac{3}{2} \leq -6a$ $a \leq -0.25$

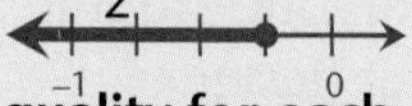

15. $-\dfrac{4}{5}y > 8$ $y < -10$

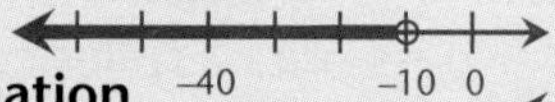

16. $\dfrac{x}{-2} \geq \dfrac{3}{4}$

$x \leq -\dfrac{3}{2}$

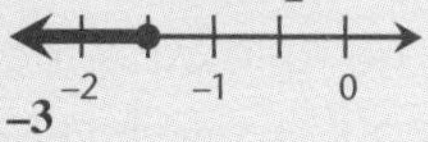

Write and solve an inequality for each situation.

17. Five more than a number is greater than two. $n + 5 > 2; n > -3$

18. Three minus twice a number is less than eight. $3 - 2n < 8; n > -\dfrac{5}{2}$

19. You will spend at least $10 if you buy a melon for $.98 and 3 lb of grapes. What do grapes cost per pound?
$3c + 0.98 \geq 10; c \geq 3.006; \$3.01$

20. A land owner has 200 acres of land and wants to keep at least 20 acres. The rest will be divided and sold in 12-acre lots. How many of these lots can the land owner offer for sale?
$200 - 12l \geq 20; l \leq 15;$ at most 15 lots

Solve each inequality.

21. $3x - 5 \leq 6$ $x \leq \dfrac{11}{3}$

22. $-4w - 18 \geq 2$ $w \leq -5$

23. $2 > 6 + 7c$ $c < -\dfrac{4}{7}$

24. $-36x + 15 < 24$ $x > -0.25$

25. $14 \leq -112a - 42$ $a \leq -0.5$

26. $4.5x + 0.8 > 3.5$
$x > 0.6$

27. $4.5 - 0.25x \geq 3.25$ $x \leq 5$

28. $7.8 - 2.3n < 3.2$ $n > 2$

29. $1.875 > 1.25z - 1.25$ $z < 2.5$

30. $\dfrac{x}{3} - 1 < \dfrac{3}{4}$ $x < \dfrac{21}{4}$

31. $\dfrac{7}{5} + \dfrac{y}{10} \leq -\dfrac{2}{5}$ $y \leq -18$

32. $12 - \dfrac{1}{2}m \geq 3\dfrac{1}{4}$ $m \leq 17\dfrac{1}{2}$

33. $\dfrac{a}{-2} + 7 < 8$ $a > -2$

34. $\dfrac{n}{3} - 2 \geq -3$ $n \geq -3$

35. $\dfrac{1}{2} \leq -8x - \dfrac{3}{2}$ $x \leq -\dfrac{1}{4}$

Answers (side column):

1. $x \leq -2$

2. $y \leq -6$

3. $a > 0.125$

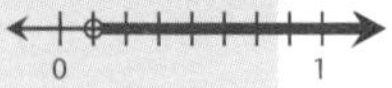

4. $x < 5$

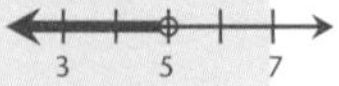

5. $a \geq 6$

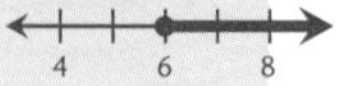

6. $x \geq 12$

7. $u > -40$

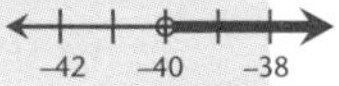

8. $c > -15$

9. $m \leq 45$

10. $x \geq \dfrac{13}{3}$

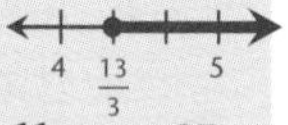

11. $n > -27$

12. $q > -16$

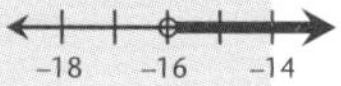

Standardized Testing ◀▶ **Free Response**

1. The edges of the base of a square pyramid are each 14 in. long. For what values of the height h will the volume of the pyramid be less than 5880 in.^{3}? less than 90 in.

2. A camera shop charges $12 to develop a roll of film plus $.45 for each extra print. How many extra prints can Stephanie get if she has $20 to spend for photographs? 17 or fewer prints

Section ⑥ Scale Drawings and Similar Figures

IN THIS SECTION

EXPLORATION 1
◆ Scale Drawings

EXPLORATION 2
◆ Perimeters and Areas of Similar Figures

BUILDING MODELS

WARM-UP EXERCISES

Write each ratio as a fraction.

1. 1 to 8 $\frac{1}{8}$

2. 4 : 9 $\frac{4}{9}$

3. 7.5 to 3 $\frac{7.5}{3}$ or $\frac{5}{2}$

Find (a) the perimeter and (b) the area of each figure.

4. a rectangle with a length of 3.5 cm and a width of 1.4 cm
   (a) 9.8 cm;
   (b) 4.9 cm^2

5. a square with side lengths of 9 in.
   (a) 36 in.; (b) 81 in.^{2}

6. a right triangle with side lengths of 3 yd, 4 yd, and 5 yd
   (a) 12 yd; (b) 6 yd^2

Setting the Stage ▸▸▸▸▸▸▸▸▸▸▸▸▸▸▸▸▸▸▸▸▸▸▸▸▸▸▸

An architect designing a building will draw a floor plan to show the rooms of the building in proportion to one another. You may have used such a floor plan to help you locate an exhibit in a museum, a store in a mall, or even a classroom in your school. The floor plan below is for the first floor of the Cesar Chavez Elementary School in Chicago, Illinois.

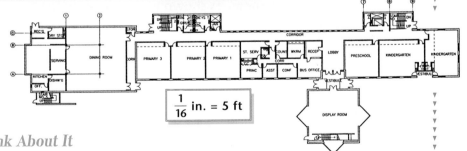

$\frac{1}{16}$ in. = 5 ft

Think About It

1 How does the plan designate a doorway? **by an arc**

2 How many feet are represented by 1 in. on the drawing? **80 ft**

3 Estimate the length of the long corridor from the dining room to the kindergarten at the other end of the building. **about 265 ft**

Exploration 1

SCALE DRAWINGS

SET UP *Work in a group. You will need:* • *tape measure* • *ruler* • *plain or graph paper*

▶ The floor plan on page 451 is an example of a *scale drawing* with a *scale* of 1 in. to 80 ft. The **scale** is the ratio of a length in the drawing to the corresponding length in the actual room.

To make a scale drawing, you need to choose a scale and convert the actual measurements to those for the drawing. You'll practice these skills by making scale drawings of your classroom.

4 **Estimation** Estimate and then find the dimensions of the walls, the door(s), and any other features of your classroom that you want to include in your scale drawings. Also measure the position of each feature relative to the floor and a corner of the room.
Answers will vary. Check students' work.

5 Based on the measurements from Question 4, choose a convenient scale that will allow you to fit a scale drawing of the floor plan of your classroom onto a standard sheet of paper.
Answers will vary. Check students' work.

▶ You can use proportions to help you figure out how long to make the outlines of your classroom, as shown in the Example below.

FOR ◀ HELP

with *finding missing lengths*, see
MODULE 3, p. 207

EXAMPLE

The dimensions of a small room are 15 ft by 14 ft. The scale in a scale drawing of the room will be 0.5 in. to 1 ft.

x = length on drawing (inches) y = width on drawing (inches)

$$\text{inches} \rightarrow \frac{x}{15} = \frac{0.5}{1}$$
$$x = (0.5)(15)$$
$$x = 7.5$$

$$\text{inches} \rightarrow \frac{y}{14} = \frac{0.5}{1}$$
$$y = (0.5)(14)$$
$$y = 7$$

In the drawing, the dimensions of the room will be 7.5 in. by 7 in.

6 Draw the outline of your classroom on your paper. Write the scale on your drawing. **Answers will vary. Check students' work.**

7 Discussion Compare your scale drawing with those of your classmates. Do all the drawings use the same scale? Do they all look the same? Why or why not?
Answers will vary. Check students' work.

▶ **Before you make a scale drawing that includes any of the features of your classroom, you may want to make a sketch and label it with the actual measurements.**

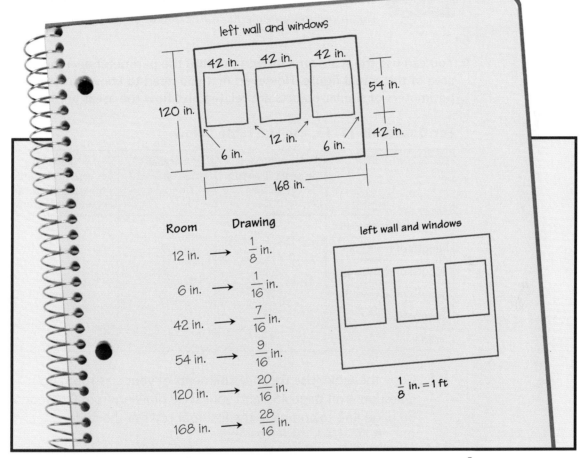

left wall and windows

Room	Drawing
12 in. →	$\frac{1}{8}$ in.
6 in. →	$\frac{1}{16}$ in.
42 in. →	$\frac{7}{16}$ in.
54 in. →	$\frac{9}{16}$ in.
120 in. →	$\frac{20}{16}$ in.
168 in. →	$\frac{28}{16}$ in.

left wall and windows

$\frac{1}{8}$ in. = 1 ft

8 Mark the positions of any doors or windows on the scale drawing you made in Question 6. **Answers will vary. Check students' work.**

9 Pick one of the walls of your classroom. What would be the dimensions of the wall in a scale drawing with a scale of 2 in. to 3 ft? Is this a good scale to use? Why or why not?

10 ✔ CHECKPOINT Make a scale drawing of one wall of your classroom. Include at least one feature, and the scale.
Answers will vary. Check students' work.

9. Sample Response: No; A drawing of an average classroom would not fit on an $8\frac{1}{2} \times 11$ in. sheet of paper.

✔ QUESTION 10

...checks that you can make a scale drawing.

HOMEWORK EXERCISES ▶ See Exs. 1–8 on p. 458.

PERIMETERS and AREAS of SIMILAR FIGURES

SET UP *Work with a partner. You will need:* • *scale drawings and classroom measurements from Exploration 1* • *ruler*

▶ You can use the scale on a drawing to find the perimeter and the area of the actual figure. However, first you need to know how the perimeters of similar objects are related and how the areas are related.

For Questions 11–13, use the table below.

	Measurement on scale drawing (in inches)	Actual measurement (in inches)	Ratio of measurement on scale drawing to actual measurement
length of front wall	?	?	?
length of back wall	?	?	?
length of right wall	?	?	?
length of left wall	?	?	?
perimeter	?	?	?
area	?	?	?

11 Copy the table. Use the measurements of your classroom from Question 4 on page 452 and your scale drawing from Question 6 on page 453 to complete the first four rows of the table.
Answers will vary. Check students' work.

12 a. Find the perimeter of your scale drawing and the perimeter of your actual classroom. **Answers will vary. Check students' work.**

b. Find the ratio of the perimeters. What do you notice?
It is the same as the ratio of the lengths.

13 a. Find the area of your scale drawing and the area of your actual classroom floor. **Answers will vary. Check students' work.**

b. Find the ratio of the areas. What do you notice?
It is the square of the ratio of the lengths.

14 Try This as a Class Based on your answers to Questions 12 and 13, how is the perimeter of a scale drawing related to the actual perimeter? How is the drawing's area related to the actual area?
The ratio of the perimeters is the scale; The ratio of the areas is the square of the scale.

▶ You can use what you have learned about the relationship between perimeters and areas of similar figures to find unknown measurements.

EXAMPLE

△ABC is similar to △DEF. Use the information in the diagram to find the perimeter of △DEF.

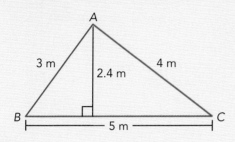 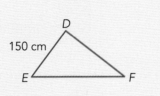

SAMPLE RESPONSE

First Find the scale. It is the ratio of *DE* to *AB*.

$$\text{scale} = \frac{DE}{AB} = \frac{150 \text{ cm}}{3 \text{ m}} = \frac{50 \text{ cm}}{1 \text{ m}}$$

Next Use the fact that the ratio of the perimeters is the same as the scale to write a proportion.

$$\frac{\text{Perimeter of } \triangle DEF}{\text{Perimeter of } \triangle ABC} = \frac{50 \text{ cm}}{1 \text{ m}}$$

Then Solve the proportion. Let *p* = the perimeter of △DEF.

$$\frac{p}{3 \text{ m} + 4 \text{ m} + 5 \text{ m}} = \frac{50 \text{ cm}}{1 \text{ m}}$$

$$\frac{p}{12 \text{ m}} = \frac{50 \text{ cm}}{1 \text{ m}}$$

$$12 \text{ m} \cdot \frac{p}{12 \text{ m}} = 12 \text{ m} \cdot \frac{50 \text{ cm}}{1 \text{ m}}$$

$$p = 600 \text{ cm}$$

The perimeter of △DEF is 600 cm.

15 Try This as a Class Use the triangles in the Example above.

a. What is the ratio of the area of △DEF to the area of △ABC? How do you know? $\frac{2500 \text{ cm}^2}{1 \text{ m}^2}; \left(\frac{50 \text{ cm}}{1 \text{ m}}\right)^2 = \left(\frac{2500 \text{ cm}^2}{1 \text{ m}^2}\right)$

b. Find the area of △ABC. Use it and your answer to part (a) to find the area of △DEF. $6 \text{ m}^2; 15{,}000 \text{ cm}^2$

16 The scale drawing below is for the offices of a small business.

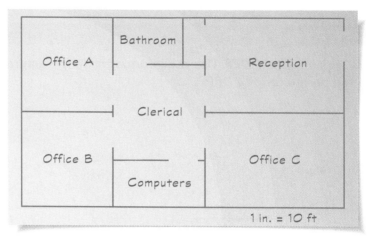

a. Measure to find the perimeter and the area of Office C in the scale drawing. **perimeter = 5 in., area = 1.5 in.²**

b. Use your answer to part (a) and the scale to find the perimeter and the area of the actual Office C.
perimeter = 50 ft, area = 150 ft²

c. The area of the actual computer room is 50 ft². Without measuring, find the area of that room in the scale drawing.
0.5 in.²

✔ **QUESTION 17**

...checks that you can use a scale to find perimeters and areas.

17 ✔ **CHECKPOINT** Each pair of figures is similar. Find each missing perimeter or area.

a. Perimeter of △ACD = 72 in.
Perimeter of △ABE = __?__

Area of △ACD = 216 in.²
Area of △ABE = __?__
24 in.; 24 in.²

b. Perimeter of WXYZ = 30 yd
Perimeter of PQRS = __?__

Area of WXYZ = 50 yd²
Area of PQRS = __?__
135 ft; 1012.5 ft²

HOMEWORK EXERCISES ▶ See Exs. 9–22 on pp. 459–460.

Key Term

Scale Drawings (pp. 452–453)

A scale drawing shows the parts of whatever it represents in proportion to one another. The ratio of each pair of corresponding lengths is the scale. To find out how long to make a segment in a scale drawing, you can use a proportion.

scale

Example A building is 30 ft high. Find the height h of the building in a scale drawing if the scale is 1 in. to 10 ft.

$$\text{inches} \rightarrow \frac{h}{30} = \frac{1}{10} \leftarrow \text{inches}$$
$$\text{feet} \rightarrow \qquad\qquad \leftarrow \text{feet}$$

$$10h = 30$$

$$h = 3$$

The height of the building in the scale drawing is 3 in.

Perimeters and Areas of Similar Figures (pp. 454–456)

If the ratio between corresponding sides of similar figures is $\frac{a}{b}$, then the ratio of their perimeters is $\frac{a}{b}$, and the ratio of their areas is $\frac{a^2}{b^2}$.

Example Parallelogram ABCD is similiar to parallelogram PQRS.

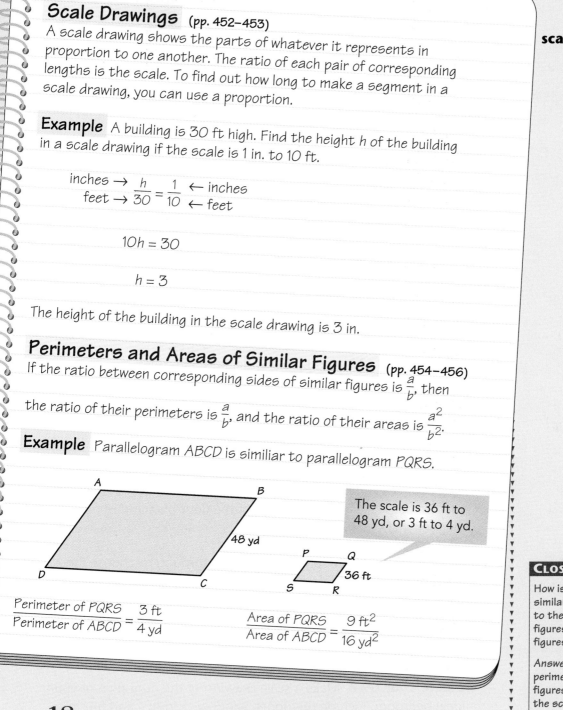

The scale is 36 ft to 48 yd, or 3 ft to 4 yd.

48 yd

36 ft

$$\frac{\text{Perimeter of } PQRS}{\text{Perimeter of } ABCD} = \frac{3 \text{ ft}}{4 \text{ yd}}$$

$$\frac{\text{Area of } PQRS}{\text{Area of } ABCD} = \frac{9 \text{ ft}^2}{16 \text{ yd}^2}$$

18 Key Concepts Question

    a. The perimeter of *ABCD* is 256 yd. Find the perimeter of *PQRS*.
    192 ft
    b. The area of *PQRS* is 1800 ft². Find the area of *ABCD*.
    3200 yd²

CLOSURE QUESTION

How is the scale of similar figures related to the perimeter of the figures? the area of the figures?

Answer: The ratio of the perimeters of the figures is the same as the scale (or the ratio of the lengths of corresponding sides), but the ratio of the areas of the figures is the square of the scale.

Section 6

Practice & Application Exercises

1. The scale drawing below uses the scale $\frac{1}{16}$ in. to 5 ft. Make a scale drawing of one of the rooms shown using the scale $\frac{1}{8}$ in. to 5 ft. Check students' work.

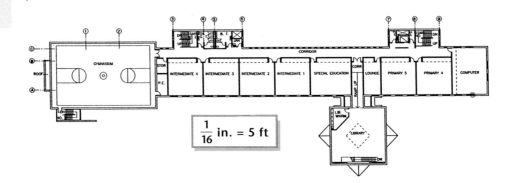

$\frac{1}{16}$ in. = 5 ft

In Exercises 2–4, the dimensions of several objects are given. Make a scale drawing of the top view, the front view, and the right-side view of each object. Include the scale. Scales and views may vary. Check students' work.

2. A dictionary is 12 in. long, 9 in. wide, and 3 in. thick.

3. A credit card is 85 mm long, 55 mm wide, and 1 mm thick.

4. The base of a rectangular pyramid is 24 ft long and 18 ft wide. The height is 36 ft.

5. **Estimation** Estimate and then find the dimensions of a room in your home. Make a scale drawing of the floor plan and of one of the four walls. Include the scale(s). Answers will vary. Check students' work.

6. **Writing** Describe the process you went through to choose the scale for one of the scale drawings you made in Exercises 2–5.

7. **Open-ended** Choose an object that is more complex than a plain rectangular prism and make detailed scale drawings of the top view, the front view, and the right-side view. Answers will vary. Check students' work.

8. **Create Your Own** Make a scale drawing of the floor plan of your ideal bedroom. Include the doors, windows, closets, and furniture in your drawing, and identify the scale. Answers will vary. Check students' work.

6. Sample Response: I decided about how big I wanted the drawing to be, then chose one measurement and decided what scale would work. Then I checked the others to be sure my drawing would be a reasonable size.

The perimeter of a room is 16 yd and the area of the room is 16 yd². What would be the perimeter and the area of the room in a scale drawing with each of the following scales?

9. 1 in. to 1 yd
16 in.; 16 in.²

10. 1 ft to 4 yd
4 ft; 1 ft²

11. 3 in. to 4 yd
12 in.; 9 in.²

12. Writing Describe the process you went through to find the answer in Exercise 11.

To find perimeter, I used the proportion $\frac{3}{4} = \frac{x}{16}$. To find area, I used the proportion $\frac{9}{16} = \frac{x}{16}$.

The two figures in each diagram are similar. Use the given information to replace each ? with the correct measurement. Round decimal answers to the nearest tenth.

13. Area of $\triangle ABC$ = 5.25 cm²
Area of $\triangle XYZ \approx$ __?__ 58.3 mm²

14. Perimeter of $STUV$ = 58 ft
Perimeter of $DEFG$ = __?__ 348 in.

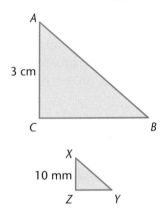

3 cm

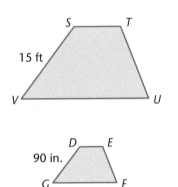

15 ft

90 in.

15. Area of $PQRSTU \approx$ 9353.1 ft²
Area of $ABCDEF \approx$ __?__
2338.3 yd²

16. Perimeter of $WXYZ$ = 16.5 m
Perimeter of $KLMN$ = __?__
2200 cm

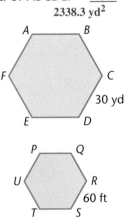

30 yd

60 ft

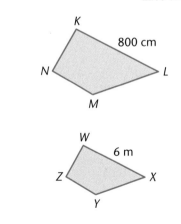

800 cm

6 m

17. Challenge Use a ruler and the trapezoids in Exercise 14.

a. Find all the unknown side lengths of the trapezoids.
ST = 8 ft, TU = 13 ft, UV = 22 ft; DE = 48 in., EF = 78 in., FG = 132 in.

b. Find the height of each trapezoid.
height of $STUV$ = 12 ft, height of $DEFG$ = 72 in.

Scale: 3 in. = 10 mi

Shingle Creek

Mississippi River

City Hall

Cedar Lake

Lake of the Isles

Lake Calhoun

MINNEAPOLIS

Lake Harriet

Lake Hiawatha

Lake Nokomis

Minnehaha Creek

Mother Lake

The scale on the map of Minneapolis is 3 in. to 10 mi.

18. Estimation Estimate the perimeter of the city on the map. Then use your answer to estimate the actual perimeter of the city.
about 10 in.; about 33 mi

19. Estimation Estimate the actual length of the section of the Mississippi River that runs through the city.
about 11.5 mi

20. The actual city covers about 58.7 mi². How many square inches is this on the map? 5.3 in.²

21. There are about 3.6 mi² of inland water in the actual city. How many square inches of water is this on the map? 0.324 in.²

RESEARCH

Exercise 22 checks that you can interpret the scale on a scale drawing.

Reflecting on the Section

22. Find a floor plan. Some possible sources are books about architecture and magazines about homes. Use the scale on the floor plan to estimate the perimeter and the area of the actual floor.
Answers will vary. Check students' work.

Spiral Review

Solve each inequality. Graph each solution. (Module 6, p. 447)

23. $2 + x \leq 6$ $x \leq 4$

24. $n - 3 > 5$ $n > 8$

25. $-2.5a < 50$ $a > -20$

26. $17 - 3m \geq 5$ $m \leq 4$

27. $1.2c - 4.6 \leq -0.4$
$c \leq 3.5$

28. $\frac{5}{12} > \frac{7}{12} + \frac{2}{3}y$ $-\frac{1}{4} > a$

The spinner is equally divided into eight sections. Use it to find the probability of each event.
(Module 4, p. 308)

29. The pointer lands in a red section on the first spin and a yellow section on the next. $\frac{3}{16}$

30. The pointer lands in the blue section on the first spin and a red section on the next. $\frac{1}{16}$

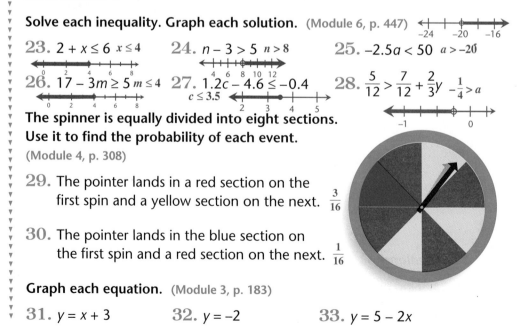

Graph each equation. (Module 3, p. 183)

31. $y = x + 3$

32. $y = -2$

33. $y = 5 - 2x$

31.
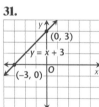
(0, 3)
y = x + 3
(−3, 0)

32.
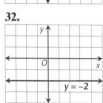
y = −2

33.
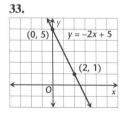
(0, 5) y = −2x + 5
(2, 1)

Working on the Module Project

Creating a Model Town

Scale Drawings You can use scale drawings to show details of the various parts of your building. **6–8. Answers will vary. Check students' work.**

SET UP

You will need:
- *graph paper (optional)*
- *ruler*

6 Use your sketch from Project Question 2 on page 416. What actual dimensions will you use for the exterior doors and the windows of your building? Explain why you chose these dimensions.

7 Make a scale drawing of each exterior wall of your building. Include doors, windows, steps, and so on. Identify the scale.

8 Compare your scale drawings with those of another student. What similarities do you notice? What differences do you notice?

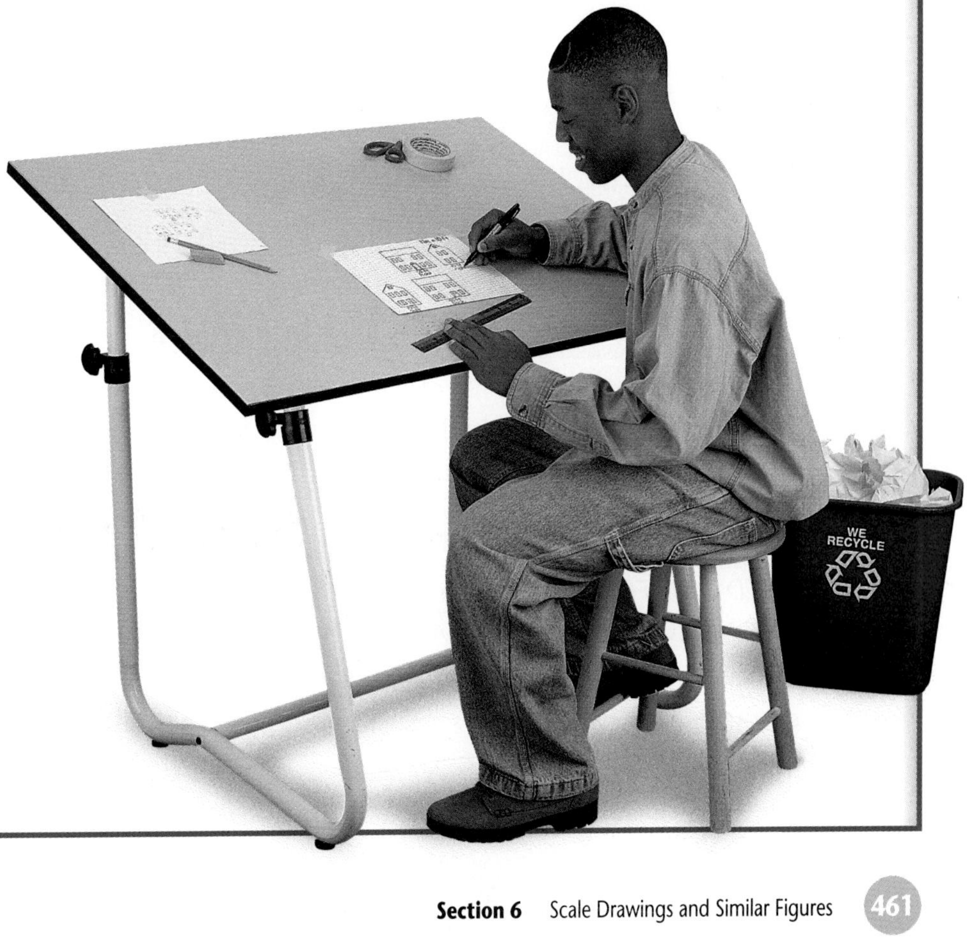

1. A 6 ft tall man is drawn 4 in. tall in a scale drawing. What is the scale?

2. The dimensions of a room in a scale drawing are 8 cm by 5 cm. The scale is 2 cm to 1 m. Find the dimensions of the actual room.
   4 m by 2.5 m

The dimensions of some objects are given. Make a scale drawing of the top view, the front view, and the right-side view of each object. Include the scale. Scales and views may vary. Check students' work.

3. A rectangular prism is 27 ft long, 12 ft wide, and 36 ft high.

4. The base of a regular square pyramid is 5 m long and 5 m wide. The height of the pyramid is 11 m.

The two polygons in each diagram are similar. Find the unknown perimeter or area.

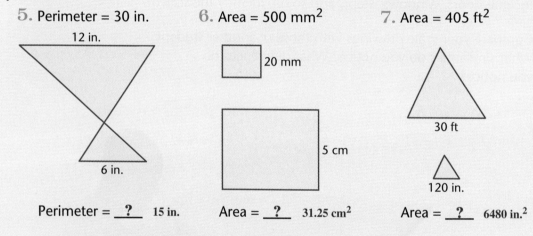

5. Perimeter = 30 in.
   12 in.
   6 in.
   Perimeter = __?__ **15 in.**

6. Area = 500 mm²
   20 mm
   5 cm
   Area = __?__ **31.25 cm²**

7. Area = 405 ft²
   30 ft
   120 in.
   Area = __?__ **6480 in.²**

Standardized Testing ▶ Multiple Choice

1. A door is 8 ft high. How high is the door in a scale drawing that uses the scale 1 in. to 2 ft? **C**

   A 0.25 in.   B 2 in.   C 4 in.   D 16 in.

2. *ABCD* and *EFGH* are similar parallelograms. If the perimeter of *ABCD* is 80 ft, the length of $\overline{AD}$ is 10 ft, and the length of the corresponding side $\overline{EH}$ is 5 ft, what is the perimeter of *EFGH*? **A**

   A 40 ft   B 20 ft   C 15 ft   D 30 ft

Completing the Module Project

Creating a Model Town

Throughout this module you have made sketches and scale drawings to describe a building. To complete your module project, you'll build a three-dimensional model of your building and help to put together your class's model town. **9–14. Answers will vary. Check students' work.**

SET UP

Work as a class.
You will need:
- *large sheets of sturdy paper*
- *ruler*
- *colored pencils or markers*
- *scissors*
- *tape*

9 Work as a class. Compare the scales you used in Project Question 7 on page 461. Together, choose a scale that you will all use to create the buildings for your model town.

10 Use the net you sketched in Project Question 2 on page 416. On sturdy paper, make a net for your building using the scale from Project Question 9.

11 Add to your net the features that you drew in Project Question 7 on page 461, such as doors and windows.

12 Use colored pencils or markers to add other details to your net.

13 Cut out your net and fold along the edges to form your building. Then tape the edges together.

14 Work as a class to arrange your buildings to form a model town. Use the same scale for the streets that you did for each building.

Review and Assessment

You will need: • *ruler* (Exs. 3, 26, and 28)

For Exercises 1 and 2, assume that the figure at the right is made of centimeter cubes. (Sec. 1, Explor. 1)

1. Find the surface area and the volume of the figure.
   surface area = 26 cm²; volume = 6 cm³

2. Find the surface area and the volume of the figure without the shaded cubes. surface area = 18 cm²; volume = 4 cm³

3. Draw flat views of the entire figure from each of the following view points: front, back, left, right, and top.
   (Sec. 1, Explor. 2)

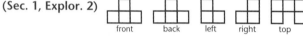
front   back   left   right   top

front   right

For Exercises 4–7, tell whether each view is the *front-right*, *right-back*, *back-left*, or *left-front* view of the figure above without the shaded cubes. (Sec. 1, Explor. 2)

4.   5.   6.   7.

right-back   front-right   back-left   left-front

8. Sketch a net for an octagonal pyramid. How many faces, edges, and vertices will the pyramid have? (Sec. 2, Explor. 1)

9 faces, 16 edges, 9 vertices

For Exercises 9 and 10, tell whether the triangles in each pair are congruent. Explain your reasoning. (Sec. 2, Explor. 2)

9. △ABE, △CBD
congruent; Two sides and the included angle of △ABE are congruent to two sides and the included angle of △CBD.

10. △PQS, △RQS
not congruent; Two sides of △PQS are congruent to two sides of △RQS, but the included angles are not congruent.

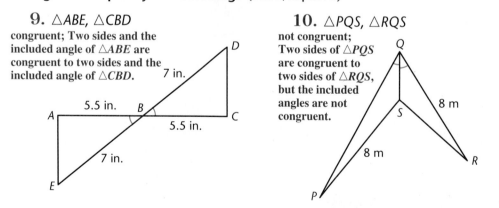

11. The radius of the base of a cone is 0.5 cm. The height of the cone is 30 cm. Find the volume of the cone. Round your answer to the nearest tenth. (Sec. 3, Explor. 2) 7.9 cm³

Find the surface area and the volume of each figure. Assume that the pyramid is regular. (Sec. 3, Explors. 1 and 2)

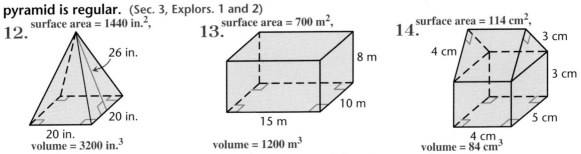

12. surface area = 1440 in.^{2},
26 in.
20 in.
20 in.
volume = 3200 in.^{3}

13. surface area = 700 m^2,
8 m
10 m
15 m
volume = 1200 m^3

14. surface area = 114 cm^2,
3 cm
4 cm
3 cm
5 cm
4 cm
volume = 84 cm^3

For Exercises 15–18, use the diagram. Line k is parallel to line n, and the measure of $\angle 3$ is 105°. (Sec. 4, Explor. 1)

15. Identify and find the measure of the alternate interior angle to $\angle 3$. $\angle 7$; 105°

16. Identify and find the measure of the corresponding angle to $\angle 6$. $\angle 8$; 75°

17. Identify and find the measure of the alternate exterior angle to $\angle 8$. $\angle 4$; 75°

18. Find the measure of $\angle 5$. Explain your method.
Sample Response: 105°; $\angle 3$ and $\angle 5$ are vertical angles, so $m\angle 5 = m\angle 3 = 105°$.

Solve each inequality. Graph each solution. (Sec. 5, Explors. 1 and 2) See Additional Answers.

19. $2a \leq 10$

20. $5 + d > -2$

21. $\dfrac{n}{3} < -3$

22. $5k + 3 \geq 9$

23. $8 - 3x > -4$

24. $-0.4n + 0.2 \leq 1.6$

25. A rectangular community garden is 100 m long by 70 m wide. The community will set aside 50 m^2 of the garden to plant trees. The rest of the garden space will be split into sections. The area of each section will be at least 20 m^2. Write and solve an inequality to find the number of sections. (Sec. 5, Explor. 2) $6950 \geq 20s$; $s \leq 347.5$; no more than 347 sections

26. Make a scale drawing of a rectangular window that is 3 ft wide and 1.5 ft high. Include the scale. (Sec. 6, Explor. 1) Sample Response: Scale: $\dfrac{1}{2}$ in. = 3 ft

27. The scale on a map is 1 cm to 2 km. The perimeter of a lake on the map is 14 cm and its area on the map is 12 cm^2. Find the area and the perimeter of the actual lake. (Sec. 6, Explor. 2) area: 48 km^2, perimeter: 28 km

Reflecting ◀▶on the Module

28. Sketch a pyramid and a prism and give the dimensions. Then make scale drawings of the figures from different views. Find the surface area and the volume of each figure, to the nearest tenth.
Answers will vary. Check students' work.

Visualizing Change

1 Graphs and Functions

As you study rainfall data:
- ◆ Use tables and graphs to model changes in data
- ◆ Use equations, tables, and graphs to represent functions

2 Linear Equations and Problem Solving

As you study different savings plans:
- ◆ Use linear equations, tables, and graphs to solve problems
- ◆ Solve equations that involve simplifying and using the distributive property

3 Modeling Exponential Change

As you learn about compound interest:
- ◆ Use tables and equations to solve problems involving exponential growth

4 Algorithms and Transformations

As you model a gymnast's change in position:
- ◆ Use algorithms to transform geometric shapes
- ◆ Reflect geometric shapes

5 Exploring Quadratic Functions

As you model the paths of aircraft, bridge cables, and basketballs:
- ◆ Explore the shape and symmetry of parabolas
- ◆ Recognize and simplify quadratic equations

The Module Project

Modeling Change in a Story

Leaves change color, caterpillars change into butterflies, and day changes into night. In this project, you'll write a story that involves changes and use mathematics to model them.

More on the Module Project
See pp. 480, 495, 519, and 531.

INTERNET
To learn more about the theme:
http://www.mlmath.com

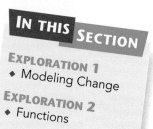

Section ① Graphs and Functions

Use the graph below.

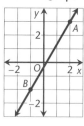

1. Give the coordinates of point A.   (2, 3)

2. Give the coordinates of point B.   (−1, −2)

3. What quadrant is point A in?
   quadrant I

4. What quadrant is point B in?
   quadrant III

5. Is the line increasing or decreasing? How do you know?

   increasing; Sample Response: The line is moving up and to the right.

Time for a Change

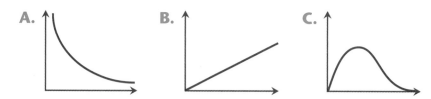

◄◄◄ *Setting the Stage*

Suppose you are asked to describe a rainfall. You might paint a picture, write a story, or compose a piece of music. Barbara M. Hales decided to write the poem shown below.

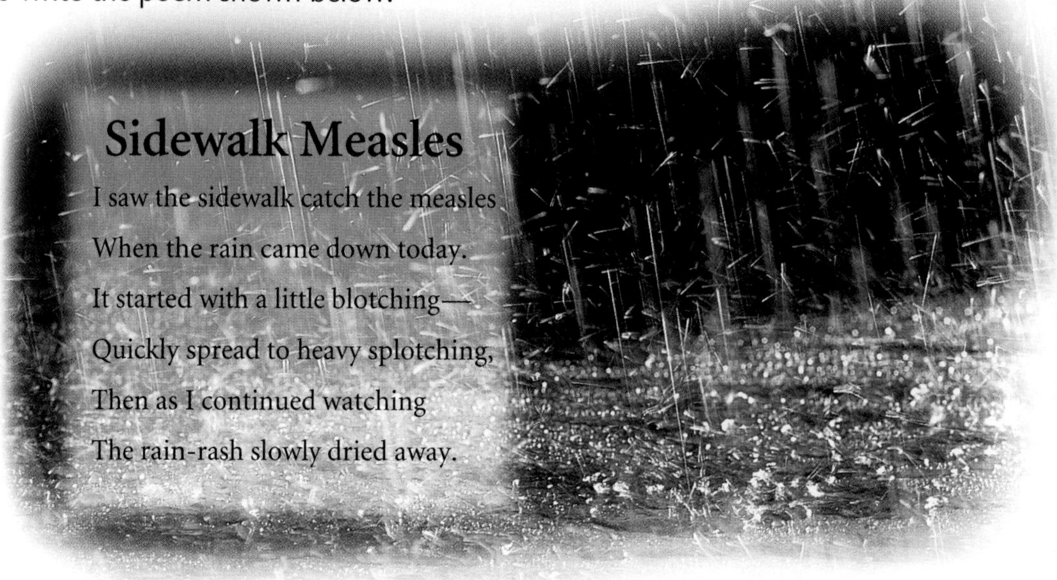

Sidewalk Measles

I saw the sidewalk catch the measles

When the rain came down today.

It started with a little blotching—

Quickly spread to heavy splotching,

Then as I continued watching

The rain-rash slowly dried away.

Think About It

1 Which graph below do you think best describes how the rainfall changes over time in the poem? **C**

A.

B.

C.

2 How did the rainfall change in the poem? How was this change shown in the graph you chose in Question 1?

3 What title would you use for the graph you chose in Question 1? What labels would you use for the horizontal and vertical axes?
Sample Response: Rainfall; Time; Amount of Rainfall

▶ **The world around you is constantly changing. A graph is one way to model change. Throughout this module you'll choose and develop mathematical models that can help you visualize change.**

2. It started slowly with scattered showers, then became heavy, and then slowly stopped; The graph starts at zero, slowly climbs, reaches a peak and then gradually drops off.

Exploration 1

Modeling Change

SET UP *Work in a group of three. You will need: • water • clear plastic cup • metric ruler • clear container • graph paper*

GOAL

LEARN HOW TO...
◆ use tables and graphs to model changes in data

AS YOU...
◆ explore how the shape of a container affects changes in water level

▶ **Rainfall can cause dramatic changes in the water level of lakes and rivers. For example, from 1873 to 1963, the water level in Utah's Great Salt Lake varied by as much as 20 ft. The surface area of the lake went from 2400 mi^2 to 1000 mi^2. These changes were due in part to the shape of the lake bed.**

In this exploration, you'll model rainfall on a lake by pouring water into a container. Each group in your class should choose a container with a different shape. As you add water to the container, your group will measure the change in water level.

4 **Discussion** Suppose you were to pour water steadily into your group's container. How can you use a graph to show the change in water level inside the container?

4. Sample Response: Show the amount of water on the horizontal axis and the height of the water in the container on the vertical axis.

5 Before you start your experiment, look at your group's container. How do you think the water level will change as water is poured into the container? Use your prediction to sketch a graph of the water level as the container is filled. Answers will vary. Check students' work.

6 Follow the steps below to perform the experiment.
Answers will vary. Check students' work.

 Step 1

Mark your cup so that the same amount of water will be poured into the container each time. This amount will be called a "unit."

 Step 2

Fill the cup with water up to the mark you made in Step 1. Pour the water into the container.

 Step 3

Measure the water level to the nearest millimeter.

 Step 4

Record the measurement in a table like the one shown.

 Step 5

Repeat Steps 2–4 until the container is almost full. As you finish filling the container, you may need to estimate what fraction of a unit you use to completely fill it. Do not let the container overflow.

7. Answers will vary. Check students' work.

7 **a.** Use your table to make a graph that shows how water level depends on the number of units of water in the container. Connect the data points with a smooth curve.

b. Compare your graph from part (a) with the one you drew in Question 5. How accurate was your prediction?

FOR◄HELP
with *choosing a scale*, see
MODULE 1, p. 29

▶ To get an idea of how something is changing, look at how one variable changes as the other variable increases by a fixed amount.

8 Try This as a Class Compare your results with other groups' results.

a. For which containers did the water level increase by the same amount each time water was added? For which containers did the water level change by a different amount?
cylinders and prisms; irregularly shaped containers

b. Which graphs are linear? Which are nonlinear?
graphs for cylinders and prisms; graphs for irregularly shaped containers

c. Suppose you repeated the experiment using the container shown at the right. Describe what you think your graph would look like. Explain your thinking.
The graph would be linear because the shape of the container is uniform.

FOR◀HELP
with *linear and nonlinear graphs*, see
MODULE 3, p. 183

9 Try This as a Class For which groups did the water level rise the fastest? How can you tell from the graphs? What does this tell you about the containers these groups used? See below.

10 ✔ CHECKPOINT Match each table with one of the graphs below. Explain why you chose that graph and tell what the labels of the vertical and horizontal axes should be.

a. Height of a ball thrown in the air as time passes
Graph 2; The graph starts at the origin and shows increase followed by decrease.

Time (seconds)	0	0.5	1	1.5	2	2.5	3
Height (feet)	0	27	40	45	42	31	12

vertical: Height (ft), horizontal: Time(s)

b. Bacteria growth in a heated swimming pool
Graph 1; The graph starts above the origin and shows increasing growth over time.

Time (days)	0	0.5	1	1.5	2	2.5
Bacteria count	1500	2121	3000	4242	6000	8485

vertical: Bacteria count, horizontal: Time (days)

c. Speed conversion chart
Graph 3; The graph starts at the origin and shows a steady rate of change.

mi/h	0	10	20	30	40	50	60	70
km/h	0	16	32	48	64	81	97	113

vertical: km/h, horizontal: mi/h

✔ QUESTION 10

...checks that you can use tables and graphs to interpret data.

9. Graphs with an upward curve show the fastest growth; Small based containers that are larger at the base than at the top would show the fastest growth.

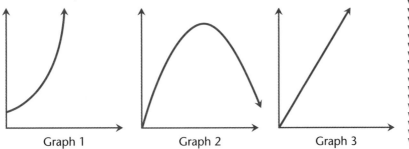

Graph 1   Graph 2   Graph 3

11 On page 469, you read about the Great Salt Lake. Suppose a lake bed is approximately cone-shaped, as shown at the right. A long, steady rain causes the water level to rise. Sketch a graph that could model the water level over time.

11.

HOMEWORK EXERCISES ▶ See Exs. 1–9 on pp. 476–477.

Exploration 2

FUNCTIONS

SET UP *Work with a partner.*

▶ In Exploration 1, you used a graph to show the relationship between the amount of water poured into a container and the water level inside the container.

12 Use the phrases *amount of water added* and *water level* to complete the following sentence. Explain your thinking.

In the experiment performed in Exploration 1, the __?__ depended on the __?__. water level; amount of water added; The water level changed as a result of changes in the amount of water.

▶ The graph you made in Question 7 modeled a *function*. A **function** is a relationship between input and output. For each input value of a function, there is *exactly* one output value. Output is a function of input.

13 a. Explain why the data you collected in your experiment modeled a function. There was only one water level for each amount of water added.

b. What was the input in the experiment in Exploration 1? What was the output? the amount of water; the water level

c. Use the phrase *is a function of* to rewrite the completed statement from Question 12. The water level is a function of the amount of water added.

14 For five days, Mei recorded the data shown at the right. She concluded that the amount of rainfall for any given day is a function of the high temperature for that day.

Daily high temperature (°F)	Amount of rainfall (in.)
81	0.4
75	0
79	0.5
80	1.2
74	0.5

  a. How do you think Mei came to this conclusion? **For each daily high temperature there is only one rainfall amount.**

  b. Suppose Mei recorded these data for a year. Do you think she would still say that daily rainfall is a function of daily high temperature? Why or why not?

14. b. No; It is likely that there would be different rainfall amounts for the same daily high temperature.

  c. In general, do you think that daily rainfall is a function of daily high temperature? Explain. **Sample Response: No; Rainfall amounts are affected by more than daily high temperature.**

15 Discussion Tell whether y is a function of x. Explain your thinking. **Sample responses are given.**

  a. x = the amount of time that the sky is cloudy
  y = the amount of rain that falls **No; Not all clouds produce rain.**

  b. x = the number of minutes someone drives at 55 mi/h
  y = the distance that person drives **Yes; The distance driven depends on the driving time.**

  c. x = the time of day today
  y = the number of people at your school at that time

15. c. Yes; at any one time today there are a certain number of people at school.

  d. x = a person's height
  y = the foot length of someone with that height
  No; Two people can be the same height but have different foot lengths.

▶ You can also think of a function as a *rule* that pairs each input value with exactly one output value. You can use an equation to write a rule for some functions.

16 Suppose it starts raining steadily at noon. The rain falls for the rest of the afternoon at a rate of 0.2 inches per hour.

  a. Let y = the amount of rain that has fallen since noon. Let x = the number of hours since noon. Explain why the value of y is a function of the value of x. **The amount of rainfall depends on the number of hours since noon.**

  b. Write an equation that models this function. **$y = 0.2x$**

▶ You can use a table of values or a graph to tell whether an equation models a function.

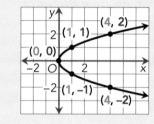

EXAMPLE

Given an equation, you can tell whether y is a function of x by comparing input and output values in a table or a graph.

a. $y = x^2$ For every value of x, there is exactly one value of y. The equation models a function.

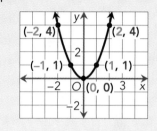

Input (x)	Output (y)
–2	4
–1	1
0	0
1	1
2	4

b. $x = y^2$ For some values of x, there are two different values of y. The equation does not model a function.

Input (x)	Output (y)
0	0
1	–1 and 1
4	–2 and 2

17. a. Both graphs are the same shape; They are in different positions. One opens upward and the other opens to the right.

17 **Try This as a Class** Refer to the Example.

a. How are the two graphs alike? How are they different?

b. Use the tables to find the value(s) of y when $x = 1$ in both equations. Then use the graphs.
For $y = x^2$, $y = 1$ when $x = 1$; For $x = y^2$, $y = –1$ and 1 when $x = 1$.

c. How can you use a table of values to tell whether an equation models a function? How can you use a graph? If there is only one value of y for each value of x in either a table or a graph, the equation models a function.

✔ **QUESTION 18**

...checks that you can identify a function.

18 ✔ **CHECKPOINT** For each equation or graph, tell whether y is a function of x. Explain your thinking.

a. $y = 7x$ function; For every value of x there is only one value of y. **b.** $2 + x = y^2$ not a function; There are two values of y for some values of x.

c. not a function; There are two values of y for some values of x.

d. function; For every value of x there is only one value of y.

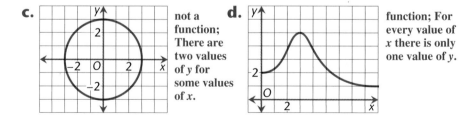

HOMEWORK EXERCISES See Exs. 10–26 on pp. 478–479.

474 **Module 7** Visualizing Change

Section 1
Key Concepts

Modeling Change (pp. 469–472)

You can use tables and graphs to model and analyze changes in data.

Example Suppose you measure the depth of snow in two different towns over the same period of time.

Town A The table shows that the snow depth increases by about the same amount each day. The data points lie almost on a straight line.

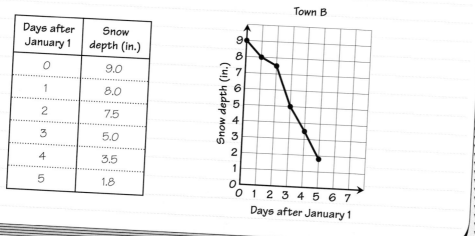

Days after January 1	Snow depth (in.)
0	2.3
1	3.3
2	4.4
3	5.4
4	6.3
5	7.4

Town A

Town B The table shows that the snow depth decreases by a different amount each day. The graph of the data is always decreasing, but not in a straight line.

Days after January 1	Snow depth (in.)
0	9.0
1	8.0
2	7.5
3	5.0
4	3.5
5	1.8

Town B

19 Key Concepts Question Sketch a container that you might fill with water. Then sketch a graph that models the water level inside the container as you fill it.

Answers will vary. Check students' work.

Continued on next page

Key Concepts

Key Term

function

Functions (pp. 472–474)

A function is a rule that pairs each input with exactly one output. You can use equations, tables, and graphs to model some functions.

Example A number y is 1 more than 3 times a number x.

Equation

$y = 3x + 1$

Table

x	y
−2	−5
−1	−2
0	1
1	4

Graph

(1, 4)
(0, 1)
(−1, −2)
(−2, −5)

20. Yes;

Input	Output
0	2.3
1	3.3
2	4.4
3	5.4
4	6.3
5	7.4

Input	Output
0	9.0
1	8.0
2	7.5
3	5.0
4	3.5
5	1.8

20 **Key Concepts Question** Do the graphs and tables on page 475 model functions? If so, list the input values and the corresponding output values. If not, explain why.

Section ①

Practice & Application Exercises

YOU WILL NEED

For Ex. 5:
♦ Labsheet 1A

For Exs. 6, 7, 25, and 29–32:
♦ graph paper

Suppose water is steadily poured into each of the containers below. Which graph models the water level in each container over time?

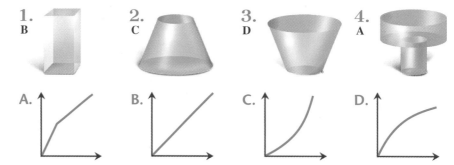

1. B

2. C

3. D

4. A

A.

B.

C.

D.

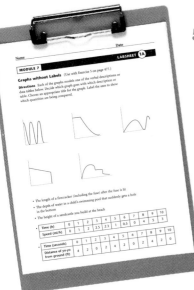

5. **Use Labsheet 1A.** You'll match a verbal description or a table with each of the *Graphs without Labels.*

6. **Open-ended** Sketch a graph that could model the following bike ride. You ride a bicycle for some time at a constant speed. Then you slow down for a stop sign, stop and look both ways, then speed up again.

7. **Create Your Own** Write a story or a poem that describes a change over time. Use a graph to illustrate your story or poem. **Answers will vary. Check students' work.**

History In ancient times, people used containers filled with water to tell time. The water steadily flowed out through a hole in the base of the water clock. People could tell the time by comparing the water level with hour marks on the container. Use this information for Exercises 8 and 9.

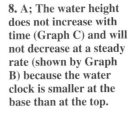

5. first graph matches second table, second graph matches second description, third graph matches first table, fourth graph matches first description, fifth graph matches third description.

6. Sample Response:

◄
The oldest surviving water clock is from Egypt, 14th century B.C.

8. Which graph would you expect to model the change in water level inside the water clock shown above? Why?

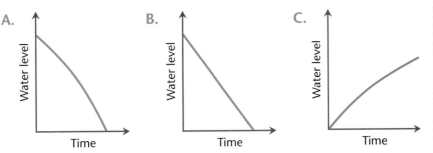

A.

B.

C.

8. A; The water height does not increase with time (Graph C) and will not decrease at a steady rate (shown by Graph B) because the water clock is smaller at the base than at the top.

9. **Challenge** An artist drew a sketch of the inside of a water clock to show that after one hour, the level is at the first hour mark, after two hours, the level is at the second hour mark, and so on. The artist makes the distances between the marks the same. Are the marks spaced correctly? Explain.

No; The marks should be farther apart toward the bottom where the water clock is narrower.

1 hour
2 hours
3 hours
4 hours
5 hours

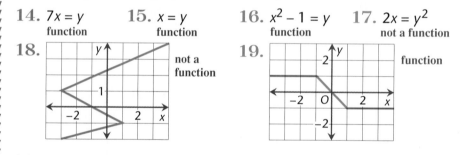

10. Suppose you have $230 saved. You get a job that pays $25 a week. You decide to add all of your earnings to your savings.

　a. Describe a function based on this situation. Identify the input and output. **Input is the number of weeks and output is the total amount in the savings account.**

　b. Write an equation to model the function. $y = 25x + 230$

Writing For each pair of variables, tell whether *y* is a function of *x*. Explain your thinking.

11. *x* = the number of $12 concert tickets sold

　y = the amount of money made from selling the tickets
　Yes; the amount of money made depends on the number of tickets sold.

12. *x* = the age of any given office building

　y = the height of that office building
　No; The height of an office building does not necessarily depend on how old it is.

13. *x* = the time of year

　y = the time at which the sun rises where you live
　Yes; In one location there is only one sunrise time for each day of the year.

For each equation or graph, tell whether *y* is a function of *x*.

14. $7x = y$　　**15.** $x = y$　　**16.** $x^2 - 1 = y$　　**17.** $2x = y^2$
　function　　　　**function**　　　**function**　　　　　**not a function**

18.　**not a function**　　**19.**　**function**

20. Geometry Connection Is the area of a square a function of its side length? Is the side length of a square a function of its area? Explain. **Yes; Yes; Sides lengths determine the area of a square and the side length of a square is its positive square root, so for each area, there is only one side length.**

For Exercises 21–23, a rule for a function is given. Write an equation to model the function.

21. Divide a number by 5. $y = \frac{x}{5}$　　**22.** Multiply a number by –1. $y = -x$

23. Multiply a number by itself, then divide the result by 2. $y = \frac{x^2}{2}$

24. Home Involvement Make up a rule for a function like those in Exercises 21–23. Keep your rule secret. Have someone give you a number to use as the input. Tell the person what the output for that number is. The person should make a table of the input and output pairs. Have the person try to guess the rule.
Answers will vary. Check students' work.

25. **Earth Science** In 1993, heavy rains in the Midwest caused the Mississippi River to flood its banks. By April 4, the water had risen 2.1 in. above the banks of the river. It continued to rise at an average rate of 0.4 in. per day for the next six days.

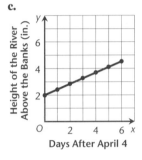

a. Let y = the height of the river above the bank x days after April 4. Write an equation for y in terms of x. $y = 0.4x + 2.1$

b. Describe reasonable values for each of the variables in your equation. Explain your thinking.

c. Graph your equation.

d. Tell whether y is a function of x. y **is a function of** x.

Reflecting on the Section

Be prepared to discuss your response to Exercise 26 in class.

26. In this section, you have seen how graphs and tables can be used to illustrate change. **Answers will vary. Check students' work.**

a. Describe a quantity that changes over time. Explain how you could use a table and a graph to model the change.

b. Is the change you described in part (a) a function? Explain.

Spiral Review

27. The perimeter of a rectangular garden is 136 m. Its area is 960 m². Find the perimeter and the area of a scale drawing of the garden with a scale of 1 cm to 2 m. (Module 6, p. 457)
Perimeter is 68 cm and area is 240 cm².

28. Find the value of x. (Module 5, p. 363)

about 6.5 m

Graph each equation. Give the slope of each line. (Module 5, pp. 337–338)

29. $y = x + 1$ 30. $y = -x$ 31. $y = -3$ 32. $y = -x - \dfrac{1}{2}$

25. b. $(0, 2.1)$, $(1, 2.5)$, $(2, 2.9)$, $(3, 3.3)$, $(4, 3.7)$, $(5, 4.1)$, $(6, 4.5)$; The values of x range from 0 to 6 since the river rose at a rate of 0.4 in./day for 6 days. The values of y will be between 2 and 5 since it started at about 2 in.

c.

Days After April 4

Discussion

Exercise 26 checks that you can model a function.

29.

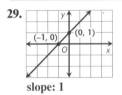

slope: 1

30.

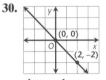

slope: –1

31.

slope: 0

32.

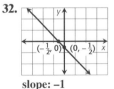

slope: –1

Beginning the Module Project

Modeling Change in a Story

In this project you'll experiment with using different mathematical models to describe changes. Then you'll write a story using these mathematical models as illustrations.

Graphing Change Over Time Many stories involve change. You may be able to model the change with a graph. An example is the story of "Jack and the Beanstalk." In the story, a poor boy named Jack sells his family's cow for some magic beans. The beans sprout into a giant beanstalk that Jack climbs. He finds a wealthy giant at the top of the beanstalk, steals the giant's riches, and then chops down the beanstalk to protect himself from the giant. The graph shown models one change in the story.

SET UP

You will need:
• *graph paper*

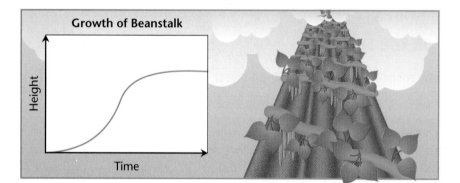

Growth of Beanstalk

Height

Time

1. Sample Response: The seed is planted. After it sprouts, it grows rapidly for a period of time then growth continues but at a gradually slower pace.

1 Describe in words the change modeled by the graph.

2 Describe at least three changes in your own life or from a story that can be modeled by graphs. Draw the graphs. Give each graph a title and label the axes.

Answers will vary. Check students' work.

Extra Skill Practice

Match each container with a graph that shows the water level as a function of the amount of water in the container.

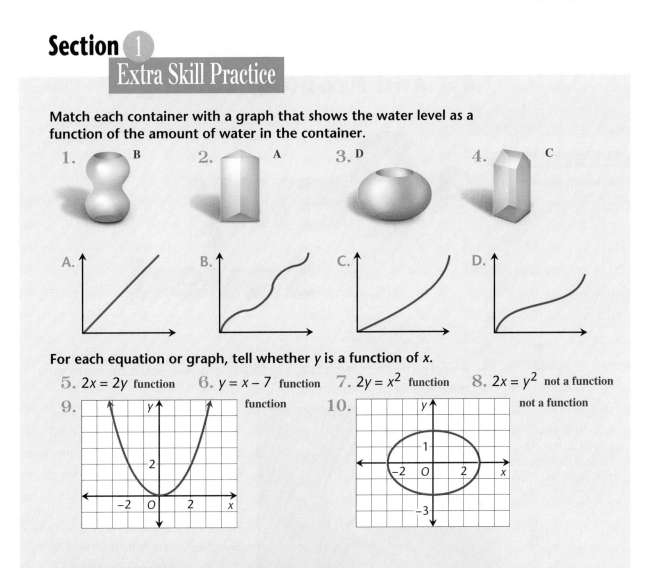

1. **B**

2. **A**

3. **D**

4. **C**

A.

B.

C.

D.

For each equation or graph, tell whether *y* is a function of *x*.

5. $2x = 2y$ function

6. $y = x - 7$ function

7. $2y = x^2$ function

8. $2x = y^2$ not a function

9. function

10. not a function

Study Skills ◀▶ Managing Your Time

Whether you are working independently or in a group to complete a short-term activity or a long-term project, time management should be part of your preparation.

1. In Exploration 1, you worked in a group to conduct an experiment to explore how the shape of a container affects water level. Did your group finish the experiment in the available time? What strategies can you use in planning your time so that you will always finish group activities?

   1. Answers will vary. Check students' work. Set specific goals in the beginning and specify the time in which they need to be completed, appoint a group leader to make sure your project is on schedule.

2. Before you begin working on the module project, make a plan for how you will complete all of the steps so that you finish the entire project on time.   Answers will vary.

Section ② Linear Equations and Problem Solving

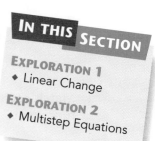

IN THIS SECTION

EXPLORATION 1
♦ Linear Change

EXPLORATION 2
♦ Multistep Equations

a **Penny** Saved

WARM-UP EXERCISES

Use the equation
$y = 2x - 5$.

1. Find the y-value when
   $x = 3$.   1

2. Find the x-value when
   $y = 11$.   8

3. What is the slope of
   the line?   2

Solve each equation.

4. $3x + 2 = 5$ 1

5. $\frac{2}{5}x = \frac{10}{13}$ $\frac{25}{13}$

◄◄◄Setting the Stage

A penny may not seem like very much, but you would be surprised at how quickly pennies add up.

► Fourth graders at Lovell J. Honiss School help count the pennies collected by the school.

Students at the Lovell J. Honiss School in Dumont, New Jersey, set a goal of filling two five-gallon jugs with pennies. Although they quickly met their goal, they continued to save pennies. In the end, they filled four jugs and raised over $1000 to help the homeless.

In Hartland, Michigan, students in the Hartland Consolidated Schools collected pennies for the Meals on Wheels program. They collected over $10,000, enough to fund the program for a year.

Think About It

1 a. About how many pennies does a five-gallon jug hold? How do you know? **about 25,000 pennies; Four jugs held about $1000 or 100,000 pennies.**

b. Suppose the Hartland students collected the pennies over 50 school days. On average, about how many pennies were collected each day? **about 20,000 pennies**

2 Would the pennies collected at the Hartland Consolidated Schools cover your classroom floor? the gymnasium floor? Explain.
Answers will vary. Check students' work. Spread out in a single layer, the pennies would cover about 307 ft²

► In this section, you'll use equations, tables, and graphs to model problems involving the growth of savings over time.

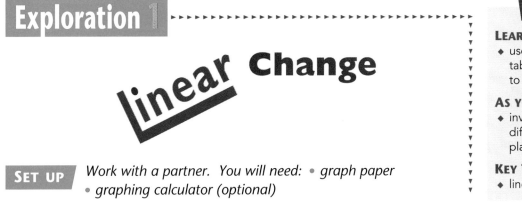

Linear Change

SET UP Work with a partner. You will need: • graph paper • graphing calculator (optional)

▶ **How quickly can you save $1000? It all depends on how much you start with, and how much you add to your savings over time.**

3 **Discussion** Read the savings plans described below. Without doing any calculations, tell which person you think will reach the $1000 goal first. Explain your thinking. See below.

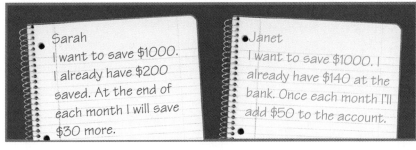

Sarah
I want to save $1000. I already have $200 saved. At the end of each month I will save $30 more.

Janet
I want to save $1000. I already have $140 at the bank. Once each month I'll add $50 to the account.

4 **a.** Copy and extend the table to show how much Sarah will save throughout the first year of her plan. See below.

Sarah's Savings	
Number of months (x)	Amount saved (y)
0	200
1	230
...	...

b. Use your table to find the number of months it will take Sarah to save $1000. Describe your method. See below.

5 **a.** Plot the ordered pairs (x, y) for the data in your table on a coordinate grid. What do you notice about the points? **5. a–c.** See Additional Answers.

b. Draw a line through the points on your graph. Extend the line and use it to find the number of months it will take Sarah to save $1000.

c. **Discussion** Find the point on the line whose x-coordinate is $6\frac{1}{2}$. Does the value of the y-coordinate of this point represent Sarah's savings after $6\frac{1}{2}$ months? Explain.

3. Sample Response: Janet; She starts with less but saves a greater amount each month.

4. a. 2, 260; 3, 290; 4, 320; 5, 350; 6, 380; 7, 410; 8, 440; 9, 470; 10, 500; 11, 530; 12, 560
b. 27 months; Sample Response: After 12 months, she still needs $440 and $\frac{440}{30} = 14\frac{2}{3}$. It will take 15 months + 12 months.

▶ The growth of Sarah's savings over time is an example of linear change. You can use a *linear equation* to represent linear change. A **linear equation** is an equation whose graph is a line.

FOR◀HELP

with *slope-intercept form*, see

MODULE 5, p. 338

6 **a.** Find the slope *m* and the *y*-intercept *b* of the line you drew in Question 5(b). Use these values to write an equation for the line in slope-intercept form. $y = 30x + 200$

b. Substitute values for *x* in the equation from part (a). Solve for *y*. Do the values you get match the values in your table? Yes.

▶ You can use equations, tables, and graphs to model problems involving linear change.

EXAMPLE

Janet has $140. She adds $50 to her savings at the end of each month. When will she have $1000?

Method 1 Use a linear equation.

$$\text{Savings after } x \text{ months} = \text{Starting amount} + \frac{\$50 \text{ per}}{\text{month}} \cdot x \text{ months}$$

$$y = 140 + 50x$$

$$1000 = 140 + 50x$$

> Substitute **$1000** for **y**. Solve the equation for **x**.

Method 2 Use a table.

Keep adding $50 to Janet's savings for each month until she reaches the $1000 goal.

Janet's Savings	
Number of months	Amount saved
0	140
1	190
2	240
...	...

Method 3 Use a graph.

Graph $y = 140 + 50x$ and $y = 1000$ on the same pair of axes.

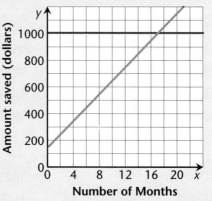

Janet's Savings

---

7 Try This as a Class Refer to the Example on page 484. You will use each model to find how long it will take Janet to save $1000.

a. Solve the equation in the Example. How can you use the solution to find out when Janet will have saved $1000? **17.2; Round up to the next whole number.**

b. Show how to use the table to find out how long it will take Janet to save $1000. **See Additional Answers.**

c. Show how to use the graph to find out how long it will take Janet to save $1000. **See Additional Answers.**

d. Which method do you prefer? Why? **Answers will vary.**

8 ✓ **CHECKPOINT** The Honiss School students collected $1000 in pennies. Suppose your class saved $35 each week. With your partner, use an equation, a table, or a graph to find out how many weeks it would take to save $1000. Explain why you chose the model you did. **See above.**

9 Discussion Find a group in your class who chose a different model than you did for Question 8.

a. Show the other group how you got your answer. **See answer to Question 8.**

b. Compare the advantages and disadvantages of using an equation, a table, and a graph to model the growth of a savings plan. **See below.**

10 Draw the graph from the Example on page 484 on the same pair of axes as the graph you made in Question 5 on page 483. What does the intersection of the two lines tell you?

See Additional Answers.

9. b. Sample responses are given. Table: gives additional information that may be helpful, but may have to be very large (as in Question 8); equation: requires less time and effort than a table or graph, but gives less information; graph: gives a visual interpretation, but may be difficult to determine exact coordinates if they are not integers.

HOMEWORK EXERCISES ▶ See Exs. 1–9 on pp. 491–492.

---

8. Possible answers: In the equation $y = 35x$, if $y = 1000$ then $x =$ about 28.6; 29 weeks;

Number of Weeks	Amount of Savings ($)
0	0
1	35
2	70
3	105
4	140
...	...
29	1015

✓ **QUESTION 8**

…checks that you can model and solve a problem about linear change.

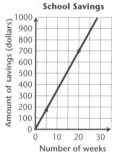

School Savings

Explanations may vary. Check students' work.

You can use a graphing calculator to make and analyze tables and graphs for Question 7 on page 485.

Step 1 Enter the equations to graph by using the Y = feature.

Step 2 Select the TABLE feature to display the *x*-values and the *y*-values of each equation you entered.

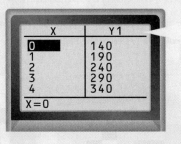

Use the arrow keys to view the entire table. Move the arrows to the right to view Y2.

Step 3 To set the *viewing window* for your graph, enter the minimum, maximum, and scale values for **X** and **Y**. The **X** values set the scale on the horizontal axis and the **Y** values set the scale on the vertical axis. Then graph.

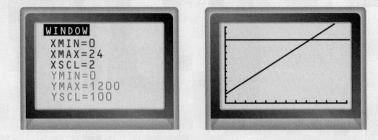

Exploration 2

Multi-step Equations

▶ On page 483, you read about two people who are each trying to save $1000. Sarah has $200 and saves another $30 each month. Janet is starting with $140 and saves an additional $50 each month.

11 Discussion In Question 10 on page 485, you used a graph to find when the two girls will have saved equal amounts of money. How could you use tables to solve this problem?

▶ You can also use an equation to find out when the girls will have the same amount.

GOAL

LEARN HOW TO...
- ◆ solve equations that involve simplifying
- ◆ use the distributive property

AS YOU...
- ◆ model savings plans

KEY TERM
- ◆ distributive property

11. Sample Response: Set up a table of input values with output values for each girl. Continue adding input values until the solution to the problem is reached.

EXAMPLE

For each plan, model the amount saved after x months.

   Sarah's savings = 200 + 30x Janet's savings = 140 + 50x

Then write a new equation.

When will **Sarah's savings** equal Janet's savings?

            Sarah's savings = Janet's savings

            200 + 30x = 140 + 50x

> To find out when the amounts saved are equal, solve the equation.

12 Try This as a Class The final equation in the Example has a variable on both sides of the equal sign.

   a. What would be your first step in solving an equation like this one? Explain your thinking. Subtract or add one of the variable terms from both sides of the equation so all variable terms will be on the same side.
   b. When will Sarah and Janet have the same amount? after 3 monthly savings deposits

13 ✔ CHECKPOINT Solve each equation.

   a. $18 + 3x = x + 24$ **b.** $9 + 2x = 12 + 5x$ **c.** $4x - 7 = 2 - 3x$ $\frac{9}{7}$
          3   −1

✔ QUESTION 13

...checks that you can solve equations with variables on both sides.

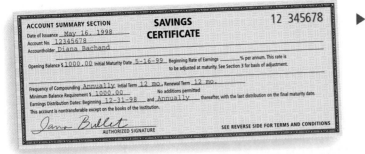

▶ One way to save money is in a savings bank *certificate of deposit* (CD). You deposit an amount of money and agree not to take any money out for a certain amount of time. In return, the bank pays a higher than usual interest rate.

14 Suppose you deposit $1000 into a one-year CD. The expression $1000 + 1000x$ models the amount of money you will have after one year. What do you think x represents? **the interest rate on the CD**

▶ You can use the *distributive property of multiplication over addition* to write the expression in Question 14 another way.

> The **distributive property** says that for all numbers a, b, and c:
>
> $a(b + c) = ab + ac$ and $ab + ac = a(b + c)$
>
> $4(1 + 5) = 4(1) + 4(5)$ $4 + 20 = 4(1 + 5)$
>
> $6(x + 2) = 6x + 6(2)$ $6x + 12 = 6(x + 2)$

15 Use the distributive property to rewrite the expression $1000 + 1000x$. **$1000(1 + x)$**

▶ You can use the distributive property of multiplication over *addition* for expressions involving *subtraction*.

EXAMPLE

To rewrite $5(3 - 2x)$ without parentheses, first write $3 - 2x$ as an addition expression.

$$5(3 - 2x) = 5(3 + (-2x))$$

> Use the distributive property.

$$= 5(3) + (5)(-2x)$$

$$= 15 + (-10x)$$

$$= 15 - 10x$$

16 **Discussion** Michael says that for all numbers a, b, and c, $a(b - c) = ab - ac$. Do you agree? Use examples to support your answer. **Yes; Answers will vary. Check students' work.**

✔ QUESTION 17

...checks that you can use the distributive property.

17 ✔ CHECKPOINT Use the distributive property to rewrite each expression.

a. $5(2x - 3)$
$10x - 15$

b. $-2(5 + x)$
$-10 - 2x$

c. $18m + 21$
$3(6m + 7)$

d. $56m - 7$
$7(8m - 1)$

▶ Sometimes you may want to use the distributive property to solve an equation.

EXAMPLE

Hector earns the same amount babysitting every week. Each week he saves all but $10 of his earnings. If he has $160 after 8 weeks, how much does he earn each week?

SAMPLE RESPONSE

Let x = the amount Hector earns each week.

$160 = 8(x - 10)$ Use the distributive property.

$160 = 8x - 80$

$240 = 8x$

$30 = x$

Hector earns $30 each week babysitting.

18   Two students tried to solve the equation $-4(2 - x) = 6$.

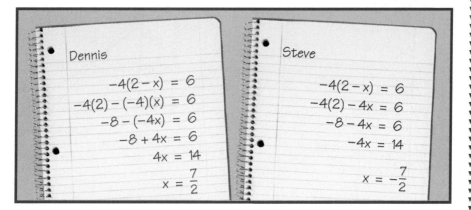

a. Which student solved the equation correctly? What mistake did the other student make? **Dennis; Steve used the distributive property incorrectly.**

b. What would be your first step in solving $-2(3 - x) = 8$? **Use the distributive property to simplify $-2(3 - x)$ or divide both sides of the equation by -2.**

19   **Discussion** How would you solve $-3(x - 1) = 2(5 - x)$?

20 ✔ **CHECKPOINT** Solve each equation.

a. $4(x - 1) = 12$ **b.** $-2(3 + x) = 3x + 1$ **c.** $3(2x - 1) = x + 13$
       4                  $-\dfrac{7}{5}$ $\dfrac{16}{5}$

▌ **HOMEWORK EXERCISES** ▶ See Exs. 10–31 on pp. 492–494.

19. Sample Response: Use the distributive property to rewrite both sides of the equation. Next get variable terms alone on one side of the equation. Finally, if necessary, divide both sides so the coefficient of the variable term is 1.

✔ **QUESTION 20**

…checks that you can use the distributive property to solve an equation.

Key Concepts

Key Term

linear equation

Modeling Linear Change (pp. 483–485)

When a quantity changes by the same amount at regular intervals, the quantity shows linear change. You can use a linear equation to model linear change. You can also use a table or a graph.

Example Lynda borrowed $175 from her parents. She pays them back $10 a week. Her sister Maria borrowed $200 and pays back $15 a week. Who will finish paying off her loan first?

Write an equation for each person. Let y = the amount the person owes after x weeks.

Lynda
$y = 175 - 10x$

Maria
$y = 200 - 15x$

Number of weeks	Amount Lynda owes	Amount Maria owes
0	175	200
1	165	185
2	155	170
3	145	155
4	135	140
5	125	125
6	115	110
…	…	…
13	45	5
14	35	0

Lynda's and Maria's Loans

Maria only has to pay $5 in the 14th week.

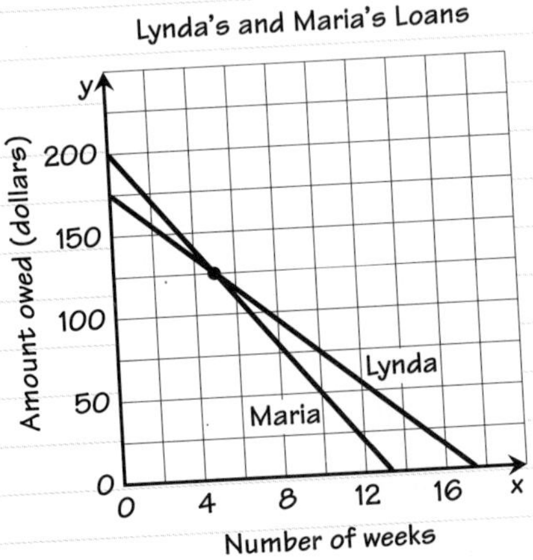

After five weeks, they owe the same amount of money. After that, Maria is paying more per week than Lynda, so she will pay off her loan first.

21 Key Concepts Question In the Example above, how does the graph show when the sisters owe the same amount of money?

It is shown by the point of intersection of the two graphs.

Section ② Key Concepts

Solving Equations (pp. 487–489)

To solve some equations, you may need to use the distributive property and combine like terms.

Example

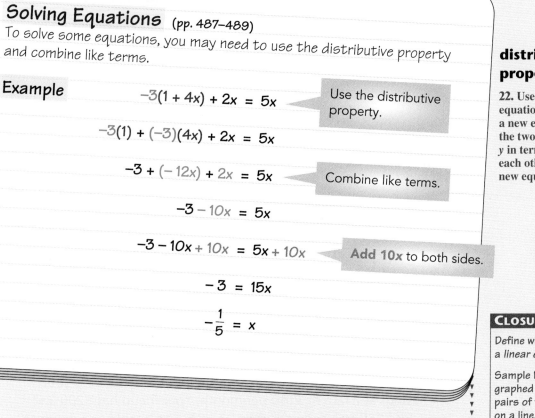

$$-3(1 + 4x) + 2x = 5x$$ — Use the distributive property.

$$-3(1) + (-3)(4x) + 2x = 5x$$

$$-3 + (-12x) + 2x = 5x$$ — Combine like terms.

$$-3 - 10x = 5x$$

$$-3 - 10x + 10x = 5x + 10x$$ — **Add 10x** to both sides.

$$-3 = 15x$$

$$-\frac{1}{5} = x$$

distributive property

22. Use the two equations given to write a new equation setting the two expressions for y in terms of x equal to each other. Solve the new equation for x.

CLOSURE QUESTION

Define what is meant by a *linear equation*.

Sample Response: When graphed the ordered pairs of the equation lie on a line.

22 Key Concepts Question Look back at the Example on page 490. Explain how to write and solve an equation to find out when the sisters owe the same amount of money. See above.

Section ② Practice & Application Exercises

YOU WILL NEED

For Exs. 2–5, 8, 18, 30, and 31:
♦ graph paper or graphing calculator (optional)

1. The equation $y = 75x + 90$ models Bruce's savings after x weeks. Describe his savings plan in words. **Bruce has $90 in his savings account and he deposits $75 each week without withdrawing any money.**

Graph each pair of equations on the same pair of axes. Find the point where the graphs intersect and label its coordinates.

2. $y = 25x$ and $y = 20x + 10$ **(2, 50)**   3. $y = 10 - 2x$ and $y = 4 - x$ **(6, –2)**

4. $y = 18 - 3x$ and $y = 6$ **(4, 6)**   5. $y = 50 - 4x$ and $y = 20 + x$ **(6, 26)**

Zoology Scientists use graphs to analyze the movements of animals. For example, the graph below shows the vertical position of a dolphin over time. Use the graph for Exercises 6 and 7.

6. **Interpreting Data** Suppose you were watching the dolphin as the data in the graph were collected. What would you expect to see the dolphin do? **Sample Response: I would expect it to swim underwater, jump out of the water, then dive back down into the water again.**

7. Explain what information the coordinates of points *A*, *B*, and *C* give you about the dolphin.

7. *A*(1.4, 0): The dolphin was at the surface (0 ft above the surface) after 1.4 s; *B*(2, 5): The dolphin was 5 ft above the surface after 2 s; *C*(2.5, 0): The dolphin was at the surface after 2.5 s.

8. Suppose you have $5000 in savings. You start spending your savings at a rate of $150 per month. Your friend has $200 and adds $150 to his savings every month. Use a table or a graph to answer the questions below.

a. When do you run out of money? How much has your friend saved by that time? **at 34 months; $5300**

b. When will you and your friend have the same amount of money? How much money will you each have then? **at 16 months; $2600**

9. Look back at Exercise 8. Show how to write and solve equations to answer part (a). **See Additional Answers.**

Use the distributive property to rewrite each expression.

10. $-5(m + 12)$ **$-5m - 60$** 11. $3 + 24p$ **$3(1 + 8p)$** 12. $8(-5 - x)$ **$-40 - 8x$**

13. $10(0.5 - 0.5w)$ **$5 - 5w$** 14. $18x - 6$ 15. $12 - 4t$

14. Possible answers: $6(3x - 1)$, $3(6x - 2)$, or $2(9x - 3)$

15. Possible answers: $2(6 - 2t)$ or $4(3 - t)$

16. **Alternative Method** Anne used a different method to solve the equation $160 = 8(x - 10)$ in the Example on page 489. She first divided both sides of the equation by 8. Why do you think she did this? What do you think she did next? Do you prefer her method or the method used in the Example? Explain. **Sample Response: to eliminate the multiplication required by the distributive property; added 10 to both sides of the equation; Preferences will vary.**

17. It costs $3 to park at Bay Beach if you buy a special sticker for your car. A sticker costs $50 and can be used all summer. It costs $8 to park without a sticker.

   a. Write two equations that model your cost of parking at the beach n times, one if you have a sticker and one if you do not have a sticker. **Let c = the cost in dollars and n = the number of times you park; c = 3n + 50, c = 8n**

   b. Writing Under what circumstances would you save money by buying a sticker? Explain your thinking. **See below.**

   18. See Additional Answers.

18. a. Use an equation to find a common solution of $y = 5x$ and $y = 2x + 3$. Are there other common solutions? Explain.

   b. Graph the equations from part (a) on the same pair of axes. How can you use the graph to find a common solution of the two equations?

   c. Graph $y = 3x + 4$ and $y = 3x - 2$ on the same pair of axes. Do these equations have any common solutions? Explain.

17. b. You would save money only if you parked at the beach more than 10 times in a summer because the cost of 10 tickets at $8 is equal to the cost of 10 tickets at $3 plus the initial $50 cost. After 10 times it would cost $5 more each time you parked at the beach.

Solve each equation.

19. $25x + 200 = 50x + 50$ **6**

20. $4t = -10t - 28$ **–2**

21. $3 = 2(m - 3)$ $\frac{9}{2}$

22. $-3 - 6h = 3(2h + 3)$ **–1**

23. $15m + 30 - 2m = 2m$ $-\frac{30}{11}$

24. $8(2x - 1) = 5(2x + 3)$ $\frac{23}{6}$

25. $2(5 - x) = -2x - 5 + x$ **15**

26. $5 - 3(1 - m) = 2(m - 5)$ **–12**

Geometry Connection For each diagram, use the given area to find the value of x.

27. Area = 25 m^2 **3 m** **28.** Area = 24 ft^2 **5 ft** **29.** Area = 35 cm^2 **3 cm**

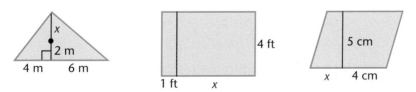

FOR ▶ HELP

with *using formulas from geometry*, see
TOOLBOX, p. 605

30. **Graphing Calculator** You can use graphs to solve equations like $3x + 8 = 2(x - 5)$.

   a. Graph $y = 3x + 8$ and $y = 2(x - 5)$ on the same pair of axes. Find the x-coordinate of the point where the graphs intersect. **–18**

   b. Check to see that the x-coordinate you found in part (a) is the solution of $3x + 8 = 2(x - 5)$. **$3(-18) + 8 = -54 + 8 = -46$; $2(-18 - 5) = 2(-23) = -46$**

   c. Use graphs to solve $-5 = -3(-1 - x) + 7$. Check your solution. **–5**

Reflecting on the Section

Write your response to Exercise 31 in your journal.

31. Suppose you have $100 in savings. How much money would you like to have saved in 10 years? Make a plan for achieving this savings goal that involves linear change. Describe your plan in words. Use an equation, a table, and a graph to model your plan. **Answers will vary. Check students' work.**

Spiral Review

32. C; The graph shows the height of the flag increasing in stages with several pulls of a rope followed by brief rest periods.

32. Suppose you raise a flag up a pole. Which of the graphs below could model this situation? Explain your choice(s).

(Module 7, p. 475)

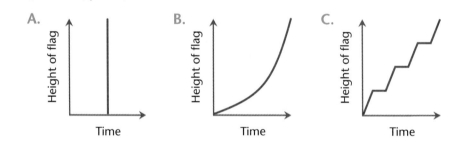

Write a rule for finding a term of each sequence when you know the previous term. (Module 4, p. 247) **Sample responses are given.**

33. 10, 70, 490, … **Multiply by 7.**   34. 1, $\frac{1}{2}$, $\frac{1}{4}$, … **Multiply by $\frac{1}{2}$.**

35. 0.3, 0.003, 0.00003, … **Divide by 100.**   36. 20, 100, 500, … **Multiply by 5.**

Rewrite each product as a power. (Toolbox, p. 600)

37. (5.2)(5.2)(5.2)(5.2) **5.2^4**   38. $3 \cdot 3 \cdot 3 \cdot 3 \cdot 3 \cdot 3 \cdot 3 \cdot 3$ **3^8**

39. $16 \cdot 16 \cdot 16 \cdot 16 \cdot 16$ **16^5**   40. $\frac{3}{5} \cdot \frac{3}{5} \cdot \frac{3}{5} \cdot \frac{3}{5} \cdot \frac{3}{5} \cdot \frac{3}{5}$ **$\left(\frac{3}{5}\right)^6$**

Modeling Change in a Story

Linear Models Many stories involve travel. You can use equations, tables, and graphs to model changes in distance over time.

3 Suppose Brad leaves his house at 3:00 P.M. and heads west on his bike. His speed is 8 mi/h. His friend John is 10 mi west of Brad's house. He starts walking toward Brad's house at 3:00 P.M. His speed is 4 mi/h.

a. Copy and complete the table to model Brad's and John's distances from Brad's house. Use the table to estimate when Brad and John will meet. **See table; between 3:45 P.M. and 4:00 P.M. (3:50)**

John
4 mi/h east →

Brad
8 mi/h west ←

|— 10 mi —|

Time after 3:00 P.M. (hours)	Brad's distance from Brad's house (miles)	John's distance from Brad's house (miles)
0	0	10
0.25	2	9
0.50	**? 4**	**? 8**
0.75	**? 6**	**? 7**
1.00	**? 8**	**? 6**

John's speed is 4 mi/h, so in 0.25 h, he travels 1 mi and is 10 – 1 mi from Brad's house.

b. Let x = the number of hours after 3:00 P.M. and y = the distance from Brad's house. Use the table to write two equations, one that models Brad's distance from his house over time, and one that models John's distance from Brad's house over time.
$y = 8x$ (Brad's distance) and $y = 10 - 4x$ (John's distance)

c. Graph your equations from part (b) on the same pair of axes. How does your graph show when John and Brad will meet?

d. Show how you can write and solve an equation to find out when John and Brad will meet. **See below.**

3. c. The x-coordinate of the point of intersection indicates the time at which they will meet and the y-coordinate indicates the distance from Brad's house.

Distance from Brad's house

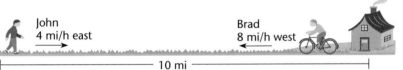

Distance (mi)

8

4

0

0   0.5   1   x

Time (h) after 3:00 P.M.

4 Describe a situation that involves a change in distance over time like the one in Project Question 3. Explain how you could model the change. **Answers will vary. Check students' work.**

3. d. $8x = 10 - 4x$
$12x = 10$
$x = \dfrac{5}{6}$; after $\dfrac{5}{6}$ h = 50 min; 3:50 P.M.

You will need: • *graph paper or graphing calculator (optional)* (Exs. 1–4)

Graph each pair of equations on the same pair of axes. Find the point where the graphs intersect and label its coordinates. 1–4. See Additional Answers.

1. $y = 10x$ and $y = 5x + 20$

2. $y = 15 - 3x$ and $y = 5 - x$

3. $y = 12 - 4x$ and $y = 3$

4. $y = 25 - 2x$ and $y = 10 + x$

Solve each equation.

5. $3x - 4 = x + 10$ 7

6. $6 + 2x = 5x + 9$ –1

7. $12 + x = -3 + 4x$ 5

8. $7x + 4 = 2x - 11$ –3

9. $-3x - 2 = -9 - 4x$ –7

10. $-7x + 5 = 8x - 1$ $\frac{2}{5}$

11. $3x = 18 - 3x$ 3

12. $14x + 6 = -2x - 2$ $-\frac{1}{2}$

13. $-5x - 9 = 3x + 17$ $-3\frac{1}{4}$

Use the distributive property to rewrite each expression.

14. $5(x - 3)$ $5x - 15$

15. $-3(2 + 3x)$ $-6 - 9x$

16. $4(-1 - 6x)$ $-4 - 24x$

17. $12x + 6$ See below.

18. $3x - 9$ $3(x - 3)$

19. $14 - 8x$ $2(7 - 4x)$

20. $x(x + 1)$ $x^2 + x$

21. $2x(x^2 - 3)$ $2x^3 - 6x$

22. $2x(5x + 10)$ $10x^2 + 20x$

23. $x^2 + 4x$ $x(x + 4)$

24. $3x^3 + 6x^2$ See below.

25. $12x^3 - 3x$ See below.

17. Possible answers: $2(6x + 3), 3(4x + 2), 6(2x + 1)$ **24.** Possible answers: $3x^2(x + 2), 3x(x^2 + 2x), 3(x^3 + 2x^2)$

Solve each equation.   **25.** Possible answers: $3x(4x^2 - 1), 3(4x^3 - x), x(12x^2 - 3)$

26. $2(x - 1) = 3x + 4$ –6

27. $6 - 2t = 3(2t + 4)$ $-\frac{3}{4}$

28. $3y + 5 + 2y = 5(2y + 1)$ 0

29. $2 - 4(h - 4) = 10(2h - 3)$ 2

30. $4k - 15(k - 2) = 17k + 9$ $\frac{3}{4}$

31. $8 + 5m(m - 3) = 12 - m(3 - 5m)$ $-\frac{1}{3}$

32. $-w + 2(5w - 6) - 4w = -3(-w - 10)$ 21

33. $3b(4 - 2b) - 6b = -b(6b + 7) + 104$ 8

Standardized Testing ◀▶ Open-ended

1. Describe a real-life situation that can be modeled by the equation $y = 5x + 30$.   Answers will vary. Check students' work.

2. Use the distributive property to write $24x^2 + 8x$ in four different ways.   Possible answers: $2x(12x + 4), 4x(6x + 2), 8x(3x + 1), x(24x + 8), 2(12x^2 + 4x), 4(6x^2 + 2x), 8(3x^2 + x)$

3. Write an equation that can be solved by using the distributive property. Then solve your equation.   Sample Response: $5(2x - 1) = 75; x = 8$

EXTENDED
E²
EXPLORATION

Accessing:// the .Web/

SET UP *You will need graph paper.*

See the Resource Book for a detailed discussion of this Extended Exploration.

The Situation

The Smith family is planning to subscribe to an Internet service. They have three payment plans from which to choose.

The Problem

The Smiths are not sure which plan they should choose. Evaluate each plan described at the right. Use mathematical models such as equations, tables, and graphs to make recommendations for choosing a plan.

Something to Think About
See Additional Answers.

◆ What factors should the Smiths consider when choosing a payment plan?

◆ How can you model the three plans using equations, tables, and graphs?

Present Your Results

Write a letter to the Smith family explaining the advantages and disadvantages of each service plan. Give useful advice to the Smiths about choosing a plan. Include the mathematical models you used to come up with your recommendations.
Answers will vary. Check students' work.

ONLY $14 per month
PLAN A
15 hours of web access
$2 for each additional hour

PLAN B
ONLY $10 per month
10 hours of web access
$2.50 for each additional hour

PLAN C
ONLY $**20** per month
UNLIMITED USE

Section ③ Modeling Exponential Change

IN THIS SECTION

EXPLORATION 1
♦ Exponential Change

EXPLORATION 2
♦ Exponential Models

WARM-UP EXERCISES

Find each value.

1. 6^2 36
2. 7.2^2 51.84
3. $3 \cdot 3 \cdot 3 \cdot 3 \cdot 3$ 243
4. $3^2 \cdot 2^3$ 72
5. Find the value of y in the equation $y = 4^x$ when x = 4.   256

How Sweet It Is

‹‹‹ *Setting the Stage*

In Roald Dahl's *Charlie and the Chocolate Factory*, Charlie Bucket's family is so poor that he only gets a chocolate bar once a year.

HAPPY BIRTHDAY CHARLIE

Only once a year, on his birthday, did Charlie Bucket ever get to taste a bit of chocolate. The whole family saved up their money for that special occasion, and when the great day arrived, Charlie was always presented with one small chocolate bar to eat all by himself.

. . . he would take a *tiny* nibble . . .

The next day, he would take another tiny nibble, and so on, and so on. And in this way, Charlie would make his ten-cent bar of birthday chocolate last him for more than a month.

Roald Dahl, *Charlie and the Chocolate Factory*

Think About It

Suppose on the first day, Charlie eats half the chocolate bar. The next day, he eats half the remaining chocolate bar, and continues to eat half the remaining chocolate each day after that.

1 Will Charlie eat the same amount of chocolate each day? Explain.
No; Each day he eats half as much as he did the day before.

2 How long do you think the chocolate bar will last? a few days; The pieces will soon become so small that he will not actually be able to divide them in half.

Exploration 1

exponential Change

SET UP *You will need:* • *a rectangular sheet of paper* • *graph paper* • *graphing calculator (optional)*

▶ **In Question 2 on page 498, you estimated how long Charlie Bucket's chocolate bar would last if he ate half of the remaining chocolate each day. In this exploration, you will use paper folding to model this situation.**

3 a. Fold a sheet of paper in half. With no folds there is one layer. After one fold there are two layers. **Check students' work.**

0 folds
1 layer
area = 1

1 fold
2 layers
area = ?

3. c. $\frac{1}{2}$; 4, $\frac{1}{4}$; 3, 8, $\frac{1}{8}$; 4, 16, $\frac{1}{16}$; 5, 32, $\frac{1}{32}$; 6, 64, $\frac{1}{64}$; 7, 128, $\frac{1}{128}$

b. If the area of the unfolded paper is one square unit, what is the area of each layer after you fold the paper once? **0.5 square units**

c. Record the number of folds, the number of layers, and the area of each layer in a table like the one shown. **See above.**

d. Fold your paper as many times as possible. Extend and fill in your table each time you fold the paper.
Check students' work.

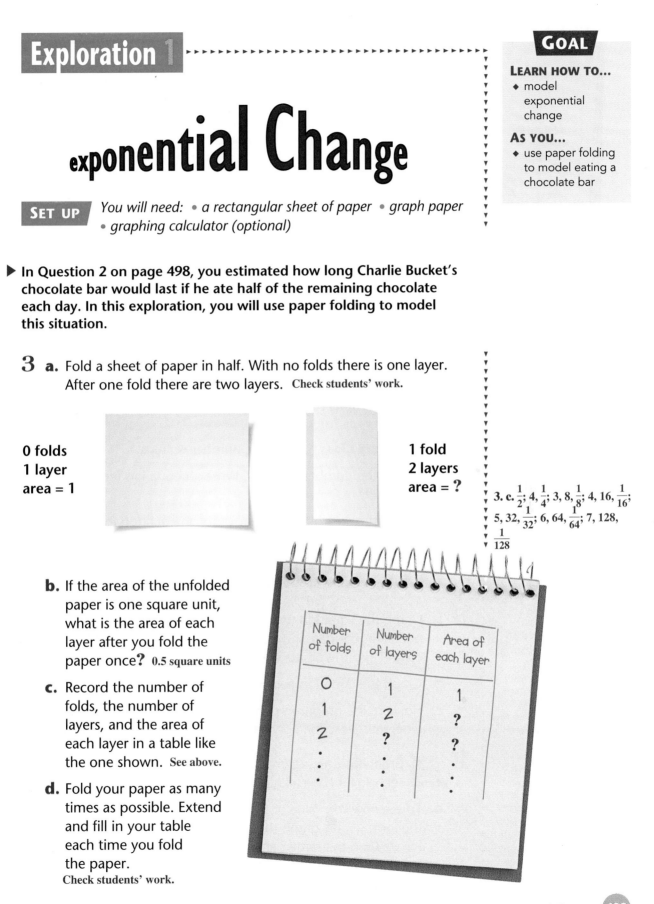

Number of folds	Number of layers	Area of each layer
0	1	1
1	2	?
2	?	?
⋮	⋮	⋮

Number of folds	Number of layers	Area of each layer	Number of layers as a power	Area of each layer as a power
0	1	1	2^0	$\left(\frac{1}{2}\right)^0$
1	2	?	?	?
2	?	?	?	?
⋮	⋮	⋮	⋮	⋮

For Questions 4–7, use your completed table from Question 3.

4 Suppose you could continue folding the paper. What would happen to the number of layers as the number of folds increased? What would happen to the area of each layer? It would increase, doubling at each stage; It would decrease halving at each stage.

5 Add two columns to your table, as shown. Write the number of layers as a power of 2 and the area of each layer as a power of $\frac{1}{2}$. See below.

6 Suppose you could fold the paper ten times. Predict how many layers there would be. Then predict the area of each layer. Explain your reasoning. 2^{10} or 1024 layers; $\frac{1}{2^{10}}$

▶ As you folded the paper, the number of layers and the area of each layer changed *exponentially*. You can use equations and graphs to model exponential change.

7 **Try This as a Class** Let x = the number of folds.

  a. Let y = the number of layers. Write an equation for y in terms of x. $y = 2^x$

  b. Let y = the area of each layer. Write an equation for y in terms of x. $y = \left(\frac{1}{2}\right)^x$

  c. How are your equations in parts (a) and (b) alike? How are they different? Both equations involve a variable exponent; In one the base is a whole number, in the other the base is a fraction

8 **a.** Graph the equation you wrote in Question 7(a) by plotting points for the data in your table from Question 3 and connecting the points with a smooth curve. 8. a–c. See Additional Answers.

  b. Graph the equation you wrote in Question 7(b).

  c. How are the graphs in parts (a) and (b) alike? How are they different? Describe how each graph changes as x increases.

9 Graphing Calculator The *exponential equations* you have seen so far have all had the form $y = b^x$, where $x \geq 0$.

  a. To see how the value of b affects the graph of an equation in the form $y = b^x$, graph the equations $y = 3^x$, $y = 4^x$, and $y = 7^x$ for $x \geq 0$ on the same pair of axes. Describe the differences and the similarities in the curves.

5. $2^0, \left(\frac{1}{2}\right)^0; 2^1, \left(\frac{1}{2}\right)^1; 2^2, \left(\frac{1}{2}\right)^2;$
$2^3, \left(\frac{1}{2}\right)^3; 2^4, \left(\frac{1}{2}\right)^4; 2^5, \left(\frac{1}{2}\right)^5;$
$2^6, \left(\frac{1}{2}\right)^6; 2^7, \left(\frac{1}{2}\right)^7$

9. a. All three curves pass through (0, 1) and rise from left to right. The greater the base, the steeper the graph.

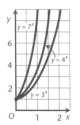

b. How would you describe the graph of an equation in the form $y = b^x$, where $b > 1$ and $x \geq 0$?

c. In Question 8(b), you graphed the equation $y = \left(\dfrac{1}{2}\right)^x$. How is this graph different from the graphs in part (a)? Why do you think the graphs are different? **It fell from left to right; The base is less than 1.**

10 ✔ **CHECKPOINT** Look back at the excerpt from *Charlie and the Chocolate Factory* on page 498. What fraction of the original candy bar would Charlie have left after 1 month (30 days) if he eats half of what is left each day? $\left(\dfrac{1}{2}\right)^{30} \approx 9.3 \cdot 10^{-10}$

HOMEWORK EXERCISES ▶ See Exs. 1–5 on pp. 505–506.

9. b. The graph is a curve that passes through (0, 1) and rises from left to right.

✔ **QUESTION 10**

…checks that you understand exponential change.

Exploration 2 ▶▶▶▶▶▶▶▶▶▶▶▶▶▶▶▶▶▶▶▶

exponential Models

SET UP *Work with a partner. You will need a calculator.*

▶ **Much has changed since 1964, when *Charlie and the Chocolate Factory* was first published. The price of a candy bar is more than five times what it was then.**

11 In 1960, a candy bar cost about $.10. Suppose this price is raised 5 times to reach $.50. Work with your partner to find a way to change 10 to 50 in 5 steps by:

a. *adding* the same number at each step. Tell what number you added. Copy and complete the table for each step.
.08; $.18, $.26, $.34, $.42

b. *multiplying* by the same number at each step. Tell what number you multiplied by. Copy and complete the table for each step.
about 1.38; $.14, $.19, $.26, $.36

Step	Price
0	$.10
1	?
2	?
3	?
4	?
5	$.50

GOAL

LEARN HOW TO…
◆ write an equation to model compound interest
◆ use tables and equations to solve problems

AS YOU…
◆ model price changes and the growth of a savings account

KEY TERM
◆ exponential equation

▶ Savings can grow as quickly as prices if you deposit money into a savings account that earns interest. The amount of money increases exponentially, even if you do not make any more deposits.

12 **a.** Suppose you deposit $1000 into an account that pays 8% annual interest. Find 8% of $1000 to determine the amount of interest you will earn in one year. $80

b. What is the new total in your account at the end of one year? $1080

▶ How much money will you have in a savings account after 10, 20, or 30 years? To find out, look for a pattern.

EXAMPLE

Suppose you deposit $2000 into an account that earns 5% annual interest. After one year, you will have 100% of your deposit plus an additional 5% interest.

Initial deposit + Interest after one year

$(1.00)(2000) + (0.05)(2000)$

You can use the distributive property to rewrite this expression:

$(1.00)(2000) + (0.05)(2000) = (1.05)(2000)$

$= 2100$

After one year, there will be $2100 in the account.

13 Refer to the situation described in the Example.

a. Suppose you leave your money in the account for two years. How much money will you have at the end of the second year? Explain how you got your answer. $2205; Multiply $2100 by 1.05.

b. Copy and complete the table below, by continuing the pattern in the *Expression* column. See table.

c. Discussion Describe the pattern in the *Expression* column.

13. c. Each year, the expression increases by 1.05.

Year	Amount in account at beginning of year	Expression	Amount in account at end of year
1	$2000	$1.05 \cdot 2000$	$2100
2	$2100	$1.05 \cdot 1.05 \cdot 2000$	? $2205
3	? $2205	$1.05^3 \cdot$? $2000	? $2315.25
4	? $2315.25	$1.05^4 \cdot$? $2000	? $2431.01
5	? $2431.01	$1.05^5 \cdot$? $2000	? $2552.56

14 a. At the end of two years, the amount of money in the account described in the Example is given by the expression 1.05 · 1.05 · 2000. Rewrite this expression using exponents.

$2000 \cdot 1.05^2$

b. 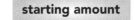 **Calculator** Use exponents to write an expression for the amount of money in your account at the end of 20 years. Use the y^x key to evaluate the expression.

$2000 \cdot 1.05^{20}$; $5306.60

▶ **The growth of money in a savings account that earns annual interest is an example of exponential change. You can model exponential change with an exponential equation which has the form:**

starting amount

amount after **x** years

$$y = a \cdot b^x$$

growth factor

15 Try This as a Class The equation $2923.08 = 1500 \cdot (1.1)^7$ gives the amount in an account after a certain number of years.

a. How much money was originally deposited into the account? $1500

b. How many years was the money in the account? How much money is in the account after this amount of time?

7 years; $2923.08

c. What is the growth factor? What is the interest rate? 1.1; 10%

16 ✔ **CHECKPOINT** Suppose you deposit $4000 into an account that earns 6% annual interest. Write an equation that models the amount y in the account after x years. How much will be in the account after 1 year? after 12 years? after 20 years?

$y = 4000 \cdot (1.06)^x$; $4240; $8048.79; $12,828.54

✔ **QUESTION 16**

...checks that you can write and use an exponential equation to solve problems.

17 Discussion Look back at Question 11 on page 501.

a. Suppose the price of a candy bar starts at $.10 and increases by $.01 each year. Write an equation for the price after x years. $y = 0.10 + 0.01x$

Price of candy bar	$.01 yearly increase	10% yearly increase
After 10 years	? $.20	? $.26
After 20 years	? $.30	? $.67
After 30 years	? $.40	? $1.74
After 40 years	? $.50	? $4.53

b. Suppose the price starts at $.10 and increases by 10% each year. Write an equation for the price after x years. $y = 0.10 \cdot (1.10)^x$

c. Use your equations to copy and complete the table. Compare the predicted price changes over time.

17. **c.** See table; Sample Response: For 10 years, the prices are not significantly different. After that, the price increases much more rapidly for the 10% increase than for the $.01 increase.

■ **HOMEWORK EXERCISES** ▶ See Exs. 6–17 on pp. 506–507.

Key Term

exponential
equation

Exponential Change (pp. 499–501)

Some exponential equations have the form $y = b^x$, where $x \geq 0$.
You can use an equation in this form to model some types of
exponential change.

Example Suppose a piece of paper
has an area of 1 square unit. You fold
the paper into thirds. Then you fold
the paper into thirds again. You keep
repeating this process.

Number of regions after x steps = 3^x

Area of each region after x steps = $\left(\dfrac{1}{3}\right)^x$

Step 0
Regions: 1
Area of
each region: 1

Step 1
Regions: 3
Area of
each region: $\dfrac{1}{3}$

Step 2
Regions: 9
Area of
each region: $\dfrac{1}{9}$

Exponential Models (pp. 501–503)

When you deposit money into a savings account that earns annual
interest, the amount of money in the account grows exponentially over
time. You can model a relationship like this one with an exponential
equation in the form $y = a \cdot b^x$.

starting amount

Amount after **x** years → $y = a \cdot b^x$ ← **growth factor**

Example Suppose you deposit $1800 into a savings account that
earns 3% annual interest. To find out how much money you will have
after 5 years, you can write and solve an equation.

$$y = 1800 \cdot (1.03)^5 \approx 2086.69$$

You will have about $2087 after 5 years.

CLOSURE QUESTION

Explain the meaning of
y, a, b, and x in the
exponential equation
$y = a \cdot b^x$.

Sample Response: y is
the amount after x time
intervals, a is the
starting amount, b is
the rate of change, and
x is the number of time
intervals.

18 Key Concepts Question In the Example above about the
savings account, how is the number 1.03 related to the interest
rate? Explain why you use 1.03 as a factor five times.

The interest rate is 0.03; 1.03 represents 100% of the initial deposited amount in
the account plus 3% interest per year for 5 years.

Section 3
Practice & Application Exercises

YOU WILL NEED

For Ex. 16:
♦ graph paper or a graphing calculator

1. In the Example about folding paper on page 504, two equations are given. Match each equation with one of the graphs below. Explain your thinking.

A.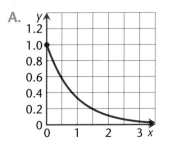

B.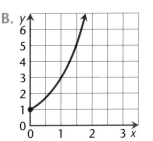

1. A: $y = \left(\frac{1}{3}\right)^x$; B: $y = 3^x$;

As x increases, $\left(\frac{1}{3}\right)^x$

decreases and 3^x increases.

2. **Geometry Connection** In the diagram at the right, the area of each regular hexagon is $\frac{3}{4}$ the area of the next larger hexagon. If the area of the outer hexagon is 1 unit, what is the area of the smallest hexagon? $\left(\frac{3}{4}\right)^5 = \frac{243}{1024} \approx 0.24$

3. Suppose someone in your class starts a rumor. This student tells the rumor to two other students. Each of these students repeats the rumor to two other students. This pattern continues. **See Additional Answers.**

   a. Suppose it takes one minute to find two students and tell them the rumor. Copy and extend the table for the first ten minutes after the rumor starts.

   b. Write and solve an equation to find the **number of new people who *hear* the rumor** one hour after it was started.

   c. How is this problem like the paper folding activity in Exploration 1?

   d. **Visual Thinking** Show how you can use a tree diagram to model this situation.

Number of minutes	Number of new people hearing the rumor	Total number of people who know the rumor
0	1	1
1	2	3

4. **Challenge** Use the information in Exercise 3. Write an equation that models the **total number of people who *know* the rumor** after x minutes. $y = (2^{x+1}) - 1$ or $2 \cdot 2^x - 1$

5. **Writing** Jane graphed three equations on the same graphing calculator screen, but cannot tell which graph goes with each equation. Explain how she can tell just by looking at the graphs. See below.

1st equation: $y = \left(\dfrac{1}{3}\right)^x$

2nd equation: $y = 4^x$

3rd equation: $y = \left(\dfrac{3}{2}\right)^x$

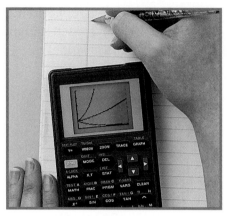

5. All three curves pass through (0, 1). $y = 4^x$ and $y = \left(\dfrac{3}{2}\right)^x$ then rise from left to right, while $y = \left(\dfrac{1}{3}\right)^x$ decreases but remains positive. The graph with the steepest slope represents $y = 4^x$ and the graph with the next steepest slope represents $y = \left(\dfrac{3}{2}\right)^x$. This is because for the same values of x, $y = 4^x$ gives the larger values of y. $y = \left(\dfrac{1}{3}\right)^x$ decreases and approaches 0 or a horizontal line because as numbers less than 1 are exponentially increased, they become smaller.

6. c. 17 years; Sample Response: I graphed my equation from part (a) and found the x value that had a y value of about 2000.

6. a. Suppose you deposit $500 into an account that earns 9% annual interest. Write an equation that shows the amount of money in the account after x years. $y = 500 \cdot (1.09)^x$

   b. How much money will be in the account after 10 years? **$1183.68**

   c. About how many years will it take for the amount of money in the account to reach $2000? How did you get your answer? See below.

7. Write an equation in the form $y = a \cdot b^x$ to model each situation. Tell what the variables x and y represent.

   a. A school with 1200 students is predicted to grow at a rate of 4% each year. $y = 1200 \cdot (1.04)^x$ **where y represents the enrollment and x represents the number of years.**

   b. Marcia is training for a marathon. She runs 5 km this weekend. For the next several weeks, she will increase her distance by 10% each weekend. $y = 5 \cdot (1.1)^x$ **where y represents Maria's distance and x represents the number of weeks.**

8. **Open-ended** Describe a situation like the ones in Exercise 7. Write a word problem about the situation that you could use an exponential equation to solve. Give the solution of your problem. **Answers will vary. Check students' work.**

9. **Algebra Connection** Are the equations you wrote in Exercise 7 functions? Explain. **Yes; For every value of x there is only one value of y.**

Evaluate each expression for the given value of the variable.

10. $4 \cdot 3^x$; $x = 3$ **108**   11. $4 \cdot \left(\dfrac{1}{2}\right)^x$; $x = 4$ **0.25**   12. $100 \cdot 0.4^x$; $x = 2$ **16**

13. $\dfrac{1}{2} \cdot 2^x$; $x = 5$ **16**   14. $\dfrac{2}{3} \cdot 6^x$; $x = 3$ **144**   15. $5 \cdot \left(\dfrac{1}{3}\right)^x$; $x = 4$ **about 0.06**

16. **Population Growth** Exponential equations in the form $y = a \cdot b^x$ are often used to model population growth. For example, suppose the population of a town is 10,000 and is predicted to grow at a rate of 3% each year.

   a. Write an equation to model the population y after x years.
      $$y = 10{,}000 \cdot (1.03)^x$$

   b.  Graphing Calculator Graph your equation. Your graph should show the town's population for the next 30 years. **See below.**

   c. In about how many years will the population double?
      about 24 years

   d. Suppose the population of the town grows at a rate of 6% each year. Predict how many years it will take the population to double. Check your prediction by writing and graphing an equation. **See below.**

Reflecting ◀▶on the Section

Be prepared to discuss your response to Exercise 17 in class.

17. **Discussion** Suppose you win a $25,000 college scholarship on a TV quiz show. You are given two options for collecting your scholarship money. What are the advantages and disadvantages of each option? Which option would you choose? Why?
    See Additional Answers.

Discussion

Exercise 17 checks that you can use an exponential equation to model a problem situation.

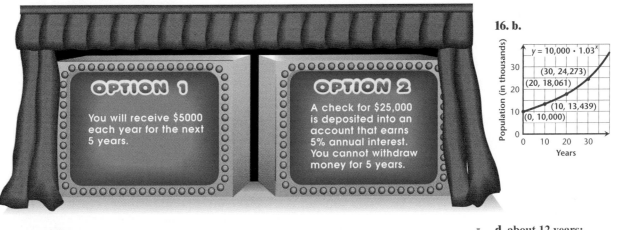

OPTION 1

You will receive $5000 each year for the next 5 years.

OPTION 2

A check for $25,000 is deposited into an account that earns 5% annual interest. You cannot withdraw money for 5 years.

16. b.

$y = 10{,}000 \cdot 1.03^x$

(30, 24,273)
(20, 18,061)
(10, 13,439)
(0, 10,000)

d. about 12 years;
$y = 10{,}000 \cdot 1.06^x$

(15, 23,966)
(10, 17,908)
(5, 13,382)
(0, 10,000)

Spiral ◀▶Review

Solve each equation. (Module 7, p. 491)

18. $13x + 15 = 185 - 4x$ **10**

19. $-6 - 2p = -(3 - 4p)$ $-\frac{1}{2}$

20. After the translation $\left(x - 2,\ y + \frac{1}{2}\right)$, the image of a point is (5, 0). What are the coordinates of the original point? (Module 2, p. 130)
    $\left(7, -\frac{1}{2}\right)$

Wildlife Veterinarian: William Karesh

As a wildlife veterinarian, William Karesh studies disease and nutrition. He may help a monkey with malaria or an elephant with an infected toe. Many infections are caused by bacteria that reproduce exponentially.

21. Suppose 2 bacteria infect an animal. In 20 min, each of these bacteria splits into 2 bacteria, so that there are 4 bacteria. In another 20 min, these 4 bacteria each split into 2 bacteria. This pattern continues over time.

   a. How many bacteria will there be after 2 h? after 6 h? How did you get your answers? **128 bacteria; 524,288 bacteria; Possible answers: Write an equation, complete a table, or sketch a graph.**

   b. How does exponential growth help explain what can happen if an infection is not treated quickly? **Sample Response: It shows how quickly the bacteria grow and, so, how rapidly the infection worsens.**

Extension ▶ ▶

Exponential Decay

Most of the situations you modeled in this section involved *exponential growth*. You can also use an equation in the form $y = a \cdot b^x$ to model *exponential decay*. For example, suppose you pay $18,000 for a new car. You plan to sell the car in a few years, but know that the car will be worth less and less as time goes on. The value of the car is *depreciating* (losing value) at a rate of 12% a year.

Used car for sale

5 years old
1 owner, a/c, airbag
am/fm
very reliable
555-0173

22. About how much will your car be worth after 1 year? after 2 years? after 3 years? How did you get your answers? **$15,840; $13,939.20; $12,266.50; Possible answers: Make a table, write an equation.**

23. Let y = the value of your car after x years. An equation for y in terms of x is $y = 18,000(0.88)^x$. The number 0.88 is the *decay factor*. How is the decay factor related to the rate of depreciation? **The decay factor is the rate of depreciation subtracted from 100.**

24. In Exploration 1, you found the area of each layer as you folded a sheet of paper. Was this an example of exponential growth or exponential decay? Explain. **exponential decay; The amount of area decreased with each fold.**

Section 3
Extra Skill Practice

Write an equation in the form $y = a \cdot b^x$ to model each situation. Tell what the variables x and y represent.

1. A baseball card worth $150 is projected to increase in value by 8% a year. $y = 150 \cdot (1.08)^x$ where y represents the value of the baseball card and x represents the number of years.

2. A TV station's local news program has 60,000 viewers. The managers of the station plan to increase viewership by 5% a month. $y = 60{,}000 \cdot (1.05)^x$ where y represents the number of viewers and x represents the number of months from the onset of the managers' plan.

3. A bakery produces 2000 loaves of bread on an average day. In order to meet demand for an upcoming holiday, the bakers want to increase production by 10% a day. $y = 2000 \cdot (1.1)^x$ where y represents the number of loaves of bread and x represents the number of days.

Evaluate each expression for the given value of the variable.

4. $18 \cdot 4^x$; $x = 6$ 73,728

5. $\frac{3}{5} \cdot 5^x$; $x = 7$ 46,875

6. $0.35 \cdot 9^x$; $x = 4$ 2296.35

7. $\frac{4}{3} \cdot 3^x$; $x = 8$ 8748

8. $8 \cdot \left(\frac{1}{4}\right)^x$; $x = 6$ $\frac{1}{512} \approx 0.002$

9. $\frac{3}{2} \cdot \left(\frac{2}{3}\right)^x$; $x = 4$ $\frac{8}{27} \approx 0.3$

Write and solve an equation to find out how much money you will have in each situation.

10. You deposit $2000 into an account for 1 year at 3% interest. $y = 2000 \cdot (1.03)^1$, $2060

11. You deposit $200 into an account for 10 years at 3% interest. $y = 200 \cdot (1.03)^{10}$, $268.78

12. You deposit $600 into an account for 4 years at 7% interest. $y = 600 \cdot (1.07)^4$, $786.48

13. You deposit $1500 into an account for 8 years at 4% interest. $y = 1500 \cdot (1.04)^8$, $2052.85

Standardized Testing ▶ Performance Task

1. A store is having a sale on sweaters. On the first day the price of a sweater is reduced by 20%. The price will be reduced another 20% each day until the sweater is sold. Gustav thinks that on the fifth day of the sale the sweater will be free. Is he right? Explain. No. Each day the new price, not the original price, is being reduced 20%, so on the fifth day the price will be about 67% off the original price.

2. Carlos has $1000 to invest for four years until he goes to college. If the money is deposited in Bank A it will earn 6% annual interest. If the money is deposited in Bank B it will earn 7% annual interest, but only on the original $1000 deposited. In which bank do you think Carlos should deposit his money? Explain.
Bank B; He will make $17.52 more than at Bank A.

Section ④ Algorithms and Transformations

IN THIS SECTION

EXPLORATION 1
◆ Using Algorithms

Moving Around

WARM-UP EXERCISES

Begin with the point (3, 1). Follow the algorithm below.

1. Add 1 to the current x-value. What is the new x-value? 4

2. Subtract 5 from the current y-value? What is the new y-value? −4

3. Write the new x-value and the new y-value as a point. (4, −4)

4. Tell where the new point is located on a graph in comparison to the original point of (3, 1).
   Sample Response: It is 1 unit to the right and 5 units down.

‹‹‹**Setting the Stage**

Computer graphics can be used to model motion. For example, Olympic gymnasts in training are videotaped performing a floor routine or vault. A computer analyzes the tape and recreates the motion. Sometimes these tapes are broken down into stick figure sequences like the one below. Sports scientists study these sequences to help improve equipment and reduce injury among athletes.

Suppose the computer simulation on page 510 is shown in a coordinate plane. You want to give instructions that will move the figure through the back flip.

1 What information do you need to include in your instructions?
direction and type of movements

2 How can you use coordinates to describe changes in the gymnast's position? Put the figures on a coordinate grid. Choose a point on the original figure and determine the coordinates of the image. Determine how the coordinates of the original point and the image are related.

▶ **Movement of a figure on a computer screen can be created by assigning coordinates to points on the figure and giving instructions for moving each point. In this section you'll explore how to model movements using a series of instructions.**

Exploration 1 ▶▶▶▶▶▶▶▶▶▶▶▶▶▶▶▶▶▶▶▶▶▶▶▶

Using Algorithms

SET UP *You will need:* • *Labsheet 4A* • *graph paper*

▶ **In Module 2 you learned how to translate and stretch objects. You can use these and other *transformations* to model simple motions. A transformation is a change in an object's shape, size, or position.**

GOAL

LEARN HOW TO...
♦ use algorithms to transform geometric shapes
♦ reflect geometric shapes

AS YOU...
♦ model a gymnast's change in position

KEY TERMS
♦ transformation
♦ algorithm
♦ reflection

3 The figures below show positions before and after a move.

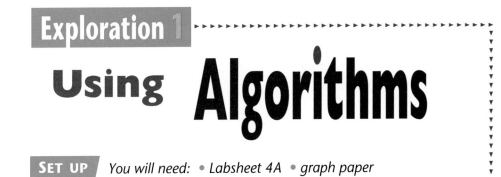

a. Are the image and the original figure congruent? Explain.
Yes; The two figures are the same shape and size.

b. How can you transform the original figure to get the image?
Sample Response: Translate it 1.5 units to the right.

FOR◀HELP
with *translations*,
see
MODULE 2, p. 130

▶ Animation that models movement may combine a series of steps. You can use an *algorithm* to describe these steps. An **algorithm** is a step-by-step set of instructions you can follow to accomplish a goal.

The Example below shows an algorithm for creating a very simple model of the key positions of a gymnast's jump.

EXAMPLE

Suppose a gymnast is videotaped jumping on a balance beam. At the peak of the jump, the gymnast is 2 units to the right and 1 unit higher than her starting position. After landing, she is 2 units to the right and 1 unit lower than when she was in the peak position.

Use an algorithm to create a simple model of the gymnast's key positions in a coordinate plane.

SAMPLE RESPONSE

Step 1	**Step 2**	**Step 3**
Plot points to show the gymnast's starting position.	Translate each point 2 units to the right and 1 unit up.	Translate each point 2 units to the right and 1 unit down.
(x, y)	$(x', y') =$ $(x + 2, y + 1)$	$(x'', y'') =$ $(x' + 2, y' - 1)$

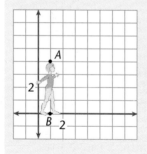 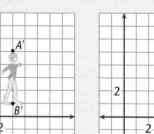 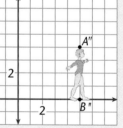

---

4 Give the coordinates of points *A*, *A'*, and *A''* in the Example.
$$(1, 4), (3, 5), (5, 4)$$

✔ QUESTION 5

...checks that you can use an algorithm to describe a series of transformations.

5 **✔ CHECKPOINT** Write an algorithm for moving a point from $(0, 0)$ to $(2, -3)$ and then to $(2, 3)$. $(x', y') = (x + 2, y - 3); (x'', y'') = (x', y' + 6)$

6 a. Write an algorithm that moves the gymnast in the Example directly from the starting position to the landing position.
$(x', y') = (x + 4, y)$

b. How is your algorithm from part (a) different from the one in the Example? How is it similar? It has only one step; The end result is the same.

▶ **Animation that models movement may be made up of different types of transformations. The Example below shows a reflection.**

EXAMPLE

The triangle is *reflected* across the **y-axis.** We say that △*A'B'C'* is the reflection of △*ABC*. Note that the triangles are congruent.

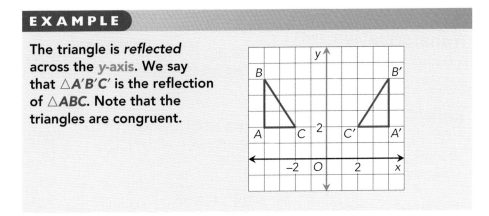

7 **Discussion** Look back at the Example. Compare the coordinates of points *A* and *A'*. Then compare the coordinates of points *B* and *B'* and the coordinates of points *C* and *C'*. Describe any patterns you see. **Sample Response: The *y*-coordinates are the same. The *x*-coordinates are opposites.**

8 **Try This as a Class** The vertices of △*JKL* are *J*(1, −4), *K*(5, −2), and *L*(3, 0).

  a. Write an algorithm for reflecting △*JKL* across the *y*-axis of a coordinate plane. Then perform the steps of your algorithm.

  b. Compare △*JKL* and its reflection. Are the two figures congruent? How do you know?

9 **Use Labsheet 4A.** Sometimes there is more than one way to write an algorithm, depending on the order in which you perform the steps. **Answers will vary. Check students' work.**

  a. Draw a figure on the blank grid to complete a *Sequence of Transformations*. Describe the steps that transform the original figure to its image.

  b. Compare your sequences with those of other students. Did everyone perform the same steps in the same order?

10 ✔ **CHECKPOINT** In a coordinate plane, draw a triangle with vertices at points *M*(−2, −4), *N*(−2, −2), and *O*(0, 0). Then write an algorithm for reflecting △*MNO* across the *x*-axis and then across the *y*-axis.

8. a. $(x', y') = (-x, y)$

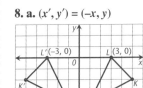

b. Yes; You could fold the graph over the *y*-axis and the two triangles would fit over each other perfectly.

10.

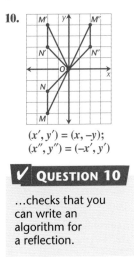

$(x', y') = (x, -y);$
$(x'', y'') = (-x', y')$

✔ **QUESTION 10**

...checks that you can write an algorithm for a reflection.

HOMEWORK EXERCISES ▶ See Exs. 1–20 on pp. 515–518.

Key Concepts

Transformation (p. 511)

A transformation is a change made to an object's shape, size, or position. Two types of transformations are translations and reflections.

transformation

Reflection (p. 513)

A reflection is a transformation where a figure is flipped across a line such as the x-axis or the y-axis. The original figure and its reflection are congruent.

reflection

Example To reflect the point $(-3, 2)$ across the x-axis, multiply the y-coordinate by -1, or find the opposite of the y-coordinate. Then plot the new coordinates.

Algorithms (p. 512)

An algorithm is a set of steps that you can follow to accomplish a goal.

algorithm

Example Write an algorithm for the transformation shown.

Step 1 Reflect each point across the y-axis.
$(x', y') = (-x, y)$

Step 2 Translate each point up 1 unit.
$(x'', y'') = (x', y' + 1)$

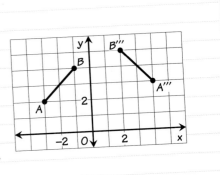

Step 3 Translate each point right 1 unit.
$(x''', y''') = (x'' + 1, y'')$

11 **Key Concepts Question** Write an algorithm that can be used to create the transformation shown.

Sample Response: $(x', y') = (x, -y)$, $(x'', y'') = (x' + 1, y' + 2)$

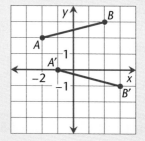

Practice & Application Exercises

For Exercises 1 and 2, sketch a person in a coordinate plane. Label a point for one foot and a point for the head. Use an algorithm to create a simple model of the foot's key positions for the movement described. If your algorithm does not model the key positions of the head, write one that does. Show the steps of your algorithm(s) in coordinate planes.

1. jumping up and down in place See Additional Answers.

2. standing in place and then doing a split See Additional Answers.

For each figure in Exercises 3–6: 3–6. See Additional Answers.

a. **Copy the figure on graph paper.**

b. **Reflect the figure across the given axis or axes. Draw the reflection(s) in the same coordinate plane.**

3. the *y*-axis

4. the *x*-axis

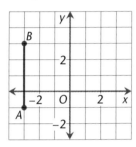

5. the *x*-axis,
   then the *y*-axis

6. the *y*-axis,
   then the *x*-axis

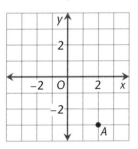

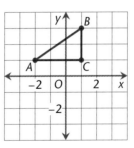

7. Copy the original figure from Exercise 6. Reflect the triangle across the *x*-axis and then across the *y*-axis. How does the final image compare to the final image in Exercise 6? See Additional Answers.

Art The first and last steps in creating a design are shown.

8. Write an algorithm that can be used to create the design.

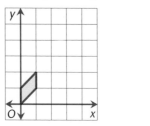

9. **Create Your Own** Sketch a repeating design and write an algorithm that can be used to create it.

Answers will vary. Check students' work.

Write an algorithm that can be used to create each transformation.

10.

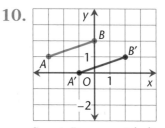

Sample Response: $(x', y') = (x + 2, y - 1)$

11.

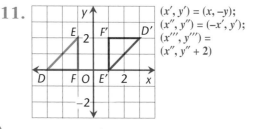

$(x', y') = (x, -y);$
$(x'', y'') = (-x', y');$
$(x''', y''') = (x'', y'' + 2)$

12. **Alternative Method** In the diagram at the right, $\triangle AB'C'$ was created by rotating $\triangle ABC$ 180° clockwise about the origin. Describe how to transform $\triangle ABC$ to $\triangle AB'C'$ using reflections.

Reflect across both axes in either order.

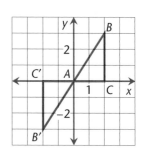

13. In the diagram at the right, $\triangle DE'F'$ was created by rotating $\triangle DEF$ 90° clockwise about the origin. Do you think it is possible to transform $\triangle DEF$ to $\triangle DE'F'$ using only reflections across the x- and y-axes? Explain.

No; Sample Response: $\triangle DE'F'$ is on the same side of the y-axis as $\triangle DEF$ and is not the image of $\triangle DEF$ reflected across the x-axis.

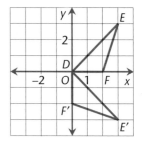

14. The diagram at the right shows a triangle and its reflection across the line $y = x$. Compare the coordinates of each point on the original figure with the coordinates of the corresponding point on the reflection. Write an algorithm for reflecting a figure across the line $y = x$. Draw a figure in a coordinate plane and use it to test your algorithm.

$(x', y') = (y, x);$ Check students' work.

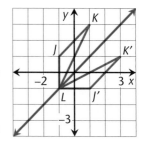

15. You can use an algorithm to model a change that involves stretching. The transformation shown is modeled by the algorithm below.

> **Step 1** Multiply the *x*- and *y*-coordinates of each point by 2.
>
> **Step 2** Translate each point up 1 unit.

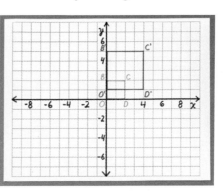

15. a.

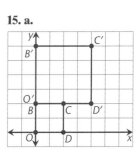

a. Draw *OBCD* with coordinates *O*(0, 0), *B*(0, 2), *C*(2, 2) and *D*(2, 0). Translate the figure up 1 unit. Then multiply each coordinate by 2. Draw the final image.

b. Compare your results from part (a) with the transformation shown. Does the order in which you perform the steps matter?

Yes.

16. Copy the figure below. Then use the algorithm to transform the figure. **See Additional Answers.**

> **Step 1** Multiply the *x*- and *y*-coordinates of each point by 3.
>
> **Step 2** Reflect each point over the *x*-axis.
>
> **Step 3** Translate each point up 12 units.

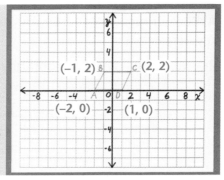

17. You already know how to stretch a figure using multiplication. You can also use multiplication to shrink a figure. Draw the figure below. Then use the algorithm to transform the figure.

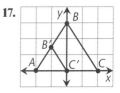

17.

> **Step 1** Multiply the *x*- and *y*-coordinates of each point by $\frac{1}{2}$.
>
> **Step 2** Translate each point to the left 1 unit.

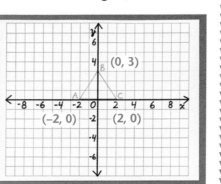

18. **Challenge** What value must you multiply each coordinate of the points on the original figure by to create the final image? $1\frac{1}{3}$

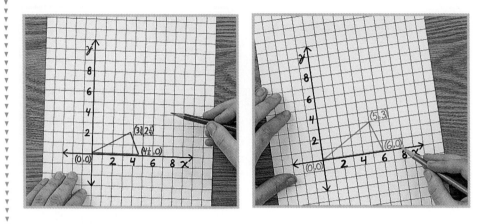

19. **Create Your Own** Work in a group of three. Agree on a figure to transform, and an algorithm with 3 or 4 steps. Each person should follow the steps in a different order. Compare your results.
    Answers will vary. Check students' work.

Reflecting ◀▶ on the Section

Write your response to Exercise 20 in your journal.

20. Write two different algorithms for the transformation shown.
    Sample Response: $(x', y') = (x, -y)$, $(x'', y'') = (x' + 3, y')$; $(x', y') = (-x, y)$, $(x'', y'') = (x', -y')$, $(x''', y''') = (x'' + 1, y'')$

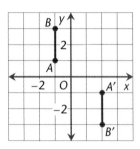

Spiral ◀▶ Review

Evaluate each of the following equations for $x = 3$. (Module 7, p. 504)

21. $y = 3^x$ 27

22. $y = 2 \cdot \left(\frac{1}{4}\right)^x$
    $\frac{1}{32} = 0.03125$

23. $y = 4^x$ 64

24. In the diagram, line s is parallel to line t. Find each angle measure.
    (Module 6, p. 436) $m\angle 1 = m\angle 4 = 95°$, $m\angle 2 = m\angle 3 = 85°$

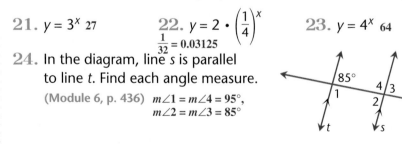

Mental Math Use mental math to find each value. (Module 3, p. 170)

25. $-\sqrt{144}$ –12

26. $\sqrt{0.0001}$ 0.01

27. $\sqrt{\frac{1}{81}}$ $\frac{1}{9}$

28. $-\sqrt{\frac{49}{225}}$ $-\frac{7}{15}$

Working on the Module Project

Modeling Change in a Story

Algorithms for Change You know how to translate, stretch, and reflect figures in a coordinate plane. Each of these transformations can create a different visual effect that you can use to illustrate a story.

SET UP

You will need:
• *graph paper*

5 Imagine that the frames below are frames of film. Describe the visual effect of each transformation. **Translation: The car is driving forward; Stretch: The motorcycle is moving toward me; Reflection: The wind is changing the direction of the sail.**

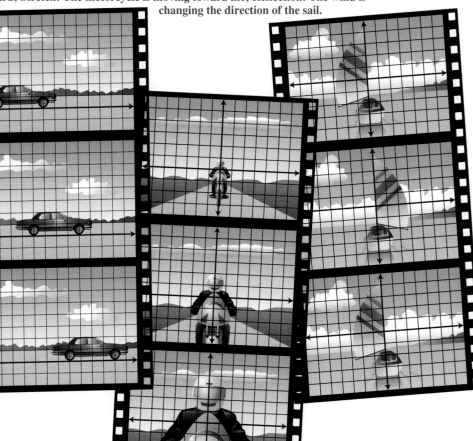

6 Create a visual effect using a series of transformations. You may use up to ten different frames. Each frame should be a coordinate plane that shows what the object looks like after each transformation. Include a written description of each transformation. **Answers will vary. Check students' work.**

Section 4
Extra Skill Practice

You will need: • *graph paper* (Exs. 7–9)

Write an algorithm for moving the point as specified.

1. from (0, 0) to (3, −3) $(x', y') = (x + 3, y − 3)$ 2. from (1, 4) to (3, 5) $(x', y') = (x + 2, y + 1)$

3. from (−2, 5) to (0, 7) and then to (2, 5) $(x', y') = (x + 2, y + 2), (x'', y'') = (x' + 2, y' − 2)$

Explain how to perform the following reflection(s). 4–6. See below.

4. reflect point (−1, 4) across the *y*-axis 5. reflect point (0, 3) across the *x*-axis

6. Describe at least three different ways to transform point *A*(2, 5) to point *A*'(2, −5).

Sketch the original figure and the final image of the reflection(s).

7. reflect across the *x*-axis

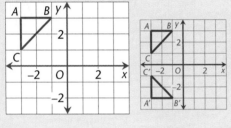

8. reflect across the *y*-axis and then across the *x*-axis

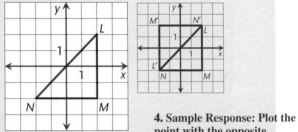

9. Write an algorithm that involves a reflection and a translation. Then sketch a figure in a coordinate plane and use the algorithm to transform it. **Answers will vary. Check students' work.**

4. Sample Response: Plot the point with the opposite *x*-coordinate and the same *y*-coordinate.

5. Sample Response: Plot the point with the same *x*-coordinate and the opposite *y*-coordinate.

6. Sample Response: Use $(x', y') = (x, y − 10)$; Reflect across the *x*-axis; Reflect across the *y*-axis then across the *x*-axis, then across the *y*-axis again.

Standardized Testing ◀▶ **Multiple Choice**

1. △*ABC* is translated 8 units to the right and 5 units down. What are the coordinates of point *A* if the coordinates of point *A*' are (6, 7)? c

    Ⓐ (8, −5)   Ⓑ (11, −1)   Ⓒ (−2, 12)   Ⓓ (14, 2)

2. Which transformation cannot be modeled by an algorithm that involves multiplication? c

    Ⓐ reflection over the *x*-axis   Ⓑ reflection over the *y*-axis

    Ⓒ a translation   Ⓓ stretching a figure

520   **Module 7** *Visualizing Change*

Section 5 Exploring Quadratic Functions

IN THIS SECTION

EXPLORATION 1
◆ Parabolas

EXPLORATION 2
◆ Quadratic Functions

It's All in the Curve

WARM-UP EXERCISES

Use the equation
$y = 2x^2 + 1$.

1. What is the value of y when $x = 0$?   1

2. What is the value of y when $x = 1$ or -1?   3

3. What is the value of y when $x = 2$ or -2?   9

4. Record your points in the table below.

x	-2	-1	0	1	2
y					

9; 3; 1; 3; 9

5. What x-value seems to be in the "middle" of the y-values?   0

Setting the Stage ▸▸▸▸▸▸▸▸▸▸▸▸

How does it feel to orbit Earth? Before NASA astronauts even leave the atmosphere, they have a chance to find out. A KC-135 aircraft is used to help astronauts get used to the near-weightless conditions they will experience in space. The KC-135 flies at a high speed, zooming upward and back down following part of a mathematical curve known as a *parabola*. As it reaches the top of the parabola, the astronauts feel weightless for 15–25 seconds.

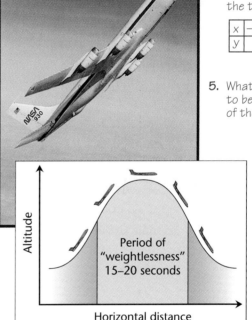

Altitude

Period of "weightlessness" 15–20 seconds

Horizontal distance

Think About It

1 During a training flight aboard the KC-135, the astronauts usually fly along the curve of 40 parabolas. About how much time do they spend feeling weightless on a training flight?
600–1000 s, or about 10–17 min

2 The section of the curve where the astronauts feel weightless is part of a parabola. Describe it. Does it show symmetry? Explain.
Sample Response: An upward curve that reaches a peak and then points downward; Yes; The parabola has line symmetry with a vertical line drawn through the peak.

▶ In this section, you'll learn about objects and situations that can be modeled by parabolas.

GOAL

LEARN HOW TO...
◆ predict the shape
  of a parabola

AS YOU...
◆ use equations and
  graphs to model
  events and
  objects

KEY TERMS
◆ parabola
◆ line of symmetry
◆ vertex of a
  parabola

Exploration 1

 Work in a group of three. You will need: • graph paper or graphing calculator (optional)

▶ A **parabola** is a type of curve. In the photos below, the main cable of the Golden Gate Bridge and the path of the water are both parabolas. You can model a parabola with an equation or a graph.

EXAMPLE

The graph of the equation $y = 0.0239x^2$ models the curve formed by a main cable on the Golden Gate Bridge.

The y-axis is the **line of symmetry** for this parabola because it divides the curve into two parts which are reflections of one another.

The **vertex** of a parabola is the point where the line of symmetry intersects the parabola.

3 Give the coordinates of the vertex of the parabola in the Example. **(0, 0)**

4 Describe the relationship between the x-coordinates of points A and A' in the Example on page 522. Describe the relationship between the y-coordinates. Are there other points with coordinates that have the same relationships? How is the line of symmetry related to these relationships between points?

▶ **All equations in the form $y = ax^2$, where $a \neq 0$, have graphs that are parabolas. The value of a determines the shape of the parabola.**

5 [Graphing Calculator icon] Graphing Calculator Graph the equations $y = x^2$ and $y = -x^2$ on the same pair of axes. How are the graphs alike? How are they different?

5.
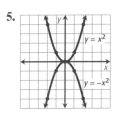

they have the same shape, vertex, and line of symmetry; one opens up, the other down.

6 [Graphing Calculator icon] Graphing Calculator Each person in your group should graph one of the following sets of equations on the same pair of axes. How do you think the value of a affects the shape of the graph of an equation in the form $y = ax^2$? See Additional Answers.

a. $y = x^2$ $y = 2x^2$ $y = 3x^2$ $y = 4x^2$

b. $y = x^2$ $y = 0.25x^2$ $y = 0.07x^2$ $y = \frac{1}{3}x^2$

c. $y = x^2$ $y = -0.5x^2$ $y = -3x^2$ $y = -4x^2$

7 **Try This as a Class** How does the graph of an equation in the form $y = ax^2$ compare with the graph of $y = x^2$ when $a > 1$? when $0 < a < 1$? when $a < 0$? The graph of $y = ax^2$ is narrower; The graph of $y = ax^2$ is wider; The graph opens down instead of up.

8 ✔ **CHECKPOINT** Predict how the graph of $y = -0.25x^2$ will compare with the graph of $y = x^2$. Check your predictions by graphing both equations on the same pair of axes. See below.

9 **Discussion** For each parabola below, give the coordinates of the vertex and find the line of symmetry. How are these parabolas different from the ones you saw in Question 6? The vertex is not $(0, 0)$.

a. $y = x^2 + 1$

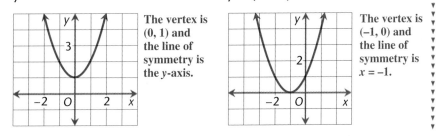

The vertex is $(0, 1)$ and the line of symmetry is the y-axis.

b. $y = (x + 1)^2$

The vertex is $(-1, 0)$ and the line of symmetry is $x = -1$.

HOMEWORK EXERCISES ▶ See Exs. 1–7 on pp. 527–528.

GOAL

LEARN HOW TO...
◆ recognize quadratic equations
◆ simplify quadratic expressions

AS YOU...
◆ explore the physics of sports

KEY TERM
◆ quadratic function

SET UP *You will need graph paper or a graphing calculator.*

▶ One common place to "see" parabolas is at a basketball, baseball, or football game. When a ball is thrown, it follows a parabolic path.

EXAMPLE

The equation $y = -0.05x^2 + 0.7x + 5$ describes the path of a basketball after it is tossed.

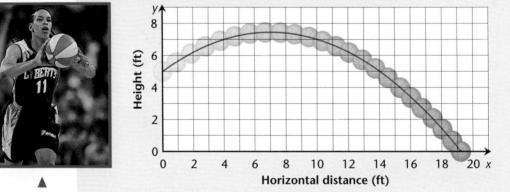

Teresa Weatherspoon, a guard for the New York Liberty women's basketball team, was named winner of the WNBA Defensive Player of the Year Award for the 1997 season.

10. a. *x* represents the distance (in feet) that the ball is thrown and *y* represents the height (in feet) of the ball.
b. No; Some players are taller than other players and basketballs are thrown at different speeds and heights depending on the player and the play.

Refer to the Example for Questions 10 and 11.

10 a. What do the variables *x* and *y* represent in the equation?

b. Does the equation model every basketball throw? Explain.

c. What was the maximum height the ball reached? about 7.5 ft

d. When it hit the floor, how far was the ball from the person who tossed it? about 19 ft

11 Why do you think part of the parabola is missing? Sample Response: The point at which the parabola crosses the *y*-axis represents the height from which the ball was thrown. The parabola is completely on or above the *x*-axis because height is never negative.

▶ The equation and graph in the Example model a *quadratic function*. A **quadratic function** can be expressed as an equation in this form:

$$y = ax^2 + bx + c, \text{ where } a \neq 0$$

12 Try This as a Class Identify the values of a, b, and c in the equation $y = -0.05x^2 + 0.7x + 5$. $a = -0.05$, $b = 0.7$, and $c = 5$

13 In Exploration 1, you explored graphs of equations in the form $y = ax^2$. What were the values of b and c in these equations? 0

14 Explain why the equation $y = 0x^2 + 5x + 3$ does *not* model a quadratic function. What kind of function is it? In the definition of a quadratic equation, $a \neq 0$; a linear equation

15 Tell whether each equation models a quadratic function.

  a. $y = 5x^2 - 3x$ quadratic function   **b.** $4x^2 + 3 - x = y$ quadratic function

  c. $y = -2 - 9x + 9x^3$ **d.** $y = -2x^2 - 3x^4 - 2x^2$
  not a quadratic function   not a quadratic function

▶ **Sometimes it is difficult to tell whether an equation models a quadratic function. In these cases, you may find it helpful to rewrite the equation.**

16. Using the distributive property makes it easier to combine like terms; Combining like terms makes it easier to tell if the equation is quadratic.

17. a single curve

EXAMPLE

To see whether $y = -x(2x + 4) - 3 + 2x^2$ models a quadratic function, rewrite the equation in the form $y = ax^2 + bx + c$.

Use the distributive property.

$y = -x(2x + 4) - 3 + 2x^2$

$= (-x)(2x) + (-x)(4) - 3 + 2x^2$

$= -2x^2 - 4x - 3 + 2x^2$

Regroup to combine like terms.

$= -2x^2 + 2x^2 - 4x - 3$

$= -4x - 3$

The equation does not model a quadratic function because it has no x^2 term.

FOR◀HELP

with *the distributive property*, see

MODULE 7, p. 491

16 Why did it make sense to use the distributive property in the Example? Why did it make sense to combine like terms? See above.

17 Graphing Calculator Predict what you would see if you graphed $y = 5x^2 - 6x$ and $y = 3x(x - 2) + 2x^2$ on the same pair of axes. Check your prediction by graphing the equations.
See above.

18 ✔ **CHECKPOINT** Tell whether each equation models a quadratic function.

  a. $y = 3x(-x - 2) + 6x^2$ **b.** $y = x^2 + x(4 - x) - 2x$
  quadratic function   not a quadratic function

✔ **QUESTION 18**

…checks that you can identify a quadratic function.

HOMEWORK EXERCISES ▶ See Exs. 8–18 on p. 528.

Key Terms

parabola

vertex

line of symmetry

19. b. quadratic function; vertex: (0.25, −1.875); line of symmetry: $x = 0.25$

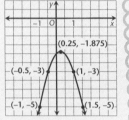

(0.25, −1.875)
(−0.5, −3)   (1, −3)
(−1, −5)   (1.5, −5)

quadratic function

Parabolas (pp. 522–523)

A parabola is a type of curve. The vertex of a parabola is the point at which the line of symmetry intersects the curve. Many parabolas are the graphs of equations in the form $y = ax^2$ where $a \neq 0$.

Example The graph of $-2x^2$ is narrower than the graph of $y = -0.5x^2$ because $|-2| > |-0.5|$. Both graphs are "upside-down" compared to the graph of $y = x^2$ because the coefficient of x^2 is negative.

x	$y = -0.5x^2$	$y = -2x^2$
−2	−2	−8
−1	−0.5	−2
0	0	0
1	−0.5	−2
2	−2	−8

> The vertex of each parabola is at (0, 0).

> The line of symmetry of each parabola is the y-axis.

Quadratic Functions (pp. 524–525)

A quadratic function can be modeled by an equation in the form $y = ax^2 + bx + c$, where $a \neq 0$. Its graph is a parabola.

Example To see whether $y = 4x^2 + 2x(-2x - 5)$ models a quadratic function, rewrite it in the form $y = ax^2 + bx + c$.

> Use the distributive property.

$$y = 4x^2 + 2x(-2x - 5)$$

$$= 4x^2 + 2x(-2x) + 2x(-5)$$

> Combine like terms.

$$= 4x^2 - 4x^2 - 10x$$

$$= -10x$$

The equation is not a quadratic function because it has no x^2 term.

CLOSURE QUESTION

How does the value of a in the equation $y = ax^2$ affect the graph of the equation as compared to the graph of $y = x^2$?

Sample Response: If $0 < a < 1$, then the graph is wider than the graph of $y = x^2$. If $a > 1$, then the graph is narrower than the graph of $y = x^2$. If $a < 0$, then the graph opens down, which is the opposite direction of the graph of $y = x^2$. If $a > 0$, then the graph opens up, which is the same direction as the graph of $y = x^2$.

19 Key Concepts Question Tell whether each equation models a quadratic function. If so, sketch the graph of the function. Identify the vertex and the line of symmetry of the parabola.

a. $y = -x^2 + x(-x - 3) + 2x^2$

not a quadratic function

b. $y = x(3 - 2x) - 2(x + 1)$

See above.

Practice & Application Exercises

YOU WILL NEED

For Ex. 6:
♦ graph paper

For Exs. 5, 8, 18, 19, and 27:
♦ graph paper or graphing calculator (optional)

Match each equation with one of the parabolas at the right.

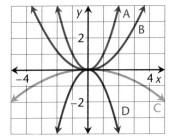

1. $y = 0.3x^2$ **B**

2. $y = x^2$ **A**

3. $y = -x^2$ **D**

4. $y = -0.08x^2$ **C**

5. ▱ Graphing Calculator The graph of an equation in the form $y = ax^2 + c$ is also a parabola.

a. Graph the four equations below on the same pair of axes.

$$y = x^2 + 1 \qquad y = x^2 + 2 \qquad y = x^2 + 3 \qquad y = x^2 + 4$$

b. Predict how the graph of $y = x^2 + 5$ will compare with the graphs from part (a).

c. Predict how the graphs of $y = 0.5x^2 - 1$ and $y = 0.5x^2 - 2$ will compare with the graph of $y = 0.5x^2$. Then check your predictions by graphing all three equations on the same pair of axes.

5. a.

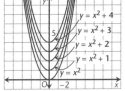

b. It will have the same shape and line of symmetry as the graphs in part (a), but its vertex will be (0, 5).

c. They will have the same shape and line of symmetry. Their vertices will be (0, −1) and (0, −2)

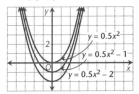

6. Physics The observation deck of the Tower of the Americas in San Antonio, Texas, is 622 ft above the ground. You can use the formula $h = 622 - 16t^2$ to find the height h (in feet) of an object t seconds after it is dropped from the observation deck.

See Additional Answers.

a. Find the values of h for $t = 0, 1, 2, \ldots, 7$.

b. Use your answer to part (a) to plot eight ordered pairs (t, h). Connect the points with a smooth curve.

c. About how long does it take an object dropped from the observation deck to hit the ground? How do you know?

d. Reflect the curve you drew in part (b) across the y-axis. Does this part of the parabola make sense in this real-life situation? Explain.

e. Give the coordinates of the vertex of the parabola you drew in parts (b) and (d).

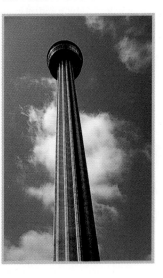

⬦ **FOR◄HELP**

with *reflections*, see

MODULE 7, p. 514

7. a. Use the graph in the Example on page 522 to estimate the height of point *A* above the road. Then use the equation $y = 0.0239x^2$ to make the same height estimate. (*Hint:* Use the scale on the *x*-axis to create a measurement scale.)
   about 500 ft; about 527 ft

   b. About how high is point *A* above the water? **about 727 ft**

   c. Estimate the length of the main cable that stretches from point *A'* to point *A*. **If the cables were tight lines, the length would be about 4330 ft (by the Pythagorean theorem).**

8. [Graphing Calculator] A ball is thrown upward with an initial speed of 80 ft/s. The equation $h = -16t^2 + 80t + 6$ gives the height *h* (in feet) of the ball *t* seconds after it is thrown.
   See Additional Answers.

   a. Explain why this equation is a quadratic function. Identify the values of *a*, *b*, and *c* in the equation.

   b. Graph the equation. Show where the graph crosses each axis. Sketch in the line of symmetry.

   c. About how high does the ball go? After about how many seconds does it begin to fall? About how long does it stay in the air?

Rewrite each equation in the form $y = ax^2 + bx + c$. Tell whether the equation models a quadratic function.

9. $y = 7x + 8 - 3x + 5$
   $y = 4x + 13$; not a quadratic function

10. $y = 3x(x - 4)$
    $y = 3x^2 - 12x$; quadratic function

11. $y = 2(x^2 - 7) - 2x^2$
    $y = -14$; not a quadratic function

12. $y = 6x^2 - 2x - 3x^2$
    $y = 3x^2 - 2x$; quadratic function

13. $y = 12x^2 - 8x(2 - 3x) + 12x$
    $y = 36x^2 - 4x$; quadratic function

14. $2x^2 + 9x(3 - x) + 7x^2 = y$
    $y = 27x$; not a quadratic function

15. $y - 3 = x^2 + 7x - 5$
    $y = x^2 + 7x - 2$; quadratic function

16. $y + x^2 = x^2 - 2x + 5$
    $y = -2x + 5$; not a quadratic function

17. **Challenge** An ordered pair of numbers that make an equation true is a solution of the equation. Find a common solution for the equations $y = x^2 - 2$ and $y = -x^2 + 2$. **Possible answers: $(\sqrt{2}, 0)$, $(-\sqrt{2}, 0)$**

Journal

Exercise 18 checks that you can identify quadratic functions and graphs.

Reflecting ◀▶ **on the Section**

Write your response to Exercise 18 in your journal.

18. You have explored linear, exponential, and quadratic functions. How can you tell from looking at an equation what type of function it models? How can you tell from looking at a graph? Include examples in your explanation. **Sample Response: equation: $y = mx + b$, linear; $y = a^x$, where $a > 0$ and $a \neq 1$, exponential; $y = ax^2 + bx + c$, where $a \neq 0$, quadratic; graph: line, linear; curve that increases from left to right or decreases from left to right, exponential; parabola, quadratic.**

19. The points $A(3, 5)$, $B(7, 4)$, and $C(6, 1)$ are vertices of a triangle. Plot $\triangle ABC$ and draw it after it has been reflected across the x-axis. (Module 7, p. 514)

19.

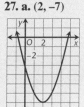

Find the complement of each angle measure. (Module 5, p. 363)

20. 16° 74°   **21.** 78° 12°   **22.** 31° 59°   **23.** 88° 2°

A survey is given to find out whether taxes should be used to build a playground. The survey is given to parents in the town. (Module 2, p. 90)

24. What is the population? What is the sample? taxpayers; parents

25. Is this a representative sample? Why or why not? No; Taxpayers who are not parents are not represented.

Extension ▶ ▶

Finding the Vertex

In this section you learned that all quadratic functions can be written in the form $y = ax^2 + bx + c$. All quadratic functions can also be written in the form $y - k = a(x - h)^2$, which is sometimes more useful.

26. Study the equations and graphs below. What do the values of h and k tell you about the vertex of each parabola?

$y - 1 = (x - 2)^2$ $y - 3 = (x + 3)^2$ $y + 2 = (x + 4)^2$
$k = 1 \quad h = 2$ $k = 3 \quad h = -3$ $k = -2 \quad h = -4$

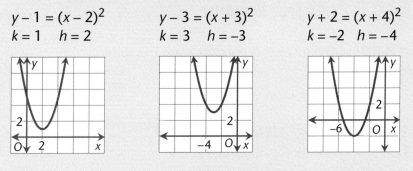

27. Graphing Calculator Make a prediction about the vertex of the graph of each equation. Then check your prediction by graphing the equation. (*Hint:* Before graphing, rewrite the equation so that y is alone on one side of the equals sign.)

    a. $y + 7 = (x - 2)^2$ b. $y - 2 = (x - 1)^2$ c. $y = (x + 3)^2$

26. The value of h is the x-coordinate and the value of k is the y-coordinate of the vertex of the parabola.

27. a. $(2, -7)$

b. $(1, 2)$

c. $(-3, 0)$

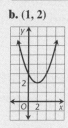

You will need: • *graph paper* (Exs. 1–6)

Predict how the graph of the equation given will compare with the graph of $y = x^2$. Then check your prediction by graphing both equations on the same pair of axes. **1–6.** See Additional Answers.

1. $y = 5x^2$

2. $y = 0.1x^2$

3. $y = x^2 + 1$

4. $y = -x^2$

5. $y = -3x^2 - 2$

6. $y = -\frac{2}{3}x^2$

For each parabola give the coordinates of the vertex and describe the line of symmetry.

7.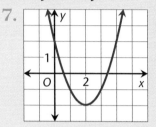
The vertex is at $(2, -2)$ and the line of symmetry is a vertical line through the point $(2, -2)$.

8.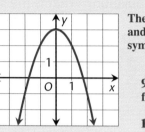
The vertex is at $(0, 3)$ and the line of symmetry is the y-axis.

9. $y = x^2 + 7x$; quadratic function

10. $y = 5x - 16$; not a quadratic function

11. $y = -x^2 - 5x + 10$; quadratic function

12. $y = 3x^2 + 12x$; quadratic function

Rewrite each equation in the form $y = ax^2 + bx + c$. Tell whether the equation models a quadratic function.

9. $y = 2x^2 + 7x - x^2$

10. $y = 3(x - 6) + 2(x + 1)$

11. $x^2 - 5x = 2(x^2 - 5) + y$

12. $y = 3x(x + 4)$

13. $y - 2x^2 = 2(3 - x^2)$

14. $2 - 3x(x + 7) = 1 - 2(x^2 + 3x) - y$

15. $y + 7 = x^2(2x - 5)$

16. $y + 8x^3 - 4 = -2x(-2x^2 + x) - 4(x^3 + 9)$

13. $y = 6$; not a quadratic function

14. $y = x^2 + 15x - 1$; quadratic function

15. $y = 2x^3 - 5x^2 - 7$; not a quadratic function

16. $y = -8x^3 - 2x^2 - 32$; not a quadratic function

Standardized Testing ◀▶ Free Response

1. Describe how the graphs of the following equations are the same and how they are different.

$$y = x^2 \qquad y = \frac{1}{2}x^2 \qquad y = 2x^2 \qquad y = x^2 + 4$$

1. Sample Response: All the graphs are parabolas that open up and have the same line of symmetry (the y–axis); the graphs of $y = x^2$, $y = \frac{1}{4}x^2$ and $y = 2x^2$ all have vertex $(0, 0)$ but the graph of $y = x^2 + 4$ has vertex $(0, 4)$.

2. Tell whether each equation models a quadratic function.

a. $y = -5x^2 + x(3x + 2) + 2(x^2 + 4)$ not a quadratic function

b. $y = 2x(3x + 1) - 7x^2 + 4$ quadratic function

c. $y = 3x - 3x(2 - x) + 4x + 5$ quadratic function

d. $y = 4x^2 + 3x^2(7 - x^2) - 2$ not a quadratic function

Completing the Module Project

Modeling Change in a Story

Illustrating a Story Any or all of the various models you have experimented with can be used to model change in a story. It all depends on the story.

7 Work with a partner to discuss possible story ideas. Each of you should write down at least three possible ideas. Your ideas do not need to be complicated, but each idea should involve at least one of the following: **Answers will vary. Check students' work.**

  • a change over time

  • a change that can be modeled by an equation, a table, or a graph

  • a simple movement that can be modeled with transformations on a coordinate plane

8 On your own, choose the story idea that appeals the most to you. Write a draft of the story. Include the mathematical models you plan to use as illustrations.

9 Exchange drafts and models with a partner. Share helpful comments and suggestions for improvement.

10 Write the final draft of your story. Include your mathematical models.

Match each situation with a graph. Explain your thinking.
(Sec. 1, Explor. 1)

1. The number of sunlight hours per day throughout the year
B; The hours increase gradually to a maximum and then decrease gradually to a minimum.

2. Your height from birth to age 18 C; Height increases at varying rates.

A; The length of the grass in the summer increases then sharply decreases each time it is cut and and then begins to grow again.
3. The length of the grass in your yard during the summer

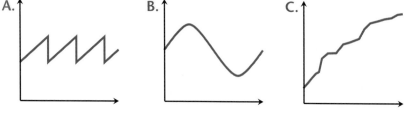

For each equation, tell whether *y* is a function of *x*. (Sec. 1, Explor. 2)

4. $y = 6x$ Yes.

5. $x = 6y^2$ No.

6. $2x = 2y$ Yes.

7. $y = x^2 - 4$ Yes.

8. $y = |x|$ Yes.

9. $x = |y|$ No.

10. Olivia Murk paid $20,000 for her car. Her car is losing value at the rate of $500 per year. Write an equation to model this situation. Then use your equation, a table, or a graph to determine what her car will be worth in 10 years. (Sec. 2, Explor. 1) See Additional Answers.

Solve each equation. (Sec. 2, Explor. 2)

11. $3x - 10 = 7 + 2x$ 17

12. $5(x - 2) = 10$ 4

13. $-4x - 7 = -2(x + 3)$ –0.5

14. $20 - (x - 5) = 3(3x + 5)$ 1

15. $7x - 2(x + 5) = 5(5x + 9)$ –2.75

16. $x(5 - 6x) = -3x(2x + 1) - 20$ –2.5

17. Joe starts walking at the rate of 3 ft/s. His total distance traveled can be modeled by the equation $y = 3x$, where y = distance in feet and x = time in seconds. Ten seconds later Lidia starts jogging at the rate of 5 ft/s. Her total distance traveled can be modeled by the equation $y = 5(x - 10)$. When will Lidia's distance traveled equal Joe's? (Sec. 2, Explor. 2) at 25 seconds

Evaluate each expression for the given value of the variable.
(Sec. 3, Explors. 1 and 2)

18. 10^x; $x = 4$ 10,000 **19.** $\left(\dfrac{3}{4}\right)^x$; $x = 2$ $\dfrac{9}{16}$ **20.** $3 \cdot 2^x$; $x = 5$ 96 **21.** $5 \cdot \left(\dfrac{1}{5}\right)^x$; $x = 3$ $\dfrac{1}{25}$

22. Irene Ehler deposits $100 into a savings account that earns 5% interest. Write an equation that models the amount of money y in the account after x years. Use your equation to determine how much money will be in the account after 25 years. (Sec. 3, Explor. 2) $y = 100 \cdot (1.05)^x$;
$338.64

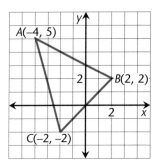

A(−4, 5)

B(2, 2)

C(−2, −2)

23. Use the triangle at the right. Write an algorithm to reflect $\triangle ABC$ across the y-axis and translate it up 3 units. Then draw the image. (Sec. 4, Explor. 1) See Additional Answers.

Make a sketch showing how you think the graphs of the given equations will compare with the graph of $y = x^2$. (Sec. 5, Explor. 1) 24–26. See Additional Answers.

24. $y = 2x^2$; $y = -2x^2$ **25.** $y = 0.5x^2$; $y = 10x^2$ **26.** $y = x^2 + 2$; $y = x^2 - 5$

27. ▨ **Graphing Calculator** A ball is thrown upward with an initial speed of 15 m/s. The equation $h = -4.9t^2 + 15t + 1$ models the height h (in meters) of the ball t seconds after it is thrown. (Sec. 5, Explor. 2) See Additional Answers.

   a. Graph the equation and sketch the line of symmetry for the parabola.

   b. About how long does it take the ball to hit the ground?

   c. Give the approximate coordinates of the vertex of the parabola.

Rewrite each equation in the form $y = ax^2 + bx + c$. Tell whether the equation models a quadratic function. (Sec. 5, Explor. 2)

28. $y = 5 - x^2$ $y = -x^2 + 5$; quadratic function **29.** $y + 7 = 2(x^2 - 3) + x$ $y = 2x^2 + x - 13$; quadratic function

30. $x^2 - 2x - y = x^2 + 7x + 4 - x^2$
$y = x^2 - 9x - 4$; quadratic function

31. $x^2 + 4(x^2 - 2x) = -2(x - 3) + y + 3$
$y = 5x^2 - 6x - 9$; quadratic function

Reflecting ◀▶ on the Module

32. Writing In this module you studied linear, exponential, and quadratic functions. Give an example of each type of equation. Describe a real-life situation that could be modeled by each type of equation. Answers will vary. Check students' work.

CONNECTING

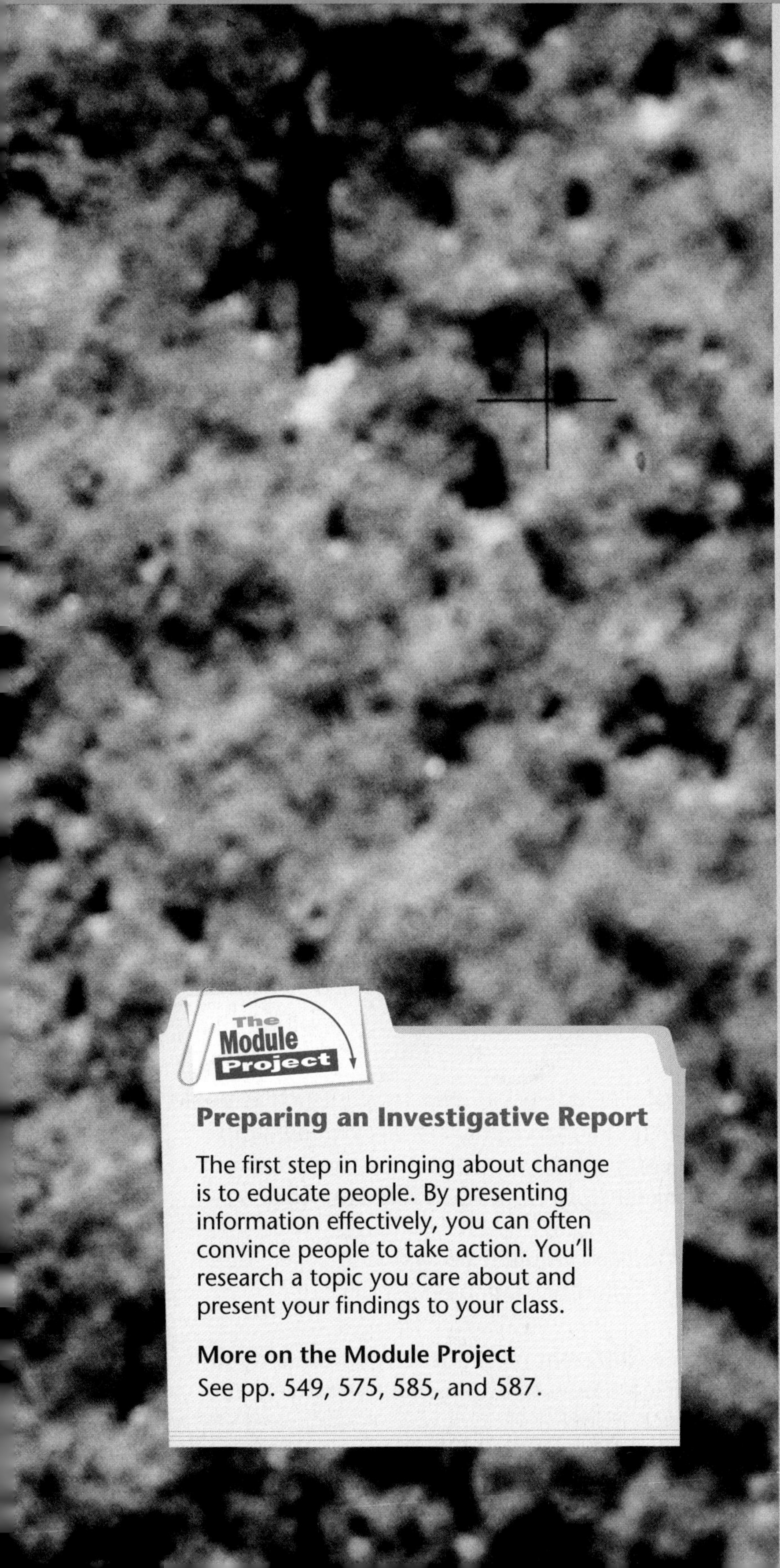

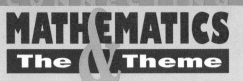

MATHEMATICS & The Theme

MODULE 8 SECTION OVERVIEW

1 Collecting Data

As you study the Florida manatee:

- Learn how to collect data by using data sources, surveys, observations, and experiments

2 Making Data Displays

As you read about school web pages:

- Draw and interpret circle graphs
- Draw and interpret histograms

3 Representing Data

As you explore national and world statistics:

- Choose the best data display for a given situation
- Recognize misleading graphs
- Illustrate facts with pictorial models and demonstrations

4 Equivalent Rates and Relative Frequency

As you analyze data about donating blood:

- Use equivalent rates to make an impact
- Find relative frequencies

The Module Project

Preparing an Investigative Report

The first step in bringing about change is to educate people. By presenting information effectively, you can often convince people to take action. You'll research a topic you care about and present your findings to your class.

More on the Module Project

See pp. 549, 575, 585, and 587.

INTERNET
To learn more about the theme:
http://www.mlmath.com

WARM-UP EXERCISES

Tell what group of people might be interested in the following categories. Sample Responses are given.

1. retirement funds
   senior citizens
2. sizes of car engines
   auto mechanics
3. number of calories in food
   people on a diet
4. weight limit of road bridges
   truck drivers

What information could be studied about each group below?
Answers will vary. Check students' work.

5. birds
6. children's toys

1. Answers will vary. Sample Response: Data sources may have been used for the report on the prairie chicken, a survey for the investigation into attitudes toward recyling, observation for the record of frog deformities, and an experiment for the study of seeds sent into space.

2. Answers will vary. Sample Response: attitudes toward recycling; sending seeds into space; It would be easy for the students to find people to interview about their attitudes toward recycling, but difficult to get access to equipment for an experiment in space.

Getting the Facts

◄◄◄ Setting the Stage

Have you ever wanted to speak out on an issue? Some students at Paul Revere Middle School in Houston, Texas, found a way to do just that. In 1991, they began publishing a magazine called *Earth Focus* to draw attention to environmental problems. Some student projects featured in recent articles include:

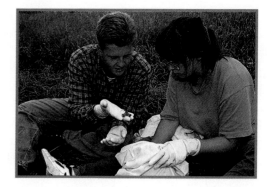

♦ a report on the endangered Attwater's prairie chicken
♦ an investigation into attitudes toward recycling
♦ a record of deformities in frogs from a Minnesota pond
♦ an experiment in which seeds were sent into space

Think About It

1 Some ways to collect data include using *data sources* (such as books and magazines), conducting a *survey*, making *observations*, and performing an *experiment*. How do you think these methods were used in the student projects from *Earth Focus* listed above?

2 For which of the projects listed would it be easiest to collect data? For which project would collecting data be most difficult?

▶ **In this section, you'll explore different methods for gathering data. Later in the module, you'll learn how to display data effectively and use data to "make an impact."**

Using **DATA** Sources

GOAL

LEARN HOW TO...
◆ find and interpret information given in data sources
◆ determine if there is a correlation between two variables

AS YOU...
◆ read about the Florida manatee

KEY TERMS
◆ positive correlation
◆ negative correlation

SET UP *You will need Labsheet 1A.*

▶ **One way to collect data is to use books, magazines, and other data sources. For example, the following passage from Gary Turbak's book *Survivors in the Shadows* contains data about the Florida manatee.**

An adult manatee can measure ten feet from end to end and tip the scale at about twelve hundred pounds—with an appetite to match. Depending on what's on the menu, a manatee may need to consume one fourth of its own weight each day.... The manatee passes away much time lounging on the bottom of turbid pools, rising to the surface for air every ten minutes or so....

[The Florida manatee] is listed as endangered by the federal government.... Humans are this species' greatest enemy. Collisions with power boats do the most damage, but additional manatees die from vandals' bullets, in flood-control structures, and by becoming entangled in nets and ropes.

Use the information in the passage to answer Questions 3–6.

3 What are the length and the weight of a typical adult manatee? **10 ft, 1200 lb**

4 About how many pounds of food does an adult manatee eat each day?
about 300 lb

5 About how many times each day does a manatee surface for air? **about 144 times**

6 ✔ **CHECKPOINT** Finish the brochure shown by listing three threats that the manatee faces from humans.

Possible answers: **power boats, vandals' bullets, flood-control structures, nets and ropes**

✔ **QUESTION 6**

...checks that you can locate information given in a data source.

▶ Data sources often present information in graphs or tables instead of in text. For example, a double line graph like the one below appears in *Population Biology of the Florida Manatee* from the United States Department of the Interior.

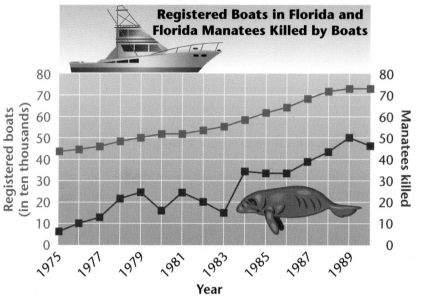

Registered Boats in Florida and Florida Manatees Killed by Boats

Year

7 Are the scales on the graph's two vertical axes the same? Explain.
No; One scale ranges from 0 to 80 and the other from 0 to 800,000.

8 **Estimation** Estimate the answers to parts (a) and (b) from the graph.

   a. About how many boats were registered in Florida in 1975? in 1980? in 1985? in 1990?
   about 450,000 boats, about 530,000 boats, about 630,000 boats, about 740,000 boats

   b. About how many Florida manatees were killed by boats in 1975? in 1980? in 1985? in 1990?
   about 6 manatees, about 16 manatees, about 33 manatees, about 47 manatees

✔ QUESTION 9

...checks that you can interpret data displayed in a graph.

9 ✔ **CHECKPOINT** Does there seem to be a rough relationship between the number of registered boats in Florida and the number of Florida manatees killed by boats? Explain.
   Yes; As the number of registered boats increased, the number of manatee deaths increased.

▶ Two variables that are related in some way are said to be *correlated*. There is a **positive correlation** if one variable tends to increase as the other increases. There is a **negative correlation** if one variable tends to decrease as the other increases.

10. a positive correlation; moderate; There are periods in which the number of manatees decreased while the number of registered boats increased.

10 Is there a *positive correlation*, a *negative correlation*, or *no correlation* between the number of registered boats and the number of manatees killed by boats? Would you describe this correlation (if any) as *strong*, *moderate*, or *weak*? Explain.

11 Use Labsheet 1A. Using a double line graph like the one on page 538 is one way to show a correlation between two variables. You can also show a correlation with a scatter plot.

    a. Labsheet 1A shows a *Table and Scatter Plot*. The table gives data from the graph on page 538. Complete the scatter plot by graphing the data pairs in the table's last two columns.
                                  See Additional Answers.

    b. Discussion Which graph—the double line graph or the scatter plot—gives more information? Which graph do you think better shows the correlation between the number of registered boats and the number of manatees killed? Explain.
the line graph; Sample Response: the scatter plot; The general trend is more apparent

12 ✔ **CHECKPOINT** Tell whether there is a *positive correlation*, a *negative correlation*, or *no correlation* between the two variables.

    a. the height and the weight of a person   **a positive correlation**

    b. the outside temperature and sales of hot cocoa
      a negative correlation
    c. an adult's salary and his or her shoe size   **no correlation**

13 The scatter plot below shows the number of Florida manatees killed by boats and the price of stocks as measured by the Dow Jones Industrial Average for the years 1975–1990.

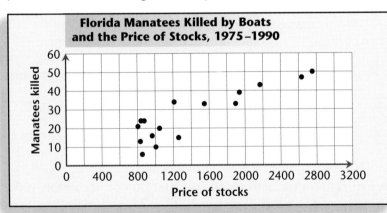

Florida Manatees Killed by Boats and the Price of Stocks, 1975–1990

y-axis: Manatees killed
x-axis: Price of stocks

    a. Is there a *positive correlation*, a *negative correlation*, or *no correlation* between the price of stocks and the number of manatees killed by boats?   **a positive correlation**

    b. Would it be correct to say that a rise in stock prices tends to *cause* an increase in the number of manatees killed by boats?
      No.

    c. Discussion If a correlation exists between two variables, does that necessarily mean there is a cause-and-effect relationship between the variables? Explain.
    No; Sample Response: It may just be a coincidence that the data correlates.

✔ **QUESTION 12**

...checks that you can determine if there is a correlation between two variables.

HOMEWORK EXERCISES ▶ See Exs. 1–10 on pp. 545–546.

GOAL

LEARN HOW TO...
- identify and correct biased survey questions
- identify representative and biased samples

AS YOU...
- read about conducting a survey to choose a fundraising activity

KEY TERMS
- biased question
- biased sample

14. a. Sara's; Kelly's; The questions imply there is a correct answer.

15. c. Using the word forced favors a negative response; Should all students take physical education?

✔ **QUESTION 16**

...checks that you can write an unbiased survey question.

Exploration 2

Surveys and Sampling

▶ Surveys are another way to gather data. For example, suppose a student group is planning an activity to raise money for manatee conservation. A talent show and a softball game are possible activities. The group will survey students to see which they prefer.

14 Kelly and Sara suggest the survey questions shown.

a. Which question is more likely to get responses favoring the talent show? Which question is more likely to get responses favoring the softball game? Explain.

Kelly: Wouldn't a softball game make a better fundraising activity than a talent show?

Sara: Do you agree that a talent show would be more fun than a softball game?

b. Which activity do you think Kelly would prefer? Which do you think Sara would prefer?
a softball game; a talent show

c. Will either Kelly's or Sara's question produce responses that accurately reflect students' opinions? Why or why not?
Probably not; Each question favors a particular response.

▶ When a question produces responses that do not accurately reflect the opinions of the people surveyed, it is a **biased question**. A good survey asks questions that are not biased.

15 Explain why each question below is biased. Then try rewriting each question so that it is not biased. Sample responses are given.

a. "Is recycling a waste of time?" The question prompts a negative attitude toward recycling; Do you think recycling is of value?

b. "Wouldn't building a new high school be a good idea?"
The question favors a positive response; Should we build a new high school?

c. "Should all students be forced to take physical education?"

16 ✔ **CHECKPOINT** Write an unbiased question that could be asked to find out whether students prefer a talent show or a softball game for a fundraising activity. Sample Response: Do you prefer a talent show or a softball game as a fundraiser?

17 Tell whether each group of students would make a good sample for the survey about a fundraising activity. Explain your thinking.

FOR◄HELP

with *surveys and sampling,* see
MODULE 2, p. 90

a. Members of the girls' softball team

b. Members of the school band

c. Every fifth student in line for lunch in the cafeteria

d. Every student who takes a survey and completes it

17. a. No; Students who are not on the girls softball team are not represented in the sample.
b. No; Students not in the band are not represented in the sample.
c. Yes; Since all students are in the cafeteria for lunch, all students in school that day have a chance of being in the sample.
d. No; Students who, for whatever reason, don't take and complete a survey are not in the sample.

18. a. biased; more likely to prefer softball than the general population.
b. biased; more likely to prefer a talent show than the general population.
c. representative; same characteristics as general population.
d. biased; probably have strong enough feelings about one response to motivate them to make an effort to respond

▶ When you conduct a survey, the characteristics of your sample should be similar to those of the population you are studying. A **biased sample** is not representative of the population.

18 **Try This as a Class** Look back at Question 17. Which of the groups shown are biased samples**?** For each biased sample, tell why you think it is biased.

19 ✔ **CHECKPOINT** Identify the intended population for each survey. Also tell whether the sample from the population is *representative* or *biased*. Explain your answers.

✔ **QUESTION 19**

...checks that you can tell whether a sample is representative or biased.

a. A pollster asks people attending a Democratic Party fundraiser whom they plan to vote for in a city council election.
voters; biased; The sample probably includes only Democratic voters.
b. A librarian asks every tenth person who enters the library what new books he or she would like the library to order.
people who use the library; representative; The sample is taken from the intended population.
c. A news program asks viewers to phone in a vote for or against building a nuclear power plant. all community members; biased; The sample represents only people who are listening to the program, have a telephone, and have the time and inclination to call in.

HOMEWORK EXERCISES ▶ See Exs. 11–15 on pp. 546–547.

GOAL

LEARN HOW TO...

◆ collect data by making observations and performing experiments

AS YOU...

◆ learn how the sizes of animal populations are estimated

Exploration 3

Observations and Experiments

SET UP *Work in a group. You will need:* • *coffee can* • *bag of dried beans* • *marker*

▶ **Because the Florida manatee is endangered, it is important to know how many manatees there are. Biologists measure the size of animal populations by making observations and by performing experiments.**

20 In winter, manatees gather in certain bays and rivers called *refuges* where the water is warmer. Biologists in airplanes fly over these refuges and count the number of manatees they observe. This gives them an estimate of the population size.

   a. The aerial counts of the manatees are all completed during a 1–2 day period. Why do you think a longer period is not used? **Sample Response: Over a longer period of time, there could be migration between refuges and some manatees would be counted twice.**

   b. Why do you think biologists count the manatees from airplanes rather than from boats? **Sample Response: Since manatees spend much of their time underwater, they are better seen from the air.**

▶ **When you make observations to collect data, be aware of factors that can affect the reliability of your observations and conclusions.**

▲

Aerial views are also used to estimate population sizes for other animals, such as African elephants.

21 The results of two aerial counts of manatees are shown below.

Date of count	Jan. 1991	Feb. 1991
Number of manatees	1268	1465

   a. Do you think the manatee population actually grew by almost 200 from January to February of 1991? What factors besides population growth could explain the observed increase? **Sample Response: No; migration into the observed refuges; better visibility**

   b. Do the counts probably *overestimate* or *underestimate* the true manatee population at the time the counts were taken? Explain your thinking. **Sample Response: underestimate; Manatees in the depths of the refuge may not be visible from the air.**

✔ QUESTION 22

...checks that you understand how observations can be used to gather data.

22 **✔ CHECKPOINT** What observations do you think biologists made to conclude that manatees travel to the refuges because the water there is warmer (and not because of some other factor)? **Sample Response: They may have looked for other common factors such as food supply, vegetation, topology, and water depth.**

▶ **Making observations is not the only way to find the size of an animal population. Experiments can also provide good estimates.**

23. Answers will vary. Check students' work.

23 Biologists can use a method called *capture-recapture* to estimate a population's size. Follow these steps to simulate this method.

Step 1 Pour a bag of beans into a can. Each bean represents one animal.

Step 2 Take out a handful of beans and mark them. Record how many beans you marked.

Step 3 Put the marked beans from Step 2 back in the can. Mix the beans thoroughly.

Step 4 Take out another handful of beans. Count these beans. Also count how many are marked.

24 The beans you removed in Step 4 represent a sample of animals from a population. Write a ratio of the number of marked beans in your sample to the total number of beans in your sample.
Answers will vary. Check students' work.

25 Let *P* = the unknown number of beans in the can (that is, the size of the animal population). Write a ratio of the number of marked beans in the can to the total number of beans in the can.
Answers will vary. Check students' work.

26 What should be true about the ratios you wrote in Questions 24 and 25? Use this fact to estimate *P*. They should be approximately the same; Answers will vary. Check students' work.

27 **Discussion** Why is the method in Question 23 called capture-recapture? How do you think biologists actually mark animals?

28 ✔ **CHECKPOINT** Design an experiment for finding out how manatee behavior is affected by the presence of humans nearby.

27. Some animals from a population are captured, marked, thrown back into the general population, and then recaptured for study; with electronic tracking devices or actual physical markings or tags

28. Answers will vary. Sample Response: Observe the behavior of manatees from a boat and from an airplane.

✔ **QUESTION 28**

...checks that you know how to use an experiment to collect data.

HOMEWORK EXERCISES ▶ See Exs. 16–19 on pp. 547–548.

Section 1
Key Concepts

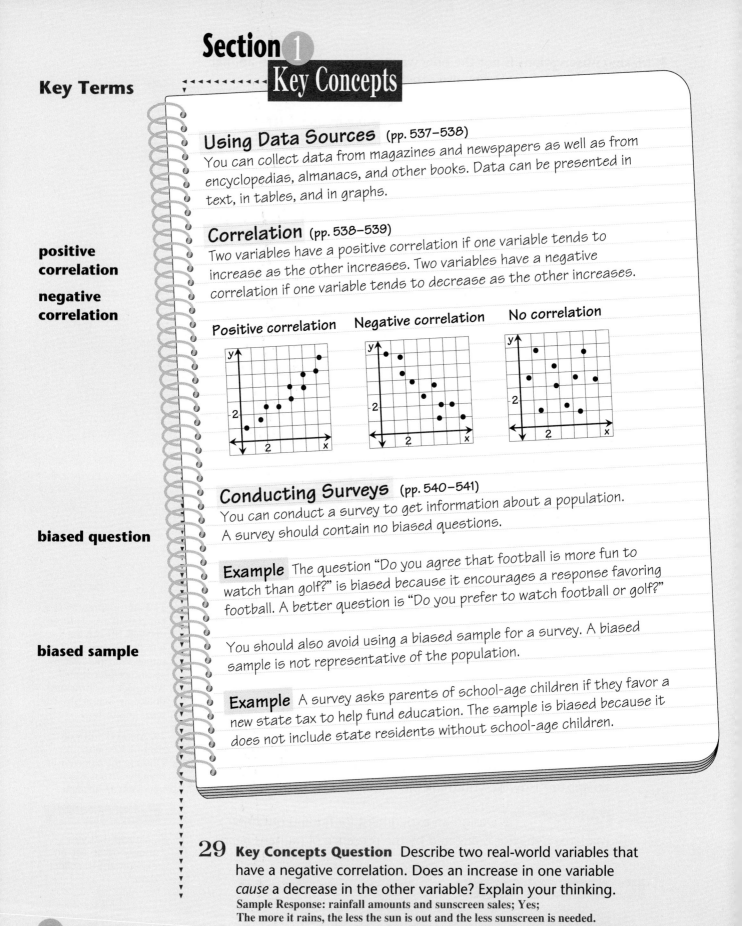

Using Data Sources (pp. 537–538)
You can collect data from magazines and newspapers as well as from encyclopedias, almanacs, and other books. Data can be presented in text, in tables, and in graphs.

Correlation (pp. 538–539)
Two variables have a positive correlation if one variable tends to increase as the other increases. Two variables have a negative correlation if one variable tends to decrease as the other increases.

Positive correlation   Negative correlation   No correlation

Conducting Surveys (pp. 540–541)
You can conduct a survey to get information about a population. A survey should contain no biased questions.

Example The question "Do you agree that football is more fun to watch than golf?" is biased because it encourages a response favoring football. A better question is "Do you prefer to watch football or golf?"

You should also avoid using a biased sample for a survey. A biased sample is not representative of the population.

Example A survey asks parents of school-age children if they favor a new state tax to help fund education. The sample is biased because it does not include state residents without school-age children.

29 Key Concepts Question Describe two real-world variables that have a negative correlation. Does an increase in one variable *cause* a decrease in the other variable? Explain your thinking.
Sample Response: rainfall amounts and sunscreen sales; Yes;
The more it rains, the less the sun is out and the less sunscreen is needed.

Section 1
Key Concepts

Observations and Experiments (pp. 542–543)

Sometimes you can collect data just by making and recording observations of events, objects, or people.

Example A city employee wants to see how frequently a new park is being used. Every afternoon for several weeks, the employee counts and records the number of people in the park.

You can also perform an experiment to generate data.

Example To see how fast a certain car can stop on dry pavement, an engineer accelerates the car to 50 mi/h, applies the brakes, and measures the length of the skid marks after the car stops.

30 Key Concepts Question List all of the data collection methods you learned about in this section. For each method, describe a question you could answer using that method.

Data sources (such as books and magazines), surveys, making observations, and performing experiments; Answers will vary.

Section 1
Practice & Application Exercises

1. **Probability Connection**
   The article at the right appeared in the *Washington Post* on November 27, 1965.

   a. How many heads did Edward Kelsey get while flipping a penny? How many tails did he get?
      8743 heads, 9207 tails

   b. What was Edward Kelsey's experimental probability of getting a head? of getting a tail?
      about 0.487, about 0.513

A3

Student Flips, Finds Penny is Tail-Heavy

Edward J. Kelsey, 16, turned his dining room into a penny pitching parlor one day last spring, all in the name of science and statistics.

In ten hours the Northwestern High School senior registered 17,950 coin flips and showed the world that you didn't get as many heads as tails....

Edward got 464 more [tails], enough to make him ... discover that the United States Mint produces tail-heavy pennies.

Tell whether each graph shows a *positive correlation*, a *negative correlation*, or *no correlation* between the two variables.

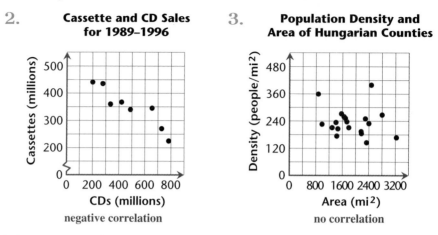

2. **Cassette and CD Sales for 1989–1996**

negative correlation

3. **Population Density and Area of Hungarian Counties**

no correlation

Biology The table shows biological data for several animals.

Animal	Body weight (kg)	Brain weight (g)	Heart rate (beats/min)	Life span (years)
mouse	0.023	0.40	630	3.2
hedgehog	0.79	3.5	250	6.0
kangaroo	35	56	130	16
pig	190	180	78	27
cow	470	420	45	30
elephant	2500	4600	30	69

▲

A baby kangaroo lives in its mother's pouch for the first 8 months of its life.

Use the table to tell whether there is a *positive correlation*, a *negative correlation*, or *no correlation* between each pair of variables.

4. brain weight, body weight
   positive correlation
5. heart rate, body weight
   negative correlation
6. heart rate, brain weight
   negative correlation
7. life span, body weight
   positive correlation
8. life span, brain weight
   positive correlation
9. life span, heart rate
   negative correlation

10. **Challenge** Suppose there is a positive correlation between x and y and a negative correlation between y and z. What kind of correlation is there between x and z? Explain.
    negative; As x increases, y increases. As y increases, z decreases. So, as x increases, z decreases.

Tell whether each question is biased. Rewrite each biased question so that it is no longer biased.

11. "Wouldn't Smith make a much better governor than Jones?"
    biased; Who do you think will make a better governor—Smith or Jones?

12. "Which kind of movie do you like better—dramas or comedies?"
    not biased

13. "Should teachers use filmstrips and movies to make their classes more interesting and effective?" biased; Should teachers use filmstrips and movies?

Entertainment Some results from a survey of decision makers in the United States entertainment industry are shown below.

Who would you say is most responsible for encouraging violence on television?

Viewers	35%
Ratings pressure	33%
Network programmers	17%
Producers	5%
Writers	3%
Advertisers	2%
Program suppliers	1%
Directors	1%
Performers	2%
Outside media pressure	5%

Note: Due to rounding, percentages do not add up to 100%.

14. Can you conclude from this survey that a majority of people in the United States think viewers and ratings pressure are most responsible for TV violence? Why or why not?

15. **Writing** How might the survey results differ if the question were asked to a representative sample of people in the United States?
Sample Response: The percentage who held viewers responsible would be less.

Tell what observations you could make to answer each question. List any factors that may affect the reliability of your conclusions.

16. On what day of the week is the Northfield mall busiest?

17. What is the most popular color for cars?

14. No; The population for the survey was decision makers in the United States entertainment industry, not people in the United States.

16. Answers will vary. Sample Response: Observe the number of cars in the parking lots on each day of the week; time of day, weather, special sale or holiday

17. Answers will vary. Sample Response: Over a period of several hours, observe the color of cars going through a busy intersection; current trends in colors

18. **Physics** You can perform an experiment to test your reaction time. Work with a partner. You will need a customary ruler.
Answers will vary. Sample responses are given.

Step 1 Hold out your hand with your thumb and index finger spread apart.

Step 2 Have your partner drop the ruler between your thumb and index finger. Catch the ruler between these fingers as quickly as you can.

Step 3 Record the length L of ruler that passed between your fingers to the nearest inch.

Step 4 Use the formula $t = \sqrt{\dfrac{L}{192}}$ to find your reaction time t in seconds.

Switch roles with your partner, and repeat Steps 1–4.

a. What could you do to be more certain that the experiment's results reflect your true reaction time?
Sample Response: Conduct the experiment 10 times and find an average of the results.

b. Design a different experiment to test reaction time.
Sample Response: Flash a red or a green light and record how much time elapses before a person touches an index card with the name of the correct color written on it.

Reflecting on the Section

19. Find a newspaper article that reports the results of a survey or an experiment. Describe what the survey or experiment showed. *Answers will vary. Check students' work.*

Spiral Review

Rewrite each equation in the form $y = ax^2 + bx + c$. Tell whether each equation models a quadratic function. (Module 7, p. 526)

20. $y = 4x(x - 3) + 7$
$y = 4x^2 - 12x + 7$; quadratic

21. $y - 8x = 15x^2 + 3x(2 - 5x)$
$y = 14x$; not quadratic

22. Find the surface area of a cylinder whose radius is 4 in. and whose height is 11 in. (Module 5, p. 324) 120π in.^{2}, or about 377 in.^{2}

23. Find 20% of 360. (Module 2, p. 90) 72

Extension ▶▶

Sampling Methods

Several ways to take a sample from a population are described below.

With *self-selected sampling*, you let people volunteer.

With *systematic sampling*, you use a pattern to select people, such as choosing every other person.

With *convenience sampling*, you choose easy-to-reach people, such as those in the first row.

With *random sampling*, each person has an equally likely chance of being chosen.

24. What are some advantages and disadvantages of each sampling method described above? *See Additional Answers.*

25. Which sampling method is most likely to produce a sample that is representative of the population? Explain. *random; Each person has an equally likely chance of being chosen and represented.*

Beginning the Module Project

Preparing an Investigative Report

Did you ever wish that you had more of a voice in the things happening around you? Would you like to learn more about a situation in order to improve it?

In this module, your group will act as investigative reporters. You'll use mathematics to collect and display data on a topic you care about. You'll then report your findings to your class.

Work in a group.

Collecting Data The first step of your project is to choose a topic and begin your research.

1 **a.** Think about the kinds of questions you would be interested in investigating for your report. Some examples are the following:

Answers will vary. Check students' work.

> Where have all the pandas gone?
>
> Does a longer school year make students "smarter"?
>
> Is there too much violence on TV?
>
> Which advertisements are misleading?

b. Of the topics your group is considering, for which would it be easiest to collect data? For which would it be most difficult?

c. Choose a topic. Explain why your group chose this topic.
Answers will vary. Check students' work.

2 Use a book, magazine, or newspaper to find at least one data set that is related to your topic. Also generate at least one data set by conducting a survey, making observations, or performing an experiment. Answers will vary. Check students' work.

3 Gather any other information you'll need for your report. As part of your research, find at least three numerical facts relating to your topic. (You'll use these facts later in the module.)
Answers will vary. Check students' work.

1. b. Sample Response: The question regarding violence on TV asks for an opinion and so could be answered by conducting a survey. The question regarding advertisements could be answered by collecting and analyzing sample advertisements. To answer the questions regarding pandas and the length of the school year would require gathering data that is not accessible to the average person.

For Exercises 1 and 2, tell whether there is a *positive correlation*, a *negative correlation*, or *no correlation* between *x* and *y*.

1. 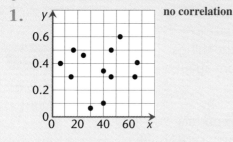 no correlation

2.

x	0	1	2	3	4
y	5	2	–1	–4	–7

negative correlation

Tell whether each question is biased. Rewrite each biased question so that it is no longer biased.

3. "Do you really think this town needs another grocery store?"
   biased; Do you think a grocery store should be opened?

4. "Wouldn't the city be a more exciting place to live than the country?"   biased; Would you prefer to live in the city or in the country?

5. "Which football team do you like better—the Green Bay Packers or the Denver Broncos?"   not biased

Tell what observations you could make to answer each question. List any factors that may affect the reliability of your conclusions.

6. Do many students buy their lunch in the school cafeteria?
   Sample Response: Count the number of students buying lunch in the cafeteria each day for two weeks.

7. How long does it take to learn a part in the drama club's spring production? Sample Response: Question each member of the cast.

Study Skills ◀▶ Synthesizing

You can often solve mathematical problems by combining, or *synthesizing,* ideas you already know.

1. In Module 7, you learned how to solve multistep equations such as $8(2x - 1) = 5(3x + 7)$. Identify at least three mathematical concepts that you used to solve this type of equation.   Sample Response: the distributive property; addition, subtraction, multiplication, and division of integers; solving equations with two operations

2. In this module, you'll analyze data and examine different ways to display data. Describe what you already know about analyzing and displaying data. As new concepts are introduced in this module, synthesize them with the knowledge you already have. Answers will vary. Check students' work.

Section ② Making Data Displays

IN THIS SECTION

EXPLORATION 1
◆ Circle Graphs

EXPLORATION 2
◆ Histograms

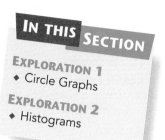

On ://the.Web/

Setting the Stage ►►►►►►►►►►►►►►►►►►►►►►►►►►►►►►►►►

Many schools have an electronic *home page* on the World Wide Web that you can access with a computer. The home page may provide information about school events or give students a place to express their views and concerns. An example of a home page is shown at the right.

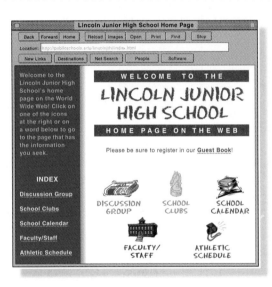

WARM-UP EXERCISES

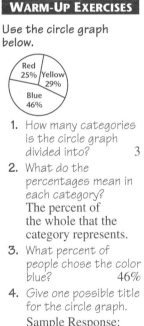

Use the circle graph below.

1. How many categories is the circle graph divided into? 3

2. What do the percentages mean in each category?
The percent of the whole that the category represents.

3. What percent of people chose the color blue? 46%

4. Give one possible title for the circle graph.
Sample Response: What is your favorite primary color?

Think About It

1 Which one of these features do you think is *most* important to include on a school home page? **Answers will vary. Check students' work.**

   A. a student discussion group   **B.** a school calendar

   C. a list of school clubs   **D.** other

2 Tally the results from Question 1 for your entire class. Copy the table below. Record the number of students who chose each feature in the table. **Answers will vary. Check students' work.**

Feature	A	B	C	D
Number of students	?	?	?	?

GOAL

LEARN HOW TO...
♦ draw and interpret circle graphs

AS YOU...
♦ read about home pages and computer software

KEY TERMS
♦ frequency table
♦ frequency
♦ circle graph
♦ sector

Circle Graphs

 Work with a partner. You will need: • Labsheet 2A
• *compass* • *protractor*

▶ The data that one class collected for Question 2 are displayed below using a *frequency table* and a *circle graph*.

frequency table

Feature	Number of students
A	8
B	4
C	5
D	3

A **frequency table** shows the **frequency**, or number, of items in each category or numerical interval.

circle graph

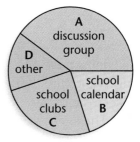

A **circle graph** shows the division of a whole into parts, each represented by a slice called a **sector**.

---

3. a–c.
40%, 144°, 40%,
20%, 72°, 20%,
25%, 90°, 25%,
15%, 54°, 15%
d. They are equal; For each item in the table, find its percent of the whole. Find the corresponding percent of 360°. Mark off a sector of the circle with this degree measure.

3 **Use Labsheet 2A.** The labsheet shows a larger version of the *Circle Graph* above.

   a. Find the percent of all students in the class who chose each feature. Record your answers in the table on the labsheet.

   b. For each feature, use the protractor to measure the angle of the corresponding sector of the circle graph. Record the angle measures in the table.

   c. Find the percent of the total measure of the circle graph (360°) taken up by each sector. Record your answers in the table.

   d. Discussion What do you notice about the percents from parts (a) and (c)? Use this observation to describe how you can make a circle graph from a frequency table.

A software company asked 60 computer owners what they use their computers for most. Of these owners, 21 said word processing, 18 said spreadsheets, 6 said Internet access, and 15 had other responses. Use a circle graph to display these results.

SAMPLE RESPONSE

Step 1 Organize the data in a table. Find the percent of computer owners giving each response. Use these percents to find the angle measures of the sectors of the circle graph.

Response	Number	Percent	Angle measure
word processing	21	$\frac{21}{60} = 35\%$	$0.35 \times 360° = 126°$
spreadsheets	18	$\frac{18}{60} = 30\%$	$0.30 \times 360° = 108°$
Internet access	6	$\frac{6}{60} = 10\%$	$0.10 \times 360° = 36°$
other	15	$\frac{15}{60} = 25\%$	$0.25 \times 360° = 90°$

To find each angle measure, multiply the percent expressed as a decimal by 360°.

Step 2 Use a compass to draw a circle. Then use a protractor to draw sectors having the angle measures found in Step 1.

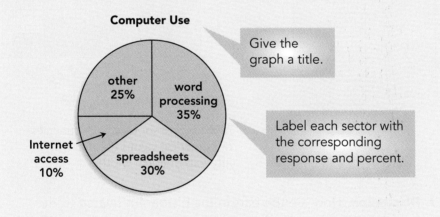

Computer Use

other 25%
word processing 35%
Internet access 10%
spreadsheets 30%

Give the graph a title.

Label each sector with the corresponding response and percent.

4 Find the sum of the percents and the sum of the angle measures in Step 1 of the Example. How does doing this help you check your work when making a circle graph? **100%, 360°; If the sums are not 100% and 360°, a mistake has been made. (Sums may not be exact due to rounding.)**

5 ✔ **CHECKPOINT** Draw a circle graph of the data you collected in Question 2 about your class's home page preferences.
Answers will vary. Check students' work.

✔ **QUESTION 5**

…checks that you can draw a circle graph.

HOMEWORK EXERCISES ▶ See Exs. 1–6 on p. 558.

GOAL

LEARN HOW TO...
◆ draw and interpret histograms

AS YOU...
◆ read about a school's home page on the World Wide Web

KEY TERM
◆ histogram

Exploration 2

HISTOGRAMS

SET UP *Work with a partner. You will need:* • *Labsheet 2B* • *compass* • *protractor*

▶ To measure demand for a school home page, the computer club at Garfield Middle School asks 50 students to estimate the number of times per month they access the World Wide Web. The results are displayed below in a frequency table and a *histogram*.

7. Both use bars of varying heights to display data; Each bar in a histogram represents the data for an interval. Each bar in a bar graph represents the data for a single value or category. The bars in a histogram touch each other; in a bar graph there are gaps between the bars.

8. No; A frequency is given for the interval 10–14 times per month, but not for the values within that interval.

9. a.

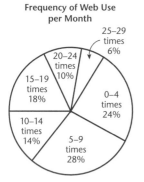

Frequency of Web Use per Month

the percentage of students who fall within particular intervals of web usage
b. The histogram gives the number of students who fall within particular intervals of web usage.

frequency table

Times per month	Frequency
0–4	12
5–9	14
10–14	7
15–19	9
20–24	5
25–29	3

histogram

A **histogram** shows the frequencies of numerical values that fall within intervals of equal width.

6 **Discussion** How are the bars in the histogram related to the frequencies in the table?
The heights of the bars correspond to the frequencies in the table.

7 How is a histogram like a bar graph? How is it different?

8 Can you tell from the histogram exactly how many students said they access the World Wide Web 10 times per month? Explain.

9 a. Draw a circle graph that displays the data in the frequency table. What does each sector of the circle graph tell you?

b. How does the information given by the histogram differ from the information given by the circle graph?

▶ **The Garfield computer club creates a school home page and monitors the number of "hits" per day the page receives. (A "hit" occurs each time a person accesses the page.) The numbers of hits per day for one month are shown.**

16, 27, 26, 5, 11, 33, 23, 17, 15, 20, 3, 14, 29, 21, 23,
31, 16, 8, 14, 28, 19, 20, 24, 35, 7, 12, 22, 27, 18, 20

Use Labsheet 2B for Questions 10–15.

10 Labsheet 2B shows two frequency tables and two sets of axes for *Histograms*. The first table and set of axes use intervals of 5.

a. For each interval in the first table, make a tally of the numbers of hits per day that lie within the interval, and record the corresponding frequency. The first two rows have been completed for you.

b. Use the table to draw a histogram on the first set of axes.
See Additional Answers.

11 The second frequency table and set of axes use intervals of 10. Complete the table and use it to draw a histogram.
See Additional Answers.

12 Compare the shapes of the two histograms you drew. How are they alike? How are they different? The heights of the bars increase and then decrease; The bars of the second histogram are fewer and broader.

13 Which histogram gives more information? Explain.
the first; The frequency is given for a greater set of intervals.

14 Can you use the first histogram to make the second? Can you use the second histogram to make the first? Explain.

15 Can you use either histogram to recover the original data values? Why or why not? No; The frequencies of individual data values are not given.

16 ✔ **CHECKPOINT** Tell whether each data set can be displayed using a histogram. If it can, draw a histogram of the data. If it cannot, explain why not.

a. Weekly high temperatures (in °F) for 20 consecutive weeks:

15, 18, 30, 22, 25, 37, 33, 35, 40, 47,
38, 49, 52, 59, 51, 62, 68, 65, 70, 74

b. Days on which weekly high temperatures occurred for 20 consecutive weeks:

Wed, Sat, Mon, Fri, Wed, Sun, Mon, Thurs, Thurs, Fri,
Tues, Fri, Wed, Sat, Sun, Fri, Mon, Tues, Sat, Sun
The 7 days of the week cannot be divided into intervals of the same width.

10. a.

Hits per day	Tally	Frequency
0–4	|	1
5–9	|||	3
10–14	||||	4
15–19	⼤||| I	6
20–24	⼤||| III	8
25–29	⼤|||	5
30–34	||	2
35–39	|	1

14. Yes; No; The frequencies of the first 2 bars in the first histogram can be combined to give the frequency of the first bar in the second histogram. However, there is no way of knowing how the frequency of the 0–9 bar should be distributed over the 0–4 and 5–9 bars.

✔ **QUESTION 16**

…checks that you know how to use a histogram to display data.

16. a.

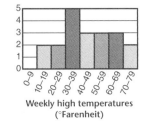

Weekly high temperatures (°Farenheit)

HOMEWORK EXERCISES ▶ See Exs. 7–15 on pp. 559–560.

You can use spreadsheet software to make a circle graph or
a histogram of the data in the frequency table on page 554.

Step 1 Enter the data into a
spreadsheet. The "times per
month" intervals should be
entered in column A. The
frequencies should be
entered in column B.

File Edit Format Calculate Options View

WORLD WIDE WEB ACCESS

B7 | × | √ | 3

	A	B	C
1	Times per month	Frequency	
2	0–4	12	
3	5–9	14	
4	10–14	7	
5	15–19	9	
6	20–24	5	
7	25–29	3	

Step 2 Highlight the data you entered. Select the spreadsheet feature that
makes charts, and choose the type of chart you want.

To make a histogram, you may need
to choose the bar graph option and
set the space between bars to 0.

A circle graph is also
called a *pie chart*.

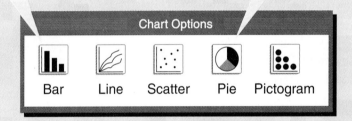

Chart Options

Bar   Line   Scatter   Pie   Pictogram

Step 3 Your spreadsheet software will make the chart you chose. Specify the
labels to use for the sectors of your circle graph or the axes of your
histogram. You can also give your graph a title.

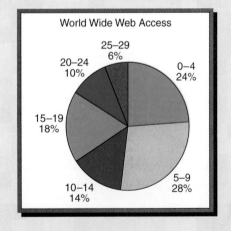

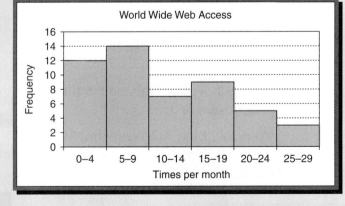

Section 2
Key Concepts

Key Terms

Circle Graphs (pp. 552–553)

A circle graph shows the division of a whole into parts. Each part is represented by a slice, or sector, of the circle graph.

circle graph

sector

Example The circle graph below compares the amounts of electricity produced in Spain by different power sources.

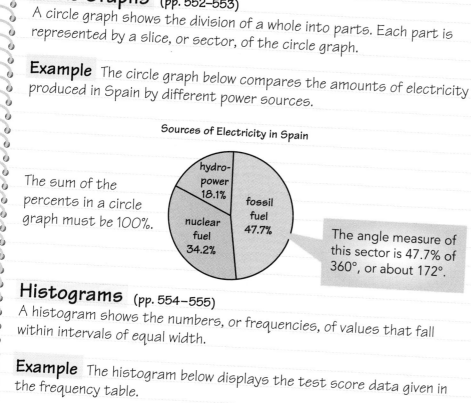

Sources of Electricity in Spain

hydro-power 18.1%

fossil fuel 47.7%

nuclear fuel 34.2%

The sum of the percents in a circle graph must be 100%.

The angle measure of this sector is 47.7% of 360°, or about 172°.

Histograms (pp. 554–555)

A histogram shows the numbers, or frequencies, of values that fall within intervals of equal width.

histogram

frequency

Example The histogram below displays the test score data given in the frequency table.

frequency table

Score	Frequency
51–60	3
61–70	6
71–80	10
81–90	8
91–100	4

Test Scores

The height of each bar is the frequency of test scores in the corresponding interval.

Frequency / Score

17 **Key Concepts Question** Can you use the circle graph shown above to draw a histogram of the electricity data? Can you use the histogram shown above to draw a circle graph of the test score data? Explain.

17. No; Yes; Since no frequencies are given in the circle graph, it cannot be used to draw a histogram. Since the percentage of frequencies that fall within a given interval can be calculated, the histogram can be used to draw a circle graph.

Section ②

1. 10%; The circle graph represents 100% and $100\% - (60\% + 30\%) = 10\%$.

5. The sizes of the sectors do not correspond to the percents they represent.

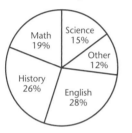

Favorite Subject

Math 19%
Science 15%
Other 12%
History 26%
English 28%

Nutrition The circle graph shows the recommended sources of calories for a person. Use the graph for Exercises 1–3.

1. What percent of calories should come from protein? How do you know?

2. Without measuring, give the angle measure of the sector that represents fat. How did you get your answer? $108°$; 30% of $360° = 108°$

3. John takes in about 2000 Cal each day. How many of these calories should come from carbohydrates? **1200 Cal**

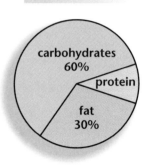

Calorie Sources

carbohydrates 60%
protein
fat 30%

4. Social Studies The gross national product (GNP) of a country is the total value of all the goods and services the country provides in a given year. For each country in the table, draw a circle graph that shows the sources of the country's GNP in 1994.

See Additional Answers.

		Sources of GNP in 1994 (in billions of U.S. dollars)		
	Country	Agriculture	Industry	Services
a.	China	132	296	202
b.	India	84	78	117
c.	Pakistan	14	14	28

6. The sum of the percents is only 90%. Sample Response: Label 10% "other."

Favorite Color

8% yellow
red 25%
10% other
green 16%
blue 41%

Tell what is wrong with each circle graph. Then draw each graph so that it is correct.

5.
See above.

Favorite Subject

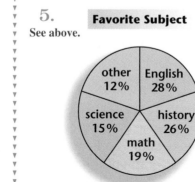

other 12%
English 28%
science 15%
history 26%
math 19%

6.

Favorite Color

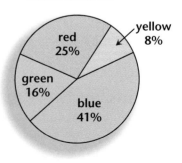

red 25%
yellow 8%
green 16%
blue 41%

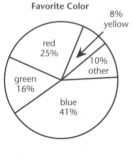

Botany In the late 1800's, Charles Darwin compared the heights of crossed corn plants and self-fertilized corn plants. The heights (in inches) of two groups of plants he grew are shown below.

Crossed plants	Self-fertilized plants
23.5, 12, 21, 22, 19.125, 21.5, 22.125, 20.375, 18.25, 21.625, 23.25, 21, 22.125, 23, 12	17.375, 20.375, 20, 20, 18.375, 18.625, 18.625, 15.25, 16.5, 18, 16.25, 18, 12.75, 15.5, 18

For Exercises 7 and 8, draw a histogram of the given data set. Use the same intervals for both histograms.

7. heights of crossed plants

8. heights of self-fertilized plants
See Additional Answers.

9. **Interpreting Data** Use the histograms from Exercises 7 and 8 to draw a conclusion about how the heights of crossed corn plants compare with the heights of self-fertilized corn plants.

10. **Challenge** In one encyclopedia, the population of the United States is given for each of these age intervals: 0–14, 15–29, 30–44, 45–59, 60–74, and 75 and over. Explain why you *cannot* use these intervals to make a histogram of the data.
The interval 75 and over is not the same width as the other intervals.

Psychology In 1978, D. H. Foster performed an experiment to see how people process visual patterns. Participants were shown 96 pairs of patterns like those at the right. They were asked if the two patterns contained the same number of dots. The numbers of correct responses for the 24 participants are given below.

55, 60, 58, 50, 57, 59, 61, 59, 65, 58, 49, 63, 54, 55, 56, 48, 50, 62, 66, 55, 51, 54, 62, 61

11. Draw a histogram of the data using intervals of 2. See below.

12. Draw a histogram of the data using intervals of 5.
See Additional Answers.

13. a. Explain how you can draw a histogram with intervals of 10 using only the histogram from Exercise 11.
See Additional Answers.
b. Explain how you can draw a histogram with intervals of 10 using only the histogram from Exercise 12.
See Additional Answers.
c. **Open-ended** Use one of the methods you described in parts (a) and (b) to draw a histogram with intervals of 10.
See Additional Answers.

14. **Writing** Explain why you *cannot* use the histogram from Exercise 11 to draw the histogram from Exercise 12.
See Additional Answers.

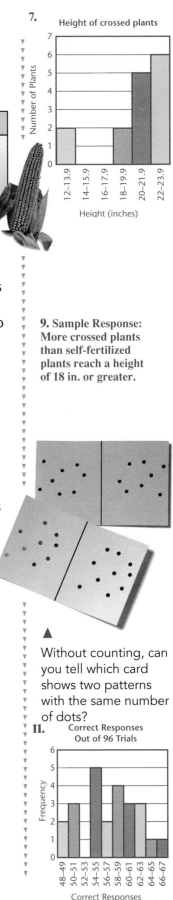

7.
Height of crossed plants

9. Sample Response: More crossed plants than self-fertilized plants reach a height of 18 in. or greater.

Without counting, can you tell which card shows two patterns with the same number of dots?

11.
Correct Responses Out of 96 Trials

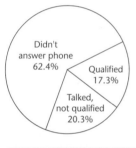

Oral Report

Exercise 15 checks that you can use circle graphs and histograms to display data.

Reflecting on the Section

Be prepared to report on the following topic in class.

15. Find a data set in a newspaper, almanac, or other source that can be displayed using a circle graph. Find a second data set that can be displayed using a histogram. Draw a circle graph of the first data set and a histogram of the second data set. Describe what the circle graph and the histogram tell you about the data.
Answers will vary. Check students' work.

Spiral Review

16. Do you think there is a *positive correlation*, a *negative correlation*, or *no correlation* between the price of apples at a grocery store and the number of apples the average shopper buys? Explain.
(Module 8, p. 544)   Sample Response: negative correlation; As the price of apples decreases, the number of apples the average shopper buys tends to increase.

Write each expression without using zero or negative exponents.
(Module 5, p. 350)

17. x^{-1} $\frac{1}{x}$ 18. c^{-5} $\frac{1}{c^5}$ 19. n^0 1   20. $3y^{-4}$ $\frac{3}{y^4}$

21. Make a box-and-whisker plot of these data values: 10, 13, 13, 15, 20, 22, 23, 25, 26, 30, 30, 30, 37, 39, 44. (Module 2, p. 152)

0 5 10 15 20 25 30 35 40 45

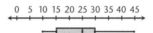

22. a.

Results of
Contacting 133 People

Didn't answer phone
62.4%

Qualified
17.3%

Talked, not qualified
20.3%

Career Connection

Market Researcher: Melissa McMillan

Melissa McMillan works for a company that provides market research to businesses. The information she gathers can determine what products the businesses will develop and how these products will be marketed.

22. For one project, Melissa tried to contact 133 people by telephone about participating in a study on meal preparation. Of these people, 23 qualified for the study, 27 talked with Melissa but did not qualify for the study, and 83 did not answer their telephones.

a. Draw a circle graph that displays the given data.
See above.

b. Can you draw a histogram that displays the data? If so, draw one. If not, explain why not. No; The data relates to categories, not intervals.

Section ② Extra Skill Practice

You will need: • *compass* (Ex. 4) • *protractor* (Ex. 4)

Cost of Joysticks

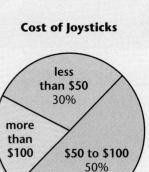

For Exercises 1–3, use the circle graph at the right.

1. What percent of joysticks cost more than $100? How do you know? **20%; The circle graph represents 100% and 100% − (30% + 50%) = 20%**

2. Ten joysticks were reviewed. How many cost $100 or less? **8 joysticks**

3. Without measuring, give the angle measure of the sector for joysticks that cost less than $50. **108°**

4. Use the table to draw a circle graph that compares the areas of the five boroughs of New York City.

Manhattan	The Bronx	Staten Island	Brooklyn	Queens
23 mi²	41 mi²	56 mi²	73 mi²	110 mi²

4.

Area of New York by Borough

The record low temperatures for each month in Phoenix, Arizona, are given below.

17, 22, 25, 32, 40, 50, 61, 60, 47, 34, 25, 22

5. Draw a histogram of the data using intervals of 10. **See Additional Answers.**

6. Draw a histogram of the data using intervals of 15. **See Additional Answers.**

7. Explain how to use the histogram you drew in Exercise 5 to make a histogram of the same data using intervals of 20.

   Use the intervals 15–34, 35–54, and 55–74. To find the frequency within each interval, add the frequencies of the intervals from Exercise 5 that fall within the range of the new intervals.

Standardized Testing ◀▶ Multiple Choice

The histogram shows a person's monthly telephone bills for a one year period.

Monthly Telephone Bills

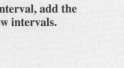

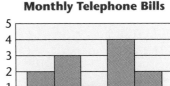

1. Which interval contains the greatest frequency of the data? **C**

   Ⓐ $30–$39   Ⓑ $40–$49

   Ⓒ $50–$59   Ⓓ $60–$69

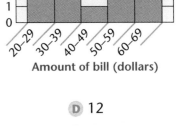

2. How many bills are for at least $40? **B**

   Ⓐ 6   Ⓑ 7   Ⓒ 10   Ⓓ 12

Section ③ Representing Data

IN THIS SECTION

EXPLORATION 1
♦ Choosing a Data Display

EXPLORATION 2
♦ Misleading Graphs

EXPLORATION 3
♦ Pictorial Models and Demonstrations

WARM-UP EXERCISES

Tell if using a graph to display the following information is beneficial.

1. temperatures in a city for a month
   Yes.
2. the favorite colors of a group of people
   Yes.
3. your shoe size
   No.
4. a book you are reading
   No.
5. families that have a computer at home
   Yes.

Displaying the News

Setting the Stage

Every day hundreds of news reports use numbers to describe the world. When you read these reports, it is important to realize that different presentations can give different impressions of the same topic. For example, both of the statements below compare the amounts of money the United States and Denmark spent on secondary education in 1991. (All dollar amounts are in U.S. dollars.)

> The United States spent $6667 per secondary student, while Denmark spent $5540 per secondary student.

> The United States spent 2.0% of its gross domestic product (GDP) on secondary education. Denmark spent 2.7% of its GDP on secondary education.

1. Sample Response: If the United States' GDP is greater than Denmark's, 2% of the United States' GDP could be more than 2.7% of Denmark's GDP.

Think About It

1 Although both statements are true, each one implies that a different country spent more on education. How is this possible?

2 Why might someone use the first statement in a report? Why might someone use the second statement? to imply the United States spends more on education; to imply Denmark spends more on education

▶ Just as two reports can give different impressions of the same topic, two data displays can give different impressions of the same data. In this section, you'll explore many ways of displaying data.

Choosing a Data Display

SET UP *Work with a partner. You will need Labsheet 3A.*

▶ In 1991, students from around the world took a test called the International Assessment of Educational Progress. The data displays below show the average mathematics scores of 13-year-old students for 15 different countries.

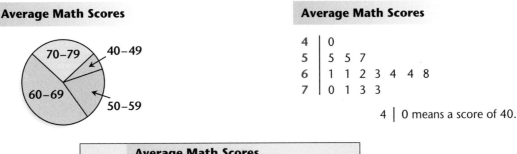

Average Math Scores

Average Math Scores

4	0
5	5 5 7
6	1 1 2 3 4 4 8
7	0 1 3 3

4 | 0 means a score of 40.

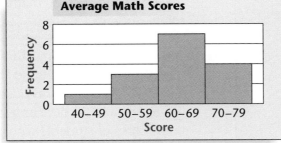

Average Math Scores

3 Which display best shows that almost half the average scores are from 60 to 69? **the circle graph**

4 How are the histogram and the stem-and-leaf plot alike? How are they different? **Both show the frequencies of scores within intervals of 10; The histogram does not show the individual average scores.**

5 Which display gives you the actual scores? List the scores.
the stem-and-leaf plot; 40, 55, 55, 57, 61, 61, 62, 63, 64, 64, 68, 70, 71, 73, 73

6 Given the 15 average scores, can you make a histogram different from the one above? Can you make a stem-and-leaf plot different from the one above? Explain. **Yes; No; You could make a histogram with different intervals; There is only one way to show the data in a stem-and-leaf plot.**

7 What information might you want that the displays do not give?
Sample Response: whether all 13-year old students in a country took the test; which scores belong to which countries

FOR ► HELP

with *box-and-whisker* plots, see

MODULE 2, p. 152

► The box-and-whisker plot below shows the same data as that given in the displays on page 563.

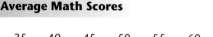

Average Math Scores

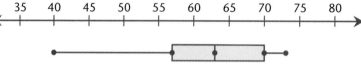

8 a. Use the box-and-whisker plot to find the median, the quartiles, the extremes, and the range of the data. 63, 57, 70, 40, 73, 33

b. Can you find the information in part (a) using the circle graph? the stem-and-leaf plot? the histogram? Explain.

8. b. No; Yes; No; Individual data values are needed to find the information in part (a). Only the stem-and-leaf plot gives those values.

9 Discussion What information can you estimate quickly from the circle graph, stem-and-leaf plot, or histogram that the box-and-whisker plot does not show? Sample Response: the percentage or number of scores between 60 and 69

12. Sample Response: Since the median of the scores is 63, separate the countries into two groups, those with scores below 63 and those with scores 63 or above. Then compare the number of school days for each group.

► The table below gives the actual average mathematics scores for the 15 countries. It also shows the number of days that students in each country spend in school each year.

Country	Days of school	Math score
Canada	188	62
France	174	64
Hungary	177	68
Ireland	173	61
Israel	215	63
Italy	204	64
Jordan	191	40
Korea	222	73
Scotland	191	61
Slovenia	190	57
Soviet Union	198	70
Spain	188	55
Switzerland	207	71
Taiwan	222	73
United States	178	55

10 Make a conjecture about the relationship between a country's number of school days and the average mathematics score of its students. Sample Response: The greater the number of days spent in school, the higher the math score.

11 You can test your conjecture from Question 10 by separating the scores into two groups: scores of students who go to school 190 days or less each year, and scores of students who go to school more than 190 days each year.
See Additional Answers.

a. Draw a box-and-whisker plot for each group of scores. Use the same number line for both plots.

b. Do the box-and-whisker plots support your conjecture from Question 10? Explain.

12 Discussion Explain how you can also test your conjecture from Question 10 by making box-and-whisker plots of two groups of numbers of school days (rather than mathematics scores). See above.

▶ A scatter plot of the data in the table on page 564 is shown below.

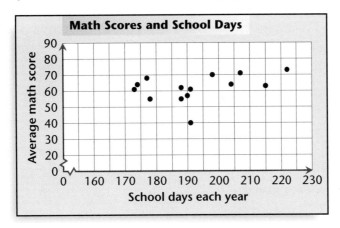

Math Scores and School Days

13 What information does the scatter plot give that the displays shown on pages 563 and 564 do not?
the relationship between the test scores and number of school days

14 **Discussion** Do you think the scatter plot shows an obvious correlation between a country's number of school days each year and the average mathematics score of its students?
Sample Response: No; there is no strong trend shown in the plot.

Use Labsheet 3A for Questions 15 and 16.

15 Labsheet 3A shows a table of data about the *Longevity of United States Presidents*. You'll make a display to show some or all of this information. **See Additional Answers.**

   a. Decide what information you want your display to emphasize. Tell what type or types of displays can show this information.

   b. Draw the data display from part (a) that you think *best* shows the information you chose. Why do you think this display works best?

16 ✔ **CHECKPOINT** Tell which type of data display best does each of the following.

   a. compares the ages at death of Eisenhower, Kennedy, L. Johnson, and Nixon **table**

   b. gives the median age at death of presidents born before 1800
   box-and-whisker plot
   c. shows the relationship between age at death and year of birth
   scatter plot
   d. shows the percentage of presidents who died in their eighties
   circle graph
   e. shows that three presidents died at age 67 **stem-and-leaf plot**

✔ **QUESTION 16**

...checks that you understand when to use different types of data displays.

▌ **HOMEWORK EXERCISES** ▶ See Exs. 1–7 on p. 572.

Choosing a Data Display

Use a **bar graph** to compare numbers of data items that are grouped into categories.

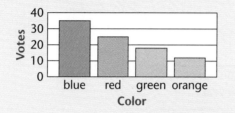

Votes for School Color

Use a **histogram** to compare numbers of data items that are grouped into numerical intervals.

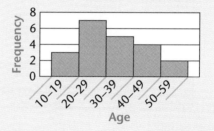

Ages of Actors in a Play

Use a **box-and-whisker plot** to show the median, the quartiles, and the extremes of a data set.

Ages of Actors in a Play

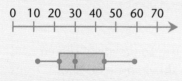

Use a **stem-and-leaf plot** to show each value in a data set and to group the values into intervals.

Ages of Actors in a Play

1	2 5 8
2	1 3 4 4 7 9 9
3	0 2 5 8 9
4	3 6 6 7
5	5 9

4 | 3 means 43 years old.

Use a **scatter plot** to show a relationship between two sets of data.

Corn Production

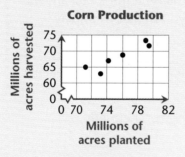

Use a **line graph** to show how data values change over time.

Corn Production

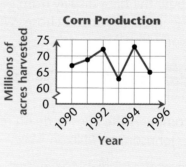

Use a **circle graph** to show the division of a whole into parts.

Votes for School Color

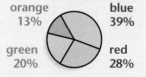

orange 13%   blue 39%

green 20%   red 28%

Exploration 2

Mis**leading** GRAPHS

GOAL

LEARN HOW TO...
◆ recognize a misleading graph
◆ interpret graphs with different vertical scales

AS YOU...
◆ look at the amount of waste generated in the United States

SET UP *Work with a partner. You will need graph paper.*

▶ As you learned in Exploration 1, each type of data display has a specific purpose. Many displays are chosen for their visual impression.

17 Suppose the height of one bar in a bar graph or histogram is twice the height of another bar. What would you expect to be true about the values that the bars represent? One value is twice the other.

▶ Bar graphs and histograms can sometimes give a misleading impression of data. For example, look at the graph shown.

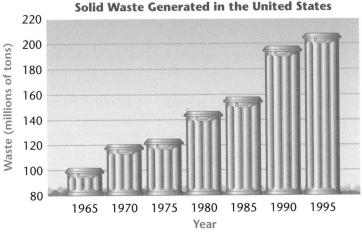

Solid Waste Generated in the United States

18. See Additional Answers.

18 a. Estimation Cover the vertical scale of the graph. Use the heights of the bars to estimate the year when the amount of waste generated was twice the amount generated in 1965.

b. Uncover the vertical scale. Use the scale to solve the problem in part (a). Does your answer agree with your answer to part (a)?

c. Explain why this graph is misleading. Then draw a bar graph that gives an accurate visual impression of the data.

When you draw a line graph, the scale you choose for the vertical axis may affect the conclusions readers draw from the graph. For example, although both of the graphs below are accurate, each gives a different impression of the same data.

▲
In 1995, about one quarter of the solid waste generated was recycled at plants like the one above.

19 Which graph do you think would be used to convince people that the amount of waste generated is rising fairly slowly? **the first**

20 Which graph do you think is more likely to convince people to recycle? Why? **the second; The graph appears to show that the amount of solid waste being generated is increasing rapidly.**

21 a. Estimation Use one of the graphs to estimate the amounts of waste generated in 1965, 1980, and 1995. Your partner should use the other graph to estimate the amounts of waste for these years. **See below.**

b. Switch graphs with your partner, and repeat part (a). Which graph helps you make more precise estimates? **Sample Response: the second; Estimates are made over a range of 40, rather than 100, million tons of waste.**

✔ **QUESTION 22**

...checks that you understand how two graphs can give different impressions of the same data.

21. a. Sample Responses (estimates are given in millions of tons): For the first graph, 1965: about 100, 1980: about 150, 1995: about 210; For the second graph, 1965: about 105, 1980: about 145, 1990: about 210

22 ✔ **CHECKPOINT** The table gives United States budget deficit data.

(*Note:* You may want to use graphing technology.) **See Additional Answers.**

a. Draw two bar graphs of the data that show the difference between a misleading graph and a graph that gives an accurate visual impression.

b. Draw two line graphs of the data with different vertical scales. Describe the impression that each graph gives.

Year	Budget deficit (billions of dollars)
1990	221
1991	269
1992	290
1993	255
1994	203
1995	164

HOMEWORK EXERCISES ▶ See Exs. 8–11 on p. 573.

Pictorial Models
and DEMONSTRATIONS

▶ Graphs are often a very effective way to display data. Sometimes, though, a picture or drawing can illustrate data more dramatically than a graph. Look at the *pictorial model* shown.

The water in the jug represents the total amount of water on Earth.

The water in the tablespoon represents the amount of freshwater on Earth available for human use.

23 Discussion Describe what this model is trying to illustrate.

24 Does this model tell you how much water there is on Earth? Does it tell you how much freshwater is available for human use? No; No.

25 Can you use this model to find the ratio of freshwater to total water? Explain. No; The number of tablespoons of water in the jug is not known.

26 a. In what way is this model more effective than a graph?

b. What would a graph tell you that this model does not? the actual amounts of water

27 Describe a situation where you would want to use this model.

28 There are 1.36 billion km³ of water on Earth, of which 5.3 million km³ is freshwater available for human use. Suppose you want to set up a physical model similar to the one above. If you use a tablespoon of water to represent the freshwater available, how many gallons of water will you need to represent all the water on Earth? (1 gallon = 256 tablespoons) 1 gallon

23. the quantity of freshwater available for human use as compared to the total amount of water on Earth

26. a. The relatively small amount of freshwater available is immediately evident.

27. Sample Response: in explaining the scarcity of freshwater to someone who doesn't understand graphs

▶ Sometimes the best way to explain a concept or display data is with a *demonstration*. Taking part in a demonstration often makes more of an impression on the participants than looking at a graph.

29 Try This as a Class Your class will demonstrate how the world population has grown over the last 350 years.

a. Choose one area of your classroom to represent Earth. Use tape, yarn, or chairs to mark off this area.

b. Let each student in your class represent 100 million people. In 1650, the world population was about 500 million people. The appropriate number of students should stand in the marked-off area of your classroom to represent this population. **5 students**

c. Your teacher will read off years and the world population for those years. The appropriate number of students should stand in the marked-off area for each year. One student should keep a record of the year, the population, and the number of students in the marked-off area. For which year(s) do you not have enough students to represent the population? **1650: 5 students; 1700: 6 students; 1750: 8 students; 1800: 10 students; 1850: 13 students; 1900: 17 students; 1950: 25 students; 2000: 62 students; Sample Response: for the year 2000.**

DATA FOR TEACHER TO READ FOR EX. 29(c)

Year	World Population
1650	500,000,000
1700	600,000,000
1750	800,000,000
1800	1,000,000,000
1850	1,300,000,000
1900	1,700,000,000
1950	2,500,000,000
2000	6,200,000,000 (estimated)

30 How does the world population today compare with the population in 1650? How does the demonstration show this? **It is about 12.5 times as big; The number of students would have grown from 5 to 62.**

31 What did you notice about the number of students that were added each time your teacher read off a year? What does this tell you about the rate of population growth? **The number of students added each time steadily increased; The rate of population growth is increasing.**

32 The world population is expected to be about 10 billion in 2050. How many students would be needed to represent this number? **100 students**

33 Discussion Discuss how you could make this demonstration more powerful. **Sample Response: Have each student represent fewer people.**

34 ✔ **CHECKPOINT** Give an example of information that can be illustrated more effectively with a pictorial model or a demonstration than with a graph. **Sample Response: the distances of planets from the sun**

QUESTION 34

...checks that you understand when to use pictorial models and demonstrations.

HOMEWORK EXERCISES ▶ See Exs. 12–16 on pp. 574–575.

Choosing a Data Display (pp. 563–566)

You can use bar graphs, histograms, box-and-whisker plots, stem-and-leaf plots, scatter plots, line graphs, and circle graphs to display data. When deciding what type of display to use, consider the type and number of data sets you have as well as the aspect of the data you want to emphasize.

Misleading Graphs (pp. 567–568)

Sometimes graphs can give a misleading impression of the data they display. For example, a bar graph or histogram can be misleading if the heights of the bars are not proportional to the values they represent.

The vertical scale of a line graph can be adjusted to make changes in data values seem small or large.

Example

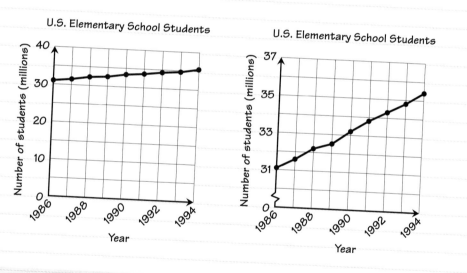

Pictorial Models and Demonstrations (pp. 569–570)

Pictorial models and demonstrations can be used to present information in a very visual and dramatic way.

35 Key Concepts Question Explain how each of the concepts you learned about in this section could help a researcher present his or her data effectively. Answers will vary. Check students' work.

CLOSURE QUESTION

Explain how you would choose a display to represent data values.

Sample Response: I would need to decide what values or aspects of the data I want to display and then select a type of display that best illustrates those values.

Science The tables below give the dimensions (in centimeters) of the petals from 20 different irises.

Length	Width
4.7	1.4
4.5	1.5
4.9	1.5
4.0	1.3
4.6	1.5

Length	Width
4.5	1.3
4.7	1.6
3.3	1.0
4.6	1.3
3.9	1.4

Length	Width
3.5	1.0
4.2	1.5
4.0	1.0
4.7	1.4
3.6	1.3

Length	Width
4.4	1.4
4.5	1.5
4.1	1.0
4.5	1.5
3.9	1.1

For Exercises 1–4, make a data display that shows the information specified. Tell why you chose that type of display.

1. the number of irises whose petals are 4.0–4.1 cm long
   a histogram; It shows the frequencies within intervals.

2. the percent of irises whose petals are 1.3 cm wide
   a circle graph; It shows what percentage a part is of the whole.

3. the relationship between the length and the width of the petals
   a scatter plot; It shows the relationship between 2 sets of data.

4. the median petal length compared to the median petal width
   box-and-whisker plots; Each shows the median of its data.

5. **Open-ended** Describe a data set that can be shown using the given type of display. **See above.**

   a. line graph

   b. stem-and-leaf plot

   c. circle graph

   d. scatter plot

6. **Open-ended** Suppose you conduct a survey to find out how often people ride bicycles. You decide to give sample responses for people to choose from.

   a. What are four sample responses you could give if you want to display your survey results in a histogram?

   b. What are four sample responses you could give if you want to display your survey results in a bar graph?

   c. Why must your sample responses for part (b) be different from your sample responses for part (a)? **Data for a bar graph is given in categories. Data for a histogram is given in intervals.**

7. **Challenge** Given a stem-and-leaf plot of a data set, can you always make a box-and-whisker plot of the data set? Given a box-and-whisker plot of a data set, can you always make a stem-and-leaf plot of the data set? Explain.

8. Visual Thinking Explain why the graph below is misleading.

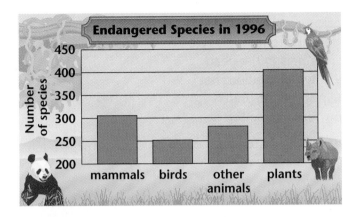

Endangered Species in 1996

8. Since the vertical scale does not start at 0, the proportion of endangered species within each category is misrepresented.

Economics The graphs show the unemployment rate in the United States for 1989–1995. Use the graphs for Exercises 9 and 10.

9. Writing Describe how the two graphs give different impressions.

10. Which graph would you use to persuade people that unemployment increased significantly from 1989 to 1992 and decreased significantly from 1992 to 1995? **the second**

9. Sample Response: The first graph implies gradual change in unemployment and the second suggests radical change.

11. Consumer Spending The table gives the percent of money spent on reading materials in the United States for 1985–1994.

See Additional Answers.
a. Draw a line graph implying that the money spent on reading materials has decreased sharply since 1985.

b. Draw a line graph implying that the money spent on reading materials has decreased only slightly since 1985.

c. Explain how a bar graph of the data could be misleading. Give an example to support your answer.

Year	Percent
1985	0.60
1986	0.59
1987	0.59
1988	0.58
1989	0.57
1990	0.54
1991	0.55
1992	0.55
1993	0.54
1994	0.52

12. World Records In 1980, Shakuntala Devi of India performed what is thought to be the most difficult mental calculation ever done. She took only 28 seconds to multiply two 13-digit numbers in her head. Describe a demonstration that would help someone understand how remarkable this is.

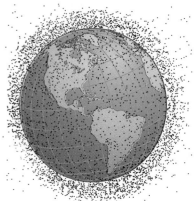

13. Astronomy The picture at the right appeared in the magazine *Science World* on November 18, 1988. It shows the amount of space junk orbiting Earth as of April, 1988.

a. Does the picture tell you exactly how many objects were orbiting Earth in 1988? Explain.

b. The pieces of space junk range in size from 2 in. to more than 100 ft. Could you show this accurately in the picture? Why or why not?

c. The article that featured this picture stated that about 48,000 pieces of space junk were orbiting Earth in 1988. Why do you think the article's author included the picture in addition to this number? to help the reader visualize how dense the mass of space junk is

Geography Although Alaska is the largest state in the United States, it has the fewest people per square mile. New Jersey, the fifth smallest state, has the most people per square mile. Use the data in the table for Exercises 14 and 15.

14. a. Describe or draw a pictorial model that compares the populations of the two states.

State	Area (mi²)	Population in 1996
Alaska	587,875	607,007
New Jersey	7,790	7,987,933

b. Describe or draw a pictorial model that compares the areas of the two states.

15. a. For each state, find the *population density* (the number of people per square mile). Describe a demonstration that compares the population densities of the two states.
See Additional Answers.

b. Find the number of square miles per person in each state. Describe a demonstration that compares these numbers.
See Additional Answers.

Reflecting ◀▶ on the Section

Write your response to Exercise 16 in your journal.

Journal
Exercise 16 checks that you know when to use each type of data display.

16. Give one advantage of using each of the following: bar graph, histogram, box-and-whisker plot, stem-and-leaf plot, scatter plot, line graph, circle graph, pictorial model, and demonstration.
See Additional Answers.

Spiral ◀▶ Review

Displaying Data Use the circle graph.
(Module 8, p. 557)

17. What percent of the memberships are lifetime memberships? **21%**

18. Without measuring, give the angle measure of the sector that represents 1 year memberships.
115.2°

Health Club Memberships

1 year
32%

life-time

6 months
47%

Copy and complete each equation. (Module 1, p. 9)

19. 25 mi/h = __?__ mi/min **0.42**   20. $.17/oz = $_?_ /lb **$2.72**

Working on the Module Project

Preparing an Investigative Report

Choosing Data Displays Many publications use graphs and illustrations to display large amounts of data clearly and compactly.

SET UP

Work in a group.

Use the data you collected in Project Questions 2 and 3.
4–7. Answers will vary. Check students' work.

4 What would you like each data set to show? Use your answers to choose a display for each data set. Explain your choices.

5 Make the data displays you chose in Project Question 4.

6 Are any of your displays potentially misleading? If so, fix them.

7 Describe a pictorial model or demonstration that you can use to illustrate a numerical fact you found in Project Question 3.

Section ③
Extra Skill Practice

**Tell which type of data display best does each of the following.
Explain your thinking.**

1. shows the relationship between height and shoe size
   scatter plot; A scatter plot shows a relationship between two sets of data.
2. compares the populations of New York, Los Angeles, and Chicago
   bar graph; A bar graph compares data items grouped into categories.
3. shows that a company's profit has increased each year since 1992
   line graph; A line graph shows how data values change over time.
4. tells what percent of the United States population is self-employed
   circle graph; A circle graph shows the division of a whole into parts.

**Tell what impression each graph gives about the price of gold from
1990 to 1994.**

5.
Price of Gold

the price remained steady.

6.
Price of Gold

the price decreased sharply from 1990–1992, then increased sharply.

7. The diameter of the sun is 864,950 mi. The diameter of Jupiter is
   88,736 mi. Sketch or describe a pictorial model that compares the
   size of Jupiter to the size of the sun.
   Sample Response: Let a pea represent Jupiter and an orange represent the sun.

Standardized Testing ◀▶ Open-ended

1. Use the data in the table below to make a data display of your choice. See Additional Answers.

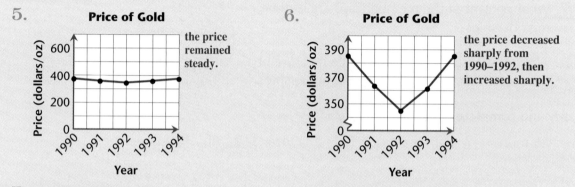

	1986	1987	1988	1989	1990	1991	1992	1993	1994	1995
New One-Family Houses Sold (thousands)										
Northeast	136	117	101	86	71	57	65	60	61	55
Midwest	96	97	97	102	89	93	116	123	123	125

2. Give one piece of information that is shown in your display. Name
   a type of display that would *not* show this information. Sample Response: number of
   new one-family houses sold in the northeast and midwest in 1990; box-and-whisker plot

3. Describe an aspect of the data that your display does *not* show.
   What type of display would show this information?
   Sample Response: median number of new one-family houses sold in the Northeast; box-and-whisker plot

The Situation   See the Resource Book for a detailed discussion of the Extended Exploration.

The table shows the amounts of paper and glass municipal waste generated and recycled for various years. All amounts are given in millions of tons. Sample responses are given.

Paper and Glass Municipal Waste				
Year	Paper waste generated	Paper waste recycled	Glass waste generated	Glass waste recycled
1970	44.2	7.4	12.7	0.2
1975	43.0	8.2	13.5	0.4
1980	54.7	11.9	15.0	0.8
1985	61.5	13.1	13.2	1.0
1990	72.7	20.3	13.2	2.6
1995	81.5	32.6	12.8	3.1

The Problem

Make a new type of data display that uses all the data in the table.

Something to Think About

♦ How is the given data set different from the data sets you have displayed so far in this book? Four different categories, paper and glass, generated and recycled, are given for each year.

♦ Can you modify a type of data display you have already learned about so that it uses all of the given data? If so, how? Yes; Use different colors on a bar graph to denote the different categories.

♦ Can you somehow combine values from different columns of the table so that the data are easier to display? If so, how? Yes; Combine the 2 types of waste generated and the 2 types of waste recycled.

Present Your Results

Make a poster that shows your data display. On a separate sheet of paper, discuss any trends that your display suggests and any conclusions you can make. Present your work to your class.

See Additional Answers.

Section ④ Equivalent Rates and Relative Frequency

State Your CASE

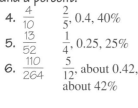
Write each rate as a unit rate.

1. 8 teaspoons of water for every 2 cups of flour
   4 tsp/cup

2. 125 miles in 2.5 hours
   50 mi/h

3. 5 times in a 24-hour period
   5 times/day

Write each fraction in lowest terms. Then write the fraction as a decimal and a percent.

4. $\frac{4}{10}$ $\frac{2}{5}$, 0.4, 40%

5. $\frac{13}{52}$ $\frac{1}{4}$, 0.25, 25%

6. $\frac{110}{264}$ $\frac{5}{12}$, about 0.42, about 42%

◄ ◄ ◄ *Setting the Stage*

SET UP *Work in a group. You will need Labsheets 4A–4C.*

People often rephrase facts to make a more powerful impact. However, you must make sure that any rephrasing you do causes no loss of accuracy. The *To Tell the Truth* game will help you practice "stating your case" correctly. You'll play this game in Question 2.

To Tell the Truth

- For each round of the game, your group will look at a card showing a fact and four related statements. Decide whether each statement is *equivalent* or *not equivalent* to the given fact.

Fact: An average of about 27,000 species become extinct each year.

An average of about 40 species become extinct each day. — Jean

An average of about 2250 species become extinct each month. — Deven

An average of about 10 species become extinct each hour. — Elisa

On average, a species becomes extinct about every 20 min. — Brian

- Your group will receive 1 point for each statement correctly identified as equivalent or not equivalent.

Think About It ▸▸▸▸▸▸▸▸▸▸▸▸▸▸▸▸▸▸▸▸▸▸▸▸▸▸▸▸▸▸▸▸▸▸

1 **Try This as a Class** Look at the sample card from *To Tell the Truth* shown on page 578. Which statements on the card are equivalent to the given fact? Which are not equivalent? Explain.

2 **Use Labsheets 4A–4C.** Play a game of *To Tell the Truth* using the cards on the labsheets. Write *equivalent* or *not equivalent* next to each statement. When you are done, your teacher will tell your class the correct answers. Compute your group's score.
See Additional Answers.

1. Brian's and Deven's; Elisa's and Jean's; since $\frac{27,000}{12} = 2250$, Brian's statement is equivalent. Since $\frac{27,000}{365} \approx 74$, Elisa's statement is not equivalent. Since $\frac{27,000}{24 \cdot 365} \approx 3$, Jean's statement is not equivalent, but Deven's is since 3 per hour is one every 20 min.

Exploration 1 ▸▸▸▸▸▸▸▸▸▸▸▸▸▸▸▸▸▸▸▸▸▸▸▸▸▸▸▸▸▸

RATES and Frequency

GOAL

LEARN HOW TO...
◆ use equivalent rates to make an impact
◆ find relative frequencies

AS YOU...
◆ analyze data about donating blood

KEY TERMS
◆ equivalent rates
◆ relative frequency

▸ You can often express the same information in many different yet equivalent ways.

3 Use the information in the brochure. Write the rate of blood donation in the United States using the given units.

Each year people in the United States donate about **14 million pints** of blood.

a. pints per month
about 1.2 million pints/month
b. pints per day
about 38,400 pints/day
c. gallons per minute about 3.3 gal/min
d. gallons per second about 0.06 gal/sec

▸ The rates you wrote in Question 3 are *equivalent rates*. **Equivalent rates** are equal rates that may be expressed using different units. For example, 1 gal/s and 60 gal/min are equivalent rates.

4 ✔ **CHECKPOINT** Tell whether the given rates are equivalent rates.

a. 50 mi/h; 1 mi/min not equivalent **b.** 5 mL/s; 432 L/day equivalent

c. $1.20/gal; 15¢/pt equivalent **d.** 3 oz/in.; 1728 lb/yd not equivalent

✔ **QUESTION 4**

...checks that you can recognize equivalent rates.

▶ Sometimes you may want to replace a given rate with an equivalent rate to make information more understandable or impressive.

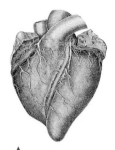

▲

A human heart

6. c. Sample Response: 10.2 pt/min; 14,688 pt/day; The first rate is easy to visualize and the second contains a large number.

✔ **QUESTION 7**

...checks that you can use equivalent rates to present information effectively.

5 The human heart pumps blood at a rate of about 0.17 pt/s. Explain why someone might have trouble visualizing this rate.
Sample Response: Seventeen-hundredths pt is not a usual quantity.

6 a. Write the rate in Question 5 in pints per minute. **10.2 pt/min**

b. Write the rate in Question 5 in pints per day. **14,688 pt/day**

c. Discussion Which of the rates from parts (a) and (b) gives you a better idea of how fast the heart pumps blood through the human body? Which rate would you use to impress upon someone how hard the heart works? Explain your answers.

d. Scientists often use metric units for rates. What units might a scientist use to explain how fast the heart pumps blood?
Sample Response: mL/s or L/day

7 ✔ **CHECKPOINT** Blood is transfused to patients in the United States at a rate of about 23 million pt/year. Write an equivalent rate that makes it easiest for you to visualize the amount of blood transfused. Explain your thinking.
Sample Response: about 44 pt/min; Smaller quantities are easier to visualize.

▶ You have probably heard statements like "2 out of every 3 dentists recommend baking soda toothpaste" or "10% of the population is left-handed." Both of these statements express *relative frequencies*. The **relative frequency** of an item is defined as:

$$\text{Relative frequency} = \frac{\text{Number of occurrences of item}}{\text{Total number of occurrences}}$$

EXAMPLE

Each year about 8,000,000 people in the United States donate blood. The total population of the United States is about 268,000,000. Therefore:

$$\begin{aligned}\text{Relative frequency of blood donors} &= \frac{\text{Population of blood donors}}{\text{Total population}} \\[6pt] &= \frac{8,000,000}{268,000,000} \\[6pt] &= \frac{2}{67}\end{aligned}$$

The relative frequency of blood donors is about $\frac{2}{67}$. You can also express the relative frequency as a decimal (about 0.03) or as a percent (about 3%).

8 In the Example, which way of expressing the relative frequency of blood donors—as a fraction, as a decimal, or as a percent—do you think is most effective? Explain.

Sample Response: as a percent; 3% is easily visualized and used in calculations

9 a. Use the Example to find numbers that make this statement true: "About __?__ out of every __?__ people in the United States donate blood each year."   2, 67

b. Is there more than one correct way to complete the statement in part (a)? If so, which way do you think is most effective? Explain your thinking.   Yes; the way that uses numbers that are easy to relate to

▶ **You can interpret a relative frequency as a probability. For example, since about 3% of people in the United States donate blood, the probability that a randomly selected person donates blood is about $\frac{3}{100}$, or about 0.03.**

The bar graph shows the number of people in the United States that have each blood type. Use the graph for Questions 10–12.

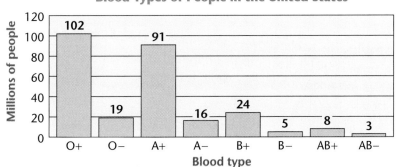

Blood Types of People in the United States

10 Find the probability that a randomly selected person has the given blood type.

a. O+ about 0.38   **b.** AB− about 0.01   **c.** A+ or A− about 0.4

11 Sara knows she has type B blood, but she is not sure whether it is B+ or B−. Which blood type does she probably have? Explain.

B+; The probability of having type B+ is 4.8 times the probability of having B−.

12 ✔ **CHECKPOINT** Suppose 200 people are expected to each donate a pint of blood at a blood drive. About how many pints of O− would you expect to get? About how many pints of AB+ would you expect to get? Explain how you obtained your answers and any assumptions you made.

about 14 pints; about 6 pints; The probability of having type O− is about 0.07 and 0.07 • 200 = 14. The probability of having type AB+ is about 0.03 and 0.03 • 200 = 6.

✔ **QUESTION 12**

...checks that you can use relative frequencies to solve problems.

HOMEWORK EXERCISES ▶ See Exs. 1–16 on pp. 583–585.

Key Terms

equivalent rates

Equivalent Rates (pp. 579–580)

Equivalent rates are equal rates that may be expressed using different units. You can use equivalent rates to rephrase data in more powerful or more understandable ways.

Example According to one book, each person in the United States eats an average of 3 oz of sugar per day. To impress upon someone just how much sugar this is, you might convert to pounds per year:

$$3 \text{ oz/day} = \frac{3 \text{ oz}}{1 \text{ day}} \cdot \frac{1 \text{ lb}}{16 \text{ oz}} \cdot \frac{365 \text{ days}}{1 \text{ year}} \approx 68.4 \text{ lb/year}$$

relative frequency

Relative Frequency (pp. 580–581)

The relative frequency of an item is defined as:

$$\text{Relative frequency} = \frac{\text{Number of occurrences of item}}{\text{Total number of occurrences}}$$

Example The table shows the results of the 1996 presidential election. You can find the relative frequency of voters who cast votes for Bob Dole:

Candidate	Votes
Bill Clinton	46,020,089
Bob Dole	38,219,266
Ross Perot	7,936,247
others	1,470,082
Total	**93,645,684**

$$\text{Relative frequency} = \frac{\text{Votes for Bob Dole}}{\text{Total votes}}$$
$$= \frac{38,219,266}{93,645,684}$$
$$\approx 0.408, \text{ or } 40.8\%$$

CLOSURE QUESTION

What is meant by an equivalent rate? by relative frequency?

Sample Response: Equivalent rates are equal ratios of two quantities that may or may not be expressed using the same units. Relative frequency is the ratio of the number of occurrences of one item to the total number of occurrences of all items.

13. Sample Response: 1 oz/ meal; An ad campaign is being developed to encourage people not to worry about eating too much sugar.

Key Concepts Questions

13 Use a rate other than ounces per day or pounds per year to specify the average amount of sugar eaten by each person in the United States. Describe a situation where it would make sense to use the rate you chose.

14 Find the probability that a randomly selected voter did *not* vote for Bill Clinton or Bob Dole in the 1996 presidential election. Explain how you got your answer.

about 0.1 or 10%; (7,936,247 + 1,470,082) ÷ 93,645,684 ≈ 0.1

Practice & Application Exercises ▸▸▸▸▸▸▸▸▸

For Exercises 1–8, you may need to use the Table of Measures on page 610.

Tell whether the given rates are *equivalent* or *not equivalent*.

1. 5 cars/min; 300 cars/s
   not equivalent

2. 20 lb/day; 3.65 tons/year
   equivalent

3. 108 lb/ft³; 1 oz/in.³
   equivalent

4. 8 pt/day; 2.29 gal/week
   not equivalent

5. **Open-ended** Use an equivalent rate to rewrite this statement so that it makes a more powerful impact: "A person must take in about 2.5 quarts of water per day in order to survive." **Sample Response: A person must take in about 80 oz of water per day in order to survive.**

6. **Open-ended** Use an equivalent rate to rewrite this statement so that it is easier to visualize: "The three-toed sloth moves along the ground at an average speed of about 0.07 mi/h." **Sample Response: The three-toed sloth moves along the ground at an average speed of about 6 ft/min.**

Science In a thunderstorm, you see flashes of lightning before you hear the thunder from the lightning. This is because sound travels much more slowly than light.

7. The speed of sound through air is about 1100 ft/s.

   a. Suppose you want to explain to a friend how the speed of sound compares to the speed of a car. What units would you use to express the speed of sound to your friend? Explain. **km/h or mi/h; The speed of a car is usually given in km/h or mi/h.**

   b. Express the speed of sound in the units you chose in part (a). **about 1250 km/h or 750 mi/h**

8. On page 54, you learned this rule of thumb: To estimate how many miles you are from a thunderstorm, count the number of seconds between the lightning and the thunder and divide by 5.

   a. **Challenge** Express the speed of sound from Exercise 7 in miles per second. Use this rate to justify the given rule of thumb. (Since light travels so fast, you can assume that there is no delay between when the lightning strikes and when you see the lightning.)

   b. **Writing** Why do you think the given rule of thumb expresses distance and time in miles and seconds rather than in, say, feet and hours? **Sample Response: The sound of the thunder will take seconds, not hours to travel over a distance best expressed in miles, not feet.**

8. a. about 0.21 mi/s; Since sound travels about 0.21 mi/s or about $\frac{1}{5}$ mi/s, it takes about 5 seconds to travel 1 mile.

Write the relative frequency expressed by each sentence as a fraction, as a decimal, and as a percent.

9. Spanish is the native language of about 3 out of every 40 people in the United States. $\frac{3}{40}$, 0.075, 7.5%

10. About 2 of every 5 mi^2 of land in the United States is farmland. $\frac{2}{5}$, 0.4, 40%

Transportation The table shows how people commuted to work in 1980 and in 1990. Use the table for Exercises 11–15. Write all relative frequencies and probabilities as decimals or percents.

Means of transportation	Number of people in 1980	Number of people in 1990
car, truck, or van	81,258,496	99,592,932
public transportation	6,175,061	6,069,589
motorcycle	419,007	237,404
bicycle	468,348	466,856
walked	5,413,248	4,488,886
other means	703,273	808,582
worked at home	2,179,863	3,406,025
Total	96,617,296	115,070,274

11. In 1980, what was the relative frequency of workers who commuted:

   a. using public transportation? 0.06, or 6%   b. using a motorcycle? 0.004, or 0.4%

   c. using a bicycle? 0.005, or 0.5%   d. by walking? 0.056 or 5.6%

12. Repeat Exercise 11 for the year 1990.
   a. 0.05, or 5%; b. 0.002, or 0.2%; c. 0.004, or 0.4%; d. 0.04, or 4%

13. For which category in the table did the number of people increase but the relative frequency decrease from 1980 to 1990? other means

14. What is the probability that a randomly selected worker:

   a. took a car, truck, or van to work in 1980? 0.84, or 84%

   b. walked to work or worked at home in 1990? 0.069, or 6.9%

   c. did not use public transportation to get to work in 1990? 0.947, or 94.7%

15. $\frac{6,069,589}{115,070,274} = \frac{p}{1200}$; about 63 workers

15. **Algebra Connection** A pollster plans to survey 1200 workers in the United States to see how they feel about raising taxes to pay for public transportation projects. Write and solve a proportion to find the number of workers the pollster should survey who take public transportation themselves. (Use the data for 1990.)

Reflecting ◀▷ on the Section

Be prepared to discuss your response to Exercise 16 in class.

16. Describe a situation where you would choose the given units to express a rate. Explain your thinking. **Sample responses are given.**

     a. ft/s   the speed of a person walking   **b.** mi/h   the speed of a bicyclist   **c.** mi/s   the speed of a spacecraft

Spiral ◀▷ Review

Choose a type of data display that you could use for each data set. Explain each choice of display. (Module 8, p. 571)

17. the amounts of rainfall during the months of a certain year
     Sample Response: a bar graph; The data falls into categories.
18. the percentages of people who voted for various candidates in a student council election
     Sample Response: a circle graph; The data is given in percentages.

Find the complement and the supplement of each angle.

(Module 5, p. 363)

19. $10°$ 80°, 170°   20. $88°$ 2°, 92°   21. $57°$ 33°, 123°   22. $45°$ 45°, 135°

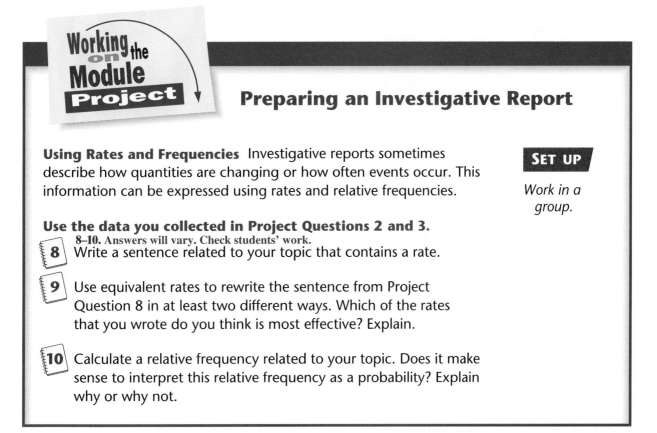

Working on the Module Project

Preparing an Investigative Report

Using Rates and Frequencies Investigative reports sometimes describe how quantities are changing or how often events occur. This information can be expressed using rates and relative frequencies.

SET UP

Work in a group.

Use the data you collected in Project Questions 2 and 3.

8–10. Answers will vary. Check students' work.

8 Write a sentence related to your topic that contains a rate.

9 Use equivalent rates to rewrite the sentence from Project Question 8 in at least two different ways. Which of the rates that you wrote do you think is most effective? Explain.

10 Calculate a relative frequency related to your topic. Does it make sense to interpret this relative frequency as a probability? Explain why or why not.

Tell whether the given rates are *equivalent* or *not equivalent*. You may need to use the Table of Measures on page 610.

1. 600 mi/h; 10 mi/min equivalent
2. $29,000/year; $100/day not equivalent
3. 15 gal/min; 2.5 pt/s not equivalent
4. 34 kg/m², 3.4 g/cm² equivalent

4. 34 kg/m^2; 3.4 g/cm^2 equivalent

5. Use an equivalent rate to rewrite this statement so that it makes a more powerful impact: "Tanya reads about 2 books per week."
   Sample Response: Tanya reads about 104 books per year

The table shows the number of students enrolled in each of the engineering programs offered at a certain university.

Type of engineering	chemical	civil	electrical	mechanical	undecided
Number of students	258	430	792	640	505

For Exercises 6–9, find the relative frequency of engineering students enrolled in the given program(s). Write each answer as a decimal or as a percent.

6. mechanical engineering about 0.24, or 24%
7. civil engineering about 0.16, or 16%
8. chemical or electrical engineering
   0.4, or 40%
9. undecided about 0.19, or 19%

Standardized Testing ◀▶ Free Response

1. Use three equivalent rates to describe approximately how much time you spend watching television. Which rate do you think communicates this information most effectively? Which rate do you think is least effective? Explain.

2. The table below gives the enrollment by grade at a certain school. If 250 students from the school are selected at random to take a standardized test, about how many of the students taking the test would you expect to be in eighth grade? about 29 students

1. Sample Response: 1 h/day, 30 h/month, 2.5 min/h; I think the rate 1 h/day communicates this information most effectively because it also describes fairly accurately about how much I watch on a typical day. I think the rate 2.5 min/h is least effective because it suggests that I turn the television on and off once an hour.

Grade	K	1	2	3	4	5	6	7	8
Enrollment	110	115	121	123	93	112	114	95	117

Completing the Module Project

Preparing an Investigative Report

Throughout this module, you have explored ways of collecting and presenting data. Now you'll share information with your class about the topic your group chose to report on.

Work in a group.

11–14. Answers will vary. Check students' work.

11 Make an outline for your report. Include the following:

- ◆ a brief description of the topic of your report

- ◆ a list of the main points you plan to address in the order you want to present them

- ◆ the data displays you made in Project Question 5 along with notes about where in your report they should appear

- ◆ a list of conclusions based on your research

12 Data displays are often accompanied by captions. Write a caption for each of your data displays explaining what the display shows.

13 You can present your report to your class orally or in writing. If you plan to give an oral report, prepare a set of index cards, posters, and other aids to use during your presentation. If you plan to give a written report, choose a format to use, such as a brochure or a magazine article.

14 Present your report to your class. Explain what you could do to improve or extend your report.

A health magazine gives the advice below. Use this information for Exercises 1 and 2. (Sec. 1, Explor. 1)

If you plan to do 20–30 min of moderate exercise, you should stretch for 5–10 min before you begin. You should also stretch for 5–10 min afterwards. Each stretch should be held for 10–20 s.

1. At most, how many stretches should you do in one minute? 3 to 6 stretches

2. What is the minimum amount of time it should take to complete a workout that includes 25 min of exercise? 35 min

Tell whether there is a *positive correlation*, a *negative correlation*, or *no correlation* between the two variables. (Sec. 1, Explor. 1)

3. the diameter of a pizza and its price
   positive correlation

4.
x	1	2	3	4	5	6
y	1	0	1	0	1	0

no correlation

5. Is the following question biased? If so, rewrite the question so that it is no longer biased. (Sec. 1, Explor. 2)

   "Do you agree that students should have access to the Internet in order to improve their education?" Yes; Should students have access to the internet?

6. The Austin Middle School for grades 5–8 is conducting a survey to decide whether its spring dance should be open to all students or just seventh- and eighth-graders. Tell whether each group of students would be a *biased sample* or a *representative sample* for the survey. Explain your thinking. (Sec. 1, Explor. 2)

   a. all students whose last names begin with the letter "A"
      representative; This group should have the same characteristics as the rest of the population.
   b. the students in Mr. Marshall's eighth grade English class
      biased; Students in grades 5-7 are not represented.

7. Suppose you want to know how lack of sleep affects a person's coordination. Tell what observations you could make or describe an experiment you could perform to find out. (Sec. 1, Explor. 3)

7. Sample Response: Give a simple test of coordination, such as catching a ball. Repeat the test over several days, with the participant sleeping for shorter periods each night.

The circle graph shows the types of art classes offered at a museum. (Sec. 2, Explor. 1)

8. What percent of classes study mixed media? 10%

9. If there are a total of 20 classes, how many are painting or drawing? 16 classes

10. Without measuring, give the angle measure of the sector that represents sculpture. 36°

Art Classes at a Museum

sculpture 10%

drawing 35%

painting 45%

mixed media

11. The heights (in feet) of the nine highest mountain peaks of the Pamir mountain range in Tajikistan are given below. Draw a histogram of these heights. (**Sec. 2, Explor. 2**) See Additional Answers.

22,067	24,406	21,686	24,590	22,260
23,310	21,637	22,880	20,118	

For Exercises 12–14, tell which type of data display would best show the given information. (**Sec. 3, Explor. 1**)

12. the percent of students who choose soccer as their favorite sport
circle graph

13. the five highest scores on a test stem-and-leaf plot

14. the relationship between rainfall and crop yield scatter plot

15. The bar graph shows the numbers of motorcycles registered in five states in 1994. Is the bar graph misleading? Explain your thinking.
(**Sec. 3, Explor. 2**) See above.

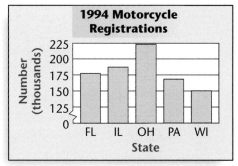

15. Yes; Sample Response: Because the vertical scale doesn't start at 0, it appears that the number of motorcycles registered in Ohio is more than twice that in Wisconsin.

16. The United States Postal Service delivers about 180 billion pieces of mail annually, but only about 900 million pieces are priority mail. Describe a pictorial model or a demonstration that would help somebody understand how much of the mail delivered is priority mail. (**Sec. 3, Explor. 3**)

16. Sample Response: Mark off 180 squares on a piece of graph paper to represent the number of pieces of mail delivered annually. $\frac{9}{10}$ of one square represent the number of pieces of priority mail delivered.

17. Use an equivalent rate to rewrite this statement so that it is easier to visualize: "Fingernails grow at approximately 0.15 mm/day."
(**Sec. 4, Explor. 1**) Sample Response: Fingernails grow at approximately 1 mm/week. (1.05 mm)

18. There are 46 members of a school band: 19 seventh-graders, 14 eighth-graders, and 13 ninth-graders. Find the relative frequency of band members who are in the eighth grade. (**Sec. 4, Explor. 1**) 0.3, or 30%

Reflecting ▶on the Module

19. Writing Suppose you are asked to give a report comparing the cost of living in different regions of the United States. Describe how you could use what you learned in this module to prepare your report. Answers will vary. Check students' work.

CONTENTS

STUDENT RESOURCES

STUDENT RESOURCES

TOOLBOX

Decimal Place Value

To compare two numbers in decimal form, first write each number using the same number of decimal places.

EXAMPLE

Replace each ? with >, <, or =.
   a. 0.63 __?__ 0.8   b. 0.02 __?__ 0.002

SOLUTION   a. 0.63 __?__ **0.80**   ◄ Rewrite **0.8** as **0.80.**

   0.63 < 0.80

   b. **0.020** __?__ 0.002   ◄ Rewrite **0.02** as **0.020.**

   0.020 > 0.002

EXAMPLE

Round each number to the nearest tenth.
   a. 0.846   b. 6.371

SOLUTION   Look at the digit in the hundredths place. Is it 5 or greater?

   a. 0.8**4**6   ◄ Not 5 or greater. Do not change.
   0.8   Drop the final digits.

   b. 6.3**7**1   ◄ Greater than 5. Add 1 to the tenths place.
   6.4   Drop the final digits.

Replace each __?__ with >, <, or =.

1. 0.4 __?__ 0.83 <   2. 0.65 __?__ 0.9 <   3. 0.750 __?__ 0.750 =

4. 0.163 __?__ 0.16 >   5. 0.12 __?__ 0.120 =   6. 0.8 __?__ 0.08 >

7. 0.5 __?__ 0.49 >   8. 0.3 __?__ 0.285 >   9. 0.1375 __?__ 0.18 <

10. 0.060 __?__ 0.06 =   11. 0.428 __?__ 0.73 <   12. 0.35 __?__ 0.25 >

Round each number to the nearest tenth.

13. 0.25 0.3   14. 0.81 0.8   15. 3.829 3.8   16. 1.657 1.7

Continued on next page

Round each number to the nearest hundredth.

17. 0.634 0.63   **18.** 7.852 7.85   **19.** 0.0499 0.05   **20.** 5.927 5.93

Round each number to the nearest thousandth.

21. 1.0375 1.038   **22.** 0.9932 0.993   **23.** 8.3096 8.310   **24.** 0.02405 0.024

Multiplying Whole Numbers and Decimals

To multiply by a number with more than one digit, you can break the number into parts.

EXAMPLE

Find each product.

    a. 425 · 312

                                  b. 0.081 · 0.02

SOLUTION

a.

$$
\begin{array}{r}
425 \\
\times\ 312 \\
\hline
850 \\
4250 \\
127500 \\
\hline
132{,}600
\end{array}
$$

← Multiply 425 by 2 ones.
← Multiply 425 by 1 ten.
← Multiply 425 by 3 hundreds.
← Add the partial products.

b.

$$
\begin{array}{r}
0.081 \\
\times\ 0.02 \\
\hline
0.00162
\end{array}
$$

← 3 decimal places
← 2 decimal places
← 5 decimal places in the product

Find each product.

1.
$$\begin{array}{r} 62 \\ \times\ 21 \\ \hline 1302 \end{array}$$

2.
$$\begin{array}{r} 48 \\ \times\ 25 \\ \hline 1200 \end{array}$$

3.
$$\begin{array}{r} 263 \\ \times\ 109 \\ \hline 28{,}667 \end{array}$$

4.
$$\begin{array}{r} 3704 \\ \times\ 58 \\ \hline 214{,}832 \end{array}$$

5.
$$\begin{array}{r} 1696 \\ \times\ 43 \\ \hline 72{,}928 \end{array}$$

6.
$$\begin{array}{r} 75{,}080 \\ \times\ 243 \\ \hline 18{,}244{,}440 \end{array}$$

7.
$$\begin{array}{r} 1.8 \\ \times\ 3 \\ \hline 5.4 \end{array}$$

8.
$$\begin{array}{r} 5.7 \\ \times\ 2.2 \\ \hline 12.54 \end{array}$$

9.
$$\begin{array}{r} 9.07 \\ \times\ 5 \\ \hline 45.35 \end{array}$$

10.
$$\begin{array}{r} 4.61 \\ \times\ 1.7 \\ \hline 7.837 \end{array}$$

11.
$$\begin{array}{r} 8.95 \\ \times\ 2.36 \\ \hline 21.122 \end{array}$$

12.
$$\begin{array}{r} 92 \\ \times\ 4.73 \\ \hline 435.16 \end{array}$$

13.
$$\begin{array}{r} 0.06 \\ \times\ 0.03 \\ \hline 0.0018 \end{array}$$

14.
$$\begin{array}{r} 5.004 \\ \times\ 1.01 \\ \hline 5.05404 \end{array}$$

15.
$$\begin{array}{r} 0.048 \\ \times\ 0.04 \\ \hline 0.00192 \end{array}$$

16.
$$\begin{array}{r} 640.8 \\ \times\ 0.012 \\ \hline 7.6896 \end{array}$$

Multiplying and Dividing by 10, 100, and 1000

To multiply by a power of 10, move the decimal point to the right.
To divide by a power of 10, move the decimal point to the left.
Use zeros as placeholders if necessary.

EXAMPLE

Find each product or quotient.

a. 143.628 · 100

b. 0.057 ÷ 1000

SOLUTION

a. 143.628 · 100 = 143.628 ◄ Move the decimal point **two** places to the right.

= 14,362.8

b. 0.057 ÷ 1000 = 0000.057 ◄ Move the decimal point **three** places to the left. Add zeros as placeholders.

= 0.000057

To convert from one metric measure to another, multiply or divide by a power of 10. Use the Table of Measures on page 610.

EXAMPLE

Complete the equation: 15 mm = _?_ cm

SOLUTION

10 mm = 1 cm

15 mm = (15 ÷ 10) cm ◄ Millimeters are a smaller unit than centimeters, so divide.

15 mm = 1.5 cm

For Exercises 1–6, find each product or quotient.

1. 51.83 · 10 518.3
2. 9.8 · 100 980
3. 30.042 ÷ 10 3.0042
4. 0.067 · 1000 67
5. 29.4 ÷ 100 0.294
6. 0.056 · 10 0.56

7. To convert from kilometers to meters, should you *multiply* or *divide* by 1000? Multiply.

Complete each equation. Use the Table of Measures on page 610.

8. 68 cm = _?_ m 0.68
9. 13 km = _?_ m 13,000
10. 27 m = _?_ cm 2700
11. 3560 m = _?_ km 3.56
12. 4.8 m = _?_ mm 4800
13. 4540 mg = _?_ g 4.54

Dividing Whole Numbers and Decimals

When you divide, you may have to add zeros to the dividend. When dividing by a decimal, move both decimal points the same number of decimal places to the right, until the divisor is a whole number. Then follow the same rules as for dividing whole numbers.

EXAMPLE

Find the quotient 6)83. Round your answer to the nearest tenth.

SOLUTION

$$\begin{array}{r} 13.83 \\ 6\overline{)83.00} \\ \underline{6} \\ 23 \\ \underline{18} \\ 5\,0 \\ \underline{4\,8} \\ 20 \end{array}$$

To round to the nearest tenth, carry out the division to the hundredths place. Then round.

To the nearest tenth, the quotient is 13.8.

EXAMPLE

Find the quotient: 0.05)4.8

SOLUTION

0.05)4.80

Move the decimal point two places to the right. Write a zero.

Divide. ⟶
$$\begin{array}{r} 96 \\ 5\overline{)480} \\ \underline{45} \\ 30 \\ \underline{30} \\ 0 \end{array}$$

The quotient is 96.

Find each quotient. Round each answer to the nearest tenth.

1. 8)198 24.8
2. 15)265 17.7
3. 32)488 15.3

Find each quotient. Round each answer to the nearest hundredth.

4. 9)68 7.56
5. 16)851 53.19
6. 11)547 49.73

Find each quotient. If necessary, round each answer to the nearest tenth.

7. 1.8)25.2 14
8. 5.4)243 45
9. 6.4)54.4 8.5
10. 4.5)1180 262.2
11. 0.32)308 962.5
12. 0.027)26.136 968

Divisibility Rules

A number is divisible by another number if the remainder is zero when you divide the second number by the first. It is not possible to divide a number by zero. The table shows divisibility tests you can use to tell if a number is divisible by another number.

Divisible by	Test
2	The last digit is 0, 2, 4, 6, or 8.
3	The sum of the digits is divisible by 3.
4	The number formed by the last two digits is divisible by 4.
5	The last digit is 0 or 5.
6	The number is divisible by both 2 and 3.
8	The number formed by the last three digits is divisible by 8.
9	The sum of the digits is divisible by 9.
10	The last digit is 0.

EXAMPLE

Is 79,120 divisible by 8?

SOLUTION The number formed by the last three digits, 120, is divisible by 8.
Yes, 79,120 is divisible by 8.

EXAMPLE

Is 5742 divisible by 9?

SOLUTION The sum of the digits, $5 + 7 + 4 + 2 = 18$, which is divisible by 9.
Yes, 5742 is divisible by 9.

EXAMPLE

Is 818 divisible by 6?

SOLUTION 818 is divisible by 2, because the last digit is 8. 818 is not divisible by 3, because $8 + 1 + 8 = 17$, which is not divisible by 3.
No, 818 is not divisible by 6.

Test each number for divisibility.

1. Is 378 divisible by 4? No.
2. Is 657 divisible by 3? Yes.
3. Is 4695 divisible by 5? Yes.
4. Is 5934 divisible by 2? Yes.
5. Is 3511 divisible by 10? No.
6. Is 2178 divisible by 6? Yes.
7. Is 2043 divisible by 9? Yes.
8. Is 80,256 divisible by 8? Yes.

Finding Factors and Multiples

A common factor of two numbers is a number that is a factor of both numbers. For example, 4 is a common factor of 60 and 100, because 60 = 4 · 15 and 100 = 4 · 25.

The greatest common factor (GCF) of two numbers is the greatest number that is a common factor of the two numbers.

EXAMPLE

Find the GCF of 60 and 100.

SOLUTION Write the prime factorizations of 60 and 100.

$$60 = 2 \cdot 2 \cdot 3 \cdot 5$$
$$100 = 2 \cdot 2 \cdot 5 \cdot 5$$

Circle the numbers that are in *both* factorizations.

Multiply the numbers you circled.
The GCF of 60 and 100 is 2 · 2 · 5 = 20.

A common multiple of two numbers is a number that is a multiple of both numbers. For example, 72 is a common multiple of 12 and 9, because 12 · 6 = 72 and 9 · 8 = 72.

The least common multiple (LCM) of two numbers is the least number that is a common multiple of the numbers.

EXAMPLE

Find the LCM of 9 and 12.

SOLUTION Find the GCF of 9 and 12.

$$9 = 3 \cdot 3$$
$$12 = 2 \cdot 2 \cdot 3$$

The GCF is 3.

Multiply the GCF by the numbers you did not circle.
The LCM of 9 and 12 is 3 · 3 · 2 · 2 = 36.

Find the GCF and the LCM of each pair of numbers.

1. 42, 60 6; 420
2. 24, 36 12; 72
3. 33, 110 11; 330
4. 80, 120 40; 240
5. 30, 90 30; 90
6. 125, 420 5; 10,500
7. 165, 315 15; 3465
8. 114, 138 6; 2622
9. 275, 495 55; 2475
10. 50, 98 2; 2450
11. 77, 81 1; 6237
12. 46, 69 23; 138

Finding Equivalent Fractions and Ratios

Fractions that name the same part of a whole are **equivalent fractions**. A fraction is in **lowest terms** if the GCF of the numerator and the denominator is 1.

A **ratio** is a comparison of two numbers using division. The ratio of a and b, $b \neq 0$, can be written a to b, $a : b$, or $\dfrac{a}{b}$. To compare ratios, first write them as fractions. Then compare the fractions.

Replace each $\underline{\ ?\ }$ with the number that will make the fractions equivalent.

1. $\dfrac{2}{7} = \dfrac{?}{21}$ 6

2. $\dfrac{14}{15} = \dfrac{?}{60}$ 56

3. $\dfrac{12}{20} = \dfrac{?}{10}$ 6

4. $\dfrac{15}{45} = \dfrac{?}{9}$ 3

Write each fraction in lowest terms.

5. $\dfrac{9}{15}$ $\dfrac{3}{5}$

6. $\dfrac{4}{12}$ $\dfrac{1}{3}$

7. $\dfrac{18}{20}$ $\dfrac{9}{10}$

8. $\dfrac{6}{9}$ $\dfrac{2}{3}$

Replace each $\underline{\ ?\ }$ with >, <, or =.

9. $\dfrac{3}{10} \ \underline{\ ?\ } \ \dfrac{9}{30}$ =

10. $5 : 12 \ \underline{\ ?\ } \ 7 : 8$ <

11. 15 to 36 $\underline{\ ?\ }$ 1 to 27   >

Multiplying and Dividing Fractions

To multiply two fractions, multiply the numerators and the denominators.

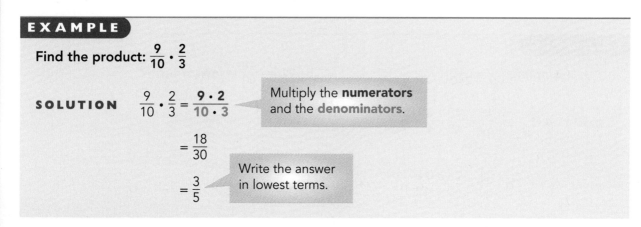

EXAMPLE

Find the product: $\dfrac{9}{10} \cdot \dfrac{2}{3}$

SOLUTION $\dfrac{9}{10} \cdot \dfrac{2}{3} = \dfrac{9 \cdot 2}{10 \cdot 3}$ — Multiply the **numerators** and the **denominators**.

$= \dfrac{18}{30}$

$= \dfrac{3}{5}$ — Write the answer in lowest terms.

To divide by a fraction, multiply by its reciprocal. Change mixed numbers to fractions before multiplying or dividing.

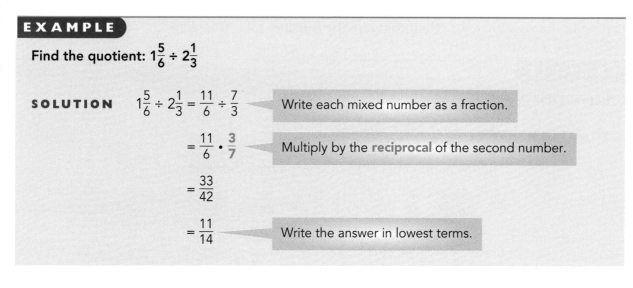

EXAMPLE

Find the quotient: $1\dfrac{5}{6} \div 2\dfrac{1}{3}$

SOLUTION $1\dfrac{5}{6} \div 2\dfrac{1}{3} = \dfrac{11}{6} \div \dfrac{7}{3}$ — Write each mixed number as a fraction.

$= \dfrac{11}{6} \cdot \dfrac{3}{7}$ — Multiply by the **reciprocal** of the second number.

$= \dfrac{33}{42}$

$= \dfrac{11}{14}$ — Write the answer in lowest terms.

Find each product. Write each answer in lowest terms.

1. $\dfrac{4}{5} \cdot \dfrac{1}{3}$ $\dfrac{4}{15}$

2. $\dfrac{1}{14} \cdot \dfrac{2}{7}$ $\dfrac{1}{49}$

3. $\dfrac{1}{3} \cdot \dfrac{9}{10}$ $\dfrac{3}{10}$

4. $\dfrac{7}{12} \cdot \dfrac{8}{21}$ $\dfrac{2}{9}$

5. $\dfrac{3}{8} \cdot 16$ 6

6. $\dfrac{8}{15} \cdot 1\dfrac{1}{2}$ $\dfrac{4}{5}$

7. $1\dfrac{4}{5} \cdot 1\dfrac{2}{3}$ 3

8. $18 \cdot \dfrac{5}{6}$ 15

Find each quotient. Write each answer in lowest terms.

9. $\dfrac{1}{4} \div \dfrac{1}{2}$ $\dfrac{1}{2}$

10. $\dfrac{3}{10} \div \dfrac{2}{5}$ $\dfrac{3}{4}$

11. $\dfrac{1}{3} \div \dfrac{1}{8}$ $\dfrac{8}{3}$ or $2\dfrac{2}{3}$

12. $\dfrac{3}{10} \div \dfrac{6}{25}$ $\dfrac{5}{4}$ or $1\dfrac{1}{4}$

13. $6 \div \dfrac{4}{5}$ $\dfrac{15}{2}$ or $7\dfrac{1}{2}$

14. $\dfrac{3}{10} \div 3$ $\dfrac{1}{10}$

15. $1\dfrac{1}{2} \div \dfrac{1}{4}$ 6

16. $2\dfrac{2}{9} \div 1\dfrac{1}{4}$ $\dfrac{16}{9}$ or $1\dfrac{7}{9}$

Writing Fractions, Decimals, and Percents

You can write a fraction as a decimal or as a percent. Percent means "per hundred," so to write a fraction as a percent, start by finding an equivalent fraction with 100 as the denominator.

EXAMPLE

Write $\frac{2}{5}$ as a decimal and as a percent.

SOLUTION

$\frac{2}{5} = \frac{2 \cdot 20}{5 \cdot 20}$ — Find an equivalent fraction with 100 as the denominator.

$= \frac{40}{100}$

$\left. \begin{array}{l} = 0.40 \\ \\ = 40\% \end{array} \right\}$ $\frac{2}{5} = 0.40 = 40\%$

EXAMPLE

Write 72% as a decimal and as a fraction in lowest terms.

SOLUTION $72\% = 0.72$

$= \frac{72}{100}$

$= \frac{18}{25}$ — Write the fraction in lowest terms.

The chart shows some common percent, decimal, and fraction equivalents.

$1\% = 0.01 = \frac{1}{100}$	$33\frac{1}{3}\% = 0.\overline{3} = \frac{1}{3}$	$66\frac{2}{3}\% = 0.\overline{6} = \frac{2}{3}$
$10\% = 0.1 = \frac{1}{10}$	$40\% = 0.4 = \frac{2}{5}$	$75\% = 0.75 = \frac{3}{4}$
$20\% = 0.2 = \frac{1}{5}$	$50\% = 0.5 = \frac{1}{2}$	$80\% = 0.8 = \frac{4}{5}$
$25\% = 0.25 = \frac{1}{4}$	$60\% = 0.6 = \frac{3}{5}$	$100\% = 1$

Write each fraction as a decimal and as a percent.

1. $\frac{19}{20}$ 0.95; 95%   2. $\frac{4}{25}$ 0.16; 16%   3. $\frac{1}{1000}$ 0.001; 0.1%   4. $\frac{31}{50}$ 0.62; 62%

Write each percent as a decimal and as a fraction in lowest terms.

5. 80% $0.8; \frac{4}{5}$ 6. 87.5% $0.875; \frac{7}{8}$ 7. 64% $0.64; \frac{16}{25}$ 8. 120% $1.2; \frac{6}{5}$ or $1\frac{1}{5}$

Write each decimal as a percent and as a fraction in lowest terms.

9. 0.48 $48\%; \frac{12}{25}$ 10. 0.85 $85\%; \frac{17}{20}$ 11. 0.125 $12.5\%; \frac{1}{8}$ 12. 3.5 $350\%; \frac{7}{2}$ or $3\frac{1}{2}$

Using Order of Operations

When you evaluate an expression that contains more than one operation, perform the operations in the order shown below.

1. First do all work inside parentheses.

2. Then evaluate any powers.

3. Then do all multiplications and divisions in order from left to right.

4. Then do all additions and subtractions in order from left to right.

A power is the product when a number or an expression is used as a factor a given number of times. For example, $3 \cdot 3 \cdot 3 \cdot 3 \cdot 3$ is the fifth power of 3 and can be written as 3^5. In 3^5, 3 is the base and 5 is the exponent.

Sometimes multiplication is written with parentheses. For example, $3(4) = 3 \cdot 4$.

EXAMPLE

Find each answer.

a. $2(11) + 20 \div (7 - 5)$

b. $5 \cdot 2^3 - 6$

SOLUTION

a. $2(11) + 20 \div (7 - 5) = 2(11) + 20 \div 2$ ← Do work inside parentheses first.

$= 22 + 10$ ← Do multiplication and division.

$= 32$ ← Add.

b. $5 \cdot 2^3 - 6 = 5 \cdot 8 - 6$ ← Evaluate the power first: $2^3 = 2 \cdot 2 \cdot 2 = 8$

$= 40 - 6$ ← Multiply.

$= 34$ ← Subtract.

Find each answer.

1. $4^2 - 1$ 15

2. $6(8 - 5)$ 18

3. $7 \cdot 2^3$ 56

4. $5 \cdot 6 - 17$ 13

5. $3 \cdot 10 \div 6$ 5

6. $(9 \div 3)^2$ 9

7. $9 \div 3^2$ 1

8. $15 + 42 \div 7 - 17$ 4

9. $15 + 2(11 - 4)$ 29

10. $4^2 + 5(2^3 - 3)$ 41

11. $2 \cdot 3^2 - 4(7 - 3)$ 2

12. $3(6 + 2) \div 4(9 - 7)$ 3

Comparing Integers

Integers are the numbers ... –3, –2, –1, 0, 1, 2, 3, ... To compare two integers, use a number line. The greater number is to the right of the lesser number on a horizontal number line.

EXAMPLE

Graph each pair of integers on a number line. Then replace each ? with > or <.

    a. –3 __?__ 2   **b.** 2 __?__ –3

SOLUTION

The greater number is always to the right of the lesser number.

Since 2 is to the right of –3, 2 is the greater number and –3 is the lesser number.

    a. –3 < 2   **b.** 2 > –3

EXAMPLE

Use a number line to write the integers 3, 5, and –2 in order from least to greatest.

SOLUTION   Graph each number on a number line.

           –2, 3, 5

Replace each __?__ with > or <.

1. 4 __?__ –6 >
2. –3 __?__ –1 <
3. –5 __?__ 0 <
4. –2 __?__ 4 <
5. 0 __?__ –7 >
6. –1 __?__ –4 >
7. 5 __?__ 1 >
8. –8 __?__ 8 <
9. –4 __?__ 2 <

Use a number line to write each group of integers in order from least to greatest.

10. –5, 1, –4 –5, –4, 1
11. 0, –3, 2 –3, 0, 2
12. –2, –4, –1 –4, –2, –1
13. 3, 4, –5 –5, 3, 4
14. –3, 0, –6 –6, –3, 0
15. 2, –2, 6 –2, 2, 6
16. 1, –1, 0, –2 –2, –1, 0, 1
17. 0, –4, –7, –2 –7, –4, –2, 0
18. 5, –3, 2, –6 –6, –3, 2, 5

Locating Points in a Coordinate Plane

You can use an ordered pair to describe the location of a point in a coordinate plane. The first number in an ordered pair is the **horizontal coordinate** and the second number is the **vertical coordinate**.

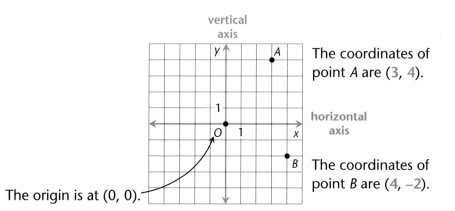

The coordinates of point *A* are (3, 4).

The coordinates of point *B* are (4, –2).

The origin is at (0, 0).

EXAMPLE

Graph each point.

   a. (–5, –1)

   b. (0, 3)

SOLUTION   **a.** From the origin, move **5 units left** and **1 unit down**.

b. From the origin, move 3 units up. **10–18.**

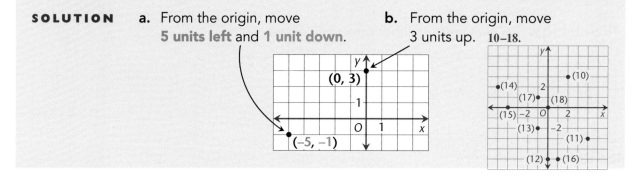

Use the diagram at the right. Give the coordinates of each point.

1. *A* (–5, 2)
2. *B* (–3, –2)
3. *C* (–3, 1)
4. *D* (1, 4)
5. *E* (3, 0)
6. *F* (0, –2)
7. *G* (2, –4)
8. *H* (–2, 4)
9. *K* (–1, 1)

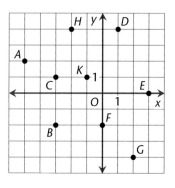

Graph each point in a coordinate plane. 10–18. See graph above.

10. (2, 3)
11. (4, –3)
12. (0, –5)
13. (–1, –2)
14. (–5, 2)
15. (–4, 0)
16. (1, –5)
17. (–1, 1)
18. (0, 0)

Measuring Angles

An angle is formed by two rays, called *sides* of the angle, with the same endpoint, called the *vertex*. Angles are measured in degrees. You use a protractor to measure an angle.

An angle whose measure is between 0° and 90° is an acute angle.	An angle whose measure is 90° is a right angle.
An angle whose measure is between 90° and 180° is an obtuse angle.	An angle whose measure is 180° is a straight angle.

EXAMPLE

Use a protractor to measure ∠S.

SOLUTION

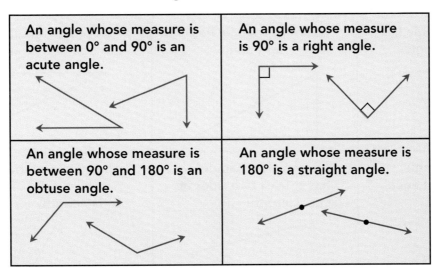

Step 1 Place the center mark of the protractor on the vertex.

Step 3 Read the number where the other side of the angle crosses the scale. Read the number on the bottom scale since you used its 0° mark. **The measure of ∠S is 65°.**

Step 2 Place the 0° mark on one side of the angle.

Use a protractor to measure each angle. Then tell whether the angle is *acute, right, obtuse,* or *straight.*

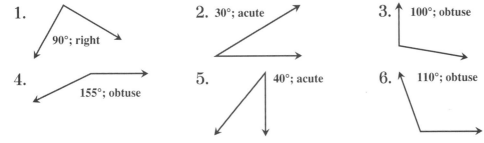

1. 90°; right

2. 30°; acute

3. 100°; obtuse

4. 155°; obtuse

5. 40°; acute

6. 110°; obtuse

Classifying Triangles

To classify a triangle, you can use the measures of its angles or the relationship between the lengths of its sides. The sum of the measures of the angles of a triangle is 180°.

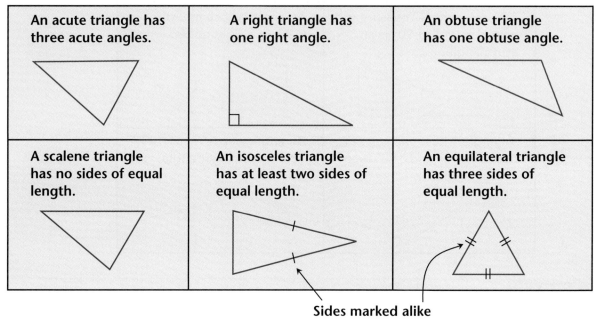

An acute triangle has three acute angles.	A right triangle has one right angle.	An obtuse triangle has one obtuse angle.
A scalene triangle has no sides of equal length.	An isosceles triangle has at least two sides of equal length.	An equilateral triangle has three sides of equal length.

Sides marked alike
are equal in length.

Tell whether each triangle is *acute*, *right*, or *obtuse*.

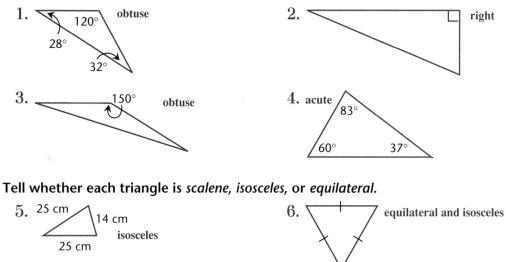

1. 120° 28° 32°   obtuse

2. right

3. 150°   obtuse

4. acute 83° 60° 37°

Tell whether each triangle is *scalene*, *isosceles*, or *equilateral*.

5. 25 cm 14 cm 25 cm   isosceles

6. equilateral and isosceles

7. 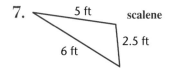 5 ft 2.5 ft 6 ft   scalene

8. isosceles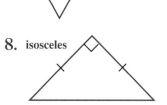

Using Formulas from Geometry

To find the perimeter, area, or volume of a figure, use the
Table of Formulas on page 611.

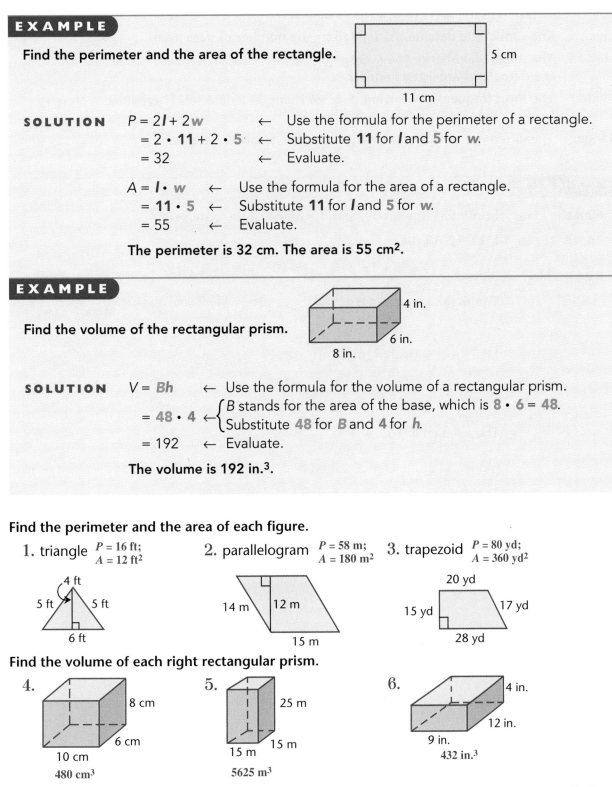

EXAMPLE

Find the perimeter and the area of the rectangle.

5 cm

11 cm

SOLUTION $P = 2l + 2w$ ←   Use the formula for the perimeter of a rectangle.
                   $= 2 \cdot 11 + 2 \cdot 5$ ←   Substitute **11** for *l* and **5** for *w*.
                   $= 32$ ←   Evaluate.

                   $A = l \cdot w$ ←   Use the formula for the area of a rectangle.
                   $= 11 \cdot 5$ ←   Substitute **11** for *l* and **5** for *w*.
                   $= 55$ ←   Evaluate.

The perimeter is 32 cm. The area is 55 cm².

EXAMPLE

Find the volume of the rectangular prism.

4 in.

6 in.

8 in.

SOLUTION $V = Bh$ ←   Use the formula for the volume of a rectangular prism.
                   $= 48 \cdot 4$ ← $\begin{cases} B \text{ stands for the area of the base, which is } 8 \cdot 6 = 48. \\ \text{Substitute } 48 \text{ for } B \text{ and } 4 \text{ for } h. \end{cases}$
                   $= 192$ ←   Evaluate.

The volume is 192 in.³.

Find the perimeter and the area of each figure.

1. triangle $P = 16$ ft;
             $A = 12$ ft²

2. parallelogram $P = 58$ m;
                  $A = 180$ m²

3. trapezoid $P = 80$ yd;
              $A = 360$ yd²

4 ft

5 ft   5 ft

6 ft

14 m   12 m

15 m

20 yd

15 yd   17 yd

28 yd

Find the volume of each right rectangular prism.

4.

8 cm

6 cm

10 cm

480 cm³

5.

25 m

15 m   15 m

5625 m³

6.

4 in.

12 in.

9 in.

432 in.³

Finding the Mean, Median, Mode, and Range

You can use different numbers to describe a data set.

Mean: The sum of the data items, divided by the number of data items.

Median: The middle number or the average of the two middle numbers when the data items are listed in order.

Mode: The most frequently occurring item, or items, in a data set. There may be more than one mode or no mode.

Range: The difference between the largest and the smallest data items.

EXAMPLE

Find the mean, the median, the mode, and the range of the data set.

14, 18, 19, 16, 14, 20, 12, 18, 14

SOLUTION Mean $= \dfrac{14 + 18 + 19 + 16 + 14 + 20 + 12 + 18 + 14}{9} \approx 16.1$

The mean is about 16.1. There are **9** data items.

Median: 12 14 14 14 **16** 18 18 19 20 ◂ List the numbers in order.

Find the **middle** number.

The median is 16.

Mode: 14 appears more often than any other number.

The mode is 14.

Range: The smallest number is 12. The largest number is 20.
Subtract to find the range: $20 - 12 = 8$.

The range is 8.

Find the mean, the median, the mode, and the range of each data set.

1. 29, 38, 32, 37, 29
mean: 33; median: 32; mode: 29; range: 9

2. 18, 14, 15, 16, 20, 17
mean: $16\frac{2}{3}$; median: 16.5; mode: none; range: 6

3. 3.6, 2.5, 4.2, 3.3, 5.4
mean: 3.8; median: 3.6; mode: none; range: 2.9

4. 34, 34, 34, 34, 34, 34, 34
mean: 34; median: 34; mode: 34; range: 0

5. 4, 1, 1, 0, 2, 3, 5, 2
mean: 2.25; median: 2; modes: 1 and 2; range: 5

6. 145, 95, 90, 120, 105, 85, 95
mean: 105; median: 95; mode: 95; range: 60

Using Self-Assessment Scales

One way to improve your problem solving skills is to use the Student Self-Assessment Scales on page 608. Use whichever scales apply to a problem you have solved to assess your work in mathematics.

EXAMPLE

PROBLEM

Five people are hired to work at a new store. As they are introduced they shake hands exactly once. How many handshakes take place?

A STUDENT'S SOLUTION

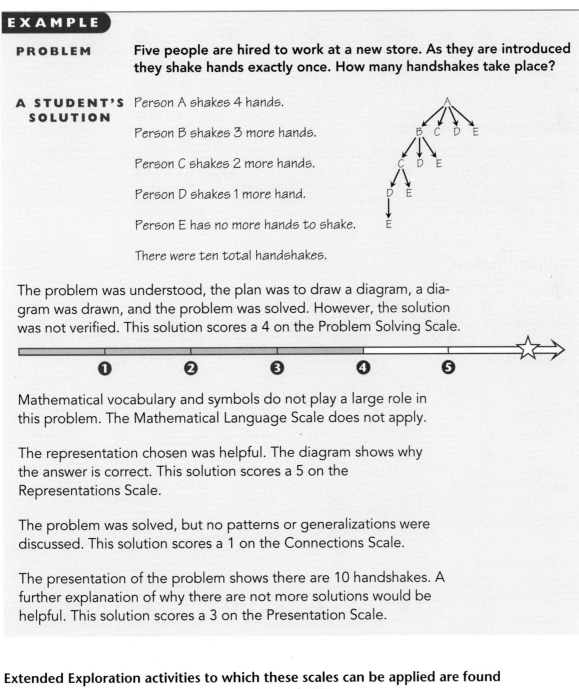

Person A shakes 4 hands.

Person B shakes 3 more hands.

Person C shakes 2 more hands.

Person D shakes 1 more hand.

Person E has no more hands to shake.

There were ten total handshakes.

The problem was understood, the plan was to draw a diagram, a diagram was drawn, and the problem was solved. However, the solution was not verified. This solution scores a 4 on the Problem Solving Scale.

❶   ❷   ❸   ❹   ❺

Mathematical vocabulary and symbols do not play a large role in this problem. The Mathematical Language Scale does not apply.

The representation chosen was helpful. The diagram shows why the answer is correct. This solution scores a 5 on the Representations Scale.

The problem was solved, but no patterns or generalizations were discussed. This solution scores a 1 on the Connections Scale.

The presentation of the problem shows there are 10 handshakes. A further explanation of why there are not more solutions would be helpful. This solution scores a 3 on the Presentation Scale.

Extended Exploration activities to which these scales can be applied are found on pages 53, 106, 200, 255, 330, 441, 497, and 577.

Student Self-Assessment Scales

If your score is in the shaded area, explain why on the back of this sheet and stop.

The star indicates that you excelled in some way.

Problem Solving

1 I did not understand the problem well enough to get started or I did not show any work.

3 I understood the problem well enough to make a plan and to work toward a solution.

5 I made a plan, I used it to solve the problem, and I verified my solution.

Mathematical Language

1 I did not use any mathematical vocabulary or symbols, or I did not use them correctly, or my use was not appropriate.

3 I used appropriate mathematical language, but the way it was used was not always correct or other terms and symbols were needed.

5 I used mathematical language that was correct and appropriate to make my meaning clear.

Representations

1 I did not use any representations such as equations, tables, graphs, or diagrams to help solve the problem or explain my solution.

3 I made appropriate representations to help solve the problem or help me explain my solution, but they were not always correct or other representations were needed.

5 I used appropriate and correct representations to solve the problem or explain my solution.

Connections

1 I attempted or solved the problem and then stopped.

3 I found patterns and used them to extend the solution to other cases, or I recognized that this problem relates to other problems, mathematical ideas, or applications.

5 I extended the ideas in the solution to the general case, or I showed how this problem relates to other problems, mathematical ideas, or applications.

Presentation

1 The presentation of my solution and reasoning is unclear to others.

3 The presentation of my solution and reasoning is clear in most places, but others may have trouble understanding parts of it.

5 The presentation of my solution and reasoning is clear and can be understood by others.

TABLE OF SYMBOLS

SYMBOL		Page
...	and so on	4
·	times	7
=	equals	7
%	percent	12
$\frac{1}{2}$	1 divided by 2	14
>	is greater than	24
<	is less than	24
−6	negative 6	24
(x, y)	ordered pair of numbers	29
°	degrees	38
≈	is approximately equal to	41
π	pi, a number approximately equal to 3.14	41
+	plus	42
×	times	43
r^2	r used as a factor 2 times	44
−	minus	48
( )	parentheses—a grouping symbol	50
÷	divided by	50
P(A)	the probability of event A	115
|x|	absolute value of x	124
−x	the opposite of x	124
A′	A prime—point A goes to point A′ after a transformation	125
≥	is greater than or equal to	146

SYMBOL		Page
≤	is less than or equal to	146
√	positive, or principal, square root	166
∠A	angle A	202
m∠A	the measure of angle A	202
$\overline{AB}$	segment AB	202
AB	length of segment AB	202
~	is similar to	203
⊿ ⊿	equal angle measures	203
△ABC	triangle ABC	203
⌐	right angle	205
	equal side lengths	205
2 : 1	ratio of 2 to 1	212
≠	is not equal to	217
≅	is congruent to	243
$0.\overline{63}$	repeating bar—the digits 6 and 3 repeat	261
	parallel sides	273
‖	is parallel to	273
7^{-2}	$\frac{1}{7^2}$	348
tan A	tangent of angle A	361
sin A	sine of angle A	366
cos A	cosine of angle A	366
[ ]	brackets—grouping symbol	420

TABLE OF MEASURES

Time

60 seconds (s) = 1 minute (min)
60 minutes = 1 hour (h)
24 hours = 1 day
7 days = 1 week
4 weeks (approx.) = 1 month

$\left.\begin{array}{l}\text{365 days}\\\text{52 weeks (approx.)}\\\text{12 months}\end{array}\right\} = 1\ \text{year}$

10 years = 1 decade
100 years = 1 century

METRIC

Length

10 millimeters (mm) = 1 centimeter (cm)
$\left.\begin{array}{l}\text{100 cm}\\\text{1000 mm}\end{array}\right\} = 1\ \text{meter (m)}$
1000 m = 1 kilometer (km)

Area

100 square millimeters = 1 square centimeter
(mm^2) (cm^2)
$10,000\ cm^2 = 1$ square meter (m^2)
$10,000\ m^2 = 1$ hectare (ha)

Volume

1000 cubic millimeters = 1 cubic centimeter
(mm^3) (cm^3)
$1,000,000\ cm^3 = 1$ cubic meter (m^3)

Liquid Capacity

1000 milliliters (mL) = 1 liter (L)
1000 L = 1 kiloliter (kL)

Mass

1000 milligrams (mg) = 1 gram (g)
1000 g = 1 kilogram (kg)
1000 kg = 1 metric ton (t)

Temperature — Degrees Celsius (°C)

0°C = freezing point of water
37°C = normal body temperature
100°C = boiling point of water

UNITED STATES CUSTOMARY

Length

12 inches (in.) = 1 foot (ft)
$\left.\begin{array}{l}\text{36 in.}\\\text{3 ft}\end{array}\right\} = 1\ \text{yard (yd)}$
$\left.\begin{array}{l}\text{5280 ft}\\\text{1760 yd}\end{array}\right\} = 1\ \text{mile (mi)}$

Area

144 square inches $(in.^2) = 1$ square foot (ft^2)
$9\ ft^2 = 1$ square yard (yd^2)
$\left.\begin{array}{l}43{,}560\ ft^2\\4840\ yd^2\end{array}\right\} = 1\ \text{acre (A)}$

Volume

1728 cubic inches $(in.^3) = 1$ cubic foot (ft^3)
$27\ ft^3 = 1$ cubic yard (yd^3)

Liquid Capacity

8 fluid ounces (fl oz) = 1 cup (c)
2 c = 1 pint (pt)
2 pt = 1 quart (qt)
4 qt = 1 gallon (gal)

Weight

16 ounces (oz) = 1 pound (lb)
2000 lb = 1 ton (t)

Temperature — Degrees Fahrenheit (°F)

32°F = freezing point of water
98.6°F = normal body temperature
212°F = boiling point of water

TABLE OF FORMULAS

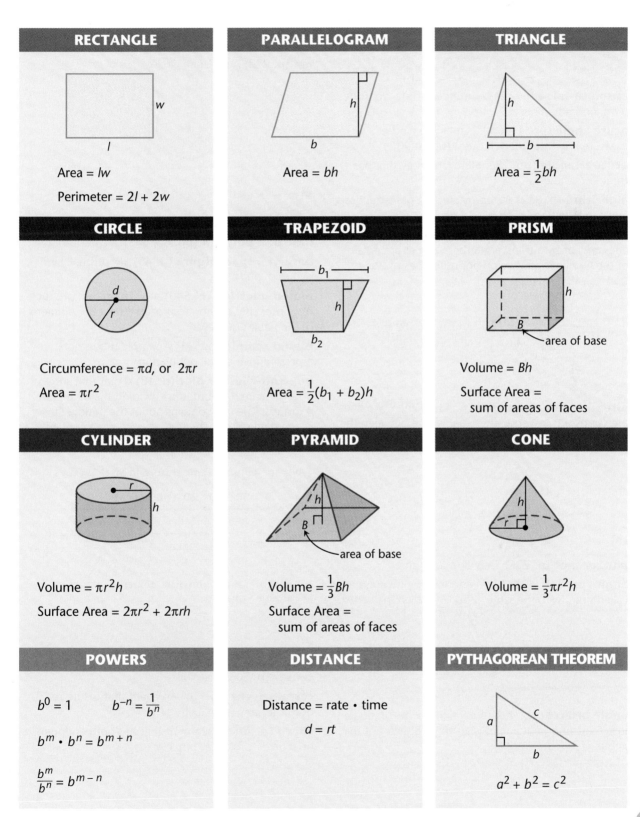

RECTANGLE

Area = lw

Perimeter = $2l + 2w$

PARALLELOGRAM

Area = bh

TRIANGLE

Area = $\frac{1}{2}bh$

CIRCLE

Circumference = πd, or $2\pi r$

Area = πr^2

TRAPEZOID

Area = $\frac{1}{2}(b_1 + b_2)h$

PRISM

Volume = Bh

Surface Area =
   sum of areas of faces

CYLINDER

Volume = $\pi r^2 h$

Surface Area = $2\pi r^2 + 2\pi rh$

PYRAMID

area of base

Volume = $\frac{1}{3}Bh$

Surface Area =
   sum of areas of faces

CONE

Volume = $\frac{1}{3}\pi r^2 h$

POWERS

$b^0 = 1$ $b^{-n} = \frac{1}{b^n}$

$b^m \cdot b^n = b^{m+n}$

$\frac{b^m}{b^n} = b^{m-n}$

DISTANCE

Distance = rate · time

$d = rt$

PYTHAGOREAN THEOREM

$a^2 + b^2 = c^2$

GLOSSARY

absolute value (p. 124) A number's distance from 0 on a number line.

acute angle (pp. 119, 603) An angle whose measure is greater than 0° but less than 90°.

acute triangle (pp. 288, 604) A triangle that has three acute angles.

algorithm (p. 512) A step-by-step set of instructions you can follow to accomplish a goal.

alternate exterior angles (p. 434) When two lines are cut by a transversal, these angles are outside of the two lines and are on opposite sides of the transversal.

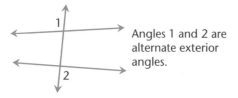

Angles 1 and 2 are alternate exterior angles.

alternate interior angles (p. 434) When two lines are cut by a transversal, these angles are between the two lines and are on opposite sides of the transversal.

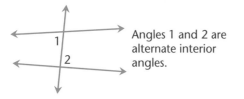

Angles 1 and 2 are alternate interior angles.

and, or, not (p. 226) *See* Venn diagram.

angle (pp. 119, 603) A figure formed by two rays, called sides, with the same endpoint, called the vertex.

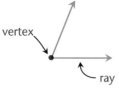

vertex

ray

angle bisector (p. 407) A ray that divides an angle into two congruent angles is an angle bisector of the angle.

arc (p. 242) A part of a circle.

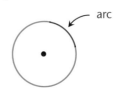

arc

base (pp. 346, 600) *See* exponent.

base of a polygon (pp. 66, 605) *See* trapezoid.

base of a space figure (p. 43) *See* prism, cylinder, pyramid, *and* cone.

biased question (p. 540) A question that produces responses that do not accurately reflect the opinions of the people surveyed.

biased sample (p. 541) A sample that is not representative of the population.

box-and-whisker plot (p. 18) A plot that shows how data are distributed by dividing the data into 4 groups. The *box* contains about the middle 50% of the data values. The two *whiskers* each contain about 25% of the data values.

Average January Temperature in 50 U.S. Cities

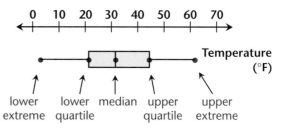

center (p. 206) *See* circle.

certain event (p. 110) An event that is sure to occur. It has a probability of 1.

chord (p. 205) A segment that has both endpoints on a given circle. *See also* circle.

circle (p. 206) The set of all points in a plane that are a given distance from a point called the center of the circle.

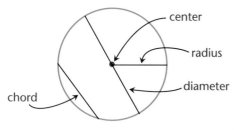

circle graph (p. 552) A graph that shows the division of a whole into parts, each represented by a sector.

circumference (p. 40) The distance around a circle.

coefficient (p. 61) The numerical factor of a term.

combination (p. 375) A selection of items in which order is not important.

complement (p. 359) One angle is the complement of a second angle if the two angles are complementary angles.

complementary angles (p. 359) Two angles whose measures have a sum of 90°.

complementary events (p. 305) Two events where one or the other must occur but they cannot both occur.

concave (p. 283) A polygon that is not convex is concave. *See also* polygon.

cone (p. 424) A space figure with one curved base and a vertex.

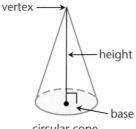

circular cone

congruent (p. 241) Having the same shape and size.

convex (p. 283) A polygon is convex when all of its diagonals lie in the interior of the polygon. *See also* polygon.

coordinate grid or plane (pp. 180, 602) A grid with a horizontal axis and a vertical axis that intersect at a point called the *origin* with coordinates (0, 0). Each point on the grid is identified by an ordered pair of coordinates that give the point's location left or right of the vertical axis and up or down from the horizontal axis.

corresponding angles (p. 435) When two lines are cut by a transversal, these angles are in the same position with respect to the two lines and the transversal.

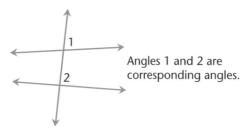

Angles 1 and 2 are corresponding angles.

corresponding parts (p. 202) When two figures are similar, for each angle or side on one figure there is a similar angle or side on the other figure. The corresponding angles have the same measure. The corresponding sides are in proportion.

counting principle (p. 372) The total number of ways a sequence of decisions can be made is the product of the number of choices for each decision.

cross products (p. 86) Equal products formed from a pair of equivalent ratios by multiplying the numerator of each fraction by the denominator of the other fraction.

cube (p. 169) A prism with six square faces.

cylinder (p. 44) A space figure that has a curved surface and two parallel, congruent bases.

circular cylinder

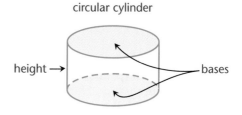

D

decimal notation (p. 214) A number is in decimal notation when it is written as a decimal, without using any powers. *See also* scientific notation.

dependent events (p. 109) Events for which the probability of one is affected by whether or not the other event occurs.

diameter (p. 41) A segment whose endpoints are on a given circle and that passes through the center of the circle. The length of a diameter is called *the* diameter. *See also* circle.

distributive property (p. 488) For all numbers a, b, and c: $a(b + c) = ab + ac$ and $ab + ac = a(b + c)$.

E ▸

edge of a space figure (p. 169) A segment where two faces of a space figure meet. *See also* prism *and* pyramid.

equally likely (p. 108) Two outcomes that have the same chance of happening are equally likely.

equation (p. 55) A mathematical sentence stating that two quantities or expressions are equal.

equilateral triangle (pp. 288, 604) A triangle that has three sides of equal length.

equivalent rates (p. 579) Equivalent rates are equal rates that may be expressed using different units. For example, $\frac{8 \text{ oz}}{25¢}$ and $\frac{2 \text{ lb}}{\$1}$ are equivalent rates.

evaluate (p. 42) To find the value of an expression for given values of the variables.

event (p. 108) A set of outcomes of an experiment.

experiment (p. 108) An activity whose results can be observed and recorded.

experimental probability (p. 112) A probability determined by repeating an experiment a number of times and observing the results. It is the ratio of the number of times an event occurs to the number of times the experiment is done.

exponent (pp. 44, 600) A raised number that tells the power of the base.

$$2^3 = 2 \cdot 2 \cdot 2 = 8$$

exponent · base · 8 is the 3rd power of 2.

exponential equation (p. 503) An equation of the form $y = a \cdot b^x$, where a is the starting amount, b is the growth factor, and y is the amount after x units of time.

expression (p. 41) A mathematical phrase that can contain numbers, variables, and operation symbols.

F ▸

face of a space figure (pp. 47, 169) A flat surface of a space figure. *See also* prism *and* pyramid.

fair game (p. 119) A game in which every player has an equal chance of winning.

fitted line (p. 31) A line drawn on a scatter plot to show a pattern in the data. *See also* scatter plot.

flat view (p. 398) A view of an object straight on from any side.

fractal (p. 238) An object that contains smaller and smaller copies of the whole object.

frequency (p. 552) The number of items in a category or numerical interval.

frequency table (p. 552) A table that shows the frequency of items in each category or numerical interval.

function (p. 472) A rule that pairs each input value with exactly one output value.

G ▸

geometric probability (p. 304) A probability based on length, area, or volume.

greatest common factor (GCF) (pp. 103, 596) The greatest number that is a factor of each of two or more numbers.

growth factor (p. 503) *See* exponential equation.

H ▸

half-life (p. 213) The amount of time it takes for a radioactive substance to reduce to half of its original amount.

height of a polygon (p. 420) *See* trapezoid.

height of a space figure (p. 43) *See* prism, cylinder, pyramid, *and* cone.

histogram (p. 554) A graph that shows the frequencies of numerical values that fall within intervals of equal width.

hypotenuse (p. 294) In a right triangle, the side opposite the right angle. *See also* right triangle.

I ▸

image (p. 130) The figure that results from a transformation.

impossible event (p. 110) An event that cannot occur. It has a probability of 0.

included angle (p. 408) An angle of a polygon whose vertex is the shared point of two sides of the polygon.

independent events (p. 109) Events for which the probability of one is not affected by whether or not the other event occurs.

inequality (p. 146) A mathematical sentence that compares two quantities using the symbol $>$, $<$, $\geq$, or $\leq$.

integer (pp. 122, 601) Any number in the set of numbers ... −3, −2, −1, 0, 1, 2, 3, ...

interquartile range (IQR) (p. 145) The range of the values in the box of a box-and-whisker plot: IQR = upper quartile – lower quartile.

inverse operations (p. 57) Operations that undo each other, like addition and subtraction or multiplication and division.

irrational number (p. 261) A number that cannot be written as the quotient of two integers.

isosceles triangle (p. 604) A triangle that has at least two sides of equal length.

L ▸▸▸▸▸▸▸▸▸▸▸▸▸▸▸▸▸▸▸▸▸▸▸▸▸▸▸

leaf (p. 16) *See* stem-and-leaf plot.

least common denominator (pp. 91, 597) The least common multiple of the denominators of two or more fractions.

least common multiple (LCM) (pp. 103, 596) The least number that is a multiple of each of two or more numbers.

legs (p. 294) In a right triangle, the sides adjacent to the right angle. *See also* right triangle.

like terms (p. 61) Terms of an expression that have identical variable parts.

line symmetry (p. 264) When one half of a figure is the mirror image of the other half, the figure has line symmetry.

line of symmetry (p. 522) A line that divides a figure into two parts that are reflections of each other. *See also* parabola.

linear (p. 181) When the graph of an equation is a straight line, the equation and its graph are linear.

lower extreme (p. 18) The least data value in a data set. *See also* box-and-whisker plot.

lower quartile (p. 18) The median of the data in the lower half of a data set. *See also* box-and-whisker plot.

lowest terms (pp. 12, 597) A fraction is in lowest terms when the greatest common factor of the numerator and the denominator is 1.

M ▸▸▸▸▸▸▸▸▸▸▸▸▸▸▸▸▸▸▸▸▸▸▸▸▸▸▸

mean (pp. 16, 606) The sum of the data in a numerical data set divided by the number of data items.

median (pp. 16, 606) When the data in a data set are ordered in numerical order, the median is the middle number or the mean of the two middle numbers.

midpoint (p. 245) The point of a segment that divides it into two congruent segments.

minimum rotational symmetry (p. 259) The smallest number of degrees a figure can be rotated and fit exactly on itself. *See also* rotational symmetry.

mode (pp. 16, 606) The most frequently occurring item, or items, in a data set. A data set can have no mode.

multistage experiment (p. 306) An experiment that involves two or more events happening.

N ▸▸▸▸▸▸▸▸▸▸▸▸▸▸▸▸▸▸▸▸▸▸▸▸▸▸▸

negative correlation (p. 538) The relationship between two variables when one variable tends to decrease as the other increases.

net (p. 405) A two-dimensional pattern that can be folded into a space figure.

prism   prism net

"nice" fraction (p. 85) A fraction that can easily be converted to a decimal or a percent or that makes computations easier.

nonlinear (p. 181) When the graph of an equation is not a straight line, the equation is nonlinear.

O ▸▸▸▸▸▸▸▸▸▸▸▸▸▸▸▸▸▸▸▸▸▸▸▸▸▸▸

obtuse angle (pp. 119, 603) An angle whose measure is between 90° and 180°.

obtuse triangle (pp. 288, 604) A triangle that has one obtuse angle.

opposite (p. 124) A number and its opposite are the same distance from 0 on a number line but on opposite sides. The opposite of 3 is –3.

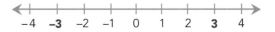

order of operations (pp. 56, 600) The correct order in which to perform mathematical operations in an expression: operations inside grouping symbols first, exponents next, then multiplication or division from left to right, and finally addition or subtraction from left to right.

outcome (p. 108) The result of an experiment.

outlier (p. 145) A data value that is significantly different from other values in a data set.

P ▸

parabola (p. 522) The graph of a quadratic function.

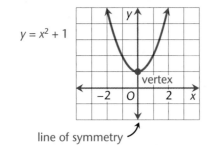

line of symmetry

parallelogram (p. 274) A quadrilateral that has two pairs of parallel sides.

percent (pp. 12, 599) Percent means "per hundred" or "out of one hundred."

percent of change (p. 99) The percent by which an amount increases or decreases from its original amount.

percent of decrease (p. 98) The ratio of the amount of decrease to the original amount.

percent of increase (p. 99) The ratio of the amount of increase to the original amount.

perfect square (p. 166) A number whose principal square root is a whole number.

permutation (p. 373) An arrangement of a group of items in which order is important.

perpendicular bisector (p. 205) A segment, line, or ray that forms a right angle with a segment and divides the segment in half.

polygon (p. 69) A closed plane figure formed by three or more segments that do not cross each other.

convex   concave   regular

population (p. 84) The entire group being studied.

positive correlation (p. 538) The relationship between two variables when one variable tends to increase as the other increases.

power (pp. 345, 600) *See* exponent.

principal square root (p. 166) The positive square root.

prism (p. 43) A space figure with faces shaped like polygons. Two of the faces, the bases, are parallel and congruent. The other faces are parallelograms. In a *right* prism, the other faces are rectangles.

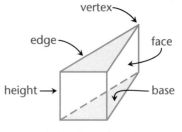

right triangular prism

probability (p. 109) A number from 0 to 1 that tells how likely it is that an event will happen.

product of powers rule (p. 346) To multiply powers with the same base, add the exponents: $b^m \cdot b^n = b^{m+n}$.

proportion (p. 86) A statement that two ratios are equal.

pyramid (p. 405) A space figure with one base that can be any polygon. The other faces are triangles that meet at a common vertex.

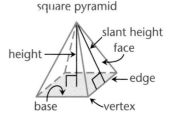

Pythagorean theorem (p. 294) In a right triangle, the square of the length of the hypotenuse is equal to the sum of the squares of the lengths of the legs.

Q ▸

quadratic function (p. 524) A function that can be modeled by an equation in the form $y = ax^2 + bx + c$, where $a \neq 0$.

quadrilateral (p. 272) A polygon with four sides.

quotient of powers rule (p. 346) To divide powers with the same base, subtract the exponents: $\frac{b^m}{b^n} = b^{m-n}$, where $b \neq 0$.

R ▸

radius (plural: radii) (p. 206) A segment whose endpoints are the center and any point on a given circle. The length of a radius is called *the* radius. *See also* circle.

range (pp. 17, 606) The difference between the greatest data value and the least data value in a data set.

rate (p. 6) A ratio that compares two quantities measured in different units.

ratio (pp. 6, 597) The quotient you get when one number is divided by a second number not equal to zero.

rational number (p. 260) A number that can be written in the form $\frac{a}{b}$, where a and b are integers and $b \neq 0$.

reciprocals (p. 271) Two numbers whose product is 1.

rectangle (p. 274) A quadrilateral that has four right angles.

reflection (p. 513) A transformation where a figure is flipped across a line such as the *x*-axis or the *y*-axis.

regular polygon (p. 69) A polygon with all sides of equal length and all angles of equal measure. *See also* polygon.

regular pyramid (p. 421) A pyramid with a base that is a regular polygon and whose faces are congruent isosceles triangles.

relative frequency (p. 580) The ratio of the number of occurrences of an item to the total number of occurrences.

repeating decimal (p. 260) A decimal that contains a number or a group of numbers that repeats forever.

representative sample (p. 88) A sample whose characteristics are similar to those of the entire population.

rhombus (p. 274) A quadrilateral that has four sides of equal length.

right angle (pp. 119, 603) An angle whose measure is 90°.

right triangle (pp. 288, 604) A triangle that has one right angle

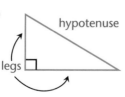

rise (p. 191) *See* slope.

rotation (p. 258) A turn of a figure about a fixed point, the center of rotation, a certain number of degrees either clockwise or counterclockwise.

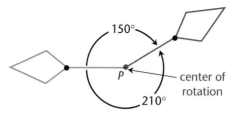

rotational symmetry (p. 258) When a figure fits exactly on itself after being rotated less than 360° around a center point, the figure has rotational symmetry.

The minimum rotational symmetry is 72°

run (p. 191) *See* slope.

S ▸

sample (p. 84) A small group from the population.

scale of a drawing (p. 452) The ratio of a length on a drawing to a corresponding length on the actual object.

scale on a graph (p. 29) The numbers written along the axis of a graph.

scalene triangle (p. 604) A triangle that has no sides of equal length.

scatter plot (p. 30) A graph that compares two sets of data. It can be used to look for relationships between data sets.

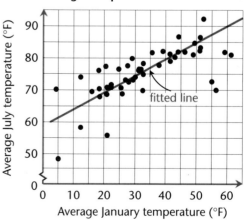

Average Temperature in 50 U.S. Cities

scientific notation (p. 214) A number is in scientific notation when it is written as the product of a number that is at least one but less than 10 and a power of ten.

decimal notation $\longrightarrow 5263.4 = 5.2634 \cdot 10^3 \longleftarrow$ scientific notation

sector (p. 552) A wedge-shaped region in a circle bounded by two radii and an arc. Can be used to refer to part of a circle graph.

sector

self-similar (p. 240) When a figure is made up of smaller pieces that are similar to the whole figure, the figure is self-similar.

sequence (p. 240) An ordered list of numbers or objects.

similar (p. 202) Figures that have the same shape, but not necessarily the same size.

slant height (pp. 295, 421) The height of a triangular face of a pyramid. In a regular pyramid, the slant heights are all the same length. *See also* pyramid.

slope (p. 191) The ratio of the vertical change to the horizontal change along a line. Slope is a measure of a line's steepness.

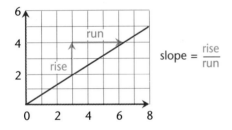

$$\text{slope} = \frac{\text{rise}}{\text{run}}$$

slope-intercept form (p. 336) An equation of a line in the form $y = mx + b$, where m is the slope and b is the y-intercept.

solution of an equation (pp. 57, 180) A value of a variable that makes an equation true. Also an ordered pair of numbers that make an equation with two variables true.

solution of an inequality (p. 443) All the values of a variable that make an inequality true are the solution of the inequality.

solve an equation (p. 57) Find all the solutions of an equation.

solve an inequality (p. 444) Find all the solutions of an inequality.

square (p. 274) A quadrilateral that has four right angles and four sides of equal length.

square root (p. 166) If $s^2 = n$, then s is a square root of n. For example, 5 and –5 are square roots of 25.

stem (p. 16) *See* stem-and-leaf plot.

stem-and-leaf plot (p. 16) A display of data where each number is represented by a *stem* (the left-most digits) and a *leaf* (the right-most digits).

straight angle (pp. 119, 603) An angle whose measure is 180°.

supplement (p. 359) One angle is the supplement of a second angle if the two angles are supplementary angles.

supplementary angles (p. 359) Two angles whose measures have a sum of 180°.

surface area (p. 320) The combined area of a figure's outer surfaces.

T ▸

tangent (p. 361) In a right triangle, the tangent of an acute angle is the ratio of the length of the leg opposite the acute angle to the length of the leg adjacent to the angle.

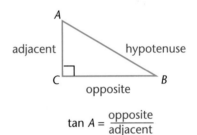

$$\tan A = \frac{\text{opposite}}{\text{adjacent}}$$

term of an expression (p. 60) The parts of an expression that are added together are called terms.

term number (p. 240) A number indicating the position of a term in a sequence.

term of a sequence (p. 240) A number or object in a sequence.

terminating decimal (p. 260) A decimal that contains a limited number of digits.

tessellation (p. 288) A covering of a plane with polygons that has no gaps or overlaps.

tetrahedron (p. 405) A pyramid with four triangular faces, including the base.

theoretical probability (p. 109) The ratio of the number of outcomes that make up the event to the total number of possible outcomes if all the outcomes are equally likely. Theoretical probability can be determined without actually doing an experiment.

transformation (p. 511) A change in an object's shape, size, or position. *See also* reflection, rotation, and translation.

translation (p. 125) A transformation that moves each point of a figure the same distance in the same direction.

transversal (p. 434) A line that intersects two or more lines in a plane at separate points.

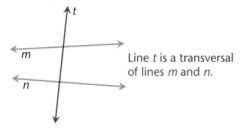

Line *t* is a transversal of lines *m* and *n*.

trapezoid (p. 274) A quadrilateral that has exactly one pair of parallel sides, called *bases*.

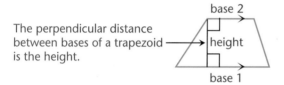

The perpendicular distance between bases of a trapezoid is the height.

tree diagram (p. 113) A diagram that can be used to show all the possible outcomes of an experiment.

triangle inequality (p. 243) The sum of the lengths of any two sides of a triangle is greater than the length of the third side.

U ▸

unit rate (p. 7) A ratio that compares a quantity to one unit of another quantity.

unlike terms (p. 61) Terms that do not have identical variable parts.

upper extreme (p. 18) The greatest data value in a data set. *See also* box-and-whisker plot.

upper quartile (p. 18) The median of the data in the upper half of a data set. *See also* box-and-whisker plot.

V ▸

variable (p. 41) A quantity, usually represented by a letter, that is unknown or that changes.

Venn diagram (p. 225) A diagram used to model relationships among groups.

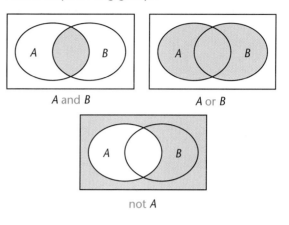

vertex of a parabola (p. 522) The point where a parabola intersects its line of symmetry. *See also* parabola.

vertex of a plane figure (pp. 203, 603) A point where sides of a figure, such as an angle or a polygon, come together. *See also* angle.

vertex of a space figure (plural: vertices) (p. 405) A point where three or more edges of a space figure meet. *See also* prism *and* pyramid.

vertical angles (p. 435) Angles that have the same vertex and whose sides are opposite rays.

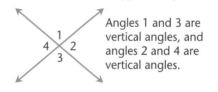

Angles 1 and 3 are vertical angles, and angles 2 and 4 are vertical angles.

Y ▸

y-intercept (p. 335) The *y*-coordinate of the point where a line crosses the *y*-axis.

INDEX

Polygon, 69
concave, 283
convex, 283
exterior angles, 287
interior angles, 283–285,
287–288
regular, 69, 284, 287
See also Quadrilateral *and*
Triangle.
Polynomials, simplifying,
60–62, 64–66
Population, 84
Portfolio, *See under* Assessment.
Powers, 345–346, 350–352, 600
product of powers rule, 346,
350, 352, 354
quotient of powers rule, 346,
350–352, 354
See also Exponents *and*
Scientific notation.
Practice, *See* Extra Skill Practice
and Spiral Review.
Prediction
using an equation, 193–195,
197, 198, 216–217
using exponential growth,
503–504, 506–507
using a fitted line, 31–32, 34
using percent, 89
using probability, 111–112
using samples and surveys,
83–89
shape of a graph, 470, 529
Prism
net for, 411
rectangular, 43, 45, 47–50
sketching, 395, 400
surface area, 419–420, 425,
427
volume, 44, 47–48, 50,
422–424, 426–427, 429
Probability, 109, 382
of complementary events, 305
of compound events, 109, 306
and counting techniques,
383–387
experimental 111–112,
117–118
geometric, 304, 308–309
of a multistage experiment,
306–310
and relative frequency,
581–582, 584
theoretical, 108–110, 115–117
Probability Connection, 142,
171, 353, 545
Problem solving, 607–608
four-step approach, 3–5, 9,

10, 13
See also Applications,
Connections, Extended
Exploration, *and* Project.
**Problem solving, choosing a
method,** 309, 364
Problem solving strategies
*Students are expected to apply
problem solving strategies
throughout the course.*
act it out, 9
examine a related problem, 9
guess and check, 9
make a model, 9
make an organized list, 9
make a picture or diagram, 9
try a simpler problem, 9
use logical reasoning, 9
work backward, 9
Project
Building a Ramp, 317, 328,
342, 367, 389
Creating a Model Town, 393,
416, 430, 461, 463
Creating a Pattern, 237, 253,
266, 300, 313
Designing a Game, 81, 94, 104,
134, 157
Fact or Fiction?, 1, 13, 25, 51,
77
Modeling Change in a Story,
467, 480, 495, 519, 531
Preparing an Investigative
Report, 535, 549, 575, 585,
587
Solving a Mystery, 161, 187,
198, 222, 231, 233
**Properties of addition and
multiplication,** 488–489,
491–493, 525
Proportional reasoning, 86,
90–92
and scale drawings, 451–453,
457–458
and similar figures, 451–460
See also Proportions.
Proportions, 86, 90–92
and similar figures, 202, 204,
207–209, 454–457, 459–460
See also Ratio *and* Scale
drawings.
Pyramid, 405
base, 405
edge, 405
face, 405
net, 405, 407, 411
regular pyramid, 421
slant height, 295, 421

surface area, 420–422, 425,
427
tetrahedron, 405
vertex, 405
volume, 423, 426, 428–429
Pythagorean theorem,
294–299

Q ▸ ▸ ▸ ▸ ▸ ▸ ▸ ▸ ▸ ▸ ▸ ▸ ▸ ▸ ▸ ▸ ▸

Quadratic functions, 524–526,
528
Quadrilaterals, 272–278
classifying, 272–278
parallelogram, 272, 274–278
rectangle, 272, 274–278
rhombus, 272, 274–278
square, 272, 274–278
trapezoid, 272, 274–278
Quartile
lower, 18
upper, 18

R ▸ ▸ ▸ ▸ ▸ ▸ ▸ ▸ ▸ ▸ ▸ ▸ ▸ ▸ ▸ ▸

Range, 606
Rate(s), 6–12
equivalent, 579–583
and slope, 190–192, 195–196
unit, 7–8, 10
See also Ratio.
Ratio(s), 6, 321–324, 326–327
See also Proportion *and* Rate.
Rational numbers, 260–262,
264–265, 281–282, 285–286
See also Fractions.
Reasoning, *See* Critical thinking,
Logical reasoning, Patterns, *and*
Proportional reasoning.
Reciprocal, 271, 275
Rectangle, 272, 274–278
Repeating decimal, 260, 266
Research, 11, 12, 37, 65, 103,
155, 221, 230, 278, 299, 326,
366, 460, 548
Reviews, *See* Assessment,
module, *and* Spiral Review.
Rhombus, 272, 274–278
Right angle, 603
Right triangles, 294–299, 604
hypotenuse, 294
legs, 294
Pythagorean theorem, 294–299
Rotational symmetry,
258–259, 262, 264, 266
minimum rotational symmetry,
259, 262, 264

U

Undefined slope, 337
Unit rate, 7–8, 10

V

Variable, 41, 46
Venn diagrams, 225–230
Vertex (vertices)
    of a cone, 424
    of a parabola, 522, 529
    of a pyramid, 405
Visual representations,
    fitted line, 31–34, 36, 194, 198
    locating points in a coordinate
      plane, 602
    self-assessment scales, 607–608
    tree diagram, 113–114,
      116, 118–119, 371–372,
      376–378

Venn diagrams, 225–230
See also Data displays,
    Modeling, *and* Visual
    thinking.
Visual thinking, 66, 75, 133,
    210, 249, 251, 265, 280, 281,
    283, 298, 309, 318, 327, 387,
    402, 505, 516, 573
Volume
    cone, 424, 426, 428–429
    cube, 169
    cylinder, 44–45, 47–50
    prism, 422–424, 426–427, 429
    pyramid, 423, 426, 428–429
    rectangular prism, 43, 47–48,
      50
    relationship to surface area,
      321–322, 324, 326

W

Writing, 22, 35, 73, 79, 92, 102,
    118, 119, 132, 140, 155, 159,
    172, 173, 235, 251, 264, 326,
    339, 352, 364, 379, 386, 391,
    400, 413, 438, 458, 459, 478,
    493, 506, 533, 547, 559, 573,
    583, 589
See also Journal.

Y

y-intercept of a line, 335–337,
    341

Z

Zero, as an exponent,
    347–348, 350, 352
Zero slope, 337

CREDITS

ACKNOWLEDGMENTS
302 Excerpt from *Exploring the Titanic* by Robert D. Ballard. Copyright © 1988 by Madison Press. Reprinted by permission of Scholastic Inc. **369, 370, 374** Excerpts from *Seeing Fingers: The Story of Louis Braille* by Etta DeGering. Copyright © 1962 by Etta B. DeGering. Reprinted by permission of Gertrude L. A. Johnson on behalf of the author. **468** "Sidewalk Measles" by Barbara M. Hales, from *The Sky Is Full of Song*, selected by Lee Bennett Hopkins. Reprinted by permission of Barbara M. Hales. **574** Graphic from "Far-Out Junk" by Phoebe Weseley, *Science World*, November 18, 1988 issue. Copyright © 1988 by Scholastic Inc. Reprinted by permission of Scholastic Inc.

COVER PHOTOGRAPHY
Front (*clockwise*) Bob Allen; Tom Bean; Rob Crandall/ Houghton Mifflin Company; Charles Feil/Stock Boston; George Steinmetz; NASA; Renee Lynn/Tony Stone Images; Holway & Lobel/Stock Market. **Back** Photo of STEM pilot students: Phil Schofield.

PHOTOGRAPHY
iii RMIP/Richard Haynes; **iv** Bob Allen; **v** Rob Crandall/ Houghton Mifflin Company; **vi** Tom Bean; **vii** Renee Lynn/Tony Stone Images; **viii** George Steinmetz; **ix** Charles Feil/Stock Boston; **x** Holway & Lobel/Stock Market; **xi** NASA; **xvi** Rich Kane/Sportschrome; **1** Bob Allen; **2** NASA; **4** NASA; **5** RMIP/Richard Haynes; **8** NASA; **10** Sipa/Zullo/Leo de Wys (t); Stephen Frisch/ Stock Boston (b); **11** RMIP/Richard Haynes; **13** RMIP/ Richard Haynes; **15** AP Worldwide Photos, Inc. (t); Bettmann (b); **18** School Division/Houghton Mifflin Company; **20** School Division/Houghton Mifflin Company; **23** PhotoDisc, Inc.; **24** Natsuko Utsumi/ Gamma-Liaison; **25** Courtesy Kelly Martino (t); Chuck Rydlewski/Sports Photo Masters (b); **27** PhotoDisc, Inc. (t); Mike Powell/Allsport (l); Sportschrome (c); Mitchell B. Reibel/Sports Photo Masters (r); **28** RMIP/Richard Haynes; **31** Gerard Vandystadt/Allsport; **35** Ben Radford/Allsport; **36** RMIP/Richard Haynes; **37** Mitchell Reibel/Sports Photo Masters; **40** RMIP/Richard Haynes; **42** RMIP/Richard Haynes; **49** Gerry Goodstein/ Huntington Theatre Company (t); **49** Paul Guy/New Albion Records (b); **50** RMIP/Richard Haynes; **51** NASA; **53** Bob Allen; **54** RMIP/Richard Haynes; **63** Betty Crowell/Faraway Places; **64** Tom Carroll Photography, Inc.; **68** Missouri Division of Tourism; **70** RMIP/Richard Haynes; **73** Wolfgang Kaehler; **77** RMIP/Richard Haynes; **79** Corbis-Bettmann; **80–81** Rob Crandall/Houghton Mifflin Company; **82** © 1997 Reprinted Courtesy of Bunny Hoest and Parade Magazine; **84** Jose Carrillo/ PhotoPhile; **89** Bob Daemmrich/Stock Boston; **92** Paul Chesley/Photographers/Aspen, Inc.; **94** School Division/ Houghton Mifflin Company; **96** RMIP/Richard Haynes; **101** School Division, Houghton Mifflin Company (tl, tc, tr, bl); Courtesy of Specialized Bicycle Components (c); PhotoDisc, Inc. (cr); Richard Hutchings/PhotoEdit (b); **104** Courtesy of Christopher Dyson; **106** Jason Hawkes/Tony Stone Images (t); Steve Welsh/Liaison International (b); **107** RMIP/Richard Haynes; **111** RMIP/Richard Haynes; **117** Mitchell B. Reibel/Sports Photo Masters; **118** RMIP/Richard Haynes; **119** PhotoDisc, Inc.; **125** School Division/Houghton Mifflin Company; **127** RMIP/Richard Haynes; **133** Rich Kane/Sportschrome; **134** RMIP/Richard Haynes; **136** Courtesy of West Edmondton Mall; **138** RMIP/ Richard Haynes; **144** Yoshikazu Tsuno/Agence France-Presse; **148** RMIP/Richard Haynes; **153** Mark Gibson/ Stock Market (tl); PhotoPhile (tr); Gale Zucker/Stock Boston (bl); Phillip Roullard (br); **157** RMIP/Richard Haynes; **160–61** Tom Bean; **162** David Muench; **164** David Muench; **171** NASA; **172** School Division/ Houghton Mifflin Company; **175** Eric R. Berndt/Unicorn Stock Photo; **178** Kent & Donna Dannen; **179** School Division/Houghton Mifflin Company; **180** School Division/Houghton Mifflin Company; **181** Charles Krebs/Tony Stone Images; **184** EROS Data Center; **185** National Motor Museum; **189** Reporters/Broze/Leo deWys, Inc.; **193** RMIP/Richard Haynes; **205** Eliot Cohen; **206** RMIP/Richard Haynes; **213** Ellen Druffel/ Department of Earth System Science/UC, Irvine; **215** School Division/Houghton Mifflin Company; **220** Bob Daemmrich/Stock Boston; **225** RMIP/Richard Haynes; **231** Courtesy of Georgia Griffith; **236–37** Renee Lynn/Tony Stone Images; **238** Loren Carpenter/Pixar; **242** RMIP/Richard Haynes; **251** Sisse Brimberg/National Geographic Image Collection; **252** Courtesy of Junpei Sekino; **253** Photographer: David Lubarsky/Walter de Maria Enterprises (t); RMIP/ Richard Haynes (b); **259** RMIP/Richard Haynes (tl); Clyde H. Smith/Peter Arnold, Inc. (l); Roland Birke/ OKAPIA/Photo Researchers, Inc. (c); E.R. Degginger (r); **263** Scott Camazine/Photo Researchers, Inc.; Brownie Harris/Stock Market (inset); **264** Andrew G. Wood/ Photo Researchers, Inc. (tl); Jim Solliday/ Biological Photo Service (tc); Rod Planck/Photo Researchers, Inc. (tr); Archive Photos (bl); Dr. E.R. Degginger/Color-Pic, Inc. (bc); Richard C. Walters/ Visuals Unlimited (br); **265** RMIP/Richard Haynes; **266** Adison Doty; **268** Richard Yapkowitz; **269** RMIP/Richard Haynes; **272** Chris Carroll/Outline Press Syndicate Inc.; **276** Garden State Pops Youth Orchestra (1997); **277** Special Collections, California Polytechnic State University (t); Courtesy of Szyszkowitz & Kowalski Architeckturburo, Graz, Austria (bl); California

Polytechnic State University (br); **280** © L&M Services B.V. Amsterdam 980105/Art Resource, New York (l); © Richard Anusziewicz/Licensed by VAGA, New York, NY (r); **283** HGM Composition 17, 1919 by Theo van Doesburg (1883–1931), Haags Gemeentemuseum, Netherlands/Bridgeman Art Library, London/New York; **286** M. Siluk/Image Works; **287** PhotoDisc, Inc.; **290** Hugh Sitton/Tony Stone Images; **291** RMIP/Richard Haynes; **292** RMIP/Richard Haynes; **294** Tibor Bognar/Stock Market; **302** Hulton Getty/Tony Stone Images (l); Illustration by Ken Marshall © 1988 from *Exploring the Titanic*, a Scholastic/Madison Press Book (r); **305** Emory Kristof/National Geographic Image Collection; **313** RMIP/Richard Haynes; **316–17** George Steinmetz; **318** Jean-Loup Charmet; **319** RMIP/Richard Haynes; **320** RMIP/Richard Haynes; **321** RMIP/Richard Haynes; **325** Super Kamiokande Experiment; **326** Andre Jenny/Unicorn Stock Photo; **331** Corbis-Bettmann; **339** Papul Freed/Animals Animals; **340** Runk/Schoenberger/Grant Heilman Photography; **344** Smithsonian/IMAX, Lockheed, and NASA; **347** Jay Hoops/Leo de Wys (tl); PhotoDisc, Inc. (tr); PhotoDisc, Inc. (bl); T.E. Adams/Visuals Unlimited (br); **348** School Division/Houghton Mifflin Company (l); Andrew Syred/Tony Stone Images (c); Stanley Flegler/Visuals Unlimited (r); **349** NASA; **351** Phillip Roullard; **352** Mark Wilson/Boston Globe; **354** Courtesy of France Cordova; **356** Werner Forman/Art Resource (l); Ronald Sheridan/Ancient Art and Architecture (r); **357** RMIP/Richard Haynes; **358** RMIP/Richard Haynes; **360** RMIP/Richard Haynes; **364** School Division/Houghton Mifflin Company; **365** School Division/Houghton Mifflin Company; **369** Roger-Viollet; **373** American Printing House for the Blind Inc.; **382** School Division/Houghton Mifflin Company; **392–93** Charles Feil/Stock Boston; **394** Glenn Short/Tony Stone Images; **398** RMIP/Richard Haynes; **401** School Division/Houghton Mifflin Company; **404** School Division, Houghton Mifflin Company (Construction from *Spooner's Moving Animals* by Paul Spooner.); **406** W.B. Finch/Stock Boston; **407** School Division/Houghton Mifflin Company; **408** RMIP/Richard Haynes; **413** School Division/Houghton Mifflin Company; **416** RMIP/Richard Haynes; **418** David Hiser/Photographers/Aspen, Inc. (l); B&C Alexander/Photo Researchers, Inc. (r); Gerben Oppermans/Tony Stone Images/PNI (bkgd); **419** Lawrence Migdale/Stock Boston; **422** Smithsonian Institution; **424** Smithsonian Institution; **427** Tom Bean/Stock Boston; **428** Ira Kirschenbaum/Stock Boston (t); Christa McAuliffe Planetarium (b); **430** School Division/Houghton Mifflin Company; **432** Bassignac/Deville/Gaillard/Gamma-Liaison; **433** RMIP/Richard Haynes; **437** Stacy Pick/Stock Boston; **439** Courtesy of Lonnie Bitsoi; **441** School Division, Houghton Mifflin Company; **442** Dan McCoy/Rainbow/PNI; **451** Seward Hedges Area School/Hedrich Blessing (t); Courtesy of Ross Barney & Jankowski Architects (b); **452** RMIP/Richard Haynes; **458** Courtesy of Ross Barney & Jankowski Architects; **461** RMIP/Richard Haynes; **463** RMIP/Richard Haynes; **467** Holway & Lobel/Stock Market; **468** Wulf Maehl/Stock Market; **469** School Division/Houghton Mifflin Company;

470 RMIP/Richard Haynes; **472** Joe Bensen/Stock Boston; **473** School Division/Houghton Mifflin Company; **476** School Division/Houghton Mifflin Company; **477** Corbis-Bettmann; **479** Larry Mayer/Gamma-Liaison; **480** RMIP/Richard Haynes; **482** Val Piatkowski/Honiss School; **483** RMIP/Richard Haynes; **485** RMIP/Richard Haynes; **487** RMIP/Richard Haynes; **492** Daniel McCulloch/Tony Stone Images; **494** Young Americans Bank; **506** RMIP/Richard Haynes; **507** Jonathan Nourok/PhotoEdit; **508** Courtesy of William Karesh; **510** Peak Performance Technologies, Inc., Engelwood, Colorado (t); Globus Bros./Stock Market (b); **515** RMIP/Richard Haynes; **518** RMIP/Richard Haynes; **521** NASA; **522** Deborah Davis/PhotoEdit (l); Kunio Owaki/Stock Market (r); **524** Jed Jacobsohn/Allsport; **527** Wernher Krutein/Liaison International; **528** Joe Sohm/Photo Researchers, Inc.; **531** RMIP/Richard Haynes; **534–35** NASA; **536** Shattil/Rozinski Photography; **537** Jeff Foott; **538** Fred Bavendam; **539** Silver Images Photography; **541** David Young-Wolff/PhotoEdit (tl); Bob Daemmrich/Stock Boston (tr); John Maher/Stock Boston (bl); RMIP/Richard Haynes (br); **542** Patrix Ravaux/Masterfile; **543** RMIP/Richard Haynes; **546** John Banagan/Image Bank; **547** RMIP/Richard Haynes; **552** RMIP/Richard Haynes; **559** Grant Heilman Photography; **560** Courtesy of Melissa McMillan; **568** Dugald Bremmer/Tony Stone Images; **569** Chuck Carter/National Geographic Image Collection; **570** RMIP/Richard Haynes; **572** Gail Shumway/FPG International; **579** Rhoda Sidney/Stock Boston; **580** Custom Medical Stock Photo; **583** Jeffrey Muir Hamilton/Stock Boston; **584** Steve Elmore/The Stock Market; **587** RMIP/Richard Haynes.

ILLUSTRATIONS
60 (t), **578** Jeremy Spiegel; **163, 164, 165** Chris Costello; **168, 175, 189, 201, 213, 216, 222, 224** Betsy James; **413** Ken Hanson; **434, 437** Magellan Geographix; All other illustrations by School Division, Houghton Mifflin Company, or by McDougal Littell Design Group. **Electronic Technical Art** Network Graphics or McDougal Littell Electronic Production Group.

SELECTED ANSWERS

MODULE 1

Section 1, Practice and Application

1. a. Sample Response: Divide the photograph into equal sections, count the number of stars in one section and multiply by the number of sections. **b.** Sample Response: 196 stars **3. a.** Sample Response: Weigh 4 rocks on each side; take the heavier side, divide it in half, and weigh 2 rocks on each side; take the heavier side, divide it in half, and weigh 1 rock on each side. **b.** 3 weighings **5.** miles per hour; 60 mi/hr **7.** cost in dollars per lb; $2/lb **9.** 60 **11.** 480,000 **13.** Sample Response: 1.38 gal/min; It is easier to think of about $1\frac{1}{3}$ gal because gallon containers are used frequently. **19. a.** 10 in. **21. a.** about 29,523,810 mi/month; about 971,178 mi/day based on 30.4 days in a month; about 40,465 mi/h **b.** Sample Response: miles per hour; It is more common to measure speed in miles per hour.

Spiral Review

23.

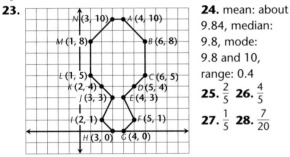

24. mean: about 9.84, median: 9.8, mode: 9.8 and 10, range: 0.4 **25.** $\frac{2}{5}$ **26.** $\frac{4}{5}$ **27.** $\frac{1}{5}$ **28.** $\frac{7}{20}$

Extra Skill Practice

1. a. Possible answers: one 12-person tent, two 6-person tents, and one 2-person tent; one 12-person tent and seven 2-person tents; one 12-person tent, two 5-person tents, and two 2-person tents; one 12-person tent, one 6-person tent, and four 2-person tents **b.** Possible Answers: four 6-person tents and one 2-person tent; three 6-person tents and four 2-person tents; two 6-person tents and seven 2-person tents; one 6-person tent and four 5-person tents; one 6-person tent, two 5-person tents, and five 2-person tents; one 6-person tent and ten 2-person tents; thirteen 2-person tents; two 6-person tents, two 5-person tents, and two 2-person tents **c.** Possible Answers: one 12-person tent, two 5-person tents, and two 2-person tents; one

6-person tent and four 5-person tents; one 6-person tent, two 5-person tents, and five 2-person tents; two 6-person tents, two 5-person tents, and two 2-person tents. **3.** 0.2 **5.** about $.15 **7.** 21 times

Section 2, Practice and Application

1. a.

Ages of Winners of Grammy Award for Best Female Country Performance, 1975–1996	
1	4
2	4 7 8 9 9
3	0 1 1 2 2 3 4 5 5 6 6 7 7 8
4	6 7

Ages of Winners of Grammy Award for Best Female Pop Performance, 1975–1996	
1	9
2	1 3 4 4 4 8 9
3	0 1 1 2 3 5 5 8
4	0 1 2 4 5
5	
6	4

b. Sample Response: Most country performers are in there 30's when they receive this award. Most pop winners are in their 20's and 30's. **3. a.** Class A: 54; Class B: 45 **b.** Class A: 100; Class B: 100 **c.** Class A: 65; Class B: 70 **d.** Class A: 95; Class B: 85 **7.** Plot C; lower extreme is 36, upper quartile is 81, upper extreme is 184

Spiral Review

10. 288 **11.** about 0.92 **12.** about 0.06 **13.** $5.25 **14.** 3 and 5 only **15.** none **16.** 2 only **17.** 3 only **18.** > **19.** > **20.** >

Career Connection

21. lower box; upper whisker

Extra Skill Practice

1.

Age of Academy Award Winners for Best Actor, 1976–1995	
3	0 0 2 5 7 7 8 9
4	0 2 2 3 5
5	1 2 2 4
6	0 1
7	6

Age of Academy Award Winners for Best Actress, 1976–1995

2	1 6 9
3	1 1 3 3 3 4 5 8
4	1 1 2 5 9 9
5	
6	
7	2 6
8	0

Sample Response: Most Best Actor and Best Actress awards are given when the actors and actresses are in their thirties and forties. The range of ages for Best Actress is greater than the range of ages for Best Actor. **3.** Best Actor: a) 30, b) 76, c) 37, d) 52; Best Actress: a) 21, b) 80, c) 32, d) 47

Standardized Testing, Multiple Choice
1. C and D **2.** A, B, C, and D

Section 3, Practice and Application
1. 88 years: 480 min, 92 years: 564 min **5.** Scatter Plot A has a straight line pattern. Scatter Plot B has a curved pattern.

Spiral Review
9. a. True; The upper extreme for linebackers is less than 250 lb. **b.** False; The median weight for offensive linemen is more than 10 lb heavier than the heaviest defensive lineman. **c.** False; The upper extreme for linebackers is about 245 lb and the lower extreme for offensive linemen is about 285 lb. **d.** True; The lower quartile for defensive linemen is less than 260 lb. **10.** 16 **11.** 16 **12.** 24 **13.** 7.85 **14.** 36 cm^2 **15.** 36 m^2 **16.** about 153.9 in.^{2}

Extra Skill Practice
1. about 125,000 ft; about 1955

3. a, b.

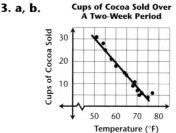

Cups of Cocoa Sold Over A Two-Week Period

Sample Response: I chose a horizontal scale of 40 to 90 because the temperatures range from 51° to 77°. I chose a vertical scale of 0 to 35 because the cups of cocoa sold range from 4 to 31. **c.** 3 pots; 4 pots

Standardized Testing, Open-ended
1. approximately 7 through 22; approximately 35 through 52 **2.** curved pattern; Sample Response: The data decreases, then levels off, then increases. This creates a curve.

Section 4, Practice and Application
1. a. smallest bicycle: about 2.39 in.; largest bicycle: about 31.4 ft **b.** smallest bicycle: about 2.39 in., largest bicycle: about 31.4 ft **c.** about 68 **d.** 2135.2 ft **3.** 100 **5.** 2 **7.** 18 **9.** $n - 4$ **11.** $10n$ **15.** about 42.39 in.^{3} **17.** about 125.6 cm^3 **19.** about 5306.6 cm^3 **21.** 1274 cm^3 **25. a.** 1000; 1750; 490,625; 1,406,720 **b.** It doubles the volume. **27. a.** 275.625 in.^{3} **b.** about 41,503; Multiply the volume of the large popcorn box by $12^3 = 1728$ to convert it to in.^{3}. Then divide that volume by the volume of the regular size box to get an estimate. Models or a drawing would probably be needed to get a more accurate answer because the regular size boxes would leave gaps that could not be counted as usable space.

Spiral Review
29.

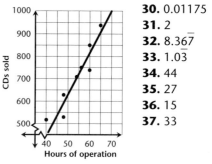

30. 0.01175 **31.** 2 **32.** $8.36\overline{7}$ **33.** $1.0\overline{3}$ **34.** 44 **35.** 27 **36.** 15 **37.** 33

Extension
39. Yes.

Extra Skill Practice
1. about 94.2 cm **3.** about 37.68 ft **5.** about 31,400 **7.** 30 **9.** about 125.6 **11.** $n + 28$ **13.** $15n - 3$ **15.** 192 mm^3 **17. a.** 55 ft^3 **b.** 92.925 m^3

Standardized Testing, Free Response
1. Sample Response: Both use the formula $V = Bh$, or volume equals area of the base times the height. The base of a prism is a polygon, so the formula for the area of its base, B, varies. The base of a cylinder is a circle, so the formula for the area of its base, B, is always $B = \pi r^2$. **2.** Sample Response: A cereal box has a length of 10 in., a width of 3 in., and a height of 14 in. What is the volume of the cereal box? Answer: 420 in.^{3}

Section 5, Practice and Application
1. A **3.** Let d = distance and n = the number of days; $\frac{d}{50} = n$ **5.** Let f = the length of the finished product and ℓ = the length of each cord; $\ell = 8f$ **7.** 1) 30°F, 2) 32°F; 1) 60°F, 2) 59°F; 1) 230°F 2) 212°F; The rule of thumb gives the best estimate for 15°C. **9. a.** 5 **b.** 1 **c.** 4 **d.** 2 **15.** $17x + 1$ **17.** $15w + 3$ **19.** no like terms **21.** $15y^2 + 7x$ **23. a.** $P = 2\ell + 2w$ **b.** 26 in. **c.** 7 cm **d.** 4.5 m **25.** equilateral triangle: 12 yd; square: 9 yd

Spiral Review

28. 25 cm **29.** 11 in. **30. a.** 24 in.^{2} **b.** 26 m^2

Extra Skill Practice

1. Let t = total amount of hamburger used in lb and c = the number of campers; $t = 0.25c + 5$ **3.** Let r = rent and a = area of the apartment; $r = 0.9a$ **5.** 31 **7.** 208 **9.** 148 **11.** 5y **13.** 10$t - 4$ **15.** 36$r - 18rd$ **17.** 9$v + 25k^3$ **19.** 7 + $w + w^2$

Standardized Testing, Multiple Choice

1. D **2.** A

Section 6, Practice and Application

1. a. perimeter: 790 mi, area: 3474 mi^2 **b.** perimeter: 872 mi, area: 19,300 mi^2 **c.** It is about in the middle; Sample Response: Yes; I would expect the average width to be about 30 mi which would make the area of this lake about 12,000 mi^2. **d.** It is greater; There are many inlets. **3. a.** $V = Bh$

c.

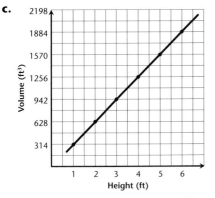

d. almost 6.5 ft; Sample Response: The graph gives a quick estimate of the height of the water.

Spiral Review

7. 6n **8.** $r - 1$ **9.** $5x^2 + 9x$ **10.** $\frac{1}{4}$ **11.** $1\frac{1}{12}$ **12.** 99 **13.** $\frac{56}{101}$ **14.** $13\frac{26}{27}$ **15.** $\frac{3}{28}$ **16.** 0.75; 75% **17.** 0.6; 60% **18.** 0.6$\overline{6}$; $66\frac{2}{3}$ **19.** 0.3$\overline{3}$; $33\frac{1}{3}$% **20.** 0.53; 53% **21.** 0.8$\overline{3}$; 83% **22.** 0.3$\overline{6}$; 36% **23.** 0.8$\overline{6}$; 86%

Extra Skill Practice

1. Should have 2 of each of the rectangles that are 1 by 48, 2 by 24, 3 by 16, 4 by 12, and 6 by 8.

3.

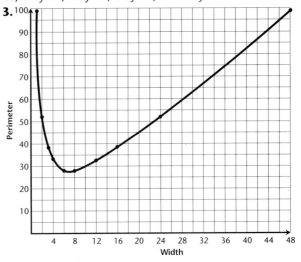

5. 19 units; Sample Response: I used the equation $p = 2\ell + 2w$ and substituted the values given for the variables p and ℓ to find w.

Standardized Testing, Performance Task

Step 1 $9 \div 2 = 4.5$ **Step 2** $4.5 + 2 = 6.5$
Step 3 The area of the polygon is 5.5, so subtract 1.

Review and Assessment

1. 2064 **2.** 10,800
3. a.

Ages of Company A Airplanes

0	2 3 5 6 9
1	2 3 5 5 7 7 7 8 9
2	0 0 1 6

Ages of Company B Airplanes

0	1 2 3 3 5 6 7 7 8 9
1	2 4 6 6 6 9
2	0 5

b. Sample Response: Most of the planes owned by Company A are older than the planes owned by Company B. **c.** Company A: mean: about 14.2, median: 16, mode: 17; Company B: mean: 10.5, median: 8.5, mode: 16 **4. a.** Company A: lower extreme: 2, upper extreme: 26, lower quartile: 9, upper quartile: 19; Company B: lower extreme: 1, upper extreme: 25, lower quartile: 5, upper quartile: 16 **b.** Sample Response: The median age of the planes at Company B is less than the median age of planes at Company A. **5.** the box
6. 21.82 ft **7. a.** $t = 0.50a + 0.25c$ **8. a.** no like terms
b. 8y **c.** $t + 4$ **d.** $x + 7xy$ **9. a.** $5\frac{1}{3}$ **b.** 7 **c.** 9 **d.** 1

10. a.

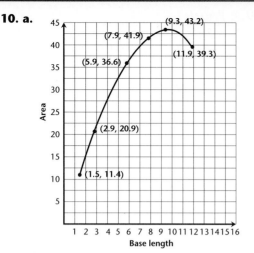

smooth curve **b.** 9.3 cm

MODULE 2

Section 1, Practice and Application

1. Possible answers: about 150, nice fraction or using multiples of 10% **3.** Possible answers: about 32, nice fraction; about 35, using multiples of 10% **5. a.** about 400 teens **b.** about 371 teens **c.** Yes **7.** 132 **9.** 126 **11.** 72 **13.** 32 **15.** 24% **17.** 130% **19.** 60
25. a. $45 = 0.6x$, 75 people **b.** Sample Response: No; The increase was only 5 people. **c.** Sample Response: No; On an average night the theater takes in $420. After the cost of the posters they only took in $360 on the night of the promotion.

Spiral Review

27. 24 m **28.** 19.2 **29.** 377.8 **30.** 2.4 **31.** 1.8 **32.** 0.062 **33.** 30 **34.** 150

Extra Skill Practice

1. about 675 **3.** about $3.30 **5.** about 18,500 **7.** about $26 **9.** about 567 **11.** 6 **13.** 1348.9 **15.** 50 **17.** 19 **19.** 132 **21.** 40% **23.** 1862 **25.** 2032

Section 2, Practice and Application

1. Sample Response: Change 69% to the "nice" fraction $\frac{2}{3}$, then find $\frac{2}{3}$ of 60; Find 10% of 60, then multiply by 7. **3.** about 48; 52.8 **5.** about 119.5; 107.55 **7.** About 1000, 964; about 650, 656; about 900, 923; about 500, 533; about 200, 226 **9.** imports: about 16% increase; domestics: about 8% increase; total: about 11% **11.** about 41,216 shopping centers

Spiral Review

15. 1456 **16.** 9.7 **17.** 639.1 **18.** 61 **19.** 300.2 **20.** 332.5 **21.** GCF 5, LCM 30 **22.** GCF 4, LCM 48 **23.** GCF 3, LCM 90 **24.** GCF 7, LCM 147 **25.** < **26.** < **27.** = **28.** >

Extension

29. about 43%; 30%

Career Connection

31. No.

Extra Skill Practice

1. about 170; 187 **3.** about 4.8; 3.36 **5.** about 64; 60.8 **7.** about 2.7% **9.** about 11.8% **11.** about 99.4% **13.** about 97.2% decrease

Standardized Testing, Performance Task

Sample Response: Rosa is right. Alaska had about a 10% increase in population. Alabama had about a 5% increase.

Section 3, Practice and Application

1. 0; 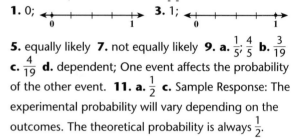 **3.** 1;

5. equally likely **7.** not equally likely **9. a.** $\frac{1}{5}$; $\frac{4}{5}$ **b.** $\frac{3}{19}$ **c.** $\frac{4}{19}$ **d.** dependent; One event affects the probability of the other event. **11. a.** $\frac{1}{2}$ **c.** Sample Response: The experimental probability will vary depending on the outcomes. The theoretical probability is always $\frac{1}{2}$.

13. a.

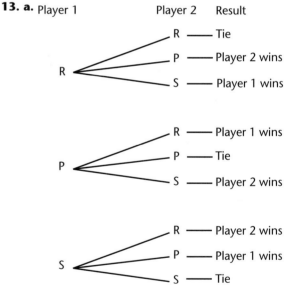

b. 9 **c.** RR, RP, PP, PS, SR, SS **d.** "Player 1 does not win" includes ties and "Player 1 loses" does not.
17. $\frac{1}{8}$ **19.** $\frac{1}{2}$

Spiral Review

21. about 3400% increase **22.** about 94% decrease **23.** acute **24.** obtuse **25.** straight **26.** obtuse **27.** −10, −7, −2 **28.** −2, −1, 3 **29.** −18, 13, 17

Extra Skill Practice

1. $\frac{1}{8}$ **3.** $\frac{5}{8}$ **5. a.** $\frac{2}{5}$; $\frac{7}{25}$; $\frac{18}{25}$ **b.** $\frac{6}{23}$; $\frac{7}{23}$ **c.** The events are independent if the first apple is replaced before the second apple is taken. If the first apple is not replaced, the events are dependent. **7.** $\frac{3}{10}$

Standardized Testing, Free Response

1. 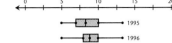 **2.** $\frac{1}{4}$; $\frac{1}{8}$; $\frac{1}{16}$; $\frac{1}{2^{49}}$

Section 4, Practice and Application

1. –31 **3.** –8 **5.** –100 **7.** 15 **9.** –74 **11.** 47 **13.** $8\frac{1}{2}$
15. 7, –7 **17.** –2 **19.** 5 **21.** –4 **23.** 13 **25.** –14
27. 41°F **29.** (7, 14) **31.** –72 **33.** –56 **35.** –3 **37.** 8
39. 64 **41.** –3 **43.** 3(–5); 15 yards lost

Spiral Review
47. $\frac{2}{7}$ **48.** $\frac{3}{7}$ **49.** $\frac{1}{5}$ **50.** $1\frac{1}{2}$ **51.** $\frac{7}{10}$ **52.** 1 **53.** $\frac{30}{49}$ **54.** 6
55. 8 **56.** 56 **57.** 33 **58.** 28 **59.** 96

Extension
61. 6, –10 **63.** –2, 2

Extra Skill Practice
1. 4 **3.** –57 **5.** –512 **7.** 1 **9.** 29 **11.** $3\frac{3}{4}$ **13.** –77
15. 6 **17.** 250 **19.** –42 **21.** –6 **23.** 18 **25.** 42 **27.** 4
29. –4 **31.** –16 **33.** –26

Standardized Testing, Open-ended
1. a. Sample Response: –7 and 5 **b.** none; Two numbers with a sum of 0 are opposites. The product of opposites is always less than or equal to 0.
c. Sample Response: 10 and –5 **2.** Sample Response: A(3, 2), B(3, –2), C(–3, –2), D(–3, 2); A′(–1, 8), B′(–1, 4), C′(–7, 4), D′(–7, 8)

Section 5, Practice and Application

1. –1 **3.** $-1\frac{1}{5}$ **5.** $-\frac{9}{14}$ **7.** $-\frac{11}{42}$ **9.** $-\frac{53}{60}$ **13.** –7 **15.** 3
17. $\frac{3}{8}$ **19.** $-\frac{2}{3}$ **21.** $-4\frac{3}{4}$ **23.** $2\frac{1}{2}$ **25.** $19\frac{3}{8}$ in. by 27 in.
27. $-\frac{3}{4}$ **29.** $\frac{1}{9}$; $-1\frac{1}{2}$; Yes.

Spiral Review
33. –13 **34.** 96 **35.** –9 **36.** –112 **37.** 10; 45; 20

Extra Skill Practice
1. $-2\frac{9}{10}$ **3.** $1\frac{1}{8}$ **5.** $-\frac{2}{3}$ **7.** $2\frac{1}{10}$ **9.** $-3\frac{1}{9}$ **11.** $-\frac{14}{33}$
13. a. $4\frac{2}{3}$ in. by $6\frac{2}{3}$ in. **b.** Possible answers: $4\frac{2}{3}$ in. by $13\frac{1}{3}$ in. or $9\frac{1}{3}$ in. by $6\frac{2}{3}$ in.

Standardized Testing, Multiple Choice
1. D **2.** A **3.** A

Section 6, Practice and Application

1. $p > 25$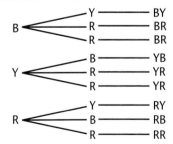

3. $e < 50$

5. Texas, Florida, and California
9. a–b.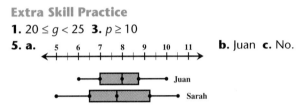

T-Shirt Prices (dollars)

c. Sample Response: No; The range is the same and the median price increased by only $1.00. **11. b.** Yes; The 1994 data contain 2 outliers, $108.97 and $112.98.
c. The costs are about the same.

Spiral Review
13. $-\frac{2}{3}$ **14.** $-3\frac{7}{8}$ **15.** $5\frac{7}{30}$ **16.** $-6\frac{2}{3}$ **17.** $2x + 1$ **18.** n^2
19. $8s + 4st$ **20.** Sample Response: There are many different pairs of numbers with a product of 9500.

Extra Skill Practice
1. $20 \le g < 25$ **3.** $p \ge 10$
5. a. **b.** Juan **c.** No.

Standardized Testing, Multiple Choice
1. C **2.** A

Review and Assessment
1. a. about 525 **b.** about 770 **2. a.** 500 New England teenagers; Sample Response: No; the sample is too small and only from one region of the country. **b.** 450 youths
3. about 50%; markup is $153 and $\frac{153}{322} \approx 50\%$.
4. about $44.50; 30% $\approx \frac{1}{3}$ and $\frac{1}{3}$ of $66.50 $\approx$ $22, $66.50 – $22 = $44.50. **5.** amount of income: 46%; amount spent: 13%; amount saved: 335%
6. Sample Response: dependent; The outcome of Event 1 affects the probability of Event 2. **7.** $\frac{1}{6}$
8.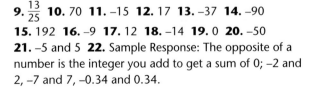

First Ball   Second Ball   Outcomes

9. $\frac{13}{25}$ **10.** 70 **11.** –15 **12.** 17 **13.** –37 **14.** –90
15. 192 **16.** –9 **17.** 12 **18.** –14 **19.** 0 **20.** –50
21. –5 and 5 **22.** Sample Response: The opposite of a number is the integer you add to get a sum of 0; –2 and 2, –7 and 7, –0.34 and 0.34.

23.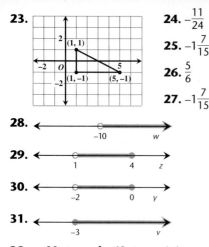

24. $-\frac{11}{24}$

25. $-1\frac{7}{15}$

26. $\frac{5}{6}$

27. $-1\frac{7}{15}$

28.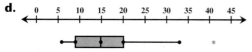

29.

30.

31.

32. a. 28 stores **b.** 60 stores; It is an outlier.
c. about 50%

d.

Sample Response: There are fewer men's stores than women's stores.

MODULE 3

Section 1, Practice and Application

1. 10 **3.** 60 **5.** $\frac{2}{5}$ **7. a.** 93.5 in.^{2} **b.** about $9\frac{1}{2}$ in.
9. about 6.2 **11.** about 3.5 **15.** $\frac{1}{10}$ **17.** –900; exact
19. about –5.7; estimate **21.** about 31.6; estimate
23. Length is about 97 yd, perimeter about 388 yd.
25. $c = 10a + 3000$ where c represents cooling capacity and a represents area.
27. a. ⬜ 18 ft cooling capacity: 7320 Btu/h
24 ft

⬜ 18 ft cooling capacity: 5160 Btu/h **b.** No; Sample
12 ft Response: The cooling capacity needed for the larger room is about 1.5 times greater than the capacity needed for the smaller room.

Spiral Review

30. Amounts raised by Students at a Charity Dance Marathon (dollars)

50 100 150 200 250 300 350 400 450 500

31. –4, 4 **32.** –11, 11 **33.** –19 **34.** 6 **35. a.** $A(-2, -2)$, $B(-2, 1)$, $C(1, 1)$, $D(2, -1)$ **b.** $A'(0, -2)$, $B'(0, 1)$, $C'(3, 1)$, $D'(4, -1)$

Extra Skill Practice

1. 700 **3.** $\frac{1}{10}$ **5.** 0.06 **7.** 0.02 **9.** about 7.1 **11.** about 11.7 **13.** about 6.6 **15.** about 5.7 **17.** about 5.3; estimate **19.** 2.5; exact **21.** about 2.2; estimate **23.** 0.8; exact **25.** The volume will be divided by 8.

Section 2, Practice and Application

1. 15 **3.** 3 **5.** 3 **7.** The addition was done before the division. **9.** The 5 in the numerator was divided by 5 but the 3 was not. **11.** 1.6 **13. a.** about 39.5
b. Sample Response: No; The length of the shoreline is very large compared to the surface area. **15.** –23.5
17. –0.1 **19.** 7.5 **21. a.** 11.75 mi/h; $d = 11.75h$
b. 6 mi/h; $d = 6h$ **c.** about 8 h

23. 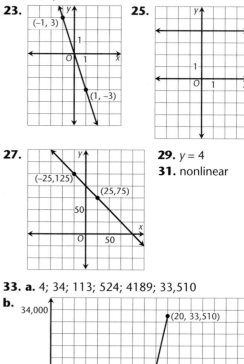 **25.**

27. 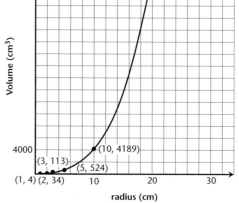 **29.** $y = 4$
31. nonlinear

33. a. 4; 34; 113; 524; 4189; 33,510
b.

nonlinear **c.** about 1150 cm^3

Spiral Review

35. about –2.8 **36.** about 3.3 **37.** about –3.9
38. about 0.4 **39.** $A(-2, -3)$, $B(0, -1)$, $C(1, 0)$, $M(-2, 2)$, $N(1, -1)$ **40.** $.14/oz **41.** 0.3 mi/h **42.** $74.67/h

Extension

43. a. Substitute 0.8 for f and 150 for d. Multiply both sides of the equation by 4500, then find the square root of each side. The speed is about 60 mi/h. **b.** about 60.2; They are about the same.

Extra Skill Practice

1. 4 **3.** 0.47 **5.** 1 **7.** 5 **9.** –3.5

11.

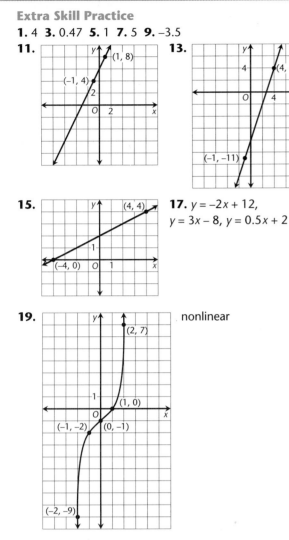

13.

15.

17. $y = -2x + 12$, $y = 3x - 8$, $y = 0.5x + 2$

19. nonlinear

Standardized Testing, Multiple Choice

1. A **2.** C **3.** B

Section 3, Practice and Application

1. 5 **3.** 0.5 **5. a.** the upper line; The slope is steeper so the rate is greater. **b.** Segura: about 0.27 km/min; Peterson: 0.2 km/min **c.** Segura: $d = 0.27t$; Peterson: $d = 0.2t$ where d = distance (km) and t = time (min) **9.** A; slope is 0.75, (0, –10) is on the line. **11.** about 50%; Sample Response: Subtract the amount of Vitamin C in the cooked vegetables from the amount in the raw vegetables and divide by the amount in the raw vegetables. **13.** 295 mg

Spiral Review

15. $10\frac{2}{3}$ **16.** 12 **17.** $\frac{3}{4}$ **18.** 12 **19.** multiplication; 136 **20.** 13.5 **21.** 26.55 **22.** 0.068

Extra Skill Practice

1. $\frac{3}{2}$ **3.** $\frac{1}{3}$ **5.** $\frac{5}{3}$

Section 4, Practice and Application

1. $\frac{5}{3.3}$ **3. a.** 65° **b.** 7.26 cm **c.** 7.58 cm **5.** Sample Response: $\triangle LMN \sim \triangle PQN$ **7.** Sample Response: $\triangle QSR \sim \triangle UTP$ **9.** Sample Response: Each angle of one trapezoid has the same measure as an angle of the other. **11.** No. **15.** Yes; If you fold along one diagonal you'll see the top and right sides are the same length. Fold along the other and you'll see the top and left sides as well as the bottom and right sides are the same length. **17.**

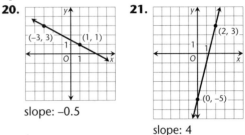

Yes.

Spiral Review

20.

21.

slope: –0.5

slope: 4

22. $33\frac{1}{3}$% decrease **23.** 37.5% increase **24.** about 34% decrease **25.** 360 **26.** 4 **27.** 249,000 **28.** 0.7 **29.** 753,000 **30.** 987,000 **31.** 16 **32.** 10,180,000

Extra Skill Practice

1. $\frac{3}{8}$ **3. a.** 90° **b.** 12 **c.** 40 **5.** Use the proportion $\frac{20}{40} = \frac{15}{x}$ then solve for x; The length of $\overline{CE}$ is not needed.

Standardized Testing, Free Response

1. $\overline{CP}$, $\overline{PD}$; any two of $\angle CPA$, $\angle CPB$, $\angle BPD$, and $\angle DPA$
2. Sample Response: 14 cm by 6 cm and 7 cm by 3 cm

Section 5, Practice and Application

1. 4,500,000,000 **3.** 186,000 **5.** A and B; The numbers are written as the product of a number greater than or equal to 1 and less than 10 and a power of ten. In C, 82.1 is greater than 10; in D, 2^{10} is not a power of 10. **7.** Approximate distances Large Cloud of Magellan: $9.7 \cdot 10^{17}$ mi; Small Cloud of Magellan: $1.1 \cdot 10^{18}$ mi; Ursa Minor dwarf: $1.4 \cdot 10^{18}$ mi; Draco dwarf: $1.5 \cdot 10^{18}$ mi; Sculptor dwarf: $1.6 \cdot 10^{18}$ mi; Fornax dwarf: $2.5 \cdot 10^{18}$ mi; Leo II dwarf: $4.4 \cdot 10^{18}$ mi; Leo I dwarf: $4.4 \cdot 10^{18}$ mi; Barnard's Galaxy: $1.0 \cdot 10^{19}$ mi **9. a.** the average depth **b.** average depth: 3.795 km; deepest point: 11.033 km **11.** 5 **13.** 2.4 **15.** 24 **17.** 0 **19.** 1.02 **21.** 11 in. **23.** size $8\frac{1}{2}$ or 9

Spiral Review

27. about 3 m **28.** –1 **29.** 17 **30.** 90 **31.** 6 **32.** 0 **33.** 12 **34.** –13 **35.** 6 **36.** about 80 **37.** about 95

Extra Skill Practice

1. $5.18 \cdot 10^6$ **3.** $2.89 \cdot 10^7$ **5.** $3.629 \cdot 10^{11}$
7. 350,000,000 **9.** 810,000 **11.** 480,000,000,000,000
13. 47,600 **15.** 60,000,000,000 **17.** 132.84 **19.** 1.1
21. 67.07 **23.** 71.97 **25.** 301.5 **27.** 1.33 **29.** 3.20

Standardized Testing, Multiple Choice

1. D **2.** B

Section 6, Practice and Application

1. exclusive **3.** Florence Griffith Joyner, Renate Stecher
5. 14 **7.** 42 students **9.** She is off by about 2%.
11.

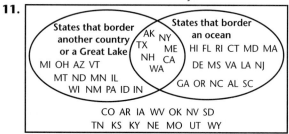

Spiral Review

15. 83 **16.** 0.6 **17.** −53.14 **18. a.**
b. $\frac{1}{6}$ **19.** equilateral and isosceles
20. scalene **21.** isosceles

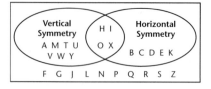

Career Connection

25. OR; AND; NOT

Extra Skill Practice

1. moose, raccoon, skunk, deer **3.** 7 animals **5.** in the
blue part of the oval labeled "Mammals"

Standardized Testing, Performance Task

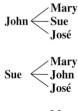

Review and Assessment

1. Sample Response: 0.3; mental math; exact
2. Sample Response: about 126.5; calculator; estimate
3. Sample Response: about −9.8; calculator; estimate
4. Sample Response: $\frac{2}{9}$; mental math; exact **5.** Sample
Response: He is comparing linear dimensions. Since the

radius and the height of the large can are twice those of
the small can, the volume is 8 times greater. **6.** 3 **7.** $\frac{2}{3}$
8. $\frac{1}{3}$ **9.**

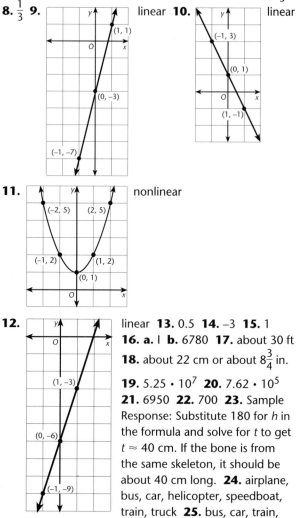

linear **10.** linear

11. nonlinear

12. linear **13.** 0.5 **14.** −3 **15.** 1
16. a. I **b.** 6780 **17.** about 30 ft
18. about 22 cm or about $8\frac{3}{4}$ in.
19. $5.25 \cdot 10^7$ **20.** $7.62 \cdot 10^5$
21. 6950 **22.** 700 **23.** Sample
Response: Substitute 180 for h in
the formula and solve for t to get
$t \approx 40$ cm. If the bone is from
the same skeleton, it should be
about 40 cm long. **24.** airplane,
bus, car, helicopter, speedboat,
train, truck **25.** bus, car, train,
truck **26.** Sample Response: raft (neither), motorcycle
(both)

MODULE 4

Section 1, Practice and Application

1. b. They are the total number of points of the stars at
each step; $t_n = 6t_{n-1}$; 1296; 7776; 46,656; 279,936;
1,679,616 **3.** Sample Response: Divide the previous
term by 2; 11.75, 5.875, 2.9375 **5.** Sample Response:
Divide the previous term by 4; 0.5, 0.125, 0.03125
7. Sample Response: Multiply the previous term by −3;
−567, 1701, −5103 **9. a.** I: Multiply the term number
by 2; $2n$; II: Multiply the term number by 2 and add 1;
$2n + 1$ **b.** Sample Response: They are based on the term
number instead of the previous term **11.** No; $k + m < n$
13. Yes; $x + w > y$ **15.** Yes. **17.** Yes. **19.** Yes.
21. △s 1 and 3, △s 2 and 5, △s 4, 6, and 7; △s 2 and 5;

△s 4 and 6; For similar △s check the shape, for congruent △s use the side-side-side rule. $\triangle GHK \cong \triangle EFD$, $\triangle STV \cong \triangle QPR$

Spiral Review
26. 26 students **27.** 28 students **28.** 3 students
29. about 0.42 **30.** $2.72 **31.** 204 **32.** about $.09

Career Connection
33.

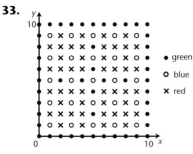

green
blue
red

Extra Skill Practice
1. Sample Response: Add 1 to the previous term. $4 + x$, $5 + x$, $6 + x$ **3.** Sample Response: Divide the previous term by 3. $1\frac{8}{9}, \frac{17}{27}, \frac{17}{81}$ **5.** No. **7.** Yes.

Study Skills, Test-Taking Strategies
1. Sample Response: (1) Choices A and C are not correct because they are not in scientific notation. Choice B is not correct because 16.6 is not between 1 and 10. Choice D is correct because it is in scientific notation. (2) Choices A, C, and D do not make the equation true. **2.** Sample Response: Draw a rectangle. Inside the rectangle draw two intersecting ovals. Put letters with no vertical or horizontal symmetry in the rectangle outside the oval. Put letters with only horizontal symmetry in one oval and letters with only vertical symmetry in the other oval. Put letters with both horizontal and vertical symmetry in the intersection of the ovals.

Section 2, Practice and Application
1. a. 5 black keys **b.** 8 white keys **c.** 13 keys **d.** They are terms 5–7 of the Fibonacci sequence. **3.** 60°, 90°, 120°, 150°, 180°, 210°, 240°, 270°, 300°, 330°
7. a. 2.6 **b.** $0.\overline{81}$ **c.** $0.2\overline{96}$ **d.** 0.35 **9.** $0.\overline{12}$, $0.1\overline{25}$, $0.12\overline{5}$, 0.125; I wrote the repeating forms and compared them. **11. a.** 111112 **b.** $0.\overline{12}$ is a repeating decimal and 0.12112111211112111112… is not. **13.** Sample Response: It is easier to calculate and compare rational numbers.

Spiral Review
15. Yes. **16.** No. **17.** Yes. **18.** $-2\frac{4}{5}$ **19.** $-6\frac{5}{8}$ **20.** $-3\frac{5}{12}$
21. 21 mm

Extension
23. $\frac{2}{9}$

Extra Skill Practice
1. no rotational symmetry **3.** no rotational symmetry **5.** minimum: 180°; none **7.** no rotational symmetry **9.** rational **11.** irrational **13.** rational **15.** irrational
17. $-0.\overline{3}$, $-\frac{3}{10}$, $\frac{1}{3}$, 0.35, $\frac{2}{5}$ **19.** > **21.** =

Standardized Testing, Multiple Choice
1. C **2.** B

Section 3, Practice and Application
1. a. 72 members **b.** $\frac{17}{72}$; $1 - \left(\frac{1}{24} + \frac{5}{9} + \frac{1}{6}\right)$ **3.** 25 **5.** 72
7. 76 **9.** 22 ft **11.** False; A quadrilateral can have two pairs of parallel sides, or no parallel sides.
13. A: parallelogram, rectangle (most precise); B: parallelogram, rhombus (most precise); C: trapezoid; D: quadrilateral; E: quadrilateral; F: parallelogram, rectangle, rhombus, square (most precise); G: trapezoid; H: quadrilateral; I: trapezoid **15. a.** trapezoid, parallelogram, trapezoid **b.** square, trapezoid, rectangle

Spiral Review
18. rational **19.** rational **20.** irrational **21.** rational
22. Yes. **23.** No. **24.** No. **25.** No. **26.** 8.84
27. –59.84 **28.** 12.17 **29.** –20.2

Extension
31. to eliminate fractions; $3x = 50$, $x = 16\frac{2}{3}$

Extra Skill Practice
1. –24 **3.** $\frac{12}{7}$ **5.** 1 **7.** 10 **9.** $\frac{55}{4}$ **11.** quadrilateral, parallelogram **13.** quadrilateral **15.** True; A trapezoid has exactly one pair of parallel sides and a square has two pairs of parallel sides.

Standardized Testing, Open-ended
1. Sample Responses are given. **a.** Kelly saves $\frac{3}{5}$ of every dollar she earns. How much must she earn to put $30 in her savings account? **b.** Moses paid $40 for a full-price CD at $12 and a half-priced boxed set. Find the regular price of the boxed set. **2.** Possible answers are given. **a.** trapezoid, parallelogram, rhombus, rectangle, square **b.** rectangle, square **c.** parallelogram, rhombus, rectangle, square

Section 4, Practice and Application
1. A, C, and D **3.** 5 **5.** $\frac{11}{9}$ **7.** –1.2 **9. a.** Let $k =$ the number of kilometers and $m =$ the number of miles; $k = 1.6m$ **b.** 88 km **c.** 75 mi **11. a.** 100 mi **b.** Let $d =$ distance, $r =$ rate of speed, and $t =$ time; $d = rt$ **c.** about 37 mi/h **13.** 360° **15.** 540° **17.** 120° **19.** 150° **21.** 140° **23. b.** Yes; Yes; Yes, a regular hexagon; Their interior angle measures are factors of 360. **c.** Sample Response: octagons and squares, triangles and squares

Spiral Review

25. 30 **26.** 92 **27.** 32 **28.** 96°; obtuse **29.** 72°; obtuse
30. 62°; acute **31.** 3.57 **32.** 14.92 **33.** 0.89

Extra Skill Practice

1. −124.2 **3.** A and C **5.** −1.1 **7.** $-\frac{5}{4}$ **9.** −15 **11.** 1620°
13. 100°

Standardized Testing, Free Response

1. $-13\frac{5}{16}$ **2. a.** 4 sides **b.** 12 sides **c.** 35 sides

Section 5, Practice and Application

1. right **3.** acute **5.** acute **7.** Yes; The square root
of the sum of the squares of the legs is about 20.81,
which is close to 21. Allowing for measurement errors,
the angle is probably a right angle. **9.** 14.7 mm
11. 8 cm **13.** 12 mm **15.** No; The diagonal is only
about 12.8 ft.

Spiral Review

19. 135° **20.** 125° **21.** 110° **22.** 739.44 cm³
23. $\frac{7}{12}$ **24.** $\frac{4}{11}$

Extra Skill Practice

1. obtuse **3.** acute **5.** obtuse **7.** 8.3 in. **9.** 10 cm
11. No; $3^2 + 3^2 \ne 5^2$

Standardized Testing, Performance Task

1. Possible answers are given. **a.** $6 < x < 7.5$, 7.5,
$7.5 < x < 10.5$ **b.** $5.5 < x < \sqrt{34.25}$, $\sqrt{34.25}$,
$\sqrt{34.25} < x < 7.5$ **2.** 48 ft²

Section 6, Practice and Application

1. $\frac{24}{49} \approx 49\%$ **3.** $\frac{1}{\pi} \approx 31.84\%$ **5.** $\frac{11}{21} \approx 52.4\%$ **7. a.** 0.4
b. 0.5 **c.** 0.3 **9. a.** 0.01 **b.** 0.81 **11. a.** $\frac{1}{9}$ **b.** $\frac{1}{4}$ **c.** $\frac{1}{3}$

Spiral Review

13. acute **14.** obtuse **15.** right
16.

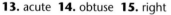
linear

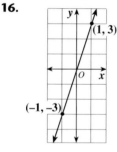

17.
nonlinear

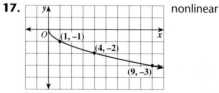

18.

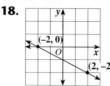
linear
19. about 1884 mm³
20. about 186.04 in.³
21. about 930.19 cm³

Extra Skill Practice

1. 50% **3.** 25% **5.** 50% **7.** 6.25% **9.** 18.75%

Standardized Testing, Multiple Choice

1. C **2.** C

Review and Assessment

1. Sample Response: Multiply the previous term by $\frac{1}{y}$;
$\frac{1}{y^5}, \frac{1}{y^6}, \frac{1}{y^7}$ **2.** Sample Response: Add 9 to the previous
term; 37, 46, 55 **3.** Sample Response: Multiply the
previous term by 10; 100,000, 1,000,000, 10,000,000
4. Sample Response: Divide the previous term by 2;
0.0625, 0.03125, 0.015625 **5.** Yes. **6.** No. **7.** Yes.
9. 60°, 120°, 180°, 240°, 300°, 360°; 60° **10.** irrational
11. rational **12.** rational **13.** rational **14.** $-\frac{3}{4}, -\frac{8}{11}$,
$-0.72, -0.7, \frac{5}{7}, 0.72, 0.7\overline{2}, 0.\overline{72}, \frac{3}{4}$ **15.** 15 **16.** 12
17. 24 **18.** parallelogram or rhombus **19.** $0.88\overline{3}$
20. 3.25 **21.** $-\frac{1}{8}$ **22.** Possible answers: Measure all the
angles with a protractor and add; Divide the polygon
into $n − 2$ triangles and multiply the number of triangles
by 180°. **23.** Yes. $7.5^2 + 4^2 = 8.5^2$, so both triangles
are right triangles and the garden is a rectangle.
24. 13 mm **25.** 6 ft **26.** $\sqrt{2} \approx 1.4$ in. **27.** 50%
28. 25% **29.** 25%

MODULE 5

Section 1, Practice and Application

1. 113.04 cm² **3.** 452.16 in.² **5.** about 103.56 m²
7. about 30 in.² **9. a.** about 1282 frames **b.** about
15,384 light detectors **11.** about 0.84 **13.** water
chestnuts, olives, chili peppers

Spiral Review

20. 50% **21.** about 20 **22.** about 700 **23.** about 528
24.

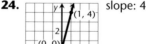
slope: 4

25.
slope: 2

26. 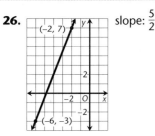 slope: $\frac{5}{2}$

Extra Skill Practice
1. 251.2 in.² **3.** 3523.08 cm² **5.** about 90.43 m²
7. 2.3 **9.** 1.73 **11.** 1.5 **13.** The cylinder with a radius of 2.5 in. and a height of 3 in.; The ratio of surface area to volume is lowest.

Study Skills, Comparing and Contrasting
1. Sample Response: The two formulas are alike in that they both use π, r, and h. They are different in that the formula for surface area ($2\pi r^2 + 2\pi rh$) uses both multiplication and addition and has an answer in square units, while the formula for volume ($\pi r^2 h$) uses only multiplication and has an answer in cubic units.

2. 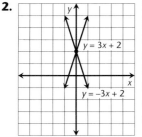 Sample Response: the lines both intersect the y-axis at 2 and have the same steepness. The first equation has $3x$ and slopes up to the right, but the second equation has $-3x$ and slopes down to the right.

Section 2, Practice and Application
1. $-\frac{3}{5}$ **3.** $\frac{1}{3}$ **5.** 0 **7.** $-\frac{9}{7}$

9.

Kemp's Ridley Turtle Nests (1970–1995)	
Time period	Rate of change (number of turtle nests/year)
1970–1975	–350
1975–1980	–75
1980–1985	–50
1985–1990	65
1990–1995	200

13. $y = 2x$ **15.** $y = -5x + 7$ **17.** $y = -\frac{3}{4}x + \frac{5}{4}$ **19.** It got worse; The line shows a decrease in pH which means that the acidity of the rain increased. **21.** about 4.58; I assumed the trend would continue, so I solved the equation for $x = 170$.

23. a. 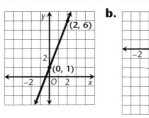 **b.**

c. **25.** slope: 0

27. slope: undefined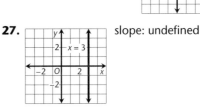

Spiral Review
30. 351.68 in.² **31.** 55% **32.** 4.5 **33.** $7 \cdot 10^2$
34. $2.593 \cdot 10^3$ **35.** $1.01 \cdot 10^5$

Extra Skill Practice
1. 3 **3.** $-\frac{1}{3}$ **5.** 0 **7.** line B **9.** line A **11.** $y = 2x - 3$
13. $y = 1$ **15.** $y = -x + 5$

Standardized Testing, Open-ended
1–4. Sample responses are given. **1.** $y = -5x + 4$
2. $y = 3x - 2$ **3.** $y = 2$ **4.** $y = -3x + 7$

Section 3, Practice and Application
1. 10^6 **3.** 2^9 **5.** 3^{10} **7.** a^4 **9.** b^8 **11.** w^{80}
13. a. $E = 0.002888s^4$ **b.** Yes; in the equation, s is raised to the fourth power. **c.** 462.08 ft-lb; 7393.28 ft-lb; It is 16 times the wave energy. **15.** 10^2
17. 2^4 **19.** 7^9 **21.** a^3 **23.** c^6 **25.** u^{43} **29.** 1.16 lb; I substituted 0 for t in the equation. **31.** $\frac{1}{9}$ **33.** $\frac{1}{5}$ **35.** $\frac{1}{b^6}$
37. $\frac{4}{w^2}$ **39.** 0.9 **41.** 0.00018 **43.** 0.00000265
45. $s < 2 \cdot 10^{-3}$; $2 \cdot 10^{-3} \le s \le 6.4 \cdot 10^{-2}$; $6.4 \cdot 10^{-2} \le s \le 2.56 \cdot 10^{-1}$; $s > 2.56 \cdot 10^{-1}$
47. $3 \cdot 10^{-1}$ **49.** $2.5 \cdot 10^{-4}$ **51.** $6 \cdot 10^{-9}$
53. a. about $3 \cdot 10^{-8}$ **b.** The probability is about 2.5 times greater that you will win the lottery than that you will get 25 heads in 25 flips.

Spiral Review
55. slope: –2; y-intercept: 9 **56.** between 7 and 8
57. 12 **58.** 65 **59.** 510

Career Connection
61. $1.56 \cdot 10^{-3}$ s

Extension

63. 2^2 **65.** a^{-4} **67.** 3^{-2} **69.** b^{-5}

Extra Skill Practice

1. 6^7 **3.** 11^{34} **5.** b^{12} **7.** k^{81} **9.** 10^{10} **11.** 8^2 **13.** p^3
15. m^4 **17.** 1 **19.** $\frac{1}{121}$ **21.** $\frac{1}{13}$ **23.** $\frac{1}{p^8}$ **25.** $\frac{3}{r^7}$
27. 0.008 **29.** 0.000000614 **31.** $6 \cdot 10^{-2}$
33. $1.013 \cdot 10^{-6}$

Standardized Testing, Multiple Choice

1. A **2.** C **3.** D **4.** D

Section 4, Practice and Application

1. 27° **3.** 42° **5.** 78° **7.** 54° **9.** ∠CED **11.** ∠DCE
13. 120° **15.** 90° **17.** 135° **19.** 60° **21.** $x + 35 = 180$;
$x = 145$ **23.** 1 **25.** about 0.53 **27.** 173.2 yd
29. 37.7 cm

Spiral Review

32. 3^{13}; a^7 **33.** Multiply the previous term by 2; 88,
176, 352 **34.** Add $x + 1$ to the previous term; $4x + 5$,
$5x + 6$, $6x + 7$
35.

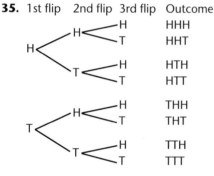

1st flip	2nd flip	3rd flip	Outcome

Extension

37. Sample Response: $\tan A = \frac{\text{opposite}}{\text{adjacent}}, \frac{\sin A}{\cos A} =$

$\frac{\text{opposite}}{\text{hypotenuse}} \div \frac{\text{adjacent}}{\text{hypotenuse}} = \frac{\text{opposite}}{\cancel{\text{hypotenuse}}} \cdot \frac{\cancel{\text{hypotenuse}}}{\text{adjacent}} = \frac{\text{opposite}}{\text{adjacent}}$

Extra Skill Practice

1. 58° **3.** 37° **5.** 82° **7.** 32° **9.** 78° **11.** 28° **13.** 168°
15. 71° **17.** 1.80 **19.** 2.75 **21.** 12.60 in.

Standardized Testing, Multiple Choice

1. B **2.** B

Section 5, Practice and Application

1. a.

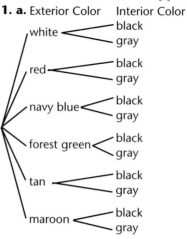

Exterior Color	Interior Color	Combination
white	black	white, black
	gray	white, gray
red	black	red, black
	gray	red, gray
navy blue	black	navy blue, black
	gray	navy blue, gray
forest green	black	forest green, black
	gray	forest green, gray
tan	black	tan, black
	gray	tan, gray
maroon	black	maroon, black
	gray	maroon, gray

b. 12 ways

3. a.

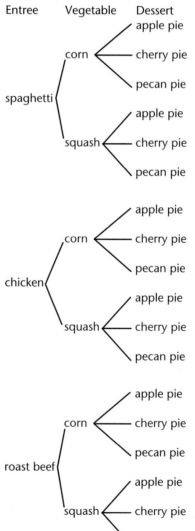

Entree	Vegetable	Dessert	Combination
spaghetti	corn	apple pie	spaghetti, corn, apple pie
		cherry pie	spaghetti, corn, cherry pie
		pecan pie	spaghetti, corn, pecan pie
	squash	apple pie	spaghetti, squash, apple pie
		cherry pie	spaghetti, squash, cherry pie
		pecan pie	spaghetti, squash, pecan pie
chicken	corn	apple pie	chicken, corn, apple pie
		cherry pie	chicken, corn, cherry pie
		pecan pie	chicken, corn, pecan pie
	squash	apple pie	chicken, squash, apple pie
		cherry pie	chicken, squash, cherry pie
		pecan pie	chicken, squash, pecan pie
roast beef	corn	apple pie	roast beef, corn, apple pie
		cherry pie	roast beef, corn, cherry pie
		pecan pie	roast beef, corn, pecan pie
	squash	apple pie	roast beef, squash, apple pie
		cherry pie	roast beef, squash, cherry pie
		pecan pie	roast beef, squash, pecan pie

b. 18 dinners

5. 2 **7.** 24 **9.** 5040 **11.** 40,320 orders
13. 6 combinations **15. a.** 5 **b.** 10 **c.** 10 **d.** 16

Spiral Review
20. 72° **21.** 36° **22.** 9° **23.** 720° **24.** 540° **25.** $\frac{1}{2}$
26. $\frac{2}{3}$

Extension
29. 70 ways

Extra Skill Practice
1. 144 ways **3.** 30 ways **5.** 24 ways **7.** 1024 ways
9. 40,320 ways

Standardized Testing, Performance Task
1. 3 ways; combination; The order in which she selects her sketches is not important. **2.** 6 ways; permutation; The order in which she hangs her sketches is important.

Section 6, Practice and Application
1. HHH, HHT, HTH, HTT, THH, THT, TTH, TTT
3. $\frac{7}{8}$ = 0.875 **5. a.** 80,318,101,760, or about
$8 \cdot 10^{10}$ license plates **b.** MATH4YOU: about
$\frac{1}{8 \cdot 10^{10}}$; MATH as first four letters: about
$\frac{1 \cdot 1 \cdot 1 \cdot 1 \cdot 10 \cdot 26^3}{8 \cdot 10^{10}}$; the latter is 175,760 times more
likely. **7. a.** $\frac{511}{512}$ = 0.998

Spiral Review
11. 6 combinations
12. Possible answers:

Stem	Leaves
4	1, 8
5	2, 3, 9
6	1, 4, 6, 8
7	0, 2, 5, 5, 7, 8
8	1, 1, 1, 5, 6, 7
9	3, 4, 6, 8, 9

Science Test Scores

40 45 50 55 60 65 70 75 80 85 90 95 100

13. surface area: 294 cm²; volume: 343 cm³

Extra Skill Practice
1. $\frac{1}{100}$ = 0.01 **3.** $\frac{64}{125}$ = 0.512 **5.** $\frac{999}{1000}$ = 0.999
7. $\frac{1}{7776}$ ≈ 0.00013 **9.** $\frac{5}{54}$ ≈ 0.093 **11.** $\frac{3125}{7776}$ ≈ 0.40

Standardized Testing, Free Response
1. $\frac{1}{16}$ = 0.0625 **2. a.** $\frac{1}{1296}$ ≈ 0.00077 **b.** $\frac{625}{1296}$ ≈ 0.48

Review and Assessment
1. 131.88 cm² **2.** 100.48 in.² **3.** 127.17 ft² **4.** 0.8$\overline{3}$
5. 0.7 **6.** 0.8 **7.** r = 4 cm, h = 10 cm; r = 5 cm,
h = 5 cm; r = 3 cm, h = 12 cm; The cans are ranked from

lowest to highest value of $\frac{S.A.}{V}$. **8.** slope: $-\frac{1}{4}$;
y-intercept: 2; $y = -\frac{1}{4}x + 2$ **9.** slope: 3; y-intercept: −1;
$y = 3x - 1$ **10.** slope: 0; y-intercept: −2; $y = -2$ **11.** 10^{11}
12. a^9 **13.** 2^7 **14.** b^4 **15.** 1 **16.** $\frac{1}{121}$ **17.** $\frac{1}{27}$ **18.** $\frac{1}{64}$
19. 0.05 **20.** 0.000803 **21.** 0.0000001266
22. $2.4 \cdot 10^{-3}$ **23.** $7.52 \cdot 10^{-5}$ **24.** $3.061 \cdot 10^{-7}$
25. ∠QTR **26.** ∠SQT **27.** 130° **28.** 6.49 mm
29. 20.26 in. **30.** 10.25 yd **31. a.** 6 uniforms
b. 120 ways **c.** Armand and Cathy, Armand and Ishana, Armand and Jim, Armand and Susan, Cathy and Ishana, Cathy and Jim, Cathy and Susan, Ishana and Jim, Ishana and Susan, Jim and Susan **32. a.** 10,000 numbers
b. $\frac{9}{100}$ = 0.09

MODULE 6

Section 1, Practice and Application

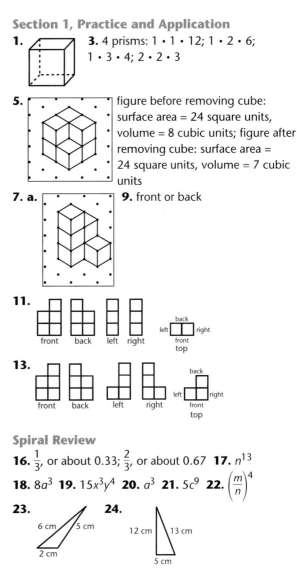

1.

3. 4 prisms: 1 · 1 · 12; 1 · 2 · 6;
1 · 3 · 4; 2 · 2 · 3

5. figure before removing cube: surface area = 24 square units, volume = 8 cubic units; figure after removing cube: surface area = 24 square units, volume = 7 cubic units

7. a. **9.** front or back

11.

front back left right
left [back / front / top] right

13.

front back left right
left [back / front / top] right

Spiral Review
16. $\frac{1}{3}$, or about 0.33; $\frac{2}{3}$, or about 0.67 **17.** n^{13}
18. $8a^3$ **19.** $15x^3y^4$ **20.** a^3 **21.** $5c^9$ **22.** $\left(\frac{m}{n}\right)^4$

23. **24.**

6 cm 5 cm
2 cm

12 cm 13 cm
5 cm

Extra Skill Practice

1. Sample Response: **3.**

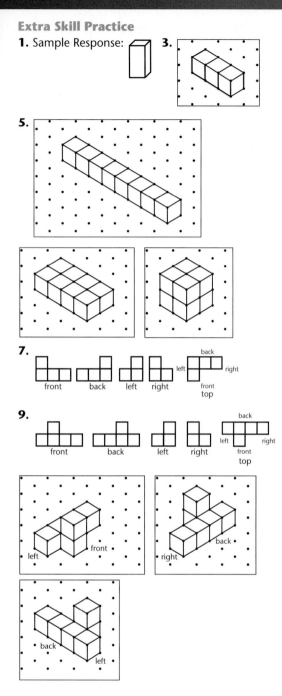

5.

7.

9.

Section 2, Practice and Application

1. 8 faces, 18 edges, and 12 vertices **5. b.** a trapezoid
c. a triangle **7.** Sample Response:

9. B **11.** A **13.** congruent: Two sides and the included
angle of △ABC are congruent to two sides and the
included angle of △DEF. **15.** not congruent; The
corresponding sides are not congruent.

Spiral Review

17.

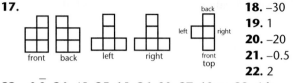

18. −30
19. 1
20. −20
21. −0.5
22. 2

23. −0.$\overline{3}$ **24.** 45 **25.** 15 **26.** 30 **27.** 13 m **28.** 6 ft

Extension

29. 9, 9, 16; 4, 4, 6; cube, 6, 8, 12; square pyramid, 5,
5, 8; hexagonal prism, 8, 12, 18 **31.** 15 edges

Extra Skill Practice

1.   10 faces, 24 edges,
                                             16 vertices

3. a. 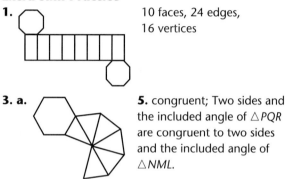   **5.** congruent; Two sides and
the included angle of △PQR
are congruent to two sides
and the included angle of
△NML.

Standardized Testing, Performance Task

6, 9, 5; 8, 12, 6; 10, 15, 7; 200, 300, 102; Sample
Response: The number of faces is twice the number of
sides on the base, the number of edges is 3 times the
number of sides on the base, and the number of vertices
is 2 more than the number of sides on the base.

Section 3, Practice and Application

1. 54.0 m² **3.** 1249.2 in² **5.** 175.0 cm² **9.** 4 in³
11. 4.7 m³ **13.** 3014.4 mm³ **15. a.** a cylinder and a
cone **b.** 339.9 ft³ **17.** surface area = 240 in.²,
volume = 264 in.³

Spiral Review

22. not congruent; Corresponding sides $\overline{PR}$ and $\overline{DF}$ are
not congruent. **23.** congruent; Two sides and the
included angle of △WZX are congruent to two sides
and the included angle of △YZX. **24.** y = 3x + 2
25. y = −4x + 5 **26.** 168° **27.** 90° **28.** 64° **29.** 27°

Extension

31. a. s; Each section is a sector of a circle with radius s.
b. πr; Each base has length one half the circumference
of the partial circle. **c.** A = πrs

Extra Skill Practice

1. 520 m² **3.** 75 cm² **5.** 0.75 ft³
7. surface area ≈ 730.4 ft², volume = 1342.7 ft³

Standardized Testing, Open-ended

1. Sample Response:

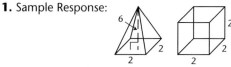

2. Sample responses are given.

a. **b.**

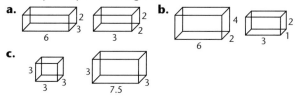

c.

Section 4, Practice and Application

1. $\angle 8$ **3.** $\angle 7$ **5.** $30°$ **7.** $30°$ **9.** $m\angle 1 = m\angle 3 = m\angle 5 = 110°$, $m\angle 2 = m\angle 4 = m\angle 6 = 70°$ **11.** $180°$

Spiral Review

17. 301.4 m^3 **18.** 8.4 ft^3 **19.** 192 in.^3

20.

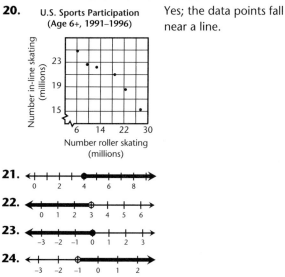

U.S. Sports Participation (Age 6+, 1991–1996)

Yes; the data points fall near a line.

21.
22.
23.
24.

Career Connection

25. a. They are parallel; The alternate interior angles formed by the transversal $\overline{CB}$ are congruent. **b.** $60°$

Extra Skill Practice

1. Line k **3.** $\angle 1$ and $\angle 3$, $\angle 2$ and $\angle 4$, $\angle 5$ and $\angle 7$, $\angle 6$ and $\angle 8$ **5.** $\angle 1$ and $\angle 5$, $\angle 4$ and $\angle 8$ **7.** $50°$ **9.** $50°$

Standardized Testing, Multiple Choice

1. C **2.** B

Section 5, Practice and Application

1. Yes; The statement $-8 + 6 < 2$ is true.

3. $w \geq 2$

5. $x \leq 5$

7. $z < 13$

9. $q \geq 10.5$ **11.** $n + 7 < 7$; $n < 0$

13. $1.75s \geq 95$; $s \geq 54.3$; at least 54.3 mi/h

15. a. up to 40 in. **b.** 4 in. **c.** 86.4 in.; The rows would have to be so far apart that they would lose too much seating if they used a sloped floor. **d.** More rows are possible with a stepped floor because of a higher rise and shorter row depth, but a sloped floor may be safer, since people may be less likely to trip in low light.

17. $24 - 0.5n \geq 132$; $n \leq -216$ **19.** $12.50h + 25 < 90$; $h < 5.2$; less than 5.2 h

21. $z \leq -10.25$

23. $a < 3$

25. $m > \frac{1}{9}$

27. $y \leq -25$

Spiral Review

30. $105°$ **31.** $105°$ **32.** $105°$ **33.** 60 **34.** 13.5 **35.** 2.25

Extra Skill Practice

1. $x \leq -2$

3. $a > 0.125$

5. $a \geq 6$

7. $u > -40$

9. $m \leq 45$

11. $n > -27$

13. $x < -3$

15. $y < -10$ **17.** $n + 5 > 2$; $n > -3$

19. $3c + 0.98 \geq 10$; $c \geq 3.006$; \$3.01 **21.** $x \leq \frac{11}{3}$ **23.** $c < -\frac{4}{7}$ **25.** $a \leq -0.5$ **27.** $x \leq 5$ **29.** $z < 2.5$ **31.** $y \leq -18$ **33.** $a > -2$ **35.** $x \leq -\frac{1}{4}$

Standardized Testing, Free Response

1. less than 90 in. **2.** 17 or fewer prints

Section 6, Practice and Application

9. 16 in.; 16 in.^{2} **11.** 12 in.; 9 in.^{2} **13.** 58.3 mm^2 **15.** 2338.3 yd^2 **19.** about 11.5 mi **21.** 0.324 in.^{2}

Spiral Review

23. $x \le 4$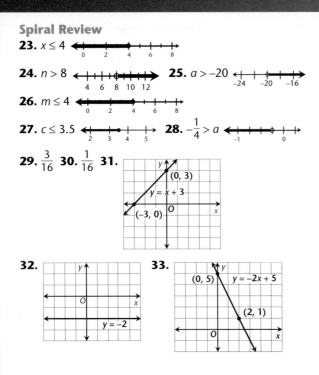

24. $n > 8$

25. $a > -20$

26. $m \le 4$

27. $c \le 3.5$ **28.** $-\frac{1}{4} > a$

29. $\frac{3}{16}$ **30.** $\frac{1}{16}$ **31.**

32.   **33.**

Extra Skill Practice

1. Answers must be equivalent to $\frac{4 \text{ in.}}{6 \text{ ft}}$ or $\frac{1 \text{ in.}}{1.5 \text{ ft}}$.

3. Sample Response: Scale: $\frac{1}{4}$ in. = 12 ft

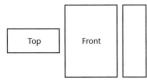

| Top | Front | |

5. 15 in.   **7.** 6480 in.^{2}

Standardized Testing, Multiple Choice

1. C   **2.** A

Review and Assessment

1. surface area = 26 cm^2; volume = 6 cm^3
2. surface area = 18 cm^2; volume = 4 cm^3
3.

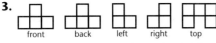

front   back   left   right   top

4. right-back   **5.** front-right   **6.** back-left   **7.** left-front

8. 9 faces, 16 edges, 9 vertices
9. congruent; Two sides and the included angle of $\triangle ABE$ are congruent to two sides and the included angle of $\triangle CBD$.   **10.** not congruent; Two sides of $\triangle PQS$ are congruent to two sides of $\triangle RQS$, but the included angles are not congruent.   **11.** 7.9 cm^3
12. surface area = 1440 in.^{2}, volume = 3200 in.^{3}
13. surface area = 700 m^2, volume = 1200 m^3
14. surface area = 114 cm^2, volume = 84 cm^3
15. $\angle 7$; 105°   **16.** $\angle 8$; 75°   **17.** $\angle 4$; 75°

18. Sample Response: 105°; $\angle 3$ and $\angle 5$ are vertical angles so $m\angle 5 = m\angle 3 = 105°$.   **19.** $a \le 5$

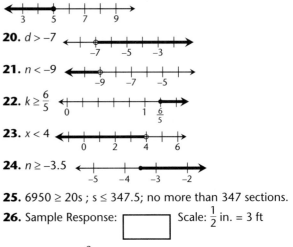

20. $d > -7$

21. $n < -9$

22. $k \ge \frac{6}{5}$

23. $x < 4$

24. $n \ge -3.5$

25. $6950 \ge 20s$; $s \le 347.5$; no more than 347 sections.

26. Sample Response: ☐   Scale: $\frac{1}{2}$ in. = 3 ft

27. area: 48 km^2; perimeter: 28 km

MODULE 7

Section 1, Practice and Application

1. B   **3.** D   **5.** first graph matches second table, second graph matches second description, third graph matches first table, fourth graph matches first description, fifth graph matches third description.   **15.** function
17. not a function   **19.** function   **21.** $y = \frac{x}{5}$ **23.** $y = \frac{x^2}{2}$
25. a. $y = 0.4x + 2.1$ **b.** (0, 2.1), (1, 2.5), (2, 2.9), (3, 3.3), (4, 3.7), (5, 4.1), (6, 4.5); The values of x range from 0 to 6 since of the river rose at a rate of 0.4 in./day for 6 days. The values of y will be between 2 and 5 since it started at about 2 in.

c.   **d.** y is a function of x.

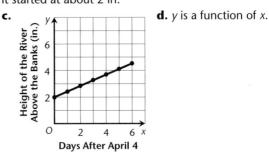

Height of the River Above the Banks (in.)

Days After April 4

Spiral Review

27. Perimeter is 68 cm and area is 240 cm^2.
28. about 6.5 m

29.   **30.**

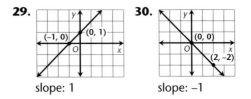

slope: 1   slope: −1

31.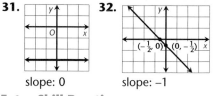

slope: 0

32. slope: −1

Extra Skill Practice

1. B **3.** D **5.** function **7.** function **9.** function

Study Skills, Managing Your Time

1. Sample Response: Set specific goals in the beginning and specify the time in which they need to be completed, appoint a group leader to make sure your project is on schedule.

Section 2, Practice and Application

1. Bruce has $90 in his savings account and he deposits $75 each week without withdrawing any money.
3. (6, −2) **5.** (6, 26) **7.** $A(1.4, 0)$: The dolphin was at the surface (0 ft above the surface) after 1.4 s; $B(2, 5)$: The dolphin was 5 ft above the surface after 2 s; $C(2.5, 0)$: The dolphin was at the surface after 2.5 s.
9.
$$5000 - 150x = 0$$
$$5000 - 150x + 150x = 0 + 150x$$
$$5000 = 150x$$
$$33\frac{1}{3} = x; \text{ 34 months}$$
$$y = 200 + 150(34)$$
$$y = 200 + 5100$$
$$y = 5300; \$5300$$
11. $3(1 + 8p)$ **13.** $5 - 5w$ **15.** Possible answers: $2(6 - 2t)$ or $4(3 - t)$ **17. a.** Let c = the cost in dollars and n = the number of times you park; $c = 3n + 50$, $c = 8n$
19. 6 **21.** $\frac{9}{2}$ **23.** $-\frac{30}{11}$ **25.** 15 **27.** 3 m **29.** 3 cm

Spiral Review

32. C; The graph shows the height of the flag increasing in stages with several pulls of a rope followed by brief rest periods. **33.** Sample Response: Multiply by 7.
34. Sample Response: Multiply by $\frac{1}{2}$ **35.** Sample Response: Divide by 100. **36.** Sample Response: Multiply by 5. **37.** 5.2^4 **38.** 3^8 **39.** 16^5 **40.** $\left(\frac{3}{5}\right)^6$

Extra Skill Practice

1. **3.**

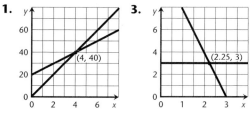

5. 7 **7.** 5 **9.** −7 **11.** 3 **13.** $-3\frac{1}{4}$ **15.** $-6 - 9x$
17. Possible answers: $2(6x + 3)$, $3(4x + 2)$, $6(2x + 1)$
19. $2(7 - 4x)$ **21.** $2x^3 - 6x$ **23.** $x(x + 4)$
25. Possible answers: $3x(4x^2 - 1)$, $3(4x^3 - x)$, $x(12x^2 - 3)$

27. $-\frac{3}{4}$ **29.** 2 **31.** $-\frac{1}{3}$ **33.** 8

Standardized Testing, Open-ended

2. Possible answers: $2x(12x + 4)$, $4x(6x + 2)$, $8x(3x + 1)$, $x(24x + 8)$, $2(12x^2 + 4x)$, $4(6x^2 + 2x)$, $8(3x^2 + x)$
3. Sample Response: $5(2x - 1) = 75; x = 8$

Section 3, Practice and Application

1. A: $y = \left(\frac{1}{3}\right)^x$; B: $y = 3^x$; As x increases, $\left(\frac{1}{3}\right)^x$ decreases and 3^x increases. **3. a.** 2, 4, 7; 3, 8, 15; 4, 16, 31; 5, 32, 63; 6, 64, 127; 7, 128, 255; 8, 256, 511; 9, 512, 1023; 10, 1024, 2047 **b.** $y = 2^{60}$ **c.** Sample Response: It shows exponential growth with powers of 2.
d.

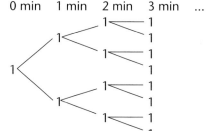

7. a. $y = 1200 \cdot (1.04)^x$ where y represents the enrollment and x represents the number of years.
b. $y = 5 \cdot (1.1)^x$ where y represents Maria's distance and x represents the number of weeks. **9.** Yes; For every value of x there is only one value of y. **11.** 0.25
13. 16 **15.** about 0.06

Spiral Review

18. 10 **19.** $-\frac{1}{2}$ **20.** $\left(7, -\frac{1}{2}\right)$

Career Connection

21. a. 128 bacteria; 524,288 bacteria; Possible answers: Write an equation, complete a table, or sketch a graph.
b. Sample Response: It shows how quickly the bacteria grow and, so, how rapidly the infection worsens.

Extension

23. The decay factor is the rate of depreciation subtracted from 100% with the result written as a decimal.

Extra Skill Practice

1. $y = 150 \cdot (1.08)^x$ where y represents the value of the baseball card and x represents the number of years.
3. $y = 2000 \cdot (1.1)^x$ where y represents the number of loaves of bread and x represents the number of days.
5. 46,875 **7.** 8748 **9.** $\frac{8}{27} \approx 0.3$ **11.** $y = 200 \cdot (1.03)^{10}$, $268.78 **13.** $y = 1500 \cdot (1.04)^8$, $2052.85

Standardized Testing, Performance Task

1. No. Each day the new price, not the original price, is reduced 20% so on the fifth day the price will be about 67% off the original price. **2.** Bank B; He will make $17.52 more than at Bank A.

Section 4, Practice and Application

1. Sample Response: $(x', y') = (x, y + 5)$; $(x'', y'') = (x', y' - 5)$

3.

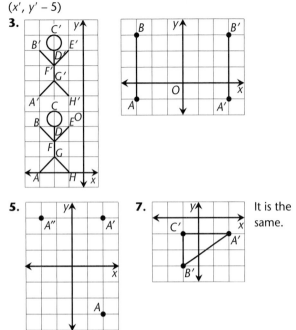

5.

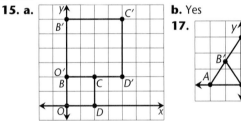

7.

It is the same.

11. Sample Response: $(x', y') = (x, -y)$; $(x'', y'') = (-x', y')$; $(x''', y''') = (x'', y'' + 2)$ **13.** No; Sample Response: $\triangle DE'F'$ is on the same side of the y-axis as $\triangle DEF$ and is not the image of $\triangle DEF$ reflected across the x-axis.

15. a.

b. Yes

17.

Spiral Review

21. 27 **22.** $\frac{1}{32} = 0.03125$ **23.** 64 **24.** $m\angle 1 = m\angle 4 = 95°$, $m\angle 2 = m\angle 3 = 85°$ **25.** −12 **26.** 0.01 **27.** $\frac{1}{9}$

28. $-\frac{7}{15}$

Extra Skill Practice

1. $(x', y') = (x + 3, y - 3)$ **3.** $(x', y') = (x + 2, y + 2)$, $(x'', y'') = (x' + 2, y' - 2)$
5. Sample Response: Plot the point with the same x-coordinate and the opposite y-coordinate.

7.

Standardized Testing, Multiple Choice
1. C **2.** C

Section 5, Practice and Application

1. B **3.** D **5. a.**

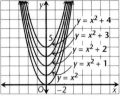

b. It will have the same shape and line of symmetry as the graphs in part (a), but its vertex will be (0, 5).
c. They will have the same shape and line of symmetry. Their vertices will be (0, −1) and (0, −2).

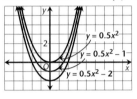

7. Sample responses are given. **a.** about 500 ft; about 527 ft **b.** about 727 ft **c.** If the cables were tight lines, the length would be about 4330 ft (by the Pythagorean theorem). **9.** $y = 4x + 13$; not a quadratic function **11.** $y = -14$; not a quadratic function **13.** $y = 36x^2 - 4x$; quadratic function **15.** $y = x^2 + 7x - 2$; quadratic function

Spiral Review
19.

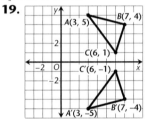

20. 74° **21.** 12° **22.** 59° **23.** 2° **24.** taxpayers; parents **25.** No; Taxpayers who are not parents are not represented.

Extension
27. a. (2, −7)

b. (1, 2)

c. (−3, 0)

Extra Skill Practice
1. same vertex and axis of symmetry, narrower

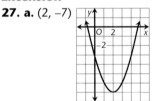

3. same shape and axis of symmetry, vertex (0, 1) instead of (0, 0)

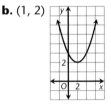

5. same axis of symmetry, narrower, vertex at (0, –2) instead of (0, 0), opens in opposite direction

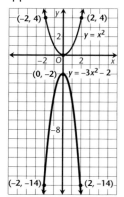

7. The vertex is at (2, –2) and the line of symmetry is a vertical line through the point (2, –2). **9.** $y = x^2 + 7x$; quadratic function **11.** $y = -x^2 - 5x + 10$; quadratic function **13.** $y = 6$; not a quadratic function **15.** $y = 2x^3 - 5x^2 - 7$; not a quadratic function

Standardized Testing, Free Response
1. Sample Response: All the graphs are parabolas that open up and have the same line of symmetry (the y-axis); the graphs of $y = x^2$, $y = \frac{1}{4}x^2$ and $y = 2x^2$ all have vertex (0, 0) but the graph of $y = x^2 + 4$ has vertex (0, 4). **2. a.** not a quadratic function **b.** quadratic function **c.** quadratic function **d.** not a quadratic function

Review and Assessment
1. B; The hours increase gradually to a maximum and then decrease gradually to a minimum. **2.** C; Height increases at varying rates. **3.** A; The length of the grass in the summer increases then sharply decreases each time it is cut and then begins to grow again.
4. Yes. **5.** No. **6.** Yes. **7.** Yes. **8.** Yes. **9.** No.
10. $y = 20{,}000 - 500x$; $15,000; Possible methods:

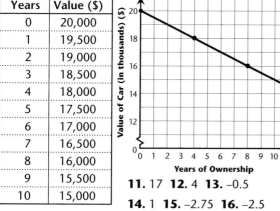

Years	Value ($)
0	20,000
1	19,500
2	19,000
3	18,500
4	18,000
5	17,500
6	17,000
7	16,500
8	16,000
9	15,500
10	15,000

11. 17 **12.** 4 **13.** –0.5
14. 1 **15.** –2.75 **16.** –2.5
17. at 25 seconds **18.** 10,000 **19.** $\frac{9}{16}$ **20.** 96 **21.** $\frac{1}{25}$
22. $y = 100 \cdot (1.05)^x$; $338.64
23. $(x', y') = (-x, y)$; $(x'', y'') = (x', y' + 3)$

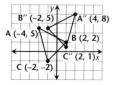

24.

25.

26.

27. a.

b. about 3.1 seconds
c. (1.5, 12.5) **28.** $y = -x^2 + 5$; quadratic function **29.** $y = 2x^2 + x - 13$; quadratic function **30.** $y = x^2 - 9x - 4$; quadratic function **31.** $y = 5x^2 - 6x - 9$; quadratic function

MODULE 8

Section 1, Practice and Application
1. a. 8743 heads, 9207 tails **b.** about 0.487, about 0.513 **3.** no correlation **5.** negative correlation **7.** positive correlation **9.** negative correlation **11.** biased; Who do you think will make a better governor–Smith or Jones? **13.** biased; Should teachers use filmstrips and movies? **17.** Sample Response: Over a period of several hours, observe the color of cars going through a busy intersection; current trends in colors

Spiral Review
20. $y = 4x^2 - 12x + 7$; quadratic **21.** $y = 14x$; not quadratic **22.** 120π in.^{2}, or about 377 in.^{2} **23.** 72

Extension
25. random; Each person has an equally likely chance of being chosen and represented.

Extra Skill Practice
1. no correlation **3.** biased; Do you think a grocery store should be opened? **5.** not biased **7.** Sample Response: Question each member of the cast.

Study Skills, Synthesizing
1. Sample Response: the distributive property; addition, subtraction, mulitplication, and division of integers; solving equations with two operations

Section 2, Practice and Application
1. 10%; The circle graph represents 100% and 100% – (60% + 30%) = 10%. **3.** 1200 Cal

5. The sizes of the sectors do not correspond to the percents they represent.

Favorite Subject

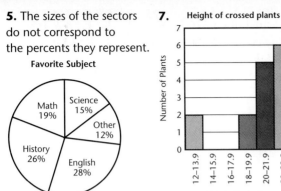

7. Height of crossed plants

9. Sample Response: More crossed plants than self-fertilized plants reach a height of 18 in. or greater.

11.

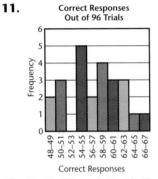

Correct Responses Out of 96 Trials

13. a. Use the intervals 40–49, 50–59, and 60–69. To find the frequency within each interval, add the frequencies of the intervals from Exercise 11 that fall within the range of the new intervals. **b.** Use the intervals 40–49, 50–59, and 60–69. To find the frequency within each interval, add the frequencies of the intervals from Exercise 12 that fall within the range of the new intervals.

Spiral Review

16. Sample Response: negative correlation; As the price of apples decreases, the number of apples the average shopper buys tends to increase. **17.** $\frac{1}{x}$ **18.** $\frac{1}{c^5}$ **19.** 1

20. $\frac{3}{y^4}$ **21.**

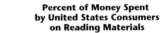

Extra Skill Practice

1. 20%; The circle graph represents 100% and 100% − (30% + 50%) = 20% **3.** 108°

5. Phoenix, AZ, Temperatures

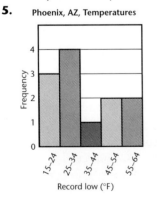

7. Use the intervals 15–34, 35–54, and 55–74. To find the frequency within each interval, add the frequencies of the intervals from Exercise 5 that fall within the range of the new intervals.

Standardized Testing, Multiple Choice
1. C **2.** B

Section 3, Practice and Application

1. a histogram; It shows the frequencies within intervals. **3.** a scatter plot; It shows the relationship between 2 sets of data. **11.** Sample responses are given.

a. Percent of Money Spent by United States Consumers on Reading Materials

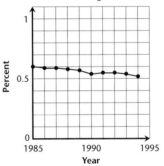

b. Percent of Money Spent by United States Consumers on Reading Materials

c. By starting the vertical scale with a number other than 0, the relative values of the bars can be misrepresented.

Percent of Money Spent by United States Consumers on Reading Materials

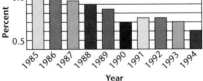

13. a. No; The dots are too small to be counted. **b.** No; Sample Response: If, for example, a scale of 0.1 cm = 1 in. were used, the smallest pieces would be 0.2 cm long and the largest would be 120 cm long. **c.** to help the reader visualize how dense the mass of space junk is **15. a.** Alaska: 1 person/mi², New Jersey: 1025 persons/mi²; Sample Response: Cut out a piece of newspaper that contains approximately 1025 characters to represent New Jersey. Use the same size paper with 1 character written on it to represent Alaska. **b.** Alaska: 1 mi²/person, New Jersey: 0.001 mi²/person. Let the floor area of the classroom represent the square miles per person in Alaska. Mark off an area $\frac{1}{1000}$ that size in the classroom to represent the square miles per person in New Jersey.

Spiral Review
17. 21% **18.** 115.2° **19.** 0.42 **20.** $2.72

Extra Skill Practice
1. scatter plot; A scatter plot shows a relationship between two sets of data. **3.** line graph; A line graph shows how data values change over time. **5.** the price remained steady. **7.** Sample Response: Let a pea represent Jupiter and an orange represent the sun.

Standardized Testing, Open-ended
1. Possible answers: double bar graph

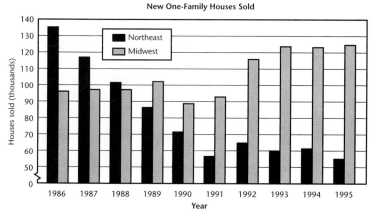

New One-Family Houses Sold

double line graph

2. Sample Response: number of new one-family houses sold in the northeast and midwest in 1990; box-and-whisker plot **3.** Sample Response: median number of new one-family houses sold in the Northeast; box-and-whisker plot

Section 4, Practice and Application
1. not equivalent **3.** equivalent **5.** Sample Response: A person must take in about 80 oz of water per day in order to survive. **7. a.** km/h or mi/h; The speed of a car is usually given in km/h or mi/h. **b.** about 1250 km/h or 750 mi/h **9.** $\frac{3}{40}$, 0.075, 7.5% **11. a.** 0.06, or 6% **b.** 0.004, or 0.4% **c.** 0.005, or 0.5% **d.** 0.056 or 5.6% **13.** other means **15.** $\frac{6,069,589}{115,070,274} = \frac{p}{1200}$; about 63 workers

Spiral Review
17. Sample Response: a bar graph; The data falls into categories. **18.** Sample Response: a circle graph; The data is given in percentages. **19.** 80°, 170° **20.** 2°, 92° **21.** 33°, 123° **22.** 45°, 135°

Extra Skill Practice
1. equivalent **3.** not equivalent **5.** Sample Response: Tanya reads about 104 books per year **7.** about 0.16, or 16% **9.** about 0.19, or 19%

Standardized Testing, Free Response
1. Sample Response: 1 h/day, 30 h/month, 2.5 min/h; I think the rate 1 h/day communicates this information most effectively because it also describes fairly accurately about how much I watch on a typical day. I think the rate 2.5 min/h is the least effective because it suggests that I turn the TV on and off once an hour. **2.** about 29 students

Review and Assessment
1. 3 to 6 stretches **2.** 35 min **3.** positive correlation **4.** no correlation **5.** Yes; Should students have acess to the internet? **6. a.** representative; This group should have the same characteristics as the rest of the population. **b.** biased; Students in grades 5–7 are not represented. **7.** Sample Response: Give a simple test of coordination, such as catching a ball. Repeat the test over several days, with the participant sleeping for shorter periods each night. **8.** 10% **9.** 16 classes **10.** 36°
11.

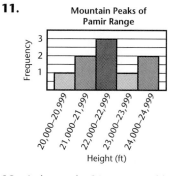

12. circle graph **13.** stem-and-leaf plot **14.** scatter plot **15.** Yes; Sample Response: Because the vertical scale doesn't start at 0, it appears that the number of motorcycles registered in Ohio is more than twice that in Wisconsin. **16.** Sample Response: Mark off 180 squares on a piece of graph paper to represent the number of pieces of mail delivered annually. $\frac{9}{10}$ of one square represents the number of pieces of priority mail delivered. **17.** Sample Response: Fingernails grow at approximately 1 mm/week. (1.05 mm) **18.** 0.3, or 30%

TOOLBOX ANSWERS

NUMBERS AND OPERATIONS

Decimal Place Value
1. < **2.** < **3.** = **4.** > **5.** = **6.** > **7.** > **8.** > **9.** < **10.** =
11. < **12.** > **13.** 0.3 **14.** 0.8 **15.** 3.8 **16.** 1.7
17. 0.63 **18.** 7.85 **19.** 0.05 **20.** 5.93 **21.** 1.038
22. 0.993 **23.** 8.310 **24.** 0.024

Multiplying Whole Numbers and Decimals
1. 1302 **2.** 1200 **3.** 28,667 **4.** 214,832 **5.** 72,928
6. 18,244,440 **7.** 5.4 **8.** 12.54 **9.** 45.35 **10.** 7.837
11. 21.122 **12.** 435.16 **13.** 0.0018 **14.** 5.05404
15. 0.00192 **16.** 7.6896

Multiplying and Dividing by 10, 100, and 1000
1. 518.3 **2.** 980 **3.** 3.0042 **4.** 67 **5.** 0.294 **6.** 0.56
7. Multiply. **8.** 0.68 **9.** 13,000 **10.** 2700 **11.** 3.56
12. 4800 **13.** 4.54

Dividing Whole Numbers and Decimals
1. 24.8 **2.** 17.7 **3.** 15.3 **4.** 7.56 **5.** 53.19 **6.** 49.73
7. 14 **8.** 45 **9.** 8.5 **10.** 262.2 **11.** 962.5 **12.** 968

Divisibility Rules
1. No. **2.** Yes. **3.** Yes. **4.** Yes. **5.** No. **6.** Yes. **7.** Yes.
8. Yes.

Finding Factors and Multiples
1. 6; 420 **2.** 12; 72 **3.** 11; 330 **4.** 40; 240 **5.** 30; 90
6. 5; 10,500 **7.** 15; 3465 **8.** 6; 2622 **9.** 55; 2475
10. 2; 2450 **11.** 1; 6237 **12.** 23; 138

Finding Equivalent Fractions and Ratios
1. 6 **2.** 56 **3.** 6 **4.** 3 **5.** $\frac{3}{5}$ **6.** $\frac{1}{3}$ **7.** $\frac{9}{10}$ **8.** $\frac{2}{3}$ **9.** = **10.** <
11. >

Multiplying and Dividing Fractions
1. $\frac{4}{15}$ **2.** $\frac{1}{49}$ **3.** $\frac{3}{10}$ **4.** $\frac{2}{9}$ **5.** 6 **6.** $\frac{4}{5}$ **7.** 3 **8.** 15 **9.** $\frac{1}{2}$
10. $\frac{3}{4}$ **11.** $\frac{8}{3}$ or $2\frac{2}{3}$ **12.** $\frac{5}{4}$ or $1\frac{1}{4}$ **13.** $\frac{15}{2}$ or $7\frac{1}{2}$ **14.** $\frac{1}{10}$
15. 6 **16.** $\frac{16}{9}$ or $1\frac{7}{9}$

Writing Fractions, Decimals, and Percents
1. 0.95; 95% **2.** 0.16; 16% **3.** 0.001; 0.1% **4.** 0.62;
62% **5.** 0.8; $\frac{4}{5}$ **6.** 0.875; $\frac{7}{8}$ **7.** 0.64; $\frac{16}{25}$ **8.** 1.2; $\frac{6}{5}$ or $1\frac{1}{5}$
9. 48%; $\frac{12}{25}$ **10.** 85%; $\frac{17}{20}$ **11.** 12.5%; $\frac{1}{8}$ **12.** 350%;
$\frac{7}{2}$ or $3\frac{1}{2}$

Using Order of Operations
1. 15 **2.** 18 **3.** 56 **4.** 13 **5.** 5 **6.** 9 **7.** 1 **8.** 4 **9.** 29
10. 41 **11.** 2 **12.** 3

Comparing Integers
1. > **2.** < **3.** < **4.** < **5.** > **6.** > **7.** > **8.** < **9.** <
10. −5, −4, 1 **11.** −3, 0, 2 **12.** −4, −2, −1 **13.** −5, 3, 4
14. −6, −3, 0 **15.** −2, 2, 6 **16.** −2, −1, 0, 1 **17.** −7, −4,
−2, 0 **18.** −6, −3, 2, 5

GEOMETRY AND MEASUREMENT

Locating Points on a Coordinate Plane
1. (−5, 2) **2.** (−3, −2) **3.** (−3, 1) **4.** (1, 4) **5.** (3, 0)
6. (0, −2) **7.** (2, −4) **8.** (−2, 4) **9.** (−1, 1)
10–18.

Measuring Angles
1. 90°; right **2.** 30°; acute **3.** 100°; obtuse
4. 155°; obtuse **5.** 40°; acute **6.** 110°; obtuse

Classifying Triangles
1. obtuse **2.** right **3.** obtuse **4.** acute **5.** isosceles
6. equilateral and isosceles **7.** scalene **8.** isosceles

Using Formulas from Geometry
1. P = 16 ft; A = 12 ft^2 **2.** P = 58 m; A = 180 m^2
3. P = 80 yd; A = 360 yd^2 **4.** 480 cm^3 **5.** 5625 m^3
6. 432 in.^{3}

DATA ANALYSIS

Finding the Mean, Median, Mode, and Range
1. mean: 33; median: 32; mode: 29; range: 9
2. mean: $16\frac{2}{3}$; median: 16.5; mode: none; range: 6
3. mean: 3.8; median: 3.6; mode: none; range: 2.9
4. mean: 34; median: 34; mode: 34; range: 0
5. mean: 2.25; median: 2; modes: 1 and 2; range: 5
6. mean: 105; median: 95; mode: 95; range: 60

ADDITIONAL ANSWERS

MODULE 1

Section 1, Exploration 1

4. a. Sample Response: A diagram could be used to plan how to build the model; acting it out could have helped the engineers prepare for their description to the astronauts. **b.** Sample Response: They would have to go back and check the astronaut's air scrubber against the engineer's air scrubber to determine why one worked and the other did not.

Spiral Review

23.

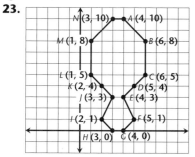

Beginning the Module Project

1. Sample Response: Find the average distance between Earth and the moon (238,857 mi). Find out how many pennies are needed to reach a height of 1 in. (17 pennies). Use this fact to determine how many pennies are needed to reach a height of 1 mi (1,077,120 pennies). Multiply this number by 238,857. (257,777,651,840 pennies) Check the answer using this method: Divide the final number of pennies by 17, then determine the number of inches in 238,857 miles. Divide the second result by the first. The results should be the same. (The answer checks.) Compare the two lengths to determine if the claim is reasonable. (It is not.)

Extra Skill Practice

1. a. Possible Answers: one 12-person tent, two 6-person tents, and one 2-person tent; one 12-person tent and seven 2-person tents; one 12-person tent, two 5-person tents, and two 2-person tents; one 12-person tent, one 6-person tent, and four 2-person tents
b. Possible Answers: four 6-person tents and one 2-person tent; three 6-person tents and four 2-person tents; two 6-person tents and seven 2-person tents; one 6-person tent and four 5-person tents; one 6-person tent, two 5-person tents, and five 2-person tents;

one 6-person tent and ten 2-person tents; thirteen 2-person tents; two 6-person tents, two 5-person tents, and two 2-person tents **c.** Possible Answers: one 12-person tent, two 5-person tents, and two 2-person tents; one 6-person tent and four 5-person tents; one 6-person tent, two 5-person tents, and five 2-person tents; two 6-person tents, two 5-person tents, and two 2-person tents

Section 2, Exploration 1

8.

Ages of Top 20 Country Artists When They Had Their First #1 Record, 1993	
2	4 5 5 7 7 8 8 8 9
3	0 1 1 3 4 5 6 8 8 9
4	2

9. a. Sample Response: Country artists are more apt to have hit singles in their 20s and 30s and pop artists are apt to have hit singles in their 20s. **b.** Sample Response: There is a slightly wider range of ages for pop artists than for country artists. **c.** Yes; No; Her age is on the high range for pop artists and near the middle range for country artists.

Practice and Application

1. a.

Ages of Winners of Grammy Award for Best Female Country Performance, 1975–1996	
1	4
2	4 7 8 9 9
3	0 1 1 2 2 3 4 5 5 6 6 7 7 8
4	6 7

Ages of Winners of Grammy Award for Best Female Pop Performance, 1975–1996	
1	9
2	1 3 4 4 4 8 9
3	0 1 1 2 3 5 5 8
4	0 1 2 4 5
5	
6	4

b. Sample Response: Most country performers are in their 30s when they receive this award. Most pop winners are in their 20s and 30s.

Extra Skill Practice

1.

Age of Academy Award Winners for Best Actor, 1976–1995

3	0 0 2 5 7 7 8 9
4	0 2 2 3 5
5	1 2 2 4
6	0 1
7	6

Age of Academy Award Winners for Best Actress, 1976–1995

2	1 6 9
3	1 1 3 3 3 4 5 8
4	1 1 2 5 9 9
5	
6	
7	2 6
8	0

Sample Response: Most Best Actor and Best Actress awards are given when the actors and actresses are in their thirties and forties. The range of ages for Best Actress is greater than the range of ages for Best Actor.

2. Actor: mean: 44.8 years, median: 42 years, modes: 30, 37, 42, and 52; Actress: mean: 41.95 years, median: 36.5 years, mode: 33; Sample Response: The median best describes the data on actor's ages because there are no major gaps in the data. The mean best describes the data on actress' ages because of a large gap between 49 and 72.

Section 3, Practice and Application

4. a, b.

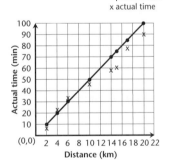

• planned time
x actual time

c. Sample Response: Both times are within a few minutes of each other until about 14 km, when the planned time is about 10 to 15 minutes greater than the actual time.
d. Between the 14th and 15th km; Sample Response: I divided the number of miles covered in each time period by the amount of time lapsed between the two distances.

6. a.

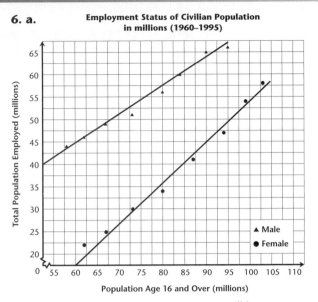

Employment Status of Civilian Population in millions (1960–1995)

b. Sample Response: How many women will be employed when the total female population is 110 million? Extend the line for females to 110 million.

Extra Skill Practice

3. a, b.

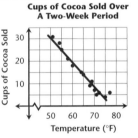

Cups of Cocoa Sold Over A Two-Week Period

Sample Response: I chose a horizontal scale of 40 to 90 because the temperatures range from 51° to 77°. I chose a vertical scale of 0 to 35 because the cups of cocoa sold range from 4 to 31. **c.** 3 pots; 4 pots

Section 4, Exploration 1

11. a. Possible answers: quarter: 2.4 cm in diameter, circumference = 7.536 cm; dime: 1.7 cm in diameter, circumference = 5.338 cm; nickel: 2.1 cm in diameter, circumference = 6.594 cm; penny: 1.8 cm in diameter, circumference = 5.652 cm **b.** Possible answers: quarter: 7.536 cm, 75.36 cm; dime: 5.338 cm, 53.38 cm; nickel: 6.594 cm, 65.94 cm; penny: 5.652 cm, 56.52 cm

29.

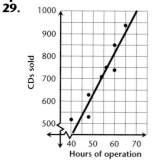

Section 5, Exploration 2

12. a.

b. $n = 9$

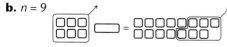

Section 6, Exploration 1

6. Check students' work for drawings.

Rectangles with an Area of 24 Square Units		
Length	Width	Perimeter
6	4	20
4	6	20
3	8	22
8	3	22
12	2	28
2	12	28
1	24	50
24	1	50

7.

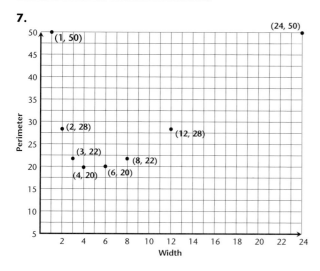

9. a.

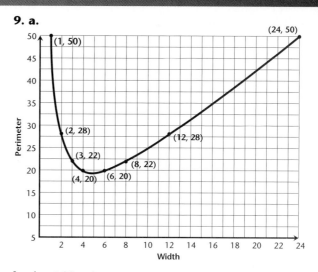

b. about 25 units

c.

4.9

4.9

Practice and Application

2. a.

Rectangles with an Area of 30 square units		
length	width	perimeter
1	30	62
2	15	34
3	10	26
5	6	22
6	5	22
10	3	26
15	2	34
30	1	62

b.

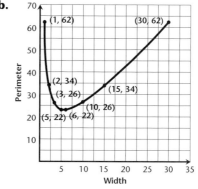

c. about 5.5 units; about 5.5 units; They are the same.

d. 180 units; Sample Response: the equation; An exact answer is needed. I can only estimate from the graph or the table. **e.** about 24 units; Sample Response: the table and the graph; There are perimeters given for 3 and 5 unit widths, so it was easy to find a perimeter about midway between them. **f.** Sample Response: No; As the width gets closer and closer to 0, the rectangle gets very long and thin, and I can see from the graph that this makes the perimeter greater and greater.

3. a. $V = Bh$ **b.** Answers will vary

c.

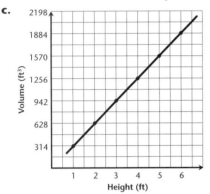

d. almost 6.5 ft; Sample Response: The graph gives a quick estimate of the height of the water.

4. a.

Rectangles with Perimeters of 28 units		
Width	Length	Area
1	13	13
2	12	24
3	11	33
4	10	40
5	9	45
6	8	48
7	7	49
8	6	48
9	5	45
10	4	40
11	3	33
12	2	24
13	1	13

b.

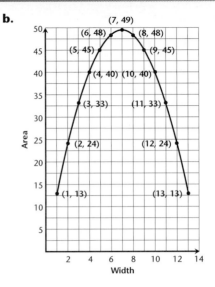

c. The length and width of the rectangle with the greatest area is 7 units and the area is 49 square units.

Extra Skill Practice

2.

Rectangles with an area of 48 square units		
Length	Width	Perimeter
1	48	98
2	24	52
3	16	38
4	12	32
6	8	28
8	6	28
12	4	32
16	3	38
24	2	52
48	1	98

3.

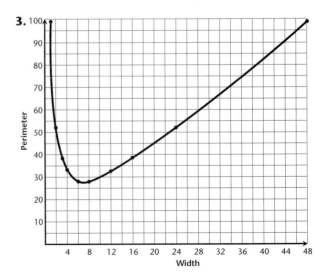

Review and Assessment

3. a.

Ages of Company A Airplanes	
0	2 3 5 6 9
1	2 3 5 5 7 7 7 8 9
2	0 0 1 6

Ages of Company B Airplanes	
0	1 2 3 3 5 6 7 7 8 9
1	2 4 6 6 6 9
2	0 5

b. Sample Response: Most of the planes owned by Company A are older than the planes owned by Company B. **c.** Company A: mean: about 14.2, median: 16, mode: 17; Company B: mean: 10.5, median: 8.5, mode: 16

4. a. Company A: lower extreme: 2, upper extreme: 26, lower quartile: 9, upper quartile: 19; Company B: lower extreme: 1, upper extreme: 25, lower quartile: 5, upper quartile: 16 **b.** Sample Response: The median age of the planes at Company B is less than the median age of planes at Company A.

10. a.

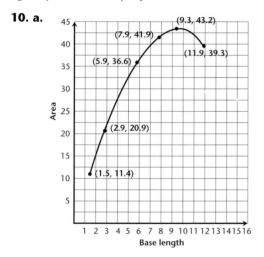

smooth curve

b. 9.3 cm

MODULE 2

Section 3, Exploration 3

23. a.

	R2 W1 R1 W1 W2
R2	W1 — W2 R1 R2 W1 W2
	W2 — W1 R1 R2 W2 W1
W1	W2 — R1 R2 W1 W2 R1
	R1 — W2 R2 W1 R1 W2
W2	W1 — R1 R2 W2 W1 R1
	R1 — W1 R2 W2 R1 W1
R1	W1 — W2 R2 R1 W1 W2
	W2 — W1 R2 R1 W2 W1

26.

1st Roll	2nd Roll	Outcome
1	1	1–1
	2	1–2
	3	1–3
	4	1–4
	5	1–5
	6	1–6
2	1	2–1
	2	2–2
	3	2–3
	4	2–4
	5	2–5
	6	2–6
3	1	3–1
	2	3–2
	3	3–3
	4	3–4
	5	3–5
	6	3–6
4	1	4–1
	2	4–2
	3	4–3
	4	4–4
	5	4–5
	6	4–6
5	1	5–1
	2	5–2
	3	5–3
	4	5–4
	5	5–5
	6	5–6
6	1	6–1
	2	6–2
	3	6–3
	4	6–4
	5	6–5
	6	6–6

$\frac{3}{36}$, or $\frac{1}{12}$

Key Concepts

28. a.

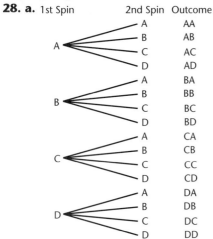

Practice and Application

13. a.

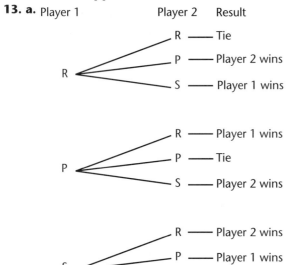

15. a.

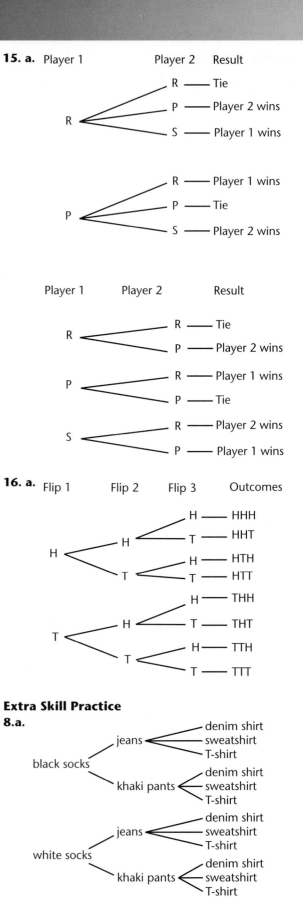

16. a.

Extra Skill Practice

8.a.

Section 4, Exploration 3
24–25. a.

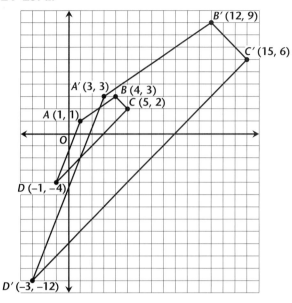

Practice and Application
30. a–c.

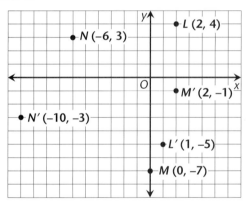

Section 6, Practice and Application
9. a–b.   T-Shirt Prices (dollars)

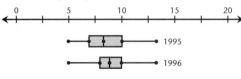

c. Sample Response: No; The range is the same and the median price increased by only $1.00.

Review and Assessment
8.

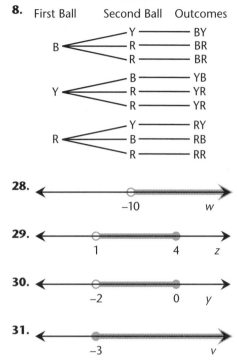

First Ball | Second Ball | Outcomes

28.

29.

30.

31.

MODULE 3

Section 1, Practice and Application
30.

Amounts raised by Students at a Charity Dance Marathon (dollars)

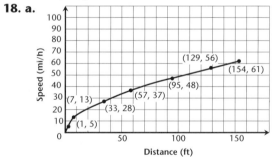

Section 2, Exploration 2
18. a.

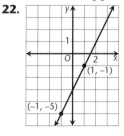

Practice and Application
22.

23.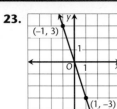

24.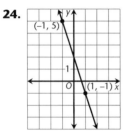

25.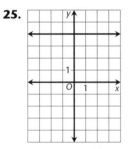

26.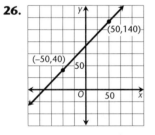

27.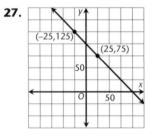

33.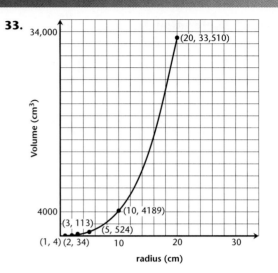

Extra Skill Practice

10.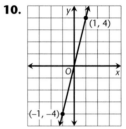

11.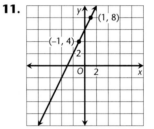

12.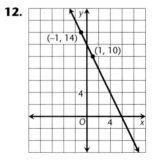

13.

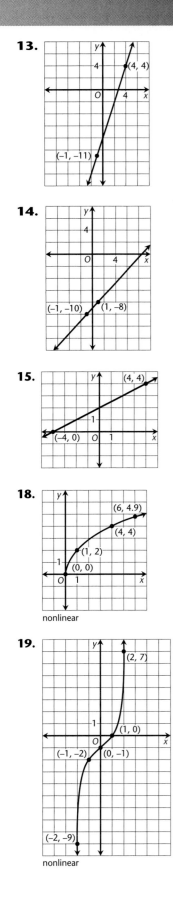

14.

15.

18.

nonlinear

19.

nonlinear

20.

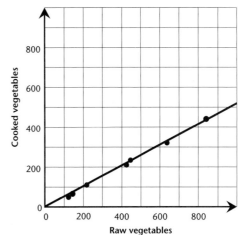

linear

Section 3, Practice and Application

12. a.

Vitamin C in Green Leafy Vegetables, (mg)

Extended Exploration
The Problem
No matter what number you start with, the result is 6. Only one state's name begins with F, Florida. The third letter of Florida, o, is the first letter of orange, a fruit closely associated with Florida.

Something to Think About
Sample Response: It would allow you to think about a simpler problem and make it easier to see the pattern involved. Yes; yes; yes; yes.

Present Your Results
The puzzle works for any number.

3.

Decay Pattern of Carbon-14			
Number of years	Number of half-lives	Fraction remaining of the original amount of carbon-14	Visual model
17,190	3	$\frac{1}{2}$ of $\frac{1}{4} = \frac{1}{8}$	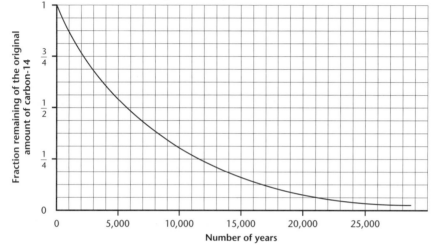
22,920	4	$\frac{1}{2}$ of $\frac{1}{8} = \frac{1}{16}$	
28,650	5	$\frac{1}{2}$ of $\frac{1}{16} = \frac{1}{32}$	

Change in Amount of Carbon-14 Over Time

Section 6, Exploration 1

3.

Blood type A — Kelley, Perlman

Blanco, Chee, Foley, Martinez, Pappas, Seowtewa, Suarez, Sullivan, Weatherwax

Absent from field trip — Chan, Sakiestewa, Valenzuela(Pedro)

Alvarado, Cordero, Fuentes, Mendoza, Nordquist, Puente, Stein, Valenzuela(Martina)

7.

Mexico & Canada

Mexico

Canada

Dan, Jim | Paolo, Maria | Stacey

Neither Mexico nor Canada ⟶ Rob

Practice and Application

10.

5

Hello Dolly 20

7

A Midsummer Night's Dream

2

13

The Marriage Proposal 1

11.

States that border another country or a Great Lake
MI OH AZ VT MT ND MN IL WI NM PA ID IN

AK NY TX ME NH CA WA

States that border an ocean
HI FL RI CT MD MA DE MS VA LA NJ GA OR NC AL SC

CO AR IA WV OK NV SD TN KS KY NE MO UT WY

Working on the Module Project

14.

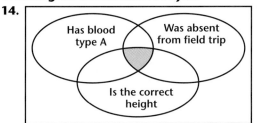

Extra Skill Practice

6.

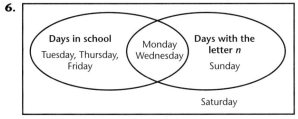

Standardized Testing

Answers may vary based on writing style.

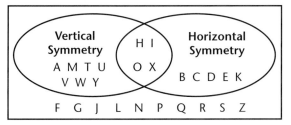

Completing the Module Project

16. Answers will vary depending on which Clues Handout Set is used. In each case, the two suspects both have access to the closet, both have cuts on their heads, and both know the area well; the person who is exonerated does not know the area well and cannot be the thief. Sample Responses: **(1)** Using Clues Handout Set #1 and information from the *Mystery of Blacktail Canyon:* **Either Alice Weatherwax or Perry Martinez is the thief**; Teresa Seowtewa cannot be the thief.
(2) Using Clues Handout Set #2 and information from the *Mystery of Blacktail Canyon:* **Either Perry Martinez or Teresa Seowtewa is the thief**; Alice Weatherwax cannot be the thief. **(3)** Using Clues Handout Set #3 and information from the *Mystery of Blacktail Canyon:* **Either Teresa Seowtewa or Alice Weatherwax is the thief**; Perry Martinez cannot be the thief.

17. Answers will vary depending on which Clues Handout Set and corresponding Interview Transcripts are used. In each case, the final suspect has the right blood type and height, was not on the field trip, and knows the area well, and another witness's statement

indicates that the suspect lied during his or her interview with the police. Sample Responses: **(1)** Using Clues Set #1 and Martinez 113-2 and Weatherwax 111-7 transcripts: **Alice Weatherwax is the thief**; another witness's statement indicated that she lied about the rain during the conference she was attending; Perry Martinez was at the Rodeo all day and cannot be the thief. **(2)** Using Clues Set #2 and Martinez 222-2 and Seowtewa 112-4 transcripts: **Perry Martinez is the thief**; another witness's statement indicated that he lied about the rain during the Rodeo; Teresa Seowtewa was at the Library all day and cannot be the thief. **(3)** Using Clues Set #3 and Seowtewa 333-4 and Weatherwax 223-7 transcripts: **Teresa Seowtewa is the thief**; another witness's statement indicated that she lied about the rain at lunchtime; Alice Weatherwax was at a conference in Crownpoint all day and cannot be the thief.

Review and Assessment

5. Sample Response: He is comparing linear dimensions. Since the radius and height of the large can are twice those of the small can, the volume is 8 times greater.

9.

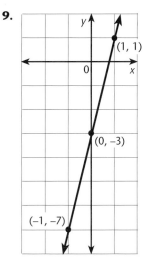

10.

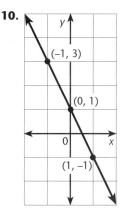

11.

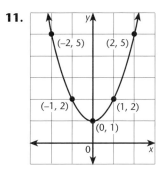

12.

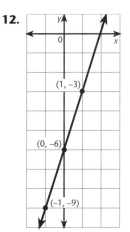

24.

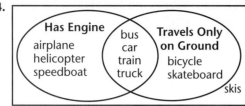

MODULE 4

Section 1, Career Connection

33.

34. The outside edge is green dots, inside the green dot edge the following patterns occur from left to right: blue, red, blue, red, blue, red, blue, red, blue—rows 1, 3, 7, and 9; red, red, red, red, green, red, red, red, red—rows 2, 4, 6, and 8; blue, green, blue, green, blue, green, blue, green, blue—row 5; The pattern would repeat itself every 10 rows.

Study Skills, Test Taking Strategies

1. Sample Response: (1) Choices A and C are not correct because they are not in scientific notation. Choice B is not correct because 16.6 is not between 1 and 10. Choice D is correct because it is in scientific notation. (2) Choices A, C, and D do not make the equation true.

2. Sample Response: Draw a rectangle. Inside the rectangle draw two intersecting ovals. Put letters with no vertical or horizontal symmetry in the rectangle outside the ovals. Put letters with only horizontal symmetry in one oval and letters with only vertical symmetry in the other oval. Put letters with both horizontal and vertical symmetry in the intersection of the ovals.

Section 2, Think About It

1.

	Number of Rabbit Pairs			Total Number of
Month	Newborn	Growing	Adult	Rabbit Pairs
Start	1	0	0	1
1	0	1	0	1
2	1	0	1	2
3	1	1	1	3
4	2	1	2	5
5	3	2	3	8
6	5	3	5	13

Practice and Application

2. a.

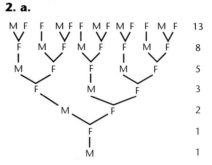

Section 3, Exploration 2

14.

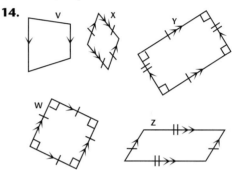

MODULE 5

Section 2, Practice and Application

9. Accept reasonable estimates.

Kemp's Ridley Turtle Nests (1970–1995)	
Time period	Rate of change (number of turtle nests/year)
1970–1975	−350
1975–1980	−75
1980–1985	−50
1985–1990	65
1990–1995	200

24. a.

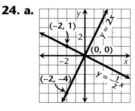

b.

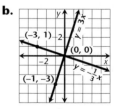

c.

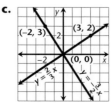

d. The lines in each pair are perpendicular; Sample Response:
$$y = \frac{2}{5}x, \ y = -\frac{5}{2}x$$

25. 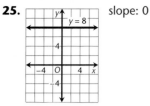 slope: 0

26. 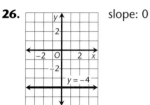 slope: 0

27. 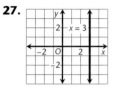 slope: undefined

28. 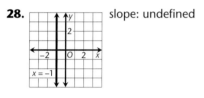 slope: undefined

Section 4, Spiral Review

35.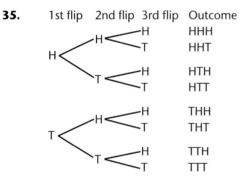

Section 5, Exploration 1

4. a.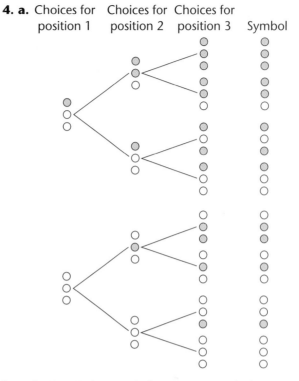

b. 2 choices; 2 choices; 2 choices **c.** 8 symbols

d. Multiply the number of choices for each position to get the number of different symbols; Yes

7. e.

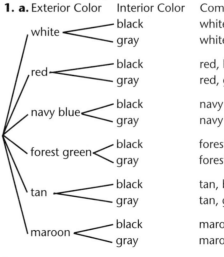

Practice and Application

1. a.

Exterior Color	Interior Color	Combination
white	black	white, black
	gray	white, gray
red	black	red, black
	gray	red, gray
navy blue	black	navy blue, black
	gray	navy blue, gray
forest green	black	forest green, black
	gray	forest green, gray
tan	black	tan, black
	gray	tan, gray
maroon	black	maroon, black
	gray	maroon, gray

b. 12 ways

3. a.

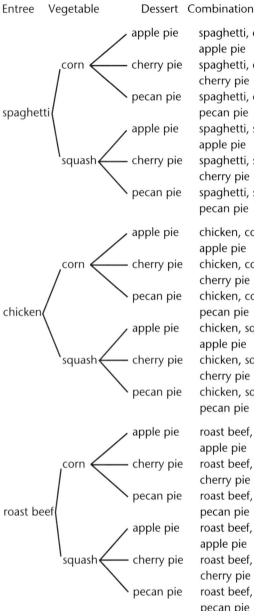

Entree   Vegetable   Dessert   Combination

spaghetti
- corn
  - apple pie — spaghetti, corn, apple pie
  - cherry pie — spaghetti, corn, cherry pie
  - pecan pie — spaghetti, corn, pecan pie
- squash
  - apple pie — spaghetti, squash, apple pie
  - cherry pie — spaghetti, squash, cherry pie
  - pecan pie — spaghetti, squash, pecan pie

chicken
- corn
  - apple pie — chicken, corn, apple pie
  - cherry pie — chicken, corn, cherry pie
  - pecan pie — chicken, corn, pecan pie
- squash
  - apple pie — chicken, squash, apple pie
  - cherry pie — chicken, squash, cherry pie
  - pecan pie — chicken, squash, pecan pie

roast beef
- corn
  - apple pie — roast beef, corn, apple pie
  - cherry pie — roast beef, corn, cherry pie
  - pecan pie — roast beef, corn, pecan pie
- squash
  - apple pie — roast beef, squash, apple pie
  - cherry pie — roast beef, squash, cherry pie
  - pecan pie — roast beef, squash, pecan pie

b. 18 dinners

Section 6, Reflecting on the Section

10. a. Sample Response: The color in the top triangle in each square is the color the first person chose, and the color in the bottom triangle is what the second person chose. The table shows that there are 9 possible ways.

b. $\frac{2}{3} \approx 0.67$; $\frac{1}{3} \approx 0.33$

c. Sample Response: See below; $\frac{1}{9} \approx 0.11$

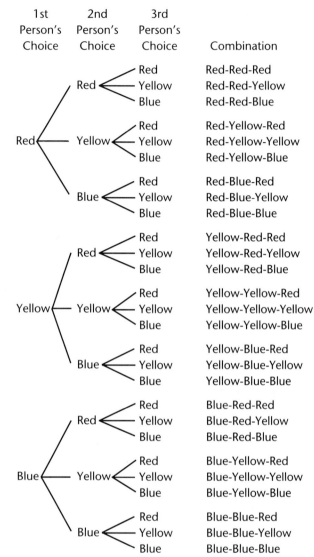

1st Person's Choice	2nd Person's Choice	3rd Person's Choice	Combination
Red	Red	Red	Red-Red-Red
		Yellow	Red-Red-Yellow
		Blue	Red-Red-Blue
	Yellow	Red	Red-Yellow-Red
		Yellow	Red-Yellow-Yellow
		Blue	Red-Yellow-Blue
	Blue	Red	Red-Blue-Red
		Yellow	Red-Blue-Yellow
		Blue	Red-Blue-Blue
Yellow	Red	Red	Yellow-Red-Red
		Yellow	Yellow-Red-Yellow
		Blue	Yellow-Red-Blue
	Yellow	Red	Yellow-Yellow-Red
		Yellow	Yellow-Yellow-Yellow
		Blue	Yellow-Yellow-Blue
	Blue	Red	Yellow-Blue-Red
		Yellow	Yellow-Blue-Yellow
		Blue	Yellow-Blue-Blue
Blue	Red	Red	Blue-Red-Red
		Yellow	Blue-Red-Yellow
		Blue	Blue-Red-Blue
	Yellow	Red	Blue-Yellow-Red
		Yellow	Blue-Yellow-Yellow
		Blue	Blue-Yellow-Blue
	Blue	Red	Blue-Blue-Red
		Yellow	Blue-Blue-Yellow
		Blue	Blue-Blue-Blue

Spiral Review

12. Possible answers:

Stem	Leaves
4	1, 8
5	2, 3, 9
6	1, 4, 6, 8
7	0, 2, 5, 5, 7, 8
8	1, 1, 1, 5, 6, 7
9	3, 4, 6, 8, 9

Science Test Scores

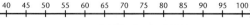
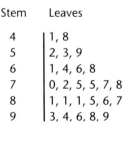

MODULE 6

Section 1, Exploration 2

14. a. No; If there were another cube, it would be visible.

b.

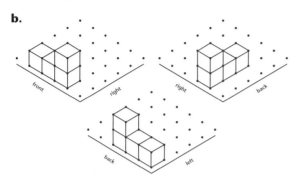

Practice and Application

2. a.

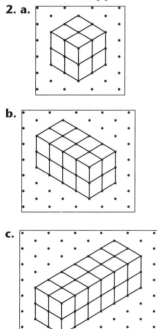

b.

c.

d. Figure a: cubes = 8, surface area = 24 square units , volume = 8 cubic units; Figure b: cubes = 16, surface area = 40 square units, volume = 16 cubic units; Figure c: cubes = 24, surface area = 56 square units, volume = 24 cubic units; when you multiply one of the dimensions by *n*, the volume (or number of cubes) is also multiplied by *n*.

12.

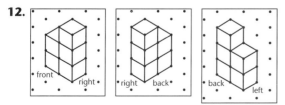

13.

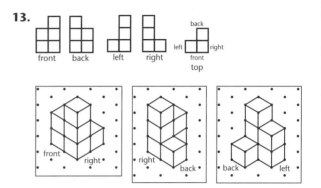

Extra Skill Practice

5.

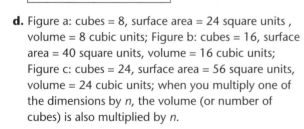

6.

Prism	Cubes	Surface Area	Volume
3 × 1 × 1	3	14	3

The number of cubes and the volume are the same.

8.

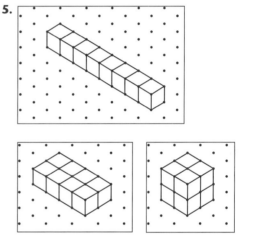

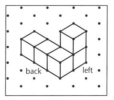

9.

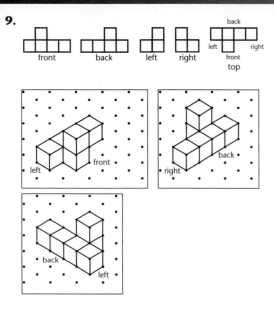

Section 3, Exploration 2

12. Labsheet 3B: 3, 9, 27, 3, 9, 14, 14 ÷ 27 ≈ 0.519; 4, 16, 64, 4, 16, 30, 30 ÷ 64 ≈ 0.469; 5, 25, 125, 5, 25, 55, 55 ÷ 125 = 0.44; 36, 216, 6, 36, 91, 91 ÷ 216 ≈ 0.421; 49, 343, 7, 49, 140, 140 ÷ 343 ≈ 0.408; 64, 512, 8, 64, 204, 204 ÷ 512 ≈ 0.398; 81, 729, 9, 81, 285, 285 ÷ 729 ≈ 0.391; 100, 1000, 10, 100, 385, 385 ÷ 1000 = 0.385

Practice and Application

7. a. 576 in.^{2}

b. Possible answers:

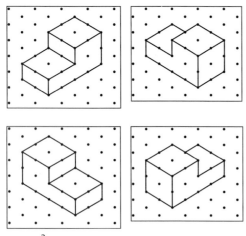

c. 768 in.^{3}

Section 4, Exploration 1

8. ∠5 and ∠6 are supplementary, so m∠5 = 180° − 56° = 124°; p and q are parallel and ∠2 and ∠6 are alternate interior angles, so m∠2 = 56°; ∠8 and ∠6 are corresponding angles, so m∠8 = 56°.

Key Concepts

10. 50°; 50°; 50°; ∠2 and ∠8 are vertical angles, so m∠2 = m∠8; The lines are parallel, so corresponding ∠'s 8 and 6 are congruent, and alternate interior ∠'s 8 and 4 are congruent.

Review and Assessment

19. $a \leq 5$

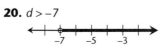

20. $d > -7$

21. $n < -9$

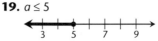

22. $k \geq \frac{6}{5}$

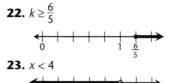

23. $x < 4$

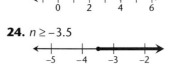

24. $n \geq -3.5$

MODULE 7

Section 2, Exploration 1

5. a–b. They lie on a line; 27

Sarah's Saving Plan

c. No; Sarah deposits the money at the end of each month.

7. b. In month 18 the $50 she adds to her savings makes it more than $1000.

Number of months	Amount saved
0	140
1	190
...	...
17	990
18	1040

7. c. The point where the graphs intersect is when she has saved $1000. When $y = 1000$, the x-coordinate is a little more than 17, so she has saved $1000 in month 18.

10. It shows when Sarah and Janet had the same amount of money in the bank.

Savings Plan

Practice and Application

9.
$$5000 - 150x = 0$$
$$5000 - 150x + 150x = 0 + 150x$$
$$5000 = 150x$$
$$33\frac{1}{3} = x; \ 34 \text{ months}$$
$$y = 200 + 150(34)$$
$$y = 200 + 5100$$
$$y = 5300; \ \$5300$$

18. a. $(1, 5)$; No; There is only one solution for the equation $5x = 2x + 3$.

b.
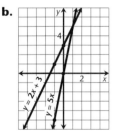
Find the point of intersection of the two graphs.

c.
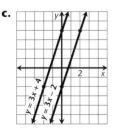
No; The graphs are parallel lines and do not intersect.

Extra Skill Practice

1.
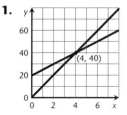

2.
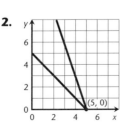

3.
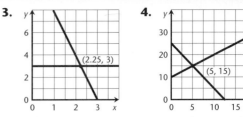

4.

Extended Exploration, Something to Think About

Possible answers: the length of time they plan to spend on the web each month, their personal budget

Plan A		Plan B		Plan C	
Time	Cost	Time	Cost	Time	Cost
0	14	0	10.00	0	20
10	14	10	10.00	10	20
11	14	11	12.50	11	20
12	14	12	15.00	12	20
13	14	13	17.50	13	20
14	14	14	20.00	14	20
15	14	15	22.50	15	20
16	16	16	25.00	16	20
17	18	17	27.50	17	20
18	20	18	30.00	18	20
19	22	19	32.50	19	20

Plan A: $y = 14$ for $0 \le x < 15$ and $y = 14 + 2(x - 15)$ for $x \ge 15$
Plan B: $y = 10$ for $0 \le x < 10$ and $y = 10 + 2.5(x - 10)$ for $x \ge 10$
Plan C: $y = 20$

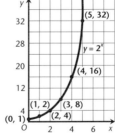

Section 3, Exploration 1

8. a.
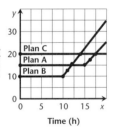

b.

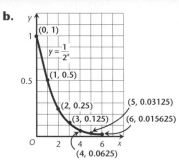

c. They are both curves; The graph of $y = 2^x$ increases rapidly and becomes very steep. The graph of $y = \left(\frac{1}{2}\right)^x$ decreases and flattens out gradually, getting closer and closer to the x-axis.

Practice and Application

3. a. 2, 4, 7; 3, 8, 15; 4, 16, 31; 5, 32, 63; 6, 64, 127; 7, 128, 255; 8, 256, 511; 9, 512, 1023; 10, 1024, 2047

b. $y = 2^{60}$

c. Sample Response: It shows exponential growth with powers of 2.

d.

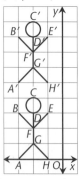

17. The advantage of Option 1 over Option 2 is having the cash now. The disadvantage is that the total amount over 5 years is almost $7000 less; Answers will vary. Check students' work.

Section 4, Practice and Application

1. Sample Response: $(x', y') = (x, y + 5)$; $(x'', y'') = (x', y' - 5)$

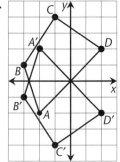

2. Sample Response: head $(x', y') = (x, y - 1)$; left foot $(x', y') = (x + 1, y)$; right foot $(x', y') = (x - 1, y)$

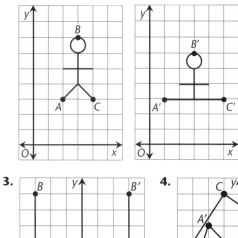

3.

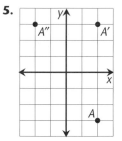

4.

5.

6.

7.   It is the same.

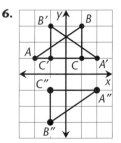

16.

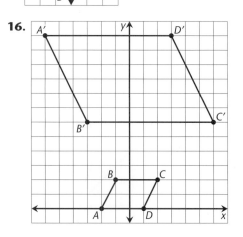

Section 5, Exploration 1

6. a. Sample Response: I think it determines whether the parabola opens up or down, and how wide or narrow the parabola is.

b.

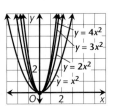

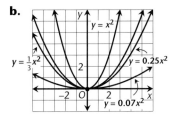

c.

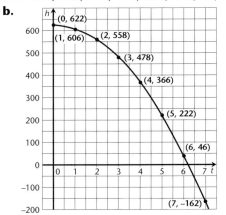

Practice and Application

6. a. 622, 606, 558, 478, 366, 222, 46, –162

b.

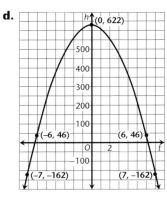

c. about 6.25 s; The graph crosses the x-axis at about x = 6.25.

d.

No; When the object is dropped, t = 0. Negative time values do not make sense in this situation.

e. (0, 622)

8. a. It is in the form $y = ax^2 + bx + c$ and $a \neq 0$; $a = -16$, $b = 80$, $c = 6$

b.

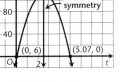
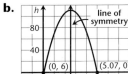

c. 106 ft; 2.5; about 5 s

Extra Skill Practice

1. same vertex and axis of symmetry, narrower

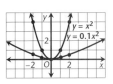

2. same vertex and axis of symmetry, wider

3. same shape and axis of symmetry, vertex (0, 1) instead of (0, 0)

4. same shape, vertex, and axis of symmetry, but opens in opposite direction

5. same axis of symmetry, narrower, vertex at (0, –2) instead of (0, 0), opens in opposite direction

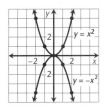
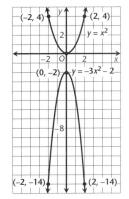

6. same vertex and axis of symmetry, wider, and opens in opposite direction

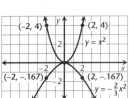

Review and Assessment

10. $y = 20,000 - 500x$; $15,000;
Possible methods:

Years	Value ($)
0	20,000
1	19,500
2	19,000
3	18,500
4	18,000
5	17,500
6	17,000
7	16,500
8	16,000
9	15,500
10	15,000

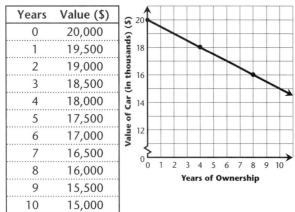

23. $(x', y') = (-x, y)$; $(x'', y'') = (x', y' + 3)$

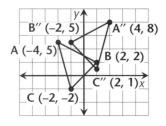

24. 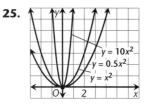 **25.**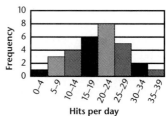

26. 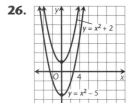 **27. a.**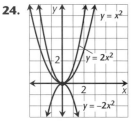

b. about 3.1 seconds

c. (1.5, 12.5)

MODULE 8

Section 1, Exploration 1

11. a.

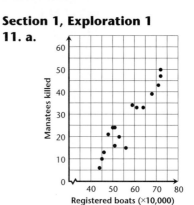

Extension

24. Answers will vary. Sample Response: Getting a self-selected or convenience sample is easier, but the sample is unlikely to be representative of the entire population. Not all those chosen using systematic or random sampling may be available or willing to participate in the survey. However, the sample is more likely to be representative.

Section 2, Exploration 2

10. b.

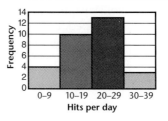

11.

Hits per day	Tally	Frequency
0–9	IIII	4
10–19	ⅢⅡ ⅢⅡ	10
20–29	ⅢⅡ ⅢⅡ III	13
30–39	III	3

Practice and Application

4. a. Source of China's 1994 GNP **b.** Source of India's 1994 GNP

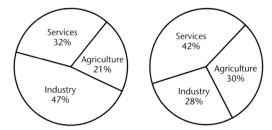

c. Source of Pakistan's 1994 GNP

8.

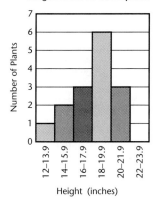

Height of self-fertilized plants

12.

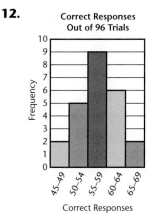

Correct Responses Out of 96 Trials

13. a. Use the intervals 40–49, 50–59, and 60–69. To find the frequency within each interval, add the frequencies of the intervals from Exercise 11 that fall within the range of the new intervals.

b. Use the intervals 40–49, 50–59, and 60–69. To find the frequency within each interval, add the frequencies of the intervals from Exercise 12 that fall within the range of the new intervals.

c.

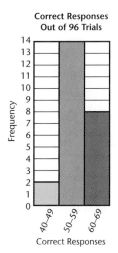

Correct Responses Out of 96 Trials

14. The frequencies of the 50–51 and 52–53 intervals, for example, could be added to find the number of responses that fall within the interval 50–53. However, we can't expand that interval to 50–54 because we can't tell how many responses within the 54–55 interval were 54 and how many were 55.

Extra Skill Practice

5.

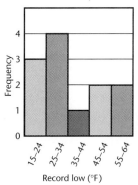

Phoenix, AZ, Temperatures

6.

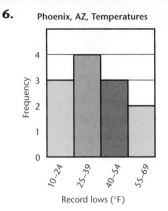

Phoenix, AZ, Temperatures

Section 3, Exploration 1
11. a.

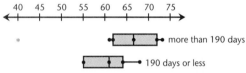

b. Sample Response: Yes; About 75% of the scores for students who go to school more than 190 days were higher than 60, while only 50% of the other group scored higher than 60.

15. Sample responses are given. **a.** median, minimum and maximum ages at death; box and whisker plot

b.

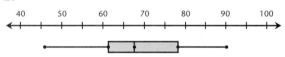

Exploration 2
18. a. 1975; The height of the bar for 1975 is twice the height of the bar for 1965.

b. 1995; No.

c. The vertical scale doesn't start at 0.

Solid Waste Generated in the US

22. a. Sample Response:

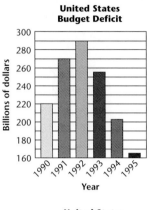

United States Budget Deficit

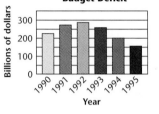

United States Budget Deficit

b. Sample Response:

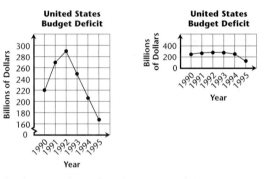

United States Budget Deficit

United States Budget Deficit

The first graph implies there was a dramatic increase, followed by a dramatic decrease, in the budget deficit. The second implies there has been little change over the years.

Practice and Application
11. Sample responses are given.

a.

Percent of Money Spent by United States Consumers on Reading Materials

b.

Percent of Money Spent by United States Consumers on Reading Materials

c. By starting the vertical scale with a number other than 0, the relative values of the bars can be misrepresented.

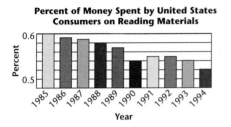

Percent of Money Spent by United States Consumers on Reading Materials

15. a. Alaska: 1 person/mi^2, New Jersey: 1025 persons/mi^2; Sample Response: Cut out a piece of newspaper that contains approximately 1025 characters to represent New Jersey. Use the same size paper with 1 character written on it to represent Alaska.

b. Alaska: 1 mi^2/person, New Jersey: 0.001 mi^2/person. Let the floor area of the classroom represent the square miles per person in Alaska. Mark off an area $\frac{1}{1000}$ that size in the classroom to represent the square miles per person in New Jersey.

Reflecting on the Section

16. Sample Response: A bar graph represents data values in categories, a histogram, data values within intervals, and a circle graph, data values as percentages. Stem-and-leaf plots and box-and-whisker plots are useful for finding or displaying statistical data such as median, maximum, and minimum. Scatter plots and line graphs represent the relationships between two sets of data. Pictorial models and demonstrations help in visualizing and appreciating the data.

Standardized Testing, Open-ended

1. Possible answers: double bar graph

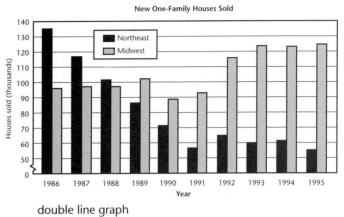

New One-Family Houses Sold

double line graph

New One-Family Houses Sold

Extended Exploration
Present Your Results

Sample responses are given.

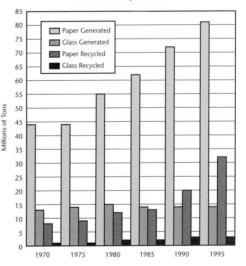

Generated and Recycled Waste

The amount of paper waste has nearly doubled, the percent recycled has quadrupled, but more than $\frac{1}{2}$ the paper waste is not yet being recycled.

Section 4, Think About It

2. Labsheet 4A, top: Jean and Brian–equivalent; Deven and Elisa–not equivalent

Labsheet 4A, bottom: Deven, Elisa, and Jean–equivalent; Brian–not equivalent

Labsheet 4B, top: Elisa and Jean–equivalent; Brian and Deven–not equivalent

Labsheet 4B, bottom: Deven and Jean–equivalent; Elisa and Brian–not equivalent

Labsheet 4C, top: Elisa–equivalent; Brian, Jean, and Deven–not equivalent

Labsheet 4C, bottom: Deven and Elisa–equivalent; Jean and Brian–not equivalent

Review and Assessment

11.

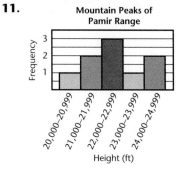